LINES to TORRINGTON

The Southern Railway Route between Barnstaple Junction, Bideford, Torrington, Hatherleigh and Halwill Junction

by John Nicholas and George Reeve

Torrington station and the fireman pays final attention to the 4.38pm Torrington to Barnstaple Junction service in August 1959. John Eyers, courtesy South Western Circle.

Irwell Press Ltd.

Copyright IRWELL PRESS LIMITED
ISBN 1-906919-69-6

ACKNOWLEDGEMENTS

This book would not have been possible without the generous help of a large number of individuals and organisations. Harry Beer, Don Bradley, Henry Casserley, Richard Casserley, Colin Chivers , Derek Clarke, the late Derek Clayton, Fred Cooper, George Copp, George Facey, Clive Fairchild, Martin Friendship, R.T.Hart, Roger Hateley, Owen Hatherell, D.Helyar, Ernest Holwill, Barry Hoper of the Transport Treasury, Barry Hughes, M.Hutchings, the late Mick Hutson, Andrew Jarrowson, R.Joanes, Mike King, Ken Ley, N.B.Martin, Mrs J.Medley, E.J.M McLaughlan, a special thanks to Roger Merry Price for the use of his working timetable and engine and carriage workings, Michael Messenger, Keith Miles, Harold Mock, E.V.Morgan, Nick Pomfret, Sid Pring, the late George Pryer, Mr Pyke, Reg Randell, J.B.Reed, the late Dick Riley, Alan Ruston, Michael Sampson, Allan Shelley, Malcom Snellgrove, Mike Squire, Peter H. Swift, Spencer Taylor, David St John Thomas, the late Bill Trigg, Harold Tumilty, Ray Tustin, Gordon Weddell, the late Ted West, Roger Whitehouse, David Wigley, R.A.Williams, Eric Youldon, Public Record Office Kew, Devon Record Office, Torrington Museum Society.

BIBLIOGAPHY

London & South Western Railway R.A.Williams
Locomotives of the LSWR, LBSCR, SECR, Southern Railway, Beattie, Adams, Drummond locomotives D.Bradley
South Western Carriages Weddell
South Western Wagons, Southern Wagons & Carriages King
Industrial Locomotives of South Western England Hateley
Southern Signals G Pryer
Southern Sheds Hawkins & Reeve
North Devon Clay M. Messenger
North Devon & Cornwall Junction Light Railway Whetmath & Stuckey
Bideford, Appledore & Westward Ho Railway Stuckey
Bideford, Appledore & Westward Ho Railway Garner
North Devon Railway Report Thomas
Canals of South West England Hadfield
Devon Hoskins
Strongs industries of North Devon Hughes

Track Layout Diagrams SR Pryer
Signalling Diagrams SR Pryer
Register of Closed Stations Clinker
Inspecting Officers & Accident Reports Board of Trade
Minute Books North Devon, LSWR, Southern Railways
Contracts for railway construction
Ordnance Survey maps
Devonshire Association Proceedings
NDR, LSWR, SR, BR Public & Working Timetables
Locomotive Duties & Carriage Working Diagrams
North Devon Journal
North Devon Journal-Herald
Bideford Gazette
Railway Magazine
Southern Railways Group Notebook
South Western Gazette
South Western Circular
Southern Railway Magazine
The Locomotive

First published in the United Kingdom in 2014
by Irwell Press Limited, 59A, High Street, Clophill,
Bedfordshire MK45 4BE
Printed by Melita Printing, Malta.

CONTENTS

Ancient wooden lamp post and loading gauge at
Barnstaple Junction in September 1967. John Eyers,
courtesy South Western Circle.

4

Chapter 1
Introduction to the Second Edition

It is now more than 30 years since publication of the First Edition in 1984, shortly after the line was closed. Fortunately when I first researched the line in the 1970s several of the men who worked on the line, including Harold Mock at Fremington, Owen Hatherell at Bideford, Sid Pring at Torrington, Fred Cooper at Petrockstow, and Ernest Holwill of the North Devon Clay Company kindly contributed reminiscences of their work on the line which extended back to the South Western era. Originally research was concerned with construction of a model of the line in the Edwardian period, the model has been completed but the amount of information gathered resulted in the book.

In recent years George Reeve and I have collected much more information, original documents and photographs deciding therefore to write a second edition. The original format was smaller and consisted of 192 pages. The scope of this work has required rewriting chapters including much more detail and information. The order and contents of the chapters has also changed since 1984 to bring this book into a similar format to our recent books. Thus we have expanded the work to some 368 pages. A little of the broad gauge content, concerning the North Devon Railway between Crediton and Barnstaple, has been published in our North Devon Line book (Irwell Press 2010) so is not included here.

John Nicholas and George Reeve
September 2014.

Left. Great Western interloper at Barnstaple Junction in 1958. In the foreground is the Torrington line with the lines to the extensive stock yards of the Devon Concrete Works behind the locomotive. *Below.* E1R 0-6-2T shunting stock at Barnstaple Junction in 1958 and seen from Sticklepath Road Bridge. Both John Eyers, courtesy South Western Circle.

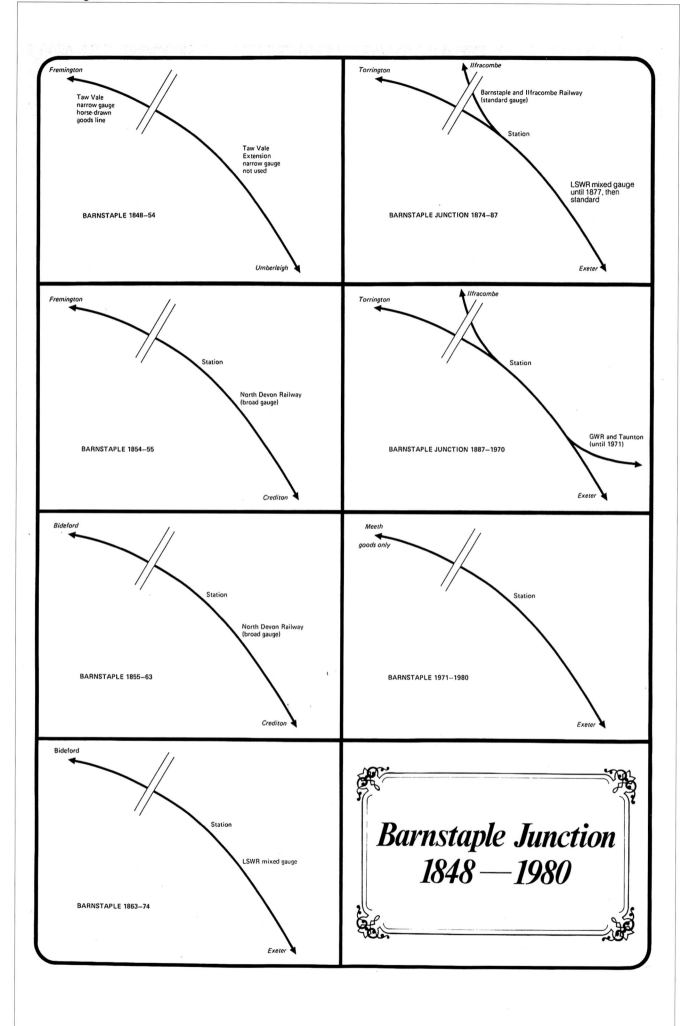

Fremington

Taw Vale
narrow gauge
horse-drawn
goods line

Taw Vale
Extension
narrow gauge
not used

BARNSTAPLE 1848—54

Umberleigh

Torrington

Ilfracombe

Barnstaple and Ilfracombe Railway
(standard gauge)

Station

LSWR mixed gauge
until 1877, then
standard

BARNSTAPLE JUNCTION 1874—87

Exeter

Fremington

Station

North Devon Railway
(broad gauge)

BARNSTAPLE 1854—55

Crediton

Torrington

Ilfracombe

Station

GWR and Taunton
(until 1971)

BARNSTAPLE JUNCTION 1887—1970

Exeter

Bideford

Station

North Devon Railway
(broad gauge)

BARNSTAPLE 1855—63

Crediton

Meeth

goods only

Station

BARNSTAPLE 1971—1980

Exeter

Bideford

Station

LSWR mixed gauge

BARNSTAPLE 1863—74

Exeter

---

*Barnstaple Junction
1848 — 1980*

Chapter 1
The Line Described

Barnstaple Junction

The development of the railways in North Devon confirmed the position of Barnstaple as the principal town in the area. It had a population of 22,500 in 1971, the shopping area is the fourth largest in Devon, and it is the centre for a population of more than 100,000 people in North Devon. At the zenith of the railway age at the beginning of the twentieth century, the town was the focus of the railway network, with five different routes operated by three different pre-grouping companies, each with its own station, goods yard, locomotive depot and staff. A full treatment of the railway history of Barnstaple is beyond the scope of this book (for that, see *The North Devon Line*, Nicholas and Reeve, Irwell Press, 2010) so only that which relates to the Torrington line is included here.

The station, the first and last to function in the town, was titled Barnstaple Junction from 1874 to 1970, the period of the Ilfracombe line, whereas before 1874 and after 1970 it was simply called Barnstaple. The main station building, constructed in local stone to a standard design of the North Devon Railway, but with additions providing extra accommodation, was the administrative centre of the railways in the area for many years. From here, in 1854, Robert Ogilvie managed the line between Bideford and Crediton when it was first leased by Thomas

Brassey, and many men have supervised the lines from here until 1974 when the British Rail Area Manager, Mr E.J.M. McLauchlan, moved on and local control passed to Exeter. Initially, in 1854, there was only the one platform and two running lines but a third line and second platform were added later. The footbridge incorporated a stone carrying the inscription 'L and S W Ry 1878', and was built to accommodate the increasing traffic after the opening of the Ilfracombe line, but the 'down' platform was not converted into an island platform until 1924. Incidentally, Barnstaple Junction was the only station in North Devon to boast a footbridge, as elsewhere passengers had to cross the tracks on the level. The layout has now reverted to one platform road. A refreshment room was provided on the 'up' platform and, in 1981, a new modern 'travel centre' was opened to replace the old and draughty booking hall.

The early freight facilities at Barnstaple junction included warehouses and lime-

kilns, leased by William Thorne, when he operated the line to Fremington with horses in 1848. The sidings in the extensive yard curve away to terminate near Barnstaple Bridge, where a slaughterhouse used to provide considerable traffic for the railway. During LSWR days, there were several wagon turntables and spurs which were later taken out of use while in the yard were a saw mill, timber yard and arrangements for all types of goods traffic. The goods shed next to the 'up'

TABLE OF REFERENCE	
RADII OF CURVES IN CHAINS	25
BRICK BUILT STATIONS	◎
BRICK & TIMBER BUILT STATIONS	◑
TIMBER BUILT STATIONS	○
WATERING STATIONS	◇
COALING STATIONS	☑
ENGINE SHEDS	⊕
ENGINE TURNTABLES	⊖
MILEAGE GIVEN THUS 86 M 23 CHS = REVISION MILEAGE	
SIGNAL BOXES	■
PUBLIC ROAD LEVEL CROSSINGS	X
ELECTRIC POWER STATIONS	⊠
GRADIENTS	660
W.I. OR STEEL BRIDGES	
DO & BRICK BRIDGES	
CAST IRON BRIDGES	
DO & BRICK BRIDGES	
TIMBER BRIDGES	
BRICK ARCHES	
STATION FOOTBRIDGES, STEEL	
DO DO , TIMBER	
TUNNELS	
BRIDGE NUMBERS	25

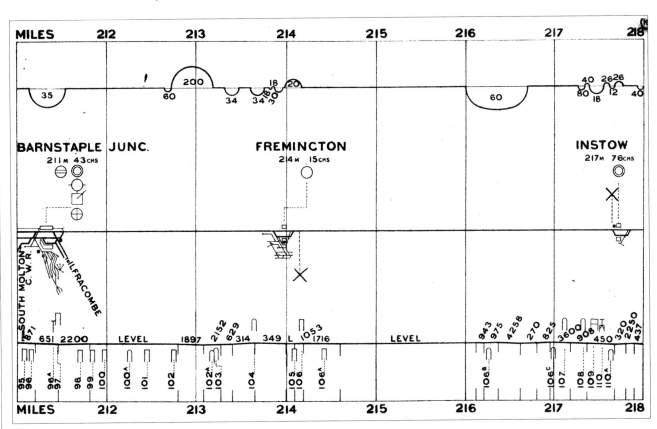

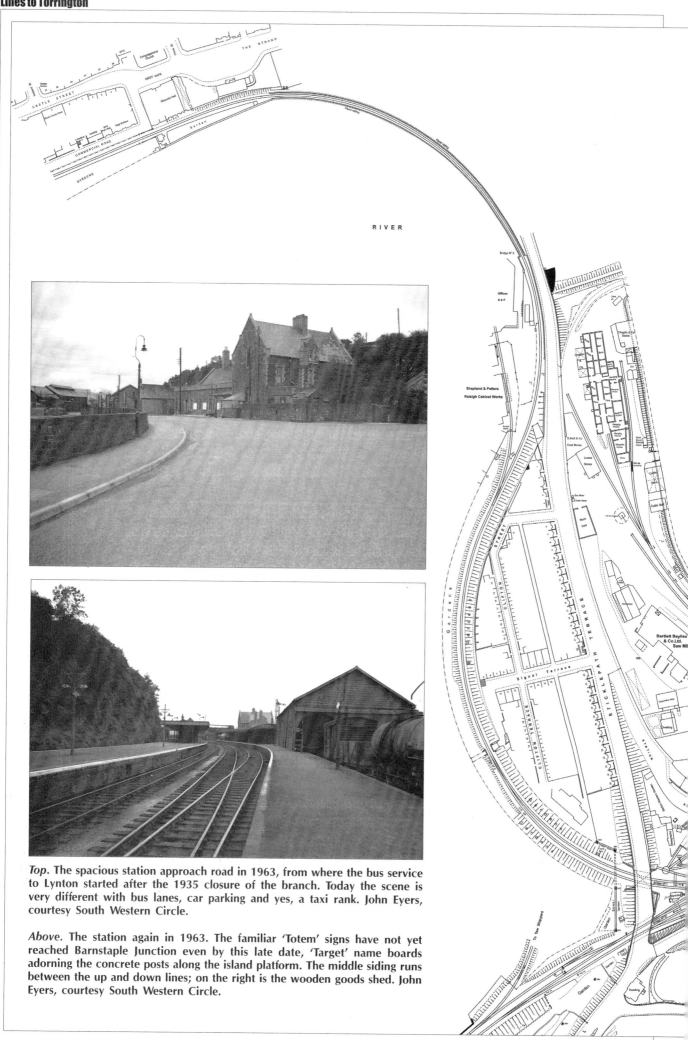

Top. The spacious station approach road in 1963, from where the bus service to Lynton started after the 1935 closure of the branch. Today the scene is very different with bus lanes, car parking and yes, a taxi rank. John Eyers, courtesy South Western Circle.

Above. The station again in 1963. The familiar 'Totem' signs have not yet reached Barnstaple Junction even by this late date, 'Target' name boards adorning the concrete posts along the island platform. The middle siding runs between the up and down lines; on the right is the wooden goods shed. John Eyers, courtesy South Western Circle.

Looking north off the end of the island platform with West signal box in the distance; to its right is the line to Barnstaple Town and Ilfracombe, to the left the line to Torrington. Most passenger trains to Taunton started from Barnstaple Junction, with a GWR 2-6-0 hauling the train tender-first to the Victoria Road terminus, where the locomotive ran round. Here we see GWR brake 3rd W2210W at the rear of a Taunton train. John Eyers, courtesy South Western Circle.

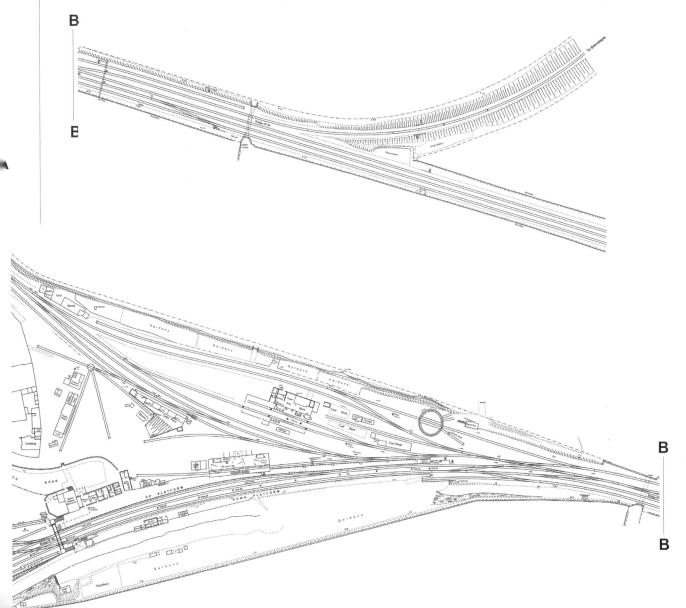

BARNSTAPLE JUNCTION c1920

M7 0-4-4T 30671 shunts some empty coal wagons by the old coal stage at Barnstaple Junction shed in July 1956. The loco had spent the best part of its time in the West Country at Exmouth Junction, arriving there in 1937; it had only been transferred here to Barnstaple the previous month. John Eyers, courtesy South Western Circle.

M7 30256 at the shed between turns on station pilot duties in July 1956. It had arrived at Barnstaple Junction from Feltham in 1931 but was transferred away to the parent shed, Exmouth Junction, in 1937. It worked the lines out of Exeter to Exmouth for some fourteen years before returning to Barnstaple in May 1951. John Eyers, courtesy South Western Circle.

34015 EXMOUTH taking coal at Barnstaple Junction shed in July 1956. For many years there was only the simple open platform, where coal was manhandled into bunkers and tenders. A primitive homemade conveyer belt was set up but this collapsed and instead, with steam in its final decade, this mechanical bucket hoist was installed. It does not seem to be quite operational yet but by the time it came fully into use a much-needed shelter had also at last been erected. John Eyers, courtesy South Western Circle.

platform was a wooden structure, which leaned slightly away from the vertical in later years. After 1971, this was the only British Rail goods depot in North Devon dealing with full loads, the main types of traffic including cement for a road distribution depot and on the closure of Bideford (Goods) in 1965, steel plate for Appledore Shipbuilders. A collection and delivery service for goods was operated from here until the national withdrawal of the service by British Rail in 1980.

In the yard was the two road wooden engine shed and stone outbuildings, its associated coaling stage and a 50ft. LSWR turntable, which replaced a North Devon Railway predecessor. Barnstaple was the principal shed in North Devon, with outstations at Ilfracombe and Torrington, and had stores, smithy, lathes, milling machines, etc. More than a hundred men were employed at the depot, mainly footplatemen, but also fitters, cleaners, boilersmiths and storemen. Increasingly decrepit, the place closed in 1964; by then, the shed had even lost its roof.

The station was controlled by two signal boxes, one at each end. The East or 'A' box controlled the line to Exeter and the junction leading to the GWR, while the West or 'B' box dealt with the Torrington and Ilfracombe lines. The

'B' box was the second to stand on the site, the first having been a very tall stone structure with a good view over the Sticklepath road bridge. The signalling was of LSWR origin with the distinctive lattice signal posts, and the junction signals at the west end of the station came into use at the time when

the Torrington line was the main, and Ilfracombe the branch line, although the roles reversed in 1925. When the layout was simplified in 1971, after the closure of the Ilfracombe line, the 'B' box was closed and the station completely resignalled using GWR pattern signals, which looked

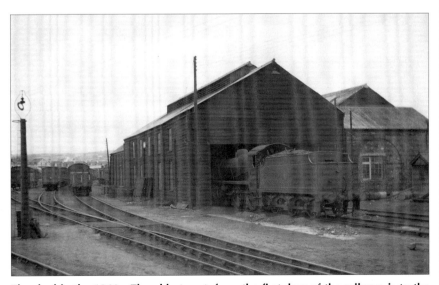

The shed in the 1960s. The oldest part, from the first days of the railway, is to the right, with its original arch entrance now bricked up with a window inserted. Behind this edifice is a large wooden structure for workshops offices and stores; on the left is the wooden shed erected when the standard gauge arrived in the 1860s. John Eyers, courtesy South Western Circle.

New arrival at Barnstaple from Exeter, the summer Saturday 8.35 Waterloo-Ilfracombe service behind 34070 MANSTON in August 1963. Passengers seem in no great hurry to get aboard while a gentleman struggles with what looks like an early version of the wheeled suitcase. John Eyers, courtesy South Western Circle.

BARNSTAPLE EAST

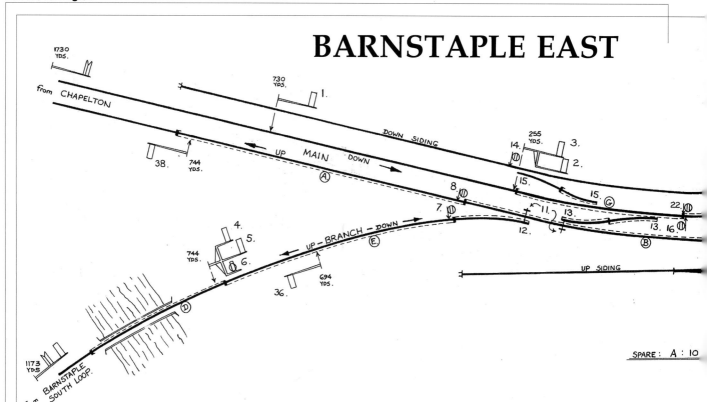

BARNSTAPLE WEST

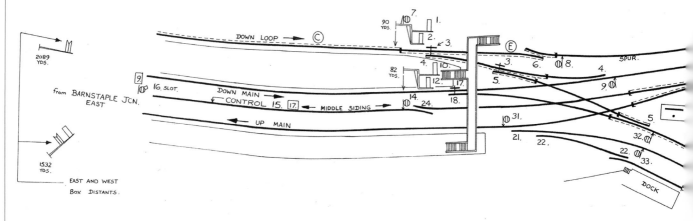

EAST BOX No's. THUS; - 9

SOUTHERN RAILWAY

Signal
Instruction
No. 28, 1924.

Instructions to all concerned as to

NEW AND ALTERED SIGNALS, ETC.

BARNSTAPLE JUNCTION WEST.

To be carried out on Tuesday, 23rd December.

The down main to Fremington and Barnstaple Town starting signals will be raised 5 feet.

The work will be in progress from 8.0 a.m. Mr. Heath to provide flagman, as required.

(R. 74.)

Signalling diagrams undated.

The dilapidated engine shed and the wooden extension at its rear. Asbestos tiles had replaced slates at some time in the 1950s but in the last years fire or tempest had left it in this desperate condition, in which the building saw out its last days. It certainly made it easier to demolish at the end... John Eyers, courtesy South Western Circle.

somewhat incongruous in their LSWR setting.

In Southern and British Railways days the typical procedure for 'up' trains was as follows. The first train to arrive was the branch train from Torrington which arrived at the 'up' platform. The locomotive, often an M7 0-4-4T, ran round the train to recouple and, with passengers and luggage safely on the platform or away, took the train back under the road bridge and waited on the branch. It was now time for the arrival of the train from Ilfracombe (in later years, invariably behind a light Pacific) which ran slowly over the bridge from Barnstaple Town station into the same 'up' platform, pulling well forward. The Torrington branch train was now propelled into the 'up' platform to enable the through coaches for Waterloo, marshalled at the front of the branch train, to be attached to the rear of the Ilfracombe train. After this, the branch train ran across to one of the 'down' platforms and the principal train departed for Exeter. In the 'down' direction, the Torrington

'A' Box, formerly East box, by the turntable in 1963 with what looks like a new set of steps. It controlled the lines to Exeter and the GWR route over the Taw River to Victoria station as well as access to the goods shed sidings and engine shed. John Eyers, courtesy South Western Circle.

SOUTHERN RAILWAY

Signal
Instruction
No. 12, 1924.

Instructions to all concerned as to

NEW AND ALTERED SIGNALS, etc.

BARNSTAPLE JUNCTION.

To be brought into use on Sunday, 29th June.

The existing loop siding behind the down platform will be extended to the western end of the station, and be available in future for passenger traffic, and known as the down loop line.

The down platform will in future be an island platform to serve both the down loop and down main lines.

EAST BOX.

A new home signal has been provided on the existing down inner home signal bracket post for controlling movements from the down main to the down loop line. (See diagram).

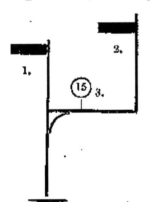

No. 1. Down main to down loop inner home signal (new signal).

No. 2. Down main inner home signal.

No. 3. Speed indicator, numbered 15, applicable to all down trains.

The existing ground signal controlling movements to the loop siding or along the down main line westward will be removed.

WEST BOX.

New facing connections have been provided at the western end of the platform between the down loop line and the down main and down branch lines with trailing points in the latter lines opposite West Box.

The down loop line has been extended at the western end to form a short dead-end siding, and catch points have been provided in the siding at the fouling point with the running line.

2

BARNSTAPLE JUNCTION.

WEST BOX—continued.

A new half bracket signal post has been provided outside the down loop line, at the western end of the down platform. (See diagram).

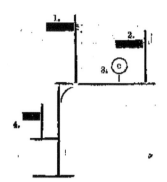

No. 1. Down loop to down main starting signal.

No. 2. Down loop to down branch starting signal.

No. 3. Speed indicator, lettered " C."

No. 4. Down loop to down siding ground signal.

A new ground signal controlling movements to the down loop has been provided at the catch points in the down siding.

A new ground signal controlling movements to the down loop or down main eastward has been provided at the new trailing points in the down main line.

A new ground signal controlling movements to the down loop or down main eastward has been provided at the new trailing points in the down branch line.

The existing ground signal controlling movements from the down branch to down main line will be removed.

The work will be in progress from 6.0 a.m. Mr. Heath to provide flagman, as required.
(R. 74.)

The West box, now Barnstaple Junction B, in 1963. It controlled the lines to Torrington and Barnstaple Town as well as the up main siding on the other side of the Sticklepath bridge. It has a unique set of concrete steps and an extended gallery for signalmen handing over and collecting the tablets for the single line working to Town and Fremington. This signal box was built in 1912, but in 1924 was lifted and moved several feet to make room for the widened layout, as seen in the photograph on p252 of the North Devon Line.John Eyers, courtesy South Western Circle.

branch coaches were marshalled at the rear of the Ilfracombe train and, on arrival, were uncoupled. Following the departure of the Ilfracombe train, the Torrington branch train backed on to the through coaches, coupled up and departed. Before 1925, the roles were reversed with the through trains running between Exeter and Torrington, Ilfracombe then being 'the branch'.

Although GWR stock and locomotives ran between Taunton and Ilfracombe through Barnstaple Junction, they do not appear to have worked through on to the Torrington line. In the 1950s, there was a regular van working between Torrington and Paddington and, in 1964, there were also through workings of diesel multiple units, but this was just before

Top. In August 1956 M7 30247 reverses its Torrington branch train into the up platform to couple up the through Waterloo coaches to the rear of the waiting Ilfracombe train. Apart from a brief two month transfer to Nine Elms in 1956, 30247 had been a Barnstaple engine since arriving from Bournemouth in 1937. John Eyers, courtesy South Western Circle.

Middle. M7 30256 backs down under Sticklepath Bridge to its train, the 5.50 all stations to Torrington service in August 1956. John Eyers, courtesy South Western Circle.

Bottom. The 'B' box from the footbridge and the prospect north and east. Reflecting an earlier lineage, the Sticklepath Road bridge to the left was numbered 97 in the sequence from Coleford Junction; the bridge to the right, over the line to Barnstaple Town and Ilfracombe, was numbered 1. John Eyers, courtesy South Western Circle.

The sweeping reverse curves of the line to Ilfracombe, from Sticklepath Road in July 1956. In the foreground is the Torrington line with the extensive stock yards of the Devon Concrete Works between. John Eyers, courtesy South Western Circle.

Looking towards Fremington from Sticklepath bridge in September 1961. On the right is the gated private siding of the Devon Concrete Works; the up main siding and headshunt disappear into the distance. The up main siding was often known as the "shipyard siding" because concrete ships had been constructed here on the banks of the Taw in 1914-18. Permanent way changes are imminent. John Eyers, courtesy South Western Circle.

Above and below. Anchor Wood bridge (No.99) nearly a mile along the line from Barnstaple Junction in July 1956. Passing is Ivatt tank 41297 with the 8.30 pm Barnstaple Junction-Torrington train. John Eyers, courtesy South Western Circle.

41297 and its train has passed and we are looking back to Barnstaple (above) and towards Fremington (below). John Eyers, courtesy South Western Circle.

closure. Victoria Road station closed in 1960 but most trains had long reversed there, to run tender first round to the Junction station, where the Taunton locos (usually 43XX 2-6-0s) turned. Victoria Road shed itself closed as early as January 1951 and its turntable taken out of use some two years later. On weekdays in 1957 for instance, seven trains ran Taunton-Barnstaple of which only one terminated at Victoria. In the up direction eight trains ran Barnstaple-Taunton of which three (only) started from Victoria Road.

Barnstaple Junction station was not the most convenient for the town, for it was separated from the town centre by Barnstaple Bridge over the Taw estuary. Barnstaple Town station, on the Ilfracombe line, was better situated for the town centre and was used by more passengers including, in earlier days, those from the Lynton and Barnstaple Railway which it also served.

Fremington opened for horse drawn goods traffic in1848, and passenger services began in 1855 with a single platform on the new line to Bideford. The tall post to the left carried navigation lights for shipping.

Town station was supervised by the Barnstaple Junction stationmaster.

On departure from one of the 'down' platforms, the Torrington train passed under the footbridge, past the 'B' signal box and here collected the token for the single line section to Fremington. Beyond the Sticklepath road bridge, carrying the main A39 road, the four running lines converged into one, with a long headshunt on the north side of the track, which provided access to a private siding curving away towards Barnstaple Bridge. This siding was used by the Raleigh Cabinet Company, the Devon Trading Company, and Saw Milling & General Supplies, at various periods. Leaving Barnstaple, a number of signals were passed, the 'up' home (on an LSWR lattice bracket post with a shunting arm), the 'down' advanced starting signal, the 'up' outer home and, finally, the 'up' distant signal, which was fixed at danger.

For most of the 3½ miles to Fremington, the line runs on a low embankment just above the marshes of the Taw Estuary, punctuated by the odd culvert. On the other side of the estuary, at some points only half a mile distant, was the Ilfracombe line and, after the Barnstaple Town stop, the branch train had often come abreast of the main train, and for several miles it was possible to observe the progress of one train from the other across the estuary. After a straight run almost due west for a couple of miles, the line slowly turned to the left into a slight

cutting, past Fremington 'down' distant signal, under an occupation bridge giving access to Penhill Point, then past Fremington 'down' home signal and into the station. 'Down' trains were required to whistle continuously for 200 yards to warn persons using the crossing in the station. This then was the first railway built in North Devon along which horses plodded, in 1848, with 'waggons' of coal and limestone imported at Fremington Quay.

Fremington

Quay and standard gauge goods line to Barnstaple opened August 1848
Line to Barnstaple converted to broad gauge July 1854
Passenger services began 2nd November 1855
Standard gauge services began 2nd March 1863
Signal box (214 miles 15 chains from Waterloo) opened about 1873
Broad gauge taken out of use 30th April 1877
Passenger services withdrawn 3rd October 1965
Loop taken out of use, signal box replaced by 2 ground frames 3rd November 1968
Quay closed 30th March 1970, but weighbridge sidings retained
Weighbridge, sidings and ground frames taken out of use 1979
Line closed 7th November 1982

At Fremington, the fortunes of the railway and quay were bound closely together. The Taw Vale Railway & Dock Company had built the quay and the railway to Barnstaple, as an

improvement to the port there. Fremington Quay came about because of the difficulties in navigating the Taw Estuary up to Barnstaple, and some of the earliest imports included limestone and coal, both from South Wales, burned in lime-kilns at Barnstaple leased by William Thorne. Later imports, from April 1852, included iron rails for constructing the North Devon Railway between Crediton and Barnstaple, and one of the last stages in the construction was the conversion to broad gauge of the existing narrow gauge tracks between Umberleigh and Fremington. For the first seven years, there were no passenger services at Fremington, and passenger trains did not run until the opening of the Bideford Extension Railway in 1855.

Fremington Quay was constructed on the south bank of the Taw Estuary just to the east of the mouth of Fremington Pill. Fremington Pill was navigable for about a mile up to Muddlebridge, and, for many years, sailing ships came right up here to collect cargoes of clay and pottery. When the Bideford Extension Railway was built, the Pill was crossed by a wooden viaduct, with an opening span for vessels. A description of the viaduct by Lt. Col. Yolland in 1855 is given in Chapter Three and, as we see in Chapter Four, the LSWR replaced this with a conventional iron girder bridge in 1880, thus closing the Pill to all but the smallest of craft.

Passenger services at Fremington commenced in 1855 with the opening

BRITISH TRANSPORT COMMISSION

THE RAILWAY EXECUTIVE

FREMINGTON QUAY

REGULATIONS RELATING TO STEMMING, LOADING AND DISCHARGING OF VESSELS

1. This Quay is the property of the British Transport Commission and permission to use it will only be granted by the Railway Executive upon condition that vessels belonging to the Commission or conveying cargo for despatch by railway shall have precedence in the Order of loading or discharge over all other vessels.

2. Subject to Regulation 1, and as is hereinafter provided, vessels which may be permitted to use this Quay will be loaded or discharged in the order of their arrival, but a steam vessel shall have precedence over a sailing vessel, notwithstandng that the sailing vessel may have arrived first at the Quay or her loading or discharge may have commenced. In any such case, the Master shall promptly remove the sailing vessel from the Quay, so that the steam vessel can be berthed thereat.

3. Subject to Regulation 2, in the case of two or more vessels arriving at the Fairway Buoy, the first to arrive at such Buoy may claim the stem for berthing and labour at the Quay. In the case of two or more vessels coming from Bideford, the first to arrive at the Pool at Appledore may claim the stem provided such vessel has arrived at the Pool before any vessel arrives at the Fairway Buoy.

4. The Railway Executive reserve the right to vary the order of precedence for the loading or discharge of any vessel in any case in which they deem it reasonable so to do, and they will not in any circumstances accept liability for any breach of the order of precedence whether in accordance with these Regulations or otherwise.

Printed in England by Joseph Wones Ltd., West Bromwich ; also Birmingham and London.

of the Bideford Extension Railway. In a Board of Trade accident report in 1869 (following a collision) Lt. Col. Hutchinson described the station: *Fremington being used as a passing place, it is provided with a loop, and also has extensive sidings, connected with coal wharves on the Taw. There are low standard signals at the points at each end of the crossing loop which serve as the ordinary station signals, and also distant signals in both directions.*

At this stage, Fremington had only one platform, on the 'down' side, but later the LSWR built an 'up' platform.

Top. Fremington signal box, in February 1956, in its lofty position on the up side of the station. Site restriction often necessitated this type of building and here the platforms were of a particularly narrow construction. The decision to build it here resulted in a unique (in the widely accepted Signalling Study Group's classification) 'Type 1' box on a tall brick base with an 'over sailing' structure on top. Windows on all sides gave the signalman a 180 degree view, necessary with the quay siding behind. The various unloading cranes and Taw estuary can be seen in the background. The passing loop was taken out in 1968; the box subsequently closed and two ground frames provided instead. R.M. Casserley.

Middle. A tactical discussion is ensuing whilst the Grafton Steam crane dispatches another grab of clay onto a modern motor vessel.

Bottom. Two vessels moored at the quay after the railway closure.

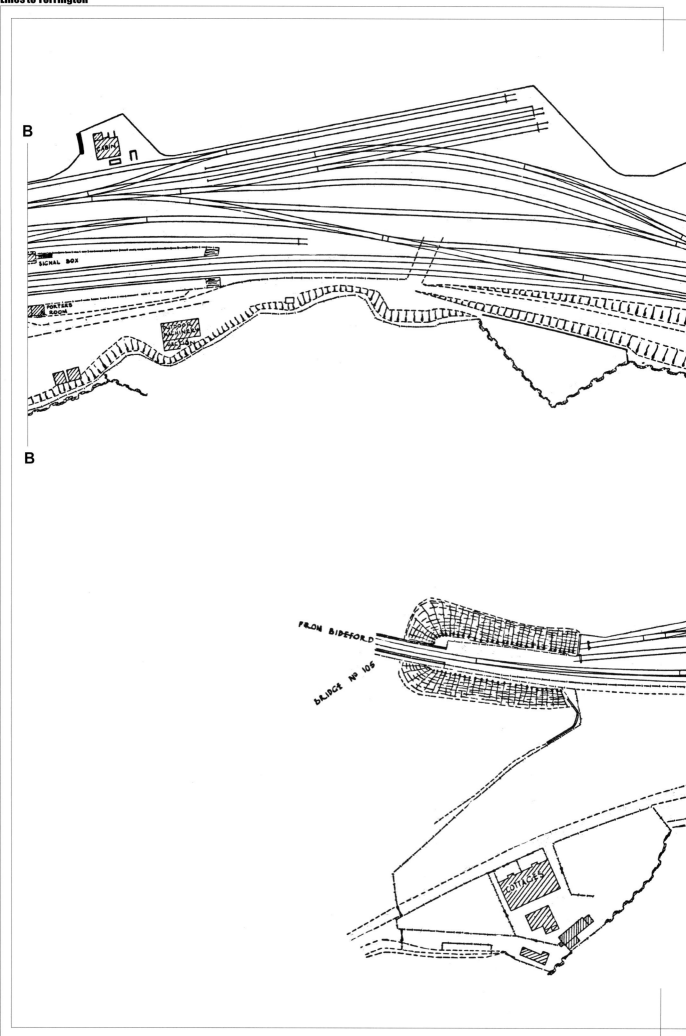

B

B

SIGNAL BOX

PORTERS ROOM

STODDY MACHINERY DEPOT

FROM BIDEFORD

BRIDGE Nº 105

COTTAGES

CABIN

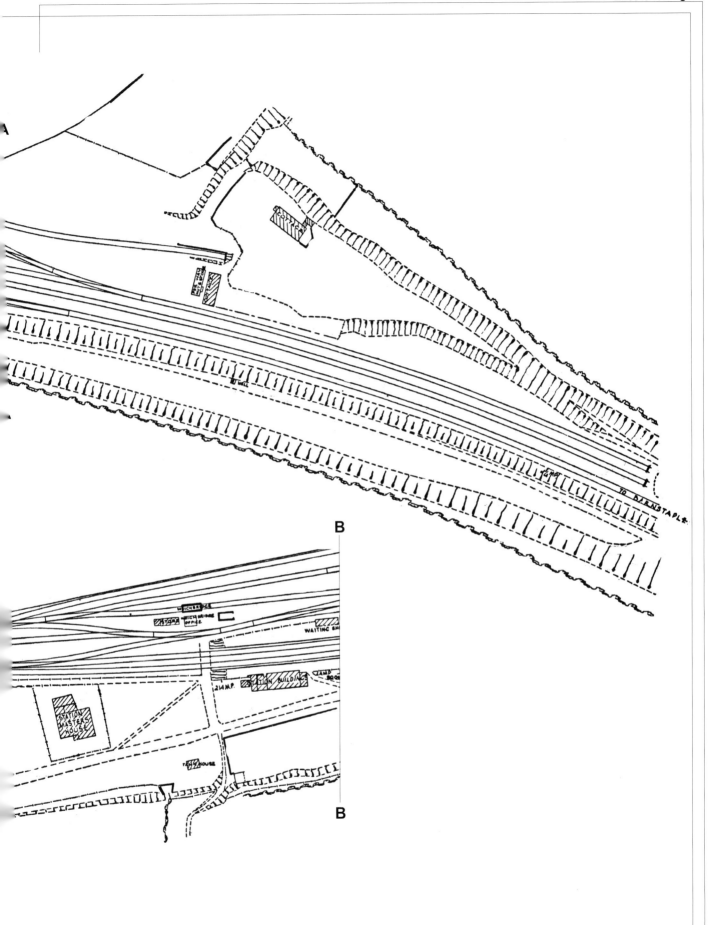

FREMINGTON c1955

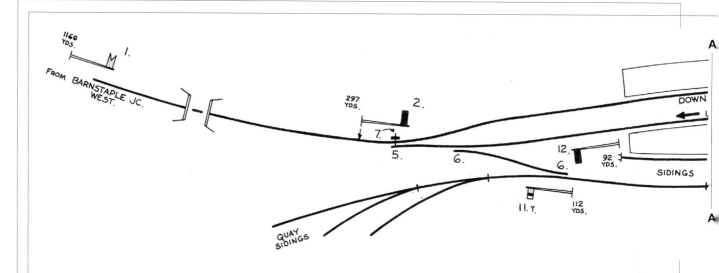

Most of the station buildings were non-descript wooden structures, painted in the standard LSWR or Southern Railway livery, the exception being the signal box which was a wooden cabin perched high up on a brick column in the centre of the 'up' platform. With windows on all four sides, the signalman had an excellent view of the running lines and quay sidings. The signalling on the running lines was simple enough with distants, homes and starters in both directions though there were a couple of unusual shunting signals in the yard, with yellow arms to control movements from the yard to the main line. These were operated by levers Nos.4 and 11 in the fourteen lever frame. Tyer's No.3 electric train tablet instruments were in use on both the single line sections from Fremington to Barnstaple and to

Top. The SS Mari Eli departs from Fremington Quay with a load of clay. In 1934 she took load of 1,300 tons to Spain, the largest shipment ever from Fremington Quay.

Above. The station and dock in June 1965, the three cranes and a small ship in one of the berths. Here railway wagons were loaded with coal for both locomotives and domestic hearths and sand dredged from the estuary, and clay from Marland and Meeth was exported by ship. The peak for Fremington was in the 1940s when nearly 100,000 tons of coal was taken off ships. A.E. West, courtesy Mike King.

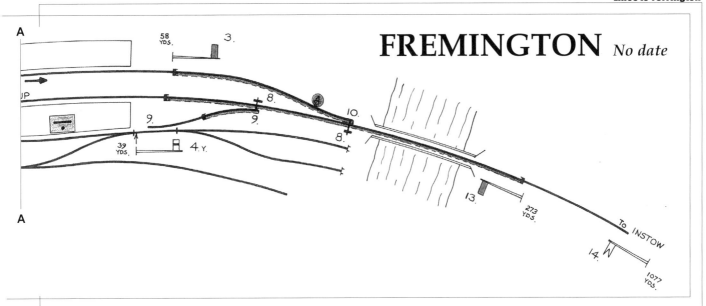

FREMINGTON *No date*

58 YDS.   3.

8.

9.   9.

10.

8.

39 YDS.   4. Y.

UP

A

A

13.   273 YDS.

To INSTOW

14. W   1077 YDS.

SOUTHERN RAILWAY

Signal
Instruction
No. 26, 1925.

Instructions to all concerned as to

NEW AND ALTERED SIGNALS, Etc.

FREMINGTON.

To be brought into use on Wednesday, 12th August.

A down starting signal erected close to, and 12 feet higher than, the existing signal, which will be removed.

A post carrying a ringed arm, erected on the right-hand side of the points from the up siding to down loop, to be known as the up siding to down loop starting signal, and apply to trains leaving the up sidings for Instow.

The down advanced starting signal will be removed.

The work will be in progress from 8.30 a.m. Mr. Breach to provide flagman, as required.

(R. 7438).

An unfortunate accident with one of the steam cranes.

The various screens and chutes for the coal, the inevitable gloomy office and (left) unloading a clay wagon in 1965; an indication of the hard, messy labour involved.

Station Master and Quay Superintendent Harold Mock.

The 'oversailing' Fremington signal box in 1963. Activity on the quayside in the mid 1930s (below) went on apace with the Grafton steam cranes seldom idle. Apart from coal there was limestone and culm from South Wales in great quantity. Culm is a form of coal whilst the lime was heated in local lime-kilns and used in agriculture. Imports of gravel, mixed with Fremington clay was used in the pottery industry and seed potatoes arrived from Ireland. Granite came from Lundy Island and was dressed in a small works by the quay and lead ore from the Mendips, via the Port of Bristol was used in the manufacture of pottery. Petersmarland ball clay, won from the pits near Torrington, was shipped out in bulk.

Instow, but were later replaced with electric key token apparatus. There were the usual huts and cabins, and a wagon weighbridge of 35 tons capacity in the yard, but no goods shed or cattle loading dock. The crossing loop was long enough to take a locomotive and twenty four wagons, and the stationmasters house lay between the 'down' platform and Fremington Pill. The house was demolished in the early 1950s, and the site later occupied by a large abattoir.

The station at Fremington was not well situated for the village, being three quarters of a mile away on the other side of the Pill. The shortest route for pedestrians was by way of a footbridge incorporated in the LSWR girder bridge across the Pill, but road access was via Muddlebridge, a two mile journey between the village and the station. Indeed by road from Fremington, it was almost as easy to travel to Barnstaple Junction and, in consequence, the passenger traffic at Fremington station was rather sparse. The bus service, established as long ago as 1924, ran on the main A39 road and was more convenient. As early as 1930, the number of tickets issued at Fremington station was under ten a day, with about the same number collected. In LSWR and Southern

Right. **The single line token apparatus. A.E. West, courtesy Mike King.**

Below. **Fremington's main station building on the down side of the line in September 1963. A small ticket office and waiting rooms were all accommodated inside this wooden building whilst the gents was in the small building at the end. Shipping navigation light can be seen beyond the station buildings. John Eyers, courtesy South Western Circle.**

Two railway cottages occupied at various times by the signalmen, gangers and quayside workers. John Eyers, courtesy South Western Circle.

A quiet moment at the station in September 1963. The water tank in the background was for station and quay use as there were no water columns on the platforms. John Eyers, courtesy South Western Circle.

Two views of the iron bridge over Fremington Pill in 1956 and 1980. In the top photograph two of the six ton Grafton steam cranes are idle awaiting their next task; below, a family enjoy a picnic and the fresh autumn wind beside the Taw River estuary. John Eyers, courtesy South Western Circle and John Nicholas.

A last look at Fremington station in 1969 with the loop removed and general dereliction everywhere including the smashed windows of the signal box. Passenger services were withdrawn in 1965 and the loop removed in 1968. John Eyers, courtesy South Western Circle.

Railway days, the principal expresses to and from Waterloo had no advertised stops at Fremington; its main business remained the transhipment of freight between ships and wagons.

The two principal commodities handled at Fremington Quay were clay and coal, the latter for the LSWR's own use too. In the summer of 1909 for instance, a train of empties left Exeter (Queen Street) in the morning to take on locomotive coal 'when required'. During the Southern Railway period the quay facilities at Bideford (Goods) at Cross Parks were taken out of use and the maritime traffic concentrated at Fremington Quay. Between 1928 and 1936, the amount of coal imported rose from 16,015 tons to 28,602 tons per annum. The peak year for imports was 1942 when 354 vessels used the port discharging 93,893 tons of goods, made up of coal (88,205 tons), fertiliser (1,936 tons), gravel (932 tons) and 2,820 tons of potatoes. Under these wartime conditions there were no exports and, after the war, the imports of coal were about 50,000 tons per annum. At this stage, the tiny quay at Fremington boasted the largest turnover in shipping tonnage between Land's End and Bristol, and the second largest in Devon, after Plymouth. Later, this distinction passed to East Yelland jetty where large quantities of coal were brought in by sea for the power station.

The major export from Fremington Quay was clay, mined at Marland and Meeth, and brought in by train. Before the war, the peak year was 1929 when more than 20,000 tons were exported, but it was usually less than this. During World War Two exports ceased but resumed after the end of hostilities; in the final year of operation of the Quay in 1969, some 14,264 tons of clay were sent to Rotterdam, Bayonne, Calais, Gravelines, Amsterdam, Antwerp, La Spezia, Ghent and Cork. The ships involved in the trade were fairly small, carrying only a few hundred tons.

Including locomotive coal for Exeter, Fremington forwarded some twenty wagons of the stuff a day to various inland destinations, and received an average of about twenty wagons a week of clay for export. The daily freight trains spent some time at Fremington delivering and collecting wagons and, when required, Barnstaple supplied a shunting engine for the yard. There was no supply of water for the engines at Fremington so these shunting trips were limited to a couple of hours or so, after which the locomotives returned to Barnstaple for replenishment.

The small ships came over Bideford Bar into Fremington on a high tide, mooring at one of the two berths which were separated by a short pier and cabin. The former stationmaster and Quay Superintendent, Mr Harold Mock, describes the operation of the Quay in later years: *Staffing levels at Fremington had been run down over the* *years in an attempt to reduce expenditure and improve productivity, and was reduced to two dock crane drivers, a leading dock porter, three dock porters and a rail man who manned the 35 ton truck weighbridge, did the number taking, assisting with shunting and similar duties. When there was no shipping traffic the crane drivers and dock porters were gainfully employed elsewhere and sometimes would travel as far as Watchet or Dunball to assist on cargoes there. There were three 6 ton Grafton steam-cranes with swan necks at Fremington. The cranes had to be steamed up before work could start and, with a cold boiler, this would take two hours, and on following days 1½ hours. The best Welsh steam coal was use; there was no forced draught or steam blower, so it was essential to have good coal to maintain 100lb. pressure, and the performance of these cranes was such that in an eight hour day it was not uncommon for a 650 ton cargo of domestic coal to be completed, and this would also involve a screening process which separated the small coal from the large. Whilst this was in operation, the whole area of the station would be literally enveloped in dust and the staff would go home from work with blackened faces.*

Over the years there were various cranes in use at Fremington, as illustrated in period photographs. In August 1898 the LSWR decided to transfer a steam travelling crane from Nine Elms. About 1900 Grafton Cranes Ltd. supplied two of their 6 ton steam

cranes to Fremington Quay, and a third was later added. The cranes normally worked on a crane road, close to the harbour wall. In 1966 the Barnstaple Area Manager re-issued instructions for the tow roping of vehicles by steam cranes at Fremington. Steam cranes could tow one or two wagons on an adjacent track, starting very gently and slowly. Since this was a repeated instruction it would appear that steam cranes had been towing wagons for some years previously.

Although Fremington station had no facilities for livestock, in both 1937 and 1938 it received from the Alexandra Docks, London, two full trains of horseboxes. These carried polo ponies, imported from Argentina for Mr George Cooper who leased the Manor House at Fremington. Mr Cooper trained the ponies on a field which was used in the last century for international polo matches.

When the passenger services at Fremington were withdrawn in 1965,

the railwaymen working at the station were Mr Harold Mock, Quay Superintendent, the two signalmen, W. Hill and D. Barrable, one porter, T. Rockhey, and the seven men previously mentioned who worked on the Quay. Mr Mock had joined the Southern Railway as a temporary junior clerk at Fremington in 1936 and, after holding posts at Bideford, Braunton, Ilfracombe, Torrington and Exeter Central, returned to Fremington where he became stationmaster in 1953. In

Above and top. The tidal creek at Fremington Pill in 1963. Before the iron bridge there had been a wooden viaduct with a central lifting span for small vessels to reach Muddlebridge. This was dispensed with when the new iron bridge was erected as a replacement in 1880. John Eyers, courtesy South Western Circle.

1964, he was made responsible for Instow and Bideford as well, reporting also to the newly appointed Area Manager at Barnstaple for the sidings at East Yelland and the operation of Fremington Quay.

After withdrawal of passenger services in 1965, there were no major changes at Fremington until 1968, when the signalling and 'down' loop were taken out of use. After the Quay was put out of use in 1969 the sidings were retained, giving access to the weighbridge, which served for checking the loads of clay wagons from Marland and Meeth for another ten years. The approach road from Muddlebridge along the east bank of Fremington Pill was then used by traffic to the abattoir. On leaving Fremington station, the line runs almost straight in a direction just south of west for a couple of miles through the marshes of the Taw estuary, with the 'up' home signal positioned at the far end of the viaduct over the Pill. The line passed under a bridge, since demolished, and through a cutting, past the Fremington 'up' distant signal and then along a slight embankment for most of the way.

East Yelland Power Station crossing in 1981. John Nicholas.

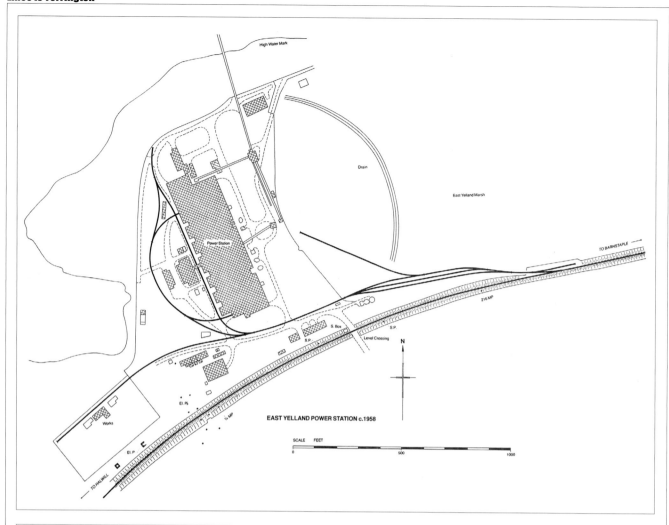

EAST YELLAND POWER STATION c.1958

SCALE FEET

Locomotives of East Yelland Power-Station

Construction — Taylor Woodrow and Co.

No.	Wheel arrangement	Builder	In use	Remarks
Standard Gauge				
SL2	0-4-0T	LSWR	1949-1952	Works No. 101

Central Electricity Generating Board

No.	Wheel arrangement	Builder	In use	Remarks
Standard Gauge				
	0-6-0DM	Andrew Barclay	1958-1968	Works No. 422
3	4 Wheel DM	Motor Rail	1970-1974	Works No. 3966

Information kindly supplied by Roger Hateley and the Industrial Railway Society.

Along this stretch of line was a modern distraction, the aircraft and helicopters of Chivenor RAF station, a mile or so away on the opposite bank of the estuary. The airfield was built shortly before World War Two, providing extra business for the Ilfracombe branch. Towards the end of this straight stretch of line, the 'down' distant signal for the post-war East Yelland crossing was passed, followed by the ground frame and points for East Yelland Sidings serving the power station.

East Yelland

After the Second World War the Central Electricity Generating Board built a new coal-fired power station at East Yelland, between the railway and the sea. The CEGB placed the contract for the power station with Taylor Woodrow & Co. and other firms in the late 1940s, and it started to supply power to the national grid in 1953. East Yelland was a 180mW station, employing 175 staff in 1979. Eleven boilers and six turbines were installed between 1952 and 1957. East Yelland had been built to receive

seaborne fuel from the South Wales mines via Barry, Newport and Swansea, and no facilities were provided for the discharge of coal from railway wagons. The sidings were there so that heavy pieces of plant, including boiler drums and transformers, could be delivered by rail direct from the manufacturers. During construction Taylor Woodrow employed an ex-LSWR B4 0-4-0T, No.101, now renumbered SL2. The CEGB had a small diesel for internal shunting within the power station, until it was disposed of in 1974. In the event coal was delivered to the power station by rail, on three occasions. In 1953 the No.1 boiler was ready for commissioning but the cranes on the jetty had not been completed; during a seamen's strike coal was again brought in by rail, and in the early 1970s when there were heavy loadings for a period, coal was brought in simultaneously by both sea and rail to prevent stocks from falling.

East Yelland crossing, which gives road access to the power station, had two manually operated gates which were normally kept shut against rail traffic, and in high winds, often required a second man with a rope in

The short Instow tunnel, only eighty three yards long, was provided to avoid cutting the village in two. This southern portal was designed with a certain ornateness to please local residents at the time. John Eyers, courtesy South Western Circle.

order to control their movement. Leaving East Yelland, the line passed the 'up' stop signal for the crossing, and continued to follow the shoreline round a very gentle curve until heading almost due south past the 'up' distant signal for the crossing. For a mile or so it continued at ground level, or just above, and gave the traveller excellent views of Appledore Pool where the estuaries of the Taw and Torridge converge, and beyond to the white breakers marking Bideford Bar, a hazard to navigation, particularly in the days of sail.

As the line approaches Instow, it passes between a military depot to the left and a row of beach huts on the edge of Instow sands to the right, and then runs a couple of hundred yards inland. The main A39 road from Barnstaple to Bideford, since bypassed, passes over the railway and the line stays in a cutting while passing the Instow 'down' distant signal. It then passes under two more road bridges

and through a short (84 yards) tunnel, constructed as a cutting and then covered in. A few yards outside the southern mouth of the tunnel was the Instow 'down' home signal, which protected not only the station, but also the level crossing. This last stretch of the Bideford Extension Railway had been expensive to build, but there can be no doubt that the character of the seafront at Instow would have been adversely affected had the railway been built along it.

Instow

**Station opened (broad gauge)
2nd November 1855
Standard gauge services began
2nd March 1863
Signal box (217 miles 71 chains from Waterloo) opened 1873-74
Broad gauge taken out of use
30th April 1877
Goods closed 8th December 1962
Passenger services withdrawn
3rd October 1965
Loop taken out of use, signal box**

**reduced to ground frame
3rd November 1968
Signal box closed 17th January 1979
Line closed 7th November 1982**

Instow station was small and the village produced little traffic, yet the Instow signalman was perhaps one of the busiest on the line. This was the middle station between Barnstaple and Torrington and trains leaving these places at about the same time crossed at Instow, nine times daily in the summer of 1909, compared with only three times a day at Bideford. The signalman had to deal with the tokens for the single line sections to Fremington and Bideford, and also with the crossing gates over what became a very busy main road, the A39 between Bideford and Barnstaple. Tyer's No.3 electric train tablet instruments were provided for the Instow to Fremington section, and No.7 instruments for the Instow to Bideford (New) section, in connection with the intermediate

INSTOW 1912

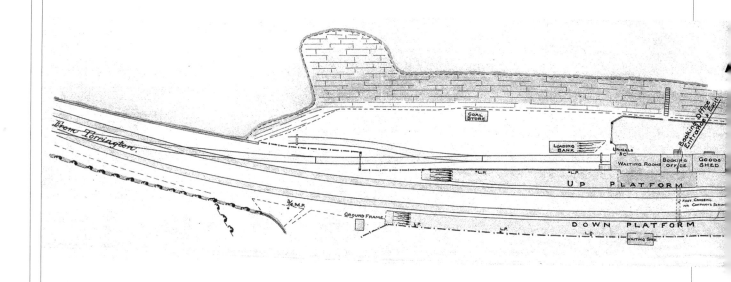

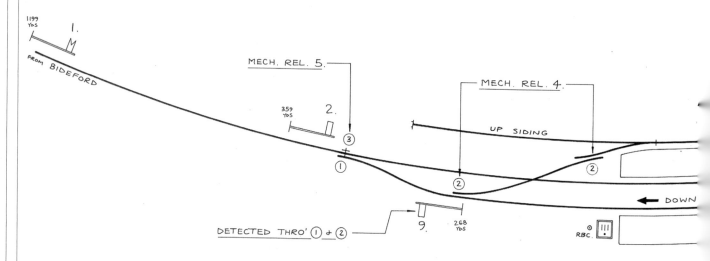

NOTES - GROUND FRAME Nº ①, WHEN PULLED, SO INDICATES
IN SIGNAL BOX BY S.W. PATTERN INDICATOR, AND
TAKES LOCK OFF Nº 9 LEVER.

  4. HALFWAY RELEASES ② AND HOLDS 9 LOCKED.

  4. RIGHT OVER LOCKS ② FOR CROSSING & RELEASES 9

  5. HALFWAY RELEASES ③.

  5. RIGHT OVER LOCKS ① FOR DOWN LOOP & RELEASES 9.

GROUND FRAME
NUMBERS THUS ①

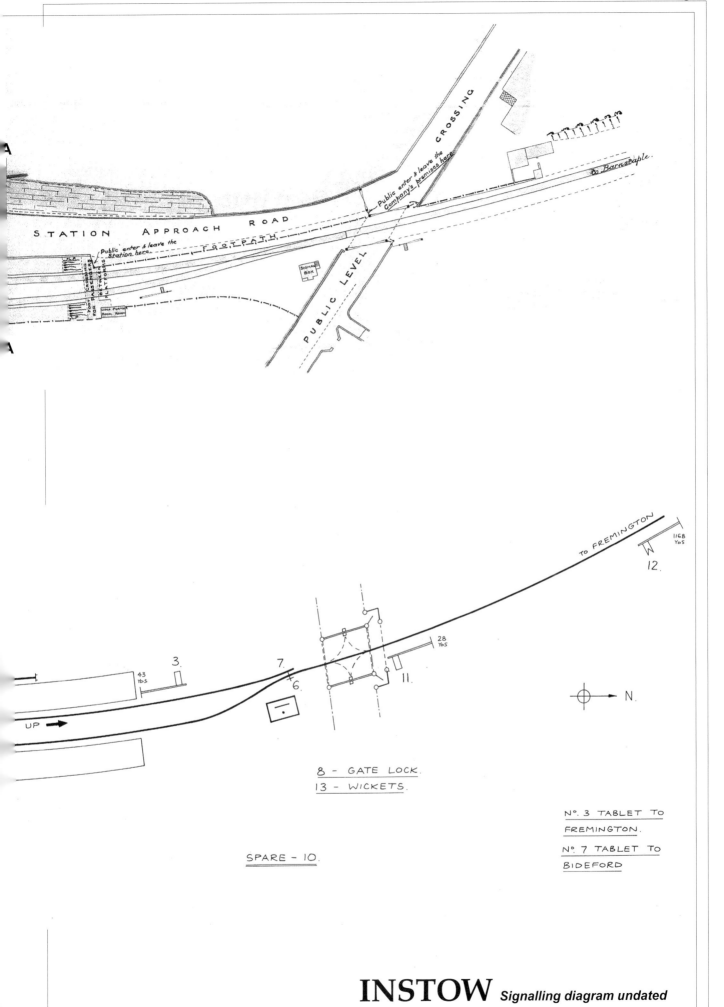

8 - GATE LOCK.
13 - WICKETS.

SPARE - 10.

N°. 3 TABLET TO
FREMINGTON.
N°. 7 TABLET TO
BIDEFORD

INSTOW *Signalling diagram undated*

Above. Instow signal box and crossing in 1963. *Below.* Instow signal box and crossing in October 1978 only three months before closure. Instow was the last box on the line to close and had its gates replaced by flashing lights, activated by an approaching train.

Left. The station from the Barnstaple end, in September 1963. It had opened as long ago as 1855 and was by now only two years away from closure to passengers. The up loop was removed in November 1968 when the signal box was downgraded. Interestingly a ferry for foot passengers operated near here to the small town of Appledore on the west bank of the estuary. John Eyers, courtesy South Western Circle.

Bideford (Goods) station. Later, both were replaced by electric key token instruments. The frame (originally 13 lever, later lengthened to 15 levers) had one lever to lock the crossing gates and another to lock the wicket gates used by pedestrians. Unusually for such a small section, there was a three lever ground frame, interlocked with the signal box, controlling access to the 'up' siding, which was reached from the 'down' road via a diamond crossing over the 'up' road. The crossing loop could accommodate a locomotive and twenty seven wagons. In LSWR days, the 'up' starting signal was located at the end of the 'down' platform, presumably to give a better view for drivers of 'up' goods trains coming round the curve, but this was later relocated more conventionally at the end of the 'up' platform. Instow signal box was the last one on the line to be closed, as late as 17th January 1979, along with its collection of ancient LSWR signals – replaced by automatic flashing lights, activated by approaching trains. As we will see in Chapter 11 the signal box itself has been preserved; one of the oldest structures remaining on the line, it had replaced an earlier gatekeepers lodge erected in 1855.

Left. The standard LSWR signal box, of 'Type 1' style, housed a 13-lever Stevens frame and the gate wheel. The small platform was used by the signalman to exchange tablets, No.3 to Fremington and No.7 to Bideford. The building survives today; beautifully restored, it boasts a Grade II listing.

Below. A quiet moment at Instow station in September 1963. The waiting room and toilet and a small booking office were on the up side. The door behind the hand trolley is in fact a small goods shed used by road vehicles, and in earlier times, a horse and cart. John Eyers, courtesy South Western Circle.

The village of Instow, a community of several hundred people, looks out over the Torridge estuary to Appledore, on the other side. Since the road journey between the two places covers several miles, via Bideford Bridge, there is a ferry between the two. The view from the station platforms was one of the most picturesque in Devon, with added interest whenever there was maritime activity, and the wide spacing between the platforms reflect that this was once a broad gauge line. The simple wooden station buildings on the 'up' platform were reminiscent of those at Fremington, but Instow also boasted a short canopy with an arc roof, from LSWR days. There was no other LSWR design quite like it. In 1912 it was reported that at Instow station 30,000 tickets were issued annually and 75,000 collected; many of these would be visitors to Instow beach.

Top. Instow some years earlier but nevertheless unchanged. A small siding on the up side was more than enough to cope with the limited goods traffic; this was shunted by a down goods train as and when required. Colin Caddy.

Right. A view of the up side looking back towards Fremington. The passing loop extended well past the platforms at the Bideford end of the layout.

A small wooden waiting shelter had been supplied in the early years but by the early 1950s it had become life expired. This concrete replacement was cobbled together at Exmouth Junction works from spare hut sections in 1955. The profile of this unusual canopy on the main building is seen to good effect in this view of 1963, a strange design hailing from earlier times. John Eyers, courtesy South Western Circle.

SR brake van S56284, of the type known colloquially as the 'Queen Mary', at Instow in 1963; they were built on redundant underframes from ex-LBSCR coaches. John Eyers, courtesy South Western Circle.

The bus service between Bideford and Barnstaple introduced in the 1920s greatly reduced the passenger traffic at Instow, with 6,859 tickets issued in 1930. The traffic figures for 1928-36 show that there was no great volume of passenger traffic originating at Instow, with usually only a score or so tickets being sold in a day. However, Instow sands were an attraction for day trips and holidays and, consequently, many more tickets were collected than sold. Indeed, one of the first excursions from Torrington when the line opened in 1872 was run for 170 children on a Sunday school outing to Instow.

The single siding (normally served only by 'down' trains) at Instow sufficed for the limited amount of freight, which in the 1928-36 period averaged about one wagon forwarded, and three or four received, per week. Messrs F.T. Molland & Sons had a coal store at Instow served by the siding, and pit props were loaded in limited

Left. An ancient remnant. The Instow up distant with wooden post and lower quadrant spectacle plates. Peter Swift.

Above and right. Two glorious views over the river from Bideford looking across to Old Bideford station and Quay in July 1965. The yard is full of wagon even at this late time. The huge warehouse on Victoria Wharf to the right is that of the Western Counties Agricultural Cooperative; to the left is a substantial 'provender store' supplied from the Exmouth Junction works. The yard had formally been the site of the broad gauge passenger station of 1855 on the line from Barnstaple, but it was cramped and inconveniently sited for the East-the-Water area let alone for the town itself on the other side of the Torridge River. In 1872 a new station was opened just a half a mile south leaving the site to become Bideford (Goods). John Eyers, courtesy South Western Circle.

quantities. The main produce forwarded was sugar beet. In 1949, record consignments of mussels, packed in containers, were forwarded from Instow to customers in the North East of England.

The identity of the first stationmaster at Instow is not known but by 1874 the post was held by a Mr Ridge, who then moved to Braunton on the newly-opened Ilfracombe line. His post at Instow was then taken by a Mr Bidgood, who was formerly a guard on the North Devon line but in later years the station did not have its own stationmaster. From 1953 to 1964, Mr W.J.O. Hatherell, the stationmaster at Bideford was in charge, followed by Mr H. Mock from Fremington. In the mid-1950s, the station employed four men, two signalmen including H. Frost, and two porters, R. Bettes and R. Harris. On closure in 1965 the signalmen were J. Frost and W. Jenkins and there was one porter, R. Harris. The signal box continued in use for another fourteen

years, the last signalman in 1979 being Mr Arthur Taylor. The station itself was later used by the North Devon Yacht Club.

The passing loop at Instow extended some distance beyond the platforms at the Bideford end of the station. Here were the 'down' starting signal, the 'up' home and finally the 'up' distant. The first two were of conventional LSWR lattice post construction, but the 'up' distant was a real Victorian antiquity, a rare example of an LSWR signal mounted on a wooden post. This was possibly the last working example of its type when taken out of use in 1979. From Instow, the line ran almost due south to Bideford with the Torridge estuary a few yards away on one side, and the main A39 road on the other. There are excellent views across the estuary to Appledore, Northam and Bideford, with shipyards and a variety of vessels. Indeed, the views from the railway are better than those from the main road, which in places are obscured

by the railway embankment. Opposite Northam, at Westleigh, there was once a lime kiln which in broad gauge days boasted its own jetty and siding. As the bridge came into sight upstream, Bideford 'down' distant signal was passed followed by the long headshunt for Bideford Goods station at Cross Parks.

Bideford (Goods) Station

Station opened (broad gauge passenger and goods) 2nd November 1855
Standard gauge services began 2nd March 1863
Passenger services withdrawn 9th June 1872
Signal box (220 miles 6 chains from Waterloo) opened 1872
Broad gauge taken out of use 30th April 1877
Signal box replaced with ground frame circa 1900
Goods closed 6th September 1965
Line closed 7th November 1982

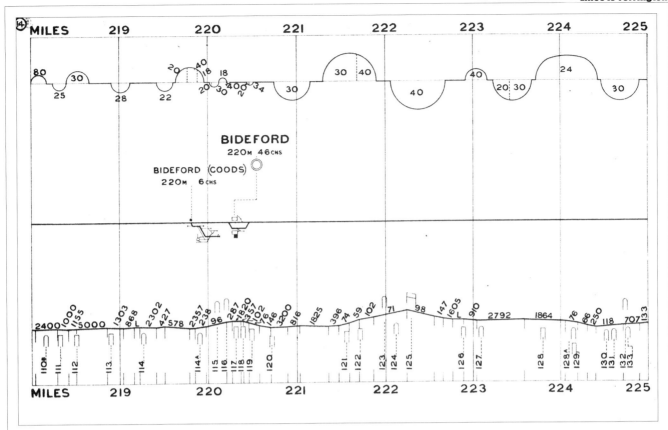

The ancient port of Bideford is the largest town on the line between Barnstaple and Halwill, and indeed had a greater maritime trade than Barnstaple. The station at Bideford served not only the town but also the many other communities situated on the other side of Bideford Bridge. The town had three stations, two on the Barnstaple to Torrington line, at Cross Parks and Bideford (New), and the third on Bideford Quay for the Bideford, Westward Ho! & Appledore Railway.

The station known in the twentieth century as Bideford (Goods) was for seventeen years the terminus of the broad gauge line from Exeter and Barnstaple. Built at Cross Parks, it was inconvenient even for the East-the-Water area of Bideford, let alone the heart of the town across the river, and road access was no better. Contemporary reports tell of a poor and inadequate station, built when

The sweeping approach curve to Bideford Goods. The tracks to the left are the siding and headshunt of the goods depot; in the background is a scrapyard and PW dump. The road to the right is the A39 and just below the wall the main line. John Eyers, courtesy South Western Circle.

money was hard to raise, but the town desperately needed the railway. Because of this, few tears were shed locally when Bideford (New) station replaced Cross Parks for passenger

services in 1872. The old broad gauge station was laid out as a terminus with the necessary facilities, including a turntable, engine shed, water for locomotives and a goods shed. There

was, apparently, one platform, and passenger facilities included a waiting room. The LSWR commenced running narrow gauge trains through to Bideford (Cross Parks) from 2nd March 1863, but passenger services here ended on Sunday 9th June 1872; on the following day Bideford (New) Station was opened. All broad gauge services ended in 1877, and the now redundant third rail was taken out of use. It seems probable that the broad gauge turntable was taken out of use at about this time, and the station was converted into the better known 'Bideford (Goods)'. The nearby Bideford Junction signal box was similar in design to that at Instow. The signalling included a 'down' bracket signal on a wooden post, with separate arms for the routes to Bideford (New) and Bideford (Goods). The LSWR later replaced this box with a ground frame, and took out all the signalling. The new block section was the single line between Instow and Bideford (New), controlled by Tyer's No.7 electric train tablet instruments. This was a rather unusual arrangement which permitted goods trains or shunting engines to enter Bideford (Goods) clear of the running line, enabling other trains to use the single line section. The Bideford (Goods) ground frame had four levers and was released by the single line tablet. Later Bideford (Goods) became an intermediate key token post when the Tyer's instruments were replaced.

The Western Counties Agricultural Cooperative offices and stores to the right is only some six feet above river level. It would have suffered flooding at some time over the years, another good reason to move the station to higher ground. In the far distance is the static yard crane (see next page) and on the right the Provender Stores which would have housed a variety of farm goods, grain and fertiliser.

The fixed 10 ton yard crane in 1955. A.E.West, courtesy Mike King.

Above. The reverse side of the WC&AC offices and stores with the bay windowed office no doubt reserved for the foreman. To the right is a fertiliser van and beside that what looks like a newly erected 'provender store'. The British Transport Commission sign issues a stern warning: 'Drivers of all vehicles are warned to place their vehicles well clear of all sidings.' John Eyers, courtesy South Western Circle.

Below. The ancient goods shed still in place in 1965. There was an office attached to it and to the right were cattle pens and a loading dock. At the far end of the yard were the delivery agents quarters, stores and some stables for the shunting horse, of course now long gone. John Eyers, courtesy South Western Circle.

BIDEFORD GOODS STATION 1959

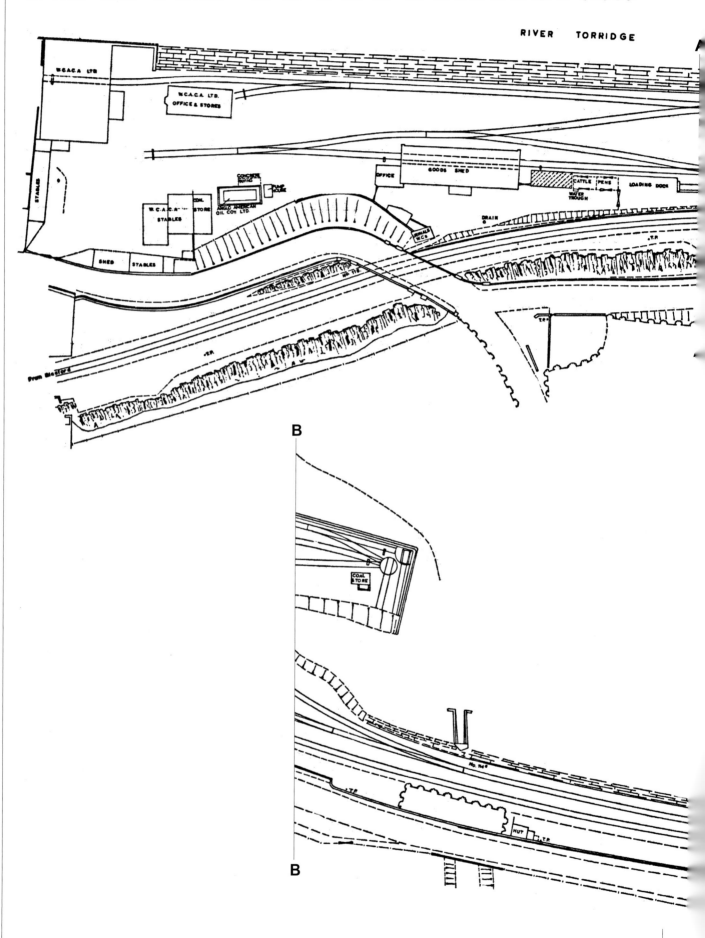

B

B

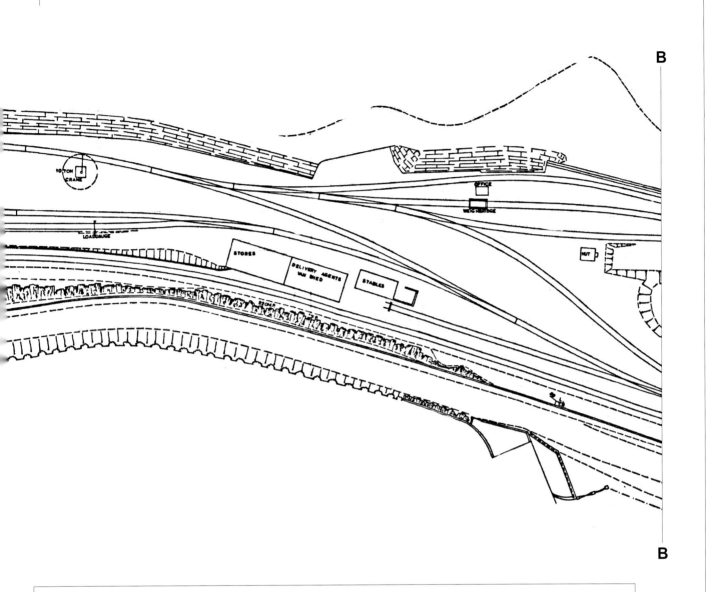

BIDEFORD.

Bideford Goods.—A competent man will be provided by the Station Master at Bideford to attend to the working of the siding.

A train or engine shunted at Bideford Goods may afterwards return to the starting point or proceed forward to the other end of the section, but when a train returns to the starting point the engine must run round the train at Bideford Goods, and draw it on the return journey.

Under no circumstances must the engine propel the train from Bideford Goods to Bideford or Instow.

Tyer's No. 7 intermediate tablet instruments are installed in connection with this siding, and when it is necessary for a train to be shunted clear of the running line in order that other trains may pass through the section, the instructions contained in Regulation 34A of the Electric Train Tablet Regulations must be observed.

RIVER TORRIDGE

C

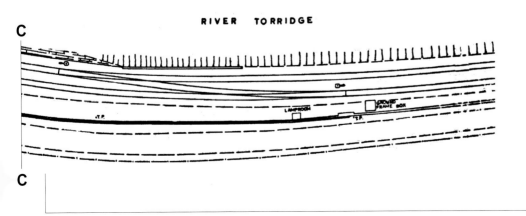

C

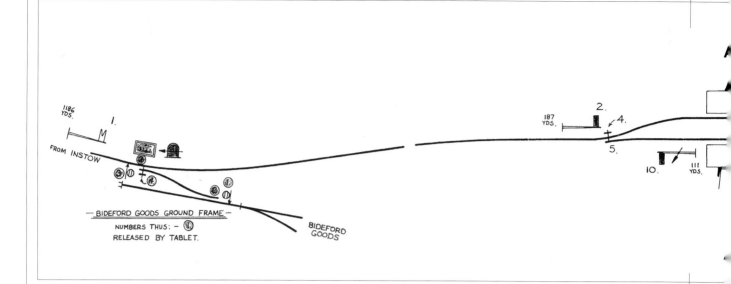

'Bideford Goods' is noted thus in the 1911 LSWR Working Timetable Appendix of 1911: *This goods yard is situate on the Up side of the single line about ½ mile east of Bideford passenger station (between Instow and Bideford), with points in the main line facing for Down trains, which are controlled by the tablet for the Instow and Bideford section.*

A competent man will be provided by the station master at Bideford to attend to the working of the points, which must be carried out in accordance with the regulation for controlling sidings by means of the electric train tablet.

Both Up and Down goods trains stop at this goods yard to do work as necessary, and should a Down goods train be shunted there the tablet must be conveyed to Bideford New by a competent man and handed to the signalman to enable the section to be cleared. In the case of an Up train, when it is shunted for another train to pass, the tablet must be returned to Bideford New in charge of a competent person. In either case it must again be conveyed there when a train requires to leave and the signalman at Bideford New is in a position to allow it to do so.

Telephone communication exists between the signal box at Bideford New and the Bideford goods ground frame, and when a train restarts from Bideford Goods, after having been shunted there, the signalman at Bideford New must be promptly advised.

When the Bideford Extension Railway was built it was intended that it should work in conjunction with the maritime trade of the port, and so the station was sited next to the river where the Cross Parks railway quay was incorporated in the works. Traffic handled at the quay included coal and limestone from South Wales, some of which was transhipped into railway wagons and forwarded to Torrington. Other traffic included clay from Marland and Meeth which was brought in by rail and loaded into small ships here until the closure of the quay during the Southern Railway period,

Above. The line swings into Bideford new station having climbed steeply through a cutting and around a 5 chain curve before the station loop was reached. *Below.* Looking back to Bridge No.117 (numbered from Coleford Junction); the line had crossed the Alverdiscott Road on Bridge No.118, plate girdered with stone abutments. John Eyers, courtesy South Western Circle.

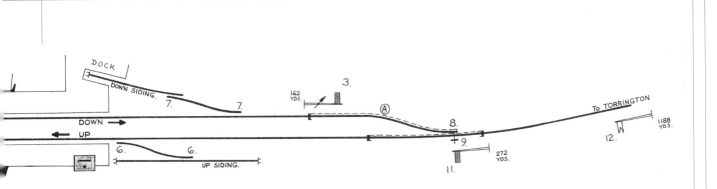

BIDEFORD *Signalling diagram undated*

As the text describes, the Torrington Extension Railway was expensive to build as it ran literally through the gardens which finally backed onto the railway on Barnstaple Road. The large building on the left is the Royal Hotel which took advantage of its close proximity to the line by building an entrance, from its second floor, to the up platform. To the right of the Royal Hotel is the former Station Masters house. John Eyers, courtesy South Western Circle.

whereupon the work passed up the line to Fremington.

In the 1920s there were no cranes for loading or unloading ships berthed at the quay, so ships derricks would have been employed for unloading timber or coal. Wooden chutes could have been used for clay shovelled out of wagons down into a ship's hold. There were cranes on Bideford Quay on the other side of the Torridge, but this had no main line railway connection. Incidentally from here there was a good view of operations at Bideford Goods, where the long head shunt was used for 'fly shunting' wagons into sidings, with a clatter of buffers that could be heard across the river.

From the start Bideford Goods handled all the needs of the town and surrounding area, from general merchandise to fertiliser, livestock and meat, though coal normally came into Bideford by sea until the closure of the Cross Parks railway quay, and only then did the coal come by rail, mainly from Fremington Quay. The LSWR had modified the track layout at Bideford Goods in 1922 and, in Southern days, the facilities were extensive. In the yard was a crane of 7½ tons capacity, and in the goods shed another of 1½ tons capacity. There was a wagon weighbridge 14ft. in length of 17 tons capacity, and there were two wagon turntables on the quay sidings of 13ft. 3in. diameter. There was also a water column, for locomotives often spent some time here shunting the yard. The Southern Railway's 1928-36 traffic returns show Bideford to be a very

Train Summer 1932	Bideford (Goods)	
	Arrive	Depart
2.10 a.m. freight and mail Exeter-Torrington	5.47 a.m.	6.10 a.m.
Engine from Torrington	6.19 a.m.	9.18 a.m.
10.10 p.m. freight Nine Elms-Torrington	10.11 a.m.	10.49 a.m
Engine from Barnstaple	11.15 a.m.	see footnote
12.45 p.m. freight from Torrington to Nine Elms	1.10 p.m.	1.53 p.m.
4.53 p.m. freight Torrington-Salisbury	5.00 p.m.	5.35 p.m.
Footnote: **It would appear that this locomotive worked back to Fremington or Barnstaple double-heading the 1.53 p.m. departure.**		

busy goods station, forwarding an average of about twelve loaded wagons and receiving about thirty a day. General merchandise, minerals, meat and fish were all represented and a good flow of coal was now coming in by rail. The two daily freight trains each way and the shunting engines were kept busy with this substantial traffic.

In British Railways days there was still a considerable business in general merchandise, some collected and delivered by the four railway lorries and some by private carriers, including Mr Walter Redclift of Hartland and Mr Roy Short of Clovelly. A major item of freight was steel plate for Appledore Shipyard; arriving by rail, the plate was delivered to the customer by railway lorry. Occasionally, the railwaymen in the yard unloaded the steel plate in a rather unorthodox way by parking the road trailer alongside the wagon,

attaching a clip and steel wire to the steel plate and pulling it on to the trailer. In the 1950s there was a 4.15 p.m. freight train from Bideford Goods to Nine Elms, in addition to the Torrington services, the M7 locomotive working to Barnstaple where the train was taken over by a Pacific.

Fertiliser was important, for the firms of Fulford Trumps and North Devon Farmers; delivered by rail, it was stored and collected from the yard by the firms' own lorries. At one stage, hundreds of tons of fertiliser in polythene bags were stored in the yard under straw and tarpaulins. Eventually, this large stack became infested with rats which caused considerable difficulties for the men working there, despite the presence of the goods yard cat.

The Devon Trading Company and the Western Counties Agricultural Association had their own private siding at the end of one of the yard sidings, the boundary being marked with a

Looking towards the station and Torrington in June 1965 with the grand entrance to the Royal Hotel on the right and the elevated Springfield Terrace on the left. John Eyers, courtesy South Western Circle.

gate. Wagons were delivered and collected by the shunting engine which was not allowed past the gate. The Devon Trading Company employed its own men but latterly, the Western Counties Agricultural Association and Silcocks, who both dealt in animal feedstuffs, arranged for all the work in the yard, and the deliveries to the farms, to be performed by the railwaymen and railway lorries. In British Railways days, the traffic in livestock had virtually disappeared.

In the mid-1950s there were about a dozen men employed at Bideford Goods under the foreman, J. Easterbrook, and the goods office chief clerk, R. Jones. These included four clerks, three lorry drivers, two checkers and two porters. At one stage, the principal local employer, Appledore Shipyard, closed for a time and a number of men who were thrown out of work were employed at Bideford Goods. One morning the staff arrived at their cabin alongside the river to be greeted by the sight of a wartime mine, that had been brought up the estuary on the previous night's high tide. There was a speedy evacuation, but it was subsequently found that the mine was harmless. When Bideford Goods closed in 1965, there were ten men employed, several of whom, together with the delivery lorries, were transferred to Barnstaple.

After closure the tracks were removed but the site was left derelict for some sixteen years before redevelopment began in 1981 when Ethelwynne Brown Close was constructed. It seems rather strange that this valuable site, convenient for the town and with an incomparable situation on the bank of the picturesque Torridge Estuary, should have been left to the weeds for so long.

Once past the ground frame at the junction for Bideford Goods, the main line curved away from the Torridge and climbed up a short stretch on a gradient of 1 in 88 past a stone retaining wall, and passed under the main Barnstaple to Bideford A39 road, through a cutting, and under a minor bridge, past

Three views of Bideford new station in June 1965. *Top.* **The up side showing the extended canopies on both sides; built at different periods they are nevertheless thought to both date from before the Grouping.** *Middle.* **The main buildings were on the down side but the building on the up side was of a substantial construction, in stone. There was a waiting room and toilets and covered steps down to Barnstaple Street.** *Bottom.* **Bideford was the principal station on the line, 220 miles from Waterloo and the railhead for a large area including Appledore, Northam, Westward Ho!, Clovelly and Hartland. John Eyers, courtesy South Western Circle.**

Bideford signal box in 1965. Another 'Type 1' it opened with the station in 1872 and had a 12 lever Stevens frame. The up distant signal was some 1186 yards from the box, near the entrance to Bideford Goods station, which needed a tablet from the Bideford signalman to unlock the Ground Frame as and when required.

the Bideford 'down' home signal and into Bideford (New) station. 'Down' trains were required to whistle continuously for 260 yards to warn pedestrians using the Bideford foot crossing. This short section of line from Cross Parks was built as part of the LSWR Torrington Extension Railway and opened to Bideford (New) station on the narrow gauge on 10th June 1872.

Bideford (New) Station
Station and signal box (220 miles 45 chains from Waterloo) line opened from Barnstaple 10th June 1872
Line opened to Torrington 18th July 1872
Passenger services withdrawn 3rd October 1965
Loop taken out of use, signal box closed 26th February 1967
Line closed 7th November 1982

When Lt. Col. Yolland from the Board of Trade first came to inspect the Torrington Extension Railway, the works were incomplete but he was able to sanction the opening of the line to Bideford (New) station which, for some six weeks, was the terminus for passenger services on the North Devon line. There were only two very short sidings for the odd van or horsebox, the one on the 'down' side terminating in an end loading dock, so it would appear that during this six week period, the turntable and sidings at Bideford (Goods) would have been used for stabling empty stock and locomotive requirements. Bideford New became a through station when the line was opened to Torrington on 18th July 1872.

Bideford New station, some 220 miles from Waterloo, was the principal passenger station on the line and although in some years the number of tickets sold at Torrington slightly exceeded the Bideford total, those collected at Bideford were usually double the number at Torrington. Bideford New was the railhead not only for the town, but also a large area on the other side of Bideford Bridge including Appledore, Northam, Westward Ho!, Clovelly and Hartland. Although the railway was on the wrong side of the river for most of Bideford, the station was situated right at the end of the bridge, which minimised the inconvenience. In Edwardian days, there was a motor bus

Bideford in July 1956 with its original wooden name board; in the view above it has been replaced by a BR metal example. On the down side the steps to Springfield Terrace can just be discerned under the canopy. **John Eyers, courtesy South Western Circle.**

In days gone by the yard would ring to the clatter of carriage wheels on the cobbled court yard. Things have changed dramatically by July 1956 with a solitary motor taxi parked ready for its next customer. John Eyers, courtesy South Western Circle.

service between the station and Westward Ho!, with the Bideford, Westward Ho! & Appledore Railway running a connecting bus service between their terminus on the quay and the LSWR station complete with through bookings. The LSWR public timetable of 1914 advertised a service of horse brakes and coaches between the station and Clovelly in connection with the principal trains. Later, the Clovelly service was operated by a motor bus run by Mr Braund of Clovelly, which unloaded its passengers at the foot of the steps leading to the 'up' platform. In later years, the Southern National buses operated from the quay on the other side of the river but continued to call at the station. In British Railways days, special buses ran between the station and Westward Ho! to take holiday makers to the resort.

The main station buildings on the 'down' platform were built in the same local stone and to a similar attractive design to those at Torrington. Whereas

the stationmasters house at Torrington was part of the same structure, at Bideford, there was a separate house near the line a few yards away from the end of the 'up' platform. Adjoining the station buildings on the 'down' side was a spacious cab yard and station approach, and there was often a full complement of horse drawn vehicles assembled here waiting for the arrival of an express from Waterloo. The station buildings on the 'up' side were more restricted in size and were approached from the road below by steps. Early photographs show a small awning on each platform painted in the LSWR striped pattern but, later, the LSWR provided a much larger awning on both sides which covered the steps to the 'up' platform. A W.H.Smith bookstall was incorporated in the new works on this platform. Between 1915 and his retirement in 1946 the bookstall was managed by Mr Frederick Steele, who had worked for W.H.Smith & Sons for a total of 53 years.

The Torrington Extension Railway had been expensive to build, and part of the reason for this was the difficulty in pushing the line through the narrow strip of Bideford East-the-Water, between the hill and the estuary. Quite literally, the line was built through the back gardens of a number of properties in Barnstaple Street, and access to Springfield Terrace, up above the 'down' platform, was by means of steps from the street below up to the cab yard, over the street on the railway bridge at the back of the platform, and up a further flight of steps to the houses. The Royal Hotel, on the corner of Barnstaple Street, turned the proximity of the station to its advantage and built an entrance into its second floor from the 'up' platform. In LSWR days, it boasted a large refreshment room notice, making Bideford the only station on the line with bookstall and refreshment facilities.

The signal box was at the Torrington end of the 'up' platform, and was a typical LSWR weatherboarded structure on a stone base. The twelve lever frame controlled the points and basic signalling with distant, home and starting signals in each direction. Tyer's No.7 electric train tablet instruments controlled the single line section to Instow while, in LSWR days, No.3 instruments controlled the section to Torrington. These were later replaced by No.6 instruments to permit the return trips from Bideford to Bartlett's Siding. The Tyer's instruments were later replaced by electric key token instruments. This small signal box was busier than might be expected, since there were the operational complications of Bideford (Goods) Bideford (New) and Bartlett's Siding, although, back in LSWR days, a shunting horse had been employed at Bideford New to move vans and horseboxes.

In the British Railways era, passenger traffic initially remained substantial, particularly in the summer and at weekends. The summer 1955 Saturday service, which provided twenty four corridor coaches to and from Waterloo, brought most of its holiday-makers to Bideford station, from where special buses were provided running to Westward Ho! and other resorts. There were also children at the three boarding schools at Bideford, Grenville College, Edgehill College and Stella Maris Convent. At the end of term, lorries collected the luggage from the schools

The station approach and the down side building. The Palace Theatre is showing two new films of 1956. *The Bold and the Brave*, starring Wendell Corey, Don Taylor and Mickey Rooney, who also directed it and Max Bygraves, Dennis Price and Michael Medwin in *Charley Moon*. John Eyers, courtesy South Western Circle.

BIDEFORD (New) *1959*

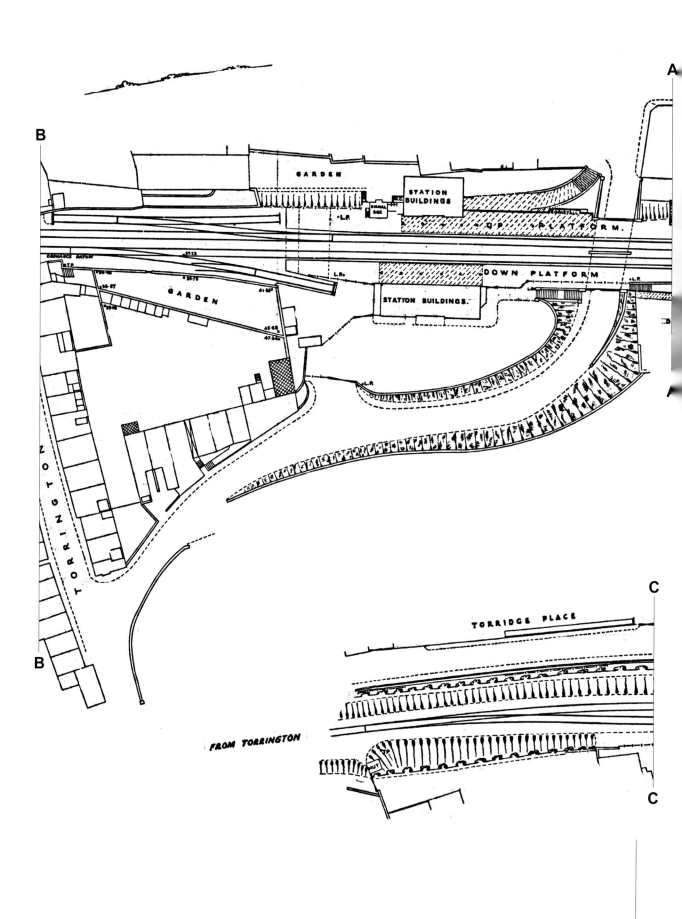

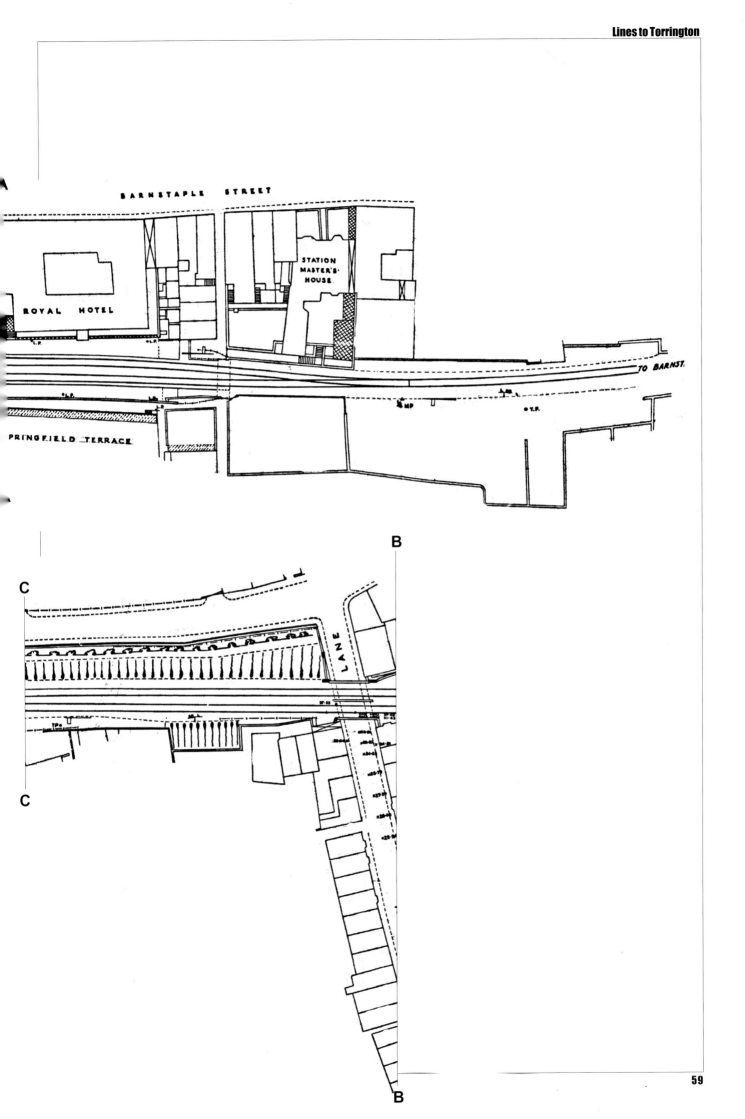

The prospect south to Torrington with the line passing over Bridge No.119 and Torrington Lane. John Eyers, courtesy South Western Circle.

and brought it to the station for loading into vans, which were specially provided for the traffic. Reservations were made for the pupils to travel to Exeter, Waterloo and other destinations, and the whole process was reversed at the start of the term.

Mr W.J.O. Hatherell was stationmaster at Bideford from January 1953 to May 1964 when he retired, and his place was taken by Mr H. Mock, who supervised the station from Fremington. In Mr Hatherell's early days at Bideford, he had twelve men working under him at the passenger station.
Signalmen: F. Bennett and F. Lovell
Parcel Porter: J. Ireland
Relief Porter: L. Hare
Leading Porters: G. Craner and R. Palmer
Porters: H. Steer and one other
Booking Clerks: F. Holwill, H. J. Parkhouse and P. Colwill
Motor driver for parcel deliveries: Mr Bettes.

When the station closed in 1965, Mr Mock was in charge of ten men:
Signalmen: E. Prouse and F. Harvey
Parcels Porters: G. Craner and R. Palmer
Porters: E. Backway, R. Elkin and one other
Booking Clerks: H.J. Parkhouse, P. Colwill and G. Tolley.

Mr Hatherell's railway career had commenced after attending the head offices of the Somerset & Dorset

Railway at Bath (Green Park) station, where he took, and passed, the Company's entrance examination. He started work as a clerk in the goods office at Bridgwater in 1915, and worked subsequently at Blandford, Bridgwater (again), Edington Junction, Ashcott and Glastonbury. He became relief stationmaster, home station Blandford, and then stationmaster at Glastonbury until leaving the Somerset & Dorset line altogether to become stationmaster at Bideford, from where he also supervised Instow station. When he retired in 1964, Mr Hatherell had served on the railway for 49 years.

Most of the staff went after the withdrawal of passenger services in 1965, but the signalling was retained until 1967 when the signal box was closed and only the 'down' road remained. Practically everything else was demolished after closure except the main station buildings on the 'down' platform, which were subsequently taken over by the Midland Bank. Much of the station at Bideford was built on an embankment, and three roads pass under the line in rapid succession with the first bridge, No.117 in the Southern Railway system of numbering structures, supporting both the tracks and the platforms. The long crossing loop, which could accommodate a locomotive and thirty two wagons, then passed over Torridge Lane on bridge No.118, and past the Bideford 'down' starting signal. The two lines then converged and passed over the third

bridge, No.119, over Torridge Place and past the 'up' home signal. Bridge No.119 was rebuilt in 1974 to give 15ft. 3in. headroom for road vehicles underneath, this road being the only suitable access to the commercial area of Bideford East-the-Water. The extra 5ft. or so of headroom was achieved by raising the track, building new concrete abutments and installing a new steel deck. Beyond bridge No.119 the line continued south along the bank of the Torridge with good views over the estuary to the right; on the left were the gasworks and the premises of Messrs Bartletts, a timber firm which, for half a century, had its own private siding.

Kynock's, later Bartlett's Siding
Kynock's Siding was laid in 1915 during the First World War jointly by the Ministry of Munitions and Kynock's munitions company. Traffic during the war must have been heavy because Kynock Ltd. employed an 0-4-0ST, built by Dick Kerr, for shunting, until sold by auction in 1922. Messrs Bartlett Bayliss and Co also had the use of the siding under an agreement of 31st December 1917 with the LSWR. In 1925 the Southern Railway approved the use of the siding by the Devon County Council in connection with its tar macadam depot recently established on Bartlett's property. Southern Railway documents record that as well as Devon County Council, by 1926 the siding also served British Petroleum and Shell Mex.

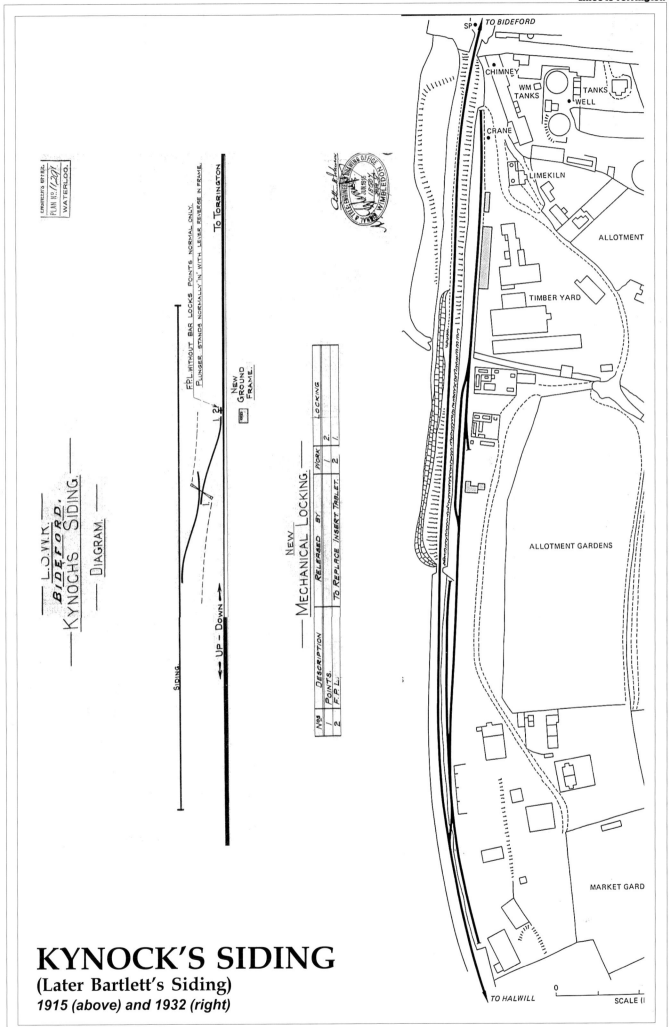

L.S.W.R.
BIDEFORD.
KYNOCH'S SIDING.
— DIAGRAM. —

ENGINEER'S OFFICE.
PLAN NO. 11291.
WATERLOO.

SIDING.

← UP — DOWN →

To Torrington

FPL WITHOUT BAR LOCKS POINTS NORMAL ONLY.
PLUNGER STANDS NORMALLY IN WITH LEVER REVERSE IN FRAME.

NEW GROUND FRAME.

NEW
— MECHANICAL LOCKING. —

Nos	DESCRIPTION	RELEASED BY	WORK		LOCKING	
1	POINTS.		1	2	2	
2	F.P.L	TO REPLACE INSERT TABLET.	2		1	

SP

TO BIDEFORD

CHIMNEY
WM TANKS
TANKS
WELL
CRANE
LIMEKILN
ALLOTMENT
TIMBER YARD
ALLOTMENT GARDENS
MARKET GARD

TO HALWILL

0   SCALE (1

KYNOCK'S SIDING
(Later Bartlett's Siding)
1915 (above) and 1932 (right)

Bartlett's (W. Slee) and Devon County Council siding.—A competent man must be sent from Bideford station to attend to the working of the siding.

The Company's engines must not pass beyond the points situated about 14 yards from the Bideford side of underbridge No. 120 leading to the siding loop.

Vehicles for the siding off a down train should be placed by means of one shunt at a spot near (but not beyond) the loop points in the siding, the responsibility for moving vehicles beyond that spot, for traders other than the Devon County Council, resting with Mr. W. Slee, who will also arrange for outgoing vehicles from the siding, other than Devon County Council wagons, to be placed in the dead end of the siding and such vehicles should be taken thence by the Company's engine by means of one shunt.

Vehicles off up trains for the siding must be left at the Torrington end of the siding whence they will be moved by Mr. W. Slee or the Devon County Council's employees.

A movable crane is in use on the portion of the siding occupied by the Devon County Council which may be used on certain portions of the siding for the purposes of loading, unloading or moving wagons. When this crane is in use on the loop portion of the siding for loading or unloading traffic, its jib is liable to foul the telegraph wires and the running line, and 24 hours notice will be given to the Station Master at Bideford by the staff of the Devon County Council of their intention to so use the crane on this portion of the siding, and the Station Master must, if necessary, post a flagman for the protection of the running line during the time the crane is so used.

The siding must be used for traffic for Mr. W. Slee, Devon County Council, British Petroleum Coy., Shell Mex Coy., Bideford Gas & Coke Coy., and Bideford Electric Supply Company, and no traffic for any other firm or individual should be placed therein, nor must traffic placed on rail by any other firm or individual be accepted from the siding except upon special instructions from the Traffic Manager or Divisional Superintendent.

By 1934 no less than six customers had the use of Bartlett's Siding; Bartletts (Mr W. Slee), Devon County Council, British Petroleum, Shell Mex, Bideford Gas & Coke Company and the Bideford Electric Supply Company. The Devon County Council employed a movable crane on their portion of the siding which, on occasions, was used in such a way as to foul the telegraph wires and running lines, resulting in special regulations for such use.

When the Southern Railway agreed to the use of the siding by the Devon County Council in 1925, it was subject to a special haulage charge of one shilling per loaded wagon. It seems probable that this charge was levied because the siding was served by 'down' goods trains, and all wagons leaving the siding had to circulate via Torrington, an extra distance of some nine miles. However, later on, it was permissible for the Bideford (Goods) shunting engine to clear the siding of outgoing traffic, returning as far as Bideford (New) station propelling the wagons. Access to Bartlett's Siding was by means of points operated by a ground frame released by the Bideford to Torrington electric train tablet, and later it became an intermediate key token post. There were gates across the entrance to the siding, with the keys kept at Bideford signal box.

In later years, Bartlett's Siding was used by three concerns; the gasworks, Bayley Bartletts and Shell Mex. At the buffer stops was a tar wagon which was used to take away tar produced at the gasworks, but there is no evidence that coal was ever delivered by rail to the gasworks. Indeed, the gasworks had been built here before the railway came. Bayley Bartletts, as the timber firm had become, forwarded timber pallets to various destinations, and Shell Mex unloaded petrol tank wagons. Wagons were shunted in and out of the siding by main line locomotives, although after Kynocks had disposed

of its shunting engine, movement of wagons on the siding was by hand, or by a tractor and wire in the timber yard. Revised Southern Railway instructions in 1946 allowed special trip workings between Bideford Goods and Bartlett's Siding, under control of the shunter or guard. An engine and two brake vans, with wagons between, ran from Bideford Goods and detached the rear brake van on the main line. After shunting wagons in and out of the sidings the train was coupled up to the brake van on the main line, and the locomotive propelled the train, with the guard or shunter in the leading brake van controlling the train by hand signals, into the up loop at Bideford station. Here the locomotive was detached and ran round, before pulling the train to Bideford Goods. The train was restricted to 25 vehicles including the brake vans, and another customer at Bartlett's Siding was listed as the Ideal Concrete Company. It would appear that these trips were authorised to cope with heavy traffic post-war.

For the purposes of ordering wagons, accountancy, and so on, Bartlett's Siding came under Bideford station. It was taken out of use on 6th July 1965 but was by then overgrown with weeds and obviously already abandoned. After Bartlett's Siding, the line passed the Bideford 'up' distant signal and, leaving industrial Bideford behind, began a stretch of several miles through country of outstanding beauty. For another mile or so the line ran along the east bank of the Torridge Estuary, which now became narrower, until it crossed the estuary on Landcross Viaduct. This is about 400ft. long, consisting of seven spans supported on eight pairs of piers sunk into the river bed. The curved viaduct is built of iron, with the cylindrical piers filled with masonry. In the SR system, Landcross Viaduct was No.121. It was followed by underbridge No.122 after which the line, level almost all the way from

Barnstaple, begins to climb on gradients as steep as 1 in 64. Next comes a cutting spanned by overbridge No.123, carrying the main A386 road from Bideford to Torrington, and here, for a mile or so, the line leaves the Torridge Estuary which takes a long eastward detour and follows the River Yeo, tidal at this point. Back in 1932, as a result of correspondence between the Devon County Council and the Southern Railway, the eastern parapet wall and boundary wall of bridge No.123 were lowered, in order to afford drivers of road vehicles a better view while negotiating the sharp bend. Incidentally, Landcross was the starting point for a number of unsuccessful proposals for a railway to Hartland and Clovelly. In fact, a Bideford & Clovelly Railway managed to get its Bill, but this scheme was abandoned in 1901.

Still climbing, the line runs over an embankment and underbridge into a cutting and then through Landcross Tunnel, 196 yards in length and now level. Above the tunnel is the divergence of the A386 and A388 roads, to Torrington and Holsworthy respectively, and the ancient Landcross chapel. The line emerges from the southern portal of Landcross Tunnel to regain the valley of the River Torridge. Near here, at Annery, was the sea-lock and shipyard of the old Rolle Canal. After passing the site of the canal inclined plane, for the next 1½ miles the railway is level along the canal bed. The railway clings to the A386 road and passes over a minor road, which itself crosses the Torridge at its tidal limit, on a bridge that formerly had a toll of one halfpenny. A long bend in the Torridge Valley slowly changes the direction of the line from east to south, as the attractive long village of Weare Giffard, on the opposite bank, is passed. The railway then leaves the old alignment of the canal to cross the Torridge on a four arch masonry bridge. This gives a good view upstream of the original canal aqueduct over the Torridge, the Beam Bridge, since converted into a drive to Beam House. The railway now passes under the bridge carrying this drive and then twice more over the meandering River Torridge on four arch masonry bridges, past the fixed Torrington 'down' distant signal and up a 1 in 66 gradient. The Torrington 'down' home signal is passed at the end of the headshunt

Ivatt 2-6-2T 41283 takes water at Torrington in September 1963. Torrington opened to the public in 1872 and served the small market town which lay a mile away at the top of the hill above the River Torridge. Through Waterloo passenger services ran from the outset, clay and milk were soon dealt with, milk despatched in churns at first but later in tank wagons.

above the running line on the left and the station is reached through an occupation overbridge.

Torrington

Station and signal box (225 miles 57 chains from Waterloo) line opened from Bideford 18th July 1872
Torrington & Marland line opened 1st January 1881
Line opened to Halwill 27th July 1925
Passenger services to Halwill withdrawn 1st March 1965
Passenger services to Barnstaple withdrawn 3rd October 1965
Signal box closed 20th September 1970
Line closed 7th November 1982

Since its opening in 1872, Torrington has always been the principal station on the line for operational purposes and, in 1980, was the last station on the line to be manned by British Rail. Before 1872, the Rolle Canal had curved round the site where the station was subsequently built at Staplevale, following the contours of the hillside. The railway contractors levelled as good a site as they could, culverting a small watercourse, but the site was rather limited in accommodation for what was, for the next 53 years, the terminus of a secondary main line. The station, as described by Lt. Col. Yolland in his report, changed little for more than a century. The first Station Master at

Torrington in 1872 was Mr King who, in 1874, moved on to become the Superintendent of the newly opened station at Ilfracombe, his place at Torrington being taken by Mr Dalby, a clerk from Waterloo.

From the start, Torrington had all the necessary facilities for an important terminus, albeit on a limited scale. Local stone had been used in the construction of the attractively designed station buildings, incorporating the stationmasters house, goods shed, water tower, signal box and platforms, although the single road engine shed had been built of wood. It had a 45ft. turntable and could house two tender locomotives. In the yard were three long sidings, one passing right through the goods shed, and a long headshunt. A local merchant in coal and wool, Mr J. B. Reed of Staplevale, had two private sidings laid in, both radiating from the turntable. The first, a coal siding, was laid shortly after the line opened in 1872, and the second longer siding, serving a lime-kiln, was laid in 1884. The 3ft. gauge Torrington & Marland Railway siding, between the two standard gauge sidings in the yard, was brought into use in 1881, together with associated offices and a shelter for the North Devon Clay Company. There was also a stone warehouse, served by a spur from a wagon turntable.

Torrington could become congested, such was the traffic; in 1913 for example, two restaurant car trains stabled overnight and two goods trains arrived early in the morning. Goods traffic forwarded included clay, which was transferred from narrow gauge to standard gauge wagons in the yard, and traffic received included coal and limestone, together with general merchandise and cattle. The *South Western Railway Magazine* of March 1919 recorded that during the Great War, several thousand tons of timber (sawn and round), and large quantities of hay, had been dealt with. The station agent, Mr E.A. Willcocks, had joined the LSWR in 1881 at Brockenhurst, and, after serving at Ascot, Elsted and Bow, had in 1909 come to Torrington as stationmaster.

Although the main line of the Torrington & Marland Railway closed as long ago as 1925, Mr E.A. Holwill, who joined the North Devon Clay Company in 1923, has been able to supply details of its operations at Torrington – see Chapter 5. The clay company forwarded about one hundred tons of clay per day, carried from the works to Torrington in about thirty narrow gauge 3½ tons capacity wagons, and then transferred to about ten main line wagons, usually of the LSWR open type with raised rounded

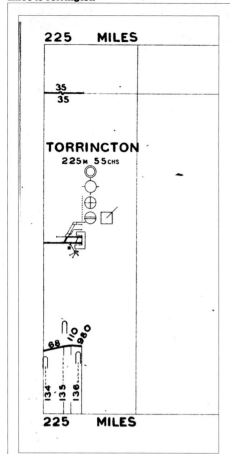

ends, and covered with a tarpaulin. The clay was forwarded by regular SR freight trains to a variety of destinations including Stoke-on-Trent, London, Bristol and the railway quays at Bideford and Fremington. There was a Torrington & Marland workmens train which left Torrington at 6.30 a.m. arriving back at 6 p.m. At Torrington station the clay company employed six or eight men to transfer clay between the narrow gauge and main line wagons, a driver to operate the Torrington to Yarde section, and two men to maintain the long wooden viaduct over the Torridge.

All this came to an end when the North Devon and Cornwall Junction Light Railway (ND&CJLR) opened in July 1925. There were major changes at Torrington station which overnight had lost its main line status and become instead a double terminus for two branch line services. Congestion in the yard was now a thing of the past, with only a few through carriages from Waterloo, and no long rakes of wagons being loaded with clay. The two terminal platform roads had been extended under the main road through a new bridge, Southern Railway No.137, to converge into a single track the other side, the crossing loop so formed having a capacity for a locomotive and thirty one wagons. The crossover between the 'up' and 'down' tracks was retained for running-round purposes, and also facilitated some snappy connections between passenger services on the two lines. For example, in the summer of 1932, the 'Atlantic

TORRINGTON *1901*

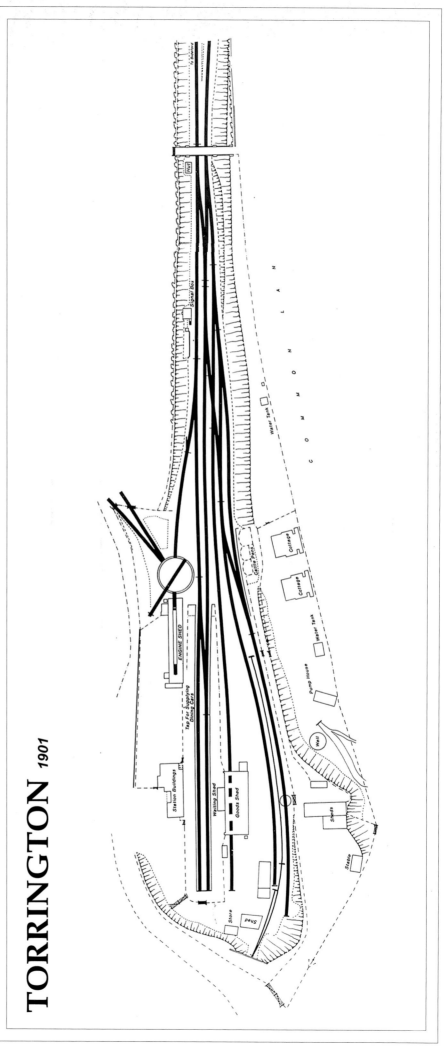

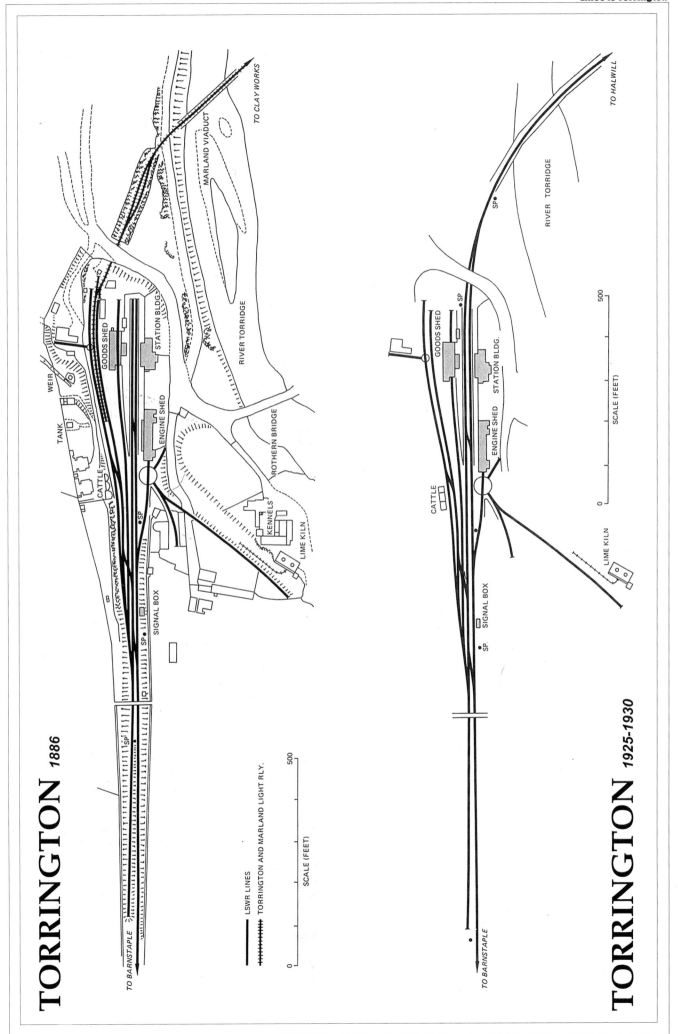

TORRINGTON *1886*

TO BARNSTAPLE

SP

SP

SIGNAL BOX

ENGINE SHED

STATION BLDG.

GOODS SHED

CATTLE

TANK

WEIR

SP

KENNELS

LIME KILN

ROTHERN BRIDGE

RIVER TORRIDGE

MARLAND VIADUCT

TO CLAY WORKS

LSWR LINES

TORRINGTON AND MARLAND LIGHT RLY.

SCALE (FEET)

0   500

TORRINGTON *1925-1930*

TO BARNSTAPLE

SP.

SIGNAL BOX

ENGINE SHED

STATION BLDG.

GOODS SHED

CATTLE

SP

LIME KILN

SP

RIVER TORRIDGE

TO HALWILL

SCALE (FEET)

0   500

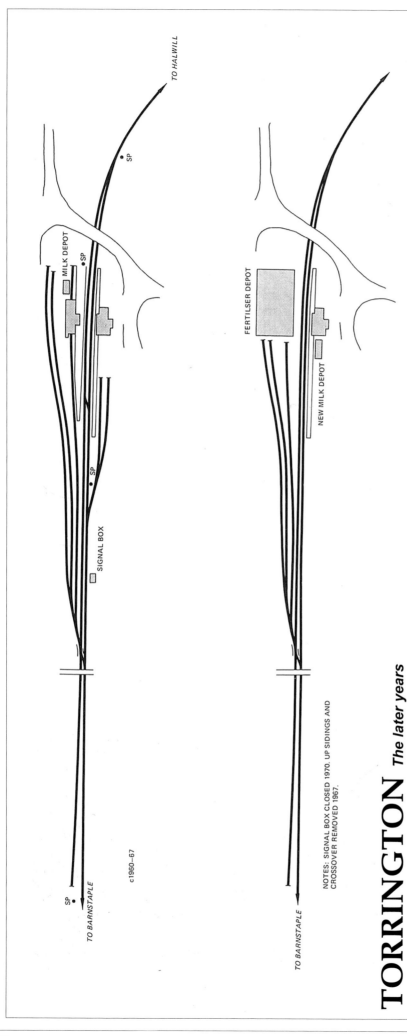

TO HALWILL

SP

MILK DEPOT

SP

FERTILSER DEPOT

NEW MILK DEPOT

SP

SIGNAL BOX

SP

TO BARNSTAPLE

c1960–67

TO BARNSTAPLE

NOTES: SIGNAL BOX CLOSED 1970. UP SIDINGS AND
CROSSOVER REMOVED 1967.

TORRINGTON *The later years*

Coast Express' arrived at 4.11 p.m. at the 'down' platform and, when all the passengers and luggage were safely on the platform, the train was backed out on to the 'down' line. The Halwill train had been waiting on the 'up' line near the engine shed and when the road was clear, ran into the 'down' platform via the crossover, collected any passengers and luggage, and departed at 4.22 p.m.

During the 1920s, the horse bus service between the station and the town, run in connection with every train, was taken over by a motor bus. The horse bus, run by the delivery agent, had seated about five passengers inside and another two or three outside with the driver. Luggage and mail bags were carried on top.

By about 1930 most services to Torrington were operated by tank engines and the redundant turntable was taken out, with access to Reed's Sidings and the engine shed then made via new points. Pointwork in the goods yard was also simplified, with a double slip at the line into the station. There was a 5 ton crane in the yard and a 2 ton crane in the goods shed, a loading dock behind the goods shed and two water columns, one at the end of each platform. Water was supplied from the tower overlooking the yard, the tank at the top being filled with water from an adjacent well by a pump worked by a steam engine. Its operation was the responsibility of the pump engineman until it was replaced by a pair of automatic electric pumps operated by the station staff, who would switch from one to the other in case of emergency.

The train services and traffic handled at Torrington remained more or less the same from the 1930s to the early 1960s, except for the familiar wartime peaks and troughs. The Barnstaple trains remained busy with through coaches to Waterloo, but the single coaches to Halwill carried only a few passengers. Contrary to popular belief, there was one daily passenger train south from Torrington which regularly loaded well. This was the 6.25 a.m. workmens train to Petrockstow, which carried about fifty men from Torrington, six from Watergate and twenty from Yarde to Dunsbear Halt, from where they walked down to the Marland clay works. The return trip was by means of a carriage, attached to the afternoon goods train from Halwill, which ran as a mixed train from Petrockstow. This was an inheritance from the Torrington & Marland Railway.

The staff at Torrington were responsible for freight traffic not only at the station itself, but also on the public sidings at Watergate and Dunsbear and the private siding of the North Devon Clay Company at Marland. The clay company ordered wagons from staff at Torrington who in turn ordered them from the

The view north from an occupational crossing bridge and the extensive head shunt in 1963. The 1 in 68 gradient into the station can be appreciated as the siding is almost on level ground. John Eyers, courtesy South Western Circle.

Looking off the end of the down platform in 1963 with some old farm buildings in the background. One J.B. Reed had traded largely in wool and coal since 1884, bringing it in by sea from South Wales via Bideford and there were two sidings on the up side, the longer of which served a lime-kiln. It was worked by a John Balch until 1907 followed by a Mr Babb and finally Mr Charles Short until closure in 1913. John Eyers, courtesy South Western Circle.

Torrington goods shed and down sidings in 1963 with Bibby's store nearest the camera; railway cottages to the right. On the arrival of the 3ft gauge Torrington and Marland Railway in 1881 an exchange siding had been laid between the two sidings seen here. The Devon Clay company also set up offices and a waiting shelter for its staff (they were just about the only passengers) at the same time. John Eyers, courtesy South Western Circle.

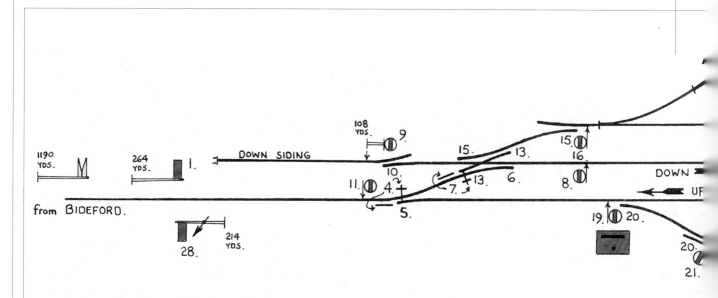

TORRINGTON *undated signalling diagram*

Barnstaple office where there were full particulars of rolling stock available in the district. Special flows of traffic at Torrington went in and out of 'Reed's Sidings' laid in for Mr J. B. Reed in 1884; cattle and, later on, milk in tanker wagons. General merchandise handled at Torrington reflected the commerce of the town and district. The glove trade, including the factories of Messrs Vaughans and Tapscotts, received raw materials and forwarded gloves on most days. Messrs Robec also forwarded children's wear which, together with the gloves, were normally despatched by passenger train. In the yard, Messrs Cobbledeck received coal and animal feedstuffs and, at the back of the goods shed, Messrs Bibbys had a store, a wooden building with an asbestos roof. The animal foodstuffs, including cattle cake, came in by goods train and were unloaded by the checker and goods porter. The weekly stock account for Bibbys was kept by the checker, F. Cornish, and the firm also had a local representative, Mr Olley.

The station in 1963, with its 'non-standard' signal box – it did not conform to the 'Types' identified by the Signalling Study Group. The extension of the line from Bideford had opened on 18 July 1872 and under the provisions of an 1871 Act the LSWR was required to install interlocking signals here at Torrington. This box had preceded the arrival of the much more common 'Type 1' boxes installed from 1873. The box was also extended by the Southern Railway when it opened its North Devon & Cornwall Junction Railway line to Halwill Junction in 1925, with the frame enlarged to 30 levers. The box closed in September 1970 whereupon all points converted to hand operation. John Eyers, courtesy South Western Circle.

TORRINGTON.

Shunting operations.—Before a shunting movement is made from the down to the up line through No. 24 crossover road whilst a train is standing at the up platform, the Driver of such train must be advised of the intended shunting movement and instructed not to move his engine forward until the crossing movement has been completed and the line is clear.

In consequence of the severe gradient from Torrington falling in the direction of Bideford, which commences a short distance the station side of the signal box, no vehicle must be permitted to stand on the up line at any point beyond the up platform ramp at the Bideford end of Torrington station, unless an engine or brake van with a man in attendance is attached at the Bideford end of the vehicle.

J. B. Reed & Co's sidings.—Traffic for the sidings must be placed immediately beyond the gates, and traffic from the sidings accepted at the same point. Messrs. J. B. Reed & Coy. will arrange to work traffic beyond this point, and under no circumstances must the Company's engine pass inside the gates.

The portions of the sidings situated on the Railway Company's premises may be used for any traffic in connection with the railway.

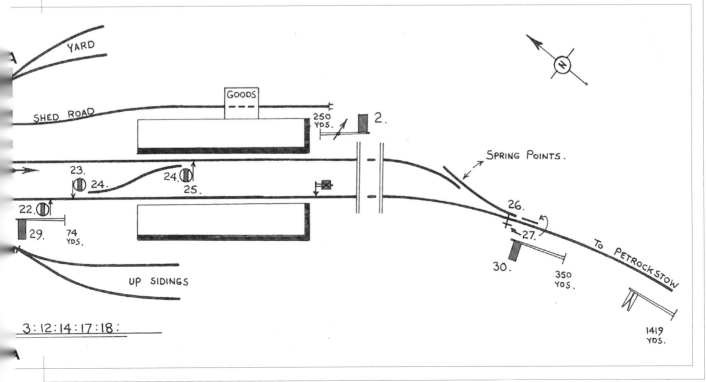

SOUTHERN RAILWAY

Signal
Instruction
No. 21, 1924.

Instructions to all concerned as to

NEW AND ALTERED SIGNALS, etc.

BALHAM INTERMEDIATE SIGNAL BOX.

To be carried out on Wednesday, 8th October.

The crossover road between the down and up local lines will be put out of service.

The work will be in progress from 9.0 a.m. Mr. Jury to provide flagman, as required.　　　　　　　　　　　　　　　(R. 3255.)

TORRINGTON.

To be brought into use on Tuesday, 7th October.

An up advanced starting signal, 30 feet in height, with a repeating arm 10 feet from rail level, erected 94 yards nearer Bideford than the existing signal, which will be removed.

The left-hand ground signal situate at the Bideford end of No. 1 crossover road will be removed, and the remaining ground signal will control movements to the arrival or departure roads.

The left-hand ground signal situate at the platform end of No. 1 crossover road will be removed and the remaining ground signal will control movements to the single line or siding.

The left-hand ground signal situate at the Bideford end of the connection leading from the arrival road to the Goods Yard will be removed and the remaining ground signal will control movements to the arrival road or goods yard.

The right-hand ground signal situate at the Bideford end of the Loco. siding points will be removed and the remaining ground signal will control movements to the departure road or Loco. siding.

The left-hand ground signal situate at the Bideford end of No. 2 crossover road will be removed and the remaining ground signal will control movements to the arrival or departure roads.

The left-hand ground signal situate at the buffer stops end of No. 2 crossover road will be removed and the remaining ground signal will control movements along the arrival road or to the departure road eastward.

The work will be in progress from 7.30 a.m. each day from Tuesday, 7th, until Friday, 10th October inclusive. Mr. Willcocks to provide flagman, as required.　　　　　　　　　　　　　(R. 1,796.)

J.B. Reed's son, also J.B. Reed, has been able to describe the business at Torrington. Coal from the collieries in the Forest of Dean and South Wales was purchased and shipped from Lydney and Newport to the railway dock at Cross Parks, Bideford, where it was loaded into wagons and despatched to Torrington. After the closure of the Cross Parks railway dock, the coal was shipped via Fremington in the same way. From the mid-1920s, most of the house coal came from Yorkshire, some travelling all the way by rail in colliery wagons and some, purchased through coal factors, by sea via Fremington. Steam coal and smokeless fuels came from South Wales, via Fremington and also all the way by rail. Coal was dealt with in its own siding, the shorter of the two nearer the signal box. From here, Mr Reed's men delivered coal to customers in the town and district using first a horse and cart, and later a lorry.

The longer of Reed's Sidings served lime-kilns which were in production until 1913. The kilns were worked by John Balch up to 1907, then by a Mr Babb, and finally by Charles Short. They burned a mixture of limestone and culm (a low grade of anthracite) to

The modest station building (Station Masters house to the left) in July 1956. Constructed in local stone it provided the usual waiting room, booking office, parcels office and toilets. Notice the milk churns, a trade the station came to be associated with for many years. John Eyers, courtesy South Western Circle.

The main up side building in 1963. There is a tap and hose on the wall, long out of use for its original purpose, which supplied water to dining cars - none seen here since 1925. John Eyers, courtesy South Western Circle.

The water tank and the water column it supplied. The tank was on the east side of the station high on the embankment to provide the necessary 'head' of pressure to serve the station and water columns. Nearby was a pump house which drew water from a deep well; originally powered by a steam engine it was replaced by an electric motor in the 1950s. John Eyers, courtesy South Western Circle.

Left. Ivatt tank 41295 ready to leave with a single coach train for Halwill in August 1960. Passenger facilities on the down side at Torrington were very sparse indeed amounting to a stone built lean-to against the goods shed wall. D. Wigley.

produce lime, a fertiliser widely used on the fields of North Devon. Both these commodities were shipped to the railway dock at Cross Parks, Bideford, and transferred to wagons for onward transit to Torrington, the limestone coming from Caldy Island, off South Wales, and the culm from the South Wales Coalfield, via Newport.

The traffic received at Reed's Sidings was generally about four to six wagons a week in the coal siding and about the same in the lime siding. Mr Reed also received fertilisers and animal feedstuffs and despatched wagons of wool, mainly to the West Riding of Yorkshire. After the engine turntable was taken out, the sidings were reached by points and locomotives were able to shunt wagons to the coal siding and to the top of the lime siding where they ran down a slight gradient. Empty wagons were pulled out by horse or tractor. Gates were provided at the entrance of each siding, the keys for which were kept at the signal box. When Mr Reed retired from the business in 1956, he sold the goodwill to Messrs Fulford Trumps of Bideford, although he continued to farm at Staplevale. The sidings were taken out of use and removed a couple of years later.

Milk traffic at Torrington station was only moderate for many years, the churns were brought to the station first by horse and cart and then by lorry and loaded into passenger vans. It was not until the mid-1940s that the milk loading depot was built at the back of the goods shed, with traffic then increasing substantially. The tanker wagons, from a variety of owners including United Dairies, Express Dairies and CWS, usually arrived at Torrington on the morning goods or mail train. At one stage, there was a shortage of tanker wagons, so the railway also used flat wagons with road tankers permanently loaded on them. At Torrington a shunting engine would place railway tanker wagons in the depot where they were loaded with milk pumped from road tankers. The Torridge Vale Dairies would advise the station staff how many tankers were required, and their destinations, which were in the London area and included Mottingham, Stewarts Lane, Vauxhall and Wood Lane. Sometimes Torrington held a few spare tankers for emergencies, but siding space was limited. Loaded milk tankers were usually despatched at the rear of passenger trains.

At Torrington considerable numbers of cattle were shipped from the loading dock in the yard, where three cattle wagons could be loaded at once. When the animals were being forwarded the whole place was very busy for several hours, with cattle herded down a long narrow track from a gate on the main road above the station, and an engine shunting more empty cattle wagons every few minutes to the cattle dock

Above. Unusual visitor to the branch was ex-GWR 0-6-0T No.3669. As we will see on page 258 Barnstaple based ex-GWR 0-6-0Ts were occasional visitors to shunt East Yelland CEGB Sidings. Harry Beer worked at the station continuously between 1953 and 1980.H. Beer collection.

Below. Harry Beer on shunting duties with N class 2-6-0 31847 and old pal Steve Bedler, a fireman at Torrington for many years. H. Beer collection.

for loading. Then, after the departure of the cattle wagons, all would be quiet again for another week or two. Some cattle went forward by regular freight services and, on other occasions, lengthy cattle specials were run. Before the war, the principal buyers were Mr Watkins, who despatched cattle from Torrington on Thursdays to the market at Exeter on Fridays, and Mr Millman who forwarded cattle to Chichester twice a month. During and after the war, the Ministry of Agriculture & Food ran special trains of thirty or forty loaded wagons about twice a week for some time. The handling of cattle at Torrington was not without incident. On one occasion, at dusk, a herd broke loose on to the adjoining common land, hotly pursued by drovers and station staff. Eventually, all were rounded up, the only casualty being the stationmaster who had the misfortune to fall into a pothole made by the American tanks which had practised there during the war.

In addition to the bus services which operated between the station and the town centre for passengers, luggage and mails, there was also a collection and delivery service for goods traffic. Back in 1873, Messrs Copp & Son acted as carriers at the station and, on one occasion, their horse drawn luggage wagon was ascending the steep hill from the station to the town when the horse, which had apparently been in good, condition, dropped dead. Later, the railway company was responsible for its own collection and delivery service, initially using horse-drawn vehicles, and then lorries. There were three rounds made to the town at

approximately 9.30 a.m., 12.30 p.m. and 4 p.m. It seems safe to assume that in the days of horse-drawn transport, the long steep hill from the station to the town made very hard work for the horses.

The engine shed at Torrington was in use from the opening of the line in 1872 through to its closure in 1959. Two or three locomotives were allocated to this outstation from Barnstaple Junction. Up to the late 1920s, these were usually tender locomotives, for many years Adams 4-4-0s but after this period, the locomotives were invariably tanks; E1R 0-6-2Ts, M7 0-4-4Ts and Ivatt 2-6-2Ts. Up to the opening of the ND&CJLR in 1925, Torrington locomotives and crews worked services to Barnstaple and Exeter and afterwards took on all the regular ND&CJLR workings together with some to Barnstaple. The wooden shed boasted some additional accommodation, including a wooden extension at the back (apparently subsequently demolished to make way for the locomotive siding) and a coach body on the 'up' platform in late LSWR days. The turntable disappeared, as noted earlier and the coal stage (illuminated by a gas lamp at night) was replaced about 1930. The turntable lay immediately outside the shed; it was close to the running line too and awkward to operate, which may have been a factor in deciding to use tank engines exclusively. From this instruction issued in 1925 it is probably that the man/men pushing the table came perilously close to passing trains: *When an engine is required to be turned on the above-mentioned turntable the*

Above. Harry Beer, right, with Mr W Steer a signalman at Torrington for 45 years – the loco is again 31847. H. Beer collection.

Below. The grand wooden engine shed at Torrington in the 1930s, looking like a temporary sleeper store. It was a popular posting from Exmouth Junction with young cleaners lodging in the summer months and, as Nobby Clarke relates, a time to look forward to endless social distractions. Torrington men worked to Halwill and Barnstaple whilst Barnstaple men, for a long time, only worked to Torrington. This inevitably changed and even Exeter men worked over the line to Halwill. Torrington, as with many small establishments had a senior driver in charge; engines did not coal here but at Barnstaple.

Ivatt 2-6-2T 41292 about to leave for Barnstaple with an early evening service in June 1958. R.E. Tustin.

M7 0-4-4T 30252 at Torrington in July 1958 with an arrival from Barnstaple. Coming to the West Country for the second time in 1937 it spent the rest of its working life in Devon and Cornwall at Bude until after the War, going to Exmouth Junction in 1948. It moved to Barnstaple Junction in March 1951 and stayed until withdrawn and scrapped in 1959. Alec Swain, transporttreasury

Top. Torrington in its days as a terminus, before the extension of the line in 1925 to Halwill Junction. There is plenty of activity at the head of the yard but the platforms are empty. A small coach body has appeared on the platform near the engine shed – possibly a primitive dormitory for enginemen on summer work.

Above. Barnstaple-bound train in 1963, with inevitable Ivatt 2-6-2T.

Below. The 3.57pm Torrington to Barnstaple service formed of a single car DMU – shortly before the termination of passenger services in 1965. John Nicholas.

Locomotive Department staff must first advise the Signalman and obtain his permission before operating the turntable. Before giving permission for an engine to be turned the Signalman must satisfy himself that the up home signal is at danger, place a lever collar on the lever operating that signal and not withdraw that collar until he has received an assurance from the Locomotive Department staff that the turning operation has been completed and the turntable secured in its normal position.

The staff at the shed usually comprised four pairs of enginemen, a coaler and a cleaner, under the supervision of the senior driver who was responsible to the Shed Master at Barnstaple. Crews worked early, middle and late shifts; early turn men started at 4.15 a.m. and prepared two engines, then worked the 6.25 a.m. train to Petrockstow and return, and then the 8.52 a.m. to Halwill and return, signing off at about 12.15 p.m. when relieved by the middle turn men. The middle crew then took the locomotive on shed and prepared it for two more trips; the 1.30 p.m. to Petrockstow and return and the 4 p.m. to Halwill and return, disposing of the engine and signing off at about 8.15 p.m. The late turn men signed on at about 1.30 p.m. and their duty included shunting and a trip to Barnstaple, returning with the last 'down' train of the day and signing off about 9.30 p.m. Barnstaple footplatemen were also involved in a number of these duties. This was the case by 1958 but the ND&CJLR services had altered little over the previous quarter of a century, so this pattern was long established. It ended when, on 2nd November 1959, the little shed closed and the locomotives and men transferred to the parent depot at Barnstaple; it was demolished shortly afterwards.

There were also guards, usually three over the years; their duty rotas were similar to those of the drivers and firemen, but there were some rather unusual jobs over the ND&CJLR. The Torrington guards carried a supply of tickets for sale to those passengers joining trains at the halts, which was out of the ordinary on the Southern Railway in the 1930s. Most trains which ran on the ND&CJLR were mixed and there were few purely passenger trains, so guards had to assist with shunting duties in the sidings at the clay works and halts, where a tragic ending came for Guard Frederick Rowland in 1932, as we will see in Chapter Seven.

The signal box at Torrington came into use when the line opened in 1872, with points and signals fully interlocked. It was equipped with a 12 lever frame and Tyer's No.3 electric train tablet instruments controlling the line to Bideford, although these were replaced with No.6 instruments after the installation of Bartlett's Siding, and later electric key token apparatus. When

A glorious panorama of Torrington station in September 1962 with a train newly arrived from Barnstaple behind Ivatt tank 41310. The departing family have crossed the line to the up side via a boarded crossing at the country end of the layout as a footbridge was deemed unnecessary. The gantry on the right supports pipes to load milk into rail tankers from lorries. A short siding meant only three tankers could be filled simultaneously. R.C. Riley, transporttreasury.

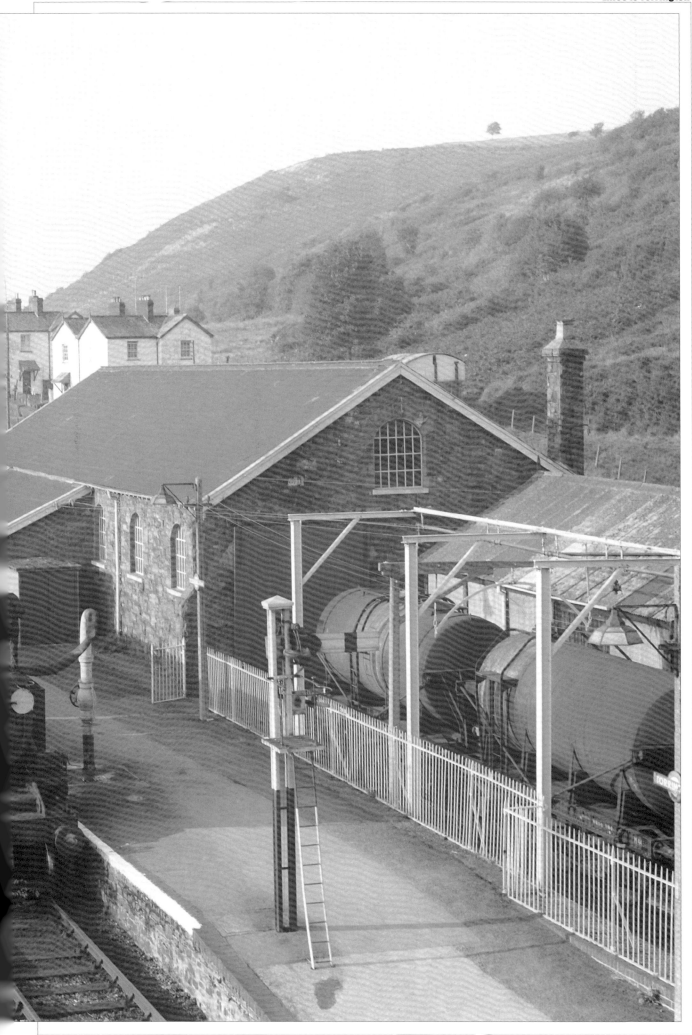

A lonely wait for the young lady in June 1960, looking hopefully towards Halwill Junction. The bridge was constructed as part of the extension southwards of the ND&CJLR in 1925, the narrow gauge trains having entered the station behind the goods shed on the left via a small bore driven through the hill. N. Browne.

Torrington was a terminus, the signalling consisted of a fixed 'down' distant and 'down' home, with 'up' starting and advanced starting signals. In 1925 the structure was extended and the frame extended to 30 levers. After the opening of the ND&CJLR in 1925, the single line section to Petrockstow was controlled by Tyer's No.6 instruments, which facilitated return trips to the North Devon Clay Company's siding at Marland from either end of the section. The 'Section Clear but Station or Junction Blocked' warning arrangement was authorised for 'down' trains between Bideford and Torrington, and between Petrockstow and Torrington for 'up' trains. There were now fixed 'up' distant, 'down' starting and 'up' home signals, and some of the existing LSWR terminal signals were re-sited, most of the new signals being on Southern Railway rail-built posts. Torrington normally had two signalmen working early and late turns; the box was taken out of use on 20th September 1970, and subsequently demolished.

The station staff at Torrington were supervised by the stationmaster who

The line burst through the hillside and almost immediately onto Torrington Viaduct which crossed over the fast flowing waters of the River Torridge, of *Tarka* fame. Just leaving the south end of the viaduct is the unadvertised 1.00pm departure for Petrockstow, a single coach behind Ivatt 41297 in August 1956. John Eyers, courtesy South Western Circle.

The steel spans of the structure are seen clearly from the banks of the Torridge in July 1964. The stumps of the Torrington and Marland viaduct stand behind; inexplicably, the girders for the new bridge were reportedly brought in by road, not rail! Peter Swift.

SOUTHERN RAILWAY.

Signal
Instruction
No. 31, (1926).

Instructions to all concerned as to the

OPENING OF A NEW HALT PLATFORM AT WATERGATE

ALSO

NEW AND ALTERED SIGNALS, ETC.

WATERGATE HALT.
(BETWEEN TORRINGTON AND PETROCKSTOW).
To be brought into use on Monday, 20th September.

A halt platform, 50 feet in length, has been constructed on the up side of the single line between Torrington and Petrockstow, situate immediately on the Torrington side of Watergate level crossing, a distance of 1 mile 68 chains from Torrington, and 6 miles 10 chains from Petrockstow. The gradient of the line at the spot is 1 in 112, rising towards Petrockstow.

The halt is provided exclusively for passenger traffic, and particulars of the trains calling thereat will be as shown in the time tables operating from the 19th September.

As the platform is only of sufficient length to accommodate one coach, care must be taken in the case of trains consisting of more than one passenger coach to load passengers for Watergate Halt in the leading coach of down trains, and in the rear coach of up trains, and Drivers must bring the trains to a stand at the halt platform accordingly. The tickets of passengers joining and alighting from trains at the Halt will be issued and collected by the Guard of the train concerned.

(R. 16,952.)

During the time these works are in progress Drivers must look out for hand signals.

EDWIN C. COX,
Chief Operating Superintendent.

Waterloo Station.
14th September, 1926.   (R. 16,978.)

Waterlow & Sons Limited, London Wall, London.

lived on the premises. In the period 1923-5, the stationmaster was Mr A. E. Willcocks, who had been there since 1909, and his staff were as follows:
Booking clerks: E. Sillifant and S. Pring
Goods agent: J. Whale
Goods clerks: F. Cornish and G. Walkey
Shunters: T. Winsborough and B. Norman
Porters: F. Weeks, F. Abbott, Mr Hunt and Mr Ridd.

At this time the North Devon Clay Company also employed eight men to transfer clay between wagons, two men to maintain their viaduct, and one driver. Mr Reed also employed three men in his sidings and Mr H. Holwill, another coal merchant, employed a man. At this time therefore, when Torrington was a Southern Railway terminus, no less than forty four men worked there, twenty seven with the Southern Railway, eleven with the clay company and six with the coal merchants. By 1939/40, the Southern Railway employed some thirty-four men under the supervision of the stationmaster, by this time a Mr F.W. Newcombe; when passenger services were withdrawn in 1965 the Stationmaster, Mr L.R. Somerfield, had a staff of sixteen.

Torrington clerk Sidney Pring joined the Southern Railway in 1923, his father being the Permanent Way Inspector at Barnstaple Junction. For several years after starting, he worked part of his turn in the booking and parcels offices in the passenger station, and the rest of his turn in the goods office. On the

Just one of a series of views taken by H.C. Casserley from the back of the 10.38am mixed train of clay wagons from Halwill in 25th September 1956. Mixed trains reduced running costs when there was a paucity of passengers so the line was perfect for such services. The train is approaching Torrington from Watergate behind Ivatt 2-6-2T 41298. H.C. Casserley, courtesy R.M. Casserley.

The tight reverse curves are evident all the way along the line to Halwill and with a speed restriction of 25mph and plenty of check rails the journey could be tediously slow. H.C. Casserley, courtesy R.M. Casserley.

Leaving Watergate Halt on the same train. H.C. Casserley, courtesy R.M. Casserley.

early turn he started at the passenger station dealing with booking office and parcels traffic until 11 a.m., and then worked for the remainder of his turn in the goods office. On the late turn he worked in the goods office from 11 a.m. to 4 p.m., and then in the parcels and booking offices until the end of his turn. There were two senior clerks, one booking and one goods. The first senior goods clerk was a uniformed man who had previously worked at Bideford, where he lost a leg, having then to come to Torrington as a warehouseman and then a clerk. When Mr Pring returned in 1946 from five years in the army, he was made booking and parcels clerk, from which post he retired in 1965 when passenger services were withdrawn.

Mr M. Hutchings was a carriage cleaner at Torrington between 1953 and 1958. It was his job to clean both the interior and exterior of the carriages and, on early turn, had sixteen coaches to deal with in time for the following departures; three for the 7.06 a.m., four for the 8.10 a.m., four for the 10.30 a.m. 'Atlantic Coast Express', three for the 12.18 p.m. and two for the 2.15 p.m. Some interior cleaning would have been done previously by late turn staff on the first two departures. On summer Saturdays there could be more than thirty coaches to be cleaned at Torrington, but then assistance would often come from dock porters from Fremington. The coach used for the workmens service between Torrington and Dunsbear was sent to Exeter Central once a week for heavy cleaning.

The LSWR had built five houses at the station for railwaymen. The stationmasters house was an integral part of the passenger station, and the stationmaster always lived there, the first being Mr King in 1872 and the last, Mr Somerfield in 1965; subsequently Mr M. Hutchings, the former carriage cleaner, lived in the house. There were also two pairs of semi-detached houses built on the embankment overlooking the station, and these were usually occupied by two clerks, the head shunter, and the pump engine man, while most of the other railwaymen lived in Torrington itself.

After closure to passengers in 1965 staffing was reduced to a signalman and a couple of shunters to deal with the still extensive milk and clay traffic. For almost a decade there was no visible sign of change, except that in 1967 the central crossover and 'up' sidings were taken out, and, in 1970, the signal box was closed and subsequently demolished, and all the signalling removed. This was followed in the mid-1970s by the construction of the new fertiliser and milk depots. By the 1970s there was only one railwayman working at Torrington station, Mr Harry Beer who joined the GWR at Taunton in 1947 after demobilisation from the RAF, and moved to

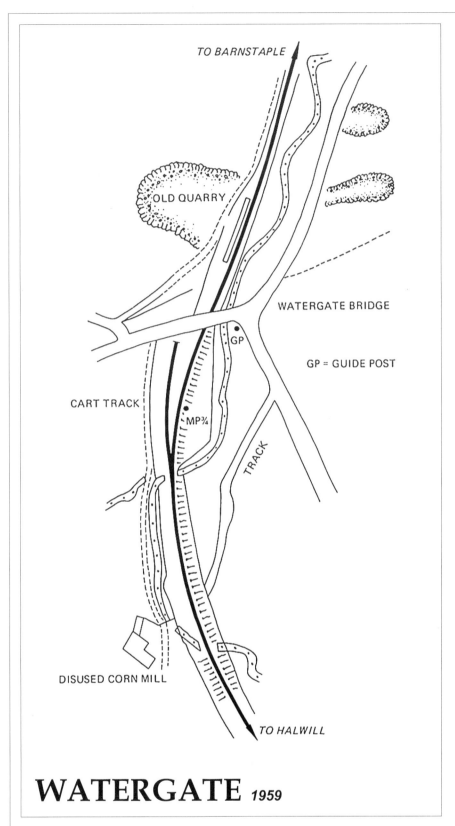

TO BARNSTAPLE

OLD QUARRY

WATERGATE BRIDGE

GP

GP = GUIDE POST

CART TRACK

MP¾

TRACK

DISUSED CORN MILL

TO HALWILL

WATERGATE *1959*

Torrington in 1953 when the station was under the control of the Western Region. Prior to 1980, his duties included accepting trains from Barnstaple, shunting, and labelling wagons from the clay works and milk tankers from the dairy. In 1980 even his post was withdrawn, when the milk and fertiliser traffic at the station came to an end. This period of 'one man' station had not been uneventful however. A TV commercial had been made, for instance and when the famous yachtsman Sir Francis Chichester died, the funeral cortege waited in the station yard for some time, complete with police escort, until they left for the funeral at Shirwell some twenty miles away. On another occasion two disabled salmon were retrieved with shunting poles from a pool in the River Torridge near the viaduct, to grace several railwaymen's tables. This remember was before the era of 'cheap' supermarket salmon.

After closure of the signal box in 1970 the Barnstaple to Torrington line was worked on the 'train staff and ticket' method but from Monday 22nd 1980 'one train only' working was introduced, with the Torrington to Meeth section under the control of the Barnstaple travelling shunter.

To Watergate, Yarde and Dunsbear

As soon as the line leaves Torrington, its character changes completely, as the expensively engineered LSWR main line was followed by a cheaply built light railway. The line, almost completely level all the way from Barnstaple, became steeply graded with 1 in 42 banks, and the gentle main line curves were followed by sharp bends of a radius as little as nine chains. Instead of using expensive bridges, the roads and tracks crossed the line at ungated level crossings.

After Torrington station the line passed under the main A386 road running up to the town, through a cutting which formerly accommodated the Torrington & Marland run-round loop, over the line of the Rolle Canal and out on to the viaduct over the Torridge, which was built with steel spans on masonry piers. From the viaduct, there were extensive views

NORTH DEVON AND CORNWALL JUNCTION LIGHT RAILWAY. WHISTLE BOARDS.

Referring to page 2 of Signal Instruction No. 25 (1925), dated 22nd July, 1925, an additional whistle board has been erected at the Torrington end of Torrington Viaduct, applicable to up trains.

Drivers to note and open the engine whistle accordingly.

(R. 7197).

The woodland of the ND&CJLR was very different from the sea and skies north of Torrington; this is Watergate Halt on 25 September 1962, 41312 having just passed over Vinney Copse crossing, a farm track near Stowford. After this the line curved away to leave the original alignment of the Torrington & Marland line. The stacked logs are larch poles used locally as pit props. R.C. Riley, transporttreasury.

Top. Looking south from the back of the mixed train at Watergate Halt in September 1956, towards one of the many ungated crossings on the line. Beyond the B3227 road is a short stub siding with a wagon, a rare sight indeed as it was only occasionally used by a local farmer and closed a year later in May 1960. H.C. Casserley, courtesy R.M. Casserley.

Left and below. Watergate Halt, its platform, fencing and signs all concrete components made at the Exmouth Junction works and taken here as a 'kit of parts'. There was no shelter, for the place saw few, if any, regular passengers. There were some of course, and the Southern Railway did issue an instruction to drivers in 1926, that 'care should be taken when passengers are boarding as the platform can only accommodate one coach which should be the leading one'.

41312 with a return service from Halwill Junction leaves Watergate Halt for Torrington on 25 September 1962, through dense conifers. R.C. Riley, transporttreasury.

upstream towards Torrington and downstream to the ancient Rothern Bridge and its modern replacement. Below, the masonry piers of the old Torrington & Marland wooden viaduct could be seen. There was a speed restriction of 10 m.p.h. over the viaduct, and 'up' trains were required to whistle as they came off the viaduct to warn staff using the crossing into the goods yard.

The line next passed the former Drummet's Corn Mill; it then left the valley of the Torridge and, after passing the Torrington 'up' distant signal, followed the valley of the stream known as Langtree Lake. Climbing and winding up the valley through the woods, the line followed the route of

the former narrow gauge line for a couple of miles until Watergate.

At Watergate Bridge the B3227 road from Torrington to Langtree and Holsworthy also crossed the railway on the level. The level crossing was of the standard ND&CJLR type, ungated with a cattle grid each side, and unattended. All trains were required to whistle continuously for 200 yards from the whistle boards, or from starting from a halt, until passing over all these level crossings on the ND&CJLR at 5 m.p.h. Over the years there was the occasional difference of opinion between the train crews and the drivers of road vehicles; yet, if the level crossings had required conventional signalling and staffing, the line would never have been built.

Watergate Halt on the Torrington side of the level crossing, its platform long enough only for the usual single coach train, opened on 20th September 1926, a year after the line itself, though it seems that trains had called here for workmen before then. The platform was constructed from standard Southern Railway prefabricated concrete components which were also used for the nameboard, notice board and lamp posts, but there was no shelter. In 1929 Langtree Parish Council asked that one be provided but in light of the small numbers of passengers this was declined. The regular passengers using Watergate Halt were the half dozen clay workers travelling to and from the works at Marland and other passengers bought their tickets from the guard whilst on the train.

On the other side of the level crossing was a short siding (the original title was Watergate Siding) used to stable a wagon occasionally for a local farmer. The gradient at this point is 1 in 45 falling towards Torrington, and the points for the siding, which was served by 'down' trains, were operated from a ground frame released by the

H.C. Casserley's train approaches Watergate Halt and blasts on its whistle to warn any motorist approaching around the corner. On these quiet rural lanes it would be startling and potentially fatal to be surprised by a steaming monster crossing the road with a train of coaches and wagons. Indeed later we will see the result of an accident at Meeth with the unfortunate coming together of the train and a bus! H.C. Casserley, courtesy R.M. Casserley.

A final view towards Watergate Halt. H.C. Casserley, courtesy Richard Casserley.

train tablet. For administrative and accountancy purposes, Watergate Siding came under Torrington station. Watergate Siding was closed to public traffic on 2nd May 1960, and removed shortly afterwards. After the withdrawal of passenger services in 1965, the nameboard and notice board were removed from Watergate Halt, but the platform remained.

From Watergate, the line passes the remains of a disused corn mill and continues to climb and turn up the wooded valley of a small stream, in a south-easterly direction. After about a mile there is a bridge over a minor road at Badslake, and then a culvert over the stream. There was another crossing over a farm track near Stowford, named Vinney Copse level crossing, after which the line left the original alignment of the Torrington & Marland line and curved away, first over a long embankment with another culvert, and then through a long cutting to arrive at Yarde Halt. This last section involved

Looking south towards Yarde from the train in September 1956; note check rails on yet another of the tight curves. H.C. Casserley, courtesy R.M. Casserley.

Above. A brief stop by our clay train at Yarde with just enough time for H.C. Casserley to snap the platform. H.C. Casserley, courtesy Richard Casserley.

Yarde Halt, a replica of the platform at Watergate from the works at Exmouth Junction.

Unlike Watergate the halt was not quite so isolated; along with clayworkers cottages there was the small community of East Yarde nearby.

SOUTHERN RAILWAY

Signal
Instruction
No. 24 (1926).

Instructions to all concerned as to the

YARDE HALT.
(BETWEEN TORRINGTON AND PETROCKSTOW.)

To be brought into use on Monday, 19th July.

A halt platform, 50 feet in length, has been constructed on the down side of the single line between Torrington and Petrockstow, situate immediately on the Torrington side of Yarde level crossing, a distance of 4 miles 42 chains from Torrington, and 3 miles 26 chains from Petrockstow. The gradient of the line at the spot is 1 in 45, falling towards Halwill.

The halt is provided exclusively for passenger traffic, and particulars of the trains calling thereat will be announced in due course.

As the platform is only of sufficient length to accommodate one coach, care must be taken in the case of trains consisting of more than one passenger coach to load passengers for Yarde halt in the leading coach of down trains, and in the rear coach of up trains, and Drivers must bring the trains to a stand at the halt platform accordingly. (R. 16,870).

During the time these works are in progress Drivers must look out for hand signals.

Through an obliging crew, R.C. Riley was also able to photograph the train to Halwill Junction, like H.C. Casserley some years before. Yarde now has a small waiting shelter, added many years after the halt was built; this is 25 September 1962 and the shelter looks new – it does not appear on the track plan of 1959, for instance. R.C. Riley, transporttreasury.

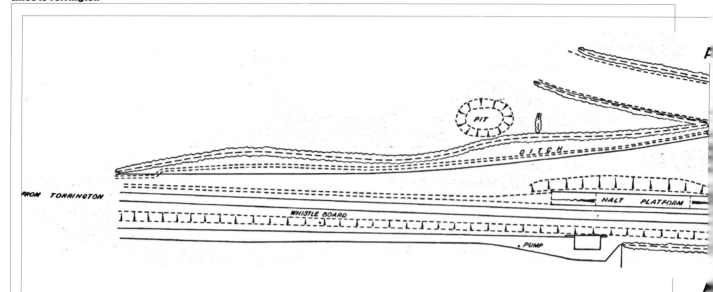

FROM TORRINGTON

WHISTLE BOARD

PIT

HALT PLATFORM

PUMP

YARDE HALT *1959*

some of the heaviest earth-works on the ND&CJLR and eased the steep gradients. The summit of the line came at more than 400 feet, just before Yarde Halt. The section from Torrington to here was continuously uphill, often as steep as 1 in 42, and required a high standard of driving when a full load of empty clay wagons was behind the

engine, particularly on a wet day. This, together with the low axle loading demanded by the civil engineer, accounted for the very limited variety of steam locomotives allowed on the line. The small community of East Yarde did not enjoy any railway facilities, apart from a standard ungated level crossing, until a year after the

opening of the line, Yarde Halt opening on 19th July 1926. This oversight seems rather strange in view of the fact that Yarde Halt provided more passengers than any other station or halt on the ND&CJLR. About twenty men travelled daily from Yarde Halt to Dunsbear Halt to work at the North Devon Clay Company's works. They

Looking back from the small lane at the halt in 1968 and a fine view of the clayworkers cottages.

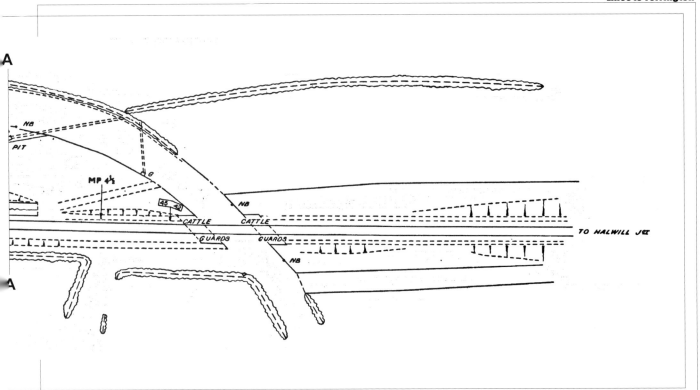

lived in a terrace of sixteen cottages, built and owned by the clay· company, next to the railway line and it seems clear that trains called before then. Yarde Halt was similar to Watergate Halt, but with a shelter, again constructed entirely of standard Southern Railway prefabricated concrete components. A little beyond the halt, a minor road to Winswell and Peters Marland crossed the line on a standard ungated level crossing. For administrative and accountancy purposes, Yarde Halt came under Torrington station, the guard issuing passenger tickets on the train. After the withdrawal of passenger services in 1965 the nameboard and notice board were removed, but the platform and shelter remained.

From Yarde Halt, the line descended as far as the Meeth clay works, dropping about 200ft. and, for a mile or so, the line continued to run approximately south-east through bleak countryside known as Willeswell Moor, over a couple of culverts and into Dunsbear Halt.

Yarde Halt in September 1982 after closure. The line begins to descend past the ungated crossing and overgrown platform towards Dunsbear. Drivers were required to whistle continuously 100 yards either side of the crossing.

Two views in September 1982 looking back towards Yarde Halt showing clearly the cattle grids fitted either side of the road. Below, a whistle board can just be discerned at the top of the 1 in 45 gradient in the distance.

Dunsbear Halt in September 1956 and two painters are in town! The chap carrying the ladders, and the one in the distance, have just finished giving the pale fence a freshen up and are now moving down the platform to make a start on one of two shelters at the halt. The halts at Watergate and Yarde were afterthoughts but Dunsbear was opened as part of the original ND&CJLR. Its platform (capped with brick) and the building nearest the road was constructed in random stone. A second shelter, in wood, was added some time later probably due to the large numbers of clayworkers using the halt who would walk along the line from the works, about a mile away. A siding was provided but was little used.

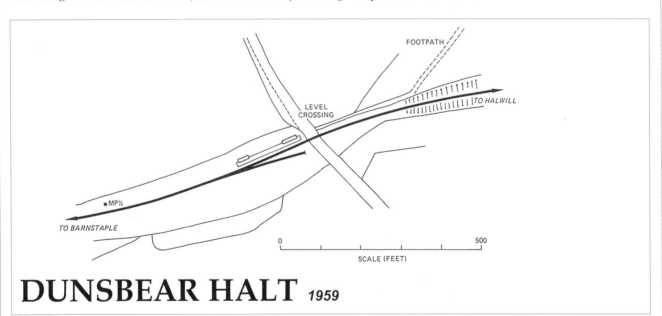

DUNSBEAR HALT *1959*

Unlike the Halts at Watergate and Yarde, Dunsbear Halt and siding were opened as part of the original ND&CJLR. The platform was built with local stone capped with brick, and boasted a small wooden waiting room, but whether it was big enough for the seventy odd clay workers, waiting for their train home to Torrington on a wet day, is another matter. From here the men had a walk of under a mile to the clay works at Marland, using the line of the Torrington & Marland Railway

The door of the Casserley train is once again ajar with the crew nicely framed in the window of the coach. H.C. Casserley, courtesy R.M. Casserley.

R.C. Riley's train waits while he records the moment at Dunsbear Halt on 25 September 1962. The little building housed a waiting room, goods store and office. R.C. Riley, transporttreasury.

THIS IS A
PRIVATE FOOTPATH
BY ORDER

It would have been the job of the crew on the last train of the day to switch out the lights, in this case an oil lamp. However, someone has removed it, maybe even as a war-time precaution.

which diverged here from the ND&CJLR. The siding was laid opposite the platform and occasionally saw wagons for local farmers or the clay works. The siding was served by 'up' trains, and the points were operated from a ground frame released by the single line tablet. At this point, the gradient was 1 in 47 falling towards Petrockstow, and the locomotives of 'up' trains of loaded clay wagons had

to work hard up the bank to Yarde. Dunsbear Halt and siding were also administered from Torrington station, passengers joining trains here again buying their tickets from the guard on the train. Dunsbear Siding was closed to public traffic on 2nd May 1960, and removed shortly afterwards. After the withdrawal of passenger services in 1965, the shelter at Dunsbear Halt was removed, but the platform remained.

Just beyond the halt was a standard ungated level crossing over the minor road linking the tiny communities of Dunsbear and Winswell.

The North Devon Clay Company Siding
On the east side of the line, a short distance after Dunsbear Halt, was the entrance to the Marland Sidings of the North Devon Clay Company. Had the

Construction work underway on the ND&CJLR with the contractor's 2ft gauge track and tipplers. The location is thought to be near Hole although Michael Messenger in his book *North Devon Clay, Twelveheads Press 2007*, suggests that it is further north, near Petrockstow.

TO TORRINGTON

PONDS

RIVER MERE

CLAY MOOR

WELL

RESERVOIRS

CLAYMOOR COTTAGES

LINE CONTINUES
TO CLAY MINE
AND PITS

0   500

SCALE (FEET)

Marland Brick and Tile Works 1904.

3ft gauge vehicles near Dunsbear Halt on 4 September 1961. Up to 1925 these unusual wagons formed part of the workmens train which departed from Torrington at 6.30am to return from Marland at 6pm. Converted horse trams were also used in the train. R. Sellick.

The North Devon Clay Company had about thirty of their own standard gauge wagons, hired around 1938-40. However, they often suffered hot boxes rendering them out of action for many days. No.114 is in the sidings at Marland Works, in a livery of black body with white lettering. *North Devon Clay Co. Ltd.*

Marland clay works not existed then, it is very unlikely that the line south from Torrington would ever have been built, but in fact the new ND&CJLR served not only the old Marland Works but also the new Meeth Works. The points to the North Devon Clay Company's siding on the main line were operated from a ground frame unlocked by the single line tablet, and the gate across the entrance to the siding was opened by a key held by the Torrington stationmaster. At this point, the gradient on the main line is 1 in 100 falling towards Petrockstow. Inside the gate the siding divided into two loops, for incoming and outgoing wagons, connected by a crossover, and then continued into the works. The locomotive would leave its train on the main line, bring in empty wagons and then depart with loaded wagons. The

siding was served by both 'up' and 'down' trains, the locomotives of 'down' trains using the release crossover in the siding; main line locomotives were banned from the remainder of the sidings which were 'dogged' and operated by the clay company's own locomotives.

Most loaded clay wagons went up to Torrington, but those destined for shipment at Fowey Docks went down to Halwill and thence travelled via Wadebridge, Boscarne Junction, Bodmin General and Bodmin Road. The North Devon Clay Company siding came under Torrington station, and the clay company advised the staff at Torrington of their requirements for empty wagons.

For a century, the Holwill family has been associated with the North Devon Clay Company and Mr E.A. Holwill

provided a very full account of the works: *In 1925, the narrow gauge railway from the works to Torrington took all the tonnage of clay and some of the bricks we produced, and the standard gauge line absorbed this traffic but it did not expand very much, as the 1926 General Strike completely cut off our supply of stoneware clay for the manufacture of jam pots. Up to then, we were supplying about 10,000 tons of clay to the jam manufacturers who had their own potteries, such as W. P. Hardey, who had two factories at St. Helens and Melling in Lancashire, and the CWS who had two at Rotherham and Ferrybridge in Yorkshire, and also to several factories in the Glasgow district making pots for various jam makers. Due to the General Strike, these potteries could not get the coal to fire their kilns and the jam makers were forced to find a substitute for the stoneware jam pots, namely cheap Belgian glass pots. The*

Marland (North Devon Clay Co.) siding.—Upon arrival of a down train at the siding the Guard must fully apply the brake in the rear van and securely apply a sufficient number of wagon brakes to ensure that the vehicles standing on the running line remain stationary. After unlocking the siding gate and operating the ground frame, the vehicles for the siding must be drawn forward into the outer loop clear of the loop facing points. The engine must then be detached and shunted to the inner loop where it must be attached to the outgoing wagons, which will be marshalled by the Marland Clay Company's employees on that loop. The outgoing wagons must then be propelled on to that portion of the train left on the running line.

Upon arrival of an up train at the siding, ingoing wagons must be propelled by the train engine on to the outer loop and outgoing wagons drawn from the inner loop.

The Company's engine must not proceed into the siding beyond the engine restriction boards which are erected on the sidings, (1) approximately 50 yards beyond the facing connection leading from the outer loop to the Clay Company's Works, (2) approximately 25 yards beyond the trailing connection on the inner loop.

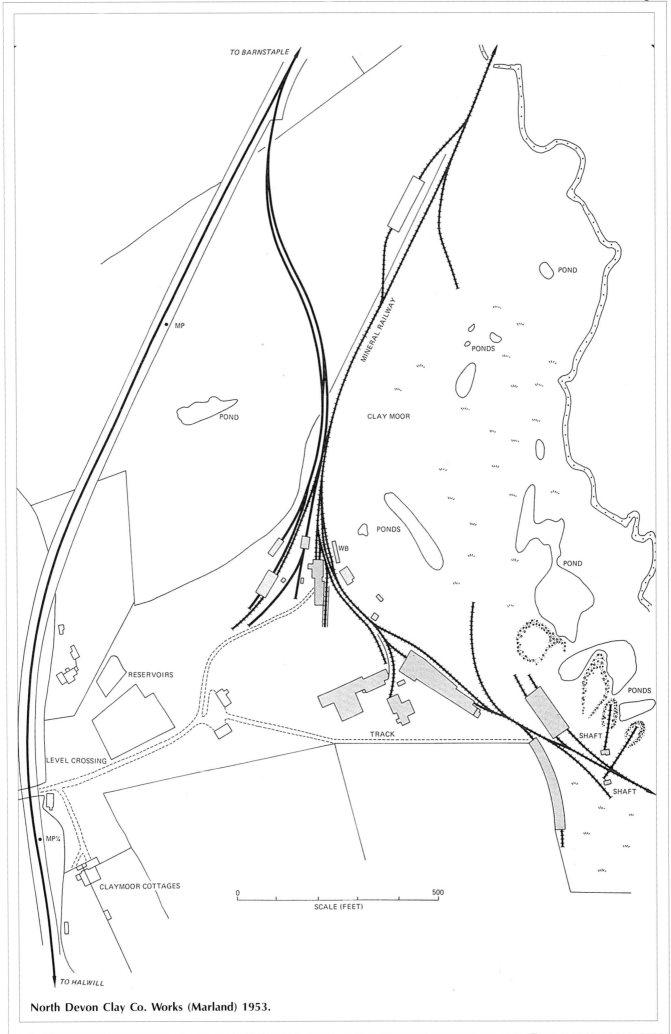

TO BARNSTAPLE

MP

POND

MINERAL RAILWAY

POND

PONDS

CLAY MOOR

POND

PONDS

WB

PONDS

RESERVOIRS

POND

TRACK

PONDS

SHAFT

LEVEL CROSSING

SHAFT

MP¼

CLAYMOOR COTTAGES

0   500

SCALE (FEET)

TO HALWILL

North Devon Clay Co. Works (Marland) 1953.

Fowler 0-4-0DM No.3900012 FORWARD on 4 September 1961, with a train of wagons containing dried and shredded clay ready for despatch. The buildings behind are constructed from Marland brick, which was formerly produced at the site. R. Sellick.

British glass industry then saw the market, and ever since jam has been sold in glass pots. Keillers marmalade still came in a white pot but this was of earthenware, made by Malings of Newcastle. The only stoneware pots produced after this were the large ones such as 7lb. sizes, etc., for the confectionery trade. Most of the stoneware potteries closed down and did not reopen. Other stoneware goods gradually disappeared, such as hot water bottles which were replaced by rubber ones, and Stephens ink bottles, replaced by glass.

When I first went to the clay company in 1923, they were about to reopen the brickworks, closed in 1914 at the outbreak of war, which used waste clay and we produced about three and a half million bricks per annum. Types of brick produced included common perforated building, solid wire cuts, bull nose, splays and squints, and also 2½in., 3in., 4in. and 6in. land drain pipes. Various housing schemes in Bideford, Barnstaple and Ilfracombe used them, but it was not difficult to get architects to specify them for engineering and other types of work. Prior to 1914, we supplied waterworks, sewerage schemes, bridges and viaducts, and we provided many thousands for the lining of the strong rooms for banks from London to the west, but of course the concrete age caught up with this in the end. The brickworks closed for good in 1942. Since the beginning of the war in 1939 we had not made any bricks as there was no building going on but we continued to make the pipes. Costs caught up with us, and we found that to produce a thousand common perforated bricks, which

had a maximum controlled selling price of 85 shillings per thousand, it took 9 cwt of coal at a cost of 25 shillings. In 1942, we had a very large slip in the open pit from which we produced the brick clay and, with costs as they were, it was decided to cease operations in this pit and close the brickyard completely. One well-known engineering work constructed of Marland Brick is Chelfam Viaduct, on the Lynton and Barnstaple Railway, which still stands to this day.

Clay production was then about 30,000 tons per annum of potters clays. The continental trade was at a standstill throughout the war, but we did still ship to the USA and Canada by way of the Liberty ships, which came over from the States with arms, etc., and they took back ball clay and china clay as ballast. Up to 1939, we used to ship to America via Bristol and Avonmouth by Charles Hill & Sons 'Bristol City Line' in ships with such names as Bristol City, New York City, Chicago City, Boston City, Montreal City, etc., and these used to load from railway wagons forwarded at Cannons Marsh or Wapping Wharf, Bristol, and later at the Royal Edward Docks at Avonmouth. They carried general cargo in addition to the clay.

After the war, the shipping was switched to Fowey and, for a time, some of the 'City' ships would go there, and now the entire cargo, not just the ballast, consisted of china clay and ball clay. Our company supplied 75 per cent of all the English ball clay shipped to the USA, which was used mainly for insulators and, to a small extent, for sanitary ware.

In the home market our share of the Staffordshire pottery requirements was small, about 4,000 tons per annum but, in 1948, research undertaken by the pottery industry found that our clays were the best in 'green strength' so our supplies were in great demand and, in 1967, production for the home market had reached 20,000 tons per annum. The continental market on the other hand did not regain its pre-war level.

The introduction of mechanical plant supplied by Watts Blake Bearne & Co. Ltd. of Newton Abbot enabled production to soar. The light railway was closed in 1970 and was replaced by lorries. Production of clay by mining ceased, and was concentrated on two opencast quarries. There had been about 54 men working in the mines and two rail packers looking after the track. When I retired from the company we were nearing the 100,000 tons mark of production with only thirty five men, which included the engineering staff of fitters, electricians, carpenters, etc.

We had great difficulties over pit props for the mines. We preferred to use English larch and this was cut into 5ft. 6in. lengths, with a 7 to 10in. diameter top. Larch would always give plenty of notice before breaking, and it would not sever in two as would oak and other species, but would break like a matchstick. It was, however, very difficult to obtain, and we cleared out all the larch in the district roundabout, after which we had to buy standing larch from Hampshire and, in the end, the Forestry Commission supplied us.

The number of railwaymen employed in

my earlier days would be two looking after the Torrington Viaduct, three rail packers for the track and three locomotive drivers and their assistants. One light railway driver and assistant ceased when the main line was put into the works, but they had to operate the standard gauge locomotive on the main line sidings. When the light railway closed, we had only one locomotive driver for the diesel which was used for shunting purposes.

When I retired in 1974, only one railwayman was left and it was his job to drive the main line locomotive for shunting in our standard gauge sidings. We had to put the loads out and then British Rail would come twice per day to take them to Torrington, thence to Barnstaple and Exeter. We maintained our own extension of the main line, which was 'dogged' and British Rail looked after their own chaired track, their engines not being allowed beyond the chaired track.

The clay company's locomotive PETER was made by Stephen Lewin of Poole, and AVONSIDE was purchased from the Avonside Engine Co. Ltd. for £250. The history of MARLAND, JERSEY No.1 and JERSEY No.2 is rather complicated. The company bought three old locomotives in 1908, which had been standing on the breakwater at St. Helier, Jersey for many years, since they had been used in the construction of the breakwater. They were brought back to the works, stripped down completely, and Marcus H. Hodges of Exeter made one good locomotive from two of them. There was also a locomotive called COFFEE POT which operated at the open pit, and like PETER this had no cab.

When we first had the main line at the works we tried out a Muir Hill/Fordson Rail Tractor, which we had obtained through Ford agents in Holsworthy. This was simply a tractor engine mounted on the floor in the centre of what was no more than a railway goods guards van. The first try-out with about five main line wagons lifted it off its wheels so it was obviously quite useless. It was then that we purchased PROGRESS with No.79 as a spare. No.79 did not last long and was replaced by PETER, which we bought from the Whitehead Engineering Co. in South Wales. The 3ft. gauge locomotives FORWARD, then ADVANCE and then EFFICIENCY were purchased about 1946-50. The latter two were Fowler/Marshall engines. Following these, we had three Ruston 48 DL locomotives and, after the closure of the light railway, we retained the last Ruston and transferred the transmission gear to the main line locomotive PETER, as we could not obtain any spares for either of these two engines.

Up to 1970 clay was brought to the transhipment shed in 3ft gauge wagons with side doors, running on a high level track, and here a side-tipping mechanism was employed to load the clay into the standard gauge trucks on the low level siding below. Prior to closure of the line, standard gauge trucks were loaded by dumpers inside a modern large clay storage shed, which incorporated its own weighbridge. The trucks were shunted between the loading shed and the interchange siding by one of the two standard gauge locomotives still in service, the 1945 Fowler, which has recently been modified and fitted with a Leyland engine and a Dowty hydrostatic drive within the original profile of the engine, and a 1958 Ruston 48DLS which was bought second-hand in 1974.

A very full account of the North Devon Clay Company and its Torrington and Marland Railway is given In *North Devon Clay* by Michael Messenger (Twelveheads Press, 2007). Leaving the North Devon Clay Company siding, the main line curved gently round the clay works which were partially visible through the trees. It then crossed Marland (Claymoor) crossing, a standard ND&CJLR level crossing over the road giving access to the clay works, and ran south-east through the open Marland Moor, crossing three streams on culverts, before reaching the Petrockstow 'down' home signal and entering Petrockstow station over another standard level crossing.

Petrockstow

Line and signalling opened
27th July 1925
Public goods services withdrawn
7th September 1964
Passenger services withdrawn
1st March 1965
Lever frame taken out of use
26th February 1967
Line closed 7th November 1982

Petrockstow station was about a mile from the village, with a crossing loop long enough to accommodate a locomotive and twenty four wagons. There were two platforms and two sidings in the goods yard, the standard arrangement for the three stations on the ND&CJLR. The platforms and station building on the 'up' platform were constructed from local stone with a small wooden awning incorporated in the building. In the yard was a cattle loading dock but no goods shed. Other standard ND&CJLR features were reduced signalling, with only home and starting signals in each direction, controlled from an outdoor seven lever frame beyond the 'up' platform. The electric train tablet instruments were in the booking office, for there was no

The first substantial station building on the line was to be found at Petrockstow; it had two sidings, one serving some cattle pens. Ivatt tank 41297 is on the 4.37pm up train to Torrington in 9th July 1962. H.C. Casserley, courtesy Richard Casserley.

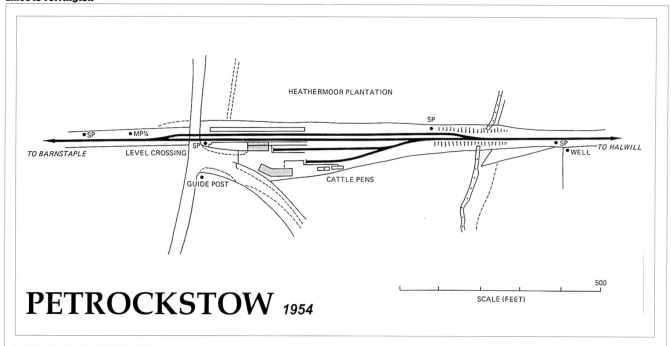

PETROCKSTOW *1954*

Left. The down platform at Petrockstow in 29th February 1956, the Heathermoor Plantation looming up behind; it had nothing in the way of creature comforts apart from this old wooden seat. Richard Casserley.

Below. The 4.37pm Torrington mixed train, with a single Maunsell coach. The Maunsell brake third coach provided 6.25am workmen's service from Torrington to Dunsbear Halt, attached to a Halwill freight service. It was stabled at Petrockstow during the day, and attached to the 2.20pm freight from Halwill seen here for the workmen's return journey from Dunsbear.H.C. Casserley, courtesy Richard Casserley.

Petrockstow in September 1956. In the down platform is 41297on the 10.30am goods from Torrington to Halwill, crossing the 10.38am up service from Halwill. There was a crossing loop here which could accommodate a locomotive and 24 wagons. H.C. Casserley, courtesy Richard Casserley.

conventional signal box. The signals were mounted on the standard SR signal post, fashioned from two lengths of old rail. Tyer's No.6 electric train tablet instruments were provided for the single line sections to Torrington (almost eight miles away) and Hatherleigh (nearly five miles) thus permitting out and back trips to the Marland and Meeth sidings from either end of the single line section.

Mr Fred Cooper joined the Southern Railway to work at Petrockstow station a few weeks after its opening in September 1925, and only retired in February 1967 when the signalling was taken out of use. He lived in the village, and must have been one of the very few railwaymen whose career covered the entire life of their station: There was no stationmaster at Petrockstow, he recalled: *The station instead was supervised by the Hatherleigh stationmaster. It was normally staffed by two railwaymen working early and late turns, who carried out all the station duties. These duties included signalling, sheeting and roping wagons, loading cattle and other merchandise, recording outwards and inwards traffic and compiling station returns and accounts. Passenger ticket sales were not large, being only eight or ten a day after opening, and falling away later as bus services developed. Petrockstow dealt with more passenger traffic than Hatherleigh or Hole, the few local*

passengers usually booking tickets through to Torrington or Bideford.

In the 1930s Petrockstow was receiving an average of about two loaded wagons per day and forwarding one. At one stage, considerable numbers of cattle were forwarded, mainly store cattle to Hampshire or Kent, and timber was another important outward traffic. Hundreds of tons of pit wood were forwarded from Petrockstow, being loaded by Messrs Chappell & Walton of Barnstaple and, during the war years, by the Ministry of Supply, and sawn timber was forwarded by Messrs Stennings of Buckland Filleigh Saw Mills. Inward traffic was mainly fertilisers and animal feed stuffs for the agricultural community and coal for local merchants. In the yard, Silcocks had a store for animal feed stuffs for which the station staff provided the labour, while the West Devon and North Cornwall Farmers of Holsworthy had a store manned by their own staff. This company built up a big business in the area and subsequently constructed an extensive new store on the other side of the road.

The yard at Petrockstow was often quite full with clay wagons brought from the North Devon Clay Company's siding and forwarded to Torrington on a mixed train, with up to eight wagons attached to the single passenger coach. The E1R 0-6-2 tank engines were restricted to sixteen loaded goods wagons between Marland and Torrington, so the mixed trains helped to spread the load at busy times. The passenger

coach used for the workmens train arrived at Petrockstow just after 7 a.m., and was berthed in the yard until about 5 p.m., when it departed behind the 'up' goods which then ran as a mixed train to Torrington.

The line at Petrockstow ran through the estates of Lord Clinton, a Director of the Southern Railway and a Chairman of the North Devon & Cornwall Junction Light Railway. His residence was at Heanton Satchville, about a mile from Petrockstow, and his estates provided employment for many local workers.

Public goods services were withdrawn from Petrockstow on 7th September 1964 and passenger services on 1st March 1965, but Fred Cooper remained working at Petrockstow to signal the clay trains until 26th February 1967; when the signalling and goods yard were taken out of use, he retired. The level crossing, passing loop and platforms survived until final closure, but the station building was demolished. The goods yard became a depot for the Devon County Council, and the West Devon and North Cornwall Farmers depot thrived on the other side of the road. The daily train serving the Meeth clay works passed through, and the loop was retained for running-round purposes.

Occasionally, the platforms at Petrockstow came to life on the arrival

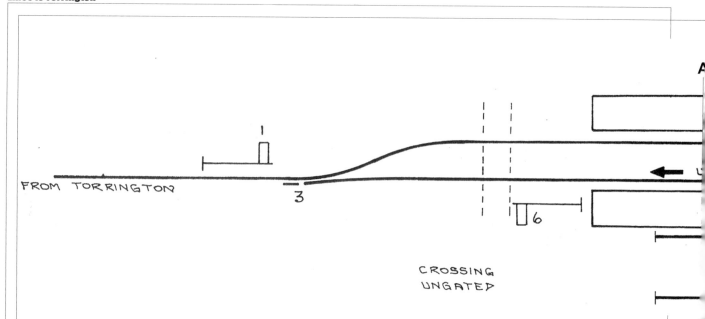

FROM TORRINGTON

3

6

CROSSING
UNGATED

PETROCKSTOW *Undated signal diagram*

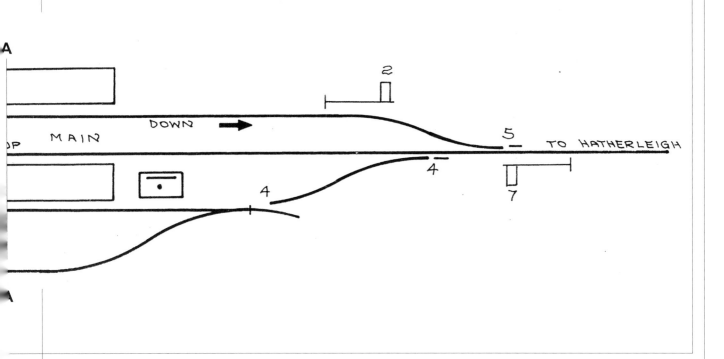

Above. Ivatt tank 41248 runs into Petrockstow over Bury Cross with the 4.40 Torrington to Halwill service in July 1964.

Left. Petrockstow's up platform building in August 1956, with that air of 'Colonel Stephens' about it. There was no signal box but instead a seven lever frame was sited on the end of the up platform with the electric train tablet located in the booking office. The Maunsell brake third coach used for the Torrington and Dunsbear workmen's service was berthed in the yard during the day. John Eyers, courtesy South Western Circle.

R.C. Riley takes time to photograph 41322 on the 8.52am Torrington to Halwill service on 25 September 1962, with the early turn porter keeping an eye on these unconventional goings-on. R.C. Riley, transporttreasury.

Above and below. Ivatt 2-6-2T 41297 arrives at Petrockstow with the 10.30am goods from Torrington to Halwill, passing 41298 on the 10.38am passenger train from Halwill to Torrington. H.C. Casserley, courtesy Richard Casserley.

of a special passenger train and. in the summer of 1981 a locally organised special train called at Petrockstow, where the local Womens Institute provided refreshments on the platform.

Beyond Petrockstow station the line ran down through wooded country, with a couple of culverts spanning the Little Mere River and another stream, at one stage running almost due east until arriving at the loop siding on the west side of the line serving the Meeth Clay Company.

Meeth Clay Company Siding

The loop siding for the Meeth Clay

Company was near a dip in the line between summits at Yarde and Meeth Halt. At the Petrockstow end, the gradient was 1 in 175 falling towards Hatherleigh and, at the Hatherleigh end, 1 in 195 falling towards Petrockstow. The points at each end of the siding were operated from two ground frames, each unlocked with the electric train tablet. The gates across each end of the siding were unlocked with a key kept by the stationmaster at Torrington, although the Meeth Clay Company siding was administered from Hatherleigh station. Wagons were ordered by the clay company from

staff at Hatherleigh, but were delivered by trains from Torrington.

Clay mining at Meeth did not start as early as at Marland, but the Meeth Clay Company, later the Meeth (North Devon) Clay Company, was formed when the North Devon & Cornwall Junction Light Railway was under construction. Some clay was sent out by lorry and some by rail before the official opening of the ND&CJLR, and the long loop siding enabled the works to be served by both 'up' and 'down' trains. Inside the works was an extensive 2ft gauge system, worked by two Ruston 4 ton diesel locomotives

Compared to other places on the line Petrockstow was relatively well provided for, with sidings and a cattle dock. Local goods out consisted mostly of timber whilst agricultural products such as animal feedstuffs and fertiliser came in. House coal also arrived in wagons, normally shunted by a down train – in the 1930s two wagons in and one out was the norm. Silcocks had an animal feed store in the yard, the station staff providing the labour. John Eyers, courtesy South Western Circle.

although in 1925 an 0-6-0WT steam locomotive, WESTERN LEA, was obtained from P&W. Anderson, the ND&CJLR contractors, who used a 2ft gauge railway in this area during construction. It therefore seems quite possible that other 2ft gauge equipment was also acquired in this way. Inside the loading shed the narrow gauge tipper wagons discharged the clay from a high level track into the standard gauge wagons below, which were then sheeted. The company never had standard gauge locomotives of its own and the last sections of the narrow gauge system were taken out of use about 1969.

The Meeth Works became part of the ECC Ball Clays Ltd., part of the English China Clays Group. Clay was then extracted by opencast quarrying, and all internal transport within the works was by lorry and dumper. After extraction, the clay was stored in a large shed until despatched to customers. Clay was then loaded into a lorry, weighed on the weighbridge, and taken to the large new rail loading shed where between 12½ and 13 tonnes were tipped into standard BR wagons which were then sheeted. This weighing procedure was adopted after the closure of the Fremington wagon weighbridge in 1979. The BR train arrived at the works at about 9.30 a.m. to deliver

empty wagons and collect loaded ones, which were then worked to Barnstaple and Exeter (Riverside) Yard and, together with despatches from South Devon and Cornwall, made up into the nightly 'Clayliner' train for Stoke-on-Trent.

After 1965 the line terminated at buffer stops shortly beyond the end of the loop siding, where an old tank wagon served as a fuel store. The track here incorporated LSWR chairs with dates as far back as 1908. The three-quarters of a mile of trackbed from the works to the A386 at the site of Meeth Halt became the road access to the works, and was BR property leased to the clay company.

Leaving the Meeth Clay Company's siding, the line ran in a south-easterly direction climbing up to the next summit near Meeth Halt. The line then crossed a culvert and an occupation crossing before arriving at Meeth Halt.

Meeth Halt

Meeth Halt and siding lay immediately to the west of the standard level crossing over the main A386 road between Torrington, Hatherleigh and Okehampton, approximately a quarter of a mile along the road from the village. Both the halt and siding were provided by the ND&CJLR when it opened in 1925; like Dunsbear, the

platform was built using local stone, the waiting-room was also stone in contrast with the workmans shelter ot Dunsbear. Unlike the other halts, Meeth had no workmens service to the clay works and so passenger traffic was sparse, passengers purchasing their tickets from the guard on the train.

The single siding at Meeth was served by 'up' goods trains, and the points operated from a ground frame released by the electric train tablet. At this point, the running line was on a gradient of 1 in 50 falling towards Petrockstow. The siding at Meeth was useful for dropping off wagons from the clay works, to be collected by other trains.

Meeth siding was closed to public goods traffic on 7th September 1964, and passenger services were withdrawn on 1st March 1965. Subsequently, the tracks were removed and the trackbed down to the Meeth clay works was converted into an access road, but the platform and shelter were left intact. Leaving Meeth Halt and its level crossing, the line ran due east through a cutting and under an occupation bridge, before taking a long sharp curve to emerge on the hillside overlooking the confluence of the rivers Torridge and Okement. The cutting marked the summit of the line at about 330ft; from here, the line fell as it ran in a south-

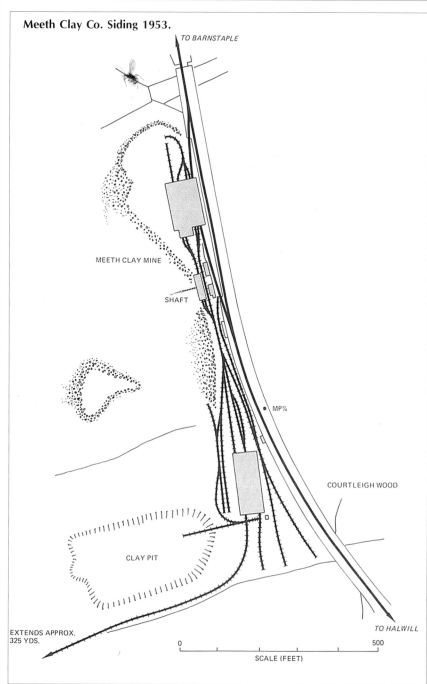

Meeth Clay Co. Siding 1953.

TO BARNSTAPLE

MEETH CLAY MINE

SHAFT

MP¾

COURTLEIGH WOOD

CLAY PIT

EXTENDS APPROX.
325 YDS.

TO HALWILL

0   500

SCALE (FEET)

Meeth Halt in September 1956; the platform was constructed, as at Dunsbear, of random stone and dressed bricks with a small waiting shelter in the same material. It opened with the line and had a small siding at the rear; the buffer stop is just discernible in the bottom left corner of the photograph. The ungated level crossing was, if you can believe it, the A386 Torrington-Okehampton main road.

Wagons being loaded at the EEC Ball Clays works at Meeth in the 1980s. Clay was collected from the storage shed by lorry, which was weighed on the road weighbridge before being discharged into the wagons. Ball Clays Ltd. Collection.

The 2ft gauge system in the Meeth clay works, which used side tipping wagons. The view is inside a storage shed where clay was stored under cover until despatched to customers. The wagons discharged directly into standard gauge wagons. E.E.C. Ball Clays Ltd. Collection.

Meeth Halt in 1960. There was a single siding and a loading gauge with a single lever ground frame released using an electric tablet. An up train would shunt the siding as and when required. The siding closed in September 1964. The shelter, although small, housed a goods store, its door just in view, with a booking hall and office out of view.

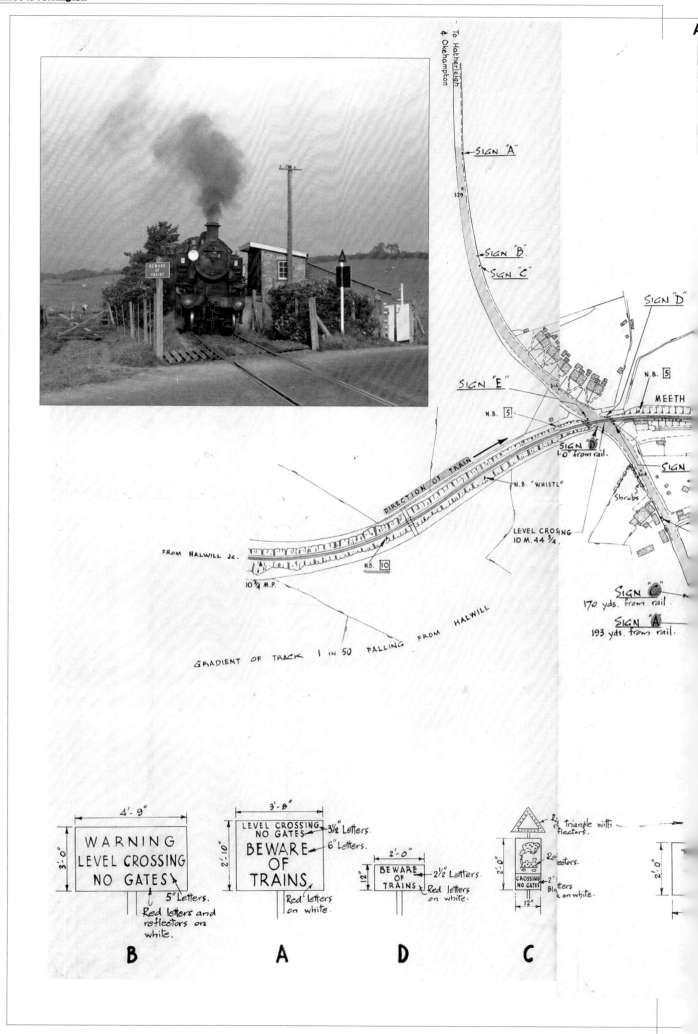

To Hatherleigh & Okehampton

SIGN "A"

329

SIGN "B"

SIGN "C"

SIGN "D"

SIGN "E"

N.B. 5

MEETH

N.B. 5

SIGN "D"
1'-0" from rail.

SIGN

DIRECTION OF TRAIN

N.B. "WHISTL"

Shrubs

LEVEL CROSING
10 M. 44 ¾.

FROM HALWILL Jc.

N.B. 10

10 ¾ M.P.

SIGN "C"
170 yds. from rail.

SIGN "A"
193 yds. from rail.

GRADIENT OF TRACK 1 IN 50 FALLING FROM HALWILL

4'-9"

3'-0"

WARNING
LEVEL CROSSING
NO GATES

5" Letters.
Red letters and reflectors on white.

B

3'-8"

2'-10"

LEVEL CROSSING
NO GATES — 3½" Letters.
BEWARE — 6" Letters.
OF
TRAINS.

Red letters on white.

A

2'-0"

12"

BEWARE
OF
TRAINS — 2½" Letters.
Red letters on white.

D

R⁴ triangle with reflectors.

Reflectors.

2'-0"

CROSSING
NO GATES — 2" B²letters k on white.

12"

C

2'-0"

Meeth on 25 September 1962 and R.C. Riley's train pauses to pick up a lone passenger. The plan records the crash of January 1960 when an up train collided with a Southern National bus. No details have been found in the relevant minutes, which is not unusual as there were no fatalities. The question seems to be, was enough warning given to the bus driver from the train crew and was the bus driver paying enough attention when approaching the crossing? Close attention is paid to the various signs and the siting thereof, doubtless in order to determine blame. R.C. Riley, transporttreasury.

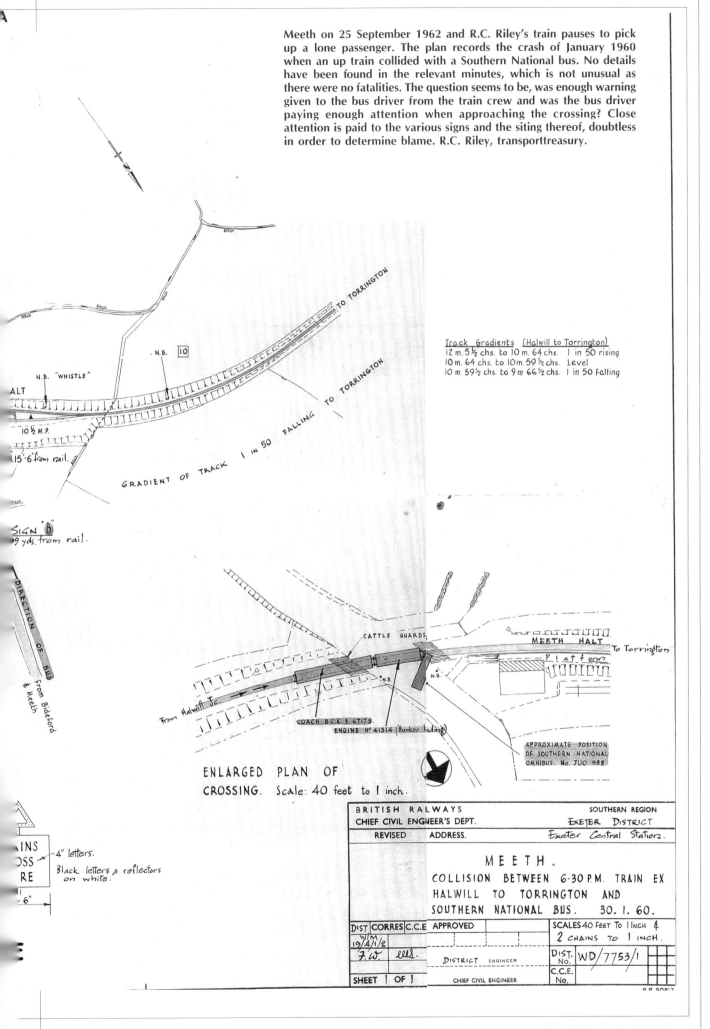

A

N.B. 10

N.B. "WHISTLE"

ALT

10½ M.P.

15'·6 from rail.

SIGN "D"
9 yds. from rail.

DIRECTION OF BUS
From Bideford
& Meeth

TO TORRINGTON
TO TORRINGTON
TO TORRINGTON

Track Gradients (Halwill to Torrington)
12 m. 5½ chs. to 10 m. 64 chs. 1 in 50 rising
10 m. 64 chs. to 10 m. 59½ chs. Level
10 m. 59½ chs. to 9 m. 66½ chs. 1 in 50 falling

GRADIENT OF TRACK 1 IN 50 FALLING

CATTLE GUARDS
MEETH HALT
To Torrington
Platform
N.B.
N.B.
From Halwill Jc.

COACH B.C.K. 3. 671/S.
ENGINE Nº 41314 (Bunker leading)

APPROXIMATE POSITION OF SOUTHERN NATIONAL OMNIBUS No. JUO 988

ENLARGED PLAN OF CROSSING. Scale: 40 feet to 1 inch.

INS
OSS
RE

4" letters.
Black letters & reflectors on white.

6"

BRITISH RAILWAYS
CHIEF CIVIL ENGINEER'S DEPT.

SOUTHERN REGION
EXETER DISTRICT

REVISED	ADDRESS.	Exeter Central Station.

MEETH.
COLLISION BETWEEN 6·30 P.M. TRAIN EX HALWILL TO TORRINGTON AND SOUTHERN NATIONAL BUS. 30. 1. 60.

DIST	CORRES	C.C.E	APPROVED		SCALES 40 FEET TO 1 INCH & 2 CHAINS TO 1 INCH.
W/M 19/4/1/2					
J.W.	ell.		DISTRICT ENGINEER		DIST. No. WD/7753/1
SHEET 1 OF 1			CHIEF CIVIL ENGINEER		C.C.E. No.

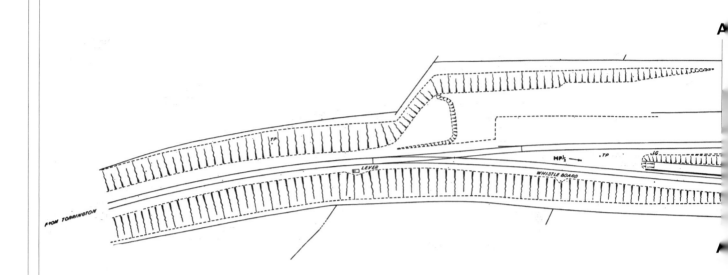

MEETH HALT *1959*

The 4.0 from Torrington with 41298 in charge, 29th February 1956. In the distance the warning sign (see crash diagram) is sign E, TRAINS CROSS HERE. H.C. Casserley, courtesy Richard Casserley.

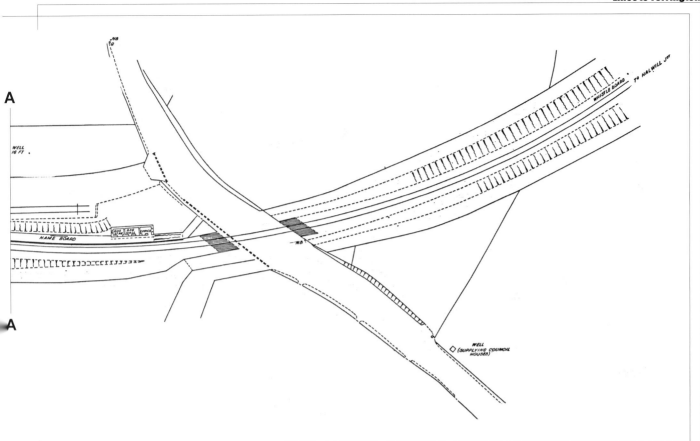

westerly direction for a couple of miles to Hatherleigh station. It passed over Wooda Lane crossing, a standard ND&CJLR type, and later crossed the A386 on a girder bridge (removed after the closure of the line) then over the Torridge, just below its confluence with the River Lew, where the 1922 ceremony of cutting the first sod of the ND&CJLR was performed, and into Hatherleigh station on an embankment.

Hatherleigh
Line and signalling opened
27th July 1925
Public goods services withdrawn
7th September 1964
Line closed 1st March 1965

The small town of Hatherleigh was the largest centre of population on the ND&CJLR, but was very poorly served by the railway. It was almost two miles from the town along hilly and inconvenient roads, or a little less by a more direct footpath through the fields. As early as 1934, only one or two

passenger tickets per day were sold, so the station had to earn its keep with the parcels and goods traffic. In 1929 Mr William Balsdon, a Hatherleigh grocer and farmer, criticised the system of clearing goods and the timing and number of trains, particularly goods.

Hatherleigh station was constructed to the same standard design as Petrockstow and Hole with a passing loop long enough to accommodate a locomotive and twenty one wagons, with two platforms and two sidings in the yard. The signals and points were

Hatherleigh was by far the largest town on the ND&CJLR but the station was inconveniently sited, some two miles from the village along hilly and winding roads. There was a shorter route by foot but this took potential passengers over often muddy fields. The 10.38 Halwill to Torrington train prepares to leave behind 41298 in September 1956. R. M. Casserley.

operated from a seven lever frame at the end of the 'up' platform, with the electric train tablet instruments in the booking office. Tyer's No.6 instruments were provided for the single line sections to Petrockstow and to Hole. The signals were of the standard SR rail-built variety with the standard home and starting signals in each direction, but there was also a fixed 'up' distant signal. The only available water for locomotives between Torrington and Halwill was at Hatherleigh and at the end of each platform was a simple water column. Water was pumped up from the River Lew to a large tank on the embankment above the station, a man from the outdoor machinery department at Barnstaple travelling down twice a week to operate the pump. When the Hatherleigh water supply was out of action, the E1R 0-6-2Ts had to be

Top. Hatherleigh's up platform in August 1962 with a lone passenger awaiting the next train. Hatherleigh's senior status on the ND&CJLR meant it had a station master who also supervised the stations at Petrockstow and Hole.

Right. The view from the cab of the Halwill-bound diesel railcar, with the starter signal in the off position.

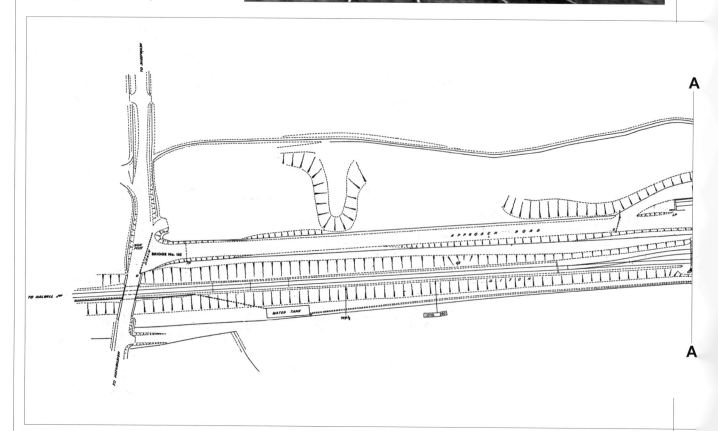

Staff gather with some lady friends at Hatherleigh for the usual group photo in the late 1930s. The original station name board will be replaced by the traditional British Railways metal version after the War.

HATHERLEIGH *1959*

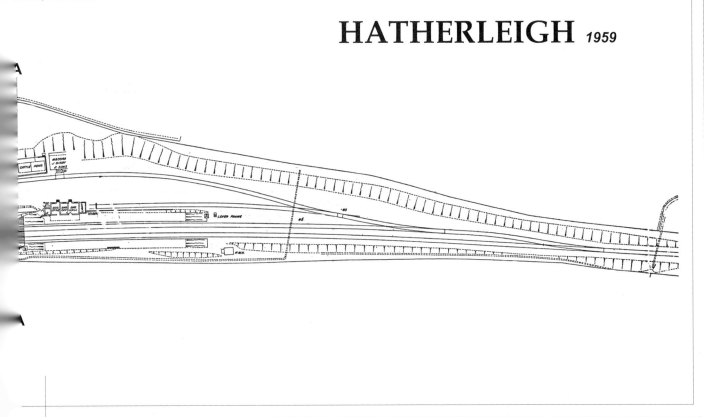

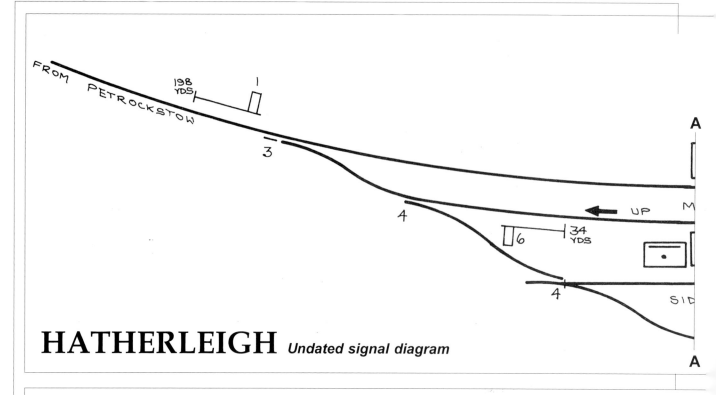

FROM PETROCKSTOW

198 YDS

1

3

4

6

34 YDS

4

UP

A

A

SID

HATHERLEIGH *Undated signal diagram*

Hatherleigh was the only intermediate station on the ND&CJLR to have water available, the columns fed from a large water tank high on the embankment on the down side near to Bridge 163 – it is just visible in the top photograph on page 116. It was fed from the nearby River Lew using a steam pump fired up twice a week by a member of staff. Like Petrockstow and Hole the buildings were of a substantial construction, random stone with brick dressings on the platforms. The 'Colonel Stephens' influence is again apparent with the simple canopies making use of the roof trusses. Although small, the building had a gents, goods store, booking office, booking hall and lamp room. With no conventional signal box the Tyer's No.6 electric train tablet instrument was housed in the booking hall for the single line section. The seven lever ground frame was at the end of the up platform. 41298 is on a goods train bound for Halwill Junction.

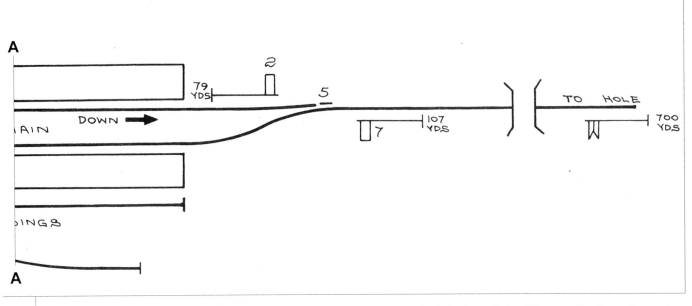

replaced by Adams 0-6-0s, which had a greater water capacity. As elsewhere on the ND&CJLR, the platforms and station building were constructed of local stone.

Hatherleigh was the 'senior' station on the ND&CJLR, the stationmaster also supervising the stations at Petrockstow and Hole. Mr E.V. Morgan occupied the post between 1954 and 1962, having previously worked at Fenns Bank on the Cambrian Section of the Western Region. One other railwayman, a porter signalman, worked at Hatherleigh on alternate early and late turns with the stationmaster. Mr Morgan was able to provide an account of operations at Hatherleigh: *In the yard, Messrs Bibbys had a large store which was run by the railwaymen for animal feed stuffs coming in by train. In early days much hay was forwarded, but later this traffic decreased. A major item of traffic forwarded was cattle,*

Railwaymen on the down platform at Hatherleigh, from left to right, Mr J. Vallence (ganger), Mr. W. Cole (platelayer), Mr. S. Yendole (guard), Mr W. Manning (fireman), Mr. G. Wonnacott (signalman), Mr. A. Snell (outdoor machinery department), Mr. T. Cockwill (platelayer) and Mr. E.V. Morgan (station master). Mr Snell travelled from Barnstaple twice a week to pump water from the River Lew for the tank and Mr. Morgan moved to become Assistant Station Master at London Bridge, which had rather more passengers! E.V. Morgan collection.

A ganger passes the time of day with the crew of a Halwill-bound train of one Bulleid brake composite coach at Hatherleigh, on 25 September 1962. Goods facilities at Hatherleigh comprised two sidings a cattle pen and the stores of Messrs Bibby and Co. who dealt in animal foodstuffs. In the early years hay was forwarded from here in large quantities with cattle forming a substantial outwards traffic. In the background to the right is the loading gauge and the replacement rail built signals with upper quadrant arms. R.C. Riley, transporttreasury.

usually consigned by Mr G. Vick on behalf of the Ministry of Agriculture. On one day, no less than forty eight trucks of sheep were loaded at Hatherleigh. Barnstaple Depot supplied a shunting engine which ran attached to the front of the 8.52 a.m. mixed train from Torrington, and this locomotive spent the whole day running special livestock trains to Halwill Junction, returning with empty cattle wagons, and shunting the yard at Hatherleigh. Such scenes at both Hatherleigh and Hole stations ceased as a result of the 1955 ASLEF strike, which lasted about three weeks, during which time the livestock traffic went by road and did not return.

A gang of permanent way staff was based at Hatherleigh Station maintaining a length of the ND&CJLR, while gangs based at Torrington and Halwill Junction covered adjacent sections. In the late 1950s, the permanent way staff were Mr J. Vallance, Mr W. Cole and Mr T. Cockwill, and the other railwayman to visit Hatherleigh regularly at this time was Mr A. Snell from Barnstaple, who came to pump water for the locomotives. The stationmaster at Hatherleigh was also responsible for the stations at Petrockstow and Hole, Meeth Halt and siding and the Meeth Clay Company's siding. Mr Morgan. visited Hole once a week, going down on the first train and returning on it when it

Above. A quiet moment at the station in July 1962. The lean-to at the end of the building housed the lamps. R.M. Casserley.

Below. The loops could hold up to twenty-one wagons and a locomotive but with the paucity of traffic probably never came near to full capacity. Ivatt 41248 is on a down train from Torrington with the 4.40 on 25 July 1964.

Hole Station, a replica of the one at Petrockstow. The year is probably 1925 shortly after the line opened with all the original features in place, lower quadrant signals and the small ground frame on the left.

came back from Halwill. He also visited Petrockstow once a week, going up on the afternoon freight train and returning on the evening passenger train from Torrington.

In 1962 he moved on to Dinton, then Wilton, Bellingham, Catford Bridge and Charing Cross, and, in 1964, to London Bridge where be became Assistant Station Manager, a considerable change from rural Hatherleigh. After closure, the tracks were removed, but the site was subsequently sold and the station building converted to a private house. A couple of signal posts and the pump house by the River Lew also remain.

After leaving Hatherleigh station the line ran through a cutting under a road bridge, and then out over the River Lew past the pump house. On the remaining eight miles of the ND&CJLR, the line rose from Hatherleigh station, at an altitude of about 200ft., to Halwill, at more than 600ft., so the gradients were almost continuously uphill, at times as steep as 1 in 50. The line passed the Hatherleigh 'up' distant signal which was fixed, and ran approximately south-west through meadows adjacent to Pulworthy Brook, over Pulworthy Road level crossing and a culvert, before turning west, and following the A3072 Hatherleigh to Holsworthy main road for some three miles, crossing it at Venton Road level crossing. Along this stretch of line were a number of level crossings over minor roads and farm tracks, including Rosemans Bower Road level crossing near the village of Highampton. Passing this village, the line continued west for a mile or so before passing through a short cutting, then under a bridge, and into Hole station.

Hole
Line and signalling opened
27th July 1925
Public goods services withdrawn
7th September 1964
Line closed 1st March 1965
Hole, for Black Torrington, rivalled Hatherleigh station for its remoteness, which again discouraged passengers.

Approached by a track, which could hardly be described as a road, half a mile long, from the main road at Windmilland Cross, the station purported to serve the villages of Black Torrington, Sheepwash and Highampton, all several miles away. Presumably, the name Black Torrington was avoided to prevent confusion with Torrington station although the tiny hamlet of Hole was, in fact, some four miles away and better served by Dunsland Cross station on the Bude line.

Much later, in 1956, and the signals have now been replaced by Southern Region rail-built examples. R.M. Casserley.

HOLE *1959*

The enamel running in board at Hole proclaimed FOR BLACK TORRINGTON – this lay a mile or so to the north, a hamlet of a few hundred people.

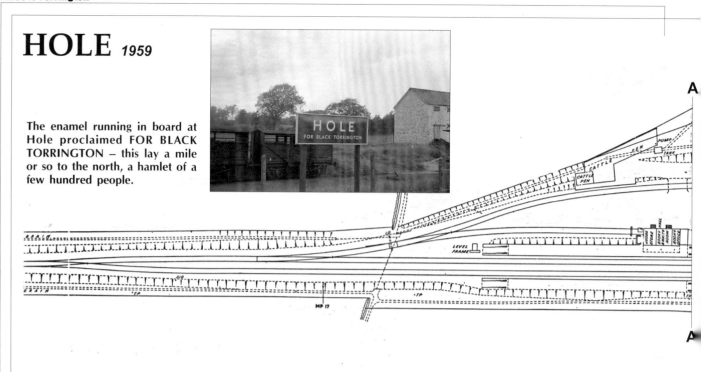

HOLE *Undated*

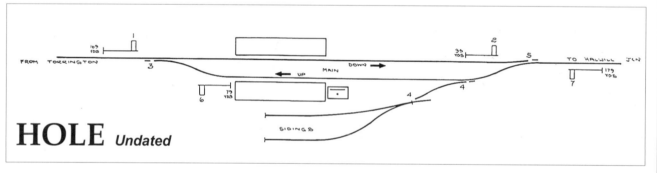

Looking towards Halwill in 1956. The station building on the up side comprised a goods store, booking hall, waiting room and booking office. A lamp room occupied the lean-to at the end. The woods to the north have been left behind and the country is more like a gentle plain. R.M. Casserley.

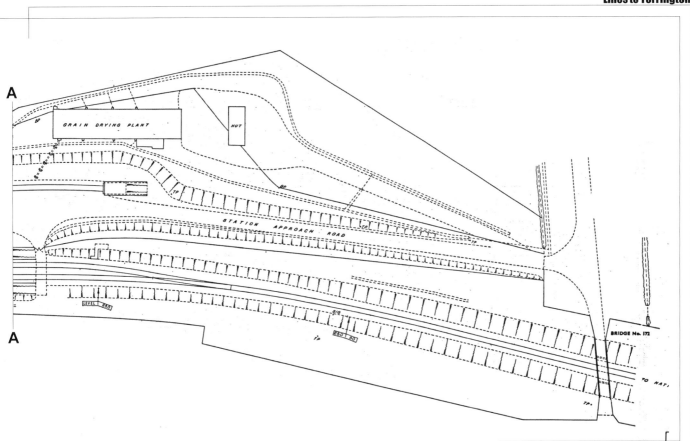

The seven lever frame was controlled by a Tyer's No.6 instrument in the station; a passing loop and small goods yard completed the arrangements at this remote station. The familiar 41298 has the 9.00am Torrington-Halwill in January 1956. R.M. Casserley.

Hole on 25 September 1962. Nothing seems to have changed much from Southern Railway days when the daily passengers in or out totalled... two, with maybe the odd wagon despatched from the yard. R.C. Riley, transporttreasury

For many years only one man was required for a shift owing to the fact there were only three trains a day, in later years a porter signalman sufficed to cover all duties. In this desolate scene in 1956 the yard seems to be busy with several cattle wagons which were shunted, when required, by a locomotive from Barnstaple, the animals destined for the slaughter house at Halwill Junction. H.C. Casserley, courtesy Richard Casserley.

The porter/signalman waits patiently for Mr Casserley to record the scene in July 1962 before waving away the 4.00pm Torrington-Halwill service. H.C. Casserley, courtesy Richard Casserley.

More cattle wagons in the yard with the pens out of sight on the far side of the yard. There was a small water tank nearby, for flushing down the pens after the cattle had departed and filling the drinking troughs. R.J. Sellick.

Hole station was built to the standard ND&CJLR pattern; stone construction, passing loop for an engine and twenty two wagons, with two platforms and two sidings. The points and signals were operated from a seven lever frame on the 'up' platform, with the electric train tablet instruments in the booking office and Tyer's No.6 instruments for the single line sections to Hatherleigh and Halwill. The elementary signalling comprised home and starting signals mounted on standard Southern Railway rail-built posts in each direction.

For many years Hole saw only three trains daily, the first being the 'down' mixed which arrived just after 10 a.m. and the last being the 'up' mixed train which departed just before 7 p.m. In this way one man could operate the station during his shift. In later years this was porter signalman Mr W. McMath. In Southern days, the average daily business at Hole was only a couple of passengers and a loaded wagon in or out. The main flow of traffic

Hole in 1963 with the huge grain drying shed in the background. Like the other stations with passing loop the one here could also accommodate an engine and twenty-one wagons.

forwarded from Hole in later years was cattle despatched by Mr Crook, a local farmer and cattle dealer. Occasionally, the traffic was sufficient to justify Barnstaple Shed supplying a locomotive to shunt cattle wagons at Hole and run trips with cattle to Halwill Junction. There was also a large store in the station yard which, in later years, was used for 'patent manure' and a wooden chute was provided to facilitate the sliding of sacks straight into the railway wagons. After closure, the tracks were removed but the station building and large store remained, and the whole area became an approved wildlife conservation area.

Leaving Hole station, the line continued to climb south-west over moorland, crossing several streams in culverts. It passed under an occupation bridge and later crossed a minor road on a stone bridge (since demolished) near Winsford Plantation. Passing the Halwill Junction 'down' distant signal, which was fixed, it converged with the Bude line running parallel to it for several hundred yards into Halwill Junction station, the end of our line. In their later days, the ageing E1R tank engines had quite a struggle to heave a train of loaded clay wagons bound

Top. 41248 pauses at Hole with the 4.40 Torrington-Halwill Junction service in August 1964. The station rivalled Hatherleigh and Petrockstow in its remoteness and was reached along a half mile lane from the main road at Windmilland Cross. It is therefore not surprising that passenger traffic was, not to put too fine a point on it, virtually non-existent. Peter Swift.

Right. The seven lever ground frame in 1964; grain drying shed behind. Peter Swift.

The ND&CJLR in September 1956; it terminated in a bay platform on the up side of Halwill Junction station. The train in the North Devon bay with the Ivatt 2-6-2T is the 10.38 departure for Torrington. The ND&CJLR was now alongside the Bude and North Cornwall lines; the T9 4-4-0 in the down platform is 30717 on the 9.56 Okehampton to Wadebridge service. R.M. Casserley.

for Fowey Docks up this gradient to Halwill Junction.

Halwill Junction (Torrington line only)

Line and signalling opened
27th July 1925
Public goods services withdrawn
7th September 1964
Line closed 1st March 1965
A small community grew up around Halwill Junction station, which flourished for almost a century. Opened in 1879 as Beaworthy station, on the branch between Okehampton and Holsworthy, it became a junction in 1886 when the LSWR reached Launceston. By the turn of the century LSWR expresses from Waterloo were split here into Bude and Padstow portions. After a period of inactivity, trains would arrive in rapid succession from Bude, Padstow and Okehampton, through coaches would be shunted on to new trains, and then they would all depart again leaving the village in peace.

The ND&CJLR from Torrington was never allowed to intrude into this bustle. It terminated in a self-contained part of the station with its own short bay platform, and a run-round loop up the line worked from its own ground frame. Thus trains from Torrington could arrive, run round and depart, completely independently of the North

Halwill Junction was one of those places that could be silent for long periods of the day to be suddenly brought into life with a flurry of arrivals and departures. On 9 July 1962 a train from the North Cornwall line behind N mogul 31835 is making its way across to the up side platform with the 3.13 Padstow to Exeter service while passengers leave the 4.00pm train from Torrington. H.C. Casserley, courtesy R.M. Casserley.

Like so many of the Southern stations in Devon and Cornwall Halwill Junction acted as a railhead and staging point for a wider area; thus the station nameboard HALWILL FOR BEAWORTHY AND TRAINS FOR BUDE, NORTH CORNWALL AND TORRINGTON. Standard 3MT tank 82024 is arriving from Bude while the Ivatt 2-6-2T has arrived on 25 September 1962 from Torrington with Mr Riley who afterwards caught a train to Launceston where he stayed overnight. R.C. Riley, transporttreasury

Cornwall and Bude trains. Admittedly, there was a connection which allowed wagons to be shunted across to the yard, but the ND&CJLR was kept at arms length. The goods traffic exchanged at Halwill Junction, between the ND&CJLR and the other lines, included loaded clay wagons travelling from Marland to Fowey, via the North Cornwall line, and cattle wagons loaded at Hatherleigh and Hole for distant markets, returning empties and some general merchandise.

The two ND&CJLR mixed trains, in the morning and evening, played their own part in the brief periods of heightened activity at Halwill Junction.

41297 arrives from Torrington in the ND&CJLR platform; in the background is an indication of Halwill Junction's importance in the fresh meat trade, insulated containers parked in the slaughterhouse siding.

SOUTHERN RAILWAY

Signal Instruction No. 27, 1925.

Instructions to all concerned as to the

HALWILL.

To be brought into use on Thursday, 20th August.

An up home signal from Dunsland Cross, erected outside the middle siding, opposite the existing signal, which will be removed.

The work will be in progress from 10.0 a.m. Mr. Bone to provide flagman, as required.

(R. 7197).

T9 4-4-0 719 after arrival at Halwill from Okehampton with a train for Bude. The extension to the signalbox (made on the arrival of the ND&CJLR in 1925) is most apparent with the signalman peering out.

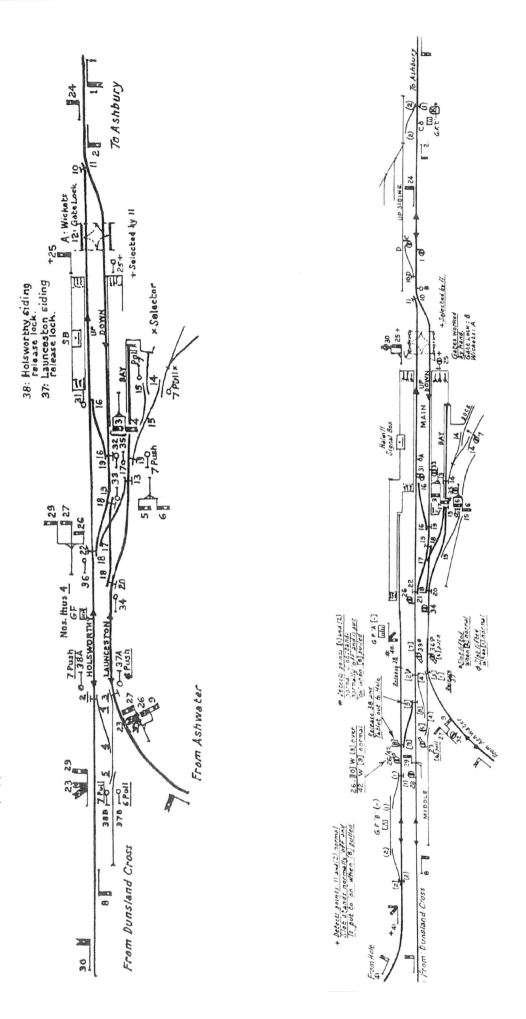

HALWILL *1900 (top) and 1956 (below)*

38: Holsworthy siding
release lock.
37: Launceston siding
release lock.

A: Wickets
12: Gate Lock

+ Selected by 11

× Selector

To Ashbury

From Dunsland Cross

From Ashwater

To Ashbury

UP SIDING

+ Selected by 11

Gates Worked
by hand.
Gate Lock: B
Wickets: A

Halwill
Signal Box

+ Detect joints (1) and (2) normal
When stands normally off 2nd
on when (8) pulled

Release 38 and
Tablet out to Hole

26. 10 W (9) over
42 W (9) normal

G F 'B' (-)

MIDDLE

+ Detect joints (1) and (2) normal
When stands normally off 2nd
To put to on when (8) pulled

From Hole

From Dunsland Cross

* Not lifted
when normal

Φ Not lifted
when normal

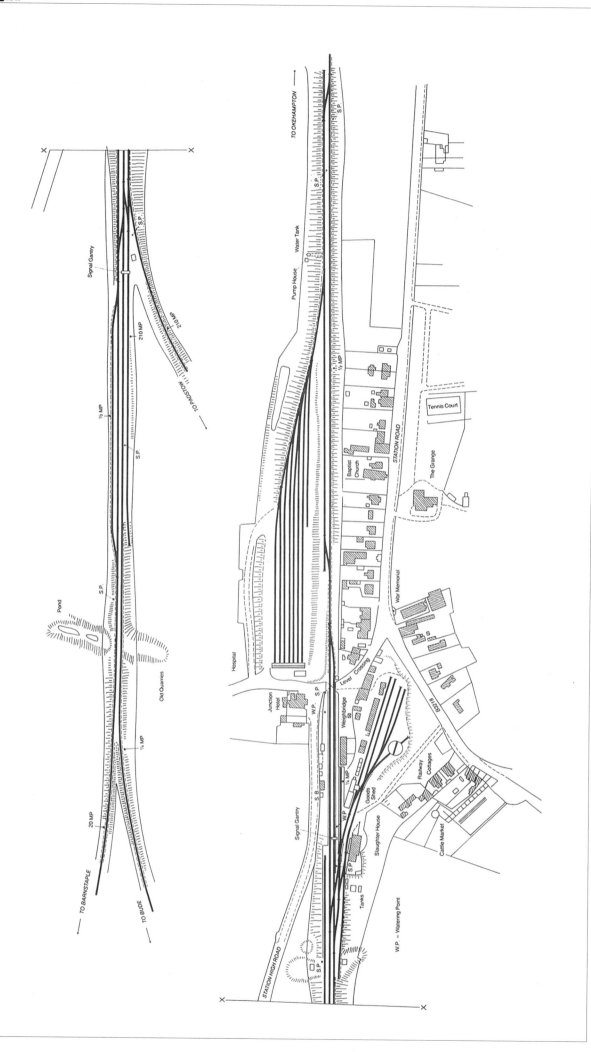

HALWILL JUNCTION *1953*

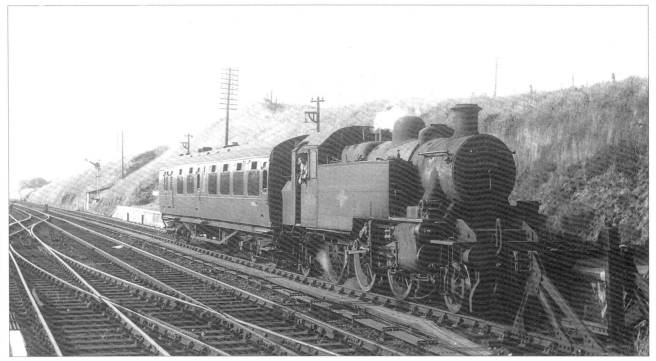

41248 has arrived from Torrington on 25 July 1964. The signal is in the off position because the train will now reverse to the run-round loop. Here the loco will detach and run-round and push the coach back into the platform ready for the return journey north. Peter Swift.

This extract from the summer 1964 timetable illustrates just how hectic things could be in the morning, with possible connections between any two of the four lines, and through coaches being shunted on to different trains.

Torrington to Halwill arr. 10.18 a.m.
Bude to Halwill arr. 10.20 a.m. through coaches to Exeter Okehampton to Padstow arr. 10.27 a.m. through coaches to Bude Padstow to Exeter arr. 10.32 a.m.
Okehampton to Padstow dep. 10.33 a.m.
Padstow to Exeter dep. 10.36 a.m.
Halwill to Torrington dep. 10.38 a.m.
Halwill to Bude dep. 10.40 a.m.

There was no engine shed at Halwill Junction but locomotives from Wadebridge, Launceston, Bude, Okehampton, Torrington and Barnstaple took water and could turn if necessary. There was a goods shed and an abattoir in the yard. which provided the railway with much business, both in receiving cattle and in forwarding meat. The station buildings were small and there were no canopies; though many passengers came through, few terminated their journeys here. A tall wooden signal box dominated the 'up' platform which had a good view of the road across the level crossing, the gates of which were worked by hand. The signal box had a 42 lever frame to control most points and signals, although its four distants were all fixed, and also released three ground frames. In 1943 an extensive yard, known as the 'up' sidings, was built on ground below the level crossing, controlled by one of the three ground frames. Ground frame 'A' had nine levers to control movements at the north end of the station including

the crossover connection to the ND&CJLR, ground frame 'B', two levers for the ND&CJLR run-round loop, and ground frame 'C', two levers for the 'up' sidings. These were interlocked with the frame in the signal box, except ground frame 'C', which was released by the single line electric train tablet. The signal box at Halwill Junction also contained single line tablet instruments for four sections; to Ashbury on the Okehampton line, to Ashwater on the Wadebridge line, to Dunsland Cross on the Bude line and to Hole on the Torrington line. It seems fair to assume that the Halwill Junction signalman was very busy at peak times, operating points, level crossing gates and signals, dealing with four different electric train tablet instruments and communicating by bell with four different adjacent signalmen.

After the withdrawal of services on the line between Meeth and Halwill in March 1965 diesel passenger trains continued to run between Okehampton, Bude and Wadebridge, though on a scale much reduced from the days of the 'Atlantic Coast Express'. All services were withdrawn on 3rd October 1966 and the tracks removed the following year. The station buildings remained standing in a derelict yard and a recreation ground has been made on the site of the 'up' sidings. Sadly, this railway village has lost its railway although it retains the name Halwill Junction.

Further details of the railway at Halwill Junction can be found in *The North Cornwall Railway*, Irwell Press 2008.

The ND&CJLR platform and buffer stops – journey's end. The Western Region had provided a final through service to Bude, but from Paddington not Waterloo, in 1965. D6342 heads BR Standard and ex-LMS corridors forming the Exeter Central to Bude portion on 21 August 1965. R.A. Lumber.

The Rolle Canal, below Castle Hill, Torrington, showing the moveable footbridge. In 1875 this part of the canal was turned into the Rolle or New Road which by-passed the town, though it was later abandoned.

Chapter 2
Before the Railways Reached North Devon

For centuries the twin ports of Bideford and Barnstaple dominated the commerce and transport of North Devon. The estuaries of the Taw and Torridge merge at Instow and flow out into the Bristol Channel at Bideford Bar, offering a haven for shipping. Bideford lies on the River Torridge and Barnstaple on the River Taw and, at the beginning of the nineteenth century, Bideford had the greater share of the maritime trade with Barnstaple at a disadvantage, owing to the difficulty of navigation in the Taw Estuary. The two ports had both a coastal and an international trade, with Bideford supporting four emigrant ships at the end of the century. There were other small ports and quays at Instow and Fremington, whilst Appledore had a shipbuilding industry which continues to this day. Culm, a form of coal, was mined at Bideford, and Barnstaple was known for its lace trade. Both towns depended for their communications on long bridges over their estuaries, which hampered the development of both road and railway links.

Inland lay mainly agricultural countryside, focussed around the small towns of Torrington, Hatherleigh, Winkleigh and Okehampton while Torrington itself, perched on a hill above the Torridge, had also a prosperous glove trade. There were stone quarries at Meldon, near Okehampton, and clay workings on the moors at Peters Marland. The area was largely self-sufficient, but goods which had to be imported included coal and limestone for burning in kilns for fertiliser and with transport inland both inconvenient and expensive, there was only limited movement of both people and goods. In order to give some idea of the size of the towns at the beginning of the railway age, we may take some figures from the 1851 census. Barnstaple had 8,667 inhabitants, Bideford 5,775, Fremington 1,350, Hatherleigh 1,710, Instow 626, Northam 3,680, Torrington 3,308 and Winkleigh 1,554.

When the railways eventually began to penetrate this part of the country, they did not always bring the anticipated benefits in the rural areas. The relatively cheap railway transport encouraged the efficient mass production of goods in distant mills and factories, so that the arrival of the railway sometimes had a catastrophic effect on the local community. For example, mills at North Tawton closed when the railway arrived throwing many people out of work. This led to emigration from the rural areas to the cities, with the inland part of North Devon suffering a reduction in population. However, the coming of the railways was a distinct advantage for agriculture, since animal foodstuffs and fertilisers could more conveniently be brought in, and timber, cattle, meat and dairy products taken out. Without the railway, the production of clay and bricks would never have reached the scale that it did. However, in mentioning these changes that were brought about by the railways, we are jumping ahead, as consideration must first be given to the state of other forms of transport at the time.

Road Transport

An extensive road system existed in North Devon before the arrival of the railways. These roads were built and maintained by the Turnpike Trusts, which gained their income from tolls collected from travellers as they passed through the toll-gates. To be more precise, the Turnpike Trusts did not collect the tolls themselves but leased the toll gates by annual auction with Barnstaple, Bideford and Torrington all having their own Turnpike Trusts.

The routes followed by the horse-drawn coaches reflected the importance of the towns and villages they served. Barnstaple was connected directly to Lynton, Ilfracombe, Instow, Bideford and Torrington on the internal services, while coaches also ran from Barnstaple to Exeter, via South Molton, Chulmleigh and Crediton, and from Bideford to Exeter, via Torrington, Winkleigh and Crediton. Another coach ran from Bideford to Plymouth, via Torrington, Hatherleigh, Okehampton and Tavistock. It is interesting that the Taw Valley route, which was to be followed later by the North Devon Railway, did not boast a coach service since it had no significant centres of population. The number of passengers that could be carried on a coach was, of course, only about a dozen and the fares were relatively high, so it is not surprising that few people travelled farther than they could walk in those days. A number of vans and wagons carried goods and were supplemented by pack-horses, particularly in districts where the roads were poor.

The main coaching firm in North Devon seems to have been Pridham and Lake, who had offices in Barnstaple and Bideford although there were also Royal Mail coaches from the Royal Mail & General Coach Office, Barnstaple. After the railways arrived, the coaching companies adapted by running connecting services firstly to Exeter and Tiverton, and then to Crediton. When the North Devon Railway line opened to Barnstaple and then to Bideford, there were connecting coach services running to the station and, at Torrington, Bideford and Barnstaple, there were also horse-drawn buses linking the town centre (usually a hotel) to the stations, connecting with all the trains. The town centres of Bideford and Barnstaple were separated from their stations by long bridges over the estuaries and, in Torrington, by a long steep hill. Local carriers also acted as agents, bringing traffic to the railways.

Coastal Shipping

Although the terrain of North Devon makes both rail and road transport less direct than in most other areas, advantage has always been taken of that great natural asset, the sea. The wide estuaries of the Taw and Torridge, though forming a considerable barrier to many road journeys, for example, between Appledore and Braunton, nevertheless enabled seagoing vessels to come right up to mooring points below the bridges at Bideford and Barnstaple. These were the major ports, but Appledore, Instow and Fremington inside the Bar, and Ilfracombe and Lynmouth, on the open coast, were all served by regular sailings, usually to Bristol. Coastal shipping used to be an important mode of transport for both passengers and goods, and continued to play an important role in conjunction with railway docks at Rolle's Quay, Barnstaple, Cross Parks, Bideford and particularly at Fremington Quay. The major commodities handled in conjunction with the railways were coal and limestone imported from South Wales, timber from the Baltic, and clay exported from Marland and Meeth.

On 15th February 1847 an Admiralty Commissioner held a court of inquiry, at Barnstaple, into the navigation on the River Taw, and the effects on navigation of railways which were then in the course of construction. Mr. Thorne stated that about 200,000 tons of merchandise came over the Bar annually, two-fifths being for Barnstaple and three fifths for Bideford. On account of the difficulties of navigation on the Taw, a great proportion of the goods intended for Barnstaple were landed at Appledore and brought up in barges of about 14-15 tons, which could go right up to the tidal limit. The difficulty of navigation on the Taw was the reason for the foundation of the Taw Vale Railway & Dock Company of 1838, which had the intention of building docks at Fremington and thence a railway to Barnstaple.

The Rolle Canal

The 'canal mania' of the 1790s produced a number of schemes for the West Country, one of which involved North Devon. The Public Devonshire Canal, as it was called, was planned to run between the port of Topsham, on the River Exe, and Okehampton, via Exeter, with a branch to Barnstaple. Later extensions were planned linking Okehampton to Bideford and to Bude, but none of these plans materialised.

In general, the county of Devon had little to gain from an extensive canal network, such as that constructed in the Midlands and the North, since most of Devon's major towns were already seaports. One seagoing vessel could take a cargo from, say, Bideford to Topsham, which would have required dozens of canal narrow boats. However, short canals inland from the estuaries were in some cases an advantage, and some of the seeds sown during the 'canal mania' era germinated at Torrington some thirty years later in the form of the Rolle Canal. Lord John Rolle, of Stevenstone House, near Torrington, built the canal at his own expense, with James Green as engineer. The first stone of the Beam Aqueduct, over the Torridge, was laid by Lord John Rolle on 11th August 1824, and the canal was completed the following year. It was built without Parliamentary authority but, in 1835,

the Rolle Canal Act was passed to regularise the situation.

The canal began at a sea lock and basin on the west bank of the River Torridge, just below its tidal limit at Weare Giffard, and the stone walls of the sea lock can still be seen from the main A386 road at Landcross, just below the south portal of the railway tunnel. At the sea lock was a small shipyard, a lime kiln which produced lime conveyed up the canal to Torrington, and nearby was the Annery Pottery, which used the Marland clay brought down the canal. In the canal basin cargoes were transferred between barges which came up from Appledore Pool and the tub boats which were horse-drawn in trains of six along the Rolle Canal. From Annery the canal was built at a level a few feet higher than the river, but a mile or so south there was an inclined plane where tub boats were transferred between levels. The upper level was 43 feet higher than the lower; the tub boats were fitted with four wheels and drawn up the incline by machinery powered by a water wheel.

From the inclined plane the canal ran along the west bank of the Torridge Valley to the Beam Aqueduct, where it crossed to the east bank and continued to its terminus at New Manor Mill, a mile above Torrington. There were several lime kilns along the line of the

canal including an extensive complex at Town Mills, and a warehouse and office at the bottom of Mill Street, Torrington. Limestone and coal for the kilns were among the products carried by the canal, these being brought in by seagoing vessels which discharged their cargoes into river barges in Appledore Pool or at Bideford. These barges were brought up at high tide under Bideford Bridge to the sea lock, which required a very high standard of navigation in the upper Torridge Estuary. It was here that the river barges were in turn discharged into canal tub boats, which were hauled by horses, in trains, up to Torrington. In the reverse direction, agricultural produce, and clay brought by pack horse from Marland, was exported.

In 1846, the joint lessees of the canal were Mr Braginton and Mr Tadrew. George Braginton was a leading local man, a banker with banks in Torrington and in Bideford and several times mayor of Torrington. He was also Chairman of the Bideford Extension Railway throughout its independent existence between 1852 and 1865. Sadly, Braginton's bank failed in 1865 and he was bankrupted, after which the canal reverted to the Rolle family.

The canal eventually closed during the construction of the Torrington Extension Railway around 1871. Parts of the canal bed were used for the

railway, from the inclined plane to near the Beam Aqueduct, and Torrington station itself was also partially built on the line of the canal. From the station to New Manor Mill, the canal was converted into a toll road called the Rolle or New Road, but this was unsuccessful and was later abandoned as Torrington had no need for a bypass in Victorian times. The aqueduct at Beam became the elegant drive for a private house, later Beam College. The Rolle Canal had, nevertheless, played a useful role in the transport system of North Devon for some forty six years.

Proposed Bideford & Okehampton Railway of 1831

The town of Torrington had to wait a long time before it eventually got a railway, but this does not imply a lack of local interest or enterprise with regard to the possibilities of railway transport. More than one attempt was made to introduce railways into Devon and, as early as 1831, a meeting was held with this purpose in mind. A subscribers' committee, consisting of John Morth Woolcombe of Ashbury, Hugh Mallet of Iddesleigh and H.C. Millett of Okehampton commissioned Mr. Roger Hopkins MI to survey and report on the possibilities of a line from Torrington to Okehampton. Hopkins' report, dated 24th October 1831, was printed in Okehampton by T.

Simmons. It was proposed that the line should run from the termination of Lord Rolle's Canal at Torrington, via Jacobstow, Iddesleigh and Okehampton to Meldon Quarries, to be 21 miles long on an average gradient of 1 in 206 and a maximum gradient of 1 in 98. The gauge was to be 4ft. 8in. and the track was to be of iron rails weighing 35lb. per yard, mounted on stone blocks. The single line would have passing loops 70 yards in length at New Bridge, Iddesleigh Bridge, Jacobstow Bridge, Okehampton and Meldon: *The whole of the trade on the railway may be carried on by two Locomotive Steam Engines, each of which may make three trips per diem from Okehampton to the other end of the railway. The engines should start at fixed times from each end of the railway, so as to pass each other at the place before mentioned (a passing loop opposite the junction of the Torridge and Okement rivers); they may perform the journey from Okehampton to the Canal in one hour and a half and return in two hours.*

The main engineering works were to be a few embankments and two short tunnels and considerable thought was given to various labour saving devices. For instance, at proposed lime kilns at Jacobstow, Iddesleigh and New Bridge the line was to be on an embankment so that limestone, coal and culm could be delivered by gravity. The capital

A view from the heights of Torrington Common. In the centre is the fifteenth century Rothern Bridge carrying the Bideford road over the River Torridge and beyond is Stapevale Farm. The station was built beyond the pine trees on the right.

required was £43,075, which would include two locomotives and sixty wagons, or approximately £2,000 per mile, a similar cost to that of the contemporary line, the Bodmin & Wadebridge.

Hopkins estimated the annual running expenses as £1,480, which would include the supply of coal and other materials, the wages of two enginemen, two assistants to attend the wagons, three blocklayers, three labourers, a part-time engineer and a clerk who would superintend the line. He estimated that the annual receipts would be £5,713 from the conveyance of limestone, culm and coal up from Lord Rolle's Canal, pipe clay and potters clay from Merton Moors, granite from Okehampton, timber and bark, slate, general merchandise and agricultural produce. He expected only about thirty passengers daily, which would yield £939 per year. His estimates were very detailed as, for example, he listed the price of coal at Okehampton as £1 15s 9d a ton but estimated that this could be reduced by at least 15 shillings.

In a second report, dated 8th November 1831, Hopkins surveyed and costed three different possible routes which would extend the line from Torrington to Bideford, a distance of about eight miles, with the costs varying from £21,000 to £26,000. The first route took the line of the Rolle Canal and terminated below Bideford Bridge on the west side of the river, while the second line took a different route to the same terminus, and the third took the same course as the first but then took the eastern bank of the Torridge Estuary. The advantage of the Bideford Extension was that ships could load directly into railway wagons, which led Hopkins to double his estimates of the volume of clay which might be carried from 3,000 to 6,000 tons per year.

In a third report, dated 11th November 1831, Hopkins dealt with a branch railway of 630 yards which would link the hilltop town of Torrington with the railway in the valley below. This branch was to take the form of an inclined plane 550 yards long on a gradient of 1 in 6, from the main line in the valley up to the top of Castle Hill, near the bowling green. There were to be three parallel rails opening out to four at a passing place, with the wagons being drawn up by a water wheel, chains and machinery. The estimated traffic would be 2,500 tons of coal, 200 tons of malt, soap, sugar, lead and other shop goods, 200 tons of ironmongery and 150 tons of malt, grain and other agricultural produce. Estimated cost of the project was £1,700.

Little progress was recorded in 1832 apart from a meeting of 'Friends and Subscribers' at the Clotworthy Arms, Winkleigh on 29th November, with John Woolcombe in the chair. In the following year, on 28th August, a meeting of shareholders and friends was told that £23,000 of the total capital of £87,000 had been raised. Robert Woolcombe suggested that in view of the capital subscribed, only the first fifteen miles from Bideford be constructed but, on 26th September, the shareholders rejected this. By the next meeting, on 24th October 1833, £25,000 had been subscribed and on 1st November notice was given in an advertisement in the *North Devon Journal* that it was intended to make application to Parliament, in the next session, for a Bill to enable the plans to be put into operation. However, despite a trio of letters to the same newspaper in December 1833 from Robert Woolcombe, the scheme died, although numerous attempts to revive it were made over the next ninety years.

Engineer Roger Hopkins may have been frustrated in his attempt to build this particular line but he was responsible for a number of early railways in other parts of the West Country, including the Plymouth & Dartmoor and Bodmin & Wadebridge lines. The year 1831 must have been very busy for him since his report on the Bodmin & Wadebridge line was dated 12th December, only a month after his second and third reports on the Bideford & Okehampton Railway. If the latter had been built, it would probably have had a similar history to that of the Bodmin & Wadebridge Railway which opened on 3rd October 1834 amid considerable difficulties, particularly with locomotives which were in their infancy. It would also have changed the pattern of railway development in northern Devon, with the line from Exeter making a junction near Sampford Courtnay instead of reaching the area by the eventual Taw Valley route.

The Taw Vale Railway & Dock Company

An advertisement for the Taw Yale Railway appeared in the *North Devon Journal* on 5th January 1837 and read; 'The object of this company is the formation of a Dock at Fremington Pill, and a Railway four miles in length, from thence to Lake, in the parish of Tawstock, with a Branch to the Bridge of Barnstaple'. The capital was £15,000 in 300 shares and the Directors were all local men, including Chairman Sir Bourchier Palk Wrey, George Acland Barber, William Long Wrey, Stephen Bencraft (who was mayor of Barnstaple), George Harris, William Thorne and a Mr Mackrell. The bankers were the West of England and South Wales District Bank, Barnstaple, the solicitors were Messrs Bembridge & Toiler of Barnstaple and the engineer was Mr D. Benyon. The Company gained its Act on 11th June 1838 as the Taw Yale Railway & Dock Company, but no construction was then undertaken. Eventually, on 21st July 1845, extensions to the quays at Fremington were authorised.

By September 1845, the project had grown to the Taw Yale Railway Extension & Dock Company from Barnstaple to Exeter with branches to Bideford, Ilfracombe and South Molton. These played a major role in the 'railway mania' and the 'battle of the gauges' which together delayed the arrival of railways in North Devon for several years, although the Fremington to Barnstaple line eventually opened in 1848 as a goods line with horse-drawn wagons.

The coming of the Bristol & Exeter Railway

The Great Western Railway opened its line between London and Bristol in 1841 and, on 1st May 1844, the Bristol & Exeter Railway opened throughout so that there was now a main line of 194 miles from Paddington to Exeter (St. David's). Both lines were built by the brilliant engineer, Isambard Kingdom Brunel to his broad gauge. On the opening day, a special train left Exeter at 5.20 p.m. and arrived at Paddington at 10.00 p.m., one of the passengers being Sir Thomas Acland MP who went immediately to the House of Commons and by 10.30 p.m. had told the House that he had been in Exeter that afternoon. The railway age had arrived in Devon.

Trains left Exeter for London at 8.15 a.m., 10.15 a.m. and 3.15 p.m. with a mail train leaving at 10.15 p.m., while trains left Exeter for Bath and Bristol at 7.00 a.m. and 5.05 p.m. To connect with these trains, coaches ran from North Devon with the 'Ruby' leaving the *Fortescue Arms*, Barnstaple at 9.45 a.m. to arrive in Exeter at 2.30 p.m. in time for the 3.15 p.m. train to London. Two coaches left the *Golden Lion*, Barnstaple (Royal Mail and general coach office, and booking office for the Great Western Railway), and ran via South Molton, Witheridge and Tiverton to connect with trains at Tiverton Station (Tiverton Junction on the main line). The 'Emerald' Royal Mail coach left at 7.45 a.m., and the North Devon Royal Mail at 4.55 p.m.

The Exeter & Crediton Railway

As early as 1831 an Exeter & Crediton Railway had been mooted but although it obtained its Act in 1832, nothing was done for a while and the powers expired. The arrival of the Bristol & Exeter line in 1844 gave it new life and on 21st July 1845, an Act was obtained for a line 5¾ miles long from a junction with the Bristol & Exeter Railway at Cowley Bridge, north of Exeter, to Crediton, with an authorised capital of £70,000. The Act also included powers for the lease or sale of the line to the Bristol & Exeter Railway or any other company forming a junction with the Exeter & Crediton line. The Chairman was J.W. Buller of Crediton, who was also Chairman of the Bristol & Exeter Railway from 1847. The Directors gave notice that the double track broad gauge line was ready for opening on 22nd December 1846, and asked the Bristol & Exeter Railway to work the line. At this stage, the line became involved in the gauge war.

Within a few days, £30,000 had been advanced by the London & South Western Railway (a standard gauge line) to the Taw Yale line to purchase 1,700 shares in the Exeter & Crediton Railway. The broad gauge Bristol & Exeter Railway had tried to defend its interests in the same way but, by 11th January 1847, when a shareholders meeting was held, the standard gauge camp controlled the majority of shares and the lease negotiated by the Directors with the Bristol & Exeter Railway was rejected. On 26th August 1847, the Taw Yale Chairman, William Thorne of Barnstaple, took over as Chairman of the Exeter & Crediton

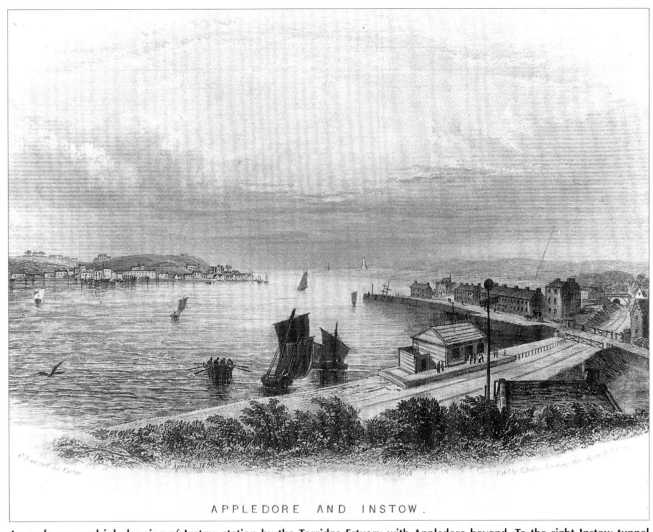

APPLEDORE AND INSTOW.

An early pen and ink drawing of Instow station by the Torridge Estuary with Appledore beyond. To the right Instow tunnel can just be glimpsed while the level crossing over Marine Parade has its gates closed. Lt. Col. Yolland, the Board of Trade Inspecting Officer, referred to it in October 1855 (see text page 148): *There is one tunnel or covered way of 84yds. in length, constructed open and then covered in, built of stone and lime mortar, with a drain through the bottom to carry off any water from the cutting.*

Railway and the new board of Directors narrowed the gauge and built a temporary station at Cowley Bridge; in the interim the Gauge Commissioners had ordered that the Taw Yale extension should be broad gauge. Eventually, five expensive years later, the Exeter & Crediton Railway was opened as a single line broad gauge railway (the second line being left standard) on 12th May 1851. Although the LSWR was the majority shareholder, the line was worked as a branch by the Bristol & Exeter Railway and later, as part of the North Devon Railway.

'Railway Mania'
The success of the first railways was well established by around 1845 and there followed a period of two or three years when it appeared that almost everyone was trying to cash in on the new transport system. Vast numbers of railways were projected, many of them highly dubious. This 'railway mania' broke a little later in North Devon but its result was to delay the arrival of the railway for years.

In the 1845 session of Parliament, authorisation had been given for the Exeter & Crediton Railway and the Tiverton branch of the Bristol & Exeter Railway, leading to the proposal of four major schemes in 1846. The first, on 8th May, was for the Bideford & Tavistock Railway, with a capital £360,000, to run from Bideford, through or near Torrington, Hatherleigh and Okehampton, to a junction with the proposed South Devon Railway branch at Tavistock. Later, branches to Barnstaple and Crediton were added. The secretary was Francis Cloves and the engineers Messrs Rice and Thomas Hopkins, sons of Roger Hopkins, who had drawn up the detailed reports on the proposed Bideford & Okehampton Railway fourteen years previously. Secondly, on 30th June, the North Devon Railway, with capital of £700,000, was launched to make an end-on junction with the Bristol & Exeter branch at Tiverton, (then authorised, but not built) to Bampton, Dulverton, South Molton, Barnstaple and Bideford, with a branch to Ilfracombe. The Chairman was Earl

Fortescue, the engineer was Brunel, and this line was intended to bring the Great Western broad gauge to the major towns in North Devon, and possibly beyond, via the Bideford & Tavistock Railway. The third proposed line, the Taw Vale Railway Extension & Dock Company, with a capital of £700,000, was launched on 18th September 1845 to link Barnstaple to Exeter with branches to Bideford, Ilfracombe and South Molton. The engineer was Joseph Locke, the Chairman Emmanuel Cooper, and there was considerable support from nominees of other companies aiming to link Exeter with the LSWR's narrow gauge system. Finally, the fourth line was the Cornwall & Devon Central Railway, another scheme backed by the LSWR, linking Exeter with Falmouth, via Okehampton, Launceston, Bodmin and Truro.

Local meetings to discuss the projected lines were held in many towns, and although apparently no public meetings were held in Torrington, several were held in Bideford Guildhall, with the Mayor in

A poor but nevertheless rare image of Cowley Bridge Junction between 1875 when track over the viaduct to the left carrying the Crediton line was doubled, and the end of the broad gauge in 1892.

the chair. It was felt that the interests of Bideford and Torrington were not best served by lines from Tiverton or Exeter, via Barnstaple, since goods imported at Bideford, to be taken inland, would have to pay for ten more miles of railway conveyance than goods imported at Barnstaple. It was thought that Bideford and Torrington would be better served by a branch of the Cornwall & Devon Central Railway, from a junction near Hatherleigh. Mr Braginton and Mr Tadrew, joint lessees of the Rolle Canal, took an active part in the discussions and pledged that they would not obstruct any move to convert the canal into a railway. On 7th March 1846, a meeting at Bideford instructed the mayor to petition Parliament in favour of the Bideford & Tavistock Railway and against the North Devon's projected Tavistock branch.

When these four schemes went to Parliament in the 1846 session, three out of the four failed in the Committee of Standing Orders, namely the Bideford & Tavistock Railway, then the Cornwall & Devon Central Railway and finally the North Devon Railway. On 7th August, however, the Taw Yale obtained its Act to go to Crediton (capital £533,000). This was one of no less than 270 Railway Bills which had been passed in that session, with the Royal Assent given to 4,540 miles of new railway involving capital of £96,000,000. Neither the capital nor the labour market could meet the demands

of this vast amount of construction, and the aftermath of the 'railway mania' was a period of depression when little was actually built. Moreover, there was another issue to be resolved before north Devon was to get its railway, and that was the question of the gauge.

The 'Gauge War'

An absolutely vital issue in railway construction in the West Country was that of the gauge, as has been mentioned previously. Brunel's broad gauge tracks from Paddington had reached as far as Exeter by 1844, and with the nearest standard gauge line not even reaching as far as Salisbury and Dorchester until 1847, one would have expected all the lines in the area to be built to the broad gauge. However, by a combination of ineptitude on the part of the broad gauge companies, and sharp practice by the LSWR, the standard gauge eventually reached Devon and Cornwall.

The Gauge Act, passed on 18th August 1846, did not affect the Taw Yale Extension which already had its own Act, but its gauge was to be as the Board of Trade approved. After the failure of the North Devon line, the Bristol & Exeter Railway supported the Taw Yale Extension in Parliament following a provisional agreement to lease the line, on the understanding that the Taw Yale Extension should be broad gauge. However, on 18th September, the Taw Yale Board of Directors opened

negotiations with the LSWR, the shareholders supported their board, and agreement was reached with the LSWR for a 1,000 year lease which was approved on 18th January 1847. During these months, the LSWR had advanced £30,000 to the Taw Yale Extension for the purchase of Exeter & Crediton shares and, as we have seen, in January 1847, the Exeter & Crediton Railway shareholders rejected the lease negotiated by their Board with the Bristol & Exeter Railway. At an Exeter & Crediton Railway meeting on 12th April 1847, a lease of the line to the Taw Yale was confirmed, which was in accordance with its Act since the Taw Yale Extension formed a junction with it.

The Railway Commissioners announced, on 8th February 1848, that the Taw Yale Extension should be broad gauge, which was hardly surprising since there was no standard gauge line for a hundred miles, apart from the original Taw Yale line from Fremington to Barnstaple, which was then under construction. The LSWR then faded out of the picture to enable the two lines to be built and opened on the broad gauge, but retained its control on the companies until it was in a position to make physical contact with them.

The aftermath of the 'railway mania' and the 'gauge war' was a delay of six or seven years before the arrival of the main railway system at Barnstaple, and this did real harm to the commerce of North Devon.

Chapter 3
Broad Gauge to Bideford

The Taw Vale Railway and Dock Company

Despite all the discussions, public meetings, reports, raising of capital and applications to Parliament over a period of fifteen years, as related in the previous chapter, it was not until 1846 that railway construction started in North Devon. On 5th January 1846 work began on the Fremington to Barnstaple line of the original Taw Yale Railway when William Thorne, a Director of the Taw Yale as well as the contractor, cut the first turf at Pentole Marsh Thorne. Construction of the single track standard gauge line was straightforward, with a few bridges and minor earthworks. In February 1847, the engineer, now Mr W.R. Neale of Crediton, reported that the line from Fremington to Barnstaple was almost completed but in June, work was still in progress on the bridge carrying the Sticklepath road over the railway at Barnstaple. On 12th February 1848, Neale reported to the half-yearly meeting of the Taw Yale Railway and Dock Company, that the works were completed, and that the rails were laid so that the line would shortly be available for traffic in coal and other goods.

William Thorne himself leased the Taw Yale line and it opened in late August 1848 for horse-drawn freight traffic. Passengers were not carried until the line was extended to Bideford in

1855. Thorne worked the line for ¾d per ton mile using his own vehicles, and the traffic included coal and limestone imported at Fremington harbour while, at Barnstaple, Thorne had leased lime kilns and warehouses on company land. After he terminated his lease in May 1850 it was found that the horses had damaged the track and, thereafter, they were banned. The Taw Vale Railway continued to run Fremington Harbour but a separate concern, the North Devon Steam Packet Company, ran a regular service between the harbour and Bristol, using the steamer *Waterwitch*. This isolated little line was North Devon's first railway, but a gap of some thirty one miles separated it from the main line railway network, which reached Crediton in 1851.

The North Devon Railway

As we have seen in the account of the 'railway mania', an unsuccessful North Devon Railway was projected in 1845, but the name was resuscitated in 1851. By an Act of 24th July 1851, the Taw Yale Railway & Dock Company was rechristened with the name of its dead rival and this new North Devon Railway was to connect Barnstaple with Crediton on the broad gauge, but was to have no branches. The Chairman was John Sharland of Croydon and the capital was reduced to £441,000, of which £50,000 had to be subscribed locally

before construction could commence. This was achieved before Christmas 1851.

Back in 1847, the Taw Yale Railway had also engaged William Thorne as contractor on the Barnstaple to Umberleigh section. When work on this was abandoned, earthworks for a double track line had been completed together with most of the masonry. About 4½ miles of single standard gauge track had been laid, but all these works had lain derelict for several years. When construction restarted, the first sod was cut at a ceremony at Copplestone on 2nd February 1852 by the Hon. Newton Fellowes of Eggesford House, an influential local supporter of the line through the Taw Valley. The contractor was Thomas Brassey, one of the most prestigious and reliable of railway builders. Brassey was the most important railway contractor in the country who, by the end of the 'railway mania', had built no less than one third of the railway mileage in Britain. He gained an international reputation by building railways all over the world.

Initially, Brassey employed more than 700 men and 100 horses on the line, and this figure rose to 1,075 men, 195 horses and a locomotive a year later, but there were delays due to heavy rain and flooding. There were also examples of the tragic mishaps associated with railway construction, such as an accident near Crediton when

A well-known engraving from the *Illustrated London News* of July 1854 depicting the celebrations surrounding the arrival of the first North Devon Railway train at Barnstaple.

The broad gauge terminus at Bideford in the period 1855-1863. Although of poor quality the image is quite unique as in 1872 it was converted into a goods station when a new station was opened some half mile away on the Torrington Extension.

a navvy was run over and killed by a spoil truck, and at Barnstaple, when two navvies were badly injured in an explosion. It would appear that the existing narrow gauge tracks from Fremington towards Umberleigh were used during construction, since rails were arriving at Fremington Harbour from April 1852. However, on 26th May 1854, the contractors commenced widening from Umberleigh to Fremington, from standard gauge to broad gauge, at the rate of half a mile per day and on 28th June 1854, a Bristol & Exeter Railway engine ran all the way from Crediton to Barnstaple, in 58 minutes. On the following day, Capt. H.W. Tyler, on behalf of the Railway Department of the Board of Trade, made his inspection of the Crediton to Barnstaple line and requested several improvements, including the erection of more signals, before the line could be opened for passenger traffic. The Barnstaple to Fremington section was not inspected at this stage, since it remained open only for goods traffic.

The North Devon Railway was ceremonially opened on 12th July 1854 and the first train, conveying the special guests from Exeter, arrived at Barnstaple at 11.30 a.m. or to be more precise, the first half of the train arrived. The other half had been left behind at Umberleigh, so the locomotive had to return there to collect it. As was the custom on such occasions, there was the usual procession and celebratory dinner at Barnstaple. Sadly, the leading local supporter of the line, the Hon. Newton Fellowes, had not lived to see its opening. He had died the previous

winter at his Eggesford home, having recently succeeded to the title Earl Portsmouth, but his name lived on at the new station near his home, Portsmouth Arms.

Public services on the North Devon Railway began on 1st August 1854 with passenger trains running between Barnstaple and Exeter calling at Chapelton, Umberleigh, Portsmouth Arms, South Molton Road, Eggesford, Lapford, Morchard Road, Copplestone and Yeoford, and thence over the Exeter & Crediton line with stations at Crediton and St. Cyres. There were four passenger trains each way on weekdays, and two on Sundays. The line was leased to Thomas Brassey for seven years; for the first year, he hired locomotives and rolling stock from the Bristol & Exeter Company, but subsequently used his own. The day to day management of the line was carried out by Robert Ogilvie from offices at Barnstaple station.

After the opening of the North Devon Railway, the local coach services ran in connection with the trains. Regular coach services linked Barnstaple station with Lynton, Ilfracombe, Braunton, Instow, Bideford and Torrington, and a van ran from Bideford and Torrington to connect with a goods train. As we shall see, in 1854, construction of the Bideford Extension Railway was well advanced, so coach services to Instow and Bideford were of a short-term nature. However, there was no immediate prospect of the extension of the railway to Torrington.

As the motorist of today will appreciate, the most direct route

between Torrington and Exeter certainly does not include the long detour northwards through Bideford and Barnstaple. To obtain the maximum benefit from the new North Devon Railway, the people of Torrington needed a direct coach service to the most convenient station at either Portsmouth Arms or Eggesford. During 1852, when the line was under construction the Trustees of the Torrington Turnpike Trust met to consider the matter. On 19th April, Mr Lock presented a £1,500 scheme to provide a direct link between Torrington and Portsmouth Arms station, via the Ebberley Arms, Diptford Cross and Kingford, including a new road on the last section. However, at another meeting of the Torrington Turnpike Trust on 22nd April 1854, it was stated that if Torrington people wanted the road they would have to pay for it. Apparently they did not, as on 30th October 1854, the North Devon coaching firm of Pridham and Lake established a new service using a light coach named *The Torrington*. The daily service left Wills Hotel, Torrington at 8.00 a.m. and ran via Beaford and Winkleigh to Eggesford station, where a connection was made with the 10.40 a.m. 'up' train. The return trip was made after the arrival of the 4.42 p.m. 'down' train and reached Torrington at 7.00 p.m. Fares were high, the charges being 5 shillings inside, 3 shillings outside and packages and parcels at 6d each.

The North Devon Railway proved to be a poor investment for its shareholders with the ordinary stock

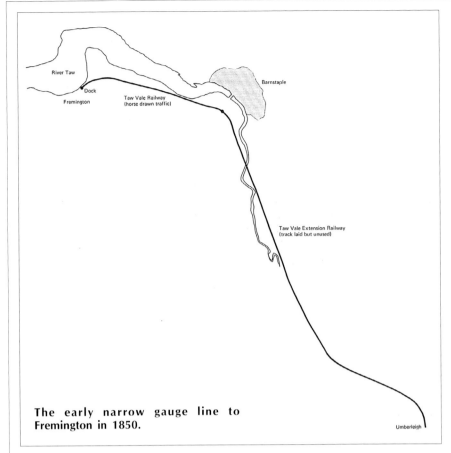

The early narrow gauge line to Fremington in 1850.

following spring to push the works vigorously forward.

The contractor, Thomas Brassey, had taken over a quarry at Appledore, from where a quantity of stone was removed for construction work. In September it was reported that the massive foundations for the sea wall, below Cross Parks at Bideford, were being laid, and considerable progress was made on the line over the next year. Neale's next report from his Crediton office was dated 24th August 1855 in which he said: *The lift bridge over the navigable creek at Fremington will be finished in about ten days. The delay here has much interfered with our progress. This obstacle is now overcome, and as a locomotive engine will be able to pass over the bridge, the ballasting and all incomplete works will be rapidly pushed forward. All the earthworks and masonry are finished. The permanent way is within half a mile of Bideford. The electric telegraph and signals are fixed. The station and station works are all in hand. Looking at the present advanced condition of the line I fully believe that we shall be ready for traffic by the end of September.*

Neale was rather optimistic, because ballasting was still in progress in mid-October when there was a fatal accident at Instow. An engineman attempted to jump on to a locomotive as it moved off with a ballast train, but he slipped and fell under the wheels of the tender. At the subsequent inquest the driver was absolved of any blame, since he was stopping the engine and had cautioned the man against the reckless jump.

On 20th October 1855 Lt. Col. Yolland from the Board of Trade made his inspection of the line between Barnstaple and Bideford. Two reports were necessary, since the Barnstaple to Fremington section of the North Devon line had not yet been passed for passenger services. His reports were dated 22nd October, and his short report on the North Devon Railway section stated: *...the line is in good order and has been worked over for some time for goods traffic, and it only requires to have the distant signal at Barnstaple raised, and that at Fremington Pill connected with the handle from which it is worked, to render it complete...* but he declined to sanction its opening until this had been done. His report on the Bideford Extension Railway was longer and more detailed stating: *The line commences at a junction with the North Devon Railway at Fremington Pill and terminates at Bideford, making its length six miles and four chains. It is laid single throughout, with sidings at Bideford and Instow, the land having only been purchased and the works constructed for a single line on the 7ft. gauge.*

The permanent way is laid upon longitudinal timbers 13in. x 6½in. tied together by transoms 6in. x 4in., bolted to

paying a dividend of only 1¾ per cent for most of its existence. When the LSWR amalgamated with the North Devon Railway from 1st January 1865, the holders of £100 worth of North Devon ordinary stock received only £49 of LSWR ordinary 4 per cent stock.

The Bideford Extension Railway

After the North Devon Railway was re-structured without branches in 1851, local people considered how to extend the railway from Fremington to Bideford through the formation of a separate company. On 11th August 1852 a meeting to discuss the project was held at Bideford Town Hall and on 8th November, the prospectus of the Bideford Extension Railway was published, showing that capital of £50,000 was required for a line six miles in length. The list of fifteen provisional Directors was headed by George Braginton and Stephen Willcock, the Mayors of Torrington and Bideford and included many local men. Five of these were also Directors of the North Devon Railway, including its Chairman, John Sharland. The close relationship with the North Devon Railway extended to sharing an engineer, W.R. Neale and the same contractor and lessor, Thomas Brassey, who had agreed to build the line and rent it for seven years.

The Bideford Extension Railway Company obtained its Act, with its capital increased to £55,000, on 4th August 1853, and on the 5th St. Mary's Church bells, Bideford, rang out to signal the Royal Assent. On 20th August 1853 there was a procession to the station site at Cross Parks, Bideford, about half a mile below the bridge. Here the ceremony of cutting the first sod was performed by Sir Bourchier Wrey and, afterwards, a dinner for 200 guests was held. Presiding over the proceedings was George Braginton, a banker and businessman of Torrington, who was Chairman of the Company throughout its existence. Thomas Brassey contracted to build the line for a price of £44,000 and subsequently, to rent it for seven years at an annual rent of £2,250. Construction of the Bideford Extension Railway was relatively straightforward along the southern shore of the Taw and Torridge estuaries, the only major engineering features being the lifting bridge over Fremington Pill, the dock wall at Bideford and the short tunnel at Instow.

The engineer, W.R. Neale, reported to the half-yearly Company meeting on 27th February 1854 that: *Since obtaining the Act of Parliament in the autumn of last year, the centre line and half-width of the railway have been staked out, and the necessary steps taken to put the contractor in possession of the land. So many difficulties have arisen in obtaining that object, added to the severe weather and continued rains throughout the winter, that up to the present time the progress made with the works is inconsiderable. However, a great proportion of the property is at last purchased or in a fair way of being settled for, and a commencement has been made at the Fremington and Instow cuttings and at the diversion of the turnpike road between Instow and Bideford, and the contractor will now be enabled during the*

A very early view of Barnstaple station. The period is considered to be between its opening in 1854 and the laying down of the mixed gauge tracks of 1863.

them at intervals of 11ft., with the exception of about 6 chains at the junction with the North Devon line at Fremington Pill, where the traverse sleepers and chairs have been continued up to the commencement of the viaduct over Fremington Pill.

The width of the line at formation level is 18ft. on embankments and 17ft. in cuttings: the ballast is composed of gravel, sand and shaley rock averaging 1ft. 9in. in depth. The rails, which are of the bridge pattern, weigh 60lb. to the lineal yard, and vary in length from 16ft. to 24ft. They are fastened to the longitudinal timbers by screws and fang bolts. The switches are not self-acting.

There are four over and three under bridges which appear to be well constructed and sufficiently strong, and a wooden viaduct over Fremington Pill, 117ft. in length, having one opening movable, to lift up for the passage of vessels – the superstructure rests upon piles driven on average 25ft. below the bed of the creek. This viaduct appears to be well constructed, but from its length and proximity to some lime kilns, I have suggested that there should be a light footway with handrails on each side, for persons on foot who might be there on duty or as trespassers, whilst a train was in the act of passing over the viaduct.

There is one tunnel or covered way of 84yds. in length, constructed open and then covered in, built of stone and lime mortar, with a drain through the bottom to carry off any water from the cutting. The fencing is complete throughout.

There is only one public level crossing at Instow, the gates for closing the road or the rail were being erected as I passed over

the line. Stations are provided at Bideford and Instow but the distant signals to cover the station at Instow, and the swing bridge in the viaduct over Fremington Pill, are not yet connected with the handles from which they are to be worked. A stop buffer is also required at Instow station at the end of the siding which abuts against the public road. A turntable has been provided at Bideford.

Again, Lt. Col. Yolland declined to sanction the line for opening until his requirements had been met. When the outstanding work on both the North Devon and Bideford Extension lines had been completed, engineer Neale notified Yolland by letter and on 2nd November 1855, he duly authorised the public opening of the line provided only one engine in steam was on the line at one and the same time. Only the pedestrian footbridge alongside the Fremington Viaduct was incomplete. In his last report of 5th December 1855, Lt. Col. Yolland dealt with the anxieties expressed by the Trustees of the Barnstaple Turnpike Roads, whom he had met during his inspection on 20th October. They were concerned that engines and trains would frighten horses on the road and cause accidents, but he felt that horses would very soon become accustomed to the passing of engines and trains. The Bideford Extension Railway proposed to build a wall 5ft. high and 19 chains long at Bideford station, and wooden screens at Instow, and to plant a screen of trees between the road and railway at several places. Lt. Col. Yolland was satisfied

with these proposals, provided that they were carried out within a month.

The ceremonial opening of the Bideford Extension Railway took place on Monday, 29th October 1855. It was estimated that some 4,000 people visited Bideford that day with many being brought free by the railway, the principal contingent travelling by the 1.40 p.m. train from Barnstaple. A special train, gaily decorated with colours and evergreens, left Barnstaple at 2 p.m. carrying the Directors, local dignitaries and Binney's Band. At Instow station, the train passed through a triumphal arch, and its arrival at Bideford was greeted by a large crowd, the bells of the parish church and the booming of cannon. The town of Bideford was decorated for the occasion with triumphal arches and banners, and the Mayor and Town Council arranged a dinner at the Guildhall, the tickets costing 12s 6d. As usual on these occasions, there were numerous toasts and speeches. the Chairman, George Braginton, referred to difficulties encountered with local landowners and said that if the line was to be extended beyond Bideford, then they should give their land and not demand ten times its value. Mr Snell, Mayor of Torrington, said that his townsmen would do all in their power to promote such an extension. A ball was held in the evening, but afterwards a number of Barnstaple people, who had turned up at the station for an advertised free trip home, were left behind.

The station at Cross Parks was limited in extent and the buildings were unfinished. The local landowner, Lewis William Buck MP, had been uncooperative and was blamed for the delays. He had refused access to a stream running through his grounds and the Company had been compelled to sink wells and drive adits for its water supply. The station was also inconvenient for the town centre, with the journey between them involving about half a mile of turnpike road, a turnpike gate and the long bridge over the Torridge, 677ft. long and supported on 24 arches. This was to be Bideford's station for the next seventeen years.

Public services began immediately after Board of Trade authorisation on 2nd November 1855, serving stations at Fremington (on the North Devon Railway), Instow and Bideford. The initial train service consisted of four trains each way between Bideford and Exeter, and one between Bideford and Barnstaple. By 31st December 1855, the Bideford Extension Railway had carried 13,499 passengers. Details of passenger traffic carried during the early years were given by the Company Secretary Mr Chanter, to a half yearly Company meeting on 22nd February 1860:

	1857	1858	1859
Passengers	98,267	105,346	116,056
Receipts (£)	2,945	2,969	3,189

The Bideford Extension Railway proved to be a good investment for its shareholders who received a 3 per cent dividend for most of its existence, almost twice that received by the less fortunate North Devon Railway shareholders. The LSWR leased the line from 1st August 1862 and amalgamated with it from 1st January 1865. The £55,000 worth of Bideford Extension ordinary stock was exchanged for LSWR 4 per cent preference stock.

Early Years on the Broad Gauge
After the anticipation of construction and all the excitement of opening ceremonies, the early years of the broad gauge line to Bideford saw the quiet establishment and expansion of railway business in North Devon. The North Devon & Bideford Extension lines were leased by Thomas Brassey until the LSWR took over on 1st August 1862. Although these were two separate companies, Brassey operated the lines as a single railway system from Bideford to Crediton. Brassey himself was so busy with many projects both at home and abroad that his Manager, Robert Ogilvie, ran the line from his office at Barnstaple station. The local people were obviously well pleased with his work as on 6th January 1857, a dinner in honour of Robert Ogilvie was held at the *Kings Arms Hotel*, Barnstaple, when he was presented with two pieces of silver plate. Two years later, at the half-yearly meeting of the Bideford Extension Railway on 22nd February 1859, the Chairman, George Braginton, paid tribute to the manner

in which the business was conducted by Robert Ogilvie and the Traffic Manager, Mr Patey, who were overseeing a gradual increase in traffic on the line.

By 1857 the initial passenger service of four trains daily between Bideford and Exeter had been increased to five trains. All trains conveyed first and second class passengers, but only the inconvenient 6.30 a.m. train from Bideford catered for third class passengers, who were further discouraged by having to wait almost eight hours at Exeter for the 5.35 p.m. train to Bristol. However, from February 1857, they were permitted to rebook at Crediton for Bristol, leaving Exeter at 10.50 a.m. First class passengers, including Earl Fortescue of Castle Hill, Filleigh, were not exempt from inconvenience either. He, and others, had arrived at Exeter on one occasion by express train from Bristol, intending to catch the 3.30 p.m. train to North Devon and on their arrival they found that the train had gone, and that the next one was six hours later, at 9.30 in the evening.

Robert Ogilvie encouraged the use of trains by the issuing of market tickets at reduced fares. These facilitated travel to the weekly markets at Bideford and Barnstaple, the most important regular events of the period in rural North Devon, and also to the new Eggesford periodical cattle fair and market held at the *Fox and Hounds Inn*, near the station. Market tickets were also sold for travel to Bideford Fair Day, and to Crediton when a horse-racing meeting was held there. Cheap fares to and from Bristol by specified trains were also introduced, at £1, 15 shillings, and 9 shillings for first, second and third class passengers respectively.

Another encouragement for potential passengers was the excursion train. One of the first excursions was run in conjunction with the Barnstaple Freehold Land Society, on Wednesday, 30th July 1856. The train left Bideford at 6.15 a.m. and, after calling at all stations to Crediton, arrived at Torquay at 9.45 a.m. It later departed at 7.35 p.m. to arrive back at Bideford by 11.50 p.m., giving a good day out for fares of 3s 6d, 4s 6d and 6s 6d for travel at third, second and first class respectively. The summer of 1857 saw a number of excursion trains run from Bideford, to a Grand Masonic Fete at Torquay on 28th May, to Plymouth on 20th June and again to Plymouth for a Grand Fancy Fair and Fete at Mount Edgcumbe Park on 19th and 20th August. There were also excursions into North Devon, one of which set the pattern for the next hundred years. This was a train which left Paddington at 8 a.m. on Monday, 17th August 1857 for Barnstaple and Bideford, returning from Bideford at 6 a.m. on Saturday, 29th August. The fares were £1 10s first class and £1, second class. This London

holiday excursion was repeated, and, by the summer of 1860, Robert Ogilvie was advertising family excursion tickets to Bideford and Barnstaple with cheap rates from London, Leeds, Sheffield and Birmingham. The era of the family travelling by train to enjoy a summer holiday at the seaside in North Devon had begun.

Events of special interest in North Devon provided the railway with extra business. For example, when Barnstaple Fair was held on 22nd, 23rd and 24th September 1858, additional trains were run, and third class accommodation was added to some timetabled trains. The following years, Barnstaple staged the Bath and West of England Agricultural Show, during the week of Monday, 30th May to Friday, 3rd June 1859. For this week, the passenger service was augmented to eight trains each way between Barnstaple and Exeter, another one between Barnstaple and Crediton and no less than eleven between Barnstaple and Bideford. On Wednesday, 1st June, the steamer *Prince of Wales* brought a contingent of visitors from Swansea to Instow, from where they took a train to the agricultural show at Barnstaple. This was one of the few boat trains to be run on the line. The show also brought extra goods traffic to the line, and additional sidings were laid at Barnstaple for this and other increasing traffic.

For towns and villages not served by the railway there were coach services run in connection with the trains, as we have already seen with the service between Torrington and Eggesford station. Messrs Blatchford & Co. operated a service between Copplestone station and Holsworthy, via North Tawton, Hatherleigh and Black Torrington, while Pridham and Lake operated services from Bideford Station to Plymouth, via Holsworthy, Launceston and Tavistock, and to Bude, via Clovelly and Stratton. Also, the 'Warrior' coach ran from Bideford station to Bude, via Holsworthy and Stratton, all these services running on alternate days. Later on, in the early LSWR period, Pridham and Lake ran a daily coach service between Bideford station, Clovelly and Hartland. At Bideford, buses plied between the station and the town, usually to inns and, in 1870, an accident occurred on the bridge when the horse pulling the New Inn bus shied and hit a lamp post, injuring itself.

The first serious derailment on the line took place at Yelland, between Fremington and Instow on the Bideford Extension Railway, on 4th January 1859. Fortunately, the only injury was to the fireman, who was slightly hurt. Lt. Col. Yolland investigated the accident on behalf of the Railway Department of the Board of Trade, visited the scene of the accident in a special train, and held his enquiry in the Manager's room at Barnstaple station. His subsequent report was dated 28th January 1859: *It appears that as the 6.15 'down' passenger train, consisting of engine and tender and two carriages, was on its way between Fremington and Instow, and about two miles from the former place, the engine suddenly quitted the rails when travelling about 25 miles per hour; the tender and one of the carriages also got off the rails, and was capsized, and remained with its wheels in the air, close to but uncoupled from the engine, the drawbar having broken; and the engine appeared to have run only 43 yards beyond a slight mark in the left rail, where it is supposed it got off. The accident occurred at about 9. 15 p.m. On examination the tire of the left leading wheel was found broken; and the driver states that he heard a report something like a fog signal at the moment the engine quitted the rails; three of the transoms were broken by the engine as it diverged, and the rails laid according to the broad gauge system on longitudinal sleepers were slightly thrown out of gauge.*

Lt. Col. Yolland went on to say that the accident was caused by the fracture of the tire, and that it was fortunate that none of the thirty passengers had been injured. The locomotive was a 2-2-2, with 4ft. diameter leading and trailing wheels, and 5ft. 6in. diameter driving wheels with no flanges. It was originally a narrow gauge engine which was converted to broad gauge by Stothert, Slaughter & Co. of Bristol. He stated that the lack of flanges on the driving wheels had been a contributory cause of the derailment

and recommended against the method of construction of the wheel tire.

The London & South Western Railway took over the lease of the Exeter & Crediton Railway from the Bristol & Exeter Railway on 1st January 1862, and the leases of the North Devon & Bideford Extension Railways from Thomas Brassey on 1st August 1862. The whole line from Exeter to Bideford up to then had been virtually a branch line of the Bristol & Exeter Railway, and a part of the broad gauge railway system which had monopolised the West of England until the standard gauge LSWR reached Exeter in 1860. The LSWR took over Brassey's motley collection of broad gauge rolling stock and continued to use it to run services for a time. Although LSWR standard gauge trains ran to Bideford in 1863, some local train services were operated with broad gauge rolling stock until the abolition of the broad gauge on the North Devon line in April 1877.

Arrival of the LSWR

The London & South Western Railway always had ambitions to extend its business to Devon and Cornwall and during the 'railway mania', the LSWR had bought shares in the Exeter & Crediton and the Taw Vale companies. Both these companies were in the standard gauge camp, but had been forced to open on the broad gauge due to reasons of railway geography as at that time, the nearest standard gauge lines were one hundred miles away. However in 1860, the railway map of

Devon changed when the LSWR standard gauge line from Waterloo opened to Exeter (Queen Street) station. At the banquet celebrating the opening, the guests on the top table included William Tite and George Braginton, Chairmen of the North Devon and Bideford Extension lines and Thomas Brassey, contractor and lessee of both. A connecting line was built down to Exeter (St. David's) station, and from there a third rail was laid along the Bristol & Exeter line to Cowley Bridge Junction and on to Crediton. On 1st February 1862, LSWR standard gauge trains ran to Crediton and, on 2nd March 1863, right through to Bideford. The latter event was marred by the derailment of the 8 a.m. 'down' train from Exeter to Bideford, but a makeshift passenger train of broad gauge trucks ran back to Barnstaple, the passengers sitting on chairs taken from the waiting room.

A surviving South Western Traffic Notice provides much detail for the Bideford Regatta on Wednesday 12th August 1863. The South Western provided a standard gauge special train, leaving Exeter Queen Street at 10.5am and returning from Bideford at 8.0pm. There were also broad gauge special trains leaving Barnstaple at 2.20pm, 4.0pm, 9.30pm (empty), returning from Bideford at 3.0pm (empty), 9.0pm, 10.5pm. The small Bideford station at Cross Parks was very busy that day.

Until April 1877 the North Devon line remained mixed gauge, and a few

Crowds gather for the opening of the Bideford Extension Railway, as recorded in the *Illustrated London News* in November 1855.

The Exeter and Crediton line remained mixed gauge to accommodate Great Western broad gauge goods trains until their demise in 1892. Here we see the replacement of a girder Bridge No.549 just to the east of Crediton station. The locomotive is Adams 0-6-0 No.509 of 1885.

local services continued to run using the old broad gauge rolling stock inherited from Thomas Brassey. An illustration of the services operated is given by the LSWR service timetable for February 1865. There were five passenger trains and one goods daily between Exeter (Queen Street) and Bideford, together with one passenger train between Barnstaple and Bideford, all standard gauge. The only broad gauge trains were the 7.45 a.m. goods and passenger from Crediton to Bideford, which started on its return journey at 3.05 p.m., and the 1.15 p.m. empty wagon train from Barnstaple to Fremington, which returned as a coal train at 1.55 p.m. A service of three broad gauge goods trains between Crediton and Exeter St. David's was operated by the Bristol & Exeter Railway. In 1869, the 'up' broad gauge goods and passenger train from Bideford to Crediton was involved in a collision at Fremington, as we shall see later. Although all through services to Exeter Queen Street and the rest of the LSWR system were composed of standard gauge stock, it was also possible to use broad gauge wagons for through traffic between the North Devon line and the Bristol & Exeter, South Devon and Great Western lines, which remained faithful to Brunel's broad gauge until its demise in 1892. However, when the North Devon line was extended to Bideford (New) and Torrington in 1872, the line was built to the standard gauge, and since most passenger services ran through to Exeter Queen Street from Torrington, it would appear that few, if any, broad gauge passenger trains ran after 1872.

Indeed, between 1870 and 1877, only four broad gauge locomotives remained in service, and they were well past their prime so, by the end, there was probably only the single broad gauge goods train running between Bideford and Crediton. Certainly the LSWR would not have encouraged broad gauge traffic. In April 1877, the broad gauge section between Bideford and Crediton was taken out of use, and any necessary transhipment of goods, between standard gauge and broad gauge wagons, was carried out at Crediton where the Great Western retained a broad gauge goods service from Exeter until 1892.

The arrival of the LSWR in North Devon also saw the end of the local companies and their rather impoverished existence. The LSWR had built an expensive main line to Exeter and needed to develop the through traffic from the North Devon line and beyond. Over a period of years, the LSWR spent considerable capital sums in North Devon both to bring the line up to LSWR standards and to extend the system to Torrington, Ilfracombe, Okehampton and beyond. Eventually, the lines between Exeter and Copplestone, and between Umberleigh and Barnstaple, were doubled.

Nonetheless the LSWR had ambitions beyond the North Devon line and from a junction at Coleford, between Yeoford and Copplestone, built the Okehampton Railway. This was opened in stages between 1865 and 1871, and was extended to Lidford in 1874. Eventually, LSWR standard gauge trains started running to Plymouth in 1876, over the mixed

gauge South Devon branch. In 1879, the LSWR opened a branch from Meldon Junction to Holsworthy with intermediate stations at Ashbury, Beaworthy (later named Halwill & Beaworthy) and Dunsland Cross, and in 1898 extended the branch to Bude. Halwill became a junction when a branch was built from there to Launceston, this being extended in stages to Wadebridge and Padstow. However, the final chapter in the expansion of Halwill Junction did not occur until Southern Railway days when the North Devon & Cornwall Junction Light Railway was built from Torrington, opening in 1925.

On 23rd September 1869, there was a collision between two trains at Fremington when four or five passengers were shaken and slightly injured. The subsequent enquiry was held by Lt. Col. Hutchinson, who made his report to the Railway Department at the Board of Trade on 23rd October 1869: *On the 23rd ult. an 'up' mixed goods and passenger broad gauge train, consisting of engine and tender, break van without guard, two loaded wagons, one composite carriage, and one second class carriage with break compartment, in which there was a guard, left Bideford for Crediton at 3.15 p.m. five minutes late, and arrived at*

PRIDHAM AND LAKE

BEG respectfully to inform the Inhabitants of North Devon and the Public in general, that they have made arrangements to work

COACHES

And other Conveyances to and from the BARNSTAPLE RAILWAY STATION, on and after WEDNESDAY, AUGUST 2nd, as follows:—

BARNSTAPLE TO LYNTON.

New Coach "Sea Bather," Monday, Wednesday, and Friday, at 5 P.M. on the arrival of the Express Train and the Mail from Bideford.

BARNSTAPLE TO ILFRACOMBE, via BRAUNTON.

"Queen" Coach, daily, at 12.35 P.M. after its arrival, from Bideford, and arrival of Down Train.

BARNSTAPLE TO ILFRACOMBE.

"MAIL," daily, at 5 P.M., from Express Train and Mail from Bideford.

BARNSTAPLE TO INSTOW AND BIDEFORD.

Daily, "The Mail," at 8.30 A.M., on the arrival of Cheap Train, and on its arrival from Ilfracombe.

BARNSTAPLE TO INSTOW AND BIDEFORD.

"Monarch" Omnibus, Daily, 12.35 P.M., from Train and Coaches from Ilfracombe and Lynton.

BARNSTAPLE TO INSTOW, BIDEFORD, AND TORRINGTON

Daily, "Hero" Coach, at 5 P.M., from the Express Train.

BARNSTAPLE TO INSTOW, BIDEFORD, AND TORRINGTON.

Daily, Van, 10 A.M. from Goods Train.

LYNTON TO BARNSTAPLE.

Monday, Wednesday, and Friday, the New Coach "Sea Bather," from the 'Castle Hotel,' at 7 a.m., for the Express Train, and "Monarch" Omnibus to Bideford.

ILFRACOMBE TO BARNSTAPLE

"Mail" Daily, at 6.45 a.m., for the Cheap Train, and thence to Instow and Bideford.

ILFRACOMBE TO BARNSTAPLE, via BRAUNTON.

The "Queen" Coach Daily, 8.15 a.m. for Express Train, thence on to Bideford.

TORRINGTON TO BIDEFORD, INSTOW, AND BARNSTAPLE.

"Hero" Coach Daily, from Wills's Hotel, Torrington, 7.45 a.m., from Pridham and Lake's Office, Bideford 8.45 a.m. for the Express Train and Coach to Ilfracombe.

BIDEFORD TO INSTOW AND BARNSTAPLE.

"Monarch" Omnibus, Daily, 10.30 A.M., for 12.55 up Train, and Coach to Ilfracombe.

BIDEFORD TO INSTOW AND BARNSTAPLE.

"Mail" Daily, at 2.30 P.M., for 5.30 P.M, up Train, and Coaches to Lynton and Ilfracombe.

TORRINGTON TO BARNSTAPLE.

Van Daily, at 5 P.M., for Goods Train.

BIDEFORD TO BARNSTAPLE.

Van Daily, at 7 A.M., for Goods Train.

☞ *Parcels Conveyed at Cheap Rates.*

For further particulars, see Small Bills.

Dated Barnstaple, August, 1854.

The firm of Pridham and Lake ran a network of coach services in North Devon and the advertisement above details the services run in connection with the newly-opened North Devon Railway. Torrington, Instow, Bideford, Ilfracombe and Lynton are all served. The advertisement appeared in the *North Devon Journal* of 8th August 1854.

Fremington platform at 3.33 p.m. also five minutes late, having been admitted through the points at the Bideford end of the loop by the Fremington points man. Although Fremington is a passing point for certain trains, it is provided with only one platform on the 'down' side; and 'up' trains therefore use the 'down' or wrong line in passing from one end of the loop to the other. The pointsman followed the train up to the platform, and as soon as the passengers had alighted told the driver to go and shunt, meaning that he was to go forward to the points at the Barnstaple end of the loop, and back through them into the loop or sidings, so as to get out of the way of the 'down' passenger train due at Fremington Station at 3.35 p.m. The points man rode up to the points on the step of the front van, in order to be ready to lower the signals (now at danger) and hold the points for the admission of the Barnstaple train as soon as the other train should have backed out of the way. As the engine was passing through the points (at about 3.34 or 3.35 p.m.) the driver caught sight of the engine of the 'down' train coming round the curve about 200yds. off; he immediately reversed, got his engine into backward motion, and had moved his train back about an engine's length when he was struck by the other engine. His leading and driving wheels were at once knocked off the road, but his trailing and tender wheels kept it. The front break van left the road with all its wheels, but no couplings gave way. The broad gauge engine came to a stand about 70yds. from the point of collision, with no serious injury either to engine or carriages, and none to the Company's servants; only one passenger complained of being slightly hurt.

The 'down' train which caused the collision was the 1.25 p.m. narrow gauge passenger train from Exeter to Bideford. It had started from Exeter five minutes after time; but, although generally late during the summer months, had on this occasion made up its time on reaching Barnstaple, from which it started at 3.29 p.m. (its correct time), consisting of a four-wheel coupled tank engine, two second class, two first class, two third class carriages, and two break vans with a guard in the last but one, it having to stop and cross the broad gauge train at Fremington. The driver stated that he shut off steam about half a mile from the Fremington distant signal (which was at danger, as it always was when trains had to cross) and whistled for it to be taken off; that as it was not he had his break applied, but finding that his speed was being reduced too much (viz, to eight or ten miles an hour on passing the distant signal post) his fireman took it off again; that on rounding the curve between the two signal posts he caught sight of the broad gauge engine coming towards him; that he sounded his break whistle and had his break applied, but did not reverse his engine, as the break-blocks already had the wheels tight (it being a tank engine). The fireman and guard corroborated the driver's statement, the guard declaring that he put his break on hard on catching sight of the broad gauge engine, at which time the speed was not more than eight to ten miles an hour. All three stated that the speed on collision did not exceed four to six miles an hour; the guard of the other train and pointsman estimating it from 15 to 20 miles an hour. Nothing left the rails in the narrow gauge train; the buffer plank, and the cover and rim of one of the cylinders of the engine was broken and there was other minor damage sustained. Three or four passengers in the carriage next to the engine complained of slight injury. The narrow and broad gauge engines kept together after collision until they stopped, as stated above, about 70yds. from the point at which they first struck and about 260yds. from the point at which they first came in sight of each other. The permanent way suffered to the extent of one rail and 45 to 50 chairs being broken.

Lt. Col. Hutchinson blamed the driver of the 'down' train for passing the distant signal at danger, when LSWR single line regulations clearly stated that he should stop. He also blamed the pointsman for allowing the 'up' train to shunt when the 'down' train was due: *The present accident would not have occurred had an 'up' platform existed and been in use at Fremington station, as in this case the broad gauge train would have used its proper line and not have had to shunt. I would recommend, therefore, that an 'up' platform be constructed at Fremington, and that 'up' and 'down' trains always use the proper lines of the loop at this and other stations of the North Devon line.*

As a result of the collision, Mr and Mrs John Sweet of Bideford sued the LSWR for £2,000 damages in compensation for injuries received in the collision, and in August 1870 were awarded damages of £550. Another accident occurred at Fremington in July 1870 when Porter Hammett was run

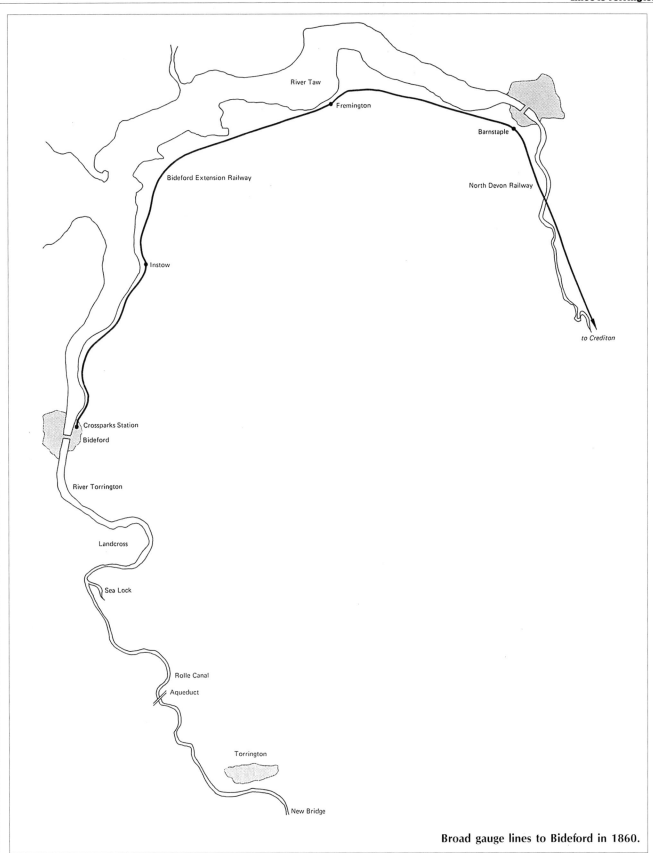

River Taw

Fremington

Barnstaple

Bideford Extension Railway

North Devon Railway

Instow

to Crediton

Crossparks Station

Bideford

River Torrington

Landcross

Sea Lock

Rolle Canal

Aqueduct

Torrington

New Bridge

Broad gauge lines to Bideford in 1860.

over by wagons during shunting operations and subsequently died of his injuries. The coroner returned a verdict of accidental death.

The decade 1864-1874 saw the authorisation, construction and opening of the remaining major railway routes in North Devon. Lines linking Bideford to Torrington, Taunton to Barnstaple and Barnstaple to Ilfracombe opened in rapid succession in 1872, 1873 and 1874. The LSWR was behind the first and last of these, while the broad gauge interests were served by the Devon & Somerset line. The railway system of North Devon was developing rapidly.

Bideford and the magnificent, and ancient, bridge over the Torridge River, around 1910. The Clovelly bus men are unloading cases and bags ready for the 10.19 train to London. Mr Braund would have been the driver.

Chapter 4
The North Devon to Torrington

Drummond L11 4-4-0 No.163 with a passenger train at Torrington carrying the headcode for Exeter Queen Street, *circa* 1919. The cross firebox water tubes and their rectangular covers were later removed. The L11s and the smaller K10 class hauled many services on this line, but from 1925 the principal North Devon passenger trains ran between Exeter and Ilfracombe, hauled by new N class 2-6-0s, with connecting services between Barnstaple Junction and Torrington.

The Torrington Extension Railway

In 1865, when the LSWR had become the only railway company operating in North Devon, it decided to extend its North Devon line up the Torridge Valley from Bideford to Torrington. By an Act of 19th June 1865, the LSWR was authorised to build the line, 5½ miles in length, at a cost of £80,000 to be paid by the LSWR. The Torrington Extension was to be a difficult and expensive line to build, the cost per mile being almost twice that of the Bideford Extension line. The Bideford Extension had been built along the edge of the estuary where land values were low, its construction was straightforward, and it terminated just outside the town. By contrast the Torrington Extension would run right through Bideford East-the-Water where compensation would be expensive, it would require engineering works including a tunnel, a viaduct and numerous bridges, and more compensation would be required for the use of the bed of the Rolle Canal, which was to be bought. Despite the additional expense, the LSWR incorporated in the line provision of a new passenger station at Bideford, more

conveniently sited right at the end of Bideford Bridge, to supersede the old broad gauge station at Cross Parks which was to be retained for goods. Additional land was acquired at Bideford for enlargement of the goods yard, while the sea wall was extended and improved. However, the station at Torrington was to be inconveniently situated at Staplevale, a mile from the town centre, and several hundred feet below it. The line was staked out and in 1867 deviations were authorised but in 1868 the LSWR sought to abandon the Torrington Extension.

There were two main reasons for this change of mind by the LSWR. The Torrington Extension line would be very expensive and the expected traffic would generate only a limited return on the outlay, but railway politics were also involved. Agreement on co-operation between the LSWR and the three broad gauge companies, the Great Western, Bristol & Exeter and South Devon Railway, had been reached. In 1866, the four companies had come to a quadruple agreement which was to be ratified by a Quadruple Bill in Parliament. However,

there was subsequent disagreement, the Quadruple Bill fell through, and the LSWR sought to withdraw the Torrington Extension as unnecessary. However, at this stage, there was a remarkable turn of events.

The Hon. Mark Rolle, owner of the Rolle Canal which was to be incorporated in the Torrington Extension Railway, led the Parliamentary opposition to the abandonment of the line by the LSWR. He and other landowners argued that although no local capital had been raised, the LSWR had virtually entered into a contract with the district to construct the line. If the Torrington Extension line were abandoned, no other company was likely to build it. The LSWR tried to abandon the Torrington Extension both in the 1868 and 1869 Parliamentary sessions but, on both occasions, they were defeated. Indeed, so successful was the Rolle's opposition, that Parliament took the unusual step of requiring the LSWR to pay his expenses. The outcome was that on 24th June 1869, the House of Commons gave the LSWR more time to build the line. The spectacle of a canal

The divergence of the Torrington and Ilfracombe lines at Barnstaple Junction in LSWR days. The original 1874 stone-built West signal box (top) is a throwback to an earlier time and has a perfect view over the top of Sticklepath road bridge. It was replaced in 1912. The box carries BARNSTAPLE JUNCTION running in boards whilst the prominent board reminds drivers that a speed restriction is 15mph across the river to Town station. Below is Barnstaple Junction before 1912 showing the original layout. There is only one down platform, which was later converted into an island platform – see page 7 in *The Line Described*.

owner insisting on the construction of a railway along his own canal was very unusual, but the Hon. Mark Rolle had performed a valuable service to the people of Torrington.

However, the Torrington Extension Railway was not the only line to Torrington to be authorised in the 1860s. The Devon & Cornwall Railway planned to build a line from the Okehampton line, near Sampford Courtnay, to run to Bude, with a branch from Hatherleigh to Torrington to connect with the LSWR Torrington Extension. This line gained its Act on 29th June 1865, only ten days after the Act for the LSWR Torrington Extension. There was difficulty in raising capital, and other Acts were obtained in 1867 and 1869, the latter renaming the line the Bude & Torrington Junction Railway, but the project came to nothing. However, the existence of this projected line does help to explain why the LSWR Torrington Extension line terminated at Staplevale, and did not run further up the bed of the Rolle Canal to a more convenient terminus at Taddiport. The Devon & Cornwall line was likely to run down the Langtree Valley which joined the

Top. The original single down platform at Barnstaple Junction. The awning is a replica of the up side which would be replaced by a simple, somewhat utilitarian, style structure under the Southern Railway.

Middle and bottom. Fremington Quay, around 1910 and, bottom, early 1920s. The steam cranes can be seen clearly in the middle photograph.

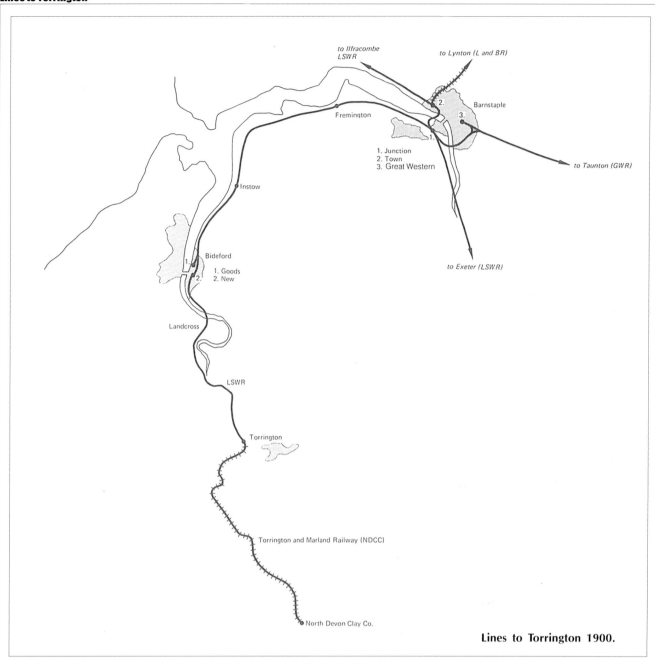

to Ilfracombe
LSWR

to Lynton (L and BR)

2.

Barnstaple

3.

Fremington

1. Junction
2. Town
3. Great Western

to Taunton (GWR)

Instow

to Exeter (LSWR)

Bideford

1.
2.

1. Goods
2. New

Landcross

LSWR

Torrington

Torrington and Marland Railway (NDCC)

North Devon Clay Co.

Lines to Torrington 1900.

Fremington Quay in 1910 showing the substantial tidal range of the Taw River, which allowed large vessels to berth.

The original wooden viaduct at Fremington. The lifting span is raised for the last time to allow the 60 ton ketch *Acorn* out to sea after discharging its cargo of coal at Muddlebridge. The span was raised by means of a chain and winch gear operated by the man behind the bows of the ship. The masts of other sailing vessels at Fremington Quay are visible in the background. S. Rogers Collection.

Torridge Valley just above Staplevale, so the LSWR terminated their line where it could be easily extended southwards up the Langtree Valley.

Construction and Opening of the Torrington Extension Railway

It took the LSWR no less than five years from gaining the Act in 1865 to starting construction of the Torrington Extension Railway in 1870. Mr Galbraith, the Chief Engineer of the LSWR, was in charge and the contractor was James Taylor, who had worked on a number of contracts for the LSWR including the Yeovil & Exeter line and the branches to Exmouth and Chard. Galbraith, Taylor, and some of his staff arrived at Bideford in April 1870 and the first sod was cut, apparently without ceremony although some local people had wished for one.

The LSWR had to compensate landowners and the property owners affected by the new line. At Torrington, there was a public meeting to agree the price for the three acres of common land to be taken for the station at Staplevale. Bideford magistrates adjudicated on a series of compensation cases and, in August 1870, awarded Mr

Daniel, an innkeeper who had claimed £100, compensation of £70 plus costs. However, Mr Taylor, a tenant, was less fortunate in getting £10 10s awarded on a claim of £22.

It was inevitable that the navvies employed on the construction of the line would suffer loss of life and limb, but their spiritual needs were attended to at the Bethel Chapel. This was adjacent to the new station at Bideford and, in June 1870, a tea was held there for them. There were two serious accidents during construction at Bideford, one when a man was buried under a heavy fall of earth and another when a man was crushed between the buffers of two wagons. In another incident, a navvy was killed at Torrington when he was buried under a heavy fall of earth at the site of the new station. There were other accidents to navvies, and also cases of drunkenness brought before the magistrates.

The LSWR Directors' Report of February 1871 included some details of progress on the Torrington Extension. All the land had been obtained, and the earth works and bridges were well advanced. The heaviest remaining

works were the tunnel and viaduct at Landcross, although most of the ironwork for the latter, and the permanent way materials, had been delivered. In October 1871, Messrs Bull & Son, contractors of Southampton, started work on the construction of the stations at Bideford and Torrington which were built to an attractive design in local stone, that at Torrington also incorporating a house for the Station Master. An LSWR Minute of May 1872 recorded that the Torrington locomotive water supply was to be provided from a wrought iron tank with the necessary engine house, boiler and pipes, cost not exceeding £395.

Lt. Col. Yolland of the Board of Trade made his inspection of the works on Friday, 7th June 1872 and made his report on 8th: *I have inspected the Torrington Extension of the London and South Western Railway from Bideford to Torrington, a length of 5 miles and 36 chains. The line is single throughout, with the exception of a loop line for a crossing place at Bideford, and a short portion of double line, and goods lines at Torrington. Land has been purchased for, and all the over-bridges have been constructed for a double line, but the under-bridges, viaducts*

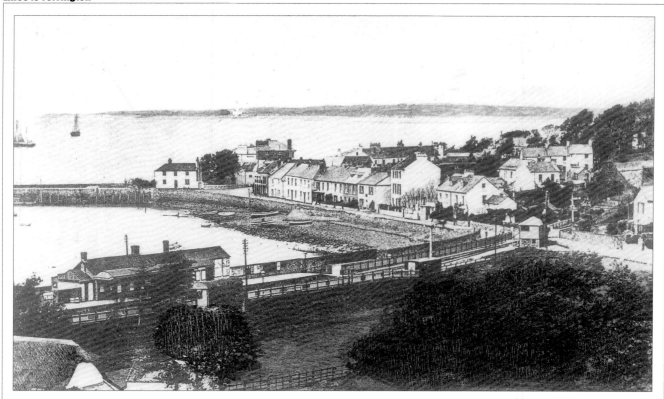

An Edwardian postcard view of Instow station showing the close proximity of the railway to the waterfront. The signal box can be seen alongside Marine Parade.

and tunnel are for a single line only, except for two under-bridges near the Bideford passenger station.

The old passenger station and lines contiguous to it are to be used as a goods station. The width of the line at formation level is 18 feet, the gauge is 4ft 8½ inches, and the width between the lines where two are laid is 6 feet. The permanent way consists of a double headed rail that weighs 75lbs per linear yard, in lengths chiefly of 24 feet, fixed in cast iron chairs that each

weigh 28lbs by compressed elm keys. The chairs are secured to transverse sleepers by Ransome and Sons patent compound treenails, and 9/16 inch iron spikes, the chairs on each side of the joints being fastened with ¾ inch fang bolts, and on the outside of sharp curves.

The sleepers are of larch or memel timber creosoted 9 feet long by 9 inch by 4½ inch for the intermediate, and 10 inch by 5 inch next to the joints which are rectangular – the average distance apart being 3 feet. The

ballast is of broken stone, and stated to be 2 feet in depth, or 12 inches under the sleepers. The steepest gradient on the line is 1 in 64 and the sharpest curve has a radius of 16 chains. An engine turntable is provided at the Torrington station.

There are 5 over and 10 under bridges, 4 viaducts and a short tunnel of 197 yards in length. The over bridges are constructed of stone or brick, the longest span being 43½ feet on the skew. One of the under bridges, for a cattle creep of small opening,

The Station Master, unmistakable in frock coat, with his staff at Instow around the turn of the century. Its broad gauge origins are evident from the great space between the tracks. Propped up against the station building is a penny farthing.

Instow station in 1913 above, and below, an Adams A12 0-4-2 No.539 with a long train of four, six wheelers, approaching Bideford new station from Torrington. Judging by the well-dressed crowd on the platform the occasion must have been of some importance and is thought to be photographed around 1890. D. Hughes Collection.

is of timber, two are constructed entirely in brick or stone, and the remainder have stone abutments with wrought iron or cast iron girders, the largest span is 40.5 feet.

Three of the viaducts are of brick and stone, and the fourth of seven spans is of wrought iron girders, resting on cast iron columns. The largest spans are of 55 feet. The whole of the works are very well executed and the iron girders are sufficiently strong by calculation, and exhibited moderate deflections under a rolling load. The tunnel has stone sidewalls and a brick arch – the workmanship being very good.

There are only two stations, viz; at Bideford and Torrington. There are no level crossings of public roads. The company are desirous of commencing to work at once with the new Bideford passenger station as it is now conveniently situated for the town traffic and there is no objection to

this being done – as the up signal worked from the junction with the goods line only requires to be reversed, so that the top signal shall be used to the left line – and the up and down signals in the goods yard require to be interlocked with each other. Mr Jacomb the Company's Engineer promised that these things should be at once attended to. Name boards are required at the station.

Torrington station and yard is still in an unfinished state, and the fencing along the line is incomplete and the fencing on the river side in places is unfinished. The cleaning out of some of the cuttings is not quite complete and the rails require lifting and regulating in some parts.

Under the circumstances I have to recommend that the Board of Trade do sanction the opening of the new station at Bideford for passenger traffic, but that in consequence of the incompleteness of the

works the opening of the remainder of the line to Torrington should not be sanctioned, with danger to the public using the same.

The LSWR immediately announced the opening of Bideford (New) station, which took place without ceremony on Monday 10th June. The first train to arrive was the early morning mail, but when the 10 a.m. train departed, the engine was decorated with flowers and evergreens, flags were flying, the church bells rang out and a crowd of several hundred cheered it off. The new station was well received by the people of Bideford, being more convenient for the town, attractive and commodious, with a carriage approach to the main buildings on the 'down' platform and steps to the 'up' platform from the street below. This new LSWR line was built to the standard gauge but the old mixed gauge station at Cross Parks was

Top. The original Bideford Junction signal box with Mr. Tolley the signalman in 1877. It was sited at Bideford Cross Parks station the town's terminus until 1872. This was the junction for the trains to run into the goods station on the left, or up to Bideford new station and Torrington. The building was a similar structure to that at Instow. When opened in 1855 the tracks were broad gauge and, in March 1863, mixed gauge was introduced. The box was demolished and replaced by a ground frame by the LSWR.

Left. The Appledore and Bideford railway light railway and quay on the other side of the Torridge River.

Laid up vessels anchored in the Torridge estuary from Bideford Goods about 1920.

Bridge No.117 with the original terminus, below, by now a goods station; the goods shed is in the middle of the photograph. The waterfront siding seen here was extended in 1893 to form a private siding for the Western Counties Agricultural Co-operative Society.

The glorious Royal Hotel had a private entrance to the station for its guests as well as steps to the refreshment rooms. On the left is Springfield Terrace which also has steps to the station; in the background a single van occupies the short up siding taken out in 1959.

retained for the extensive goods traffic. Although Bideford New was built as a through station, with a passing loop and two platforms as recommended by Lt. Col. Hutchinson in the report of the Fremington accident of 1869, it was used as a terminus for the North Devon line for some six weeks until the remaining section to Torrington was ready. There was a letter on 3rd July from Mr W.R. Malcolm at the Board of Trade to the South Western objecting to the new signalling installed at Bideford Goods, but the line was already open and Yolland did not mention it in his next report.

Lt. Col. Yolland returned to the line on Friday, 12th July 1872, and made his report the following day: *The line was not ready for re-inspection prior to yesterday, and I delayed going there until there was a reasonable prospect of the works being sufficiently advanced to render another visit unnecessary.*

Torrington station and yard is now all but complete, a crossover road at the end of the platform only being required to enable the engine to run round the train. It is covered by the proper signals, interlocked with each other, and provided with a catch siding and stop block on the 'up' and 'down' lines to prevent vehicles from escaping from the station which is partially on an incline.

I would suggest also that the lever which now works the points leading to the turntable and engine shed work on another pair of points – or even a single point in the nature of a safety switch, to prevent the engine from coming out except when required.

One of the viaducts over the River Torridge consists of wrought iron girders supported on piers formed by cast iron columns. The current in the river at times is very rapid, 10 miles an hour in, and the pillars are sheltered by wooden fenders that rise and fall with the tide and which butt against the pillars. I beg to suggest for the consideration of the company, that under these circumstances it would be expedient to drive three piles, above and below the bridge for each pier in the nature of dolphins properly braced together, to prevent these fenders being struck and forced heavily against the pillars, by barges ascending or descending the stream.

There is still some little to be done in cleaning out one or two of the cuttings and in tightening up the wire fencing where it is used. Some ditching also is still required and the name boards have to be put up but there is no reason why the Board of Trade should withhold its sanction to the opening of the line as soon as the certificate has been received. As to the mode of working the traffic – and which I understand is by only one engine in steam on the length between Bideford and Torrington.

Archibald Scott, the LSWR General Manager, and Galbraith, the engineer, who were both present at the inspection, arranged for the necessary alterations to be completed in time for public

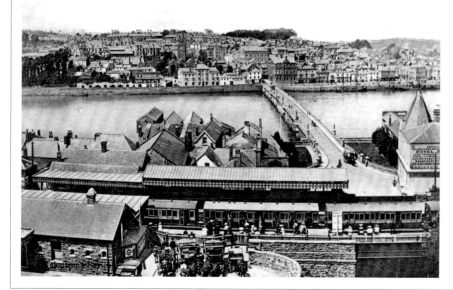

Bideford station looking across the river from 'The Grange' in 1893. Compare this view with that on the opposite page when the canopies on the down side have been extended.

Top. PW men, station staff and shunting horses thought to be at Fremington in 1910.

Middle. Horse drawn coaches were prominent at Bideford for many years despatching passengers to all parts of the town. The station was now more conveniently sited in the East-the-Water district but taxis still had to negotiate a fearsome gradient down to the river bridge. A train of dark brown coaches and a Beattie 2-4-0WT are seen here around 1872 shortly after the station had opened.

Bottom. The station in 1920 with new canopies extending along both the up and down platforms.

The covered entrance on the corner of Torrington Street allowed direct access from here to the up platform. The steep road up to the down side platform lies under the bridge.

Two local traders with their horse drawn carts, above Harris and Sons a purveyor of dairy goods and below, Chaplin and Sons contractor to the LSWR for household removals.

services to begin on Thursday 18th July again without ceremony. As at Bideford the previous month, the first arrival was the morning mail train which was welcomed by a large crowd, and a well decorated locomotive departed with the first 'up' train to Bideford, carrying a large number of passengers. The station was a well designed terminus, suitable for conversion to a through working, but some of the sheds were not complete.

Since the LSWR chose to do without a ceremony for the opening of the Torrington Extension line, the people of Torrington decided to hold their own, and a civic committee made arrangements for festivities to be held on Wednesday 24th July. The town was decorated with triumphal arches across the streets, with flags and banners of all descriptions. There was also a procession to the station with several bands, a free dinner for 600 men and tea for about 1,600 women and children in the Market House, following sports on the Castle Hill. In the evening, there was a banquet for a large number of guests in the Town Hall, presided over by the Mayor, Mr Chapple. Significant absentees from the proceedings were any representatives of the LSWR, who cited the approaching half-yearly meeting of the Company as the reason for their absence. However, Archibald Scott had recommended that the Town Council wait a few days after the public opening for the line to be worked and thoroughly tried, so this was probably a diplomatic absence since the LSWR had been forced into building the line which had eventually cost them £100,000. There were more than twenty toasts and speeches at the banquet, with great appreciation shown to the Hon. Mark Rolle who had fought so hard to ensure the building of the line. Torrington had not seen a day like this before.

A brief description of the Torrington Extension Railway line may be helpful here, to show what the local people were celebrating, in their various ways, in Torrington upon that day. The narrow gauge line commenced at a junction outside the old Cross Parks broad gauge station, controlled by the Bideford Junction signal box with junction signals mounted on a tall wooden post. The line climbed up behind the old Bideford station, which retained the extensive goods traffic, and squeezed its way through Bideford East-the-Water, between Barnstaple Street and Torrington Street on the one side by the Torridge, and the steep hill on the other. Two overbridges and three underbridges in rapid succession kept the line clear of the busy streets. The new station, with its passing loop and two platforms, had sidings enough only for the odd van or horse box, the available space being so limited. So steep was the hill that towards the

Top. Adams Goods 0395 class 0-6-0 No.83 at Torrington around 1891, possibly with a passenger train. The wagon behind the locomotive appears to contain limestone, probably for burning in the lime-kiln nearby. One of the long frame series, this locomotive's final SR number was 3083, and it was only withdrawn, as 30565, in 1953.

Middle. Torrington station in an advanced state of construction, probably in early 1872. The station building and goods shed are almost complete but the signal box and engine shed have yet to be started.

Bottom. An early view of Torrington station from Torrington Common. To the left are the down sidings with a selection of wagons and vans while in the left background is the roof of some farm buildings. The small hut in the foreground is the pump house whilst on the hill is the water tank and the station cottages.

Rothern Bridge; Torrington station to the right.

Barnstaple end of the station, the 'down' platform was overlooked by the houses of Springfield Terrace on the rock above, whilst opposite, the 'up' platform overlooked the properties below in Barnstaple Street. Leaving Bideford New, the line passed market gardens, lime kilns and the gasworks, keeping to the east bank of the Torridge Estuary until it reached Landcross. Here was the first of four bridges over the Torridge, Landcross Viaduct being a long iron structure. The line then passed through a short tunnel, and from here on it used part of the bed of the Rolle Canal, then crossed and re-crossed the River Torridge on masonry viaducts of four arches, until arriving at Torrington station near the old Rothern Bridge at Staplevale. The Rolle Canal had originally passed through the site now occupied by the station, which had been built as the new terminus of the LSWR North Devon

line with engine shed and turntable but with limited siding accommodation.

Early Years on the North Devon Line
The initial passenger train service on the North Devon line in August 1872 comprised six trains each way as far as Torrington, three from Waterloo, one from Yeovil and two from Exeter, with another between Barnstaple and Bideford. The best 'down' train from Waterloo was the 2.10 p.m. express, for first and second class passengers only, which took 6 hours 51 minutes for the journey of 225 miles to Torrington. Discrimination against the third class passenger continued, with only the inconvenient 7.05 a.m. and 7.40 p.m. 'up' trains, and the 6.45 a.m. 'down' train from Waterloo accommodating them. Extra services ran to and from Barnstaple on Fridays, which was market day. Local people started using the trains on the new line

for special events from the summer of 1872 onwards. A party of 170 travelled by train from Torrington for a Sunday school outing to Instow, and the Rifle Volunteers Corps, from Bideford and Barnstaple, travelled by train to Torrington, to parade with the Torrington and Hatherleigh Corps. The LSWR failed to anticipate the demand to travel to Torrington for the October fair on 10th October, when a large number of travellers bought tickets at Bideford intending to catch the second 'down' train of the day to Torrington, only to find there was insufficient room for them all. Some awaited the next train but others demanded their money back, and there was general dissatisfaction with the local LSWR management.

The first couple of years of the Torrington Extension was marred by a succession of unfortunate events. A carpenter was working near the turntable at Torrington when he was hit by a locomotive coming out of the shed, severing one leg just above the ankle. A platelayer was later run down and killed by a train while on duty at Instow and a trespasser was knocked down and killed by a train near Bideford. Back at Torrington, on 21st August 1874. locomotive SNAKE was shunting empty coaching stock when it ran into a loaded porter's trolley, with the porter suffering a broken arm and the locomotive being derailed.

Torrington station from Furzebeam Hill probably taken before Grouping as the signal box has yet to be extended.

Top. The original Torrington signal box; it underwent some reconstruction when the line was extended southwards to Halwill Junction in 1925.

Middle. Adams Radial tank No.524 on the turntable at Torrington in 1891. It wasn't strictly necessary to turn the tanks but running smokebox-first was always preferable. The position here was very tight as the turntable also accessed some sidings and a lime-kiln.

Bottom. Beattie 2-4-0 No.61 SNAKE on the overgirder turntable (it was eventually removed) about 1886.

An early view of Torrington station with a rake of LSWR four wheelers in mahogany livery at the departure platform. As yet, the Torrington & Marland line has not been built so the year must be some time between 1872 and 1880.

An LSWR minute of December 1876 recorded a report from the Torrington Agent, Mr Dalby, that the 9.10am 'down' train had run into a carriage and Post Office van which were standing against the stop blocks. The driver was fined 5 shillings and the fireman 2 shillings and 6 pence. It appears that the 9.10am was a local passenger train from Barnstaple and the carriage and van had arrived on the 3.20 a.m. passenger and mail from Exeter. However in March 1880 the same 9.20 a.m. 'down' passenger ran into the stop buffers, and the driver was cautioned. In October 1882 the Torrington Agent, a driver and guard were each fined 2 shillings and 6 pence for neglecting the train staff.

On the civil engineering side, a major task for the LSWR was the replacement of the original wooden viaduct over Fremington Pill. The lifting span was raised by means of chain and winch gear operated by hand, and we have already seen Lt. Col. Yolland's description of the structure back in 1855. The whole viaduct was replaced in 1880 by a fixed iron girder bridge, which was opened for traffic on 6th July 1880. However, it was not until 1883 that the LSWR Act authorising this was passed, so it would appear that the LSWR had purchased the right of way for navigation into Fremington Pill, the last vessel to use it being the ketch *Acorn*.

In 1890, as a result of a new agreement on signalmen's wages, the LSWR fitted through switches to a number of signal boxes, so that they might be closed on Sundays as an economy measure. This was a common practice on double track lines where all

points could be set normally and signals left at 'off', as occurred well into British Railways days at Chapelton and Wrafton, but this economy measure applied also to signal boxes on single lines, including those at Fremington, Bideford Junction and Bideford.

Instow Petition 1912
During 1912 there was concern at overcrowding at Instow station, resulting in a petition signed by 102 local people, representing 400 to 500 in the parishes of Westleigh, Eastleigh and Horwood, delivered to the South Western on 30th May. The request was for a more convenient footpath to the west side of the station, the up platform, the existing access over the level crossing being closed when trains were in the station or about to arrive. The organiser of the petition was Mr R.O. Hearson of Westleigh. On 1st July Herbert Walker, the newly appointed South Western General Manager, declined the request on the grounds that it would require the appointment of additional staff which the traffic could not justify.

Mr Hearson replied to Herbert Walker, but appealed unsuccessfully to Lord Clinton, a South Western Director who lived nearby at Heanton Sachville. In a second letter to Lord Clinton Mr Hearson pointed out that during the holiday season both platforms were crowded with women and children, forced to cross the lines whist two trains were in the platforms, there being no foot bridge. Also the level crossing was repeatedly closed for a considerable time, when goods trains were being loaded on unloaded at the platforms.

Mr Hearson then wrote to the Board of Trade on 2nd September, but found their reply unsatisfactory, because on 9th November a long article was published in the *Western Morning News* based on Mr Hearson's correspondence. The article reported that at Instow station 30,000 tickets were issued annually and 75,000 collected

The later LSWR Period
By the turn of the century the LSWR system was almost complete and no major new lines were built. On the North Devon, the old broad gauge tracks had been brought up to modern standards and there was a good level of traffic which was still expanding. On the Barnstaple to Torrington section, the only competition came from coastal shipping, but much of this traffic was exchanged with the railway through the wharves at Fremington and Bideford, with imports of coal and limestone and exports of clay. However, further investment was still required to expand and improve facilities. At Barnstaple Junction, a second 'down' platform road was built to turn the 'down' platform into an island, although this was not brought into use until 1924, in Southern Railway days, At Bideford the awnings on both platforms were extended, while Bideford Junction signal box was replaced by Bideford (Goods) ground frame. The expansion in railway business in North Devon was most marked on the Ilfracombe branch, which had been improved from its light railway beginnings and doubled for most of its length. Summer holiday traffic for Ilfracombe ran not only along

An Adams T3 class 4-4-0 on arrival at Torrington with a passenger train from Exeter Queen Street, *circa* 1919, with non-corridor set No.125 in the up platform. At this time T3s performed many duties between Exeter and Torrington, with Nos.571 and 575 allocated to Torrington shed in 1903, and others at Barnstaple shed.

The goods yard at Torrington and a selection of LSWR goods and passenger stock, including a distinctive clerestory roof dining saloon. There is a rake of 3ft gauge clay wagons between the two standard gauge sidings and three locomotives, including a tank engine shunting carriages, and two tender locomotives on the shed road.

Torrington from Furzebeam Hill. On the left is Rothern Bridge, in the middle distance the lime-kilns and to the right the station.

the LSWR North Devon line, but also on the GWR line from Taunton, via the Barnstaple spur line built in 1887, and the direct link opened in 1905. As we saw earlier, throughout the LSWR period, the Torrington line was the main line from Barnstaple Junction and the Ilfracombe line was the branch, but early in Southern Railway days, the roles were reversed.

First World War

During the Great War the line handled a large quantity of hay and timber traffic, much of it through Torrington station. On Monday 30 July 1917 three rather unusual consignments came down Barnstaple Street to Bideford (Goods) Yard. These were GRENVILLE, KINGSLEY and TORRIDGE, the locomotives of the Bideford, Westward Ho! & Appledore Railway, conscripted by the government for wartime service. The previous day gangers had laid temporary rails on Bideford Bridge to enable the locomotives to steam over from their terminus on the quay. The next day, temporary tracks were laid down Barnstaple Street to enable the locomotives to steam into Bideford (Goods) and away to wartime service. The Bideford, Westward Ho! & Appledore line was opened to Northam in 1901 and extended to Appledore in 1908 and, although of standard gauge, it had no connection with the LSWR system, being separated from it by the Torridge Estuary.

Projected Lines to the South

When the Torrington Extension Railway opened in 1872, several speeches at the civic celebrations referred to the need to extend the line beyond Torrington as quickly as possible. Examination of the LSWR terminus at Torrington shows that it had been designed with separate arrival and departure platforms, which could easily be converted to 'up' and 'down' lines on a single line passing loop when the line was extended under the main road. The normal LSWR terminal arrangement was rather different, being a single platform with two faces, as at Bude and Ilfracombe. This arrangement was cheaper but unsuitable for extension, so the LSWR certainly had this in mind when building Torrington station in 1872.

It was always assumed that the extension from Torrington would run south to the edge of Dartmoor, to join the LSWR main line to Plymouth near Sampford Courtnay or Okehampton. Locally, it was felt that North Devon needed a direct railway to Plymouth, which was the major centre of population and commerce in the south-western peninsular and, as we have already seen, there was, for many years, a regular coach service between North Devon and Plymouth. Such a line would also serve the Marland Clay and Brickworks, which would supply the main originating freight traffic. The narrow gauge Torrington & Marland

Railway had limited capacity, and was expensive on labour with six men employed at Torrington station loading clay into standard gauge wagons, and two more maintaining the long wooden viaduct.

As we have already seen, there were abortive attempts to link Torrington and Okehampton by a railway in 1831, 1845 and 1869, and further attempts which followed in 1888 and 1892 were again unsuccessful. In 1895, a Torrington & Okehampton Railway got its Act for a line twenty miles in length between Torrington and milepost 196, near Okehampton, with an intermediate station at Hatherleigh, with a capital of £250,000. This would have utilised part of the trackbed of the Torrington & Marland Railway, and the Act included a clause for the protection of the North Devon Clay Company. The LSWR had agreed to work the Torrington & Okehampton Railway for 50 per cent of gross receipts, but it came to nothing. Another Torrington & Okehampton Railway got its Act in 1901, and later changed its name to the Plymouth & North Devon Direct Railway. The Company had taken a delegation to meet the LSWR Traffic Committee in 1904 to seek support but, in 1906, the Plymouth & North Devon Direct Railway got its abandonment Act.

The LSWR attitude appeared to be that if a local company raised its own capital and built the line, then the

LSWR would be happy to work it for them. The LSWR was a business, and could see no good reason for spending its money on a line twenty miles long, principally to serve the small town of Hatherleigh. All existing traffic from the region under consideration eventually had to use the LSWR through its existing stations, Hatherleigh already being served by a coach service to Okehampton Station. Indeed, for the through traffic between North Devon and Plymouth, the LSWR stood to lose money if the new direct line were built, since it could not then be taken round the existing longer route, via Yeoford. However in the end. a line was built, not to main line but to light railway standards, and not to the obvious destination of Okehampton, but to the lonely junction of the Bude & North Cornwall lines at Halwill.

Bideford Wharf or Quay
The quay opened in 1855 as part of the Bideford Extension Railway, but in 1922 there was a letter from the Superintendent of the Line Geo. F. West to the company solicitor. W. Bishop:

Bideford Quay Shipping Berths
In connection with the waterside facilities which have existed at the company's Goods Yard at Bideford it has been customary for vessels to berth alongside the company's premises for the purpose of discharging or receiving cargoes.

Recently the Engineer has drawn attention to the fact that if this practice is to continue certain work will have to be carried out in the river bed which will entail an initial cost of about £200, and an annual maintenance charge of £75.

The quay and wharfage facilities in question have never been extensively used, and you will see by the papers, which I enclose for your perusal, that the only traffic which it can be confidently anticipated will be dealt with if the river approach and berths are put in good order is some 2,400 tons of china clay from Torrington upon which the Indoor Goods Manager suggests a wharfage charge of 4d per ton should be levied.

The total estimated earnings, therefore, are £310 rail charge,(and in regard of this I think we may safely assume that if the traffic is not handled at Bideford it will go to Fremington for shipment) and £40 wharfage dues which appears to be a totally inadequate return for the outlay involved in reconditioning and maintaining the berths and river approach.

W. Bishop's reply advised that there was no legal requirement for the maintenance of the river frontage, its use as a quay had grown up as a matter of mutual convenience to the company and traders. A subsequent letter from Traffic Manager Edwin C. Cox to W. Bishop advised that the company would have no objection to a firm taking over and controlling the river wharf, and sporadic correspondence continued until 1934. By 1929 the only charges made in addition to the Bideford station rates was 4d per ton for the service of placing the wagons in position, there were no charges for the use of the quay and no appliances were provided for the shipment of traffic.

The Grouping
The 1921 Railways Act organised the main line railways into four groups. The new Southern Railway comprised the London & South Western Railway, the London Brighton & South Coast Railway, London Chatham & Dover Railway and South Eastern & Chatham Managing Committee, together with a number of smaller companies. As from 1st January 1923, the Southern Railway ran the North Devon line, together with the narrow gauge Lynton & Barnstaple line. However, there were a number of other changes on the way for the lines to Torrington.

A train of empty clay wagons leaves Torrington for the Marland Clay & Brick Works, hauled by 0-6-0 tank MARY around 1913.

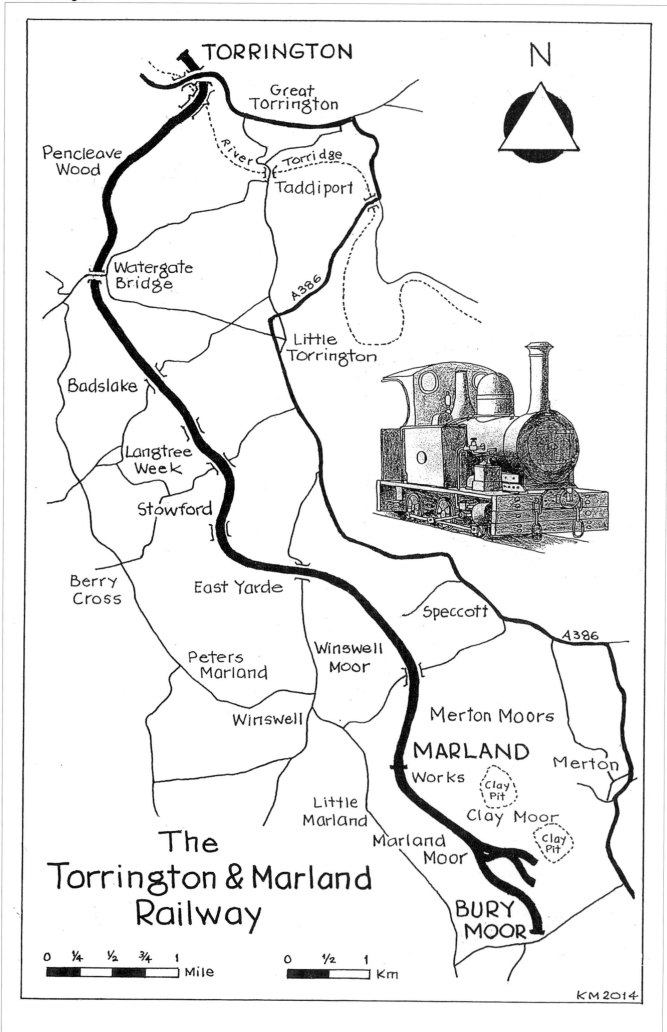

N

TORRINGTON

Great
Torrington

Pencleave
Wood

River
Torridge
Taddiport

A386

Watergate
Bridge

Little
Torrington

Badslake

Langtree
Week

Stowford

Berry
Cross

East Yarde

Speccott

A386

Peters
Marland

Winswell
Moor

Winswell

Merton Moors

MARLAND

Merton

Works

Clay
Pit

Clay Moor

Little
Marland

Clay
Pit

Marland
Moor

The
Torrington & Marland
Railway

BURY
MOOR

0 ¼ ½ ¾ 1 Mile

0 ½ 1 Km

KM 2014

Chapter 5
The Torrington and Marland Railway

When the Torrington Extension Railway had opened in 1872, it was felt locally that the line should be extended southwards, as soon as possible, to complete a through route from North Devon to Plymouth, to serve the Marland Brick and Clay Works. At that stage, clay and bricks were brought to Torrington station by road, using early traction engines, but better transport was required if the works were to prosper. Although the LSWR had designed its Torrington terminus to be easily converted into a through station, thus avoiding the expense encountered in extending from the unsuitable Bideford terminus, it soon became obvious that the LSWR was in no hurry to extend the line, and local initiative was again required.

This time, the initiative came from Mr F. Holwill, who was the manager of the Marland Clay Company. Mr Holwill contacted Mr John Fell, who was an engineer specialising in the construction of light railways, including the Mont Cenis line in Switzerland. During 1879 he surveyed a line between Torrington station and the Marland

Clay Works. This 3ft. gauge line would have a length of 6½ miles and could be built for £15,000, which contrasted very favourably with the cost of £100,000 for the 5½ miles of the LSWR Torrington Extension. An interesting feature of the line was that it was built without an Act of Parliament which kept the cost down. Mr Holwill had negotiated with the four landowners concerned and obtained their consent. The line was to commence from the goods yard of the LSWR's Torrington station and would bring increased traffic in clay and bricks to the LSWR, without expense to that company.

The ceremony of cutting the first sod of the Torrington & Marland Railway was held on Torrington Common, opposite the LSWR station, at 12 noon on Wednesday, 26th May 1880. The contractors were the Green Odd Railway & Contracting Company of Lancashire, and they started work immediately after the ceremony. The two major engineering works on the new line were a short tunnel out of the LSWR goods yard under the main road and a long wooden viaduct on stone

piers over the River Torridge, both at Staplevale. Elsewhere on the line, earthworks were kept to a minimum by following the contours (which necessitated sharp curves and steep gradients) and by the use of timber trestle structures instead of embankments. In 1880, timber was comparatively cheap and available locally in large quantities, and at the Torrington end a large quantity of timber was brought to Staplevale Farm, next to the station. Here it was cut, using a steam-powered saw, to be used in constructing the viaduct and other structures. In June, it was reported that rapid progress was being made and by December, the viaduct was finished and a locomotive had commenced running over it. Apparently, the only recorded accident occurred when a number of navvies were returning from work on a trolley, and one fell off and was run over, suffering a broken leg. The line was completed by the end of December 1880. The design and construction of the Torrington & Marland Railway, 6½ miles in length, was quite remarkable both for its low cost of £15,000 and the

Torrington and the Torridge Viaduct. A train is being backed onto by Avonside 0-6-0ST AVONSIDE ready for its journey south. Bryan Wells collection.

0-6-0 tank MARLAND built by W.G. Bagnall of Stafford, which worked the Torrington & Marland Railway. It is seen at the works with William Petherbridge as the driver in 1913.

very short seven month period of construction.

At this stage, it should be pointed out that the Torrington & Marland Railway was a private mineral line, and there was no intention of running a public passenger service. For this reason, it was not necessary for an inspecting officer of the Board of Trade to report on the line, although such a report would now be most interesting. On 1st January 1881 the first train of bricks and clay ran down the Torrington & Marland Railway from the Marland Works to Torrington goods yard. The date had been fixed in advance with the contractors, but there was no opening ceremony until 5th February when a party of local notables and press inspected the line.

The 3ft. gauge line commenced at a long interchange siding in the goods yard at Torrington, where the clay company had its office and also a shelter for its men. The line passed through a short tunnel under the road, lined with the distinctive white Marland

Torrington Viaduct during construction of the ND&CJLR in 1923. The new piers can be seen in front of the wooden viaduct, linked by temporary tracks. Power for the site comes from that vertical boiler on the left.

brick, into a cutting where there was a loop for running round purposes. It then passed on to the timber viaduct over the River Torridge, 40ft. high with three spans 45ft. in length supported on masonry piers. The viaduct was followed by a timber structure supported on trestles, which gave an overall length of almost 1,000ft. There were two similar trestle structures at other places on the line and a number of wooden bridges from 20 to 25ft. high. It was the use of these wooden structures instead of conventional earthworks and masonry that made construction of the line so cheap and quick. Leaving the Torridge Valley, the line ran up through the Langtree Valley,

Top. Locomotive MARLAND at the works around 1918, showing driver W.M. Petherbridge with a group of the Holwill family. Standing in the centre is jack Holwill then pit foreman and, on the far right, is the young E.A. Holwill who gave the authors considerable assistance in the writing of this book.

Middle. Yarde trestle viaduct, with one of contractor P&W Anderson's works train. The locomotive is No.52 GYP.

Below. Marland works and saddle tank JERSEY 1. Interestingly this Fletcher Jennings loco was rebuilt especially to work at Marland and now has its saddle tank sitting on an old wagon frame acting as a tender. The date is thought to be 1910.

Marland works had an engine shed and this is just out of view to the left of the photograph. MARLAND with loaded wagons in the stockyards in 1913; driver William Petheridge standing and William Squire on the footplate. The works engine shed is off to the left.

PETER at the works with driver Isaac Luxton on the right. Built by Stephen Lewin of Poole, the little 0-4-0T worked on the Torrington & Marland Railway for many years.

past Drummet's Flour Mill, Langtree Mill and Langtree Farm to Stowford Moor where, at Yarde, there was a passing loop at the summit. From Yarde, the line ran down over a turnpike road and followed the River Mere down to the clay and brickworks at Marland and to a depot at Bury Moor, near Petrockstow, for other goods carried by the railway.

The Torrington & Marland Railway of the North Devon Clay Company, as it became, was in use for forty four years until the opening of the North Devon & Cornwall Junction Light Railway in 1925. The ND&CJLR used much of the trackbed of the 3ft gauge line, but the narrow gauge system was retained within the clay works for another forty five years until It finally closed in 1970. The grandson of Mr F. Holwill, the Manager of the clay company when the line was first built, Mr E. A. Holwill, joined the North Devon Clay Company in 1923: *The traffic carried was mainly clay and bricks from the works to Torrington station, with return loads of goods required by the Company, such as coal and oil. The trains were normally goods trains with the exception of the 6.30 a.m. Torrington to Marland which conveyed men to work, and the return train which arrived back at 6 p.m. (Provided by the company free of charge for their employees). The men worked a 48 hour week in 5½ days. The only other 'passengers' carried were private parties and on these occasions they would*

have to sit in the open on a plank across the sides of the clay wagons. The men used to ride in two converted horse trams and later in vans. The Company had about sixty open wagons which would hold 3½ tons each and were about 11ft. long and 4ft. 6in. wide by 2ft. 6in. deep. In addition to goods carried for the Company, the line also carried various goods for the Clinton Estate and other users of agricultural produce, building materials, etc and there was a depot at Bury Moor (Petrockstow) with a man in charge to deal with these goods. The carriage charges thus earned helped towards the upkeep of the railway.

The clay and bricks were transferred to the main line wagons by six men working for the clay company at Torrington station. There was no crane available nor would it have served any useful purpose. The clay was conveyed in the main line wagons mainly to the Staffordshire pottery area at Stoke-on-Trent, to London, Bristol, the Burton upon Trent area, and also to Bideford and Fremington for shipment. The former was used by smaller motor vessels and the latter by larger steamers and motor vessels for the continent. The Bideford sailings were for the stoneware potteries in Lancashire, Yorkshire and the Glasgow district, mainly for making jam pots. Large tonnages were sent to Bristol for shipment from Bristol Docks to America; the Company used to export about 75 per cent of all the ball clay sent to the United States.

The clay company had a small office at Torrington Station and my first job on joining them in 1923 was to go to the

station twice a day to make out the various consignment notes and hand them over to the goods office where they would make out the necessary labels for the trucks. The Railway Company would also hand me a consignment note of the various items of goods which had to be carried out to the works and also for the various users such as the Clinton Estates and others. Our wagons had two coupling chains each end with a central buffer. Each wagon also had a wooden brake on one side, the brake block being made by our own carpenters from poplar. All the wagons were made at the works by our own smiths and carpenters.

The average daily traffic of clay on the Marland line was 100 tons. Not many bricks were carried by rail as most were delivered direct from the works by steam lorries to firms at Bideford and housing schemes at Bideford, Barnstaple and Ilfracombe. On average ten LSWR 10 ton open wagons were loaded with clay daily. Apart from the men employed transferring clay at Torrington Station the Company also employed two men to look after and maintain the viaduct at Torrington. There were also three rail packers for the track and three locomotive drivers and their assistants.

The Torrington & Marland line had a passing loop at the summit of the line at Yarde, which was used for a novel method of working. Normally, there were two engines at work on the main line between the works and Torrington. On the arrival at Yarde of a train of empties from Torrington the driver

Rolle Road and returning workmen in 1910, MARY heading a train more suited to a fairground ride, by the look of it! Bryan Wells collection.

waited for the arrival of a train of loaded wagons from the works. The two engines then exchanged trains, each engine working back to the point from where it started. One driver worked between Torrington and Yarde, another between Yarde and the works, and a third worked on the extensive railway system within the works. There was no signalling on the line but this method of operation appears to have worked satisfactorily without any recorded accidents. By the early 1920s, it was reported that traffic on the Torrington & Marland Railway amounted to over 42,000 tons of clay, bricks and agricultural produce per annum. Some seven steam locomotives from a variety of suppliers worked on the line, most being scrapped when the main line shut in 1925, full details being given in Chapter Ten.

Top. The wagon is apparently locally built so this photograph is fairly late in the day, nevertheless PETER is attracting the attention of several admirers at Open Pit Top. Jack Holwill far right.

Middle. Men gathered for a photograph at the Marland Clay& Brick Company, probably around 1914. The locomotives are PETER on the left and MARY on the right.

Bottom. Diesels rule the day at Marland with, from left to right, narrow gauge ADVANCE and FORWARD, standard gauge PROGRESS, narrow gauge EFFICIENCY and standard gauge PETER.

The transhipment shed (left) and the small engine shed. R. Sellick.

Pit head of Red Label mine on 4th September 1961, showing 3ft gauge wagons which are being loaded with solid lumps of clay. R. Sellick.

Construction work underway somewhere on the ND&CJLR. In days gone by many hundreds of navvies and horses would have been engaged in the backbreaking work of shifting thousands of tons of soil and rock. However, BUNTY's wagons are being loaded by a Rushton steam excavator or 'steam navvy' which made light work of shifting the heavy clay predominant in the area.

An unusual practice, but GYP seems to be engaged in filling in Yarde Viaduct to create an embankment. An incident worthy of note was the drunken brawl which occurred at Hatherleigh in 1923. In an attempt to improve rural communications, transport and alleviate unemployment Government grants and loans were available to build the line. Some inexperienced and unsuitable labour was employed culminating in a drunken riot in Hatherleigh when two local bobbies came close to losing their lives. Excessive consumption of ale was not surprisingly the culprit with some of those arrested receiving sentences of up to five months hard labour.

Chapter 6
The North Devon & Cornwall Junction Light Railway

The Light Railway Act of 1896 established the Light Railway Commissioners, who could grant Light Railway Orders without the expense of an Act of Parliament. Light railways were built to less rigorous standards and could be run more economically. On 28th February 1910 the Light Railway Commissioners held an enquiry at Torrington where there was wide support for a railway south to Hatherleigh thence west to Halwill Junction, proposed by Holman Fred Stephens, later to become Col. Stephens of light railway fame. After prolonged negotiations between the promoters, landowners and the North Devon Clay Company the Commissioners approved the application in 1913 and the North Devon & Cornwall Junction Light Railway got its Light Railway Order in 1914, allowing them to build a standard gauge line south from Torrington to Hatherleigh and then west to Halwill

Another unidentified location on the ND&CJLR with Hudswell Clarke 0-4-0ST BIRKENHEAD tipping spoil to create an embankment. The process would have been slow but quicker than horse, cart and shovel. The contracting firm P&W Anderson was engaged to build the line but went into receivership in February 1925. Colonel Stephens took over the work in July the same year, hiring direct labour.

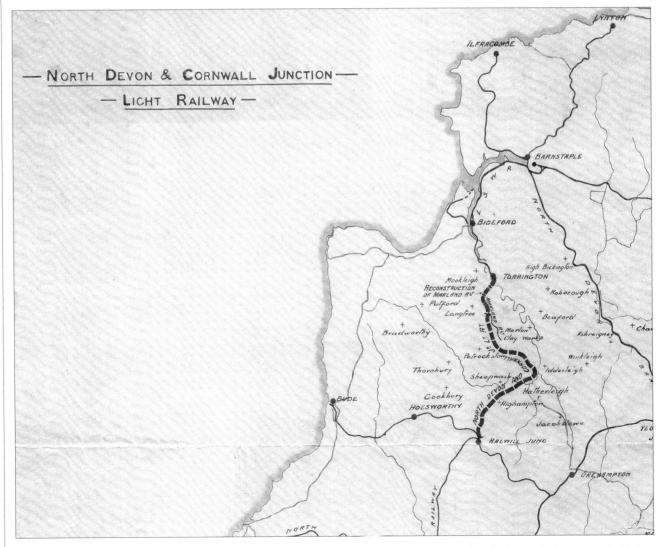

Hatherleigh, the only intermediate station to have water available for locomotives. There was no signal box here and signals and points were controlled by a small ground frame out of view to the left. The single line tablet machine was housed in the booking office.

Junction. The capital for the line, twenty miles in length, was £131,500 in 1914, which compares very favourably with the cost of the LSWR Torrington Extension some forty years before, and was little over half the authorised capital of the failed 1895 Torrington and Okehampton Railway. The engineer of the ND&CJLR, Mr Rumbold, announced in February 1914 that his firm was ready to begin building the line and then offer shares to the public. Earthworks were to be limited and most roads were crossed on the level with unattended crossings. However, the Great War intervened, and with it came the rapid inflation of the period.

North Devon & Cornwall Junction Light Railway Order 1914

This order by the Light Railway Commissioners ran to 36 pages. The directors were Holman Fred Stephens, William Arthur Wardley, Col Richard Arthur Moore Stevens and John Wilson. 'Railway No.1' ran from the LSWR Torrington station to a junction with the Torrington and Marland Railway at Little Torrington, whilst 'Railway No.2' ran thence through the parishes of Merton, Petrockstow to Hele Bridge on the River Torridge and through the parishes of Hatherleigh, Highampton and Black Torrington to Halwill, with powers for deviations. There was provision for bridges over roads at Meeth and Halwill and bridges over the railway at Torrington and Hatherleigh. There were provisions for unstaffed level crossings over roads with cattle guards.

For the protection of the South Western there were seven clauses including payment for additions or alterations at Torrington and Halwill Junction. For the protection of the North Devon Clay Company (Torrington and Marland Railway) there were 11 clauses including No.1 for the continuation of its clay traffic during construction, Nos.2, 3, 4 for conveyance of the clay traffic when the line opened, and No.6 for a passenger service for the conveyance of workmen between Torrington station, intermediate places to be agreed, and the clay works. There were powers to lease the ND&CJLR to the South Western, rates for merchandise, small parcels and passenger luggage, but there was no obligation on the company to provide shelter or convenience at any station or stopping place. The ND&CJLR was to reconstruct, repair, renew and maintain the Torrington and Marland Railway, and to pay the clay company £18,000 for its railway.

When the project got under way again after the war, the cost had rocketed to £260,000. This was raised by the sale of 130,000 shares of £2 each which were bought mainly by public bodies, with the Treasury providing £125,000, Devon County Council, Bideford Corporation, Torrington, Okehampton and Holsworthy Councils some £60,000 between them, and the balance coming from the North Devon Clay Company and local landowners, many of whom accepted payment for their land in the form of shares. A Hatherleigh grocer and farmer, William Balsdon, worked with Col. Stephens to campaign for the railway and raise funds. Under an agreement of 7th April 1922, between the LSWR and the

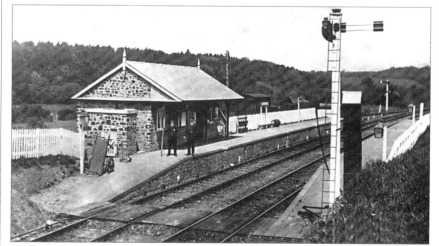

Hatherleigh new in 1925; after closure of the line it was the only station to avoid the demolition gang.

ND&CJLR, the LSWR would work the line for 75 per cent of gross receipts, and would guarantee a 5 per cent return on half the ND&CJLR stock. The engineer of the ND&CJLR was Col. Holman Fred Stephens, following his war service, who managed a number of independent light railways in Britain from his Tonbridge office.

The contractors were the Glasgow firm of & W. Anderson Ltd., Sir John Anderson being the head of the firm. The contract was dated 25th May 1922, its value being £197,000. The contract included the note ...*will from time to time employ in carrying out the works all unskilled labour that may be required from neighbouring centres in which there is unemployment in accordance with the directions to be given in that behalf by the Ministry of Labour.*

The ceremony of cutting the first sod was held on Friday 30th June 1922 at the Lewer Bridge, Hatherleigh, when Mr Arthur Neale MP, Parliamentary Secretary to the Ministry of Transport, took a new and tricoloured spade to turn a huge turf. Mr H. Montague Bates, Chairman of the ND&CJLR, introduced Mr Neale who was subsequently presented with an inscribed silver cigar box by Sir John Anderson, the contractor. There followed a luncheon with the usual speeches at the Manor Hall, and sports at Littlewood Marsh. At the time it was hoped that the ND&CJLR would be ready to open in about eighteen months.

In 1922 work soon started at the Halwill end of the line where P&W Anderson had access to the route using a siding on the up side of the Bude branch, incorporating a loop line, used for construction materials, worked from a ground frame released by the Halwill signalman. At this end of the line the contractors could work unhindered by considerations of maintaining the clay traffic at the other end. Details were given in a lengthy Southern Railway Instruction of 1924, but it was in use before then. It was cancelled by a 1925 Instruction stating that this siding now formed part of the running line of the Light Railway. Andersons used a 2ft gauge line along this section for earthworks and construction materials A standard gauge line had been laid between the Meeth Clay Company siding and Halwill Junction by April 1925 to enable the passage of the odd loaded clay wagon on to the main line.

From Torrington the first six miles of the ND&CJLR followed the line of the 3ft. gauge Torrington & Marland Railway, with some deviations to ease the gradients and curves. This brought the advantage of easier access to this part of the works for the contractors, and they ran their own 3ft. gauge locomotives and rolling stock over the Torrington & Marland tracks. However, the existing clay traffic could not be interrupted, as the light Railway Order contained a clause to protect the North Devon Clay Company from such interruption. As the standard gauge line was built south from Torrington, it incorporated a third rail for the 3ft. gauge rolling stock. The major engineering work was the new steel viaduct over the River Torridge near Torrington station. This was built alongside the old wooden viaduct of the Torrington & Marland Railway which was subsequently demolished after the opening of the new line, although the masonry piers remained. H.C. Casserley's photograph, taken on the opening day at Torrington, shows the two parallel viaducts with mixed gauge track on the new one. The old timber trestle structures erected back in 1880 were replaced by conventional earth works and masonry structures, but photographs taken during construction suggest that the timber structures were not removed, but were buried in the new embankments. A Ruston steam excavator was used during construction and on the western section of the line, 2ft. gauge tracks were used for the transport of materials. Over the twenty mile length of the ND&CJLR, only seven bridges were built to take the railway over or under roads, compared with nine level crossings protected by nothing more than wooden cattle traps.

The ND&CJLR was the last line of any length to be built in the West Country but the traditional railway navvy no longer existed in the 1920s, so almost all the labour was provided by local men. Indeed, it had been a condition of the Treasury investment in the new line that local men should be employed to reduce the very serious worklessness in the area. Many men in North Devon had been laid off by the closure of the shipbuilding yards at Bideford and the brickworks at Marland, the decline in the glove industry at Torrington and the general depression in the economy. It was reported that no less than 376,064 men working days were spent on the construction of the ND&CJLR, with more than 300 men employed on the works for some three years. Most of

Hole station in the mid-1930s. Ten Stroudley E1 0-6-0s were rebuilt in 1927/28 as 0-6-2Ts and designated E1R class. These small tanks in some ways addressed a deficiency in motive power on the line and worked the light railway for nearly thirty years. No.2610 has a down train, duty 582.

The tiny stone built halt at Meeth. Work still has to be completed with unfinished platform surfaces and unballasted track. Of interest behind the building is the contractor's loco, Manning Wardle 0-6-0ST No.244 and a number of two foot gauge wagons.

the men were supplied by the labour exchanges at Bideford and Torrington, but a few were sent from Plymouth. A number of these had too much to drink one Saturday night at Hatherleigh and sang 'The Red Flag'. They then violently attacked a policeman and the culprits subsequently received sentences of hard labour. A less serious case occurred at Torrington County Court when £3 damages were awarded to a ganger working near Watergate, who had been hit by stray shotgun pellets fired by a defendant who had been rabbiting. In February 1925 a Receiver and Manager was appointed to run P.&W.Anderson until a few weeks later Col. Stephens himself took over, completing the work with Andersons equipment.

North Devon and Cornwall Junction Light Railway Inspection and Opening
The Inspecting Officer from the Ministry of Transport, Major G. L. Hall made his visit to the line on 10th and 11th July 1925, and his report of 17th required no less than 27 minor improvements to bridges, level crossings, stations and speed restrictions. Apparently, these had been carried out by Thursday, 23rd July when Col. H. F. Stephens, the Engineer and Managing Director of the Light Railway, ran a special train over the line to celebrate its opening. The party of more than one hundred invited guests included local shareholders and civic leaders, together with a number of senior officers of the Southern Railway, which was to operate the line and guarantee its dividend. The special train started from Torrington at 11.30 a.m. and ran down the line to Halwill, two coaches and a van making up the first standard gauge passenger train to be seen in the area. The train stopped at every station and halt, and after a

lengthy interlude at Halwill, the train returned to Hatherleigh. Here a celebration lunch was held using trestle tables on the station platform, when the usual speeches were led by Mr J. Squance, a member of Devon County Council and Torrington Rural Council, who proposed a vote of thanks to Col. Stephens. After lunch, the party returned by the special train to Torrington, in time to catch the 4.35 p.m. 'up' train.

Public services on the ND&CJLR began on Monday 27th July 1925, with three trains each way between Torrington and Halwill on weekdays, but none on Sundays. There was no ceremony, although a number of journalists were invited to ride on the footplate to get a good view of the new line. For one journalist, the experience was none too pleasant due to driving rain that fell throughout the morning, there being minimal protection from the elements on the footplate of the old Adams locomotive. Work was still in progress at a couple of the stations, but public interest was limited to small crowds at the stations, and one house near the line which was decorated with flags. The fireman on the first train was Mr Tom Mill, who 57 years later witnessed the last train at Torrington.

In a press interview, Col. Stephens was enthusiastic about the new line. He declared that the clay industry would be considerably developed and permanent employment would be provided for a considerable number of men. The North Devon Clay Company at Marland had been in existence for fifty or sixty years, the new Meeth Clay Company had just been formed, and there were rumours that a third clay company would be established. Brick making had also been started, and the North Devon Clay Company proposed to reopen its brickworks, which had

been closed since the war as the old light railway had been inadequate to deal with the traffic. Brick making had also been recommended at Halwill. The Company had also been approached by Ambrosia Ltd, a firm of sweet and chocolate manufacturers, who hoped to develop a large industry in the district, and an important cattle market was developing at Petrockstow. Several stone quarries were in existence and there were good sites for others. Siding accommodation had also been provided on the line for the conveyance of cattle, agricultural produce, and heavier and more bulky goods. There had been delays in the construction of the line due to bad weather and to the employment of unskilled men who could not work as quickly as skilled railway workers. However, it had been a condition of the Treasury contribution of £125,000, that men employed on the line should be recruited from the local labour exchanges.

Having considered Col. Stephens' enthusiastic claims for the new line, perhaps some further consideration should now be given to its real value to North Devon. Although situated entirely within the county, the new line was designed to link North Devon with Cornwall, and to reduce the distances by railway between Torrington, on the one hand, and Bude and Launceston on the other. However, the traffic between North Devon and Cornwall has never amounted to much, certainly not enough to justify a railway line. The only through passenger trains were occasional Sunday excursions which ran between Bude and Ilfracombe. For a few days, the through North Cornwall line coaches of The Atlantic Coast Express passed through when the Halwill to Okehampton line was blocked by heavy snow. Much of the traffic referred to by Col. Stephens was generated on the Torrington to Hatherleigh section of the line, and the only substantial passenger business was carried by the daily workmens train between Torrington and Marland, an inheritance from the 3ft gauge line. The other local passenger traffic carried was minimal, with practically no through passenger traffic. It is not difficult to see the reasons for this as the stations, particularly at Hatherleigh and Hole, were badly situated for the local community, and few people needed to travel to Halwill Junction or beyond. Instead of striking west for Halwill, the railway should have run south from Hatherleigh, to be served by a more convenient station, to Okehampton, where local people had worked for over the previous century.

The NDCJLR saw a limited amount of freight running via Halwill. Some clay from Marland and Meeth was destined for export at Fowey Docks, and was routed via Halwill, Wadebridge, and Bodmin Road. Occasionally livestock was loaded at

Petrockstow station with what might be an inspection party. Although complete and the ground frame is in place, signals and point rodding have yet to be installed.

Hole and Hatherleigh, justifying special trains of some 40 cattle trucks which ran to London and elsewhere via Halwill Junction. Had the line been built direct to Okehampton it would have been of far more use to the local people in reaching their nearest country town, and also would have been of value as a through route between North Devon and Plymouth, where there was more traffic. One example was the daily newspaper traffic, with the *Western Morning News* being published in Plymouth and read widely in North Devon. An overnight newspaper train ran up the LSWR line from Plymouth, the North Devon papers being transferred to the 'down' newspaper train from Waterloo at Yeoford. The

distance by rail between Plymouth and Barnstaple would have been reduced by about eight miles, compared with the existing route via Yeoford, between Plymouth and Bideford by twenty six miles and between Plymouth and Torrington by thirty six miles. However, the community's gain would have been the LSWR's loss of revenue. A condition of the Treasury grant of £125,000 was that there should be a working agreement between the LSWR and the ND&CJLR, which effectively gave the LSWR a veto over the choice of route. In retrospect, it is rather sad that the new railway, built mainly with national and local Government money, should have failed to meet local transport needs as

well as it might. A third clay company did not materialise, but Ambrosia Ltd. did establish a factory in the district in the 1920s. Unfortunately for the ND&CJLR, Ambrosia Ltd. built its factory at Lapford station on the Barnstaple to Exeter line, and provided much traffic for the railway there.

The initial train service of three passenger trains each way was supplied by elderly ex-LSWR Adams 460 class 4-4-0s of Torrington Shed, hauling ex-LSWR coaches, the train crews also being supplied by Torrington. These services were timetabled as mixed trains, and it was not unusual for a train to comprise locomotive, single coach and several wagons. The trains ran at low speeds, the maximum permitted on a light railway being 25 m.p.h. This was just as well since over the years train crews were involved in several minor accidents, colliding with both animals and road vehicles on level crossings, and sometimes crews had to chase straying animals off the line. The worst accident occurred when an almost empty diesel unit collided with a full bus on a level crossing.

Halwill Junction and the ND&CJLR bay platform. There was livestock traffic off the line for the slaughterhouse on the right; a similar establishment planned for Hole was never constructed.

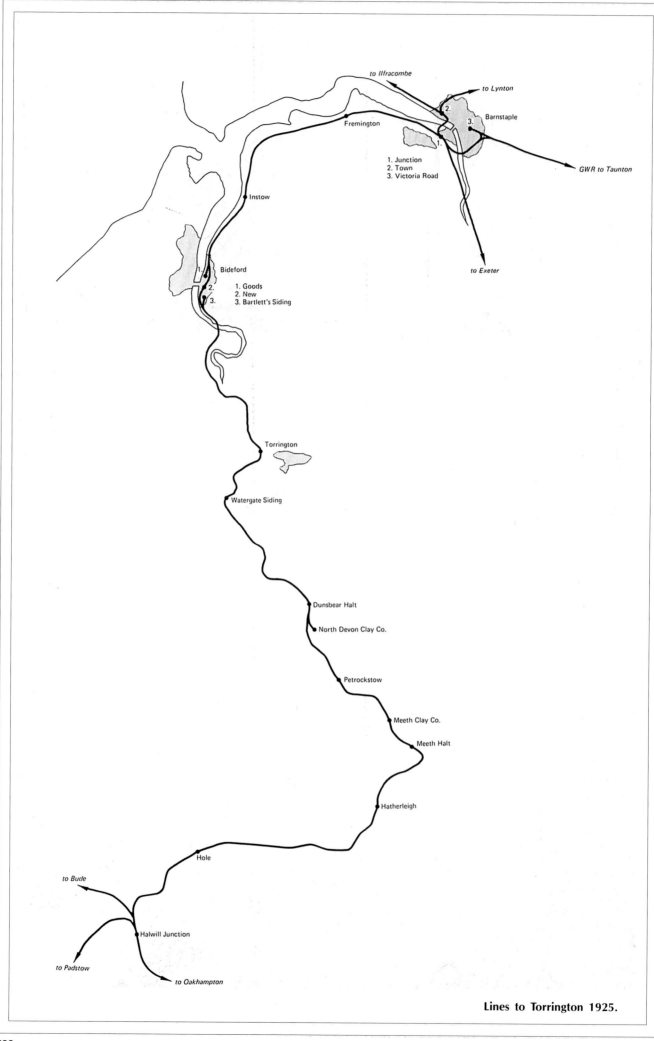

to Ilfracombe

to Lynton

Barnstaple

1. Junction
2. Town
3. Victoria Road

GWR to Taunton

to Exeter

Fremington

Instow

Bideford

1. Goods
2. New
3. Bartlett's Siding

Torrington

Watergate Siding

Dunsbear Halt

North Devon Clay Co.

Petrockstow

Meeth Clay Co.

Meeth Halt

Hatherleigh

Hole

to Bude

Halwill Junction

to Padstow

to Oakhampton

Lines to Torrington 1925.

Chapter 7
Southern Railway

The job of unifying the diverse pre-grouping companies, which constituted the new Southern Railway, fell to the dynamic ex-LSWR General Manager, Sir Herbert Walker, while the Chief Mechanical Engineer was Richard Maunsell, from the South Eastern & Chatham Railway. Soon, they had brought to North Devon a new powerful 2-6-0 locomotive of SECR design which was to change the pattern of passenger train services, and a new type of tank engine, rebuilt from an elderly LBSCR design surplus to requirements, to provide cheap motive power for the new line between Torrington and Halwill. There were also improvements to a number of LSWR stations, but the improved facilities provided at Ilfracombe resulted in the line to Bideford and Torrington being relegated to branch line status. In view of the Grouping of the railways, it is perhaps surprising that the new railway, built in the 1920s in North Devon, was independent of the Southern Railway, and remained so until nationalisation in 1948, although worked by the Southern Railway.

Branch Line Status
The new Southern Railway soon upgraded arrangements at Ilfracombe, which included the provision of a new locomotive shed and a 65ft. diameter turntable. These facilities replaced the old shed and small turntable and enabled the new N class 2-6-0 locomotives, built at Woolwich Arsenal to the SECR designs of Robert Maunsell, to take heavy trains over the 1 in 36 Mortehoe Bank with the assistance of an M7 0-4-4T banker. In June 1924 trials took place and, in July 1925, the principal North Devon line trains ran straight through to Ilfracombe, with through coaches to Torrington detached at Barnstaple Junction thus reversing the roles of the two lines. Such a change in services would not have been possible previously since the older Adams and Drummond locomotives could not have hauled the heavy loads up Mortehoe Bank. Goods services were not affected and continued to run through to Bideford and Torrington. Thus, at a stroke, in July 1925, Torrington lost its main line service and gained two

branch lines instead. At Bideford, there were heated protests against the town's relegation to branch line status. Both the Town Council and the Urban District Council protested vigorously to the Southern Railway, which had recently also offended civic pride by its opposition to the Bideford Harbour Bill. So on 10th August 1925 a meeting of the Town Council unanimously passed a protest resolution moved by Alderman Goaman. He said that he had recently taken the 11.34 a.m. fast train and found that the Bideford platform was crowded, with only three coaches arriving from Torrington. As a result there was a tremendous rush for the few seats available, and many passengers had to stand in the corridors or in the guards or luggage vans. After arrival at Barnstaple Junction the three coaches were shunted up the line for an indefinite period, and eight coaches arrived from Ilfracombe with only half the number of passengers that were on the Bideford train. The Bideford passengers had to get out of the train and wait on the platform or be shunted up the line to wait, making a long

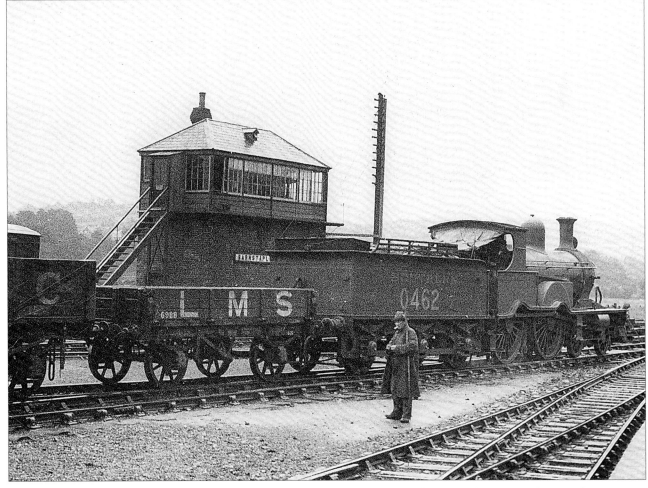

460 Class 4-4-0 No.0462 shunts Barnstaple Junction yard in front of East signal box in July 1925. H.C. Casserley, courtesy Richard Casserley.

Top. An absorbing view of Barnstaple Junction shed in July 1925 as the shed labourer goes about his business clearing the piles of clinker dumped by the side of the track by firemen. The M7s are No.30 shunting and 48 stabled on the shed road. H.C. Casserley, courtesy Richard Casserley.

Middle. Inside the ancient wooden timber shed. It ended its days in near-ruinous condition – see page 16 for instance.

Bottom. The view across Fremington Pill and the Iron Bridge towards Fremington station in the 1930s, with ships unloading alongside the quay. At the head of the goods train is an unidentified 460 class 4-4-0.

Fremington Quay at various times in the 1930s. *Top*. Some of the many workers employed at the quay with railway staff among the group. This is 1931 and safety was not of primary concern – note the sacks hanging above their heads. *Middle*. SS MARI ELI in 1934 being loaded by one of the six ton Grafton steam cranes. *Bottom*. MARI ELI again in 1934 being loaded with ball clay with three men in each wagon shovelling to keep pace. Harold Mock collection.

SS TENDER, registered at Bridgewater Somerset, comes to grief at Fremington Quay with only a hawser to stop the vessel from completely capsizing. Harold Mock collection.

journey almost intolerable. He was not asking that any harm be inflicted on Ilfracombe, but he felt that the advantages of the new arrangements to Ilfracombe were not as great as the disadvantages to the people of Bideford. Alderman Metherell said that it was strange that this should have occurred just as the Torrington to Halwill Railway was opened, and they were hoping to get through trains to Plymouth and a better service to Bude. He had been told on the highest authority that, taking all the year round, there were more bookings to and at Bideford than any station below Exeter. The Bideford and District Chamber of Trade added their own letter of protest.

The strong protests made at Bideford did not influence the Southern Railway into changing its mind. No traffic figures for North Devon appear to be available until the 1928 annual returns – see table right.

Certainly, on the 1928 figures, the decision of the Southern Railway to make Ilfracombe the main line and Torrington the branch appears to have been justified. For every passenger on the Torrington line there were two on the Ilfracombe line, and this situation had probably existed for many years previously since the LSWR had promoted Ilfracombe as a major West Country

holiday resort. Through coaches continued to be run between Waterloo and Torrington on principal trains, but with several minutes extra added to the journey times.

Bideford Corporation promoted the Bideford Harbour Act which gained the Royal Assent in 1925, despite the opposition of the Southern Railway. At about this time customers ceased to use the wharf at Bideford Goods station, and the export of clay was transferred to Fremington Quay

Southern Days
After the events of July 1925, the two branch lines to Torrington settled down to a quiet life. They were worked as separate systems connecting at Torrington, and trains did not normally

Station	No. of passenger tickets	
	Issued	Collected
Ilfracombe Line		
Barnstaple Town	79,496	149,034
Wrafton	4,080	5,090
Braunton	40,213	49,223
Mortehoe	20,806	52,145
Ilfracombe	69,218	151,641
	213,813	407,133
Torrington Line		
Fremington	3,012	3,026
Instow	9,041	28,177
Bideford	60,117	106,762
Torrington	54,687	59,719
	126,947	197,684
Figures for Torrington include journeys on the Halwill line.		

work through. Both the public and working timetables kept the lines well apart, with the Barnstaple to Torrington services incorporated in the North Devon line timetable while the North Devon & Cornwall Junction Light Railway had its own timetable. There were good reasons for this separation as few locomotive classes could comply with the weight restrictions on the ND&CJLR and the passenger numbers justified only one coach, in contrast to the much heavier passenger traffic on the main Torrington to Barnstaple line. However, both the 460 class 4-4-0 locomotives and the E1R 0-6-2Ts worked regularly on both sections, so it would have been possible to run a through service from Barnstaple to Halwill, Okehampton, or even Plymouth, as Alderman Metherell (he was also a Director of the ND&CJLR) had hoped for at Bideford in 1925.

The new Southern Railway system was concentrated in the south and south-east of England and was undertaking a massive programme of electrification, first to its inner suburban lines and then the outer

Above. Ex-LSWR K10 class 4-4-0 No.387 arrives at Instow station in SR days, probably with a through train from Exeter to Torrington. The train is a three coach set of LSWR non-corridor stock followed by at least two Maunsell corridor coaches; these are through vehicles from Waterloo. The K10 4-4-0s, together with the larger L11 class, worked on the Exeter-Torrington line for some forty years.

Middle. An E1R 0-6-2T with a Barnstaple Junction-Torrington local train at Instowe, consisting of a six wheel ex-LCDR van fitted with oil lamps and two ex-LSWR bogie coaches, the last vehicle being composite brake with the guard's compartment in the centre. A. Halls, courtesy R. Sellick.

Left. The Bideford signalman and station hand behind and the Western Region Key Tokens which replaced the Tyers instruments on the branch. Glen Woods.

E1R class 0-6-2T No.B96 pauses briefly at Bideford with a down train comprising an LSWR arc roof two coach local set, strengthened with an LSWR elliptical roof coach. The loco carries the Barnstaple shed duty disc No.583.

E1R class 0-6-2T No.2697 at the Torrington coal stage, 24 May 1935, with driver Matthews standing on the step and fireman C. Jordan on the footplate. H.C. Casserley, courtesy R.M. Casserley.

suburban and main lines to the coast at Brighton, Portsmouth and other places. The former LSWR lines west of Salisbury were not involved in the electrification programme, but did receive attention. In 1929, a party of Southern Railway Directors visited Bude, Torrington and Ilfracombe in preparation for the formation of the Southern National Omnibus Company. This was partially owned by the Southern Railway and developed a network of bus services in North Devon from a depot at Barnstaple. However, a bus service between Westward Ho!, Bideford and Barnstaple had been established by another operator as early as 1924. The Southern Railway was also responsible for major improvements to stations, including those at Ilfracombe and Exeter Central.

The economic slump of the 1920s and 1930s hit North Devon badly. One example of this was to be seen from Instow station, from where there was a good view of laid-up shipping rotting away in Appledore Pool. As we have seen, the construction of the ND&CJLR was supported with public money to provide much needed employment, and there was another scheme put forward at Barnstaple to alleviate unemployment by providing work on improvements to facilities at Fremington Quay which was, of

course, owned and operated by the Southern Railway. The initiative came from the Chairman of the Ports and Quays Committee of Barnstaple Town Council, Councillor H.S. Reavell, who went to Waterloo in December 1929 to discuss the matter with the Deputy General Manager of the Southern Railway, Mr Szlumper. After further discussions, Sir Herbert Walker wrote, in December 1930, to the secretary of the Unemployment Grants Committee, set up by an Act of 1929, requesting a grant for a series of improvements at Fremington Quay. Costing an estimated £20,000, the scheme proposed to extend the quay in a northerly direction for about 200ft. with additional siding and warehouse accommodation for traders. This would have been an improvement to the facilities of the port of Barnstaple and to the commerce of the area, and local men would have been employed. However, the project came to nothing when in November 1931 the Treasury declined to make a grant. Had the facilities been constructed they would have enabled Fremington Quay to diversify its activities, the warehouse accommodation being suitable for general merchandise in addition to the existing mineral traffic, mainly in coal and clay, and timber from the Baltic. The following year there was a tragedy

at the Marland Clay Works when a Torrington railwayman received fatal injuries. Frederick Rowland was the guard on the 6.25 a.m. mixed train from Torrington to Petrockstow on Friday September 9th 1932. All had gone well until the train stopped at Marland clay siding where some wagons loaded with clay had to be picked up. After unlocking the points and opening the gate, Guard Rowland called the driver to the wagons with a signal and proceeded down the siding to see if the road was clear. He then came back and gave the hand signal to start and a call-on signal to follow the wagons. The signals were obeyed and as the driver followed the wagons, he saw Guard Rowland's coupling pole lying on the ground. He looked back and saw Rowland lying in the four foot way and realised that the engine had passed over him but, as he was lying in the middle of the track, presumed that it did not touch him. He stopped the engine and went to Guard Rowland who said he had gone to take the brake off and had fallen underneath the wagon. Rowland added, 'It was no fault of yours, Jack'. The driver immediately sent his fireman to the clay works for assistance and Guard Rowland was taken first to Torrington Cottage Hospital and then to Bideford Hospital. His legs had been run over by the

Adams 460 class 4-4-0 No.0460 arrives at Torrington with a down train from Barnstaple in June 1926. H.C. Casserley, courtesy R.M. Casserley.

The opening day of the ND&CJLR and Adams 460 class is stabled in the stub siding at Torrington. Tender engines were permitted on the line to Halwill as there was a turntable at either end of the line. H.C. Casserley, courtesy R.M. Casserley.

The Torrington Station Master, F.W. Newcombe, chatting to the crew of the 12.20 Barnstaple train in May 1935. H.C. Casserley, courtesy R.M. Casserley.

395 class 0-6-0 E0163 at Torrington, after 1927, when it came to Exmouth Junction and before 1932 when it was renumbered into the 3000 series. These 0-6-0s were not common on this line and it was probably standing in for a 460 class or a K10 4-4-0.

E1R 2697 at Torrington in August 1935 after arrival from Barnstaple. Eight were allocated to Barnstaple with two outstationed at Torrington at any one time. 2697 is on duty 582, unsurprisingly an all stations to Halwill Junction. R.K. Blencowe collection.

trucks and one had to be amputated. He died of his injuries on 10th October 1932, but not before he had made an unsigned statement about the accident in which he said no one was to blame. The coroner returned a verdict of accidental death. This was apparently the only fatal accident to occur on the ND&CJLR.

Frederick Rowland came from a railway family and had moved to Torrington in 1926 from Woking where he had been a passenger train guard. Here he had achieved some distinction by winning the competition set to Southern Railway employees by Sir Herbert Walker to find a name for the 11 a.m. 'down' express from Waterloo to the West of England. His winning suggestion was the 'Atlantic Coast Express' which ran until 1964. Frederick Rowland was also involved in civic affairs, being elected to Torrington Town Council as a ratepayers' candidate.

The Southern carried out a number of works of improvement. These included the construction of two more halts, at Watergate and Yarde using standard Southern Railway concrete components. These halts were useful to the clay workers for their daily journeys to and from the Marland Works, Yarde Halt being brought into use on 19th July 1926 and Watergate Halt on 20th September 1926. Torrington station saw some rationalisation of the layout and facilities

around 1930, when most locomotive duties had been taken over by tank engines. The old turntable, dating back to 1872, was taken out and the entrance to the locomotive shed and to Reed's Sidings nearby was replaced with new pointwork. Up to 1925, Torrington locomotives, drivers, firemen and guards had worked trains to Barnstaple and Exeter, but the changes of July 1925 were widespread. North Devon line services between Exeter and Ilfracombe were now covered by sheds at Exeter, Barnstaple and Ilfracombe, while the Torrington locomotives and train crews took over all the regular ND&CJLR duties, together with occasional trips to Barnstaple. Most of the services between Barnstaple and Torrington were covered by Barnstaple locomotives and train crews, assisted by some from Exmouth Junction, particularly on the through freight services between Exeter and Torrington.

World War Two
During World War Two an armoured train occasionally patrolled the coastal strip of railway between Bideford, Barnstaple and Braunton. There was a minor accident during the war at Bideford when, in February 1940, the two front wheels of an engine pulling the coach forming a Barnstaple to Torrington train became derailed just outside the station. There was some alarm amongst the passengers, but they were conveyed to their destination by

bus. There had been some damage to the track and a breakdown crew was summoned from Barnstaple, but a local service was run between Bideford and Torrington while track repairs were carried out. It was suspected that the derailment was caused by children placing stones on the track.

There was a reduction in public passenger train services on the line, but there were some military specials instead. However, goods traffic increased particularly at Fremington, although exports of ball clay ceased. Fremington Quay had its busiest year in 1942 when 354 vessels used the dock, bringing in 93,893 tons of imports, mainly coal, but also fertiliser, gravel and potatoes,

During 1943-44 the estuaries of the Taw and Torridge became military training areas in preparation for the D-Day landings, requiring many additional trains for both troops and equipment. The common above Torrington station was used for training purposes by American army tanks, which resulted in a number of pot-holes appearing.

During and after the war in connection with food rationing local auction markets were closed and livestock movements determined by the Meat and Livestock Commission. This resulted in cattle trains of up to 40 wagons being forwarded monthly from Torrington and other stations. For many years an important traffic forwarded from Torrington was milk in churns carried in luggage compartments or vans. During the 1930s and 1940s, the Southern Railway built a number of glass-lined milk tank wagons in conjunction with dairy companies, together with loading and unloading facilities at the terminals. The Torrington milk loading depot with overhead pipework was built to load the 3,000 gallon milk tank wagons, together with concrete apron and hoses for cleaning the tankers, apparently in 1944 according to a surviving electricity contract with the Southern Railway. Milk arrived in tanker lorries from the Cow & Gate, later Unigate dairy, at Taddiport for loading into the rail tankers using the pipework. For many years milk tankers were worked as tail traffic on passenger trains. In London several receiving depots were built, the best known one outside Waterloo at Vauxhall.

Last Years of the Southern Railway

After 1945 traffic on the railways increased, with goods shunting at Barnstaple Junction carried on around the clock at times. Also at Bideford new regulations were brought in to facilitate the shunting of Bartlett's Siding by a special working from and back to Bideford Goods, rather than only down trains to Torrington.

During the bitter winter of 1946/47, the North Devon & Cornwall Junction Light Railway was actually used according to its title. The main line near Meldon Junction was blocked by snowdrifts for several days, closing the line between Okehampton and Halwill Junction. Some through passenger and freight services between North Cornwall and Exeter, including the through Waterloo coaches of the 'Atlantic Coast Express' were worked from Halwill Junction to Torrington thence to Barnstaple and Exeter. Apparently this was the only occasion that through services ran along the ND&CJLR, although on occasions, excursion trains also ran. It is not known if any passenger took advantage of a through carriage between Waterloo and Hatherleigh.

After twenty five years, the Southern Railway came to an end when the new nationalised British Railways came into being on 1st January 1948. The ND&CJLR was also nationalised, although most of its shares had always been in public ownership. Compared with the long LSWR period, the era of the Southern Railway was short, but much had happened in those twenty five years and many permanent records remained, including a large concrete name board which, for many years afterwards, advised travellers that they were at SOUTHERN RAILWAY - TORRINGTON STATION.

Right. The coach looks to be in private hands and the two nags have a tough journey up the hill to Great Torrington village.

E1R 2696 passes under the A386 road on its way to Halwill Junction in 1936. The little arch to the right took the narrow gauge Torrington & Marland through the hill to Torrington goods yard and the exchange siding. R.W. Kidner.

A thoroughly miserable day in June 1926 with 460 class 0473 having just arrived off the ND&CJLR with a mixed train from Halwill Junction. H.C. Casserley, courtesy R.M. Casserley.

E1R 2697 crosses Torrington viaduct on its way south to Halwill Junction in 1935. The coach had been converted from a steam rail motor of 1905.

The Torrington branch engine at Halwill Junction in June 1926. The loco had brought in an earlier service and had crossed over to the goods yard to use the turntable. Having turned it is now ready to cross back to take the next service to Torrington. H.C. Casserley, courtesy R.M. Casserley.

Halwill Junction and the ND&CJLR bay platform on the right in June 1926. E0468 has now crossed over from the goods yard to run smokebox first back to Torrington with the 5.10 service. H.C. Casserley, courtesy R.M. Casserley.

E1R 2096 at the ND&CJLR bay in 1930. The cattle wagon is SR-built to an earlier SECR design and the coach is a rebuild, as seen earlier, of an LSWR H13 rail motor.

N Class mogul 31841 arrives at Halwill Junction with the 1pm from Padstow in August 1960. Although largely controlled by ground levers the arrival of the line from Torrington necessitated the signal box here at Halwill Junction being extended to house the tablet machine. The sympathetic extension can be seen at the far end of the box. John Eyers, courtesy South Western Circle.

2096 again with a mixed train including the rail motor coach. The signal is off to allow the train to reverse to the loop, where the locomotive can run round. The wagons will then be shunted to the goods yard opposite and the coach back into the platform for the next Torrington service.

Summer in August 1963 and 34070 MANSTON in the roofless shed at Barnstaple Junction. MANSTON had earlier in the day brought in, from Exeter, the 8.35 Waterloo to Ilfracombe service. Sharing the shed is a Torrington line Ivatt 2-6-2T 41224 with a bunker full of the dreaded briquettes, a coal substitute.

Chapter 8
British Railways

The new nationalised British Railways came into existence on 1st January 1948, but it was not until the early 1960s that any significant changes were made on the lines to Torrington. Initially, the former Southern Railway lines west of Exeter were transferred to the Western Region of British Railways for commercial purposes, but reverted to the Southern Region in 1958. These changes made little difference to the operation of the lines to Torrington, which continued to enjoy services on the LSWR and Southern Railway pattern until 1962. One of the first changes to occur was in the spring of 1953 when the first LMR Ivatt 2-6-2 tank engines arrived in North Devon; over the next ten years, the new Ivatt locomotives displaced all the Brighton and Drummond tank engines.

In the early 1950s the North Devon skyline was altered by the construction of a new power station at East Yelland. Situated between the railway and the Taw Estuary, the station had extensive sidings so that heavy pieces of equipment, including boiler drums and transformers, could be delivered by rail direct from the manufacturer's works during construction. Coal for the power station was normally delivered by sea – its operations are described in more detail in Chapter 1.

It was at Barnstaple that nationalisation first made its impact, since this was the only place in North Devon where both the Southern Railway and the Great Western Railway had their own establishments. Firstly, the freight arrangements were rationalised with full loads being dealt with at Barnstaple Junction, and parcels at Victoria Road (as the GWR station became known). The GWR engine shed was then closed, the locomotives and men transferring to Barnstaple Junction shed. In 1960 the GWR station was closed to passenger traffic, and trains from Taunton then ran directly to Barnstaple Junction. Western Region rolling stock began to appear on some trains between Barnstaple and Torrington and there was a regular van working between Torrington and Paddington.

The Busy 1950s
For the first decade or so after nationalisation, the lines to Torrington were as busy as ever and, on summer Saturdays, probably carried more passengers than ever before. Post-war affluence meant that many more people could afford to take a summer holiday, but as they could not yet afford their own car, they travelled by train to their week or fortnight holiday at the seaside. Not only did the people travel

but they brought large quantities of luggage, often sent in advance by train to their holiday resort. Holiday camps and boarding houses booked their guests from Saturday to Saturday, so the railways had to press into service almost any rolling stock that could move. Some indication of the volume of traffic carried on these summer Saturdays can be found in the timetable for Monday to Saturday inclusive, with some 'Saturdays only' trains to the resorts, particularly Ilfracombe. In early British Railways days, there was a separate 'Saturday only' timetable in the summer, very different to the weekday timetable. Very little freight traffic was moved, which left the tracks, locomotives and crews available for the extra passenger trains. Additional complications were the single track North Devon line where many delays accumulated, and the bottleneck at Exeter St. David's, through which both Southern and Western Region holiday trains had to pass.

The main flow of holiday passenger traffic on the lines to Torrington was through Bideford station, the railhead for Westward Ho! and other resorts on the Atlantic Coast, with buses conveying holiday makers to their final destination. However, the trains ran to and from Torrington since there were no terminal facilities at Bideford. On

The station approach at Barnstaple Junction in 1953. The two storey house for the station master and his family is prominent to the right with the later flat roofed extension to the offices and staff accommodation to the left.

Top. M7s 30252 and 30256 at Barnstaple Junction in September 1958. A goods train has been brought in from Exeter by N class mogul 31846 and the 0-4-4Ts are busy marshalling the wagons respectively for the Torrington branch and the Ilfracombe line. John Eyers, courtesy South Western Circle.

Middle. There were eight M7s at Barnstaple Junction shed in 1947, used on shunting/station pilot work as well as passenger and goods trains to Ilfracombe and Torrington. 30247 is serving as station pilot in September 1961. John Eyers, courtesy South Western Circle.

Bottom. M7 30253 attaching the through coaches from Torrington to a Waterloo-bound train in September 1962, timed to depart at 2.15pm. Why the Plymouth Friary 632 duty disc is attached is confusing. John Eyers, courtesy South Western Circle..

Bulleid Pacifics came to dominate the passenger services along the lines to Barnstaple and Ilfracombe. In September 1962 34076 41 SQUADRON has arrived with the 12.20 Ilfracombe-Waterloo; the 12.17 service from Torrington is being attached at the rear. John Eyers, courtesy South Western Circle.

A ubiquitous N workhorse shunting empty stock from the Torrington lines in September 1962. John Eyers, courtesy South Western Circle.

The Ivatt tanks came to replace the E1R 0-6-2Ts on all duties to Torrington and along the ND&CJLR to Halwill Junction. 41297 arrives at Torrington with the 10.40 from Halwill Junction on 6 August 1956. John Eyers, courtesy South Western Circle.

2nd November 1959, Torrington shed was closed and the three locomotives and ten footplate staff transferred to the parent depot at Barnstaple Junction. As a result, there were a number of light engine workings between Barnstaple Junction and Torrington to cover services originating or terminating at Torrington.

This volume of rolling stock brought its own problems, both of berthing and cleaning, at Torrington station. There were only three sidings in the yard so, as far as possible, it was cleared of goods wagons. Even so, the railwaymen at Torrington were hard

pressed to cope with all this rolling stock. The siding situation at Torrington was eased in 1960 when, after its closure, the engine shed was demolished and the two tracks there designated 'up' sidings but, by then, the summer peak was a fading phenomenon.

Decline and Dieselisation
In the early 1960s traffic on the lines to Torrington was declining. Passengers were travelling in their own cars or on buses, particularly between Barnstaple and Bideford where there was a frequent service which was more

convenient for both town centres. Freight traffic was also declining, including much of the extensive cattle business which had been lost to road after the 1955 ASLEF strike. Inevitably, there were cuts in services.

The frequency of trains on both lines to Torrington remained about the same for some time, but the number of through coaches working between Torrington and Waterloo was cut back. In the weekday timetable of summer 1962 there were through carriages to Torrington on the 11 a.m. 'Atlantic Coast Express' and on the 1 p.m. and 3 p.m. expresses from Waterloo yet by the summer of 1963 all these had been withdrawn except on summer Saturdays. By the end of the summer 1963 timetable there were no weekday through services at all, and the Barnstaple to Torrington and Torrington to Halwill lines were both worked as self-contained branches. January 1963 also saw the transfer of all the Southern Region lines west of Salisbury, the Western Division, to the Western Region. For almost a century the Western Division had been managed from offices at Exeter, above Central station since 1933, but management was transferred to Western Region offices at Plymouth. In retrospect this can be seen as a preliminary to implementation of the recommendations of the Beeching Report published a few months later. The Western Region struck the first blow to all the Southern lines west of Exeter when the 'Atlantic Coast Express' and other through trains from Waterloo ran for the last time on Sunday, 5th

41223 comes into Instow on 15 August 1964 with the 2pm Barnstaple-Torrington train, the signalman preparing to exchange the single line tablet with the crew. E. Wilmshurst.

Top. Long-term Barnstaple resident M7 0-4-4T 30255, at Bideford in May 1951 with the branch train for Torrington.

Middle. Bideford in August 1964 with 41249 at the head of the 11.20 Barnstaple-Torrington service. The Ivatt tanks were popular with crews and in 1959 five were allocated to Barnstaple Junction, 41294, 41295, 41297, 41298 and 41314, to work services to Torrington and Halwill Junction. E. Wilmshurst.

Bottom. 41312, one of a batch of Ivatts transferred from the Eastern Section in 1960 following electrification there, takes water at Torrington with the 3.11pm from Barnstaple on 9 July 1962 H.C. Casserley, courtesy R.M. Casserley.

September 1964, thus ending a century of through train services between Bideford, Barnstaple and Waterloo.

In the early 1960s most of the trains on the lines to Torrington were in the hands of the Ivatt 2-6-2Ts, but the age of the diesels was now arriving. It began on 7th May 1963 when a North British Type 2 diesel ran up from Plymouth to Halwill, Torrington (where it suffered a failure), Barnstaple and on to Taunton and, during the following month, a cross-country diesel multiple unit was given clearance tests in North Devon. The following year saw the almost complete replacement of steam by diesels.

The new pattern of diesel services on the former LSWR lines west of Salisbury was introduced by the Western Region on Monday 6th September 1964. A semi-fast service linked Waterloo with Exeter St. David's, but there were no onward connections. Instead, diesel trains ran between St. David's and Ilfracombe in connection with the express service from Paddington, and a connecting diesel service ran between Barnstaple Junction and Torrington. To obtain the best use from the new diesel trains some interesting through workings were introduced, including two trains from Halwill Junction to Barnstaple Junction, two from Taunton to Torrington and one in the opposite direction, and one through train from Torrington to Salisbury. One, two and three car diesel multiple units were used, together with coaches hauled by the then ubiquitous but short-lived D6300 Type 2s. However, passenger services on both lines to Torrington were destined to end in a matter of months.

Reports and Closures

Faced with increasing British Railways deficits, the Government had brought in Dr Richard Beeching from ICI to make major improvements to the industry and, in March 1963, his recommendations were published in *The Reshaping of British Railways*, popularly known as *The Beeching Report*. This recommended the development of freight and fast passenger services on the main lines, concentrating on the profitable bulk flows of traffic, and the elimination of large numbers of stations and branch lines. In North Devon, the effect was devastating with the withdrawal of passenger services on three of the four routes to Barnstaple, with only the Barnstaple to Exeter line retained. The only public goods station to survive was at Barnstaple, with even the busy Bideford Goods being closed. The lines to Torrington were able to muster two bulk flows of traffic that were to be retained; clay from Meeth and Marland, and milk from Torrington. On the two lines to Torrington, passenger services were to be completely withdrawn and the line between Halwill and Meeth closed completely, but the Barnstaple to Meeth section was to be retained for the clay and milk traffic.

In the same year, 1963, the *North Devon Railway Report*, written by David St. John Thomas and sponsored by the Dartington Hall Trustees, was published. It included details of a traffic census taken on

7th May 1963, which showed that the average number of passengers between stops on the trains between Barnstaple and Torrington was just over nine. Bideford was the busiest station with 74.5 passengers joining trains and 71.5 leaving, while Torrington came next with 65.5 and 43.5 respectively, with Instow and Fremington averaging only about half a passenger per train (children being counted as 0.5 passengers). The 1962 traffic figures were given as follows:

	Bideford	Torrington
No. of tickets issued	25,918	27,000
No. of tickets collected	42,640	

The seasonal nature of the passenger traffic at Bideford was such that almost three times as many passengers used the station in July as in February. However the 50-60 clay workers travelling daily from Torrington, Watergate and Yarde were excluded because the North Devon Clay Company paid for their carriage and no tickets were issued. Had these been counted the Torrington figure would have doubled. Financial figures issued by British Railways were quoted as follows:

	Barnstaple-Torrington	Torrington-Halwill
Movement expenses	£55,000	£21,000
Terminal expenses	£15,000	£2,000
Track and signalling	£30,000	£30,000
Total expenses	£100,000	£53,000
Earnings	£10,000	£1,000
Deficit	£90,000	£52,000

Out and about on the ND&CJLR in September 1956. Bottom left, the train has crossed the relatively busy A3072 between Horraland and Holsworthy Bridge and it belongs to the cars again. Above, the tiny lane crossing between Highhampton and West Lydacott. H.C. Casserley, courtesy R.M. Casserley.

Ivatt 2-6-2T 41248, on the 4.40pm service from Torrington to Halwill, takes on water at Hatherleigh in July 1964, the only intermediate station on the line to have this facility. Peter Swift. .

34083 605 SQUADRON arrives at Halwill Junction off the North Cornwall line with the 8.30am Padstow train. In the distance a local set from the Bude branch waits to attach it to the rear. We are looking along the bay platform of the ND&CJLR; behind the signal on the right is the ground frame which controlled movements off the Torrington line. Peter Paye.

The passenger traffic at both Torrington and Bideford had dropped to only about half its pre-war level and, indeed, on the trains between Torrington and Halwill, a passenger was something of a rarity. The travelling public had taken to the roads.

However, the position on the goods traffic side was far from gloomy. At Bideford, 23,000 tons of freight was received in 1962, with the milk and cream leaving Torrington producing a revenue of £2,000 a month and the clay from Marland and Meeth rather more. However, the slow and quiet process of rationalising freight facilities had begun as early as 2nd May 1960 when Watergate and Dunsbear sidings were closed to public traffic, to be followed on 30th April 1962 by Instow. On 7th September 1964, the day after the introduction of the down-graded diesel passenger train services, the Western Region withdrew goods facilities from most former Southern Railway stations west of Exeter, including the lines to Ilfracombe, Bude and Wadebridge. On the lines to Torrington, goods services were withdrawn from Petrockstow, Meeth, Hatherleigh, Hole and Halwill Junction. This left only Barnstaple, Fremington, Bideford and Torrington open for public goods services, together with private sidings at East Yelland, Marland and Meeth, and Bartlett's Siding at Bideford.

The year 1965 proved to be a bleak one for the lines to Torrington as both passenger services and general goods services were completely withdrawn. In December 1964 the Minister of Transport, Mr Tom Frazer, had consented to the withdrawal of passenger trains on the Torrington to Halwill line, and the last train ran on Saturday 27th February 1965. This was the 6.20 p.m. from Halwill which consisted of a three coach diesel

multiple unit carrying some two hundred passengers to commemorate the event, the train being decorated with a wreath provided by the Launceston Railway Circle. An enthusiast excursion train, the 'Exmoor Ranger', comprising five coaches, hauled by Ivatt 2-6-2Ts 41291 and 41206, ran up the line from Halwill to Torrington and Barnstaple on 27th March 1965, a month after it was officially closed below Meeth, but by May 1966 the track had been lifted between Meeth and Halwill. The remaining passenger services to Halwill Junction on the North Cornwall and Bude lines were withdrawn when the lines closed on 3rd October 1966, and all the tracks were removed by December 1967.

In February 1965 it was announced that Mr Frazer had also consented to the withdrawal of passenger services on the Barnstaple to Torrington line in the following autumn. To ease the hardship for some travellers, three buses were to run daily between Torrington and Barnstaple, via Bideford, timed for the benefit of workers and school pupils. The six month delay in closure was to enable the improvement of the approach road at Barnstaple Junction station. The jobs of thirty two railwaymen were to be lost, but British Railways said that they hoped to avoid redundancies.

Meanwhile, goods services were withdrawn from Bartlett's Siding on 6th July 1965 while general goods services from Torrington, Fremington and Bideford ceased on 6th September 1965. The milk depot at Torrington and the quay sidings at Fremington remained open but Bideford Goods closed completely. All British Railways public goods services in North Devon were now operated by road transport from Barnstaple, with goods parcels handled

at the former GWR station at Victoria Road, and full loads at Barnstaple Junction. The closures made most impact at Bideford where there had been considerable goods traffic, the four railway lorries and drivers based there being transferred to Barnstaple. The closure also affected private carriers who had brought business to the railway at Bideford. At Bideford and Torrington, daily deliveries were made by British Railways lorries, but there were less frequent deliveries to the outlying areas. One substantial flow of traffic at Bideford was the supply of steel plate to Appledore Shipyard and this was continued from Barnstaple. Most of the Bideford (Goods) staff were transferred to Barnstaple but the Supervisor, Mr Jack Easterbrook, stayed on for several weeks to look after the empty depot, but even the goods yard cat had gone and he had nothing to do and no one to talk to.

When the summer season was over and the replacement bus services were ready, the passenger service between Torrington and Barnstaple was withdrawn. On Saturday, 2nd October 1965, the last regular passenger train ran from Torrington to Barnstaple. The sad occasion was witnessed by some thirty or forty passengers and the signals at Bideford were pulled off by the Mayor, Mrs Ethelwynne Browne. On the following day, the last steam train ran between Barnstaple and Torrington, a portion of the 'Exeter Flyer' from Waterloo, hauled by British Railways Standard Class 4 2-6-4T 80039.

For many branch lines at this time, such events were speedily followed by the complete closure of the line and the lifting of tracks, but the lines to Torrington were to survive and develop.

The country junction and the scene which made Halwill a special place witnessed some remarkable if often intermittent activity. First to arrive has been the 9.30 from Bude at 10.10 behind 2-6-4T 80039. After arrival the big 2-6-4T ran round and drew the coaches back onto the Bude line to await the arrival of the 8.30 Padstow service. Following its arrival 80039 would propel the coaches onto the rear ready for the off to London. During all this the Torrington train, the single coach and Ivatt 2-6-2T in the bay, had arrived at 10.18 to connect with the London service. 22 August 1964. P.W. Gray.

A wet wintry day at Torrington, February 1966. On the goods shed road is Type 2 D6323 at the head of a mixed goods train which will be attached to some milk wagons at the rear of the shed. On the former engine shed road on the right is a clay wagon. C.L.Caddy.

Chapter 9
The Freight Line

After the withdrawal of passenger train services in 1965, the goods services were reduced to a basic minimum. In the morning, a train left Barnstaple Junction conveying empty milk tankers to Torrington and empty clay wagons to Marland and Meeth, later returning with loaded clay wagons, after which there was an afternoon trip to Torrington. This was to collect loaded milk tankers and clay wagons known as 'tip ends' bound for Fowey Docks and export to South America. Initially, these trains were hauled by the NB Type 2s but they were superseded by BR Sulzer Type 2s.

Western Region 'Hymek' Type 3s also occasionally appeared but, being too heavy for the ND&CJLR, they were restricted to the Barnstaple to Torrington section.

Despite the withdrawal of passenger trains, the Barnstaple to Meeth line remained fully signalled for several years, with signalling retained at Fremington, Instow, Bideford, Torrington and Petrockstow. This was reduced, on 26th February 1967, to three signal boxes when both Bideford signal box and passing loop, and the sidings and signalling facilities at Petrockstow, were taken out of use.

The loop at Petrockstow was retained for running-round. The following year, on 3rd November 1968, the passing loops at Instow and Fremington were taken out of use and the Fremington signal box closed. The quay sidings remained in use at Fremington, and the signal box at Instow was retained with its signals of LSWR origin to control the level crossing over the main A39 Barnstaple to Bideford road. Next to go on the branch was Torrington signal box, taken out of use on 20th September 1970 when the 'down' road was converted to a siding, the central crossover and 'up' sidings having gone in 1967. Meanwhile back at Barnstaple, after the closure of the Ilfracombe branch in 1970, the west end of Barnstaple Junction was completely remodelled and the 'B' signal box closed on 25th May 1971, the whole station being controlled from 'A' box.

At Fremington Quay, traffic was declining. Following the closures of goods yards the flow of household coal imported here for distribution by rail in North Devon had ceased, and the export of clay from Marland and Meeth was the only remaining traffic for the eight railwaymen employed. The cranes were the last items of steam-operated railway equipment remaining in North Devon, and had reached the end of their working life. The quay ceased to function as from 31st December 1969 and the old cranes were taken away, but the sidings were retained to give access to the wagon weighbridge, which remained in use to check the loads of clay wagons from Marland and Meeth. Exports of clay continued using Bideford Quay, the clay being brought by lorry from the works. The traffic figures for 1969 show the freight carried on the branch before the closure of Fremington Quay:

Clay exported from Fremington Quay: 14,264 tons

Clay forwarded from Marland Sidings: 17,743 tons

Clay forwarded from Meeth Sidings: 20,051 tons

Milk forwarded from Torrington: 2,060 tanks.

During this early period (these aspects received greater attention in Chapter 1) East Yelland Power Station received some of its deliveries of coal by train. Apparently, the last year when this occurred was 1971 when 14,229 tonnes of coal were delivered by train, in comparison with 325,667 tonnes delivered by ship. Wagons were shunted into the power station sidings by British Railways locomotives, and subsequent movements were performed by a CEGB diesel shunter.

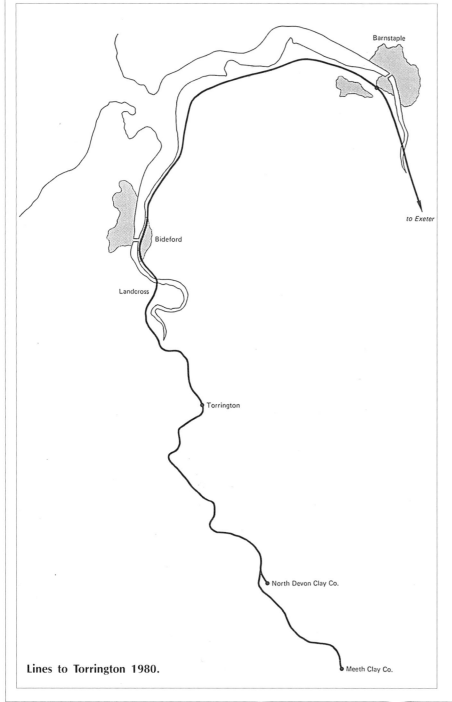

Lines to Torrington 1980.

A light engine North British Type 2 runs into Instow and collects the tablet from the signalman in 1963. I.L. Shorter.

Bideford goods yard in September 1963 with the running lines on the right. The platforms of the former station are still there even though it was abandoned some one hundred years earlier. Despite 23,000 tons of goods being received at the yard in 1963 only two years later on 6 September 1965 closure of Bideford Goods along with Fremington and Torrington was announced. John Eyers, courtesy South Western Circle.

NORTH DEVON LINE RAIL TRIPS
to & from
TORRINGTON
BIDEFORD
BARNSTAPLE
EXETER

AND NORTH DEVON LINE STATIONS

'HEART OF DEVON RAIL TOUR'

SUMMER & AUTUMN 1979

Thursday 12th. July   SEASIDE EXCURSION to Paignton

Sunday 22nd. July   TAMAR CRUISE to Plymouth & Calstock

Sunday 5th. August   TAMAR CRUISE to Plymouth & Calstock

Thursday 16th. August   GOODS LINE TOUR to Meeth

Sunday 2nd. September   HEART OF DEVON TOUR to Torrington and Dartmouth.   Part STEAM-HAULED

Saturday 20th. October   TO LONDON or HAMPTON COURT

BARGAIN FARES

TICKETS & further details from

R.N. JOANES, Old Railway Station, Filleigh, Barnstaple,
Devon. EX32 ORE. Telephone Filleigh 311.

Roger Joanes' advertisement for summer and autumn excursions in 1979.

Meanwhile at Bideford, the thriving industrial area East-the-Water, Kynocks Industrial Estate was suffering from a difficulty with its road access. The only road passed under a low railway bridge so in 1974, railway engineers rebuilt the bridge, raising the railway line by about 5ft. to allow access for the large lorries involved.

By the early 1970s, the difficult process of reducing expenses to a minimum on the line from Barnstaple to Meeth was all but over. The only remaining signalling was for the protection of the level crossing over the A39 road at Instow. British Railways sidings remained at Fremington for the weighbridge and at Torrington for the milk depot, and private sidings remained at Marland and Meeth for the clay, while those at East Yelland began to rust away. We can now give some consideration to details of the freight traffic carried on the line.

Clay Traffic
The principal reason for the survival of the Barnstaple to Meeth railway line was the clay traffic forwarded from the works at Marland and Meeth. By 1969 Meeth Works was then owned by ECC Ball Clays Ltd. of Newton Abbot, a member of the English China Clays Group. The line from Barnstaple terminated within the works, and the track bed of the ND&CJLR between the works and the main A386 road at Meeth Halt, some three quarters of a mile in length, was converted to an access road owned by British Rail but leased to the company. All shunting was carried out by British Rail locomotives, but any necessary movement of wagons on the site was manual. After closure of Fremington Quay most rail traffic was to the Midlands and amounted to approximately 20,000 tons per annum.

The North Devon Clay Company at Peters Marland became a member of the Watts, Blake Bearne Group of Newton Abbot. British Rail locomotives

An Express Dairy six wheel milk tank in the yard at Torrington in 1963. Passenger services were withdrawn between Barnstaple and Torrington in October 1965 but it was announced there would be one or two daily freights carrying clay from Marland and Meeth and milk from Torrington. The milk traffic fluctuated considerably and its eventual termination came in 1978. John Eyers, courtesy South Western Circle

delivered empty wagons and collected full wagons from the sidings, but the company had two diesel locomotives to shunt wagons between the interchange siding and the clay loading shed. Approximately 16 per cent of sales were despatched by rail to Stoke-on-Trent, Glasgow and Fowey.

A full description of the works and siding facilities at both Marland and Meeth is given in Chapter One; by the 1970s, there were changes at both works. The clay was no longer mined, but quarried from large pits, and the internal narrow gauge systems were superseded by lorries or dumpers. As a consequence, the extraction of clay became a seasonal business with peak production in the dryer summer months and low production in the wetter winter months. After extraction, the clay was shredded and stored in

large modern sheds until despatched to customers. Until 1979, loaded clay wagons were weighed on the Fremington weighbridge and it was not unknown for overloaded wagons to be returned to the works, but then both works provided their own modern loading and weighbridge facilities. When the wagons arrived at Exeter Riverside Yard, together with other clay wagons from Cornwall and South Devon, they were made up into the 'Clayliner' train for Stoke-on-Trent, and other services.

A number of factors affected the clay traffic. The Type 2 diesels were limited to thirteen loaded clay wagons between Meeth and Torrington, and the number of wagons on the 'Clayliner' train to Stoke was limited and agreed with the two companies. The delivery of clay to customers was no longer a railway

monopoly and the bulk of the clay traffic forwarded from the works went by lorry, particularly on the short hauls to Bideford Quay, for export, and to the WBB and ECC works near Newton Abbot. The wagons themselves were limited in number and near the end of their working lives, so the provision of a new wagon fleet was a crucial issue, and in 1980 a new merry-go-round wagon was given a trial run with a load of clay from Meeth, to test the discharge of ball clay from a hopper type wagon.

As far as the Meeth Works of ECC was concerned, the replacement of the life-expired wagon fleet was apparently resolved on 3rd March 1981 when the Minister of Transport, Mr Norman Fowler MP, announced a grant of £880,000 to ECC International Ltd. and Tiger Railcar Leasing (UK) Ltd. for modernising rail loading facilities at Rocks in Cornwall, Heathfield in South Devon and Meeth, the provision of a rail reception terminal at Cliffe Vale in Stoke-on-Trent, modern discharge facilities at Strood in Kent, and a fleet of specialised wagons. It was stated that the effect of the grant would be to retain, on the railways, substantial quantities of clay which would otherwise be carried by heavy lorries. The grant was made under Section 8 of the 1974 Railways Act, which enabled the Government to provide assistance towards the capital costs of facilities for loading, unloading and carriage of rail freight.

Subsequently, agreements were signed between British Rail, Tiger Railcar Leasing and ECC International Ltd. for an improved rail service between the Devon and Cornwall production works and Stoke-on-Trent. The clay would be carried in a fleet of twenty five hopper wagons, each with a capacity of 57 tonnes, owned by Tiger Railcar Leasing (UK) Ltd. and operated in conjunction with British Rail. One new hopper wagon would have the capacity to carry the same load of clay as four or five conventional 13 tonne wagons previously in use, and the new wagons would be 18 metres in length and would discharge their load through bottom doors. The size and weight of the new wagons would also necessitate some improvements by British Rail to the track on the Barnstaple to Meeth

line. However for our line this turned out to be a false dawn as we will see shortly. Meeth Clay works closed in 2004, but at the time of writing (2014) Marland was still in business.

Milk Traffic
When passenger services were withdrawn between Barnstaple and Torrington in October 1965, it was stated that the one or two daily freight trains carrying clay from Marland and Meeth, and milk from Torrington, was bringing in a monthly income of some £2,000 to British Railways. However, the milk traffic subsequently fluctuated considerably and finished in 1978.

The original milk loading depot at Torrington was inconveniently situated at the end of the siding through the old goods shed, and the pipework installed facilitated the loading of only three tankers, which then had to be shunted out of the way before three more could replace them. In the days of passenger services, there was almost always a locomotive at hand to carry out the shunting but after 1965 these operations had to be more carefully planned. The locomotive hauling the morning goods train from Barnstaple to Meeth delivered empty tankers and performed some shunting, and the afternoon Barnstaple to Torrington trip was operated to shunt the milk tankers and to take loaded tankers to Barnstaple for onward working to Exeter and London. In conjunction with other

works at Torrington in the mid-1970s, the original milk loading depot was replaced.

The new milk loading depot was built on the 'up' platform of Torrington station, and the first train of ten loaded milk tankers was despatched in March 1976, although this was the first despatch for some months. The pipework was sufficient to load some seven milk tankers which meant that far less shunting was required when the depot was in use, and the entire installation was protected from the weather by a new canopy over the platform. The milk loading depot was owned by British Rail although there was only one customer, the large creamery at Torrington, formerly the property of Unigate and later of the Milk Marketing Board, which served a wide area of North and West Devon. When in use, milk was delivered to the depot at Torrington station by lorry and pumped into the stainless steel tanker wagons, taking some twenty to thirty minutes to load a wagon. The tanker wagons were cleaned at their destination after unloading. A new feature in recent years was that, occasionally, milk was brought to Torrington by rail from another depot when the creamery there was not using it, and the whole loading procedure was then reversed. When the milk loading depot was in use, the station forecourt was sometimes packed with milk lorries delivering or collecting

The milk loading facilities at Torrington in 1963. There was a radical change in the handling of milk in 1975 when new facilities were erected on the up platform – this survived only three years.

August 1981 and the 'new' milk loading facility at Torrington can be seen on the platform as well as the canopy erected at the same time. Milk had disappeared, as mentioned, by 1978 but clay was still being shipped out in large numbers. Brush Type 2 31118 has paused with the up clay train at the station while the guard/shunter telephones the signalman at Barnstaple for permission to enter the section. John Nicholas.

loads. Apparently, the last milk loaded at Torrington was on 12th October 1978 when three tankers were forwarded to Ilford.

Torrington Fertiliser Depot

During the mid-1970s there was a most encouraging development on the Barnstaple to Meeth freight line with a major new customer establishing itself at Torrington station. Throughout the railway age in North Devon, a major undertaking had been the distribution of fertilisers, agriculture being the most important industry in the area, so the establishment of a major fertiliser depot for ICI was in keeping with the traditional role of the railway.

The entire 'down' platform, goods shed, and original milk loading depot were completely demolished and the three sidings in the yard cut back in length. A large new warehouse was built on the site, bearing the name 'ICI Fertiliser Depot'. Opened in April 1976, it was owned by South Western Storage (Torrington) Ltd. and was built on a site leased from British Rail. Attractively built in a combination of local stone and modern materials, it had a capacity of 2,000 tonnes of the full range of fertiliser produced by ICI at their Severnside Works (Bristol), Billingham Works, Cleveland and Heysham Works, Lancashire. The Torrington Depot distributed ICI fertiliser to the North Devon area; there

were also depots at Launceston, Exeter and Taunton, and the customers were local agricultural merchants who collected fertilisers from the depot in their own vehicles. Deliveries of several thousand tonnes per year to the depot were mainly by rail, using standard BR 12 ton vans. They were used to deliver the fertilisers in 50 kg. bags which were unloaded by hand on to pallets for storage in the warehouse.

During the 1970s the British fertiliser industry had developed standardised mechanical handling facilities, based on a load of 1.5 tonnes packed on a wooden pallet, which was unsuitable for loading in a standard BR 12 ton van. This development was associated with the need for improved efficiency of fertiliser manufacture and distribution, so after joint studies between ICI and British Rail, it was determined that rail transport was unsuitable for the continued transport of these products, given the costs available at the time. ICI had a total of sixty five such fertiliser depots in England and Wales, but only six of them, including Torrington, were served by rail. Accordingly, on 11th January 1980, the last five vans loaded with fertiliser arrived at the Torrington depot, and it was subsequently supplied entirely by road transport. The depot then employed two or three men who used a couple of fork lift trucks for loading and unloading the bags.

Operation of the Line

As we have seen, the volume and type of traffic on the Barnstaple to Meeth freight line varied considerably after the withdrawal of passenger services in 1965. Only the clay traffic was a constant feature, with the milk being substantial up to the mid-1970s but thereafter only occasional, and the fertiliser traffic running only between 1976 and 1980. Up to 1969, there was internal traffic on the branch, with clay wagons being delivered to Fremington Quay for onward shipment before the closure of the quay and, up to 1979, 'up' trains continued to call at Fremington to record the loads of clay wagons on the weighbridge there.

The normal pattern of operation after 1965 saw a regular weekday morning freight train between Barnstaple and Meeth, and an afternoon freight between Barnstaple and Torrington or Meeth if required. The morning freight train departed from Barnstaple about 8.30 a.m. with empty clay wagons and sometimes with empty milk tankers and loaded fertiliser vans. Up to the end of 1969, empty clay wagons were also collected from the sidings at Fremington when required. On arrival at Torrington, any empty milk tankers and loaded fertiliser vans were shunted to the appropriate sidings, and the train proceeded with the empty clay wagons which were delivered to the two clay works at Marland and Meeth. Here the loaded clay wagons were collected and the locomotive used the loop at Petrockstow to run round its train to return to Torrington, where any wagons which were ready were collected. Until 1969, the 'down' train called at Fremington to deliver any loaded clay wagons for onward shipment, and up to 1979 to check loaded wagons on the weighbridge. Arrival back at Barnstaple was at about 11.30 a.m. and, if required, a second trip departed from Barnstaple about 1 p.m. Up to the mid-1970s, this was a light engine running to Torrington to shunt the milk tanks. Departure from Torrington was at about 3.20 p.m., with a load of full milk tankers and sometimes loaded clay wagons from Marland destined for Fowey, and export to South America. Wagons went forward from Barnstaple to Exeter on the late afternoon freight train. The loads of freight trains varied considerably as demonstrated in some occasional observations:

station and cranes had to be hired to unload the wagons, so delivery by rail was not often resorted to.

As we have seen earlier, when the passenger services were withdrawn in 1965, the signalling remained for several years until it was reduced in 1971 to just the Instow signal box. In 1968, some seventeen railwaymen were still employed on the line, at Fremington, Instow and Torrington, including signalmen, crossing keepers, porters and dock staff. By the early 1970s this had been reduced to two, the Instow signalman, Mr Arthur Taylor and the senior rail man at Torrington, Mr Harry Beer. The crossing at East Yelland, giving road access to the power station, had been converted to automatic operation with flashing red lights activated by the train warning road traffic to stop and in January 1979, the Instow level crossing was also converted and the signal box closed, the road traffic having been reduced by the A39 bypass of the village

points, coupling and uncoupling wagons and so on, were then carried out by the train crews, and the permanent way was maintained by a mobile gang based at Barnstaple.

The twenty five miles of the Barnstaple to Meeth line were then operated at the minimum of expense, as part of the British Rail freight network. British Rail was obliged to operate its freight services at a profit, and to retain the traffic it had to compete with road transport. The passenger service obligation grant paid by the Government to British Rail did not of course cover freight. The retention and development of the line depended on its ability to bring valuable traffic to the national railway network at the minimum of expense.

Special Traffic
A remarkable feature of the Barnstaple to Meeth line, since the withdrawal of passenger services in 1965, was the number and variety of special passenger trains run. Fortunately, station platforms were retained on the line and not demolished as sometimes happened elsewhere. A complication was that British Rail had to obtain permission from the Department of Transport for each special passenger train to run on a goods line.

In January 1968 the railway came to the rescue of the transport system at Bideford when there was a partial collapse of Bideford Bridge. This cut the main A39 road, severing Bideford town centre from Bideford East-the-Water, Barnstaple and beyond, with the best

Day	Train	Load
Monday 9th October 1978	8.30 a.m. 'down'	About 30 wagons: half milk, half clay
Tuesday 10th October 1978	8.30 a.m. 'down'	About 15 wagons; half milk, half clay
Wednesday 11th October 1978	8.30 a.m. 'down'	3 clay wagons
Friday 29th August 1980	1.00 p.m. 'down'	18 clay wagons
	3.20 p.m. 'up'	12 clay wagons
Monday, 24th August 1981	8.30 a.m. 'down'	Light engine
	10.00 a.m. 'up'	12 clay wagons
	3.20 p.m. 'up'	Light engine

Up to 1971, when occasional deliveries of coal were made to East Yelland power station, they were made by special trains. No special discharge facilities were available at the power

seafront. The last railwayman's post on the line went on 19th September 1980 when Mr Harry Beer retired at Torrington. All necessary duties of opening and closing gates, operating

31118 earlier in the day on Torrington Viaduct, heading light engine to Meeth works to pick up its train. John Nicholas.

A distinguished group attending the 'Last Train to Torrington' in 1982; left to right, Harry Beer the last railwayman at Torrington, Councillor Clifford Quick Mayor of Torrington and finally Tom Mills fireman of the first train to Halwill in 1925. The North Devon Journal Herald

alternative route to the centre of Bideford being via the A386 road from Torrington. For a week or so, a makeshift passenger train service shuttled to and fro between Bideford and Torrington stations, connecting at Torrington with a bus running to the centre of Bideford. Freight for Bideford was also worked down to Torrington station for about a fortnight until the bridge had been repaired.

In 1980, British Rail, advertising on television to publicise the new Family Railcard, featured a most unusual train running over Torrington Viaduct. This included an experimental vehicle, carrying a 'parent', followed by four miniature vehicles, shaped in the form of a 50p piece, each carrying a member of the 'family'. The Family Railcard was promoted to allow the head of a family to pay the normal fare for any journey, with every other member of the family paying only 50p each.

Since 1965 a number of special trains for railway enthusiasts originating elsewhere, usually London but at least one from Crewe, have visited the former Southern Railway lines west of Exeter to Meldon, near Okehampton, Torrington and Meeth, and to Ilfracombe before the closure of the line

from Barnstaple in 1970. These have usually been formed of multiple units or coaches with a locomotive at each end, since the run-round loop at Petrockstow was quite short. One of these railtours took the name of the Southern's crack express to the West of England, the 'Atlantic Coast Express', and ran on several occasions organised by the Lea Valley Railway Club. An unusual working ran on 13th May 1976. This was the 'Lundy Island Boat Train' hauled by 25 207 run by Cookham Travel which arrived early in the morning to enable passengers to walk over Bideford Bridge to the Quay to board a cruise to Lundy on a high tide, returning on the next high tide for the train journey home. The empty coaching stock was worked to Torrington for berthing where the locomotive ran round before returning to Bideford.

The most interesting and very significant development in recent years has been the running of special trains originally from Bideford, and then from Torrington, for the benefit of North Devonians. There were just over forty such trains for which the public could buy tickets. Many of these were organised by Mr Roger Joanes of

Filleigh, the first being in celebration of the Silver jubilee. The special trains he organised in the period from 1977 to 1981 as shown in table opposite.

On six occasions between 1978 and 1980 special trains from London ran to Bideford and back for invited guests attending ship launches at Appledore Shipbuilders. These trains were all first class with a full meal service, and the one hundred or so passengers on each trip spent a night in Bideford and returned by train on the following day. There were also other locally organised special trains, including an excursion to Portsmouth for Bideford Football Club, to London for Bideford School and several to London for Pickfords Travel Service. The first locally organised trip from Torrington was on 29th April 1979 when a Torrington May Fair special train ran first to Barnstaple and then to Meeth, with a picnic stop at Petrockstow. There was a number of minor incidents but on approaching Landcross viaduct drivers often had to stop and sound their horn to allow fishermen with their rods and nets to leave the viaduct safely before the train could pass. There were certain problems to overcome before the local excursions could start, but with the co-

Date	Destination	Passengers	Notes
4th June 1977	Paddington	580	9 coaches Restaurant car
22nd October 1977	Paddington	450	
16th July 1978	Kingswear	500	12 coaches Restaurant car
10th September 1978	Kingswear	450	
27th May 1979	York	400	Also from Torrington
12th July 1979	Paignton	160	DMU
22nd July 1979	Gunnislake	320	DMU
5th August 1979	Gunnislake	320	DMU
16th August 1979	Meeth *(also a trip to Bideford)*	160	DMU
2nd September 1979	Kingswear	400	
3rd November 1979	Waterloo	480	
22nd August 1980	Gunnislake		DMU out, 33 return
20th July 1980	Paignton & Okehampton		DMU
27th July 1980	Paignton – Meeth – Paignton		
10th August 1980	Paignton – Meeth - Paignton		
24th August 1980	Torrington – Portsmouth		For Isle of Wight
25th October 1980	Waterloo		
13th July 1981	Bideford – Gunnislake		DMU
8th September 1981	Plymouth – Meeth - Plymouth		DMU
24th October 1981	Torrington – Dover & return		For Calais

operation of the Midland Bank who then occupied Bideford station buildings, the renovation of part of the platform and the provision of a mobile generator and engineers' lights for night trains, the passenger trains began running for the benefit of the people of North Devon. There was a considerable amount of local interest in the possibility of reopening Bideford station for regular passenger services by extending the existing train service between Exeter and Barnstaple.

Later Developments and Closure

It was in the area of passenger services that some of the most interesting later developments took place. In July 1979, Roger Joanes produced for the North Devon Railway Line Development Group a very well-documented plan for a passenger train service between Bideford and Exeter. The plan pointed out that, with some 20,000 people living in Bideford and Northam, the area suffered in comparison with the railway services provided to other Devon towns of similar size, such as Totnes. The suggested passenger service would cater principally for Inter-City passengers travelling to Exeter and beyond, and would not compete with the local bus service between Bideford and Barnstaple.

One major difficulty in reopening the passenger service between Bideford and Barnstaple was that under existing legislation, if the new service were unsuccessful, it could take several years to close it again. This would involve a very large expense which was a great disincentive to any experimental reopening. However, the Member of Parliament for North Devon, Mr Tony Speller, took this matter up in the House of Commons and, in 1981, his Private Member's Amendment to the 1962 Transport Act, to facilitate such experimental openings without these penalties, was passed with widespread support. A significant event for the railways in North Devon occurred on 10th November 1981, when a new travel centre was opened at Barnstaple station by Mr George

The 'Last Train to Torrington' on 6 November 1982, consisting of diesel 31174 (leading), fifteen coaches and 31158 trailing. The North Devon Journal Herald.

Last train to TORRINGTON

· BOOKING FORM · TRAIN TIMES · TRAVEL ITINERARY ·

SATURDAY 6 NOVEMBER

Join the farewell special train along the Barnstaple–Bideford–Torrington line

Power requested – 2 class 31 locomotives

Starting from Bristol Temple Meads and calling only at Bridgwater, Exeter St. David's and Barnstaple, with connections by scheduled services from London, the Midlands, the West Country, South Wales and the South Coast.

* RETURN PRICES (per person) *

£7.50 from Bristol Temple Meads £6.00 from Bridgwater

£5.00 from Exeter St. David's £3.00 from Barnstaple

Passengers may travel by scheduled services to join the special trains at any of its calling points, upon payment of the appropriate Awayday or other return fare from your local station. Ask for details of prices and train times.

SPECIAL TRAIN TICKETS MUST BE ORDERED IN ADVANCE – PLEASE SEE OVER

BR(W)WI 123/82

Creber, the Chairman of Devon County Council, assisted by Sir Peter Parker, the Chairman of British Rail. The County Council had contributed £30,000 towards the total cost of £108,000, and British Rail's new 1981 timetable had provided more and faster trains between Barnstaple and Exeter. At the opening, there was considerable support for the experimental reopening of the Barnstaple to Bideford line for passenger services, if the trains would pay their way, given support from local authorities and other bodies.

In June 1982, proposals for the reopening of Bideford station were put forward by British Rail. These included a service of four trains daily between Bideford, Barnstaple and Exeter in connection with Inter-City services to London and the Midlands. Trains would take seventy six minutes for the journey from Bideford to Exeter, giving an overall journey time of about four hours to London or Birmingham. The cost for the first year was given as £120,000 less fares earned, including £3,400 for improvements at Bideford, £32,700 for signalling at Barnstaple, and £1,600 per week for the train service. Mr Tony Speller hoped to persuade the Government to make a grant of 75 per cent of this cost but, in its absence, the Devon County Council and both North

Devon and Torridge District Councils were unable to find the money required, and the proposals fell.

Freight traffic on the Barnstaple to Meeth line had fallen away from its healthy levels in the mid-1970s, with the last of the milk running in 1978 and the final fertilisers in 1980, so that by 1982, the only freight traffic handled was approximately 30,000 tons of clay per annum from Marland and Meeth. New wagons were required for this as we've seen. In any event the track was not suitable for the 57 tonne Tiger Railcar wagons without major expenditure. Indeed, the track on the ND&CJLR section had deteriorated so much that, in June 1982, the civil engineer had banned excursion passenger trains south of Torrington. But 1982 proved to be perhaps the most difficult and troubled year in the history of British Rail. It started with a series of ASLEF one day strikes in protest against flexible rostering and, by the summer, had been followed by a short NUR strike and a protracted ASLEF strike. This could not have come at a better time for the road transport industry, which had much extra capacity available during a recession and road hauliers were able to offer very competitive contracts for considerable business that British Rail was then in no position to carry.

On 6th August 1982 the General Managers Saloon was hauled down the branch for an inspection; the verdict was negative, for on 31st August British Rail announced the immediate closure of the Barnstaple to Meeth freight line. Negotiations had taken place with the two clay companies, English China Clays and Watts Blake Bearne, and it was announced that all clay traffic was to be switched to road. Clay traffic did not cease immediately, since between 1st and 13th September more than a hundred loaded clay wagons had been hauled from Marland to Fowey Docks for shipment overseas. However, after this, the only revenue-earning trains seen on the line were the handful of

31174 on **The Last Train**. The North Devon Journal Herald.

specials which ran between Barnstaple and Torrington.

The main reason for the closure was the need to replace the worn out wagons. They had already been involved in several derailments on British Rail resulting in serious damage to the track; the dreamed-of replacement Tiger Railcar air-braked wagons were too heavy, and bringing the track and the Landcross viaduct up to standard would have cost £250,000. Known locally as the 'Iron Bridge', the latter had become popular for youngsters fishing the Torridge and such was its state that one boy had fallen through the decayed timbers into the river, fortunately without serious injury. The clay traffic from Meeth would fill only one wagon a day, and no arrangements for new wagons had been made at Marland. For many years the bulk of the clay from both Marland and Meeth had been despatched by· road, the choice of their customers, according to the clay companies. To finance the necessary track improvements British Rail needed more traffic from the clay companies, but this was not forthcoming and so the line was closed.

There was considerable local reaction to the closure of the Barnstaple to Meeth freight line. Back in 1965, when passenger services were withdrawn under the Beeching cuts, there was a feeling of sad resignation to the inevitable but, in 1982, it was very different. Both local Members of Parliament, Sir Peter Mills for West Devon and Mr Tony Speller for North Devon, were involved in efforts to save the line. It was suggested that the line might be used to bring in materials for forthcoming road construction in the area, and that household refuse might be brought by train to be dumped in worked-out clay pits at Meeth. It was still hoped that regular passenger services might run from Barnstaple to Bideford at some time in the future. There was concern about the extra lorry traffic on the roads around Meeth and Hatherleigh. On 8th October, there was a crowded meeting held by the North Devon Railway Line Development Group at Torrington Town Hall to discuss the closure, but a British Rail spokesman put the cost of repairs over the next five years at £1,000,000. It was agreed to ask the European Economic Community for support, and to ask

British Rail not to remove the track until all possible solutions had been exhausted.

The last few special passenger trains ran in the weeks following the closure. On Sunday, 12th September, Roger Joanes ran his last excursion from Torrington and Bideford to mid-Devon, and a six coach diesel multiple unit formed an excursion from Bristol to Bideford and Torrington. On Saturday, 16th October, the publishing firm of Ian Allan Ltd. sponsored an 'Atlantic Coast Express' from Waterloo to Barnstaple, Bideford and Torrington, consisting of first class carriages hauled by two Type 3s 33025 SULTAN and 33027 EARL MOUNTBATTEN OF BURMA. At Torrington this train pulled out on to the viaduct so that the carriages could be watered from the platform tap.

British Rail itself ran the 'Last Train to Torrington' on a wet Saturday, 6th November 1982. The train left Bristol Temple Meads at 10.08 a.m. and picked up passengers at Bridgwater, Exeter St. David's and Barnstaple. Leaving Barnstaple, the train consisted of Brush Type 2 diesel 31174 (leading), fifteen coaches carrying 843 passengers and

Harry Beer at Torrington exchanging the token with the driver of the daily goods train on Saturday 20 October 1979.

31158 (trailing). The train arrived at Torrington at 14.53, some twenty eight minutes late, where the leading locomotive halted just short of the level crossing into the yard, leaving the trailing locomotive out beyond the occupation bridge for Staplevale Farm. This was, without doubt, the longest and best patronised passenger train ever to run into Torrington station.

At the station the train was met by the Mayor, Councillor Clifford Quick, and a party of townspeople, including Mr Harry Beer, the last railwayman to work at Torrington, and Mr Tom Mill who had been the fireman on the first passenger train to Halwill in 1925. The passengers slowly disembarked to view the station and its environs, and some took the free coach trip up the long hill to the *Torrington Arms*, formerly the *Railway Inn*, for refreshment. A BBC radio team recorded interviews which were broadcast in the West Country on the following Monday. The train was due to depart at 15.15, but it was not until 16.07 that Councillor Clifford Quick was able to wave the green flag to signal the departure of the last train from Torrington.

Two developments followed. Firstly the North West Devon Railway Preservation Society was established with the aim of acquiring the Barnstaple to Bideford section of the line. Secondly the buffer stops, built across the line at Barnstaple, were temporarily removed, so that, on 27th January 1983, a single coach diesel railcar L101 ran from Barnstaple to Torrington and back to convey a party of local civic leaders, industrialists, members of the North Devon Railway Line Development Group and Lord O'Hagan, the Devon Member of the European Parliament. During the visit, the BR West of England Divisional Manager, Mr Paul Witter, announced that the track would not be lifted for at least two years to allow every opportunity for reopening. Lord O'Hagan forwarded a letter to the European Economic Community Headquarters in Brussels requesting financial assistance for the line but, at the end of March 1983, the request was turned down.

Torrington station building, which had been unoccupied for some time, was sold at a public auction in October 1983 and, in May 1984, its new owners opened it to the public as 'The Puffing Billy' restaurant. The North West Devon Railway Preservation Society was unable to raise the £313,000 required to purchase the line so in June 1984, track lifting commenced at the Meeth end of the line. However, as we will see in Chapter Twelve, subsequently there were railway related developments at four stations along the line.

Saturday 12 September 1982 and one of the last special passenger trains, an excursion from Bristol to Torrington, arrives at Bideford station. Morgan Photographic.

41324 and a solitary coach at Torrington destined for Halwill Junction in August 1958. Some passengers on the up platform have already completed their journey whilst two others wait patiently for the next up service. There were, at one time, over thirty staff at Torrington under station master, Mr F.W. Newcombe, whose residence stands on the left. A.E. Bennett, transporttreasury.

Chapter 10
Traffic and Train Services

Before passenger services from Exeter and Barnstaple to Bideford began in 1855 most people travelled very little beyond their local area. For the wealthy there were slow horse-drawn coach services but most people went by foot. The exception in this coastal area were a few travellers who took the sailing ships connecting the Taw-Torridge ports and quays with other ports in the Bristol Channel or occasionally beyond. For example in 1852 an iron-screw steamer 'Princess Royal' plied weekly, weather permitting, between Bristol, Ilfracombe, Barnstaple and Bideford. Indeed your author met one man who sailed round the world, starting and finishing at Fremington Quay. The first time that many local people could afford to travel by train was on market day at Bideford and Barnstaple when special trains with cheap fares were introduced. The North Devon Railway ran some excursions, and there were similar trains to Barnstaple and Bideford from South Devon. The first excursion from London was in 1857.

Local travel was handicapped by geography. Instow station was convenient for the village centre but Barnstaple and Bideford were separated from their town centres by long bridges over the estuaries, Fremington village was a mile away and Torrington was

more than a mile and a steep hill from the town centre. Consequently local travel did not grow to the same extent as the Ilfracombe branch with its more convenient stations, particularly at Barnstaple Town and Braunton. Moreover, in the 1920s when motor buses started running to the centres of towns and villages, people naturally found them more convenient, in particular Barnstaple, Instow, Bideford and Westward Ho! The number of tickets issued at Instow dropped from 30,000 to 5,000 between 1912 and 1932. Between Torrington and Halwill the only trains well filled with passengers took workers to Marland clay works.

Longer distance travel was a different story. From 1863 regular trains ran between Waterloo, Exeter and Bideford and from 1872 Torrington, and these were found to be attractive by the standards of the day. The service developed with reservable seats and restaurant cars, and through trains or coaches continued to run for a century until 1964, all passenger services being withdrawn in 1965.

Passenger Services 1855-1925
The initial passenger service in 1855 consisted of four trains each way between Bideford and Exeter with a fifth between Bideford and Barnstaple, by 1857 also extended to Exeter. These

were operated by the North Devon Railway, leased by Thomas Brassey, on the Bideford Extension Railway serving Bideford (Crosssparks), Instow and Fremington, to Exeter with an engine change at Crediton. At Exeter station, which became St David's, there were some connections with the Bristol & Exeter and South Devon trains, all running on the broad gauge. The 9.30am from Bideford arrived at Exeter at 12.10pm, to connect with the 12.40am express arriving at Paddington at 6.0pm. Departing from Paddington the 9.40am express gave a Bideford arrival at 6.5pm.

Following the arrival of the standard gauge South Western at Exeter in 1860 the broad gauge route to Bideford was converted to mixed gauge in 1863, and standard gauge trains began with some through carriages between Waterloo and Bideford. A bonus was that Exeter Queen Street (later renamed Central) was far more convenient for the centre of the city.

When the line was extended from Bideford in 1872 there were five daily departures from Torrington to Exeter Queen Street, the 2.10pm going forward to Waterloo, with some others having connections. Early public timetables are not reliable on which services were through carriages or connections. In addition there was a

41298's Bulleid coach has more than enough capacity for the numbers travelling south to Halwill Junction in 1958; it wasn't unusual to run with just one or two passengers. A.E. Bennett, transporttreasury.

41298 runs into Bideford with a down train in 1963, the last summer of through coaches to Waterloo. The public footpath, which crossed the line here, can just be seen at the end of the platform.

Fridays only market train, and a short working between Bideford and Barnstaple provided by attaching a carriage to the daily Crediton to Bideford (Crossparks) broad gauge goods train.

1876 Formation of Trains

In 1874 the Barnstaple & Ilfracombe line opened, in 1876 the South Western reached its Devonport terminus and began its familiar West of England service pattern with through portions of trains from Waterloo terminating at Torrington, Devonport and some at Ilfracombe. Fortunately the South Western 1876 notice of Formation of Trains between Waterloo, Exeter and the West of England survives; only the carriages to and from Torrington are detailed here.

6.45am from Waterloo: Torrington, 1 van, 2 thirds, 1 composite.
The 6.45am slow and 9.0am fast trains ran separately to Yeoford where passengers could change trains.

9.0am from Waterloo: Devonport, Ilfracombe.

10.45am from Waterloo: Devonport, Ilfracombe and Torrington, 1 composite, 1 third, 1 van.
Torrington coaches detached at Exeter, depart 4.0pm, Ilfracombe carriages detached at Yeoford, depart 4.26pm.

11.45am from Waterloo: Devonport, Torrington, 1 van, 2 composites, 2 thirds, 1 van. This train formed the 6.20pm from Exeter to Torrington. The 11.45am slow and 2.25pm express ran separately to Yeoford, where carriages were transferred.

2.25pm express from Waterloo: Devonport, Torrington, 2 composites, 1 van, attached at Yeoford to the 11.45am from Waterloo.

7.25am from Torrington: Waterloo, 1 van for 10.15 from Exeter, 2 composites, 1 van for 10.5 express from Exeter, 2 composites, 2 thirds, 1 van for 10.15 from Exeter.

10.40am from Torrington: Waterloo, 1 composite , 1 third, 1 van. Departs Exeter 1.5pm.

2.50pm from Torrington: Waterloo, 1 third, 2 composites, 1 third, 1 van. Departs Exeter 5.20pm.

In addition to these Waterloo trains there were also local services running from Torrington to Barnstaple, Torrington to Exeter, as well as an early morning Yeovil to Torrington and afternoon return train.

There was an innovation in 1881 when the 10.40am from Torrington to Waterloo acquired a Devonport portion. A compo, third and van, labelled Lidford and Devonport line, were detached at Yeoford. Here the three coaches were shunted to the front of the 11.45am from Exeter to Devonport. The coaches returned on the 4.35pm and 7.0pm from Devonport to Exeter. Just how long this Torrington

**July to September 1909
Passenger Timetable**

Down Trains	from	Torrington arr.
8.18am	Barnstaple	8.46am
8.30	Exeter	10.34
10.38	Barnstaple	11.9
6.10	Waterloo	12.45pm
1.46pm	Barnstaple	2.14
1.2	Exeter	3.20
11.10am	Waterloo	4.4
12.noon	Waterloo	5.12
5.15	Barnstaple	5.45
1.0	Waterloo	7.4
3.30	Waterloo	9.5
10.45	Barnstaple	11.12 Wed only

to Devonport service lasted is not clear, but it was probably short-lived.

Since the Waterloo to West of England expresses were some of the most important for the South Western they justified use of the best rolling stock available, developing from four wheel to six wheel to bogie carriages, and in

Up Trains from Torrington

Dep.	to	arrival
7.45am	Exeter	9.50
9.30	Exeter	11.32
10.35	Waterloo	3.37pm
11.15	Waterloo	4.40
11.40	Barnstaple	12.9
12.10pm	Waterloo	5.47
1.15	Waterloo	8.7
2.16	Waterloo	8.7
2.45	Barnstaple	3.16
3.30	Waterloo	10.34
5.13	Exeter	7.19
5.55	Barnstaple	6.26
6.30	Barnstaple	7.2
7.55	Exeter	10.4
10.0	Barnstaple	10.30 Wed only

the early 1900s to corridor trains, some with dining saloons, although some local trains were formed of older stock. By then the South Western was running passenger trains along its new lines to Plymouth (Friary), Bude and Padstow.

All Barnstaple trains ran from Barnstaple Junction, Exeter trains from Exeter Queen Street. Trains stopped at all stations between Barnstaple and Torrington, except Waterloo trains which passed Fremington.

Passenger services circa 1914

In the later LSWR period during the summer, no less than five trains, or portions of trains, ran between Waterloo and Torrington, with three more between Exeter (Queen Street)

and Torrington, and a further three between Barnstaple and Torrington. Bogie coaches were by now in almost universal use, and the principal services, such as the 'North Devon and Ilfracombe Express', were provided by corridor trains with dining cars running right through between Waterloo and Torrington. All trains now conveyed first, second and third class passengers, although the LSWR abolished second class during World War One. The trains were also faster, and in the summer of 1905 the best train from Waterloo was the 10.40 a.m. which arrived at Torrington at 3.35 p.m.; in 1907 it was the 12 noon which arrived at Torrington at 5.09 p.m., and in 1914 the 11.10 a.m. which arrived at 4.08 p.m. The time of about five hours for the 225 mile journey was quite respectable by contemporary standards with an average speed of 45 miles per hour, some of it over single line sections.

The LSWR public timetable of the summer of 1914 included details of coach and omnibus services running in connection with the trains. At Barnstaple Junction and Torrington, cabs or omnibuses ran between the station and the town centre in connection with every train, while at Bideford, services ran between the station and Westward Ho! in connection with most trains. There were also two daily coaches to and from Clovelly to connect with the principal London trains. One of the photographs of

Bideford New station illustrates just how busy the cab yard there could be at times.

Passenger Services 1925-1965

From July 1925 there were two major changes to train services. The North Devon and Cornwall Junction Light Railway opened, with three passenger trains each way between Torrington and Halwill Junction stopping at the three stations and the five halts after they opened. However the principal trains from Waterloo and Exeter to North Devon now ran through to Ilfracombe, and Torrington line passengers often had to change trains at Barnstaple Junction. More passengers used the Ilfracombe line stations, and new N class 2-6-0 locomotives could cope with the steep gradients.

Train services on the Barnstaple to Torrington section during the 1920s and 1930s followed the pattern set in the later LSWR period, with coaches running through to Waterloo on the principal services, joined with Ilfracombe trains at Barnstaple Junction. After July 1925 few passenger trains ran from Torrington beyond Barnstaple since, as we have seen, Ilfracombe had become the principal terminus of the North Devon line. If anything, the number of passenger trains on the Barnstaple to Torrington line increased, and the goods services continued to run right through to Torrington. On the section between Torrington and

Two passengers, one taking the photo, are waiting for 41314 to leave with the 10.38am service along the ND&CJLR line to Torrington. The slaughterhouse on the right was supplied with ice from Bude on a daily basis, the meat going to London and the Midlands via Templecombe.

The crew of 41294 take a break at Halwill Junction before returning with the 6.30pm Torrington train. On a train for Padstow is an unidentified N class 2-6-0 and in the distance a BR 82000 2-6-2T, the Bude branch locomotive.

July 1956 and 41297 has assembled its train at Barnstaple Junction and is now backing into the down platform. It will leave shortly with the 8.30 evening service to Torrington. John Eyers, courtesy South Western Circle.

Halwill, the original three mixed trains each way had been increased to five by 1929 but dropped back to two in 1932, together with the trains for workmen.

The 1932 working timetable shows the Torrington trains running beyond Barnstaple as the 11.0am from Waterloo and 10.30am from Torrington for which a through 'Atlantic Coast Express' coach was provided. Also the 7.10am from Torrington was a through train to Exeter, the 8.10am had a through coach to Waterloo and the 4.38pm had a through coach to Eastleigh. The 6.25am from Yeovil and 9.42am from Exeter Queen Street had a through coach to Torrington. During the peak summer months there were more through coaches or though trains scheduled. On the ND&CJLR there were two trains between Torrington and Halwill Junction, with a 6.25am from Torrington to Dunsbear Halt and 4.37pm return from Petrockstow provided for workmen at the clay works. There were connections at each end but no through carriages. The two through mixed trains each way were quite sufficient for the passenger traffic since, in 1932, Petrockstow, Hatherleigh and Hole stations between them issued only 3,141 tickets and collected 3,103, a daily average of about ten. Most of the passenger traffic consisted of clay workers conveyed to and from Dunsbear Halt.

In the 1947 public timetable the 6.25am from Yeovil through coach reached Torrington at 10.37am, and the 7.8am from Torrington included a through coach to Exeter Central. However, this timetable did not distinguish between through coaches and connections. The main flow of holiday passenger traffic on the lines to Torrington was through Bideford station, the railhead for Westward Ho! and other resorts on the Atlantic Coast, with buses conveying holiday-makers to their final destination. Trains ran to and from Torrington since there were no terminal facilities at Bideford. The extent of the holiday traffic is indicated in the figures for daily through corridor coaches between Waterloo and Torrington:
Mondays-Saturdays, summer 1913: 13,
Mondays-Fridays, summer 1955: 7,
Saturdays only, summer 1955: 24.

The summer 1955 Carriage Working Notice gives a full picture of the stock working on the lines to Torrington. Most of the corridor stock then in use was of the modern all-steel Bulleid type with some Maunsell stock, but some of the local trains were formed of much older vehicles. As late as 1954, three coach set No.126, working between Barnstaple and Torrington, consisted of LSWR non-corridor stock rebuilt on longer underframes by the Southern Railway, and an LSWR vehicle was also used on some trains between Torrington and Halwill.

The summer 1957 Carriage Working Notices provides more evidence. On weekdays the 7.6am from Torrington had three coaches to Exeter Central, the 8.10am three to Waterloo, the 10.30am and 12.18pm both two for Waterloo, and the 2.15pm one for Waterloo. In the down direction there was one coach for Torrington on the 1.15am from Waterloo, two on each of the 9.0am, 11.0, 1.0pm and 3.0pm. In every case these were portions of trains between Waterloo and Ilfracombe, attached or detached at Barnstaple Junction, except for the 7.6am Torrington to Exeter. Through services between Waterloo and Torrington ended after the summer 1963 timetable, and for the next two years until closure in 1965 there were two self-contained services from Torrington to Halwill and Barnstaple respectively.

Workmen
The North Devon Clay Company at Peters Marland was far from local towns and villages so as the company expanded it employed more men who needed transport to and from work. Some of the workmen lived at Torrington and more in NDCC cottages at Yarde. Accordingly a 3ft gauge workmen's train left Torrington for the works at 6.25am getting back about 6pm. It was a condition of the 1910 Light Railway Order for the ND&CJLR that the new railway would continue the service to and from Dunsbear Halt, the return service reaching Torrington at 5.37pm in 1932 and 4.0 in 1957. The Clay Company

Torrington station in June 1962, apparently a Saturday, with three locomotives in steam. 41297 with the 10.30am goods for Halwill Junction takes water, most of the wagons returning empty to the clay works. Meanwhile in the up platform the 10.48am departure is being marshalled, including through *Atlantic Coast Express* coaches to Waterloo. Another two coach set with locomotive waits in the up sidings. P.W. Gray.

30255 at Anchor Wood, a mile or so outside Barnstaple, with the 5.55pm service to Torrington in September 1958; it had come to Barnstaple Junction in 1951. The M7 0-4-4Ts were too heavy to work beyond Torrington on the ND&CJR.

paid the railway to put the trains on; there were no tickets issued and the clay and mud deposited made the carriage unfit for public service. This was not a unique arrangement; Whiteways Cider for instance, at Whimple paid the cost of railway tickets for employees travelling from Exeter.

Mail Services 1855-1906

One of the first railway customers was the Royal Mail, for letters could be delivered much more quickly by train than horse-drawn coach, saving days rather than hours on long distance mail. The Royal Mail made good use of the first railways, with the Dorchester mail train from Waterloo via Southampton, and the West of England mail from Paddington via Bristol and Exeter, and established sorting offices convenient to the major stations. Soon dedicated mail trains were running, and eventually they incorporated sorting carriages where Royal Mail staff sorted mail during the journey, putting off and collecting mailbags en route.

As new lines opened in the West Country they too carried letters and parcels, in conjunction with the Up and Down Paddington Royal Mail services. For North Devon for many years the Up Mail called at Exeter St David's around 10pm and the Down Mail about 3am, when mailbags were transferred between trains, and also city Post Offices. On the North Devon line there

was usually a (locked) carriage or parcels van loaded and unloaded by Royal Mail staff at station stops, or in some cases mailbags were carried in the Guards van under his care. When the line opened in 1855 the 6.30pm passenger train from Bideford , and 4.50am from Exeter were described as 'Mail', and in 1872 when the line opened to Torrington the departure times were 7.40pm Passenger and Mail from Torrington and 3.20am Passenger from Exeter Queen Street, 3.30 from St David's. For many years, up to 1900 an 'Exeter and Barnstaple Bag Tender' – a mail van – was in use, and in 1903 its route was extended to Torrington.

There would be very few passengers travelling at 3.20am from Exeter to North Devon, but the mail van had to run to meet the requirements of the Royal Mail, so it was conveyed on the Goods and Mail train instead. In 1909 this departed Exeter Queen Street at 2.35am to arrive at Torrington at 5.55am, and at Barnstaple Junction connected with a 5.25am Goods and Mail to Ilfracombe, which in turn connected with the 6.35am Passenger and Mail from Barnstaple Town to Lynton. The up service from Torrington was the 7.50pm Passenger and Mail to Exeter. This changed in 1906.

The Exeter and Torrington Sorting Carriage 1906-1917

Between 1906 and 1917 the South

Western ran an 'Exeter and Torrington Sorting Carriage', a purpose-built vehicle for the Post Office, and there was a corridor connection to an adjacent 'Bag Tender' for mailbags. Typically in 1909 this ran as part of the 2.35am Goods and Mail from Exeter Queen Street to arrive at Torrington at 5.55am. Mailbags from Exeter and beyond were loaded at Queen Street, but the train was booked to stop at St David's between 2.40 and 2.55, when mailbags were transferred from the Great Western Travelling Post Office from London, Bristol and the North, and the earlier Up Mail from Penzance. Post Office staff travelled in the Sorting Carriage to sort, frank and re-bag letter mail during the journey ready for delivery at each booked station. At Barnstaple mail from other parts of North Devon was loaded for sorting. At each station between 5 and 6am the train was met by the local postman who took the mailbags to his own Post Office where the mail was finally sorted prior to delivery to homes and businesses. The Exeter-based Post Office sorters then lodged in the town ready for the evening return journey.

Post Office sorters joined the Sorting Carriage and Bag Tender with the Torrington mail in good time for the 7.55pm Mail and Passenger train to Exeter. The morning procedures were reversed at every station where a local postman brought mailbags to the train where the mail was sorted and bagged,

41294, with the 10.38am service from Halwill to Torrington, takes water at Hatherleigh in September 1959. Clay workers used the line, the clay company paying the railway to put the trains on. There were about seventy such journeys a day in each direction with no tickets issued. It is ironic, therefore, that the very evidence which may have kept the line open was never used in the figures published by Dr. Beeching. John Eyers, courtesy South Western Circle.

Goods traffic from the Torrington line to Halwill was light although sidings were provided at Watergate, Dunsbear, Petrockstow, Meeth, Hatherleigh and Hole. 'As and when required' a locomotive would pick up a wagon or two. Petrockstow, Hatherleigh and Hole could boast the majority of the work with Hatherleigh, for instance, forwarding 1,820 loaded wagons in 1936. This is the 10.30am goods from Torrington including two loaded and sheeted clay wagons destined for Fowey and an empty van returning to fertilizer works. John Eyers, courtesy South Western Circle.

and at Barnstaple Junction the mail for other parts of North Devon was put off. The train called at St David's between 9.56 and 10.1 where mailbags for the up Great Western Travelling Post Office were unloaded, before arrival at Queen Street at 10.4pm when mailbags for Exeter were unloaded. This short-lived service was the only Travelling Post Office to operate over the South Western in the West Country.

Mail Services 1917-1965

After withdrawal of the Sorting Carriage, mail services reverted to their pre-1906 pattern. In the 1932 timetable (Down direction) was the 2.10am Freight and Mail from Exeter Queen Street, booked to call at St David's between 2.15 and 2.55, then at Yeoford between 3.21 and 3.41, with plenty of time allowed for shunting at stations from Barnstaple before a Torrington arrival at 6.29. In the Up direction was the 7.36pm Passenger and Mail from Torrington to Barnstaple Junction, where it connected with the 7.45pm Passenger and Mail from Ilfracombe to Exeter Queen Street, but it is not clear if a van carrying the mail ran through to Exeter.

By 1957 there was little change with the 2.6am Mail and Freight from Exeter Central scheduled to arrive at Torrington at 6.8am, but to convey only mail vans from Exeter Central to Yeoford. From there it could take on up to 42 loaded wagons to Barnstaple Junction, reduced to 22 wagons from Bideford Goods. The Torrington mailbags were carried in Van B stove which returned to Exeter on the 8.53am departure. The Up mail was carried in a PMV which left Torrington on the 7.38pm passenger train to Barnstaple Junction, where it was shunted on to the 7.45pm passenger from Ilfracombe to Exeter Central. The 7.38pm from Torrington was allowed four minutes at Bideford to load mailbags; during the busy Christmas period about three empty vans were detached in the down platform at Bideford from the rear of the 6.40pm passenger train from Barnstaple to Torrington. At Bideford Royal Mail vans arrived at the station forecourt to load large numbers of mailbags into the vans, which were then collected by the 7.38pm from Torrington which arrived at 7.47pm.

On the NDCJLR section, mailbags arriving at Torrington at 6.8am went forward under the care of the guard on the 8.52am to Halwill under the general Post Office contract, and left the line on the 4.0pm from Torrington and thence the 5.26 from Halwill to Okehampton.

Newspapers

By 1909 the 3.15am goods from Exeter to Torrington conveyed newspapers, passing Fremington and Instow 'at 4 miles per hour, to enable News and parcels to be put out'. It arrived at Bideford (New) at 7.55am and Torrington at 8.9am. By 1932 a portion of the 1.30am Newspaper train from Waterloo arrived at Barnstaple Junction at 6.22am, collecting Plymouth newspapers at Yeoford Junction, and newspapers for the Torrington line were transferred to the 6.48am from Barnstaple Junction, arriving at Torrington at 7.29am.

By 1955 two trains conveyed newspapers to the Torrington line. London newspapers departed Waterloo on the 1.15am service, the Ilfracombe section detaching a News Van B at Barnstaple Junction, transferred to the passenger and news train which delivered newspapers to all stations and arrived at Torrington at 7.28am. The Plymouth newspaper 'The Western Morning News' was conveyed on the 1.15am Newspaper train from Plymouth Friary to Exeter Central, and at Yeoford bundles were unloaded to be transferred to the 1.15am Waterloo service, again arriving at Torrington at 7.28am. However not all the newspapers arriving at Torrington at

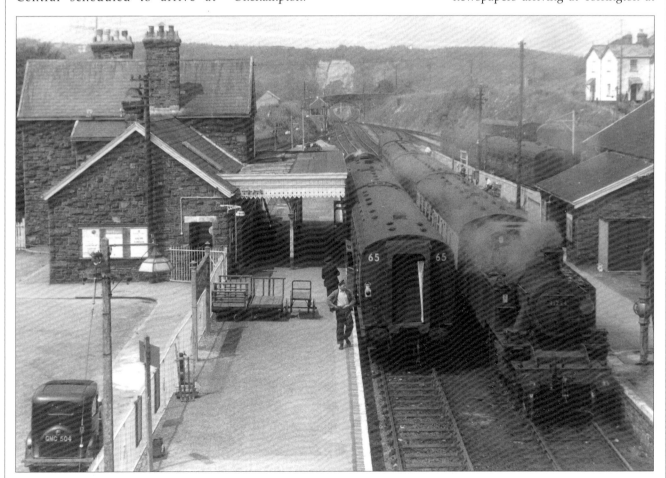

On 10th June 1963 41294 arrives at Torrington with the 1.10pm from Barnstaple Junction, including a three coach WR set. In the up platform 41214 and a two coach Bulleid set will form the 2.15pm to Barnstaple Junction. The main flow of holiday passenger traffic, so important to the line, was through Bideford, railhead for a wide area including Appledore, Westward Ho! and other resorts on the Atlantic coast. Trains ran right through to Torrington as there were no terminal facilities at Bideford and the extent of the holiday traffic can be seen in the numbers of daily through coaches in 1955. Mondays to Fridays (summer) seven, Saturdays only (summer) twenty-four. John Nicholas.

M7 30250 with a mixed train of four Maunsell coaches, a van and a milk tanker at Instow in the 1950s. Although gated the siding on the left was not private.

7.28am were destined for the town, some being sorted at the station into bundles for NDCJLR destinations. These bundles of newspapers were loaded into the guards van of the 8.52am train to Halwill Junction, and handed out by the guard at the halts and stations along the line.

Milk Traffic

In the 1870s a butter factory was established at Taddiport in Torrington by Robert Sandford, using milk carted from local farms over a wide area and in 1932 the business became associated with Cow & Gate. In the 1930s some of this milk was taken to the station and forwarded in churns, as recorded in Southern Railway traffic figures, confirmed by photographs showing milk churns on Torrington down platform. In 1930-32 some milk was also forwarded from Petrockstow. It would appear that at least some of this milk was sent to the Ambrosia creamery opened at Lapford in 1928. Churns were usually conveyed in the luggage compartments of passenger trains, but for Ambrosia churns were loaded into vans which were shunted into the factory siding at Lapford. Also occasionally some milk was received at Torrington, surplus to requirements elsewhere, to be converted into butter.

The milk depot with overhead pipework for loading the 3,000 gallon milk tank wagons was built in 1944. From then until 1965 milk tankers were worked as tail traffic on passenger trains from Torrington to Barnstaple, and thence up passenger trains sometimes collecting more tankers at Lapford and Crediton. By 1958 the milk tankers were combined into the 5.35pm Milk train from Crediton to Exeter Central, where they went

forward in the 6.48pm Milk Train from Exeter Central to Clapham Junction. From here they were worked to United Dairies and Express Dairies depots at Vauxhall, Morden and others in the London area where they were unloaded and cleaned. The empty tankers returned on the 3.54pm Milk Empties from Clapham Junction to Exeter Central and thence on morning goods trains or as tail traffic on passenger services. Following withdrawal of passenger trains milk tankers continued to run, from 1976 using a new loading depot on the former up platform, until 1978.

Other Passenger Train Traffic

In addition to mail bags, newspapers and milk churns a wide variety of other parcels traffic was carried in the luggage compartments of passenger trains, including passenger luggage in advance to and from Bideford during the holiday season, bicycles, car tyres, parcels from mail-order companies, and even cardboard boxes of day-old chicks. Many of these originated at the Otter Vale Hatcheries at Ottery St Mary and were loaded at Sidmouth Junction into the luggage compartments of vehicles destined for stations in North Devon, where they were collected by a farmer or his wife. On one occasion some boxes of day-old chicks for a customer in Hole were detained in the booking office at Halwill Junction, so to avoid further delay the branch engine made an unofficial special trip to Hole, carrying the box of chicks on the footplate.

Parcels forwarded on passenger trains normally arrived at their destination the same day and were charged at a premium rate. Less urgent small consignments were carried on

overnight 'road box' services on goods trains at a lower rate. Whilst railway collection and delivery services operated from Bideford and Torrington stations at Petrockstow, Hatherleigh and Hole customers had to collect and deliver themselves, although usually these stations dealt with more parcels than passengers.

A Survey of Freight Traffic

The first record of goods traffic on the line was in late August 1848 when coal and limestone was landed at the newly constructed Fremington Harbour. Both here and at Barnstaple new limekilns to produce lime used as fertiliser had been built and both coal and lime were loaded into trucks to be hauled by horses on the standard gauge line to Barnstaple, where a warehouse had been constructed. When construction of the North Devon Railway between Crediton and Barnstaple began in 1852 materials including iron rails and chairs from South Wales were unloaded at Fremington and conveyed by rail, the narrow gauge tracks being extended as far as Umberleigh, until conversion to broad gauge in 1854. For many years the cheapest method of delivery from South Wales for bridge girders, iron rails and chairs required for railway construction in North Devon was by ship to Fremington and delivery by rail to the nearest convenient point. This included construction materials for the Bideford Extension Railway during 1854-55, the Torrington Extension Railway in 1870-72 and the Torrington and Marland Railway in 1880.

Our line was first connected to much of the national railway system when the North Devon Railway opened in 1854, with through wagonload traffic to and from the broad gauge system including Paddington, Bristol, Plymouth and branches. However for traffic to and from the rest of the national system, on the standard gauge, wagonloads had to be transferred at one of the transfer sheds provided where the systems met, and this caused delay and extra expense. Goods traffic, on the broad gauge, was developed when the Bideford Extension railway opened in 1855. A variety of goods traffic now developed at Bideford included cargoes dealt with at the railway quay, in addition to that already seen at Fremington Harbour. The South Western took over the North Devon and Bideford Extension Railways and in 1863 opened the line to standard gauge traffic over the now mixed gauge tracks. North Devon traders now had the best of both worlds, with the ability to load traffic in both broad gauge and standard gauge wagons as appropriate, direct to all parts of the country. The South Western loaded most goods traffic on the standard gauge, but one broad gauge train ran between Bideford and Crediton where wagons were handed over to a Bristol & Exeter service, a useful facility which lasted until 1877. When required a broad gauge coal train ran between Fremington and Barnstaple.

Main Line era 1872-1925
Before the railway arrived at Fremington, Instow and Bideford there were innumerable residential, commercial and industrial premises which used coal for heating and to power machinery. South Wales coal was delivered economically by coastal shipping and this continued. Several

limekilns had been built alongside the Rolle Canal, including one adjacent to Torrington station served by Reed's Siding – coal and limestone was now unloaded from ships into railway wagons at the railway quay at Bideford Goods for Reed's limekiln. Lime had a number of uses in North Devon beyond fertiliser spread on the fields and in fact was used as mortar in construction, and as part of the treatment of animal skins in the leather trade. From 1872 traffic carried on the Rolle Canal was transferred to the railway including coal for the town and its businesses, some ball clay was carted from Marland to Torrington station instead of the canal basin and some agricultural produce was carried.

In the 1880s H.W. Strong published in the 'North Devon Journal' a series of articles on local industries, a number of which were railway customers, summarised as:

In Bideford and Appledore were four collar factories employing 600 people, of which Vincent and Duncan's Collar Factory in Bideford employed 150. The materials brought in were mainly linen from Ireland, by sea, and calico from Manchester, by train. The final products of collars, fronts and cuffs, were packed in cardboard boxes carted twice a day to the station to be forwarded by train to wholesalers in London and Manchester.

Vaughan's Glove Factory at Torrington employed more than 600 people. The raw material was leather, often locally produced, skilfully converted into high quality leather gloves of many shapes, sizes and colours. Vaughan's produced their own

custom-designed cardboard boxes to pack their gloves. These were carted to Torrington station for conveyance to Nine Elms Goods station in London and thence their wholesalers Messrs Ormes Updale & Co. Vaughan's gloves were sold to customers in Britain, Europe, America and the British Empire.

From the train between Instow and Bideford there were good views over the Torridge estuary towards the Appledore Shipbuilding Yards. There were several shipyards with different owners, some with dry docks, engaged in the construction of new ships and repair of other vessels, all wooden at this period, and between them employing several hundred men. Many of their supplies came by sea, but some of their equipment and materials arrived at Bideford Goods station and were carted over Bideford Bridge to Appledore.

Soon after the railway opened to Torrington the Torridge Vale Butter Factory was established by Robert Sandford, using milk carted from local farms over a wide area. The factory produced not only butter but also clotted cream, and the extensive factory was surrounded by market gardens growing flowers, fruit and vegetables. Butter, cream, eggs and poultry were carted to Torrington station for loading into vans destined for markets in London, the Midlands and the North

At Torrington was the yard of Nathaniel Chapple, Chamois and Skiver Dresser. Here sheepskins, calf and other animal skins previously treated with lime, were processed and split into layers of chamois leather and glovers skins. These were supplied to

30250 again on a down train at Fremington Quay with two Maunsell coaches with what appears to be one through coach at the rear.

On 21 September 1954 E1R 0-6-2T 32610 arrives at Torrington with the 2.20pm goods from Halwill, comprising a LSWR brake third from Petrockstow for the clay workers, empty van, two loaded meat containers, and two loaded and sheeted clay wagons. In the absence of cranes on the line it would appear that the containers remained on Conflat wagons in a siding, loaded with meat probably at Halwill, and destined for Nine Elms yard where the containers were lifted on to lorries for delivery to Smithfield market. R.E.Tustin

With the establishment of a semi-automated milk depot at Torrington in 1944 milk was despatched in 3000 gallon tankers; previously it had been moved in churns. N 2-6-0 31840 is at Barnstaple Junction in September 1963 with a two milk tankers and a brake van. John Eyers, courtesy South Western Circle.

M7 30254 busy shunting at Bideford Goods in November 1961.

glovers in London, Worcester and Barnstaple, first being carted to Torrington station.

At Fremington was Mr Fishley's Pottery, producing a wide range of large pots from local clay. Some of the pots were sent to Cornwall by ship, but some also went by train .

The Marland Terra-Cotta, Brick and Stoneware Pipe Works manufactured products from clay dug from the adjacent pits employing some 75 men at this period. From 1880 bricks, pipes and terra-cotta products were sent down the narrow gauge line to Torrington station where it was transferred to standard gauge wagons. The distinctive white bricks are still found all over North Devon, and the high quality terra-cotta products went to customers all over the country. In the opposite direction coal for the machinery was sent up the line. Also ball clay from Marland was loaded into standard gauge wagons at Torrington, some of it at Bideford or Fremington into ships for export, some going to the Potteries.

In 1870 construction of the standard gauge Torrington Extension Railway began, with construction materials arriving by train until it opened in 1872. Over a period of seven months in 1880 the 3ft gauge Torrington and Marland line was completed. Not only were iron rails brought in by train, but also small steam locomotives, wagons, iron components for the repair and construction of vehicles, and machinery

for the workshops at Marland, the line having to be self sufficient for most needs. The distinctive wooden viaducts of the line were constructed from Baltic red pine, so it would appear that this was shipped to Fremington Quay and loaded on to trucks for the journey to Torrington, where a steam powered saw was employed at Staplevale Farm to cut the timber to size for the viaducts.

By 1909 the goods traffic on the Barnstaple Junction to Torrington line had several major features. South Wales coal was unloaded from coastal ships at Fremington Quay and distributed to a wide area of North Devon by train, although Bideford had its own supply by ship. Best steam coal for LSWR engine sheds was delivered under contract with Stephenson Clarke & Co, as mentioned in earlier chapters. Many other local goods included timber, livestock, meat, and other agricultural produce, gloves from factories at Torrington, pit-props cut in local woods, other cargoes landed at Fremington, and the produce of many small businesses along the line. Arriving by train was a wide variety of general merchandise from London and elsewhere required by local businesses and shops.

At Torrington there was considerable traffic exchanged with the 3ft gauge Torrington and Marland line. This included ball clay, Marland bricks and a variety of agricultural produce from the sidings along the line, employing a number of men at Torrington station

to shovel loads into standard gauge wagons, some of which were owned by the clay company. Some of this clay was loaded into ships at both Bideford and Fremington, for Liverpool, thence by canal to the Potteries, Europe and America. In 1898 the barque Henriette loaded 1,000 tons of ball clay for Wilmington, Delaware USA at Bideford Crossparks Quay, probably by shovelling clay down wooden chutes into the ship's hold at low tide.

Coal was transferred from standard to narrow gauge wagons at Torrington for the steam powered machinery at the clay and brickworks. There was also coal for domestic hearths, including that supplied by B.Read & Co., coal merchant at Bury Moor. Much of it was South Wales coal imported at Fremington Quay. Much of the mechanical engineering work for the clay company was carried out by Hodges Brothers of Exeter, and their machinery and supplies arrived in standard gauge wagons and vans for transfer at Torrington. When narrow gauge locomotives and rolling stock arrived at Torrington a South Western steam crane from Exeter was required to lift them off the well wagon on to the 3ft gauge line. No photographs of this at Torrington have yet to come to light, but there are photographs of 2ft gauge Lynton & Barnstaple locomotives being transferred by steam crane at Barnstaple Town.

The pattern of goods train services developed to cater for the traffic carried, as seen in the 1909 timetable: In the down direction were the 2.35am Goods & Mail from Exeter, 3.15am Goods from Exeter and 11.0pm Fast Goods from Nine Elms, arriving at Torrington at 5.55, 8.9, 9.52am respectively, together with the 8.45am Goods Barnstaple Junction to Fremington. Of these the 11.0pm from Nine Elms catered for the premium traffic, delivered to Nine Elms goods station in the early evening, and delivered by railway horse-drawn carts from Bideford and Torrington direct to customers soon after breakfast. Much goods traffic from the Midlands and the North ran down the Midland Railway route to Bath, thence the Somerset and Dorset to Templecombe, where it was transferred to South Western trains.

In the up direction the principal train was the 12.55pm Goods from Torrington to Nine Elms, known as the 'Up Market Goods', which conveyed local produce including livestock and meat to arrive at Nine Elms at 2.0am on an Express Goods from Exeter or at 5.5am on a later Goods. North Devon meat was carted through the streets of London ready for the early morning opening of Smithfield Market. There was also a 4.20pm Goods from Torrington to Exeter, and a 12.48pm Loco Coal when required from Fremington to Exeter. As we have seen a lot of traffic was also transferred at Templecombe.

There was more railway construction in North Devon with the Bideford, Westward Ho! and Appledore Railway opened in two stages, in 1901 and 1908. Although standard gauge it was separated from the South Western by the Torridge estuary with a terminus on Bideford Quay. Most of the construction materials were unloaded from ships at Bideford Quay, but the three Hunslet locomotives arrived from Leeds and four carriages from the Bristol Carriage Works arrived at Bideford Goods. The Bideford Bridge Trustees were concerned about the heavy load and insisted that the boilers were separated from the locomotives and that they were pulled by horses on wooden carriages over the bridge to the Quay. Likewise the carriages had to be separated from their bogies. When the railway closed in 1917 a temporary track was laid for the locomotives over Bideford Bridge.

An important railway commercial facility was the wagon weighbridge used for measuring the weight of a loaded wagon. Painted on the side of every open wagon was its tare, or empty weight. Subtracting this from the weighbridge reading gave the weight of the load, of coal, clay, etc, for which the customer was charged. The only two wagon weighbridges on our lines were at Fremington, 35 tons, and Bideford Goods, 17 tons. Every loaded wagon forwarded from stations on the line with coal or minerals was weighed individually, and a shunting engine was required to move them across the weighbridge although weighing was done accurately and quickly.

In 1913 another customer started to take supplies from Fremington Quay. At Exmouth Junction the South Western Railway established a concrete works, later modernised by the Southern in 1928, for the supply of a very large number of standard concrete components including platform walls, footbridges, station nameboards and prefabricated buildings. A vital ingredient of the concrete was sand, loaded on to barges on the shores of the Taw-Torridge estuary, shipped to Fremington Quay and loaded into open wagons for delivery. One such wagon was 8 plank DS 1693 'To work between Fremington Wharf & Exmouth Junction concrete works only'.

During World War One the line handled a large quantity of hay and timber traffic, much of it through Torrington station. At Bideford, the Ministry of Munitions, in conjunction with the munitions firm Kynocks put in a private siding about half a mile to the south of Bideford (New) passenger station and details of the various firms and traffic associated with it are given earlier.

About 1925 the Southern Railway ceased to use the harbour facilities provided on the wharf at the north end of Bideford Goods station, and the loading of limestone and coal from ship to railway wagons and export of clay was transferred to Fremington Quay. About this time there was some diversification of cargoes dealt with at Fremington, including sea-dredged sand and gravel from the estuary, sack

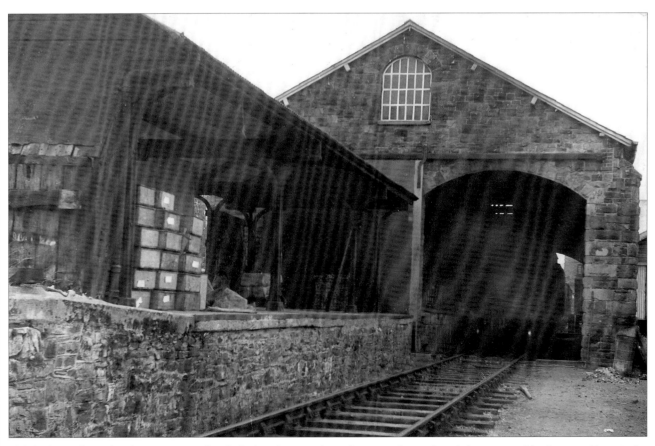

Bideford Goods station in June 1965 shortly before its complete closure and transfer of the men and business to Barnstaple. Although slightly longer the shed was otherwise identical to the one at Torrington. A.E. West, courtesy Mike King.

M7 30254 waits at Barnstaple Junction with the 9.27am goods departure, continuation of the 12.30am from Salisbury, the loaded vans being destined mainly for Bideford and Torrington.

loads of potatoes from Ireland, timber from the Baltic, and fertilisers.

Freight Traffic 1925-1964

Although Barnstaple to Torrington became a branch line for passenger services it remained the 'main' line for freight traffic. The 1932 pattern for principal freight trains altered little from 1909, with the 2.10am Freight and Mail from Exeter Queen Street arriving at Torrington at 6.29am, and the 10.10pm from Nine Elms arriving at 11.11am. Incidentally this freight was often double headed between Barnstaple Junction and Fremington. In the Up direction were the 12.45pm Freight from Torrington to Nine Elms, the 'Up Market Goods' also often double headed between Bideford and Barnstaple and the 4.52pm Torrington to Salisbury. The double-headed workings in the 1930s, involving Exmouth Junction Locomotive Duties 531, 533, enabled locomotives to shunt the busy yards at Fremington and Bideford Goods. There were also short workings between Torrington, Bideford Goods and Fremington to provide shunting engines for the goods yards.

Another feature was the gradual introduction of more vacuum braked wagons which facilitated the speeding up of Express Goods trains between Nine Elms and Exeter, initially with a 'fitted head' of vacuum braked wagons at the front of the train connected to the locomotive vacuum pipe. By 1936

the 'Tavy', the overnight fast goods to Plymouth with through wagons to North Devon, was formed entirely of vacuum braked vehicles, including the through vans to Bideford Goods and Torrington which were conveyed as tail traffic on the newspaper train from Exeter to Barnstaple Junction and thence on a passenger train.

On the Halwill line the two or three passenger trains were classified as mixed, with wagons attached to the rear of the train, the coach being parked on the main line whilst the locomotive shunted wagons in and out of the sidings. The 9.0am Mixed from Torrington to Halwill, arr.10.26pm, included an overnight Road Box, conveying small consignments from Exeter to all branch stations and halts. There was also a 10.30am freight from Torrington scheduled to shunt all the yards and sidings, if required. The formation included a Through Truck for small consignments Torrington to Halwill and eventually Nine Elms via Okehampton. It arrived at Halwill at 2.25pm, leaving at 3.6pm and collecting a coach at Petrockstow, becoming a mixed train from Dunsbear Halt to arrive at Torrington at 5.37pm for the clay miners who came to work on the 6.25am Torrington service. This was too late for the last Barnstaple line freight services, so most wagons had to wait until the next day to go forward, although vacuum braked vehicles could be attached to later passenger trains.

By the 1930s containers carried on 4 wheel Conflat wagons had been introduced, particularly for meat traffic. The yards at Barnstaple Junction and Bideford Goods were equipped with new 7½ ton cranes which could lift fully laden containers. This enabled remote rural slaughterhouses to load their carcasses directly into a container on a flatbed lorry, drive to Bideford Goods where the container could be craned on to a Conflat, and on arrival at Nine Elms the huge overhead cranes transferred the container on to another lorry for direct delivery of fresh meat to Smithfield market. At other stations the container on a Conflat could be loaded in the goods yard as a van, but transferred to a lorry at Nine Elms.

Southern Railway records during the 1930s give a very full description of how the freight traffic was handled. Many goods trains conveyed small consignments of all descriptions often packed in wooden or cardboard boxes, including goods sold in shops, such as tea, coffee, sugar, flour, cuts of fresh meat, pies, cakes, sausages, fruit, vegetables, ironmongery, china, books, glassware, cider and beer in bottles or barrels. These small consignments were loaded into box vans running to daily schedules similar to passenger services. A through truck conveyed small consignments from station A to station B only, such as that departing Nine Elms goods station in London at 9.32pm to arrive at Bideford Goods at 7.7am.

Stations with lower traffic levels were grouped together and served by a Road Box service, such as No.264 which left Torrington at 4.38pm calling at Bideford, Instow, Fremington and all stations to Crediton, to arrive at Nine Elms at 12.51am. A Road Box served specified intermediate stations where small consignments were loaded and unloaded by the guard whilst standing in the platform. At these stations such small consignments were securely stored in the booking office, or small lock-up shed on the platform when no staff were on duty. Road Boxes and Through Trucks ran overnight so that small consignments received in the afternoon could be delivered to customers soon after businesses opened next morning.

There were three principal long-distance goods trains conveying up traffic from Exeter to London and other important traffic centres, each of these being served by connecting services from North Devon, North Cornwall and Plymouth. The 7.38pm from Exeter Central arrived at Nine Elms Yard at 12.51am, the 8.37pm from Exmouth Junction Sidings arrived at 2.58am and the 10.40pm from Exmouth Junction Sidings arrived at 3.49am.

The 7.38pm Exeter Central was the fastest train for the London Markets, the 12.51am arrival allowing plenty of time for unloading and transfer of produce to Smithfield, Covent Garden and Billingsgate Market before they opened for business. This included Road Boxes from Torrington via Halwill,

Torrington via Bideford, from Bideford Goods, and other principal stations west of Exeter including Barnstaple, Ilfracombe, Plymouth, Padstow and Bude.

The first North Devon departure was a box van, scheduled as a Through Truck to Nine Elms, which left Torrington loaded with any available small consignments on the 10.30am Halwill freight, calling at Hatherleigh between 1.20 and 1.46pm to load more consignments, and more at Halwill Junction leaving there at 5.17pm on the Padstow to Templecombe perishable goods, to be transferred at Exeter Central.

Road Box service No.264 departed Torrington on the 4.38pm Eastleigh passenger train, arriving at Exeter Central at 7.1pm. A vacuum braked vehicle was scheduled and it called at almost all intermediate stations as far as Exeter to be loaded with small consignments, for Nine Elms only.

In 1930 Road Box service No.267, a vacuum vehicle to be loaded only for Nine Elms, departed Bideford Goods on the 1.55pm Nine Elms goods train (12.45pm from Torrington, arriving Nine Elms 2.58am). By 1936 it was speeded up to depart later, at 4.18pm, for a 12.51am arrival at Nine Elms.

The 8.37pm from Exmouth Junction to Nine Elms (arr.2.58am) was the continuation of the 12.55pm from Torrington, the 'Up Market Goods' which conveyed general traffic for London, livestock and perishable traffic

for the Midlands via Templecombe, for South of England via Salisbury, and Midlands, North and South east via Woking. By 1935 departure was 12.45pm. The formation of the 12.55pm from Torrington included Road Box services No.262 and 263 from Torrington to Nine Elms. No.262 ran Wednesdays Only, conveying returned empties to Nine Elms from Torrington and other intermediate stations to Copplestone, whilst No.263 was a vacuum vehicle to be loaded at Fremington and other intermediate stations for Nine Elms only. The 12.55pm from Torrington also conveyed Road Box Service No.265 to Exeter, and left Bideford Goods at 1.55pm with No.267 from Bideford Goods to Nine Elms, No.268 Bideford Goods to Plymouth Friary via Crediton, No.269 Bideford Goods to Bath & Bristol via Templecombe and No.270 from Bideford Goods to Basingstoke. The train also included a number of fully loaded box vans, through trucks to Nine Elms and elsewhere. A significant feature of the formation of the Up Market Goods were cattle trucks loaded at goods yards following periodic cattle markets. Most North Devon stations below Exeter had a market once a month, the livestock destined for centres like Maiden Lane in London. The 12.55pm Freight from Torrington arrived at Exmouth Junction at 7.58pm, and after re-marshalling left at 8.37pm for Nine Elms behind an S15 4-6-0 with a maximum load of 50 wagons, including livestock and perishable traffic

A mixed train of clay wagons, from Marland and Meeth, crosses Torrington viaduct in September 1956 with the 10.58 service from Halwill Junction. H.C. Casserley, courtesy R.M. Casserley.

Two wagons and a brake form the 5.50pm goods train from Bideford, at Anchor Wood in September 1958. M7 30247 came to Barnstaple Junction in November 1952. John Eyers, courtesy South Western Circle.

for the Midlands detached at Templecombe, for South of England detached at Salisbury, and for the Midlands, North and South east detached at Woking.

The 10.40pm from Exmouth Junction to Nine Elms (arr.3.49am) was a continuation of the 4.52pm freight from Torrington to Salisbury, with traffic for London etc. which was not ready for earlier trains. Its formation included Road Van service No.266 from Torrington to Plymouth which was transferred at Yeoford Junction.

The Down 'Tavy' 9.32pm Nine Elms to Plymouth in 1930 included Through Trucks to 15 principal destinations and six Road Boxes which served a total of another 49 stations en route. Every station west of Exeter was served, except for intermediate stations between Exeter and Barnstaple which had the 10.10pm from Nine Elms. To convey wagons to their final destinations involved not only goods trains, but also the overnight newspaper train Exeter to Barnstaple, a mixed train Barnstaple to Ilfracombe,

and several passenger trains. Overall this was a very sophisticated operation. The 10.10pm Nine Elms to Torrington called at Templecombe to detach Road Box workings Nos.33-36 to the Somerset & Dorset line, at Exeter detached Road Box working No.30 and other through wagons to Barnstaple Junction on a later stopping train. It shunted at Yeoford for almost an hour where wagons from the Plymouth line were attached, then ran almost non-stop to arrive at Barnstaple Junction at 8.7am. Departing here at 9.15am it

---

The Down 'Tavy'

9.32pm Nine Elms to Plymouth (1932)
In 1930 the formation included Through Trucks to 15 principal destinations and 6 Road Boxes which served a total of another 49 stations en route. Every station west of Exeter was served, except for intermediate stations between Exeter and Barnstaple which were served by the 10.10pm from Nine Elms. To convey wagons to their final destinations involved not only goods trains, but also the overnight newspaper train Exeter to Barnstaple, a mixed train Barnstaple to Ilfracombe, and several passenger trains. Overall this was a very sophisticated operation.

Detached at Exeter Central 3.20am Through wagon(s) thence 5.0am News Exeter Central (1.30am Waterloo) to Barnstaple Junction.
Barnstaple Junction arr.6.22am; Through wagon(s) thence 5.0am News Exeter Central (1.30am Waterloo) to Barnstaple Junction and 6.48am passenger Barnstaple Junction to Torrington.
Bideford Goods arr.7.7am; Through wagon(s) thence 5.0am News Exeter Central (1.30am Waterloo) to Barnstaple Junction and 6.48am passenger Barnstaple Junction to Torrington.
Torrington arr.7.29am; Road Box No.32 thence 5.0am News Exeter Central (1.30am Waterloo) to Barnstaple Junction and 6.48am Passenger Barnstaple Junction to Torrington.
Torrington arr.7.29am, serving 3 stations, Fremington, Instow, Torrington

Detached at Okehampton at 4.38am Road Box No.27, Ran to Okehampton on the 9.32pm, thence on the 7.48am to Bude.
Halwill Road Box No.287 from Plymouth dep. 8.7pm, also arrived at Halwill on 7.48am.
Halwill Consignments from both Nine Elms and Plymouth services for Hole, Hatherleigh, Meeth, Petrockstowe and Dunsbear. Transferred at Halwill (to the 10.46am Mixed to Torrington)

shunted every station and siding, except Bideford New, to arrive at Torrington at 11.11am. From Nine Elms it conveyed mainly fully loaded wagons and empties. By departure from Barnstaple Junction the formation included wagons from Salisbury, the Somerset & Dorset line, Exeter, Plymouth line which included empty coal wagons for Fremington Quay, empty cattle wagons, empty meat vans and containers.

During and after the 1939-45 war there were regular livestock specials of some 40 wagons loaded at Torrington for Maiden Lane in London and South Wales, trains of empty cattle trucks being worked from their base at Yeoford Junction. In the 1950s more livestock was loaded from Hole and Hatherleigh, Exmouth Junction sending an engine, usually an Adams 0-6-0 goods, with brake van and guard, to collect some 40 empty cattle wagons from Yeoford. On arrival at Halwill Junction the train was a split up and the crew worked three or four trips taking empties to Hatherleigh, loading a few at a time from the cattle dock, and returning to Halwill to berth the loaded cattle trucks. When all were loaded the complete train was marshalled and worked back to Exeter, where a more powerful locomotive was put on, although the guard sometimes worked right through to Templecombe or even Salisbury. These cattle specials had to be slotted into gaps between the regular scheduled trains. From the 1940s fertiliser and animal feedstuff traffic increased, offsetting declines in other commodities. Some of this came from factories and mills all over the country, but some was imported and packed into hundredweight sacks at ports such as Avonmouth. The Southern Railway encouraged this valuable traffic with stores in almost every goods yard for firms including Silcocks and Bibbys. Day to day unloading of railway vans and loading of farmers lorries was carried out by railway staff, who also performed all the clerical work, with a monthly visit from the local company agent to check the books and the stock.

By 1957 the freight services had changed little, although levels of traffic had declined. The 2.6am Mail & Freight from Exeter Central arrived at Torrington at 6.8am, and the 12.30am Freight from Salisbury, including wagons from Nine Elms and Feltham yard, arrived at 11.35am. In the up direction were the 12.45pm Torrington to Feltham SF Semi Fitted, the 4.15pm XF Express Fitted Bideford Goods to Nine Elms and the 5.25pm SF fitted Torrington to Nine Elms. Following the Western Region takeover of the Southern Region lines west of Salisbury in 1963 there was a review of the freight services which had become loss-making. The result was catastrophic with almost every goods station west of Exeter closed as from 7th September 1964, Bideford and Torrington surviving for only a further year.

The last timetable before passenger services and many freight services were withdrawn was 15th June 1964 to 13th June 1965, the diesel locomotives and units carrying four character train identifications. The only Exeter passenger services were the 7.4am Torrington-Exeter 2C79 and 4.19pm Exeter Central-Torrington 2C94. The self-contained passenger services between Barnstaple Junction and Torrington were all coded 2C94. These were a mixture of two and three car multiple units, single unit railcars of the 55000 series and coaches hauled by D6300 Type 2s.

The 2.6am Exeter General Mail and Freight 7C37, and 6.0am Exmouth Junction Freight 7C17 arrived at Torrington at 5.57am and 11.30am respectively , with 12.45 Torrington to Exeter Freight 7O24, 4.15pm Freight Bideford Goods to Exeter Central 6C11, and 5.25pm Freight Torrington to Exmouth Junction 5C03. Most of these were hauled by the NB Type 2s and disappeared when public goods services were withdrawn from Petrockstow,

Hatherleigh and Hole in 1964, and from Bideford, Bartletts Siding and Torrington in 1965. On the Torrington and Halwill line the mixed trains hauled by the diesels were coded 2C68, with freights 9C37, but passenger services were provided by single car multiple units although designated mixed trains. The Torrington-Dunsbear workmens service was a bus. No record has yet come to light of a 55000 hauling wagons.

After the closures of goods stations in 1964-65 and withdrawal of passenger services in 1965 there were usually two daily freight services. One left Barnstaple about 8.30am with empty clay wagons for Meeth and Marland, and milk tanks for Torrington if required. It returned to Fremington, and Barnstaple about 11.30am, and about 1pm left for Torrington to shunt the milk tankers in and out of the depot which could load only three at a time, departing about 3.30. Fremington Quay ceased to operate at the end of 1969, but the weighbridge was retained until 1979

In the 1970-71 Working Timetable the branch was regarded as a long siding and there were few locomotive-hauled trains at Barnstaple; most passenger services were provided by diesel multiple units. However the 4C15 03.00 Parcels and Freight from Exeter St David's arrived at Barnstaple Junction at 04.37, the 7C18 06.00 Freight and Milk Empties from Exeter Riverside arrived at Barnstaple Junction at 08.22. The locomotive performed shunting at Barnstaple Junction and was available for the trips to Meeth and Torrington, before being scheduled for the 6C24 16.40 Torrington Milk and Freight, arriving at Barnstaple Junction at 17.22 and Exeter St David's at 18.55. The milk tankers usually went forward to the London area and the clay to the Potteries, on Western Region services. East Yelland sidings saw very occasional use, but East Yelland Power Station itself closed in 1984.

There was another chapter in the freight story, already described, when in 1976 a large new purpose-built ICI fertiliser depot was opened at Torrington on the site of the goods shed and milk loading dock. Vans loaded with 50kg bags from several ICI factories delivered to the new Torrington depot, until the traffic came to an end in 1980. The milk depot was replaced by another on the former up platform, with a capacity to load seven tankers at a time, but the last milk traffic was forwarded in 1978. In September 1982 the last clay traffic ran.

By July 1965 the only surviving Torrington passenger service, to Barnstaple, was provided by two and three car multiple units and single unit railcars including W55026 on the 3.57pm departure. Incidentally the head code should have been 4C94." John Eyers, courtesy South Western Circle.

The majority of Bulleid coaches ran in fixed sets. They would normally stay in these formations throughout though they could be re-formed on a seasonal basis or change in response to traffic demands at any given time. These two Bulleid coaches in the up platform at Torrington in August 1958 are being readied while 41314 busies itself behind. A.E. Bennett, transporttreasury.

Chapter 11
Locomotives and Rolling Stock

Broad Gauge 1855-1877

A full account of the broad gauge locomotives and rolling stock is given in the North Devon Line by Nicholas and Reeve, Irwell Press 2010; this is a summary.

Brassey and Ogilvie took over the operation of the North Devon Railway from the Bristol & Exeter on 28th July 1855, using a variety of broad gauge rolling stock mostly second-hand, eleven were recorded in 1862. There were three new locomotives built at Brassey's Canada Works, Birkenhead; a 2-4-0 CREEDY and 2-2-2s YEO and DART. CREEDY worked the first train to Bideford on 2nd November 1855. A 2-2-2 TAW built by Robert Stephenson as a standard gauge locomotive was later converted to broad gauge by Stothert & Slaughter. TAW was derailed at Yelland after breaking a tyre on 4th January 1859, and was disposed of shortly afterwards.

When the South Western took over on 1st August 1862 the broad gauge locomotive situation was as follows:-
'Good Order (in service) CREEDY, DART, STAR
Fair Order (spare engine) YEO
Serviceable, but in store BARUM, TITE, VENUS
Not serviceable in store DEFIANCE, EXE
Derelict MOLE, DREADNOUGHT'
Brassey acquired 24 items of passenger rolling stock from the redundant Bristol & Gloucester Railway broad gauge stock. All these vehicles were passed on to the LSWR, together with 81 goods wagons, some of which had also come from the Bristol & Gloucester. After the South Western had extended its standard gauge services to Bideford in 1863 there was far less work available for the broad gauge rolling stock. This was principally coal from Fremington and the Crediton to Bideford mixed train, for which CREEDY was usually shedded at Crediton. To assist CREEDY the 2-2-2 DART was rebuilt as a 2-4-0 between 1867 and May 1868 at Barnstaple at a cost of £300, using parts supplied by Nine Elms works.

From 1870 just four engines, CREEDY, DART, YEO and STAR remained to cover the broad gauge services until April 1877 when the broad gauge was abolished north of Crediton. The North Devon Railway had engine sheds, with coal, water and turntables at Crediton, Barnstaple and Bideford, and substantial locomotive workshops at Barnstaple.

An LSWR minute of September 1876 recorded that the 3.10pm up goods was delayed due to the failure of CREEDY, Driver Hicks was at fault and fined 10 shillings.

Joseph Beattie Locomotives

The numerous classes of Beattie's standard 2-4-0WTs took over many passenger duties in North Devon after 1863; one was photographed at Bideford, No.196 involved in a collision at Fremington in 1869 and another, No.181, on a train at Crediton in 1880. In 1887-88, Nos.195, 196, 200 and 204 were working in North Devon and as late as 1894-95 Barnstaple shed had Nos.0257 and 0266, although they were scrapped shortly after.

Numerous examples of the different classes of Beattie 2-4-0 tender locomotives were employed over the years. When the Torrington extension opened in 1872 two of the first locomotives shedded there, working to Exeter and back, were 'Eagle' class No.30 VULTURE and 'Volcano' class No.89 SATURN with sister locomotive No.61 SNAKE working the line from the Exeter end. In 1872-73 the Yeovil-Torrington train was worked by Yeovil locomotives: 'Volcano' class No.84 STYX and 'Falcon' class No.25 REINDEER. The latter was joined on the roster by sister locomotive No.91 SPITFIRE in 1875-76. In the period of 1874-76 Exeter shed rostered all three members of the 'Eagle' class, Nos.27 EAGLE, 28 HAWK AND 30 VULTURE to work on the North Devon line.

The Ivatt workhorses came to Barnstaple shed to work the Torrington Branch in 1953 and were still there at the end. 41290 is in Bideford's down platform in January 1962.

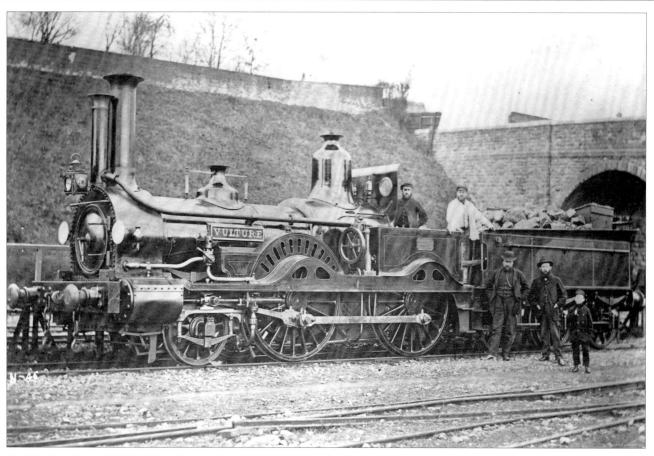

'Eagle' class No.30 VULTURE at Exeter Queen Street; it was shedded at Torrington when the extension opened in 1872.

Exeter's 4-4-2T No.489, an engine which worked to Torrington on a regular basis, at Exeter Queen Street.

Several classes of 0-6-0 goods engine were used on the line, including the 'Lion' class introduced in 1863. Among these by 1877-78 were No.3 TRANSIT and No.54 MEDEA. Standard Beyer, Peacock goods engines also appeared including a double-framed locomotive photographed at Eggesford in mixed gauge days and a single-framed locomotive at Bideford in 1922.

When the Barnstaple to Ilfracombe line was constructed as a light railway, a class of light 0-6-0 locomotives of a standard Beyer Peacock design was ordered for the line, the eponymous 'Ilfracombe Goods' engines. Those stationed at Barnstaple were likely to run to Fremington, Bideford or Torrington. In June 1881 Barnstaple shed had Nos.393 and 394, with No.300 away on repair; Ilfracombe had Nos.282 and 283, while No.394 lasted at Barnstaple until 1907. The Barnstaple shed complement in March 1878 was:
2-4-0 well tanks: 263, 298
0-6-0 Ilfracombe Goods: 300, 301
0-6-0 Single-framed Goods: 302
Two or three of the Barnstaple allocation over the years were outstationed at Torrington.

Adams Locomotives
William Adams succeeded William Beattie in 1878. He was an outstanding locomotive engineer, producing elegant, efficient and powerful locomotives for the South Western. Many South Western locomotives designed by William Adams worked in North Devon. The radial 4-4-2 tank engines were regular visitors from Exeter, and in April 1886 Nos.169, 170, 171, 480, 485, 491 and 493 were in use. No.524 was photographed on the Torrington turntable about 1891 and in 1901 No.489 of Exeter worked on a roster which took her to Torrington and Sidmouth on alternate days.

Most of the Adams 4-4-0 classes worked in North Devon at some time. In the late 1890s there were the mixed traffic 380 class, the 'Steamrollers', Nos.384, 385, 386 and 391 shedded at

Adams 4-4-2T 169, allocated to Exeter in 1886 and another regular on the line.

Barnstaple and Exmouth Junction. By 1905 Exmouth Junction was using Nos.0381, 0383 and 0384 in North Devon, and they remained in use until 1925. Earlier in the century T3 class locomotives Nos.564 and 567 were at Barnstaple in 1903, with Nos.571 and 575 at Torrington all working principal trains to Exeter. The 460 class of passenger locomotives, built in 1884, appeared in North Devon in the next century, with Exmouth Junction having Nos.0460, 0461 and 0462 in 1912. In later South Western days No 526 was shedded at Torrington

As we have seen, the Adams 460 class 4-4-0 locomotives were in use at Torrington in LSWR days, and in 1925 their numbers in North Devon were increased to also cover the ND&CJLR duties. In July and August 1925 Nos.0460, 0462, 0468, 0470, 0473, 0475 and 0476 were at Barnstaple with several at Torrington. Others recorded at Torrington were Nos.526 and 0474 and these elderly 4-4-0 locomotives worked services between Torrington and Halwill, and from Torrington to Barnstaple and beyond. These were not

the only Adams 4-4-0s to run on the ND&CJLR, since X6 class No.665 was photographed at Petrockstow, and No.666 at Hatherleigh They could cope well running chimney first with the one or two coach passenger trains, but goods trains on the 1 in 42 gradients were more demanding. Furthermore on arrival at Halwill Junction a complicated manoeuvre right across the station to the turntable and back had to be fitted in with trains on the Bude and North Cornwall lines. In the mid-1920s, the 460 class locomotives were more than forty years old, and as soon as replacements were found they were scrapped, between 1926 and 1928.

The Adams light 0-6-0 goods engines of the 395 class were regular visitors for many years, Exmouth Junction having ten of them in 1890. No.83 was photographed at Torrington about 1891; in Southern days No.0163 was recorded on a passenger train at Torrington and No.0397 at Barnstaple shed. Weight restrictions on the Torrington-Halwill line were severe, so when cattle specials were run from Halwill to Hatherleigh or Hole,

Adams 395 class 0-6-0 No.83 at Plymouth Friary shed; it was used on the branch for some years and can be seen at Torrington on page 167.

The beautifully proportioned LSWR Jubilee 0-4-2 mixed traffic locomotive came to North Devon in the late 1880s. No.539 was an early arrival and can be seen again at Bideford in the photograph on page 161.

A Beattie single framed rebuilt goods 0-6-0 with Drummond chimney, at Barnstaple shed with the crew and shunters posing for the camera.

Adams X6 class 4-4-0 No.665 is unusual motive power for this Halwill to Torrington train at Petrockstow station. The ex-LSWR railcar coach has been supplemented at this time by an ex-LSWR lavatory composite and was probably photographed here shortly after the line opened in 1925. These old but elegant locomotives were well liked and looked after at Barnstaple Junction.

X6 class 4-4-0 No.666 on a northbound freight at Hatherleigh in 1928. At this time the train would normally have been mixed.

O2 0-4-4T No.190 at Barnstaple shed in 1892. The class was permitted to work between Torrington and Petrockstow which implies that they did visit the line, although no photograph has yet come to light.

Exmouth Junction shed rostered one of the class if available, the tender providing greater water capacity than the Brighton E1R tanks which otherwise worked the traffic.

The numerous 'Jubilee' class of 0-4-2 mixed traffic locomotives of the late 1880s soon appeared in North Devon, an early arrival being No.539 photographed on a passenger train at Bideford in the early 1890s. In the Southern period, No. 628 and 637 were photographed at Barnstaple on goods trains.

The O2 0-4-4Ts were active on the Ilfracombe branch, but the SR 1932 Working Timetable authorised their use between Torrington and Petrockstow. The implication is that an O2 was given a successful trial, probably about 1926, but no record of this has come to light. About 1920 it was reported that Torrington shed normally had Adams 4-4-0 No.526 for Exeter services with a Drummond tank for local and shunting duties, and a second Adams 4-4-0 during the summer season. In March 1892 Barnstaple operated the following:

O2 class 0-4-4T: 190, 197
Ilfracombe Goods 0-6-0: 301, 324, 394
2-4-0WT: 209, 217
380 class 4-4-0: 384, 391
0415 class 4-4-2T: 483
A12 class 0-4-2: 547 (on loan)

South Western Railway Engine workings June 1919
This list of workings is not complete and a description of the trains involved has been added by the authors. Locomotives employed between Exeter and Torrington included various classes of Adams and Drummond 4-4-0s shown in the text.
LE = Light Engine

Drummond Locomotives
More than a hundred Drummond M7 class 0-4-4Ts were constructed and initially worked mainly in the London area, particularly on Waterloo suburban trains. However when electrification of these lines was gradually introduced from 1915 they became available for other duties and some arrived at Barnstaple to work on the Ilfracombe branch, No.25 being noted in 1919. The Drummond tanks, as they were known, worked in North Devon for almost half a century, in the 1920s and 1930s mainly on the Ilfracombe line, but also assisted the E1R 0-6-2Ts on the Barnstaple to Torrington line. Nos.36, 242, 250, 256, 377 and 668 were allocated to Barnstaple in 1933. Nos.23, 36, 42, 44, 247, 250, 321 and 670 were there in 1947 and Nos.30247, 30251, 30253, 30254, 30255, 30256, 30670 in 1959. By 1962 only two,

Exmouth Junction Duty 825

Exmouth Jct	5.35amLE		
5.40	Exeter	6.20	Goods & News
7.44	Barnstaple	8.13	Passenger
8.53	Torrington	9.25	Passenger
11.39	Exeter	11.45LE	
11.50	Exmouth Jcn	12.45pmLE	
12.50	Exeter	1.15	Passenger
3.35	Torrington	4.55	Passenger
7.18	Exeter	7.25LE	
7.30	Exmouth Jcn		

Exmouth Junction Duty 827

Exmouth Jcn	7.50amLE
7.55	Exeter	8.20 Passenger
10.48	Torrington	12.0 Passenger
2.1pm	Exeter	2.5LE
2.10	Exmouth Jcn	

Exmouth Junction Duty 834

Exmouth Jcn	2.5amLE
2.10	Exeter	2.35 Goods and Mail
8.15	Torrington	12.20pm Goods
7.40	Exeter	7.45LE
7.50	Exmouth Jcn	

Exmouth Junction Duty 836

Exmouth Jcn	5.15amLE
5.20	Exeter	5.40 Goods
12.47	Torrington	3.35pm Passenger
5.42	Exeter	5.50LE
5.55	Exmouth Jcn	

Torrington Duty 897

Torrington	7.25am Passenger
9.28	Exeter	11.17 Passenger
1.32	Torrington	4.0pm Goods
5.42	Barnstaple Jn	6.9 Passenger
6.40	Torrington	

Torrington Duty 898

Torrington	1.40pm Passenger
3.54	Exeter	5.48 Passenger
7.58	Torrington	

Barnstaple Duty 895

Barnstaple Jn	8.25am Goods
8.46	Fremington	
Shunt	6.30pm Goods
6.37	Barnstaple Jn	

L11 4-4-0 No.406 on the turntable at Barnstaple in the 1930s. Although primarily used on the line to Exeter *The Railway Observer* of 1937 reported that 'L11 and K10 4-4-0s had replaced M7s on the line between Barnstaple Junction and Torrington.'

M7 0-4-4Ts had gradually been drafted to North Devon as their work in London came to an end with electrification. Several were stationed at Barnstaple to work on the Ilfracombe branch but their duties extended to assisting the E1Rs on the line to Torrington. Indeed an M7 was allocated to Torrington shed in 1919 and they worked on the line to Barnstaple until 1963. No.250 at Barnstaple Junction in May 1935.

30251 and 30670, remained. In BR days the class had a number of duties on the Torrington line, including local passenger and goods trains, and yard shunting, and were the longest-serving locomotive class in North Devon. In 1957 M7 rosters included Torrington duty 588, and Barnstaple duties 576, 577, 578 and 580. M7s were not used between Torrington and Halwill.

The mixed traffic designs of Drummond 4-4-0 were widely used over the years. These were the 'Small Hopper' K10 class, 'Large Hopper' L11 class and S11 class, all of which started work in North Devon in South Western days, hauling passenger and goods trains between Exeter and Torrington. Following the 1925 timetable changes they appeared only occasionally on

passenger services, but remained in charge of goods trains. Exeter based goods engines regularly brought freight trains to Barnstaple and Torrington. S11 class 4-4-0 No.401 was photographed at Barnstaple Junction on a Torrington line freight train in the mid-1920s In the March 1937 issue of *The Railway Observer* it was reported that K10 and L11 class 4 4 0s had replaced M7s on the line; those noted included K10 No.389 and L11s Nos.134, 159 and 170. The locomotives used here by the Southern Railway included K10 class Nos.142, 153, 384, 387, 389 and 392, L11 class Nos.134, 159, 170, 175, 406 and 409 and S11 class Nos.39 and 401. The K10s were no more after 1948 and L11s similarly were gone after 1951; there had been no S11s either, since

1938, but four returned from the LMS in 1945 and found a few months work at Exmouth Junction.

The Drummond T9 'Greyhound' 4-4-0s worked in North Devon, with some reports of them on Exeter to Torrington goods trains in the 1930s. They did work some goods trains between Exeter and Barnstaple in the 1950s, with 30717 allocated to Barnstaple shed in 1952. Drummond's standard goods engines, the 700 class 0-6-0s, though absent from 1938, enjoyed a limited return from the mid-1950s, replacing 0395 0-6-0s. Both types may well have reached Torrington, but are not recorded in photographs seen so far. About 1930, following the introduction of the rebuilt 0-6-2T E1R class – see below – the small turntable

duties for the M7s included local passenger
and goods turns as well as yard shunting.
No.30247 had come to Barnstaple in 1931
and but for a brief ten months spell at Nine
Elms in 1952, saw out its days at the shed.
Withdrawn in October 1961, No.30247 is
seen here on a passenger train at Torrington
August 1953. R.K. Blencowe collection.

at Torrington was taken out and most of the tender locomotive duties taken over by tank engines. Barnstaple in March 1922 had:

    T1 0-4-4T: 68, 80
    O2 0-4-4T: 177, 216
    A12 0-4-2: 612, 616, 633
    460 4-4-0: 0460, 0472, 526
    X2 4-4-0: 586
    T3 4-4-0: 559
    X6 4-4-0: 658

The 'Brighton Bugs'

The legendary Col. Stephens had associations not only with the North Devon and Cornwall Junction Light Railway but also with the Callington line of the Plymouth Devonport and South Western Junction Railway (PD&SWJR) which opened in 1908 with

three new Hawthorn Leslie tank engines which performed well. Possibly influenced by the Col. Stephens link, in August 1926 the Southern Railway brought in the PD&SWJR 0-6-2T No.758 LORD ST LEVAN for trials on the ND&CJLR. The trials proved to be very successful, to the extent that tenders for six more were sought from Hawthorn Leslie. The Southern Railway under its Chairman Sir Herbert Walker was involved in heavy investment in the Southern Electric programme, far from the wilds of Devon. This reduced the funds available for new locomotives so although almost fifty years old, between 1927 and 1929 ten redundant ex-LBSCR E1 class goods/shunting 0-6-0Ts were rebuilt for the line as 0-6-2Ts. With new trailing pony truck, ex-N class spares from Woolwich Arsenal, and enlarged tanks they were reclassified E1R and have featured in the text a number of times already. The Southern Railway estimated a saving of £12,500 compared with the cost of new locomotives from Hawthorn Leslie. They were profoundly 'foreign' to the suspicious local crews and on arrival in North Devon were christened somewhat unkindly 'Brighton Bugs'. One retired driver declared that they were worn out before they arrived but this was untrue; they had been thoroughly refurbished and worked in North Devon for another thirty years. Initially eight of them, B95 later renumbered 2095, B96 later 2096, B124 later 2124, B135 later 2135, B608 later 2608, B610 later 2610, B695 later 2695, and B697 later 2697, were allocated to Barnstaple shed with a couple outstationed at Torrington. B94 later 2094 and B696 later 2696 mainly did banking at Exeter, though the bankers there for many years were 2124, 2135, 2695 and 2697.

Even with extended water capacity, the E1R locomotives could not run right through between Torrington and Halwill without replenishment of their tanks at Hatherleigh and, on the occasions when the water there was out of action, Adams 0-6-0 light goods locomotives had to be brought in to work the services. The E1R class locomotives were restricted to a load of sixteen loaded wagons, including the brake van, on the steeply graded section between Torrington and Marland, and twenty from Marland to Halwill.

The E1Rs otherwise monopolised all services on the Torrington to Halwill line, worked many services between Torrington and Barnstaple and very occasionally were to be found on the Ilfracombe line. When employed on the Barnstaple and Torrington passenger trains there were some complaints from passengers about the excessive fore-and-aft movement imparted to carriages at moderate speeds. This was hardly surprising considering that they were designed as goods locomotives,

but in 1936/37 five of them, Nos.2094, 2095, 2096, 2608 and 2610 were returned to works for re-balancing. On their return to North Devon these five were used for the Barnstaple and Torrington passenger trains, with the other three on the ND&CJLR or shunting at Fremington Quay and Bideford Goods. At this stage Torrington shed usually had two E1Rs and one M7, or sometimes three E1Rs.

32094, formerly 2094, was the first to be withdrawn in 1955 and 32105 the last in 1959. The new Ivatt 2-6-2Ts appeared in North Devon in 1953 and gradually replaced the E1Rs, after a working life of some 80 years. Unusually prolonged locomotive longevity due to specialised work was not unusual on the Western Division of the Southern, with the Adams radials at Lyme Regis, Beattie well tanks at Wadebridge and Hawthorn Leslie tanks at Callington famous examples.

Maunsell Locomotives

The new powerful N class 2-6-0s arrived in North Devon in 1925 and were employed mainly on the principal Exeter-Ilfracombe services inaugurated with the summer timetable. Barnstaple shed usually had several N moguls (Nos.A839, A841, A849 and A857 in 1925, Nos.1830, 1833, 1835, 1840 and 1848 in 1939; 31842 and 31843 in June 1959). The Bulleid light Pacifics took over the principal Ilfracombe services from 1945 but some Ns were still employed. In 1963-64 the 2-6-0s took over from the light Pacifics the goods train which arrived at Torrington about 11am, departing at 12.45pm, until the end of regular steam working on the line in 1964. Barnstaple shed by January 1947 housed only two types:

M7 0-4-4T: 23, 36, 42, 44, 247, 250, 321, 670
E1R 0-6-2T: 2094, 2095, 2096, 2608, 2610, 2696

Bulleid Locomotives

The West Country class were named after West Country cities, towns and localities, as you'd expect. The Southern Railway Publicity Department made the most of the opportunity and on 29th August 1946 the Mayor of Bideford Mr W.H.Chubb unveiled the nameplate of 21C119, later 34019, BIDEFORD at the station. The following day the Mayor of Barnstaple Councillor R.Berry unveiled 21C105, later 34005, BARNSTAPLE at Barnstaple Town station. It was not until 24th November 1949 that the Mayor of Torrington Alderman E.A.Holwill performed the ceremony for 34031 originally 21C131 TORRINGTON at the station. The Holwill family had long been associated with the North Devon Clay Company, and at the time the Alderman was the Manager there.

In 1945 the new Pacifics started working passenger trains between Exeter and Ilfracombe, and for many

30247 on the shed road at Torrington in 1953.

years had a regular turn on the Torrington line, Exmouth Junction Duty No.529. After working local passenger trains from Ilfracombe to Kings Nympton and back to Barnstaple Junction the 4-6-2 hauled the 11.23am passenger from Barnstaple Junction to Torrington, tender first, then the 12.45pm goods Torrington to Barnstaple Junction, and then the 5.8pm goods to Exeter (which had originated as the 4.15pm goods from Bideford). Following closure of Torrington shed in 1959 the 7.5am passenger train to Exeter was worked right through by a Pacific which had worked light tender first from Barnstaple, instead of an M7 which came off at Barnstaple where the mix had changed yet again by 1959:
M7 0-4-4T: 30251, 30253, 30254, 30255, 30256, 30671
Ivatt 2-6-2T: 41294, 41295, 41297, 41298, 41314.

Great Western Locomotives
Apparently in the 1950s, ex-GWR 0-6-0T No.3669 was photographed in the engine sidings at Torrington. Ex GWR 0-6-0Ts were occasionally used to shunt the sidings at East Yelland Power station. There are reports that ex-GWR 2-6-0s, regularly employed on the Barnstaple to Taunton line, also worked to Torrington in the mid-1950s

Modern Tank Locomotives
Starting with 41298 in July 1953 a number of LM Ivatt class 2 2-6-2Ts built for the Southern Region arrived at Barnstaple shed to take over duties on the lines to Torrington, first from the E1R 0 6 2Ts and then the M7 0-4-4Ts. Two or three were usually at Torrington until the shed closed in 1959. The following saw service in North Devon over the period 1953-1963: 41290, 41294, 41295, 41296, 41297, 41298, 41308, 41310, 41312, 41313 and 41314. After the Western Region took over the Southern Region Western Division in January 1963 these were gradually returned to the Southern Region, to be replaced by Western Region Ivatts 41208, 41210, 41213, 41214, 41216, 41223, 41224, 41230, 41245, 41248, 41249, 41276, 41283, the extra two replacing the last M7s. Barnstaple shed officially closed in November 1964 when the survivors were 41208, 41216, 41248 and 41249, but on 4th January 1965 41249 with two Bulleid coaches worked the 3.50pm passenger train from Torrington to Barnstaple, apparently the last timetabled steam-hauled train on the line.

The last steam train to traverse the ND&CJLR was the 'Exmoor Ranger' on 27th March 1965, of five coaches hauled by Ivatt 2-6-2Ts Nos.41291 and 41206, which ran from Halwill to Torrington and thence Barnstaple.

During the 1963-64 period BR class 4 2-6-4Ts and 4-6-0s from Exmouth Junction shed covered some diagrams previously covered by N 2-6-0s and West Country 4-6-2s. On one occasion in 1964 4-6-0 75022 worked the 12.45pm goods from Torrington. There were several sightings of 2-6-4Ts on this mid-day freight during 1964, including

80043. The 'last' steam trains to Torrington, on 12th September and 3rd October 1965, 'The Exeter Flyers', were hauled by 80039 and 80043, the train splitting at Barnstaple Junction into Torrington and Ilfracombe parts. By now these locomotives were allocated to far-off Templecombe, the nearest surviving steam shed

Diesel Locomotives and Units
On 7th May 1963 the first main line diesel locomotive appeared in North Devon when a North British diesel hydraulic Type 2 of the D6300 series, ran from Plymouth to Halwill, Torrington (where it promptly suffered a failure, prefiguring a life for the class that was nasty, brutish and short) Barnstaple and Taunton. Together with one, two and three car units the diesels began to replace the Ivatt 2-6-2Ts and N 2-6-0s, their duties declining following public goods station closures in 1964/65. Following withdrawal of passenger services to Halwill in February and to Barnstaple in October 1965 multiple units visited Torrington only for occasional rail tours, or special circumstances such as the Bideford Bridge collapse in 1968.

On one occasion the Barnstaple diesel shunter visited Torrington but the Type 2s dealt with the clay and milk. From 1971 there was more variety when diesel electric Sulzer Type 2s and hydraulic Hymek Type 3s also appeared, the latter being too heavy for the ND&CJLR south of Torrington. After the withdrawal of milk and clay

The E1R were rebuilds of the Stroudley 0-6-0Ts and were reconstructed in 1927-28 with additional trailing wheels. Ten were converted and came to the West Country to work out of Exmouth Junction and Barnstaple Junction sheds. At Exmouth Junction they were primarily used on banking work on the line up from St. David's station but at Barnstaple they were destined to monopolise the work on the line between Torrington and Halwill. 32608 was on shed at Barnstaple in July 1956. John Eyers, courtesy South Western Circle.

In 1950 five E1Rs were based at Torrington to work the services to Halwill Junction, 32095, 32096, 32608 and 32696. 2610 is seen at Torrington on a southbound train in September 1933 but by the end of the 1950s all had been withdrawn and replaced by Ivatt 2-6-2Ts

An undated view of E1R 32696 outside Barnstaple A box.

41224 arriving at Barnstaple Junction in September 1963 with empty stock which will form the 11.35am Torrington service. John Eyers, courtesy South Western Circle.

traffic there were several special locomotive hauled trains, as we have seen in Chapter Nine.

South Western Carriages

The first carriages used on the line were 4-wheelers, about 20-25ft in length with four or five compartments for first, second and third class passengers. There were brakes only on the engine and tender, and when braking the train the driver blew the whistle to alert the guard to screw down his brake in the brake or 'break' van. Goods wagons were sometimes included in trains of the early period. The South Western started building longer six wheelers in the late 1870s, vehicles of about 28-34ft with up to six compartments, and these more modern vehicles were soon employed on the prestigious through services from Waterloo, where there was competition from the Great Western. About this time the distinctive South Western salmon pink and umber dark brown carriage livery was introduced. These six-wheelers can be seen in a number of Victorian and Edwardian photographs and lasted on the line until about the grouping.

The South Western started building bogie carriages in the early 1880s. The first were 42 to 46ft long, with arc roofs with up to seven compartments, whilst in the 1890s 48ft vehicles were introduced, some of which boasted the luxury of lavatories adjacent to some compartments. During a six hour journey between Waterloo and Torrington lengthy stops at Salisbury, Exeter and Barnstaple had been necessary for the passengers to use the station toilets. At this stage there appeared the 'brake tricomposite' coach which boasted first, second and third class compartments, together with a brake and luggage compartment. This was an ideal vehicle for through traffic between Waterloo and the West Country branches. In the 1900s some 56ft versions were also built, and tricomposite brake No.847 has been restored at the National Railway Museum at York, a unique South Western carriage. Non-corridor bogie stock, sometimes rebuilt, could still be seen in traffic as late as the 1950s, such as three-coach set No 126 was still in use at Torrington as late as 1954.

Corridor stock arrived in the mid-1900s with several trains built specifically for the West of England expresses. The coaches were 52, 54 and 56ft long with side corridors and compartments, except for the dining cars which were saloons with distinct clerestory roofs. Out of season the Torrington portion of Waterloo expresses was a corridor tricomposite either by itself or paired with a corridor third brake, the dining car running only as far as Exeter. However, in the summer season whole North Devon corridor expresses were run, with four or five coaches for Torrington, including the dining car, the Ilfracombe coaches being detached at Barnstaple. Second class disappeared during the Great War but both the earlier wooden-panelled and later Ironclad corridor stock made appearances on the line for most of the Southern Railway period. After the 1925 timetable changes the dining cars ran through to Ilfracombe and not Torrington.

For much of the 1920s and 1930s former LSWR coaches were used on local trains at Torrington, augmented by some ex-LBSCR coaches and a LCDR van. Many of these had been rebuilt on longer underframes by the Southern Railway. The Torrington and Halwill service was provided by an ex-LSWR railmotor coach No.361 with its distinctive gates, whilst the Torrington and Dunsbear train for clay workers was an ex-LSWR corridor brake third in later years.

Maunsell Coaches

As new Maunsell corridor stock became available it replaced the older South Western corridors on the principal expresses. The olive green coaches were 59ft long and comprised the full range of first, third, composite, brake and restaurant coaches, the brake composites being the regular Torrington

In 1959 Barnstaple had five of these Ivatt class 2 locomotives, 41294, 41295, 41297, 41298 and 41314. Two or three were based here at Torrington shed through the 50s and 60s and worked primarily along the ND&CJLR but duties also included passenger and freight turns to Barnstaple.

vehicle of the Atlantic Coast Express. A 1930s period photograph at Instow shows two Maunsell through coaches, one with ACE destination board behind a three coach ex-LSWR set.

Maunsell PMVs were often in use for mail, newspaper and other traffic, and appear in many photographs.

Bulleid Coaches
After the Second World War Bulleid corridor coaches in the familiar Southern green livery appeared. The body length was 64ft 6in and there was again a full variety of types. Following South Western and Southern practice there were a number of 2, 3, 4 and 5 coach sets in addition to the individual vehicles such as the ubiquitous brake composite which usually sufficed for the weekday 'Atlantic Coast Express' to Torrington. But on Sunday 24th June 1962 typically the 10.30am from Torrington to Waterloo consisted of a five coach Bulleid rake, attached to an Ilfracombe service at Barnstaple. In the 1960s Bulleid brake composites were used between Torrington and Halwill.

British Railways Coaches
British Railways Mark 1 coaches began to arrive in the mid-1950s on Waterloo to Ilfracombe services, but in the early 1960s occasionally replaced Bulleid coaches to Torrington. However between 1965 and 1982 Mark 1s were the usual coaches for locomotive-hauled excursions.

Wagons
For freight services the usual variety of wagons were used. Numerous open wagons carrying coal and clay were seen at Fremington, rakes of cattle trucks were employed on specials at Torrington, and vans of all descriptions were used for Road Box services and in later years deliveries of bags of fertilizers. From the 1940s the milk tanker wagons served the depot at Torrington, and flat wagons were used for the conveyance of meat containers. Bartlett's Siding at Bideford was the destination for petrol wagons for Shell and British Petroleum unloading at the depots there, and the odd tar wagon took away the produce of the gas works.

In 1893 the North Devon Clay Co. owned nine standard gauge wagons, which could get no closer to the works than Torrington. In the 1920s they hired about 30 10 ton open wagons, painted in their own livery, to enable them to quote cheaper rates for trips to the Potteries. However the grease fed axle boxes sometimes overheated, so they were restricted to the Marland to Fremington run.

Other unusual wagons seen in North Devon were 8 plank opens stencilled 'To work between Fremington Wharf & Exmouth Junction Concrete Works Only', carrying sea-dredged sand.

Above. **In the years running up to closure of the line steam was replaced by single unit railcars and here at Torrington in 1963 one waits to depart for Halwill Junction.**

Top right. **One of the short-lived North British Type 2 diesel-hydraulics, D6306, waits to depart from Torrington with a train for Barnstaple in September 1964. R.E. Tustin.**

Bottom right. **Torrington in September 1954 and LSWR 3-set 126 (previously LSWR set 26) - once a 4-set including a pair of 50ft composites between the two 56ft brake thirds to SR diagram 126 (appropriate in the circumstances!). In 1935 the two 50ft coaches were removed and a 58ft rebuilt LSWR composite on a standard SR underframe took their place, to SR diagram 285. Coaches are SR nos. 3066 and 3067 for the brake thirds, 4685 for the composite. The set was withdrawn in July 1955 but the composite got a reprieve and was downrated to all third S164 in October 1955, lasting in set 410 until July 1957. R.E. Tustin.**

Not quite the original Southern Railway sign (see cover) SOUTHERN RAILWAY TORRINGTON STATION, but a fine attempt at replicating the style of Exmouth Junction concrete works.

Chapter 12
The Route Today
All photographs George Reeve taken 18 September 2014

After closure in 1982 there was an unsuccessful proposal to extend Exeter-Barnstaple trains to Bideford but funding was not available. The North West Devon Railway Preservation Society was formed to preserve the branch but by 1984 it was clear that they could not afford the purchase price. The tracks were lifted in 1985-86 and the trackbed between Barnstaple and Bideford sold by British Railways to the County Council, for much of it to be converted to a foot and cycle path. Now a new generation was able to see the magnificent scenery of the Taw-Torridge estuaries which had been a wonderful feature of the railway line. The 'Tarka Trail' was established in 1987 and runs for 30 miles from Wrafton station on the Ilfracombe line by way of Barnstaple, Bideford and Torrington to Meeth.

Railway enthusiasts had hoped that at a future stage the railway might be re-instated between Barnstaple and Bideford, with train services between Exeter and Bideford. Despite protests the Devon County Council built the Barnstaple Western By-pass in 2005-7 blocking the line just beyond Barnstaple station, although the level of the road was sufficiently high to bridge a re-opened line if the cost of a new bridge could be found. With the recent renaissance in railway travel and re-opening of lines today the decision might have been different.

Fremington Quay Cafe

From Barnstaple the Tarka Trail retains a number of features of railway interest including the Fremington Quay Cafe accommodated in replica station

Fremington Quay, first stop out of Barnstaple and the site now turned over for publice use as a cafe with glorious views across the estuary.

A look along the new cafe decking. To the left is the up platform with all buildings now gone. The present owners, or indeed the Council who restored the site, have recreated the signal box and may well have used original parts – it is certainly a good replica.

Parts of the original down building have also been used for the new café and shop.

It almost passes for the original but not quite – still, a lovely evocation of the box.

From their web site…*Paul and Charlotte would like to welcome you to The Fremington Quay Cafe. We are located overlooking the River Taw and The Tarka Trail. Fremington Quay Cafe is a family run business offering delicious wholesome food, much of which is made on the premises by us or supplied by local bakers, butchers and growers. The Cafe is located in a picture-perfect spot on the River Taw with the Tarka Trail running past our door. We are the perfect spot to pause for refreshment if you are walking or cycling from Barnstaple to Bideford on the Tarka Trail and we have parking space for those visiting us by car. The Cafe itself is in the old station building which served the quay and has been sympathetically renovated. The immediate area surrounding the cafe is a haven for wildlife and a great spot to visit if you enjoy seeing wild flora and fauna. Fremington Quay, Barnstaple, North Devon, EX31 2NH. www.fremingtonquay.co.uk*

Looking back from the iron bridge which crossed Fremington Pill.

Above and below. The tide is out at Fremington Pill and nothing has changed much from closure save the removal of the boarded footway and some new railings on the Iron Bridge.

buildings and signal box. A history and heritage display features photographs and information about the old railway port including reminiscences of the last station master Mr Harold Mock, who assisted with the writing of this book.

Instow Signal Box

Moving on, past the site of the demolished East Yelland Power Station (1955-1984) there is the short Instow tunnel before the Tarka Trail reaches Instow signal box. Opened by the LSWR about 1873 for the level crossing, Instow signal box remained in use until 1982. The signal box and its equipment was threatened with demolition but local people and enthusiasts successfully lobbied for its preservation and it was the first British signal box to be designated a listed building. It has been lovingly restored to its Southern Region condition of the 1950s, and incorporates its 12 lever frame, block instruments regulating the single track sections each side and gate wheel, though the original gates were removed in the 1970s. Replacement gates have been installed, but they do not swing across the road. This is a unique heritage building open to the public; signal boxes survive on preserved railways but are not normally accessible when working, with a signalman on duty. Initially there was a preservation group for the signal box, but now it is part of the Bideford

Railway Heritage Community Interest Company. Subject to availability of volunteers the signal box is open to visitors on Sunday and bank holiday afternoons.

South along the bank of the Torridge estuary the trackbed passes under the high level bridge opened in 1987 taking the A39 truck road over the Torridge estuary with sufficient headroom for ships navigating the estuary up to Bideford Quay on the opposite bank.

Indeed on some days there are views of coastal vessels at the quay being loaded with ball clay for export, and on other occasions the SS Oldenburg taking visitors to Lundy Island. On approaching Bideford there is an extensive housing development, Ethelwynne Brown Close, between the Tarka Trail and the estuary. This was the site of Bideford's first railway station between 1855 and 1872, then developed into the extensive Bideford

Instow's replica Totem in Western Region umber.

Charmingly, replica gates have been constructed across Marine Parade. The magnificent signal box is Grade II listed with the interior, including the lever frame, returned to original condition.

Above. To give the platform an air of realism someone has carefully placed some milk churns beside the original iron railings.

Left. The lattice post upper quadrant down home signal.

Below. Instow's signal box nameboard.

The 'up' course of the path with the box to the right; any one of the succession of walkers, if they notice it at all, might wonder at the origin of the small square platform – the signalman stood on it to exchange tablets.

A look back across the former goods yard. From the Instow Signal Box website: *Instow signal box has guarded the road crossing at Instow since 1874. It was built by the London and South Western Railway and is classified as their Type 1 box. The passenger service through Instow ceased in October 1965, with the line then only used for milk traffic from Torrington and ball clay traffic from Meeth. Rationalisation set in and the signal box only survived because of the busy level crossing and the fact that it was regarded as an operational half way point between Barnstaple and Torrington. The down loop in the station was removed in 1968 together with the small siding, and all signals were dismantled except for the 'down home', 'up starter', and the two distant signals, the 'up' one being the long-lived ex-LSWR lower quadrant arm on a wooden post. In the never-ending quest for manpower savings, BR began replacing conventional level crossings with automatic barriers and flashing lights and, as Instow's turn loomed, protests arose in the village about possible dangers to elderly people, especially from local residential homes. Nevertheless, conversion work started at the beginning of January 1979, with gates and signals removed and four sets of flashing red and amber lights mounted around the crossing. However, just three years later in 1982, the freight traffic declined, the line was closed completely and the box was threatened with demolition. The villagers came to the rescue and the Instow Box Emergency Restoration Fund came into being. IBERF managed to persuade the local authority to successfully recommend to the Department of the Environment that the box become a listed building (Grade II), thus thwarting any further attempts to demolish it or alter its outward appearance. With the purchase of the trackbed for what was to become the Tarka Trail, Devon County Council also became owners of the signal box, but immediately showed interest in preserving its heritage. During 1985 contractors lifted the track through Instow and removed the flashing lights, but the section of track across the public highway remained intact with the unsightly yellow box on it being tarred over. So that is why the signalbox is still with us today. The box eventually became under the control of BIDEFORD RAILWAY HERTITAGE CENTRE and is opened on occasional Sunday afternoons during the high season, subject to the availability of volunteers. The interior of the box contains the original lever frame and fittings, which have been reconnected to one of the reinstalled signals. The large wheel that was turned to operate the level crossing gates also remains. The décor of the box is just as it was when the line closed to traffic. In 2003 Instow Signal box received the 2003 CARILLION RAIL AWARD at the National Railway Heritage Award ceremony. www.bidefordrailway.co.uk/instow/instow-signal-box*

The original up side station buildings demonstrating the two stages of development; the rendered portion was a small goods shed.

A view across the Torridge Estuary at Appledore.

The rail-built down starting signal.

Although the lower photograph has already been produced on page 46 and 47 we thought it would be interesting for readers to do their own bit of detective work and see what remains today in the upper photograph.

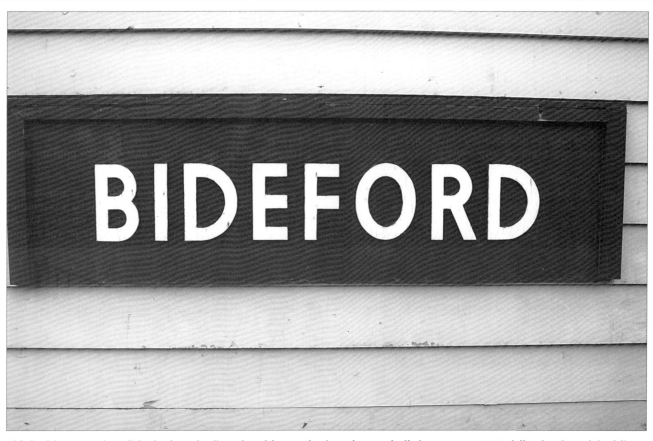

Bideford box was demolished when the line closed but enthusiasts have rebuilt it (see page 278) following its original lines: *The original Bideford signal box was demolished in 1970 but we built a replica of it in 1991. It's exactly the same apart from not having a chimney breast. In 2004 we installed a lever frame together with related signalling fittings so you can still pull the levers and imagine you're letting a train through!* www.bidefordrailway.co.uk/bideford/signal-box

Goods station which closed in 1964. The Tarka Trail now leads into the site of Bideford station, open between 1872 and 1965, and used for special passenger trains up to 1982.

Bideford Station

From the platform of the station is a splendid view right along the long Bideford Bridge. Much of Bideford station built on the hillside below Springfield Terrace and the Royal Hotel below is intact though the girders of bridge No.117 were raised in 1986 to allow full height road vehicles to pass up Station Hill below. Bridge No.119 was similarly altered in 1974. As Devon County Council started to develop the Tarka Trail it became apparent that some preserved items would be welcome at Bideford. The Bideford Railway Station Group laid two tracks through the platforms south from the raised bridge No.117 converging to a single track which terminates at Nutaberry Hill Bridge, No.119. After variously serving as bank and restaurant the 1872 stone station building was renovated and painted in Southern green, and was later used as offices for the 'North Devon Area of Outstanding National Beauty and Biosphere Service'. A replica 1872 signal box has been built on its original site on the up platform. On the tracks between the platforms are a goods brake van, passenger luggage van, BR

Mark 1 coach used for catering, and a Planet diesel, all completely or partially restored. From 2004 there have been some short train trips, subject to availability of rolling stock. Now run by the Bideford Railway Heritage Community Interest Company, together with Instow signal box, Bideford station is open to visitors.

The Tarka Trail resumes on the trackbed south of Bideford station. On the left soon after bridge No.119 is the commercial area of Bideford East-the-Water, now Kynocks Industrial Estate formerly served by Bartlett's siding, while the Torridge estuary is to the right. Here navigation is restricted to the small craft able to navigate through the arches of Bideford Bridge, including for some 40 years barges running to and from the Rolle Canal. The trail crosses the Torridge on long iron

The grand frontage of the Royal Hotel from Barnstaple Street.

The canopy at Bideford may have gone but the main down side building remains, renovated by local enthusiasts. *The station buildings next to the signal box were demolished in 1970 but the building on the other side of the line survives to this day. After the passenger service finished in 1965 as part of the Beeching cuts, it was first used as a bank, then a restaurant and finally as Devon County Council's management offices for the Tarka Trail. It is privately owned and is now empty awaiting a new use.*

Looking towards Torrington with some boundary gates and a foot crossing. To the left are some new cottages built on what was waste land; in the background is the rail-built advance starter signal.

The Royal Hotel's second floor access to the platform, still used by residents today.

Bideford's restored signalbox.

The impressive Springfield Terrace, which also had direct access to the station platforms.

Probably best described by the enthusiasts themselves… *Our train on our opening day on 15th August 2004. The train was seen off by the Mayor of Bideford, accompanied by a pipe band. Many passengers enjoyed the day, as they did over subsequent operating seasons. Our train consists of two items: an 0-4-0 Planet diesel shunter and a BR brake van. After restoration to operational condition, and the acquisition of appropriate permissions to run a train service, we commenced running our train in 2004 over our short line southwards from the station. The service ran on occasional weekends until it had to be withdrawn following a serious act of vandalism. The opportunity has been taken to subject the diesel shunter and brake van to extended maintenance so that they can be returned to the standard achieved on our opening day. Work progresses on the brake van early in 2013. The roof has been rebuilt and recovered and work is now concentrated on replacing rotten vertical planking.*

Above. The station approach road and taxi rank.

Left. The steps in the corner originally had an awning and led down from the up side platform) to the main road opposite the Royal Hotel.

Below. The plate girder bridge over Torrington road.

Torrington station and station masters house. The Tarka Valley Railway Group is now in residence, having received planning approval in March 2013 for the first phase of its plans to restore a steam railway along the valley of the River Torridge: *Attempts were made to rescue the line at the time (1982) but these sadly failed. Torrington station itself however is still remarkably well preserved with most of the main buildings still intact and serving as the Puffing Billy pub and restaurant. Both 'up' and 'down' platforms are also still in place, as is the original coal loading bay, albeit heavily overgrown. The Group was set up in July 2008 by a small group of likeminded individuals and local support was quickly achieved and a strong membership base was soon established. Whilst the planning process has taken a vast amount of effort behind the scenes, visible signs of progress were soon evident on site. Two panels of track were added to the original track in the platform and a new temporary buffer stop was installed at the end of the platform. The railway has been fenced off from the Tarka Trail ensuring the safety of all involved. The 'Thursday Gang' of volunteer members has restored the 'clay hood' wagon and work*

is now under way on the brake van. The BR Mk1 coach is undergoing heavy restoration and this will eventually be available for passenger carrying duties and will be air and vacuum braked. The Fowler 0-4-0 diesel-mechanical locomotive 'Progress' which spent most of its working life at the Peters Marland clay works was kindly donated to the group and has been repaired and refurbished to operational condition. Eventually it is planned that steam power will return to Torrington and several possible locomotives have been identified as suitable for use on the line.

Landcross Viaduct, bridge No.121, then runs through the short Landcross Tunnel with a small chapel on the hill above. Near here at Annery is the tidal limit of the Torridge.

Annery

Near the tidal limit of the Torridge estuary was the Sea Lock which is now undergoing restoration, a small shipyard and a pottery. Cargoes were transferred here between barges which came up from Appledore Pool and the tub boats which were horse-drawn in trains of six along the Rolle Canal. From Annery the canal was at a level higher than high tide and lower than the railway but a mile or so south the upper and lower levels of the canal were joined by an inclined plane where tub boats were transferred between levels. The upper level was 43 feet higher than the lower and the tub boats were fitted with four wheels and drawn up the incline powered by a water wheel. From the site of the inclined plane the railway followed the upper level of the 1825 Rolle Canal for about 1½ miles.

The Tarka Trail, following the former railway, then diverged from the flat canal bed and dropped into a dip and then back up again. The Torridge is crossed three times on masonry viaducts and there are views of the splendid Rolle Canal aqueduct over the river, subsequently converted into a private drive to Beam House. The aqueduct shows the level of the canal between the top of the inclined plane and the terminus basin at Torrington. The Beam Aqueduct was described by Henry Williamson as the birthplace of the otter, Tarka in his famous book.

Above. **The Umberleigh parcels cart and,** *below*, **the converted canopy at Torrington.** *The first phase of the extension is to extend the line just over 200 yards to the first overbridge with two sidings approximately 100 yards and 20 yards long alongside the Tarka Trail. This will provide sufficient length of track to start running short brake van rides. The sidings will provide storage space for rolling stock and trans-shipment facilities for the movement of stock onto or off the site. The Trail will be refurbished and a fence erected between it and the railway. Further phased extensions would see the line extend some half mile up the valley with restoration of Torrington's unique signal box, stores shed, permanent way trolley shed and platelayers' hut part of the project. The old signal post and lighting post which are still standing will also be refurbished for future use – some emergency work has already been completed. The line from Barnstaple to Torrington was engineered to a high standard and the track bed of the railway has been preserved generally intact, largely thanks to the presence of the Tarka Trail cycle and walking path. The Group is working closely with Devon County Council's Coast and Countryside Service to ensure the integrity of the Tarka Trail, and although there are some relatively minor engineering problems to be overcome further along the line, the establishment of an operating steam railway is perfectly feasible.*

Much work remains to be done before the sound of steam is once again heard echoing along the valley, but with the support already garnered and interest in the project growing both locally and nationally, the Group is very optimistic of the future. With the granting of planning approval the Group is now working hard on fundraising and preparation for the construction work. New members and volunteers are urgently needed to help in this exciting project. Enthusiasm rather than experience is required as we have a wide range of jobs to be done! Please get in touch via this website, or come and see us on an open day or a Thursday - you are assured of a very warm welcome. Tarka Valley Railway, Torrington Station, Station Hill, Great Torrington, North Devon, EX38   8JD www.tarkavalleyrailway.co.uk

Following the third viaduct the Tarka Trail climbs up a relatively steep incline, under a bridge and into Torrington station.

Torrington

Following the withdrawal of railway staff at the station the attractive stone building was sold and the new owners converted it into the 'Puffing Billy' restaurant which remains open for business. In 2008 the Tarka Valley Railway Group was formed with the object of establishing a heritage railway in conjunction with the restaurant, and a short length of track has been laid in the former up platform. Here the group

have a BR Mark 1 coach, a BR brake van, an open (clay hood) wagon and the 1945 Fowler diesel locomotive PROGRESS, which spent its working life at the Marland Clay Works. In 2013 the group gained planning permission to relay almost 270 yards of track parallel to the Tarka Trail, towards Bideford. The building first used as a fertiliser depot remains in the former goods yard.

The North Devon and Cornwall Junction Light Railway section

Leaving Torrington station under the A386 bridge the ND&CJLR section of the Tarka Trail continues over the

Torridge on the 1925 steel viaduct and up the valley for several miles, following the undulating countryside. The lack of habitation along the route explains why two passenger trains a day were sufficient for public services. The sites of the halts at Watergate and Yarde are marked by the remains of the concrete platforms, with the distinctive block of houses built at Yarde for clay workers. At Dunsbear Halt and Petrockstow station only the remains of the platforms survive, and between the two may be found the site of the siding running into the Marland clay works, which still operates. After Petrockstow the Tarka Trail passes the

The up side platform at Torrington.

Above. The BRMk1 coach stabled in the up platform.

Left. The 0-4-0 diesel PROGRESS. From little acorns...

Two relics of Exmouth Junction concrete works. The pub signat Torrington is in a long and noble tradition of thoroughly mangled images of locomotives, so that they look like nothing that ever existed. PUFFING BILLY itself of course came a century or so before this weird vaguely Maunsellish amalgam with its collapsing front wheels. Jesting aside – the pub, at the time of writing is awaiting new management.

closed site of the Meeth clay works, which in 2013 was acquired by the Devon Wildlife Trust, and ends at the platform remains of Meeth Halt next to the A386 road.

From here on access to the overgrown old line is limited. Hatherleigh was the only ND&CJLR station to avoid demolition, was sold after closure, and after extensions now forms the Old Station House. The site of the demolished Hole station has been developed into the Hole Station Campsite. On the B3218 road signs advise Halwill Junction but the station area has become an extensive housing development.

Top and middle. The mouldering remains of Watergate, the first halt on the Devon and Cornwall Junction Light Railway. The Exmouth Junction concrete works components are still there to be found, from the platform supports to the fencing.

Yarde, identifiable from the former clayworker cottages and a magnificently weed-colonised platform.

On the Tarka Trail; below, the original stone-built platform barely visible under the ivy.

The pleasant little station building at Petrockstow has sadly disappeared but, below, the original building of Silcocks, the animal feedstuffs supplier, remain in private use.

Left. Meeth Halt, a remarkable survivor. Some dear soul has even put up a station sign. Below, the building renovated and acting as a shelter for walkers and cyclists.

Top right. The original 'office' with notice board and map.

Right and below. Readers may wish to make their own comparisons of R.C. Riley's photo of 1956

Chapter 13
Appendices
ENGINE WORKINGS
for
PASSENGER and FREIGHT TRAINS
WESTERN DISTRICT JUNE 1953

BARNSTAPLE DUTY No. 574.
2 P.T. (M.7 Class).

—	Loco. Yard	6.35 a.m.	‖
6.40 a.m.	Barnstaple Jc.	6.50 a.m.	P
7.24 a.m.	Torrington	—	

C—Shunting 7.35 a.m. to 7.55 a.m.

—	Torrington...	8.10 a.m.	P
8.41 a.m.	Barnstaple	9.25 a.m.	
		(A.N.R.)	
9.31 a.m.	Fremington	—	

F—Shunting 9.30 a.m. to 11.30 a.m.

—	Fremington (B)	...11.37 a.m.	F
11.45 a.m.	Instow (C)... ...	...11.51 a.m.	F
12. 2 p.m.	Fremington (D)	...12.32 p.m.	F
12.40 p.m.	Barnstaple Jc.	**	‖
**	Loco. Yard	—	

SATURDAYS EXCEPTED.

**	Barnstaple Jc. Loco. ...	2.45 p.m.	‖
2.50 p.m.	Barnstaple	3.10 p.m.	P
3.40 p.m.	Torrington...	—	

C—Shunting 3.45 p.m. to 4.15 p.m.

—	Torrington...	4.38 p.m.	P
5.10 p.m.	Barnstaple Jc.	—	

C—Shunting 5.10 p.m. to 5.45 p.m.

—	Barnstaple	6.40 p.m.	P
7. 9 p.m.	Torrington	7.40 p.m.	P
8.12 p.m.	Barnstaple	8.25 p.m.	‖
8.30 p.m.	Loco. Yard	—	

SATURDAYS ONLY.

**	Barnstaple Loco. ...	3.40 p.m.	‖
3.45 p.m.	Barnstaple	3.58 p.m.	P
4.30 p.m.	Torrington...	—	

C—Shunting 4.40 p.m. to 5.10 p.m.

—	Torrington...	5.46 p.m.	P
6.19 p.m.	Barnstaple	6.40 p.m.	P
7. 9 p.m.	Torrington...	**	‖
**	Loco. Yard	8.15 p.m.	‖
**	Torrington	8.26 p.m.	P
8.59 p.m.	Barnstaple	9.10 p.m.	‖
9.15 p.m.	Loco. Yard	—	

B—Start 11.35 a.m. (M.O.).

C—Start 11.49 a.m. (M.O.).

D—Terminate at Fremington when required for F Shunting.

Barnstaple Men.

Off No. 572, prepare engine.

1st set on duty 6.20 a.m., relieved at 1.40 p.m.

2nd set on duty 1.25 p.m., relieve 1.40 p.m., work and dispose.

BARNSTAPLE DUTY No. 575.
2 P.T. (M.7 Class).

SATURDAYS EXCEPTED.

—	Loco. Yard	4.50 a.m.	
—	Barnstaple	—	

F—Shunting 5.5 a.m. to 6.50 a.m.

—	Barnstaple Jc.	7. 8 a.m.	P
7.47 a.m.	Torrington...	—	

C—Shunting 8.0 a.m. to 8.30 a.m.

—	Torrington...	8.53 a.m.	P
9.23 a.m.	Barnstaple Jc ...	....10.18 a.m.	P
10.51 a.m.	Torrington...	—	

C—Shunting 10.55 a.m. to 11.20 a.m.

Engine requirements.

—	Torrington...	...12.18 p.m.	P
12.49 p.m.	Barnstaple Jc.	1.10 p.m.	P
1.46 p.m.	Torrington...	2.15 p.m.	P
2.46 p.m.	Barnstaple Jc.	3.34 p.m.	P
4. 5 p.m.	Torrington...	—	

F—Shunting 4.15 p.m. to 4.45 p.m.

—	Torrington...	5. 0 p.m.	F
6.11 p.m.	Barnstaple Jc.	6.35 p.m.	‖
6.40 p.m.	Loco. Yard	—	

SATURDAYS ONLY.

—	Loco. Yard	4.50 a.m.	
5. 0 a.m.	Barnstaple	—	

F—Shunting 5.5 a.m. to 6.50 a.m.

—	Barnstaple	7. 3 a.m.	P
7.43 a.m.	Torrington...	—	

C—Shunting 8.0 a.m. to 8.30 a.m.

—	Torrington...	9.20 a.m.	P
9.52 a.m.	Barnstaple	10.12 a.m.	P
10.45 a.m.	Torrington...	—	

C—Shunting 10.55 a.m. to 11.20 a.m.

—	Torrington...	...11.55 a.m.	P
12.25 p.m.	Barnstaple	...12.30 p.m.	‖
12.35 p.m.	Loco. Yard	1. 5 p.m.	‖
1.10 p.m.	Barnstaple	1.28 p.m.	P
1.58 p.m.	Torrington...	2.47 p.m.	P
3.20 p.m.	Barnstaple	4.56 p.m.	P
5.29 p.m.	Torrington...	5.46 p.m.	P
		(A.N.R.)	
6.19 p.m.	Barnstaple Jc.	**	
**	Loco. Yard	—	

Barnstaple Men.

Off No. 577, prepare.

1st set (S.X.) on duty 4.35 a.m. work and relieved 12.49 p.m.

2nd set (S.X.) on duty 12.34 p.m., relieve 12.49 p.m., work and dispose and as ordered.

1st set (S.O.) on duty 4.35 a.m., and relieved in depot.

2nd set (S.O.) on duty 10.45 a.m., shunt ash wagons, as ordered and relieve in depot work and dispose.

574—575.

BARNSTAPLE DUTY No. 576.
2 P.T. (M.7 Class.)

MONDAYS ONLY.

—	Loco. Yard	...10.10 a.m.
10.15 a.m.	Barnstaple	...10.18 a.m.
		(A.N.R.)
10.53 a.m.	Torrington... ...	...11.55 a.m. P
12.25 p.m.	Barnstaple	... **
**	Loco. Yard	... —

FRIDAYS ONLY.

—	Loco. Yard	... 4.40 p.m.
4.45 p.m.	Barnstaple	... 4.56 p.m. P
5.29 p.m.	Torrington... ...	... 5.46 p.m. P
		(A.N.R.)
6.19 p.m.	Barnstaple	... **
**	Loco. Yard	... —

SATURDAYS ONLY.

—	Barnstaple Loco.	... 6.10 a.m.
6.15 a.m.	Barnstaple Jc. ...	... 6.30 a.m. E
		A.R.
7.13 a.m.	Ilfracombe	... 8.10 a.m. P
		(Bank)
8.22 a.m.	Mortehoe	... 8.38 a.m.
		(A.N.R.)
8.46 a.m.	Ilfracombe	... —
	C—Shunting 8.50 a.m. to 10.25 a.m.	
—	Ilfracombe	...10.30 a.m. P
		(Bank)
10.47 a.m.	Mortehoe	...10.58 a.m.
11. 6 a.m.	Ilfracombe	...11.30 a.m. P
		(Bank)
11.42 a.m.	Mortehoe	...11.50 a.m.
12. 0 noon	Ilfracombe	...12.35 p.m. P
		(A.R.)

Up to 29th August.

12.59 p.m.	Braunton	... 1.54 p.m. P
	(8.22 a.m. ex Waterloo)	(Bank)
2.11 p.m.	Mortehoe	... 2.35 p.m.
2.45 p.m.	Braunton	... 3.13 p.m. P
	(10.15 a.m. ex Waterloo)	(Bank)
3.30 p.m.	Mortehoe	... 4.35 p.m.
4.45 p.m.	Braunton	... 5. 1 p.m. P
	(12.0 noon ex Waterloo)	(Bank)
5.18 p.m.	Mortehoe	... 5.36 p.m.
5.46 p.m.	Braunton	... 5.50 p.m. P
	(3.36 p.m. ex Taunton.)	(Bank)
6. 7 p.m.	Mortehoe	... 6.10 p.m.
**	Ilfracombe	... 7.45 p.m. P
		(Bank)
7.57 p.m.	Mortehoe	... **
**	Braunton	... 8.42 p.m. P
	(3.0 p.m. ex Waterloo)	(Bank)
8.59 p.m.	Mortehoe	... 9. 5 p.m.
9.30 p.m.	Barnstaple	... —

[continued.

BARNSTAPLE DUTY No. 576—continued.

Barnstaple Men.

1st set (M.O.) on duty 9.25 a.m., work and dispose and as ordered.

1st set (F.O.) on duty 3.55 p.m., work and dispose and as ordered.

S.O.—Men of No. 573 prepare engine.

1st set (S.O.) on duty 5.55 a.m., relief at Braunton and home pass.

2nd set (S.O.) on duty 1.0 p.m., pass. per 1.20 p.m. to Braunton, relieve, work and dispose.

576

BARNSTAPLE DUTY No. 577.
2 P.T. (M.7 Class).

SATURDAYS EXCEPTED.

—	Loco. Yard	... 4.45 a.m.
4.50 a.m.	Barnstaple	... 5.15 a.m. **F**
6. 8 a.m.	Torrington... ...	... — ‖

    F—Shunting 6.15 a.m. to 6.30 a.m.
    C—Shunting 6.30 a.m. to 6.45 a.m.

—	Torrington... ...	... 7. 6 a.m. **P**
7.35 a.m.	Barnstaple Jc. ...	... 8. 2 a.m. **P**
8.33 a.m.	Torrington...	—

    C—Shunting 9.0 a.m. to 9.20 a.m.
    F—Shunting 9.20 a.m. to 10.0 a.m.

—	Torrington... ...	...10.30 a.m. **P**
11. 3 a.m.	Barnstaple Jc. **(B)**	...11.23 a.m. **P**
11.52 a.m.	Torrington... ...	...12. 0 noon ‖
12. 5 p.m.	Loco. Yard	...12.20 p.m. ‖
12.25 p.m.	Torrington...	—

    C—Shunting 12.30 p.m. to 1.0 p.m.
    F—Shunting 1.0 p.m. to 1.30 p.m.
    C—Shunting 1.50 p.m. to 2.30 p.m.

—	Torrington... ...	... 2.47 p.m. **P**
3.23 p.m.	Barnstaple	... 4.28 p.m. **P**
4.58 p.m.	Torrington... ...	... 5.46 p.m. **P**
6.19 p.m.	Barnstaple	... 6.25 p.m. ‖
6.30 p.m.	Loco. Yard...	—

SATURDAYS ONLY.

—	Loco. Yard	... 4.45 a.m. ‖
4.50 a.m.	Barnstaple	... 5.15 a.m. **F**
6. 7 a.m.	Torrington...	—

    F—Shunting 6.15 a.m. to 6.30 a.m.
    C—Shunting 6.30 a.m. to 6.45 a.m.

—	Torrington... ...	... 7. 0 a.m. **P**
7.30 a.m.	Barnstaple	... 8.14 a.m. **P**
8.45 a.m.	Torrington...	—

    C—Shunting 9.0 a.m. to 9.20 a.m.
    F—hunting 9.2 a.m. to 10.0 a.m.
    C—Shunting 10.0 a.m. to 10.40 a.m.

—	Torrington... ...	...10.48 a.m. **P**
11.21 a.m.	Barnstaple	...11.25 a.m. ‖
11.30 a.m.	Barnstaple Loco.	...12.35 p.m. ‖
12.55 p.m.	Braunton	... 1. 0 p.m. **P**

[continued.

BARSTABLE DUTY No. 577—continued.

From 4th July.

	(7.40 a.m. ex Waterloo)	**(Bank)**
1.29 p.m.	Mortehoe	... 1.35 p.m. ‖
1.45 p.m.	Braunton	... 2.14 p.m. **P**
	(8.35 a.m. ex Waterloo.)	**(Bank)**
2.31 p.m.	Mortehoe	... 2.35 p.m. ‖
2.45 p.m.	Braunton	... 2.56 p.m. **P**
	(8.54 a.m. ex Waterloo.)	**(Bank)**
3.13 p.m.	Mortehoe	... 3.18 p.m. ‖
3.28 p.m.	Braunton	... 4. 9 p.m. **P**
	(11.0 a.m. ex Waterloo.)	**(Bank)**
4.26 p.m.	Mortehoe	... 4.40 p.m. ‖
5.20 p.m.	Barnstaple	—

    C—Shunting 5.20 p.m. to 5.50 p.m.

—	Barnstaple	... 6. 0 p.m. **P**
6.42 p.m.	Ilfracombe	—

    C—Shunting 6.50 p.m. to 8.5 p.m.

—	Ilfracombe	... 8.10 p.m.
		(A.R.)
8.49 p.m.	Barnstaple	** ‖
**	Loco. Yard...	—

B—(M.O.) start 11.19 a.m.

Barnstaple Men.

1st set on duty 3.15 a.m., prepare No. 575, then prepare work and relieved 11.3 **(S.X.)** 11.40 a.m. **(S.O.)**

2nd set **(S.X.)** on duty 10.48 a.m., relieve 11.3 a.m., work and dispose.

S.O.—Off No. 578 relieve 11.40 a.m. to 12.35 p.m.

2nd set **(S.O.)** on duty 12.20 p.m., work and relieved in depot.

S.O.—No. 2 P. & D. men dispose.

577

BARNSTAPLE DUTY No. 578.
4 M.T. (N Class.)
M.O.—Off No. 578 (Sat.).
M.X.—Stabled off No. 592.

SATURDAYS EXCEPTED.

—	Loco. Yard	4.35 a.m. ‖
4.40 a.m.	Barnstaple	4.50 a.m. **F**
11. 3 a.m.	Exmouth Jc. ...	...11.13 a.m. ‖
11.16 a.m.	Exmouth Loco. ...	... 3.25 p.m. ‖
3.27 p.m.	Exmouth Jc. ...	... 3.50 p.m. **F**
8.47 p.m.	Yeovil Jc.	—

F—Shunting 8.50 p.m. to 9.10 p.m.
Requirements

—	Yeovil Jc.	...10.45 p.m. **F**
1.25 a.m.	Exmouth Jc. ...	... 1.30 a.m. ‖
1.33 a.m.	Loco. Yard	—

SATURDAYS ONLY.

—	Loco. Yard	7.10 a.m. ‖
7.25 a.m.	Barnstaple Jc.	7.22 a.m.
	(5.20 a.m. ex Taunton)	(**A.R.**)
8.12 a.m.	Ilfracombe	9. 0 a.m. **P**
		(**Bank**)
9.12 a.m.	Mortehoe	9.15 a.m. ‖
9.23 a.m.	Ilfracombe	9.24 a.m. ‖
9.25 a.m.	Loco. Yard	...10. 0 a.m. ‖
10. 5 a.m.	Ilfracombe	...10.12 a.m. **P**
10.55 a.m.	Barnstaple Jc. ...	...11.28 a.m. **P**
	(10.48 a.m. ex Torrington)	
12.39 p.m.	Exeter...	...12.41 p.m. ‖
12.45 p.m.	Exmouth Jc. ...	... 3.40 p.m. ‖
3.44 p.m.	Exeter...	... 4.22 p.m. **P**
5.46 p.m.	Barnstaple	**
**	Loco. Yard	—

Stable for No. 578 (**Mon.**).

Barnstaple Men.
1st set (**S.X.**) on duty 3.35 a.m., work to Yeoford, change to No. 532 (6.35 a.m., ex Exmouth Jc.) 8.45 a.m., work to Eggesford, change to No. 489 (7.40 a.m. ex Yeovil) 10.32 a.m. work, relieved Barnstaple 11.6 a.m.

Exmouth Jc. Men.
S.X.—Off No. 532 change over at Yeoford 8.45 a.m., work and dispose.
1st set (**S.X.**) on duty 2.35 p.m. work to Chard Jc. change to No. 534 (6.0 p.m. ex Templecombe) at 7.8 p.m. and work and dispose.

Yeovil Men.
S.X.—Off No. 534 change at Chard Jc. 7.8 p.m. work, relieved Yeovil Jc. 8.55 p.m. and home pass.
S.X.—Off No. 473, relieve at Yeovil Jc. 8.55 p.m., work and change with No. 474 (7.5 p.m. ex Exmouth Jc.) at 10.15 p.m. work, relieved Templecombe, 11.45 p.m. relieve No. 483 at 11.50 p.m., work relieved at 1.20 a.m., home pass. per 1.50 a.m. Freight.

[continued.

BARNSTAPLE DUTY No. 578—continued.

Exmouth Jc. Men.
S.X.—Off No. 474, change over at Yeovil Jc. 10.15 p.m. work, relieve in Loco.
S.X.—Men off No. 556 dispose

Barnstaple Men.
1st set (**S.O.**) on duty 4.40 a.m. prepare No. 584 then prepare and work, relief at 11.28 a.m., then relieve on No. 577 11.40 a.m. until 12.35 p.m.
2nd set (**S.O.**) on duty 11.13 a.m., work and dispose.

BARNSTAPLE DUTY No. 579.
2 M.T. TK. (E.1/R Class).

SATURDAYS EXCEPTED.

—	Loco. Yard	7.15 a.m. ‖
7.20 a.m.	Barnstaple	—

F—Shunting 7.20 a.m. to 10.30 a.m.
Engine requirements 10.30 a.m. to 10.50 a.m.
F—Shunting 10.50 a.m. to 1.30 p.m.

—	Barnstaple	1.30 p.m. ‖
1.35 p.m.	Loco. Yard... ...	... 2. 0 p.m. ‖ **Q**
2. 5 p.m.	Fremington	—

F—Shunting 2.5 p.m. to 4.55 p.m. **Q**

—	Fremington **B** ...	... 4.55 p.m. **Q**
5. 0 p.m.	Barnstaple Loco. ...	—

B—(**F.O.**) start 5.11 p.m.

SATURDAYS ONLY.

—	Loco. Yard	5.45 a.m. ‖
5.50 a.m.	Barnstaple	6. 2 a.m. **P**
6.34 a.m.	Torrington...	7. 0 a.m.
		(**A.N.R.**)
7.35 a.m.	Barnstaple	—

F—Shunting 7.40 a.m. to 10.30 a.m.

Engine requirements 10.30 a.m. to 10.50 a.m.
F—Shunting 10.50 a.m. to 4.0 p.m.
Engine requirements 4.30 p.m. to 4.50 p.m.
F—Shunting 4.50 p.m. to 8.5 p.m.
C—Shunting 8.5 p.m. to 8.35 p.m.

—	Barnstaple	8.35 p.m. ‖
8.40 p.m.	Loco. Yard	—

Barnstaple Men.
1st set (**S.X.**) on duty 5.45 a.m., prepare No. 580 then prepare work and relieved in Depot
S.X.—No. 1 P. and D. men, work and dispose **Q**.
1st set (**S.O.**) on duty 5.0 a.m.
S.O.—Off No. 573, relieve 12.30 p.m. to 1.30 p.m.
2nd set (**S.O.**) on duty 1.15 p.m. and dispose.

578—579

BARNSTAPLE DUTY No. 580.
2 P.T. (M.7 Class).

—	Loco. Yard ... ... 6.40 a.m.	
—	Barnstaple	—
C—Shunting 6.50 a.m. to 7.20 a.m.		
—	Barnstaple ... ... 7.30 a.m.	
7.52 a.m.	Kings Nympton... ... 8.28 a.m.	P
8.52 a.m.	Barnstaple Jc. ... ... 9.25 a.m.	F
11.33 a.m.	Torrington...	
F—Shunting 11.40 a.m. to 12.30 p.m.		
—	Torrington... ... ...12.45 p.m.	F
2.29 p.m.	Barnstaple Jc. ... ... 2.40 p.m.	
2.45 p.m.	Loco. Yard ... ... 3.20 p.m.	
3.25 p.m.	Barnstaple	—
F—Shunting 3.30 p.m. to 8. 5 p.m.		
F—Shunting 8.35 p.m. to 10.0 p.m.		
—	Barnstaple ... ...10. 0 p.m.	
10. 5 p.m.	Loco. Yard	—

SATURDAYS ONLY.

—	Loco. Yard ... ... 6.40 a.m.	
6.45 a.m.	Barnstaple	—
C—Shunting 6.50 a.m. to 7.20 a.m.		
—	Barnstaple ... ... 7.25 a.m.	E
7.47 a.m.	Kings Nympton... ... 8.28 a.m.	P
8.52 a.m.	Barnstaple Jc. ... ... 9.12 a.m.	F
10. 6 a.m.	Bideford Goods... ...	—
F—Shunting 10.20 a.m. to 11.35 a.m.		
—	Bideford Goods... ...11.40 a.m.	
12. 2 p.m.	Barnstaple ... ...12.54 p.m.	P
1.27 p.m.	Torrington... ... ... 2. 7 p.m.	P
2.41 p.m.	Barnstaple ... ... 3. 9 p.m.	
	(A.R.)	
	(12.50 p.m. ex Taunton)	
3.46 p.m.	Mortehoe ... ... 4. 0 p.m.	F
	(A.N.R.)	
4.17 p.m.	Braunton ... ... 4.44 p.m.	P
	(20/6 to 5/9).	
	(2.26 p.m. ex Taunton) (Bank)	
5. 1 p.m.	Mortehoe ... ... 5.10 p.m.	
5.20 p.m.	Braunton ... ... 5.29 p.m.	P
	(Bank)	
	(12.15 p.m. Portsmouth)	
5.46 p.m.	Mortehoe ... ... **	
**	Braunton ... ... 7.11 p.m.	P
	(A.R.)	
	(4.35 p.m. Taunton)	
7.37 p.m.	Ilfracombe ... ... 8.45 p.m.	E
	(A.R.)	
9.19 p.m.	Barnstaple Jc. ... ... **	
**	Loco. Yard	—

Barnstaple Men.

S.X.—Off No. 579, prepare.

1st set (S.X.) on duty 6.25 a.m., work and relieved 2.45 p.m.

2nd set (S.X.) on duty 2.30 p.m., relieve 2.45 p.m., work and relieved in Depot.

[continued.

BARNSTAPLE DUTY No. 580—continued

S.X.—No. 2 P. and D. men dispose.

1st set (S.O.) on duty 5.55 a.m., work and relieved 2.41 p.m.

2nd set (S.O.) on duty 2.26 p.m., relieve 2.41 p.m., work and dispose.

No. 581 SPARE.

BARNSTAPLE DUTY No. 582.
(S.X.) 4 M.T. (N Class).
(S.O.) 2 P. (T.9 Class).

—	Loco. Yard ... ... 3.45 p.m.	
3.50 p.m.	Barnstaple Jc. ... ... 4. 0 p.m.	P
5.58 p.m.	Taunton ... ... 6. 0 p.m.	
6. 5 p.m.	Loco. Yard ... ... 8.50 p.m.	
8.55 p.m.	Taunton ... ... 9.10 p.m.	P
10.55 p.m.	Barnstaple V.R.... ...11.30 p.m.	
11.40 p.m.	Barnstaple Loco. ...	—

Barnstaple Men.

S.X.—No. 1 P. and D. men prepare engine.

S.O.—Off No. 526 prepare.

1st set on duty 3.30 p.m. and commence disposal, relief 12.5 a.m.

No. 2 P. and D. men relieve 12.5 a.m. and complete disposal.

BARNSTAPLE DUTY No. 583.
2 P.T. (M.7 Class).

FRIDAYS ONLY.

—	Barnstaple Loco. ... 4.30 p.m.	
**	Braunton ... ... 5. 1 p.m.	
	(Bank)	
5.18 p.m.	Mortehoe ... ... 5.25 p.m.	
5.33 p.m.	Ilfracombe	—
Shunt " Devon Belle " Stock.		
—	Ilfracombe	**
**	Barnstaple	—

SATURDAYS ONLY.

—	Loco. Yard ... ...11.15 a.m.	
11.20 a.m.	Barnstaple ... ...11.35 a.m.	P
12.15 p.m.	Torrington... ... ...12.35 p.m.	P
1. 9 p.m.	Barnstaple ... ... 2. 0 p.m.	P
2.31 p.m.	Torrington... ... ... 4. 5 p.m.	F
5.39 p.m.	Barnstaple ... ... **	
**	Loco. Yard	—

Barnstaple Men.

1st set (F.O.) on duty 3.45 p.m., work and dispose.

S.O.—Off No. 584, prepare and work and relieved 2.0 p.m.

1st set (S.O.) on duty 1.45 p.m., relieve 2.0 p.m., work and relieved in Depot, then relieve No. 572 at 6.30 p.m., work and relieved in Depot.

580—583

TORRINGTON DUTY No. 588.
2 P.T. (M.7 Class).

SATURDAYS EXCEPTED.

—	Loco. Yard...	6.40 a.m.	‖
6.52 a.m.	Bideford Goods... ...	—	
	F—Shunting 7.0 a.m. to 9.15 a.m.		
—	Bideford Goods... ...	9.50 a.m.	‖
10. 2 a.m.	Torrington...	—	

C & F—Shunting 10.5 a.m. to 10.50 a.m.
(C 15 mins., F 30 mins.)

—	Torrington... ...	10.55 a.m.	‖
11.10 a.m.	Bideford Goods... ...	—	

F—Shunting 11.10 a.m. to 1.0 p.m.
Engine Requirements.
F—Shunting 1.45 p.m. to 3.50 p.m.
Engine Requirements.

—	Bideford Goods... ...	4.18 p.m.	F
4.54 p.m.	Barnstaple Jc.	**	‖
**	Loco. Yard...	5.37 p.m.	‖
5.42 p.m.	Barnstaple	5.52 p.m.	P
6.24 p.m.	Torrington...	—	

C—Shunting 6.30 p.m. to 6.55 p.m.

—	Torrington... ...	6.55 p.m.	‖
7. 0 p.m.	Loco. Yard	—	

SATURDAYS ONLY.

—	Loco. Yard...	6.35 a.m.	‖
**	Torrington...	6.40 a.m.	‖
6.52 a.m.	Bideford Goods... ...	—	

F—Shunting 7.0 a.m. to 9.15 a.m.

—	Bideford Goods... ...	10.52 a.m.	F

(9.12 a.m. ex Barnstaple)

11.39 a.m.	Torrington...	—	

F—Shunting 11.45 a.m. to 1.0 p.m.
Engine requirements 1.0 p.m. to 1.30 p.m.

—	Torrington... ...	1.38 p.m.	P
2.12 p.m.	Barnstaple	3.10 p.m.	P
3.39 p.m.	Torrington... ...	4.38 p.m.	P
5.10 p.m.	Barnstaple	5.52 p.m.	P
6.24 p.m.	Torrington...	—	

C—Shunting 6.30 p.m. to 6.55 p.m.

—	Torrington... ...	7.40 p.m.	P
8.12 p.m.	Barnstaple	8.32 p.m.	P
9. 1 p.m.	Torrington... ...	9. 6 p.m.	‖
9.11 p.m.	Loco. Yard...	—	

Torrington Men.

1st set (**S.X.**) on duty 5.50 a.m., work and relieved at Bideford Goods 1.35 p.m. and home pass. per 1.37 p.m.

Barnstaple Men.

1st set (**S.X.**) on duty 12.55 p.m., pass. per 1.10 p.m. to Bideford, relieve at 1.35 p.m. and work and part dispose and home pass. per 7.40 p.m.

Torrington Men.

S.X.—Off No. 590, finish disposal.

1st set (**S.O.**) on duty 5.50 a.m.

2nd set (**S.O.**) on duty 1.23 p.m., work and dispose.

TORRINGTON DUTY No. 589.
2 M.T. TK. (E.1/R Class).

—	Loco. Yard...	6.10 a.m.	‖
6.15 a.m.	Torrington...	6.25 a.m.	
		(Mixed)	
7. 4 a.m.	Petrockstow	7.15 a.m.	FQ
7.26 a.m.	Marland	7.36 a.m.	FQ
7.46 a.m.	Petrockstow	7.55 a.m.	
		(Mixed)	
8.32 a.m.	Torrington...	8.52 a.m.	
		(Mixed)	

SATURDAYS EXCEPTED.

10.18 a.m.	Halwill	10.40 a.m.	P
12. 6 p.m.	Torrington... ...	12.15 p.m.	‖
12.20 p.m.	Loco. Yard... ...	12.45 p.m.	‖
12.50 p.m.	Torrington... ...	1. 0 p.m.	F
1.45 p.m.	Petrockstow	1.55 p.m.	F
2.38 p.m.	Torrington...	—	

F—Shunting 2.55 p.m. to 3.40 p.m.

—	Torrington... ...	3.55 p.m.	P
5.21 p.m.	Halwill	6.40 p.m.	P
8. 6 p.m.	Torrington... ...	8.11 p.m.	‖
8.16 p.m.	Loco. Yard...	—	

SATURDAYS ONLY.

10.18 a.m.	Halwill	10.52 a.m.	P
12.18 p.m.	Torrington...	—	

C—Shunting 12.30 p.m. to 1.0 p.m.
F—Shunting 1.0 p.m. to 1.30 p.m.
F—Shunting 2.50 p.m. to 3.40 p.m.
C—Shunting 3.15 p.m. to 3.40 p.m.

—	Torrington... ...	4.40 p.m.	P
6. 6 p.m.	Halwill	6.40 p.m.	P
8. 6 p.m.	Torrington... ...	8.11 p.m.	‖
8.16 p.m.	Loco. Yard...	—	

Torrington Men.

1st set on duty 5.25 a.m., work until 1.0 p.m. (**S.X.**), 1.45 p.m. (**S.O.**).

2nd set on duty 12.45 p.m. (**S.X.**), 1.30 p.m. (**S.O.**) and complete, then dispose.

588—589

TORRINGTON DUTY No. 590.
2 M.T. TK. (E.1/R Class).

SATURDAYS EXCEPTED.

—	Loco. Yard... ...	...10.15 a.m. ‖
10.20 a.m.	Torrington... ...	...10.30 a.m. **F**
1.48 p.m.	Halwill	... 2.20 p.m. **F**
3.45 p.m.	Petrockstow ...	... 4.35 p.m.
		(Mixed)
5.12 p.m.	Torrington...	—

C—Shunting 5.20 p.m. to 5.40 p.m.

—	Torrington... ...	... 7.40 p.m. **P**
8.12 p.m.	Barnstaple	... 8.32 p.m. **P**
9. 1 p.m.	Torrington... ...	... 9. 6 p.m. ‖
9.11 p.m.	Loco. Yard...	—

SATURDAYS ONLY.

—	Loco. Yard... ...	...10.15 a.m. ‖
10.20 a.m.	Torrington... ...	...10.30 a.m. **F**
1.48 p.m.	Halwill	... 2.20 p.m. **F**
4.12 p.m.	Torrington... ...	... 4.23 p.m. ‖
4.30 p.m.	Loco. Yard...	—

Torrington Men.

1st set on duty 9.15 a.m. (**S.X.**), coal engine and relief 5.15 p.m. (**S.O.**) dispose.

2nd set (**S.X.**) on duty 4.55 p.m., relieve 5.15 p.m., complete, dispose and the complete disposal of No. 588.

No. 591 SPARE.

TORRINGTON DUTY No. 588.
2 M.T. T.K. (E.I/R. Class).

SUNDAYS.

—	Loco. Yard	... 8.40 a.m.	‖
8.45 a.m.	Torrington	... 8.55 a.m.	**P**
9.25 a.m.	Barnstaple	... 9.35 a.m.	**P**
9.52 a.m.	Bideford	...10. 2 a.m.	**P**
10.21 a.m.	Barnstaple	...10.40 a.m.	‖
10.45 a.m.	Loco. Yard	...11.48 a.m.	‖
11.53 a.m.	Barnstaple	...12.13 p.m.	**P**
12.46 p.m.	Torrington	... 1.55 p.m.	**P**
2.25 p.m.	Barnstaple	... 3.15 p.m.	**P**
3.46 p.m.	Torrington	... **	‖
**	Loco. Yard	... 6. 0 p.m.	‖
—	Torrington	... 6.14 p.m.	**P**
6.44 p.m.	Barnstaple	... 8. 5 p.m.	**P**
8.34 p.m.	Torrington	... 9. 5 p.m.	**P**
9.35 p.m.	Barnstaple	... 9.56 p.m.	**P**
10.25 p.m.	Torrington	... —	
	C—Shunting 10.35 p.m. to 11.0 p.m.		
—	Torrington	...11. 0 p.m.	‖
11. 5 p.m.	Loco. Yard	... —	

Torrington Men.

   1st set on duty 7.55 a.m.
   2nd set on duty 3.55 p.m.

TORRINGTON DUTY No. 589.
2 M.T. T.K. (E.I/R. Class).

EVERY SUNDAY.

—	Loco. Yard	...11.40 a.m.	‖
11.45 a.m.	Torrington	...11.55 a.m.	**P**
12.25 p.m.	Barnstaple	... **	‖
—	Loco. Yard	... 4.35 p.m.	‖
4.40 a.m.	Barnstaple	... 4.50 p.m.	**P**
5.19 p.m.	Torrington	... —	
	C—Shunting 5.20 p.m. to 5.50 p.m.		
—	Torrington	... 5.50 p.m.	
5.55 p.m.	Loco. Yard	... —	

Torrington Men.

   1st set on duty 10.55 a.m., work and dispose.

Nos. 590 and 591—SPARE.

CARRIAGE WORKING NOTICE
STEAM TRAINS
WESTERN DISTRICT JUNE 1953

BARNSTAPLE JC. (SX).

Dep	From	Vehicles	To	Time	Code
a.m.					
4F50	King's Nympton	2 lav. set	Berth.		—
5F15	Torrington	1 van B. (Stove)	Exeter Central		4F55
6 50	Torrington	1 News van B. / 1 bke. cpo. (new)	Waterloo F.P.	1.25 a.m.	6 41
6 57	Ilfracombe	1 van B. / 1 Cor. News van / 1 third MO / 1 bke. cpo. (new) MO / 1 bke. cpo. (new) MO	Exeter Central / Waterloo R.P.	2F 6 a.m. / 1.25 a.m.	4F55 / 6 41
7 8	Torrington	1 third / 1 bke. cpo. (new) MO / *3-set (770) MO	Berth. (*15/6 to 29/6)		—
8 0	Ilfracombe	2-set (63/75) MO / 1 bke. cpo. (new) MX	Berth.		—
8 2	Torrington	3 lav. set	Berth.		—
8 56R	Waterloo	*2 thirds MFO / 3-set (770) / 1 bke. cpo. (new)	Ilfracombe	8.10 a.m. / 8.10 a.m.	8 51 / 8 41
9 39	Salisbury / Waterloo / Exeter Central	3-set (770) / 1 News van B. / 1 van B. (Stove)	Torrington F.P. (*Com. 24/7)	8.55 a.m. / 8.53 a.m.	9 33 / 9 23
10 9	Ilfracombe	3-set	Yeovil F.P.	6.20 a.m.	10 2
10 18	Torrington	2 lav. set / 1 W.R. van	King's Nympton / Yeovil R.P.	8.28 a.m. / 6.20 a.m.	8 52 / 10 2
11 18R	Exeter Central / Waterloo	1 third MFO / *1 third MFO / 2-set (63/75)	Ilfracombe	10.30 a.m.	11 13
11 19MO / 11 23MX	Torrington	*1 third	Torrington F.P. (*Also Tu.W.Th. 28/7 to 27/8)	10.30 a.m.	11 3
	Torrington	*1 third / 1 third / 1 bke. cpo. (new)	Torrington R.P. / Berth. (*Tu.W.Th. until 23/7 & com. 1/9)	10.30 a.m. / 8.10 a.m.	11 3 / 8 41
11 25	Taunton W.R.	4 W.R. set	Taunton W.R.	8.30 a.m.	10 31
p.m.					
1 4R	Waterloo	1 third MFO / 3-set (770) / 1 bke. cpo. (new)	Ilfracombe	12.20 p.m.	12 59 / 12 49
1 4	Ilfracombe	1 third / 3-set	Torrington F.P. / Salisbury	12.18 p.m. / 8.5 a.m.	12 54

BARNSTAPLE JC. (SX)—continued.

5

Dep	From	Vehicles	To	Time	Code
p.m.					
1 10	Torrington	3 W.R. set / 1 P.M.V. (4)	Taunton W. R. / Salisbury	11. 0 a.m. / 8. 5 a.m.	12 48 / 12 54
1 55	Taunton W.R.	3 lav. set	Torrington R.P.	8.53 a.m.	9 23
2 59	Ilfracombe	3-set (770)	Waterloo F.P.	9. 0 a.m.	2 54
3 5R	Exeter Central / Waterloo / Exeter St. Davids	2-set (63/75) / 1 bke. cpo. (new) / 1 W.R. Stores van TUO	Ilfracombe / Torrington F.P.	2.20 p.m. / 2.15 p.m.	2 58 / 2 46
3 10	Torrington	1 third / 1 bke. cpo. (new)	Torrington R.P. / Waterloo R.P.	2.15 p.m. / 9. 0 a.m.	2 46 / 2 54
3 29	Ilfracombe	*1 third MFO / 2-set (63/75)	Waterloo F.P. (*also TWT 28/7 to 2/8/8)	11. 0 a.m.	3 25
3 34	Torrington	1 bke. cpo. (new) FX / 2-set (63/75) FO	Waterloo R.P.	11. 0 a.m.	3 25
3 47	Waterloo	1 Cor. news van / 1 third / 2 bke. cpos. (new)	Ilfracombe	3. 0 p.m.	3 40
4 0	Taunton W.R.	3 W.R. set	Torrington	2.47 p.m.	3 22
4 28	Torrington	2 lav. set	Torrington R.P.	12.18 p.m.	12 49
4 56 FO	Torrington	3-set (770)	Berth.	—	—
5 15	Ilfracombe	4 W.R. set	Taunton W.R.	2. 5 p.m.	4 12
5 35	Waterloo / Exeter Ctl. / Totnes W.R.	1 cor. P.M.V. / 3-set / 1 P.M.V. (4)	Ilfracombe / Torrington	4.48 p.m. / 4.38 p.m.	5 28 / 5 10
6 0	Ilfracombe	1 third / 1 bke. cpo. (new)	Ilfracombe	4.38 p.m.	5 10
6 35	Ilfracombe	1 third FO / 3-set (770)	Waterloo F.P.	1. 0 p.m.	6 30
6 38	Taunton W.R.	4 W.R. set	Taunton W.R.	5.45 p.m.	6 28
6 40	Torrington	3-set (770) FO / 1 bke. cpo. (new)	Berth. / Waterloo R.P.	— / 1. 0 p.m.	— / 6 30
8 26	Ilfracombe	1 restaurant car FO / 2-set (63/75) open third FO	Exeter Central	3. 0 p.m.	8 19
8 30	Exeter Ctl. / Paddington W.R.	3-set (770) / 1 van B. / 1 P.M.V. (4) / 1 W.R. van	Ilfracombe / Torrington	7.45 p.m. / 7.40 p.m.	8 24 / 8 12

BARNSTAPLE JC. (SO)—continued.

Arr.	From	Dep.	Stock	To	Time
—	Berth... (*Until 27/6)	—	2-set (63/75) / *3-set (770)	Torrington	a.m. 7 3
7 16	Taunton W.R.	5.20 a.m.	7 W.R. corrs.	Ilfracombe	7 22
—	Berth	—	2 lav. set	King's Nympton	7†25
7 30	Torrington F.P.	7. 0 a.m.	3 lav. set	Salisbury	7 36
—	Berth	—	5-set	Ilfracombe	8 0
—	Berth	—	3 lav. set	Torrington	8 14
8 51	Ilfracombe	8.10 a.m.	1 bke. cpo. (new) / 5-set ... / 3-set (770)	Waterloo	8 56
—	Berth	—	6 W.R. corrs.	Bristol T.M.	9 12 (Until 27/6)
9 6	Ilfracombe	8.25 a.m.	6 W.R. corrs.	Manchester Exchange	9 12 (Com. 4/7)
9 6	Ilfracombe	8.25 a.m.	6 W.R. corrs.	Ilfracombe	9 13 (Com. 20/6)
9 10	Taunton W.R.	7.15 a.m.	6 W.R. corrs.	Ilfracombe	
9 40	Ilfracombe	9. 0 a.m.	2-set 63/75 / 5-set ... / 3-set (770)	Waterloo	9 58 (Until 27/6)
9 52	Torrington	9.20 a.m.			
9 40	Ilfracombe	9. 0 a.m.	2-set (63/75) / 1 third / 3-set (770)	Waterloo	9 58 (Com. 4/7)
9 52	Torrington	9.20 a.m.	3-set (770) / 1 third / 3-set	Torrington	10 12
8 52 / 10 4	King's Nympton / Yeovil R.P.	8.28 a.m. / 6.20 a.m.	2. lav set / 1 W.R. van	Torrington	10 12
10 4	Yeovil F.P.	6.20 a.m.	3-set (770) / 3-set	Ilfracombe	10 13
10 11	Ilfracombe	9.25 a.m.	7 W.R. corrs.	Cardiff W.R.	10 19
10 31	Taunton W.R.	8.30 a.m.	4 W.R. corrs.	Ilfracombe	10 36
—	Berth	...	1 bke. cpo. (C.A.)	Yeoford	10 37
10 55	Ilfracombe	10.12 a.m.	4 W.R. corrs.	Taunton W.R.	11 5
—	Berth	...	1 bke. compo. (new) / 2 thirds / 1 third / 3-set (770)	Waterloo	11 28 R (Until 27/6)
11 21	Torrington	10.48 a.m.			

BARNSTAPLE JC. (SX)—continued.

Time	From	Stock	To	Time
p.m. 8 32	Torrington	1 bke. cpo. (C.A.) / 1 bke. cpo. (new)	Torrington / Waterloo R.P.	6 19 / 8 19
8 55	Taunton W.R.	3 W.R. set	Taunton W.R.	8 11
MO (Com.15/6)	Berth	3-set (770)	Torrington	12 25
FO	Berth	2-set (63/75)	Torrington R.P.	6 19
FO (until 26/6)	Berth	3-set (770)	Ilfracombe F.P.	6 28
Th.O	Berth	2 thirds	Waterloo R.P.	6 30
—	Berth	3 lav. set	Taunton W.R.	6 55
—	Berth	2 lav. set	Torrington	8 12
—	Berth	1 bke. cpo. (new) FX / 1 bke. cpo. (C.A.) FO	Torrington	8 59
—	Berth	2 thirds FX / 1 bke. cpo. (new) FO / 3-set (770) FX	Ilfracombe	9 9

BARNSTAPLE JC. (SO).

Arr.	From	Dep.	Stock	To	Time
a.m. 5F15	Torrington	2F6 a.m.	1 van B.	Exeter Ctl.	4F55
5 55 (Com. 4/7)	Ilfracombe	12.35 a.m.	3-set (770)	Waterloo F.P.	5 45
6 2 (Com. 4/7)	Torrington	12.35 a.m.	1 third / 1 bke. cpo. (new)	Waterloo R.P.	5 45
6†30	Ilfracombe	6†20 a.m.	4 W.R. corrs.	Barnstaple (Victoria Road) W.R.	6†25
6 50 (Until 29/8)	Torrington	1.35 a.m.	3-set (770) / 1 News van B.	Waterloo F.P.	6 41
6 50 (Com. 5/9)	Torrington	1.25 a.m.	3-set (770) / 1 News van B. / 1 bke. cpo. (new)	Waterloo F.P.	6 41
6 57 (Until 29/8)	Ilfracombe	2F6 a.m. / 1.35 a.m. (*Com. 4/7.)	1 van B. / 1 third / 3-set (770)φ / 5-set* / 1 Cor. News van	Exeter Ctl. / Waterloo R.P. (φ Until 27/6.)	4F55 / 6 41
6 57 (Com. 5/9)	Ilfracombe	2F6 a.m. / 1.25 a.m.	1 van B. / 1 Cor. News van / 1 bke. cpo. (new)	Exeter Ctl. / Waterloo	4F55 / 6 41

BARNSTAPLE JC. (SO)—continued.

Page 8

a.m. 11 28 R (4/7 to 29/8)	Waterloo	1 bke. compo. (new) 2 thirds 1 bke. cpo. (new) 3-set (770)	10.48 a.m.	Berth... Torrington	— 11 21
11 28 R (Com. 5/9)	Waterloo	1 bke. cpo. (new) 2 thirds 1 third 2 bke. cpo. (new) 3-set (770)	10.48 a.m.	Berth... Torrington	— 11 21
11 35	Torrington	1 bke. cpo. (new) 1 third	7. 0 a.m.	Torrington R.P.	7 30
11 44 (Com. 20/6)	Birmingham S. Hill W.R.	6 W.R. corrs.	10.55 a.m.	Ilfracombe	11 40
p.m. 12 41 (Com. 4/7)	Ilfracombe	2 thirds 3-set (770) 1 restaurant car (13) 1 open third 1 bke. cpo. (new)	7.40 a.m.	Waterloo F.P.	12 36
12 54 (Com. 4/7)	Torrington	3-set (770)	7.40 a.m.	Waterloo R.P.	7 40
1 27R (Until 27/6)	Waterloo	5-set 2-set (63/75)	12.35 p.m. 12.35 p.m.	Ilfracombe Torrington F.P.	1 18 1 18
1 27R (Com. 4/7)	Waterloo	1 third 3-set (770) 3-set (770) 1 third 2-set (63/75)	12.35 p.m. 12.35 p.m.	Ilfracombe Torrington F.P.	1 7 1 7
1 28	Torrington	4 W.R. corrs.	11. 0 a.m.	Taunton W.R.	12 52
1 52	Ilfracombe	2 thirds 5-set	8.35 a.m.	Waterloo F.P.	1 44
1 55	Taunton W.R.	3 lav. set	12.35 p.m.	Torrington R.P.	1 7
2 0	Torrington	2 lav. set 2-set (63/75)	11.55 a.m. 8.35 a.m.	Torrington Waterloo R.P.	12 25 1 44
2 29R	Waterloo	3-set (770) 1 third 1 bke. cpo. (new)	1.45 p.m. 1.38 p.m.	Ilfracombe Torrington	2 25 2 12
2 54R	Waterloo	1 third 3-set 1 bke. cpo. (new)	2.10 p.m. 2. 7 p.m.	Ilfracombe Torrington F.P.	2 50 2 41
2 56	Ilfracombe	1 third 5-set	10.15 a.m.	Waterloo F.P.	2 51

BARNSTAPLE JC. (SO)—continued.

Page 9

p.m. 3 8	Torrington	3-set (770)	10.15 a.m.	Waterloo R.P.	2 51
3 9	Ilfracombe	6 W.R. corrs.	12.50 p.m.	Taunton W.R.	3 0
3 51	Ilfracombe	2 thirds 5-set	11. 0 a.m.	Waterloo F.P.	3 45
3 58	Torrington	1 third 2-set (63/75)	11. 0 a.m.	Waterloo R.P.	3 45
4 0	Taunton W.R.	4 W.R. corrs.	2.47 p.m.	Torrington	3 20
4 28 (20/6 to 5/9)	Ilfracombe	6 W.R. corrs.	2.26 p.m.	Taunton W.R.	4 25
4 56 (Until 27/6)	Torrington	2 thirds 1 bke. cpo. (C.A.)	3†25 p.m. 2. 7 p.m.	Ilfracombe F.P. Torrington R.P.	4†5 2 41
4 56 (Com. 4/7)	Torrington	2 thirds 3-set (770)	3†25 p.m. 2. 7 p.m.	Ilfracombe F.P. Torrington R.P.	4†5 2 41
5 30 (Until 12/9)	Ilfracombe	6 W.R. corrs.	3.36 p.m.	Taunton W.R.	5 20
5 35	Waterloo Exeter Ctl.	1 P.M.V. (4) *1 open third *1 restaurant car 2 thirds 2 lav. set 1 P.M.V. (4) 1 P.M.V. (4)	4.48 p.m. 4.38 p.m.	Ilfracombe Totnes W.R. (*Com. 4/7, not staffed).	5 28 5 10
6 0	Taunton W.R.	6 W.R. corrs.	5.15 p.m.	Taunton W.R.	5 54
6 0	Ilfracombe	2 lav. set 2-set (63/75)	4.38 p.m.	Torrington F.P.	5 10
6 35	Ilfracombe	3-set (770)	1. 0 p.m.	Waterloo F.P.	6 30
6 38	Taunton W.R.	4 W.R. corrs.	5.45 p.m.	Ilfracombe	6 28
6 40	Torrington	2-set (63/75) 2-set (63/75)	5.46 p.m. 1. 0 p.m.	Torrington R.P. Waterloo R.P.	6 19 6 30
6 55	Ilfracombe	6 W.R. corrs.	4.35 p.m.	Taunton W.R.	6 50
7 37 (20/6 to 5/9)	Taunton W.R.	6 W.R. corrs.	6.50 p.m.	Ilfracombe	7 29
8 26	Ilfracombe	5-set	3. 0 p.m.	Waterloo F.P.	8 19

BARNSTAPLE JC. (SO)—continued.

Dep.	From	Formation	Time	To	Arr.
p.m. 8 30	Exeter Ctl.	3-set / 3 lav. set / 1 van B. / 1 van B. / 1 News van B. / 1 W.R. van	7.45 p.m.	Ilfracombe	8 24
	Waterloo / Paddington		7.40 p.m.	Torrington F.P.	8 12
8 32	Torrington	1 third / 1 bke. cpo. (new)	5.46 p.m.	Torrington R.P.	6 19
			3. 0 p.m.	Waterloo R.P.	8 19
8 55 (Until 12/9)	Taunton W.R.	6 W.R. corrs.	8.10 p.m.	Ilfracombe	8 49
8 55 (19/9 only)	Taunton W.R.	3 W.R. corrs.	6.15 p.m.	Taunton W.R.	8 11
9†15 (Until 12/9)	Taunton W.R.	3 W.R. corrs.	6.15 p.m.	Taunton W.R.	8 11
—	Berth	5-set / *1 bke. cpo. (new)	3†25 p.m.	Ilfracombe (*Com. 4/7)	4† 5
—	Berth	3 W.R. corrs.	2.35 p.m.	Taunton W.R.	4 45
—	Berth	3 lav. set	4.35 p.m.	Taunton W.R.	6 50
—	Berth	4-set	7.40 p.m.	Torrington	8 12
—	Berth	1 bke. cpo. (C.A.)	8.26 p.m.	Torrington	8 59
—	Berth	2 lav. set / *3-set (770)	8.30 p.m.	Ilfracombe (*Until 27/6)	9 9

BERE ALSTON (WEEKDAYS).

Dep.	From	Formation	Time	To	Arr.
a.m. 6 15	Plymouth Friary	1 stove van (400/1) / 3 lav. set / 2-set 361 / 1 bke. cpo. (C.A.)	6. 0 a.m.	Tavistock North	6 10
			5.20 a.m.	Callington	6 8
7 35	Plymouth Friary	P. & P. set / P. & P. set	7. 5 a.m.	Lydford	7 30
			7. 8 a.m.	Gunnislake	7 29
8 5	Plymouth Friary	3 lav. set / 1 third / 1 P.M.V. (4)	7.50 a.m.	Tavistock North	8 0
			7. 9 a.m.	Callington	7 52 SO
			7.16 a.m.		7 59 SX
8 24	Callington	2-set "A"	7. 9 a.m.	Callington	7 52 SO
			7.16 a.m.	Callington	7 59 SX
10 39	Plymouth Friary	3-set / 1 third / 1 P.M.V. (4) / 1 P.M.V. (4)	8.41 à.m.	Exeter Ctl.	10 34
10 50	Callington	2-set "A"	9.44 a.m.	Callington	10 27
			9.44 a.m.	Callington	10 27

BERE ALSTON (WEEKDAYS)—continued.

Dep.	From	Formation	Time	To	Arr.
p.m. 12 57 SO	Tavistock North	3 lav. set	12. 8 p.m.	Plymouth Friary F.P.	12 51
			12. 8 p.m.	Plymouth Friary R.P.	12·51
1 2 SO	Callington	P. & P. set	1. 0 p.m.	Callington	1 42
2 0 (W.Th. SO)	Gunnislake	2-set "A"	1. 8 p.m.	Plymouth Friary F.P.	1 56
2 0	Tavistock North	3 lav. set	1. 0 p.m.	Callington	1 42 (M.Tu.FO) / 2 47 (W.Th. SO)
3 15 SX / 3 22 SO	Callington	2-set "A"	2.26 p.m.	Gunnislake	1 56 (W.Th. SO)
			1. 8 p.m.	Plymouth Friary R.P.	1 56
5 23	Callington	2 P.M.V. (4)	8.46 a.m.	Tavistock North	8 57
			4.23 p.m.	Callington	5 6
6 1 SX	Gunnislake	1 bke. cpo. (C.A.) SX / 2-set (361) SO / 2-set "A"	4.53 p.m.	Plymouth Friary	5 43
7 10	Callington	2-set "A"	6.20 p.m.	Callington	7 1
8 0 SX	Callington	2-set (361)	8.46 a.m.	Tavistock North	8 57
10 5 SO	Callington	2-set "A" / 1 bke. cpo. (C.A.)	9.10 p.m.	Callington	9 53
			8.46 a.m.	Tavistock North	8 57

(2-set "A" is formed of 2 trailer bke. compos.)

BODMIN GENERAL (WEEKDAYS). (Trains to and from S.R. only.)

Dep.	From	Formation	Time	To	Arr.
a.m. 9 0 SX	Wadebridge	2-set / 1 third	8.10 a.m.	Padstow	8 55
	Ex W.R.		—		—
p.m. 4 8 SX	Wadebridge	2 W.R. set	4†43 p.m.	Wadebridge	5† 8
SX	To W.R.	2 W.R. set	5.35 p.m.	Wadebridge	5 55
SX	To W.R.	2 W.R. set			

BODMIN NORTH (WEEKDAYS).

Dep.	From	Formation	Time	To	Arr.
a.m. 7 22	Padstow	2-set / 1 third MSX	6.55 a.m.	Wadebridge	7 15
8 45	Wadebridge	2-set	8. 3 a.m.	Wadebridge	8 26
11 20 SO / 11 20 SX	Padstow / Wadebridge	2-set	9.48 a.m.	Wadebridge	10 8
p.m. 2 0	Padstow	2-set	12.28 p.m.	Wadebridge	12 52 SX
			12.10 p.m.	Padstow	12 52 SO

CALLINGTON (WEEKDAYS)—continued.

	Formation	Destination	Time	Berth	Time
p.m.	{ 2 P.M.V. (4)	Bere Alston … / Bere Alston …	3.15 p.m. / 3.22 p.m.	Berth …	3 57SX / 4 4SO
—	1 bke. cpo. (C.A.)SX / 2-set 361 SO	Bere Alston …	5.23 p.m.	Berth …	6 5
SX	2-set "A"	Bere Alston …	7.10 p.m.	Berth …	7 53
SX	2-set 361	Bere Alston …	8. 0 p.m.	Berth …	8 42
SO	2-set "A" / 1 bke. cpo. (C.A.)	Bere Alston …	10. 5 p.m.	Berth …	10 49

2 coach set "A" is formed of 2 trailer bke. compos.

EXETER CENTRAL (SX).

Formation of Exeter—Exmouth 5-Coach sets:—
2 lav. thirds
*2 lav. set
1 lav. third
*From Nos. 8, 10, 13, 14, 15, 17 & 20.

	Formation	Destination	Time	Berth	Time
a.m. 2F 6	1 B.Y. / 1 van B. / 1 van B. / 1 B.Y. (stove) (400/401)	Exeter St. Davids / Ilfracombe / Barnstaple Jc. / Torrington / Plymouth Friary	—		—
	1 B.Y. / 1 van B.	Bude / Padstow		Berth …	—
3V50MO	1 B.Y. (stove) (400/1)	Exmouth Jc.	1V25 a.m.	Plymouth Friary	3V47
5 9	1 third / 1 bke. cpo. (new) / 1 third MO / 2 set (63/75) MO	Plymouth Friary	1.25 a.m.	Berth …	5 0
	1 bke. cpo. (new) MX			Waterloo F.P. …	
5 18	1 News van B. / 1 bke. cpo. (new) / 1 Cor. News van / 1 third MO	Torrington	1.25 a.m.	Waterloo R.P. …	5 0
	1 third / 1 bke. cpo. (new) M.O.	Ilfracombe			
6 0	1 third Th.O (Com. 2/7) / 1 third MFO (Com 24/7)	Sidmouth	—	Berth…	—
6 30	2 lav. set / 1 P.M.V. (4) / 3-set (770)	Waterloo	—	Berth…	—

BUDE (SO)—continued.

	Formation	Destination	Time	Berth	Time
a.m. 11 45 (Com. 18/7)	{ 1 bke. cpo. (new) / 1 third / 1 third / 1 bke. cpo. (new) / 3-set (770)	Waterloo …	12.35 a.m.	Waterloo …	6 49
				Berth…	—
p.m. 2 1	{ 2-set / *1 third	Okehampton	10.15 a.m. / 7.33 a.m.	Okehampton / Waterloo … (* Com. 4/7)	11 33 / 1 27
3 13	1 P.M.V. (4) / 2-set / *2-set	Waterloo … / Okehampton	1.18 p.m. / 7.15 a.m.	Berth… / Okehampton / Halwill (*Until 27/6)	2 23 / 7 49
5 32	3-set (770) / 1 third	Halwill …	10.35 a.m.	Waterloo …	3 54
7 5	1 B.Y. / 2-set	Exeter Ctl. / Halwill …	2F 6 a.m. / 8.53 a.m.	Exeter Ctl. / Halwill	6F14 / 9 25
(Com. 4/7)	3-set (770)	Berth …	7.33 p.m.	Waterloo …	1 27
—	1 third / 2-set (63/75)	Berth …	11.15 a.m.	Waterloo …	5 9
—	2-set	Berth …	5.51 p.m.	Okehampton	7 0
—	2-set	Berth …	7.47 p.m.	Okehampton	8 55

BUDLEIGH SALTERTON (SX).

	Formation	Destination	Time		Time
p.m. 6 15	1 bke. cpo. (new)	Exmouth …	5.50 p.m.	Exmouth …	6 1

CALLINGTON (WEEKDAYS).

	Formation	Destination	Time		Time
a.m. 5 20	1 bke. cpo. (C.A.) / 2-set 361	Bere Alston …	—	Berth…	—
7 9SO / 7 16SX	{ 2-set "A" / 1 P.M.V. (4)	Bere Alston … / Plymouth Friary …	—	Berth…	—
9 44	1 P.M.V. (4) / 2-set "A"	Plymouth Friary … / Bere Alston …	8.24 a.m.	Berth… / Bere Alston	9 8
p.m. 1 0	2-set "A"	Bere Alston …	10.50 a.m.	Bere Alston	11 34
4 23	{ 2-set "A" / P. & P. set SO	Bere Alston … / Gunnislake …	3.15 p.m. / 3.22 p.m. / 1. 2 p.m.	Bere Alston / Bere Alston / Bere Alston	3 57SX / 4 4SO / 1 46SO
6 20	2-set "A"	Bere Alston …	5.23 p.m.	Bere Alston	6 5
9 10SO	2-set "A"	Bere Alston …	7.10 p.m.	Bere Alston	7 53

Departure	Destination	Formation	From time	From station	Arr.
a.m.					
6 40	Axminster ...	1 third / 3-set / 2-set	—	Berth...	—
6 45	Exmouth ...	5 lav. set	—	Berth...	—
7 16	Exmouth ...	5 lav. set	6.40 a.m.	Exmouth ...	7 8
7 30 R.	Waterloo ...	1 compo. MO / 1 third / 4-set (400) / 1 open third / 1 restaurant car (29) / 1 third	—	Berth...	—
7 34	Sidmouth ...	1 P.M.V. (4) / 2 lav. set / 2 lav. set MO	—	Berth...	—
7 35	Plymouth Friary ...	3-set (770) / 1 bke. cpo. MO / 2 P.M.V. (4) MX / 1 cor. P.M.V. MX / P.M.V. (4) MX / B.Y. / 1 P.M.V. (4) MX	1.25 a.m.	Waterloo ...	5 0
...	Padstow ...	2 lav. set	—	Berth...	—
...	Okehampton ...	2 lav. set			
8 0	Honiton ... / Sidmouth	5 lav. set	7.16 a.m.	Exmouth ...	7 43
8 17	Exmouth ...	3-set	6.20 a.m.	Yeovil ...	8 11
8 20	Ilfracombe ...	3-set / 1 third / 1 P.M.V. (4)	—	Berth...	—
8 41	Plymouth Friary ...	1 Cor. P.M.V. / 5-set MO / 3-set (770) MX / 3-set (770) Tu.O (Until 14/7)	6.20 a.m.	Yeovil R.P.	8 11
8 48 (Until 24/7)	Salisbury ...	3-set ... / 1 third ... / 1 P.M.V. (4)	6.10 a.m.	Plymouth Friary	8 39
...	Axminster ...	2-set MX / 2-set MO (Until 13/7)	—	Berth...	—
8 48 (Com. 27/7)	Salisbury ...	3-set (770) / 2-set MX	6.10 a.m.	Plymouth Friary	8 39
...	Axminster ...		—	Berth...	—
8 51	Exmouth ...	5 lav. set	8.10 a.m.	Exmouth ...	8 36
9 24	Exmouth ...	5 lav. set	8.50 a.m.	Exmouth ...	9 15
9 33	Templecombe ...	1 third MX / 3 set (770)	7.55 a.m. / 7. 6 a.m.	Axminster / Torrington	8 50 / 9 3

Departure	Destination	Formation	From time	From station	Arr.
a.m.					
9 40	Ilfracombe ...	3-set (770) FO / *3-set (770) FO	7.40 a.m. / —	Yeovil / Berth (*Com. 3/7)	9 29 / —
9 56	Exmouth ...	5 lav. set	9.22 a.m.	Exmouth ...	9 49
10 17 MFO (Com. 24/7)	Waterloo ...	1 third / 1 open third / 1 rest. car (15/16) / 2 thirds / 3-set (770) / 1 third / 1 bke. cpo. (new)	—	Berth...	—
			8.10 a.m.	Ilfracombe	10 11
			8.10 a.m.	Torrington	10 11
10 30 MO (Not Mons. & Fris. com. 24/7)	Waterloo ...	3-set (770) / 1 third / 1 bke. cpo. (new) / 1 refreshment sal. / 1 kitch. buff. car (7) / 3-set (770)	8.10 a.m. / 8.10 a.m.	Ilfracombe / Torrington	10 11 / 10 11
			—	Berth...	—
				Plymouth Friary	10 23
10 30 FO (Com. 24/7)	Waterloo ...	1 refreshment sal. / 1 kitch. buff. car (7) / 5-set	—	Berth...	—
			8.15 a.m.	Plymouth Friary	10 23
10 45	Exmouth ...	1 refreshment sal. / 1 kitch. buff. car (7) / 1 third / 3-set (770)	—	Berth...	—
			8.15 a.m.	Plymouth Friary	10 23
11 14	Salisbury ... / Clapham Jc.	5 lav. set	9.55 a.m.	Exmouth ...	10 23
11 27	Ilfracombe ...	3-set (770) / 1 News van B.	8.55 a.m.	Ilfracombe ...	11 4
11 40	Exmouth ...	1 third / 3-set ...	8. 5 a.m.	Salisbury F.P.	11 19
11 47	Padstow / Okehampton / Plymouth Friary	1 van B. (stove) / 5 lav. set	8.55 a.m. / 7.47 a.m.	Ilfracombe / Exmouth	11 4 / 8 14
p.m. 12 18 MFO (Also TWT 28/7 to 27/8)	Waterloo ...	1 P.M.V. (4) / 2-set / 3-set / 2-set (63/75)	8. 5 a.m. / 7.55 a.m.	Padstow / Axminster / Berth...	11 19 / 8 50 / —
...	Waterloo ...	1 third / 1 refreshment sal. / 1 kit. buff. car (4/5) / 1 third / 2 bke. cpo. (new)	— / 9.35 a.m.	Berth... / Padstow	— / 12 12
...		1 third / 1 bke. compo. (new) / 2 set (63/75)	10.20 a.m. / 9.50 a.m.	Bude... / Plymouth Friary	12 12 / 12 12

18

EXETER CENTRAL (SX)—continued

Dep.	From	Stock	Time	To	Arr.
p.m. 12 30 MFO (Also TWT 28/7 to 27/8)	Waterloo	1 bke. compo. (new) 1 refreshment sal. 1 kit. buff. car (6/28) 1 third	—	Berth.	—
		2-set (63/75) 1 third	10.30 a.m.	Ilfracombe	12 24
		1 bke. compo. (new)	10.30 a.m.	Torrington	12 24
12 30 TuWTh (until 23/7 and Com. 1/9)	Waterloo	2 bke. compo. (new) 1 bke. compo. (new)	9.35 a.m.	Padstow	12 12
		2 set (63/75)	10.20 a.m.	Bude	12 12
		1 refreshment sal. 1 kit. buff. car (6/28)	9.50 a.m.	Plymouth	12 12
		1 third	—	Berth.	—
		2 set (63/75)	10.30 a.m.	Ilfracombe	12 24
		1 bke. compo. (new)	10.30 a.m.	Torrington	12 24
12 35	Broad Clyst	1 bke. compo. (new)	9.50 a.m.	Plymouth Friary R.P.	12 12
12 45	Exmouth	5 lav. set	10.47 a.m.	Exmouth	11 16
1 0	Brighton	*1 third bke. *1 third 1 refreshment sal. 1 kit. buff. car (9/10) *1 compo *1 third bke.	11. 0 a.m.	Plymouth Friary	12 52
	Portsmouth & S.	4-set		*4-set	
1 6	Waterloo	1 P.M.V. (4) 3-set	—	Berth.	8 50
	Salisbury	3-set (770) FO (Comm. 17/7)	7.55 a.m.	Axminster	—
	Axminster	2 thirds Th.O (Comm. 2/7)		Berth.	—
	Seaton Jc.				
1 14	Plymouth Friary	4-set	9. 0 a.m.	Waterloo F.P.	1 8
1 30	Exmouth	5 lav. set	12.15 p.m.	Exmouth	12 41
1 30	Ilfracombe Torrington	3-set (770) 1 bke. cpo. (new)	9. 0 a.m.	Waterloo M.P.	1 8
1 45 MO (Com. 15/6)	Waterloo	9 Pullman cars	12. 0 noon	Ilfracombe	1 38
2 11 (MO 8/6 to 20/7 also 31/8 to 14/9, FX 27/7 to 27/8)	Padstow	1 bke. cpo. (new) 2 thirds 1 bke. cpo. (new)	1.35 p.m.	Broad Clyst	1 46
	Bude Plymouth Friary	1 third 2-set (63/75)	11. 0 a.m.	Waterloo	2 5

EXETER CENTRAL (SX)—continued.

Dep.	From	Stock	Time	To	Arr.
p.m. 2 11 (TWT 9/6 to 23/7 and 1/9 to 17/9)	Padstow	1 bke. cpo. (new) 1 third Th. O 1 bke. cpo. (new)	1.35 p.m.	Broad Clyst Berth.	1 46 —
	Bude Plymouth	2-set (63/75)	11. 0 a.m.	Waterloo	2 5
2 11 FO	Padstow	3-set (770) 1 kitchen buffet car 1 refreshment sal. 1 bke. cpo. (new) 1 third	11. 0 a.m.	Waterloo	2 5
	Bude Plymouth	4-set			
2 17	Exmouth	5 lav. set	1.30 p.m.	Exmouth	1 58
2 21 MO (Also Tu. W.Th. 28/7 to 27/8)	Ilfracombe	1 third 1 third	10.30 a.m. 11. 5 a.m.	Ilfracombe Waterloo	12 24 2 15
	Torrington	2-set (63/75) 1 bke. cpo. (new)			
2 21 (Tu.W. Th. 9/6 to 23/7 and 1/9 to 17/9)	Ilfracombe	1 third	10.30 a.m.	Ilfracombe	12 24
	Torrington	2-set (63/75) 1 bke. cpo. (new)	11. 0 a.m.	Waterloo	2 5
2 21 FO	Ilfracombe	1 third 2-set (63/75) 2-set (63/75)	11. 5 a.m.	Waterloo F.P.	2 15
	Torrington				
2 30	Waterloo	4-set 1 refreshment sal. 1 kitch. buff. car (1) 1 third MFO 3-set (770) 1 bke. cpo. (new)	11.35 a.m. 9. 0 a.m.	Plymouth Friary Waterloo R.P.	2 11 1 8
2 49	Exmouth	5 lav. set	12.20 p.m. 12.18 p.m.	Ilfracombe Torrington	2 23 2 23
3 25	Templecombe	3-set	2.15 p.m.	Exmouth	2 40
3 30	Crediton	1 van B. (stove)	11.46 a.m.	Templecombe Berth.	1 55MO —MX
3 42 FO	Ilfracombe	9 Pullman cars	8. 5 a.m. 12. 0 noon	Salisbury Waterloo	11 19 3 35
3 50	Okehampton	2-set 2-set	8.30 a.m.	Padstow	11 58
4 0	Exmouth	1 lav. third 5 lav. set	2.48 p.m.	Berth. Exmouth	— 3 15

EXETER CENTRAL (SX)—continued.

Dep. p.m.	From	Formation	From time	To	Arr.
4 12	Plymouth Friary	*1 third bke. / *1 compo. / 1 kit. buff. car (9/10) / 1 refreshment sal. / *1 third / 1 third bke. / 4-set (*4-set)	11.30 a.m.	Brighton	4 7
4 20 FX	Torrington	*1 third / 3-set (770) / 1 third MX / 1 bke. compo. (C.A.) MO	— / 12.46 p.m. / 7. 8 a.m. / 1V25 a.m. (*Tu.W.Th. 28/7 to 27/8)	Berth... / Salisbury / Plymouth Friary / Plymouth Friary	3 35 / 9 51 / 3V47
4 20 FO	Torrington	3-set (770) Com. 3/7 / 1 third / 3 lav. set	12.46 p.m. / 10.30 a.m.	Salisbury / Ilfracombe / Berth...	3 53 / 12 24
4 30	Waterloo	1 bke. cpo. (new) / 3-set (770) / 1 bke. cpo. (new) / 1 refreshment sal. / 1 kitch. buff. car (2) / 2-set (63/75) / 2-set (63/75) / 1 bke. cpo. (new)	2.15 p.m. / 12.45 p.m. / 11. 0 a.m. / 11. 5 a.m. / 7. 8 a.m. / 2.20 p.m. / 2.15 p.m.	Plymouth Friary / Padstow / Waterloo / Waterloo / Berth... / Plymouth Friary / Ilfracombe / Torrington	4 11 / 4 11 / 2 5 FX / 2 15FO / —MO / 9 51MX / 4 24 / 4 24
4 35	Portsmouth & S.	1 bke. cpo. (new) / 3-set	11.35 a.m. / 11.46 a.m.	Plymouth Friary / Templecombe	2 11 / 1 55
4 45	Exmouth	5 lav. set	11.40 a.m.	Exmouth	12 7
4 48	Plymouth Friary	1 third / 3-set (770)	2.20 p.m. / 1. 0 p.m.	Ilfracombe / Waterloo F.P.	4 24 / 4 41
5 5	Ilfracombe	1 third FO (Com. 3/7) / 3-set (770) / 1 bke. cpo. (new) / 2 thirds Th.O	— / 1. 0 p.m. / —	Berth... / Waterloo M.P. / Berth...	4 4‖
5 18	Exmouth	1 lav. third / 5 lav. set	4.40 p.m.	Exmouth	5 8
5 35	Honiton	3-set FX / 3 lav. set FO	2.23 p.m.	Plymouth Friary R.P.	5 5
5 45	Exmouth	1 lav. third / 5 lav. set	8.21 a.m. / —	Berth... / Exmouth	8 42
5 52	Okehampton	2-set	2. 5 p.m.	Axminster	3 2

21

EXETER CENTRAL (SX)—continued.

Dep. p.m.	From	Formation	From time	To	Arr.
5 55	Waterloo	1 cor. News van / 1 third / 2 bke. cpos. (new) / 1 refreshment sal. / 1 kitch. buff. car (3) / 2-set (63/75) / 4-set	3. 0 p.m. / 1. 0 p.m. / 3.50 p.m.	Ilfracombe / Waterloo R.P. / Plymouth Friary	5 24FX / 5 31FO / 4 41 / 5 48
6 15	Axminster	3-set	2.55 p.m.	Salisbury	5 56
6 18	Exmouth	5 lav. set	5.15 p.m.	Exmouth	5 41
6 45	Exmouth	5 lav. set	5.45 p.m.	Exmouth	6 13
6 46	Plymouth Friary	1 third FO / 4-set	3. 0 p.m.	Waterloo F.P.	6 38
6 48 (Perishable)	Waterloo	Milk vans / 1 Van B. (stove) / 1 P.M.V. (4) / 1 News Van B. / 1 P.M.V. (4) / * 1 P.M.V. (4)	5V36 p.m. / 3.50 p.m. / 2.55 p.m.	Crediton / Plymouth Friary / Padstow	5V59 / 5 48 / 6 38
6 57 FO	Ilfracombe	1 rest. car (29) FO / 1 open third FO / 2-set (63/75) / 1 bke. cpo. (new) / 1 bke. cpo. (new) FO (Until 3/7)	3. 0 p.m. / —	Derby / Torrington / Barnstaple Jc. / Berth...	6 38 / —
7†22MO	Exmouth	9 L.M. corrs.	7†8 p.m.	Exeter St. Davids	7†11
7 45	Exmouth	5 lav. set	6.47 p.m.	Exmouth F.P.	7 18
7 50	Waterloo	1 cor. P.M.V. / 1 P.M.V. (4) / 3-set / 1 P.M.V. (4)	4.48 p.m. / 4.40 p.m.	Ilfracombe / Plymouth Friary	7 3 / 7 24
8 7	Eastleigh / Portsmouth & S.	1 third / 2-set (63/75)	5.39 p.m.	Templecombe	7 39
8 17	Exmouth	5 lav. set	6.20 p.m. / 7.17 p.m.	Exmouth / Exmouth	6 47FX / 7 45FO
8 55	Exmouth	5 lav. set FX / 2 lav. set FO / 3-set (770) FO (Until 26/6)	8.18 p.m. / 10.20 a.m. / 12.46 p.m.	Exmouth / Sidmouth / Salisbury	8 47 / 11 13 / 3 53
9 20	Exmouth	5 lav. set FX / 2 lav. set FX / 5-set FO	7.17 p.m. / 10.20 a.m. / —	Exmouth / Sidmouth / Berth...	7 45 / 11 13 / —

EXETER CENTRAL (SO)—continued

a.m.					
6 30	Waterloo	1 cor. P.M.V. / 1 third / 3-set	—	Berth	—
6 40	Axminster	3-set / 2-set	—	Berth	—
6 45	Exeter	1 van B. (stove) / 5 lav. set	5V 0 a.m.	Exeter St. Davids / Berth	5V 3
7 16	Exmouth	4 L.M. corrs.	6.40 a.m.	Exmouth	7 8
7 30 R	Waterloo	1 compo. / 3-set (770) / 1 open third / 1 restaurant car (18) / 1 bke. cpo. (new) / 1 third	—	Berth	—
7 34	Sidmouth	1 P.M.V. (4) / 2 lav. set	—	Berth	—
7 35	Plymouth Friary	3 lav. set / 2 lav. set	—	Berth	—
	Padstow / Okehampton	1 third / 1 P.M.V. (4) / 1 P.M.V. (4)	1.25 a.m.	Waterloo	5 0
8 0	Honiton	2-set (63/75)	—	Berth	—
8 17	Exmouth	5 lav. set	7.16 a.m.	Exmouth	7 43
8 20	Ilfracombe	3-set (770) / 3-set	—	Berth / Yeovil	8 11
8 30	Waterloo	3-set (770)	6.20 a.m.	Berth	—
8 41	Plymouth Friary / Okehampton	3-set / 1 third / 1 P.M.V. (4) / 1 bke. cpo. (new)§ / 1 restaurant car (24)§ / 1 open third§	(*Not staffed. §Com. 18/7.)	Berth	—
8 48	Templecombe	3-set	6.10 a.m.	Plymouth Friary	8 39
8 51	Exmouth	4 L.M. corrs.	8.6 a.m.	Exmouth	8 36
9 12	Salisbury	3 lav. set	7. 0 a.m.	Torrington	9 4
9 24	Exmouth	5 lav. set	8.50 a.m.	Exmouth	9 15
9 35	Ilfracombe	1 third / 3-set	7.40 a.m.	Yeovil	9 29
9 55	Manchester	4 L.M. corrs. / 5 L.M. corrs.	9.22 a.m. / 8.21 a.m.	Exmouth / Exmouth	9 49 / 8 42

EXETER CENTRAL (SX)—continued

p.m.					
—	Berth	2-set / 1 third / 1 third TWT 28/7 to 27/8 / 1 third MO	11. 0 p.m.	Honiton	11 29
—	Berth	Milk tanks / 1 van B. (stove)	3V54 p.m.	Clapham Jc.	12V 3

EXETER CENTRAL (SO)

a.m.					
2F 6	Exeter St. Davids / Ilfracombe / Barnstaple Jc. / Torrington / Plymouth Friary / Bude / Padstow	1 van B. (stove) / P.M.V. (4) / 1 van B. / 1 van B. / B.Y. stove (400/1) / B.Y. / 1 van B.	—	Berth	—
4 30 (Com. 4/7)	Padstow / Bude	1 third / 2-set / 1 third / 1 bke. cpo. (new)	12.35 a.m.	Waterloo F.P.	4 20
4 40 (Com. 4/7)	Ilfracombe / Torrington	3-set (770) / 1 third / 1 bke. cpo. (new)	12.35 a.m.	Waterloo R.P.	4 20
5 9 (until 29/8)	Plymouth Friary / Padstow	3-set (770) / 2 thirds / 1 bke. cpo. (new) / 1 News van B.	1.25 a.m.	Waterloo F.P.	5 0
5 9 (Com. 5/9)	Plymouth Friary / Padstow	3-set (770) / 1 third / 1 bke. cpo. (new) / 1 News van B.	1.25 a.m.	Waterloo F.P.	5 0
5 18 (Until 29/8)	Torrington / Ilfracombe	3-set (770) / 1 News van B. / 1 third / ø3 set (770) / *5-set / 1 Cor. News van	1.35 a.m.	Waterloo	5 12
	(øuntil 27/6. *Com. 4/7).				
5 18 (Com. 5/9)	Torrington / Ilfracombe	3-set (770) / 1 News van B. / 1 bke. cpo. (new) / 1 Cor. News van / 1 bke. cpo. (new)	1.25 a.m.	Berth / Waterloo R.P.	5 0
6 0	Sidmouth	ø1 bke. compo. (new) / *2 thirds / 2 lav. set	—	Berth	—
	(øUntil 27/6. *13/6 only)				

EXETER CENTRAL (SO)—continued.

Exeter time	Station	Formation	Station	Time	Time
a.m. 11 39	Ilfracombe	2 lav. set / 1 third / 3 lav. set / 1 P.M.V. (4)	Salisbury	7.45 a.m.	10 57
11 40 (4/7 to 29/8)	Waterloo	5-set / 5-set	Mortehoe	10. 0 a.m.	11 33
11 43	Exmouth	1 lav. third / 5 lav. set	Berth / Exmouth	— / 10.47 a.m.	11 13 / —
11 49	Plymouth Friary / Okehampton	4-set / 1 third (Until 27/6)	Plymouth Friary R.P. / Berth	7. 0 a.m. / —	9 44 / —
11 56	Waterloo	1 third / 1 open third / 1 rest. car (17)	Berth	—	—
p.m. 12 10 (Until 29/8)	Ilfracombe	5-set / 2 thirds / 3-set (770)	Padstow / Bude	8.30 a.m. / 9.30 a.m.	11 50 / 11 50
12 12	Portsmouth & S.	3 thirds / 5-set	Waterloo	8.22 a.m.	12 4
12 15	Exmouth	8-set	Plymouth Friary	9.50 a.m.	12 6
12 26	Ilfracombe	5 lav. set	Exmouth	11.40 a.m.	12 7
12 30	Torrington	2 thirds / 5-set	Waterloo F.P.	8.35 a.m.	12 20
12 45 (until 27/6)	Waterloo	2 thirds / 2-set (63/75)	Plymouth Friary F.P. / Ilfracombe	7. 0 a.m. / 10.30 a.m.	9 44 / 12 21
		2 thirds / 1 open third / 1 rest. car (29) / 5-set	Berth	—	—
		3-set (770) / 1 open.third / 1 rest. car (15) / 1 bke. compo (new) / 3 thirds / 3-set (770)	Torrington	10.48 a.m.	12 39
12 45 (4/7 to 29/8)	Waterloo	1 third / 1 open third / 1 rest. car (15) / 1 bke. cpo. (new)	Waterloo / Berth	8.22 a.m. / —	12 4 / —
		2 thirds / 1 bke. cpo. (new) / 2 thirds / 3-set (770)	Torrington	10.48 a.m.	12 39

EXETER CENTRAL (SO)—continued.

Exeter time	Station	Formation	Station	Time	Time
a.m. 9 56	Exmouth	5 lav. set	Exmouth	7.47 a.m.	8 14
10 5	Waterloo	1 third / 3-set (770) / 3-set (770)	Torrington	8.10 a.m.	9 56
10 18	Waterloo	1 bke. cpo. (new) / 1 refreshment sal. / 1 kitch. buff. car (6) / 1 bke. cpo. (new) / 5-set / 3-set (770)	Yeovil / Berth	7.40 a.m. / —	9 29 / —
10 32	Waterloo	3-set (770) / 1 refreshment sal. / 1 kitch. buff. car (7) / 4-set (400) / 4-set	Ilfracombe / Berth	8.10 a.m. / —	10 11 / —
10 42	Honiton	2 lav. set	Plymouth Friary / Berth	8.15 a.m. / —	10 25 / —
10 45	Exmouth	5 lav. set	Exmouth	9.55 a.m.	10 23
11 6 (Until 27/6)	Waterloo	2-set (63/75) / 5-set / 1 third / 3-set (770)	Ilfracombe / Torrington	9. 0 a.m. / 9.20 a.m.	10 58 / 10 58
11 6 (Com. 4/7)	Waterloo	2-set (63/75) / 1 third / 3-set (770) / 1 third / 3-set (770)	Ilfracombe / Torrington	9. 0 a.m. / 9.20 a.m.	10 58 / 10 58
11 16 (Com. 4/7)	Padstow / Bude	5-set / 1 restaurant car (14) / 1 open third / 1 bke. cpo. (new) / 1 third / 3-set (770)	Waterloo	7.33 a.m.	11 10
11 26 (Com. 4/7)	Ilfracombe	2 thirds / 3-set (770) / 1 rest. car (13) / 1 open third / 1-bke. cpo. (new) / 3-set (770)	Waterloo	7.40 a.m.	11 20
11 26 (Com. 4/7)	Torrington	3-set (770) / 1 third / 2 thirds / 2-set	Wadebridge / Bude	8. 5 a.m. / 9. 0 a.m.	11 20 / 11 20

Time	Station	Formation	Destination	Time
p.m. 2 46	Plymouth Friary / Padstow / Bude	4-set / 2 thirds / 1 bke. cpo. (new) / 1 third / 2-set (63/75)	Waterloo F.P.	2 39.
2 52	Exmouth	1 lav. third / 5 lav. set	Exmouth	2 42
3 0 (Until 27/6)	Waterloo	3-set (770) / 1 bke. cpo. (new) / 1 refreshment sal. / 1 kitch. buff. car (28) / 5-set / 2-set (63/75)	Berth.. ; Waterloo R.P. ; Ilfracombe ; Torrington	— ; 1 55 ; 2 50 ; 2 50
3 0 (Com. 4/7)	Waterloo	1 bke. cpo. (new) / 1 refreshment sal. / 1 kitch. buff. car (28) / 1 third / 3-set (770) / 3-set (770) / 1 third / 2-set (63/75)	Waterloo R.P. ; Ilfracombe ; Torrington	1 55 ; 2 50 ; 2 50
3 25	Templecombe	2 lav. set / 2 lav. set	Sidmouth Jc.	12 35
3 42	Ilfracombe	9 Pullman cars	Waterloo R.P.	3 35
3 45	Exmouth	5 lav. set / 2 lav. set	Exmouth	3 17
3 55	Ilfracombe	2 thirds / 3-set	Portsmouth & S. F.P.	3 47
4 5	Waterloo	1 bke. cpo. (new) / 1 bke. cpo. (new) / 1 refreshment sal. / 1 kitch. buff. car (5) / 3-set (770) / 3-set / 1 third / 1 bke. cpo. (new)	Waterloo R.P. ; Waterloo R.P. ; Ilfracombe ; Torrington	1 40 ; 2 39 ; 3 58 ; 3 58
4 12	Plymouth Friary	4-set / *1 third bke. / *1 compo. / 1 kitch. buff. car (10) / 1 refreshment sal. / *1 third / *1 third bke.	Brighton	4 7
4 22	Torrington	4-set / 2 lav. set	Portsmouth & S. R.P. ; Axminster R.P.	3 47 ; 3 8

*4-set.

Time	Station	Formation	Destination	Time
p.m. 4 30	Waterloo	1 third / 3-set / 1 bke. cpo. (new) / 1 refreshment sal. / 1 kit. buff. car (2) / 3-set (770) / 1 third (until 29/8) / 1 bke. cpo. (new)	Ilfracombe 2.10 p.m. ; Torrington 2. 7 a.m. ; Waterloo M.P. 11. 0 a.m. ; Plymouth Friary 2.25 p.m. ; Padstow 1. 0 p.m.	4 11 ; 4 11 ; 2 28 ; 4 24 ; 4 24
4 35	Portsmouth & S.	3-set	Axminster F.P. 2. 8 p.m.	3 8
4 45	Exmouth	1 lav. third / 5 lav. set	Exmouth 3.45 p.m.	4 11
4 48	Plymouth Friary	1 third / 3-set (770)	Waterloo F.P. 1. 0 p.m.	4 41
5 5	Ilfracombe / Torrington	3-set (770) / 2-set (63/75)	Waterloo M.P. 1. 0 p.m.	4 41
5 18	Exmouth	5 lav. set / 2 lav. set	Exmouth 4.45 p.m.	5 13
5 35	Honiton	1 third / 2 lav. set	Plymouth Friary 2.35 p.m.	5 8
5 45	Exmouth	2 lav. set / 3 set / 1 third	Sidmouth 3. 9 p.m. ; Salisbury F.P. 12.56 p.m.	4 23 ; 4 27
5 52	Okehampton	2-set	Axminster F.P. 7.55 a.m.	8 50
5 55	Waterloo	1 cor. News van / 3-set (770) / 1 refreshment sal. / 1 kit. buff. car (3) / 2-set (63/75) / 4-set	Ilfracombe 2.55 p.m. ; Waterloo R.P. 1. 0 p.m. ; Plymouth Friary 3.50 p.m.	5 26 ; 4 41 ; 5 48
6 15	Axminster	3-set (770)	Salisbury 3. 5 p.m.	6 5
6 18	Exmouth	1 lav. third / 5 lav. set	Exmouth 5.15 p.m.	5 41
6 45	Exmouth	1 lav. third / 5 lav. set	Exmouth 5.45 p.m.	6 13
6 46	Plymouth Friary	1 bke. cpo. (new) / 3-set (770)	Waterloo R.P. 1. 5 p.m. ; Waterloo F.P. 3. 0 p.m.	5 37 ; 6 38
6V48 (Milk)	Clapham Jc.	Milk tanks	Berth..	—
	Templecombe	3-set (770)	Waterloo 1. 5 p.m.	5 37
	Yeovil Jc.	3-set (770) / 1 third / 1 bke. cpo. (new)	Plymouth Friary 1v25 a.m. ; Plymouth Friary 2.25 p.m. ; Waterloo 1. 5 p.m.	3v47 ; 4 24 ; 5 37

Time		From	Time	Formation		Berth/To	Time
4 27	Berth	Salisbury R.P.	12.56 p.m.	1 bke. compo.; 1 Cor. P.M.V.	p.m. —		
4 41	Berth	Waterloo R.P.	1. 0 p.m.	2-set (63/75)	—		
6 38	Berth	Waterloo R.P.	3. 0 p.m.	1 kitch. buff. car (6); 1 refreshment sal.; 1 bke. cpo. (new)	—		
7 3	Berth	Ilfracombe (* Com. 4/7)	4.48 p.m.	*1 open third; *1 restaurant car (13); 2 thirds	—		
7 12	Berth	Honiton	6.38 p.m.	2 lav. set; 1 third	—		
7 45	Berth	Exmouth	7.17 p.m.	1 third (com. 4/7); 1 rest. car. (18); 1 open third	—		
8 56	Berth	Axminster	7.55 p.m.	3-set (770)	—		
9 20	Berth	Exmouth	8.52 p.m.	1 third; 3-set	—		
9 48	Berth	Plymouth Friary	7.10 p.m.	1 open third; 1 rest. car. (14)	(Com. 4/7)		
9 59	Berth	Waterloo R.P.	6. 0 p.m.	4-set (400); 1 kitch. buff. car (7); 1 refreshment sal.; 3-set (770)	—		
10 7	Berth	Ilfracombe	7.45 p.m.	2 thirds; 3 lav set; 1 van B.	—		
10 20	Berth	Exmouth * 27/6, 4/7 & 11/7. § 18/7 only.	9.50 p.m. * 27/6, 4/7 &	*2 thirds; §1 third	—		
10 39	Berth	Waterloo	5. 0 p.m.	1 rest. car (16); 1 open third	—		
11 3	Berth	Sidmouth	10.20 p.m.	1 compo.; 2 lav. set	—		
11 25	Berth	Exmouth	10.55 p.m.	5 lav. set; 2 lav. set	—		
11 29	Berth	Honiton	11. 0 p.m.	3 lav set	—		

Time		From	Time	Formation	To	Time
p.m. 6 57	Berth	Ilfracombe / Torrington	3. 0 p.m.	5-set; 1 bke. cpo. (new)	Waterloo M.P.	6 38
7 45	Berth	Exmouth	6.20 p.m.	5 lav. set; 2 lav. set	Exmouth	6 47
7 50	Berth	Yeovil Jc. / Waterloo / Eastleigh / Portsmouth & S. / Clapham Jc.	4.40 p.m.	1 third; P.M.V. (4); 3-set; 1 cor P.M.V.; 1 News Van B.	Plymouth Friary	7 24
8 7	Berth	Plymouth Friary / Exeter St. Davids	3. 5 p.m. / —	2 thirds; 5-set; Vans (as required)	Waterloo F.P. / Berth...	7 39 / —
8 17	Berth	Exmouth	6.47 p.m.	2 set; 3-set; 1 third	Exmouth	7 18
8 55	Berth	Exmouth	8.18 p.m.	5 lav. set; 2 lav. set	Exmouth	8 47
9 20	Berth	Exmouth	7.45 p.m.	2 lav. thirds; 5 lav. set	Exmouth	8 12
10 6	Berth	Plymouth Friary	6. 0 p.m.	4-set	Waterloo F.P.	9 59
10 15	Berth	Exmouth	8.52 p.m. / 7.17 p.m.	2 lav. set; 5 lav. set	Exmouth / Exmouth	9 20 / 7 45
10 18	Berth	Honiton	7.10 p.m.	3 lav. set	Plymouth Friary F.P.	9 48
10F30	Berth	Clapham Jc.	7.10 p.m.	1 van B.	Plymouth Friary	9 48
11 0	Berth	Exmouth	9.50 p.m. / 4.48 p.m.	5 lav. set; 2 lav. set	Exmouth / Ilfracombe	10 20 / 7 3
11 5	Berth	Honiton	5. 0 p.m.	3-set (770); 1 third	Waterloo F.P.	10 39
—	Berth		1V25 a.m.	1 B.Y. (stove) (400/1)	Plymouth Friary	3V47
—	Berth		5V26 a.m.	Vans	Exmouth Jc. Sdgs.	5V29
—	Berth		8.22 a.m.	1 third (Until 27/6); 3-set (770) (4/7 and 11/7)	Waterloo	12 4
— (Until 27/6)	Berth		8.35 a.m.	1 res. car (27); 1 open third	Waterloo	12 20
—	Berth		10.15 a.m.	1 rest. car; 1 open third	Waterloo R.P.	1 40
—	Berth		11. 0 a.m.	1 bke. cpo. (new)	Waterloo R.P.	2 28
—	Berth		12. 0 noon	4 Pullman Cars	Waterloo F.P.	3 35

Dep.	To	Formation	To	Arr.
8.17 a.m.	Exeter Central	5 lav. set	Exeter Central	8 44
8.51 a.m.	Exeter Central	5 lav. set	Exeter Central	9 16
—	Waterloo	1 third MFO (Com. 24/7) / 1 bke. cpo. (new)	Berth	—
8.50 a.m.	Sidmouth	2 lav. set	Tipton St. Johns	9 15
9.24 a.m.	Exeter Central	5 lav. set	Exeter Central	9 48
9.56 a.m.	Exeter Central	5 lav. set	Exeter Central	10 22
10.45 a.m.	Exeter Central	5 lav. set	Exeter Central	11 13
9.43 a.m.	Tipton St. Johns	2 lav. set	Tipton St. Johns	10 19
11.40 a.m.	Exeter Central	5 lav. set	Exeter Central	12 7
12.45 p.m.	Exeter Central	5 lav. set	Exeter Central	1 9
11.12 a.m.	Tipton St. Johns	2 lav. set	Sidmouth	12 0
1.30 p.m.	Exeter Central	5 lav. set	Exeter Central	1 58
2.17 p.m.	Exeter Central	5 lav. set	Exeter Central	2 43
1.17 p.m.	Exeter Central	2 lav. set	Tipton St. Johns	1 45
7.38 a.m.	Exeter Central	2 lav. set	Tipton St. Johns	8 7
2.24 p.m.	Tipton St. Johns	2 lav. set	Tipton St. Johns	2 51
11.40 a.m.	Waterloo	1 van B. (stove)	Exeter Central	12 7
4. 0 p.m.	Exeter Central	5 lav. set / 1 lav. third	Exeter Central	4 26
2.49 p.m.	Exeter Central	5 lav. set	Exeter Central	3 14
4.45 p.m.	Tipton St. Johns	2 lav. set	Tipton St. Johns	5 11
4.45 p.m.	Exeter Central	5 lav. set	Exeter Central	5 11
11. 0 a.m.	Budleigh Salterton	1 bke. cpo. (new)	Waterloo..?	2 51
5.18 p.m.	Exeter Central	5 lav. set / 1 lav. third	Exeter Central	5 43
5.45 p.m.	Exeter Central	5 lav. set / 1 lav. third	Exeter Central	6 13
6.15 p.m.	Exeter Central	1 bke. cpo. (new) FO / 5 lav. set	Budleigh Salterton / Exeter Central	6 27 / 6 45
6.45 p.m.	Sidmouth	2 lav. set	Tipton St. Johns	7 12
7.45 p.m.	Exeter Central	5 lav. set	Exeter Central	8 12

EXETER CENTRAL (SO)—continued.

Dep.	To	Formation	To	Arr.
3V54 p.m.	Clapham Jc.	Milk tanks / 1 van B. (stove) / 2 lav. set	Berth	12V 3
11.50 p.m.	Exmouth	5 lav. set / 2 lav. thirds	Berth	mdt. 12 19
11†47 p.m.	Honiton	1 third / 3-set (770)	Berth	12†19

EXETER ST. DAVIDS (WEEKDAYS).

Dep.	To	Formation	To	Arr.
a.m. 5V 0 SX	Exeter Central	Vans / 1 van B.	Exeter Central	2F 0
8 28 SO	Ilfracombe / Torrington	3-set (770) / 3-set / 1 P.M.V. (4) / 1 W.R. van	Exeter Central / Berth	8 23 / 2F 0
8 31 SX	Ilfracombe / Torrington	3-set / 1 P.M.V. (4) / 1 W.R. van	Exeter Central / Exeter Central / Berth	8 23 / 2F 0 / —
p.m. 10 4	Exeter Central SO	3-set SO / 3-set / 1 news van B.	Ilfracombe F.P.	7.45 p.m. 9 53
—	Paddington	1 W.R. van	Ilfracombe R.P.	7.45 p.m. 9 53

EXMOUTH (SX).

Formation of Exmouth—Exeter 5-Coach sets :—
1 lav. third
*2 lav. set
2 lav. thirds
*From Nos. 8, 10, 13, 14, 15, 17 & 20.

Dep.	To	Formation	To	Arr.
a.m. 6 40	Exeter Central	5 lav. set	Berth	—
6 55	Tipton St. Johns	2 lav. set	Berth	—
7 16	Exeter Central	5 lav. set	Exeter Central	6.45 a.m. 7 10
7 47	Exeter Central	5 lav. set	Berth	—
8 9	Tipton St. Johns	2 lav. set	Berth	—
8 10	Exeter Central	5 lav. set	Exeter Central	7.16 a.m. 7 43
8 21	Exeter Central	5 lav. set	Berth	—

40

HALWILL (SX)—continued.

p.m. 4 35	Bude ...	2 thirds MO (Comm. 29/6). 2 thirds FO *1 third 2-set	Okehampton R.P. ... (*TWT 28/7 to 27/8)	3.55 p.m. ...	4 26
6 24	Padstow ...	2-set	Okehampton F.P. ...	5.51 p.m. ...	6 21
6 27	Bude ...	2-set	Okehampton R.P. ...	5.51 p.m. ...	6 21
6 40	Halwill ...	1 bke. cpo. (C.A.)	Torrington	3.55 p.m. ...	5 21
8 0	Okehampton Nine Elms	2-set 1 van B. 1 van fit 1 B.Y.	Padstow ...	6. 0 p.m. ...	7 56
	Exeter Ctl. ...		Bude ...	7. 5 p.m. ...	7 45
8 20	Launceston ...	2-set	Okehampton F.P. ...	7.47 p.m. ...	8 17
8 25	Bude ...	2-set	Okehampton R.P. ...	7.47 p.m. ...	8 17
—	Berth ...	2-set	Bude ...	5.32 p.m. ...	6 11
—	Berth ...	2-set	Bude ...	7. 5 p.m. ...	7 45

HALWILL (SO).

a.m. 5F17	Bude ...	1 B.Y.	Exeter Ctl. ...	2F 6 a.m. ...	4F37
5F31	Padstow ...	1 van B.	Exeter Ctl. ...	2F 6 a.m. ...	4F37
5 58 (com. 4/7)	Padstow ...	1 third 2-set	Waterloo F.P. ...	12.35 a.m. ...	5 53
6 8 (com. 4/7)	Bude ...	1 third 1 bke. cpo. (new)	Waterloo R.P. ...	12.35 a.m. ...	5 53
7 15	Bude ...	2-set	Berth...	—	—
7 18	Padstow ...	1 third (until 29/8) 1 third 1 bke. cpo. (new) 1 News van B.	Waterloo ...	1.25 a.m. ...	7 6
8 49	Okehampton	2-set 2-set 2-set	Launceston Bude ...	8.20 a.m. ... 7.58 a.m. ...	8 44 8 37
8 53	Bude ...	2-set	Berth...	—	—
9 54 (com. 4/7)	Waterloo ...	3-set (770) 1 third 2 thirds 2-set	Wadebridge Bude ...	8. 5 a.m. ... 9. 0 a.m. ...	9 49 9 42
10 28	Waterloo ...	5-set 2 thirds 3-set (770)	Padstow ... Bude ...	8.30 a.m. ... 9.30 a.m. ...	10 22 10 10

HALWILL (SO)—continued.

a.m. 10 51	Padstow ...	1 P.M.V. (4) 1 third bke. (2627) 2-set	Okehampton F.P. ...	10.15 a.m. ...	10 48
10 52	Torrington	1 bke. cpo. (C.A.)	Torrington	8.52 a.m. ...	10 18
10 55	Bude ...	2-set	Okehampton R.P. ...	10.15 a.m. ...	10 48
12 44 p.m. (until 27/6)	Waterloo	1 third 3 set (770) 1 refreshment saloon 1 kitch. buffet car (4) 1 third	Padstow ...	10.45 a.m. ...	12 34
		1 bke. compo. (new)	Bude ...	11.45 a.m. ...	12.35
12 44 (4/7 and 11/7)	Waterloo	5-set 1 refreshment sal. 1 kit. buff. car (4) 1 third 1 bke. cpo. (new)	Padstow ...	10.45 a.m. ...	12 34
		2 thirds 1 bke. cpo. (new)	Bude ...	11.45 a.m. ...	12 25
12 47 (com. 4/7)	Padstow	5-set 1 rest. car (14) 1 open third 1 bke. cpo. (new)	Waterloo F.P. ...	7.33 a.m. ...	12 42
12 52 (com. 4/7)	Bude ...	1 third 3-set (770)	Waterloo R.P. ...	7.33 a.m. ...	12 42
1 46	Bude ...	2-set	Okehampton F.P. ...	1.18 p.m. ...	1 44
1 57	Launceston	2-set	Okehampton R.P. ...	1.18 p.m. ...	1 44
2 51	Waterloo	1 third (until 29/8) 1 third	Padstow ...	1. 0 p.m. ...	2 47
	Okehampton	2-set 1 third (com. 4/7)	Bude ...	2. 1 p.m. ...	2 41
3 11	Padstow	1 third 5-set	Waterloo F.P. ...	10.35 a.m. ...	3` 7
3 16	Bude ...	1 third 3-set (770)	Waterloo R.P. ...	10.35 a.m. ...	3 7
4 29	Padstow	2 thirds 1 bke. cpo. (new)	Waterloo F.P. ...	11.15 a.m. ...	4 26
4 35	Bude ...	1 third 2-set (63/75)	Waterloo R.P. ...	11.15 a.m. ...	4 26
6 24	Padstow	1 bke. cpo. (new) (Until 27/6) 1 third 2-set	Okehampton F.P. ...	5.51 p.m. ...	6 21

HALWILL (SO)—continued.

	From	Formation	To	Arr.
p.m.				
6 27 ...	Bude ...	2-set ...	Okehampton R.P. ...	6 21
6 40 ...	Torrington ...	1 bke. cpo. (C.A.) ...	Torrington ...	6 6
8 0 ...	Okehampton ...	1 lav. third bke. 2627	Padstow ...	7 56
	Exeter Central ...	2-set ... / van B. ... / B.Y.		
8 20 SX	Bude ...	2-set ...	Bude F.P. ...	7 45
8 25 ...	Launceston ...	2-set ...	Okehampton R.P. ...	8 17
—	Berth ...	3 set (770) ... / 1 third ...	Okehampton F.P. ...	8 17
—	Berth ...	2-set ...	Bude ...	6 11
			Bude R.P. ...	7 45

HONITON (WEEKDAYS).

	From	Formation	To	Arr.
a.m.				
9† 3 SO	Sidmouth Jc. ...	2-set (63/75) ...	Exeter Ctl. ...	8 38
p.m.				
1 45 SO	Sidmouth Jc. ...	2 lav. set ...	Exeter Ctl. ...	11 17
4 0 FSX } 4 5 FO }	Exeter Ctl. ...	2 lav. set ...	Exeter Ctl. ...	8 38
4 35 SX	Sidmouth Jc. ...	2 lav. set ...	Sidmouth Jc. ...	4 28
6 38 ...	Exeter Ctl. ...	3-set FSX / 3 lav. set FO / 2 lav. set SO / 1 third SO	Exeter Ctl. ...	6 9
11 0 SX	Exeter Ctl. ...	2-set ... / *1 third ... / 1 third ... / 2 thirds MO	Exeter Ctl. ...	10 37
11 10 SO	Exeter Ctl. ...	3 lav. set ...	Exeter Ctl. ...	10 55
11†47 SO	Exeter Central ...	1 third ... / 3-set (770)	Exeter Central ...	11 34

ILFRACOMBE (SX).

	From	Formation	To	Arr.
a.m.				
8 10 R	Waterloo ...	*2 thirds MFO ... / 3-set (770)	Berth ... *Com.24/7.	—
8 55 ...	Salisbury ...	3-set (770)	Berth ...	—
10 30 R	Exeter Ctl. ... / Waterloo	1 third ... / *1 third MFO ... / 2-set (63/75)	Berth ... (also T.W.T. 28/7 to 27/8).	—

43

ILFRACOMBE (SX)—continued.

	From	Formation	To	Dep.
—	Berth ...	9 Pullman cars ...	Waterloo	noon 12 0 R MO (Com.15/6)
—	Berth ...		Waterloo	p.m. 12 20 R
1 48 —MX / 8 46 MO	Salisbury ... / Berth ... / Barnstaple Jc. ...	1 third MFO ... / 3-set (770)	Waterloo	2 20 R / 8 5 a.m. / 8 0 a.m.
7 42	Waterloo ...	1 third ... / 2-set (63/75)	Exeter Ctl. ... / Waterloo	3 0 R / 1.25 a.m.
8 46 MX / 7 42 MO	Barnstaple Jc. ... / Waterloo ...	1 cor. News van / 1 third / 1 bke. cpo. (new) / 1 bke. cpo. (new)	Waterloo	8 0 a.m. / 1.25 a.m.
1 48	Berth ... / Salisbury ...	1 P.M.V. (4) / 3-set ...	Waterloo ... / Exeter Ctl. ...	4 48 / 8 5 a.m.
12 0	Yeovil ...	*3 set (770) FO	Barnstaple Jc. ...	5 45 / 7.40 a.m. (* until 26/6)
10 52 / 7 42	Berth ... / Yeovil ... / Exeter Ctl. ...	4 W.R. set / 3-set ... / 1 van B.	Berth ... / Exeter Ctl. ...	7 45 / 6.20 a.m. / 2F 6 a.m.
6 42	Berth ... / Barnstaple Jc. ...	1 third FX / 1 third FX / 1 bke. cpo. (new) FX / 3-set (770) FO	Barnstaple Jc. ...	8 30 / — / 6. 0 p.m.
7 17	Waterloo ...	1 third	Berth MO	1. 0 p.m.
7 42	Waterloo ...	3-set (770)	Berth FX	1.25 a.m.
12 0	Yeovil ...	3-set (770) FO (com. 3/7)	Berth ...	7.40 a.m.
12 0	Yeovil ...	3-set (770)	Berth ...	7.40 a.m.
3 40	Waterloo ...	3-set (770)	Berth —	9. 0 a.m.
4 11	Waterloo ... 28/7 to 27/8	*1 third MFO / 2-set (63/75)	Berth —	11. 0 a.m. (also T.W.T.)
5 27	Waterloo ...	9 Pullman Cars	Berth FO	12. 0 noon
5 56	Barnstaple Jc. ...	4 W.R. set	Berth FO	5.15 p.m.
6 42	Barnstaple Jc. ...	1 third / 1 bke. cpo. (new)	Berth —	6. 0 p.m.
7 17	Waterloo ...	1 third FO (Com. 3/7) / 3-set (770) FX	Berth —	1. 0 p.m.
9 8	Waterloo ...	1 rest. car FO / 1 open third FO / 2-set (63/75)	Berth —	3. 0 p.m.

54

PADSTOW (SO)—continued

p.m.				
Com. 4/7	Berth ...	1 P.M.V. (4)	Okehampton ...	12 34
	Berth ...	5-set ... / 1 bke. cpo.	Waterloo ...	2 26
—	Berth ...	1 third / 5-set ...	Waterloo ...	5 0
—	Berth ...	2 thirds / 1 bke. cpo. (new) / *2 set (770)	Waterloo ...	6 22
—	Berth ...	1 bke. cpo. (new) (until 27/6) / 1 third	Okehampton F.P. ...	7 56

(* until 27/6 and com. 18/7)
5.51 p.m.

PETROCKSTOW (WEEKDAYS)

a.m.				
7 55	Torrington ...	1 bke. cpo. (C.A.)	Torrington R.P. ...	7 4
11 30 SO	Torrington ...	1 bke. cpo. (C.A.) / 1 bke. cpo. (C.A.)	Halwill / Torrington F.P.	11 41 / 7 4
p.m.				
1F55 SX	Torrington ...	1 bke. cpo. (C.A.)	Torrington ...	1F45
4 35 SX	Torrington ...	1 bke. cpo. (C.A.)	Torrington F.P. ...	6 25 a.m.

PLYMOUTH FRIARY (SX)

a.m.				
1 25 (News)	Axminster MO / Exeter Ctl. MX	1 B.Y. (stove) (400/1)	Berth...	—
5 58	Tavistock North ...	1 third / 3 lav. set	Berth...	—
6 10MO	Salisbury ...	1 Cor. P.M.V. / 5 set (until 20/7) / 3 set (770) (com. 27/7)	Berth...	—
6 10MX	Salisbury ...	1 Cor. P.M.V. / 3-set (770)	Berth...	—
7 8	Exeter Ctl. ...	1 third / 3-set (770) MO / 2-set (63/75) MX	Berth...	—
7 34	Tavistock North...	1 bke. cpo. (C.A.) / 2-set (361)	Tavistock North R.P.	6 53
8 15 R MO (until 20/7)	Exeter Ctl. / Waterloo	1 third / 3-set (770)	Berth...	—
8 15 R MO (com. 27/7)	Exeter Ctl. / Waterloo	1 third / 5-set ...	Berth...	—
8 15 R MX	Exeter Ctl. / Waterloo	ø1 third / *1 third FO / 3-set (770)	Berth...	—

*Com. 24/7. øNot Fridays com. 24/7

55

PLYMOUTH FRIARY (SX)—continued

a.m.				
9 50	2-set (63/75) ... / 1 bke. cpo. (new)	Waterloo ... / Berth... / Waterloo ...	1.25 a.m. / — / 1.25 a.m.	7 49MO / —MX / 7 49
1 0 R	*1 third bke. / *1 third / 1 refreshment sal. / 1 kit. buff. car / *1 compo. / *1 third bke. / 4-set. ...	Brighton ... / Portsmouth & S. ...	—	*4-set.
11 35 R	1 third / 4-set ...	Exeter Central / Waterloo ...	1.25 a.m. / —	7 49 / —
p.m.				
1 8	3 lav. set / 2 P.M.V. (4)	Tavistock North F.P. / Callington	6. 0 a.m. / 8.41 a.m.	6 53 / 11 25
2 15 R	1 bke. cpo. (new) / 3-set (770)	Waterloo / Exeter Ctl. / Exeter Central	7.35 a.m. / 1.25 a.m. / 7.35 a.m.	10 15MO / 7 49MX / 7 49
2 23	3-set FX / 1 third MFO	Exeter Ctl. / Waterloo / Berth... / Berth...	8.41 a.m. / 1.25 a.m. / —	11 25 / 7 49MO / —FO
3 50 R	2-set (63/75) / 4-set ...	Waterloo / Berth...	11.47 a.m. / —	2 32 / —
4 5	3 lav. set FX / 3 set FO	Brentor... / Exeter Central	8.41 a.m.	11 25
4 40	1 third / 1 P.M.V. (4) / 3-set / 1 cor. P.M.V.	Exeter Ctl. / Waterloo / Eastleigh / Portsmouth & S.	8.41 a.m. / 7.50 a.m. / 11.47 a.m. / 7.35 a.m.	11 25 / 8 46 / 2 32 / 10 15
4 53	P. & P. set	Gunnislake ...	7. 5 a.m.	8 10
5 11	P. & P. set / 3 lav. set	Tavistock North	7. 5 a.m. / 7.50 a.m.	8 10 / 8 46
6 11	1 third / 3 lav. set	Tavistock North / Tavistock North	7.50 a.m. / 4.25 p.m.	8 46 / 5 17
7 10	2 thirds MO / 1 third / 2-set ...	Exeter Central / Waterloo / Okehampton	(1)11. 0 a.m. / (1) / 11. 0 a.m. / 11. 0 a.m. / 3.20 p.m.	4 25 / FX / 4 30FO / 4 25 / 4 46
9 15	3 lav. set ... / 1 B.Y. (stove) (400/1)	Tavistock North... / Berth ...	6.55 p.m. / 6. 0 a.m.	7 45 / 6 53

(*T.W.T. 28/7 to 27/8)

60

SEATON JC. (SX)—continued.

a.m. 10 24	Templecombe	1 third MX / 3-set (770) / 1 bke. cpo. (new)	Exeter Ctl. / Seaton R.P.	9.33 a.m.	10 20 / 10 16
10 45	Seaton	P. & P. set	Seaton	10. 3 a.m.	10 16
11 55	Seaton	P. & P. set	Seaton	11.37 a.m.	11 50
p.m. 12 36	Seaton	P. & P. set	Seaton	12.15 p.m.	12 28
2 7	Seaton	P. & P. set	Seaton	1.42 p.m.	1 57
2 54	Exeter Ctl.	3-set (770) / 1 cor. P.M.V.	Salisbury F.P.	12.46 p.m.	2 50
3 15	Seaton	P. & P. set	Seaton / Salisbury R.P.	2.36 p.m. / 12.46 p.m.	2 49 / 2 50
4 48	Seaton	P. & P. set / 1 bke. cpo. (new)	Seaton / Exeter Ctl.	3.48 p.m. / 1. 6 p.m.	4 6 / 2 0
5 36	Seaton	2 thirds Th.O. (Com. 2/7) / P. & P. set	Seaton	5. 8 p.m.	5 24
6V 3	Waterloo	Vans, etc... / 1 B.Y. (stove)	Sidmouth Jc.	5V18 p.m.	5V45
6 54	Seaton	P. & P. set	Seaton	6.10 p.m.	6 26
7 55	Seaton	P. & P. set	Seaton	7.35 p.m.	7 51
8 44	Seaton	P. & P. set	Seaton	8.15 p.m.	8 31
9 23FO	Axminster	P. & P. set	Seaton	9. 3 p.m.	9 19
9 42FO	Seaton	P. & P. set	Axminster	9.33 p.m.	9 39
11V 0	Exeter Ctl.	Vans ... / Empty milk tanks / 1 van B. (stove)	Clapham Jc.	3V54 p.m.	10V35
—	Berth	3 set (770) / Empty milk tanks	Clapham Jc.	3V54 p.m.	10V35

SEATON JC. (SO).

a.m. 6F50	Seaton	3 set (770)	Berth	—	—
8 5	Seaton	P. & P. set	Seaton	7.46 a.m.	7 59
8 40	Seaton	P. & P. set	Seaton	8.23 a.m.	8 36
9 19	Waterloo	3-set (770) / 1 bke. cpo. (new) / 3-set (770)	Exeter Ctl. / Seaton R.P.	8.30 a.m. / 9. 0 a.m.	9 11 / 9 11
9 40	Seaton	P. & P. set	Seaton F.P.	9. 0 a.m.	9 11
10 35	Seaton	P. & P. set	Seaton	9.55 a.m.	10 8

61

SEATON JC. (SO)—continued.

a.m. 10 45 (until 27/6)	Waterloo	3-set (770) / 3-set (770) / 1 third / 5-set	Torrington / Seaton	8.10 a.m. / 10.10 a.m.	10 40 / 10 21
10 45 (com. 4/7)	Waterloo	1 third (new) / 3-set (770) / 3-set (770) / 2 thirds	Torrington / Seaton	8.10 a.m. / 10.10 a.m.	10 40 / 10 21
11 13 (com. 4/7)	Exmouth / Sidmouth	1 third / 3-set (770) / 1 bke. cpo. (new) / 2 thirds	Waterloo F.P.	8. 5 a.m.	11 9
11 25 (until 27/6)	Seaton	P. & P. set	Seaton	10.58 a.m.	11 11
11 25 (com. 4/7)	Seaton	P. & P. set / 3-set	Seaton / Waterloo R.P.	10.58 a.m. / 8. 5 a.m.	11 11 / 11 9
p.m. 12 58	Seaton	P. & P. set	Seaton	12. 5 p.m.	12 18
1 55	Waterloo	5-set / 1 third	Seaton	10.45 a.m.	1 45
2 20	Seaton	P. & P. set	Seaton	1.26 p.m.	1 39
2 55 (com. 11/7)	Waterloo	5-set / 1 third	Seaton R.P.	2.35 p.m.	2 48
3 20	Seaton	P. & P. set	Seaton F.P.	2.35 p.m.	2†48
4 0	Seaton	P. & P. set / 1 bke. compo	Seaton / Salisbury R.P.	3.40 p.m. / 12.56 p.m.	3 53 / 3 30
4 48	Seaton	P. & P. set	Seaton	4.20 p.m.	4 36
5 36	Seaton	P. & P. set	Seaton	5. 8 p.m.	5 24
6V 3	Waterloo	Vans ... / 1 B.Y. (stove)	Sidmouth Jc.	5V18 p.m.	5V40
6 55	Seaton	P. & P. set	Seaton	6.10 p.m.	6 26
7 55	Seaton	P. & P. set	Seaton	7.35 p.m.	7 51
8 4	Exeter Central	3-set (770)	Axminster F.P.	7.55 p.m.	8 1
8 44	Seaton	P. & P. set	Seaton	8.15 p.m.	8 31

68

TEMPLECOMBE (WEEKDAYS).

Dep.	From	Formation	Time	To	Arr.
a.m. 7 0	Bath	2 L.M. set / 3-set / 1 third	—	Berth...	—
7 15	Yeovil	P. & P. set	6.28 a.m.	Yeovil	6 55
7 28	Bournemouth W.	3-set / 1 third	—	Berth...	—
8 15	Evercreech Jc.	2 L.M. set / 1 B.Y. (stove)	—	Berth...	—
8 48 SX	Yeovil Jc.	1 bke. cpo. (new) MO / 3-set (770) / 1 third Th.FO	—	Berth...	—
9 10	Bath	3-set / 1 third	6.48 a.m.	Bournemouth W.	8 40
	Bournemouth W.	3-set / 1 third	6. 5 a.m.	Bristol T.M.	8 43
10 25 SX	Evercreech Jc.	3-set / 1 third	8.15 a.m.	Bath	10 8
10 30 SO	Salisbury	3-set	—	Berth...	—
11 45	Bournemouth W.	3-set 391/9 / 1 third	9. 5 a.m.	Bristol T.M.	11 26SX / 11 30SO
11 46 SX	Exeter Ctl.	3-set MO / 3-set	6.33 a.m.	Woking R.P.	9 45
11 55 (Until 23/7 and MFX com. 28/7.)	Waterloo	2 bke. cpos. (new) / 3-set (770) / 1 third / 1 bke. cpo. (new) / 1 refreshment sal. / 1 kitch. buff. car (7) / 3-set (770)	8.15 a.m.	Plymouth Friary (10.30 a.m. Exeter Ctl.)	11 50
	...	1 bke. cpo. (new)	9.33 a.m.	Exeter Ctl. R.P.	11 41
11 55MFO (com.24/7)	Waterloo	1 bke. cpo. (new) / 1 bke. cpo. (new) / 1 third / 1 refreshment sal. / 1 kitch. buff. car (7) / 5-set MO / 1 third FO / 3-set (770) FO / 1 bke. cpo. (new)	8.15 a.m.	Plymouth Friary (10.30 a.m. Exeter Ctl.)	11 50
11 57 SO	Axminster	3-set	9.33 a.m.	Exeter Ctl. R.P.	11 40
noon 12. 0	Bath	3-set / 1 third	6.33 a.m.	Woking	9 45
			8.48 a.m.	Bournemouth W.	10 21SO / 11 5SX
p.m. 12 23 SO	Salisbury	3 lav. set	7. 0 a.m.	Torrington	11 16

TEMPLECOMBE (WEEKDAYS)—continued.

Dep.	From	Formation	Time	To	Arr.
p.m. 12 23	Evercreech Jc. / Bournemouth W.	2 L.M. set / 3-set / 1 third	9.50 a.m.	Highbridge & B.,R.P. / Berth...	11 16 / —
12 50 SX	Salisbury	3-set	—	Berth...	—
1 13 SO	Salisbury	3-set	—	Berth...	—
2 41	Bath	3-set / 1 third	6.10 a.m.	Plymouth Friary	10 51
			12.55 p.m.	Bournemouth W.	2 26
3†15 SO	Evercreech Jc.	3-set / 1 third	8.15 a.m.	Bath	10 8
3 23 SX	Plymouth Friary / Ilfracombe / Torrington / Exeter Ctl.	3-set (770) / 3-set (770) / 1 bke. cpo. (new) / 1 kitch. buff. car (3) / 1 refreshment sal.	1. 0 p.m.	Waterloo F.P.	3 19
3 30 SX	Bailey Gate	2 L.M. set	9.50 a.m.	Highbridge & B., F.P.	11 16
3 36 SX	Exeter Ctl. / Lyme Regis	3-set (770) / 2-set (63/75) / 1 bke. cpo. (new)	7. 6 a.m.	Torrington	11 41
			1. 0 p.m.	Waterloo R.P.	3 19
4† 0SX / 4† 5SO	Evercreech Jc.	2 L.M. set	2.20 p.m.	Highbridge & B.	3 49
4 15	Bristol St. P.	3-set / 1 third	1.10 p.m.	Bath	2 55
4 45 SX	Bournemouth W.	3-set / 1 third	4.13 p.m.	Evercreech Jc.	4 37
5 10 SO	Bournemouth W.	3-set / 1 third	4.13 p.m.	Evercreech Jc.	4 37
5 27FSX	Plymouth Friary / Ilfracombe / Torrington / Exeter Ctl.	4-set / 2-set (63/75) / 1 bke. cpo. (new) / 1 rest. car (29) / 1 open third / 1 third	3. 0 p.m.	Waterloo F.P.	5 23
5 27FO	Plymouth Friary / Ilfracombe / Torrington	1 third / 4-set / 1 rest. car (29) / 1 open third / 2-set (63/75) / 1 bke. cpo. (new)	3. 0 p.m.	Waterloo F.P.	5 23
5 30	Bristol St. P.	3-set 391/9 / 1 third	3.35 p.m.	Bournemouth W.,	5 15

Western Steam—4

TEMPLECOMBE (WEEKDAYS)—continued.

Code	Origin	Set	Dep.	Destination	Arr.
p.m. 5 39SX	Exeter Ctl.	1 third; 2-set (63/75); 1 compo **FO**	7. 6 a.m.; 3. 0 p.m.	Torrington; Waterloo R.P.	11 41; 5 23
7V45	Gravesend, etc.	Vans; 1 B.Y. (stove)	5V40 p.m.	Yeovil	6V45
8V25	Bath; Derby	Vans, etc.; 2 P.M.V. (4)	—; 2V55 p.m.; 6V48 p.m.	Berth; Padstow; Exeter Ctl.	8V12**SX**; 8V28**SO**
8 50	Bath	3-set; 1 third	6.40 p.m.	Bournemouth W.	8 14
9 3	Bournemouth W.	3-set; 1 third; 3-set **SO**; 1 third **SO**	6. 0 p.m.; 4.37 p.m.	Bristol St. P.; Bath	8 50; 6 22
9V4	Exeter Central; Seaton Jc.; Exeter Central	Vans, etc. **FO**; 3 set (770) **FO**; 2 lav. set **SO**	3V54 p.m.; 4.56 p.m.; 3.25 p.m.	Clapham Jc.; Salisbury; Exeter Central	7V35; 5 50; 5 36
9V5	Clapham Jc.	1 P.M.V. (4); Vans; Milk tanks; 1 van B. (stove)	4.35 p.m.; 2V55 p.m.; 6V48 p.m.; 5V40 p.m.; 6V48 p.m.	Exeter Ctl. R.P.; Padstow; Exeter Ctl.; Yeovil; Exeter Ctl.	6 57; 8V12**SO**; 6V45; 8V12**SX**; 8V28**SO**
9V20	Semley; Waterloo	1 third **Th.F.O**; 3-set (770); 2 P.M.V. (4); 1 van B. (stove); 1 P.M.V. (4)	5V18 p.m.	Sidmouth Jc.	8V46
	Salisbury	Milk vans; 2 lav. set **SO**; 1 News van B. **SX**; 1 P.M.V. (4) **SX**	ex S. & D.; 3.25 p.m.; 6V48 p.m.	Line; Exeter Central; Exeter Central	5 36; 8V12
9V30SO	Highbridge & B.	Milk tanks	—	Berth	—
SO	Berth	2 L.M. set	9.50 a.m.	Highbridge & B. R.P.	11 16
SX	Berth	3-set; 1 third	3.15 p.m.	Bath	5 3
SX	Berth	3-set	3.25 p.m.	Exeter Ctl.	5 38
FSX	Berth	3-set (770); 1 third **W.Th.O**	4.56 p.m.	Salisbury	5 50
SO	Berth	3-set	5. 7 p.m.	Salisbury	6 0**SO**
SX	Berth	2 L.M. set; Vans	5V30 p.m.	Bailey Gate	6V41

Western Steam—4a

71

TEMPLECOMBE (WEEKDAYS)—continued.

Code	Origin	Set	Dep.	Destination	Arr.
p.m. SX	Berth	3-set; 1 third	4.37 p.m.	Bath	6 22
—	Berth	3-set; 1 third	5.18 p.m.	Bournemouth W.	7 5
—	Berth	Vans	3V20 p.m.	Highbridge & B.	7V35
SO	Berth	Vans	9V40 p.m.	Bailey Gate	10V35
SO	Berth	3-set; 1 third	10. 0 p.m.	Bournemouth W.	11 44
—	Berth	2 L.M. set	11†16 p.m.	Shepton Mallet	11†50
SO	Berth	3-set; 1 third	10. 0 p.m.	Bath	11 50
SO	Berth	3-set (770)	6V48 p.m.	Exeter Ctl. R.P.	8V28

TIPTON ST. JOHNS (SX).

Arr.	Origin	Set	Dep.	Destination	Arr.
a.m. 7 38	Exmouth	2 lav. set	6.55 a.m.	Exmouth	7 22
8 50	Exmouth	2 lav. set	8. 9 a.m.	Exmouth R.P.	8 37
9 40	Sidmouth	2 lav. set; 2 lav. set **MO**	9.25 a.m.	Sidmouth Jc. F.P.	9 36
9 43	Exmouth	2 lav. set	9.25 a.m.	Sidmouth Jc. R.P.	9 36
10 32	Exeter Ctl.; Waterloo	3-set **MFO**; I third (Com. 24/7); 1 bke. cpo. (new)	10.20 a.m.	Sidmouth	10 28
		I third **MFO** (Com. 24/7); 1 bke. cpo. (new)	9.50 a.m.	Exmouth F.P.	10 19
10 36	Sidmouth	2 lav. set	9.50 a.m.	Exmouth R.P.	10 19
11 32	Exmouth	2 lav. set	11.12 a.m.	Sidmouth	11 19
p.m. 1 17	Sidmouth	2 lav. set	11.50 a.m.	Exmouth	12 19
2 18	Exmouth	2 lav. set; 1 bke. cpo. (new)	11. 0 a.m.	Waterloo	2 14
2 24	Exmouth	2 lav. set; 1 bke. cpo. (new)	1.34 p.m.; 11. 0 a.m.	Exmouth; Waterloo	2 5; 2 14
4 45	Exmouth	2 lav. set	4. 2 p.m.	Exmouth	4 34
4 46	Sidmouth Jc.; Waterloo	2 lav. set; 1 P.M.V. (4); 1 B.Y. (stove)	4.34 p.m.; 4. 2 p.m.	Sidmouth; Exmouth	4 41; 4 34

Western Steam—4a

TIPTON ST. JOHNS (SO)—continued.

p.m.	Station	Formation		Station	Time	No.
8 0	Sidmouth	1 third; 1 bke. cpo. (new)	}	Exmouth	7.20 p.m.	7 48
8 50	Exmouth	1 third; 1 bke. cpo. (new)	}	Sidmouth	8.35 p.m.	8 42
10 7	Exmouth	1 third; 1 bke. cpo. (new)	}	Exmouth	9.25 p.m.	9 50
—	Berth	2 lav. set	}	Exmouth	1.48 p.m.	2 13

TORRINGTON (SX).

	Station	Formation		Station	Time	No.
a.m. 6 25	Petrockstow	1 bke. cpo. (C.A.)	}	Petrockstow	7.55 a.m.	8 32
7 6	Exeter Ctl.	3-set (770)	}	Berth	—	—
8 10 R	Waterloo / Barnstaple Jc.	1 third; 1 bke. cpo. (new); 1 bke. cpo. (new)	}	Berth	—	—
8 52	Halwill	1 bke. cpo. (C.A.)	}	Petrockstow	—	8 32
8 53	Waterloo / Exeter Ctl. / Barnstaple Jc.	1 News van B.; 1 van B. (stove); 3 lav. set	}	Waterloo / Exeter Ctl. / Barnstaple Jc.	1.25 a.m. / 2F6 a.m. / 8. 2 a.m.	7 28 / 6F 8 / 8 33
10 30 R	Waterloo / Barnstaple Jc.	*1 third MFO; 1 bke. cpo. (new); ¢1 third	}	Waterloo / Barnstaple Jc.	7. 8 a.m.	7 47
11 55 MO (com. 15/6)	Barnstaple Jc.	3-set (770)	}	Barnstaple Jc.	7. 8 a.m.	7 47 (until 29/6) / — (com. 6/7)
p.m. 12 18 R	Waterloo / Barnstaple Jc.	1 bke. cpo. (new); 2 lav. set	}	Waterloo / Barnstaple Jc.	1.25 a.m. / 10.18 a.m.	7 28 / 10 51
1F 0	Petrockstow	1 bke. cpo. (C.A.)	}	Halwill	10.40 a.m.	12 6
2 15 R	Waterloo / Barnstaple Jc. / Exeter St. David	1 bke. cpo. (new); 1 third; 1 W.R. stores van Tu.O	}	Barnstaple Jc.	11.19 a.m. / 11.23 a.m. / 11.19 a.m. / 11.23 a.m.	11 53 MO / 11 58 MX / 11 53 MO / 11 58 MX
2 47	Barnstaple Jc.	3 W.R. set	}	Barnstaple Jc.	1.10 p.m.	1 46
3 55	Halwill	1 bke. cpo. (C.A.)	}	Petrockstow	1F55 p.m.	2F43
4 38	Totnes W.R. / Barnstaple Jc.	1 P.M.V. (4); 1 bke. cpo. (new); 1 third	}	Barnstaple Jc. / Waterloo	1.10 p.m. / 9. 0 a.m.	1 46 / 3 39

*also T.W.T. 28/7 to 27/8.
¢T.W.Th. until 23/7 & Com. 1/9.

TIPTON ST. JOHNS (SX)—continued.

p.m.	Station	Formation		Station	Time	No.
5 56	Sidmouth	2 lav. set	}	Exmouth	5.21 p.m.	5 46
		3-set (770) (FO Com. 19/6)	}	Berth	—	—
6 45	Exmouth	2 lav. set	}	Sidmouth	6.28 p.m.	6 35
8 0	Sidmouth	2 lav. set	}	Exmouth	7.20 p.m.	7 48
8 50	Exmouth	2 lav. set	}	Sidmouth	8.35 p.m.	8 42
10 7 FO	Exmouth	2 lav. set	}	Exmouth	9.25 p.m.	9 50
MO (com. 15/6)	Berth	3-set (770)	}	Sidmouth Jc. R.P.	6.28 p.m.	6 38

TIPTON ST. JOHNS (SO).

a.m.	Station	Formation		Station	Time	No.
7 38	Exmouth	2 lav. set	}	Exmouth	6.55 a.m.	7 22
9 10	Exmouth	2 lav. set	}	Exmouth	8. 9 a.m.	8 37
10 24	Sidmouth	*2 thirds; 2 lav. set (*20/6 and 27/6 only)	}	Exmouth	9.50 a.m.	10 19
11 38	Exmouth	2 lav. set; 1 lav. third	}	Sidmouth	11.20 a.m.	11 27
11 58 (com. 4/7)	Sidmouth	2 thirds; 1 bke. cpo. (new)	}	Waterloo F.P.	8. 5 a.m.	11 54
12 5 p.m. (com. 4/7)	Exmouth	3-set (770); 1 third	}	Waterloo R.P.	8. 5 a.m.	11 54
1 29	Exmouth	5-set; 2 thirds	}	Waterloo F.P.	9. 0 a.m.	1 23
1 44	Sidmouth	5-set	}	Waterloo R.P.	9. 0 a.m.	1 23
3 18	Sidmouth	1 compo.; 3-set (770)	}	Waterloo R.P.	11.45 a.m. R	3 14
3 24	Exmouth	1 open third; 1 rest. car (18); 1 bke. cpo. (new); 2 thirds; 3-set (770)	}	Waterloo R.P.	11.45 a.m.	3 14
4 44	Exmouth	1 bke. cpo. (new)	}	Sidmouth Jc.	4. 0 p.m.	4 10
4 46	Sidmouth Jc. / Waterloo	2 lav. set; 1 P.M.V. (4); 1 B.Y. (stove); 3-set (770)	}	Sidmouth / Exmouth	4.34 p.m. / 4. 2 p.m.	4 41 / 4 34
5 35	Semley / Exmouth	1 third; 1 bke. cpo. (new)	}	Exmouth	5. 0 p.m.	5 25

Dep.	Station	Stock	Time	Station	Arr.
a.m. 10 48 (Until 27/6)	Waterloo	1 third 3-set (770)	1.35 a.m.	Berth Waterloo	— 7 24
10 48 R (4/7 to 29/8)	Waterloo	1 bke. cpo. (new) 1 third 3-set (770)	12.35 a.m.	Waterloo Berth Waterloo	6 34 — 7 24
10 48 R (com. 5/9)	Waterloo	1 third 1 bke. cpo. (new) 1 bke. cpo. (new) 3-set (770)	12.35 a.m. 1.25 a.m.	Waterloo Waterloo	6 34 7 24
11 55	Barnstaple Jc.	2 lav. set	10.12 a.m.	Barnstaple Jc.	10 45
p.m. 12 35 R	Waterloo	*1 third 2-set (63/75) 3 lav. set	7. 3 a.m. 8.14 a.m.	Berth Barnstaple Jc. Barnstaple Jc. (*Com 4/7)	— 7 43 8 45
1 38 R	Barnstaple Jc.	1 third 1 bke. cpo. (new)	11.35 a.m.	Barnstaple Jc.	12 14
2 7 (until 27/6)	Waterloo Barnstaple Jc.	1 bke. cpo (new) 1 bke. cpo. (C.A.)	10.52 a.m.	Berth Halwill F.P.	— 12 18
2 7 (com. 4/7.)	Waterloo Barnstaple Jc.	1 bke. cpo. (new) 3-set (770)	7.40 a.m.	Berth Waterloo	— 1 27
2 47	Barnstaple Jc.	4 W.R. carrs.	1.28 p.m.	Barnstaple Jc.	1 58
4 38	Barnstaple Jc. Exeter Central Totnes W.R.	2-set (63/75) 2 lav. set 1 P.M.V. (4) 1 P.M.V. (4)	8.35 a.m. 2. 0 p.m.	Waterloo Barnstaple Jc. Berth	2 31 2 31 —
4 40	Halwill	1 bke. cpo. (C.A.)	10.52 p.m.	Halwill R.P.	12 18
5 46	Barnstaple Jc.	2-set (63/75) 1 third	11. 0 a.m.	Waterloo	4 30
7 40	Exeter Ctl.	1 news van B.	1.25 a.m. (Com. 5/9) 1.35 a.m. (Until 29/8)	Waterloo	7 24 7 24
	Paddington Barnstaple Jc.	1 W.R. van 4-set	10.12 a.m. 4.22 p.m.	Barnstaple Jc. Exeter Ctl.	10 45 6 24
8 26	Barnstaple Jc.	1 bke. cpo. (C.A.)	6.40 p.m.	Halwill	8 6
	Berth	1 bke. cpo. (C.A.)	10.52 a.m.	Halwill F.P.	12 18
(com. 4/7.)	Berth	3 set (770)	10.15 a.m.	Waterloo	3 41

Dep.	Station	Stock	Time	Station	Arr.
p.m. 5 46	Barnstaple Jc.	1 bke. cpo. (C.A.) FO 2-set (63/75) FO	4.35 p.m. 11. 5 a.m.	Petrockstow Waterloo	5 12 4 5
7 40	Exeter Ctl.	1 P.M.V. (4)	11.19 a.m. 11.23 a.m.	Barnstaple Jc. Barnstaple Jc.	11 53MO 11 58MX
	Paddington Barnstaple Jc.	1 W.R. van 2 lav. set	10.18 a.m. 4.28 p.m.	Barnstaple Jc. Barnstaple Jc.	10 51 4 58
8 26	Barnstaple Jc.	1 bke. cpo. (C.A.) FO 1 bke. cpo. (new) FX	6.40 p.m. 1. 0 p.m.	Halwill Waterloo	8 6 7 9
TWT (until 23/7 & com. 1/9)	Berth	1 third	11.23 a.m.	Barnstaple Jc.	11 58
FX	Berth	1 bke. cpo. (new)	11. 0 a.m.	Waterloo	4 5
FO	Berth	3-set (770)	4.56 p.m.	Barnstaple Jc.	5 29
—	Berth	*1 third 3-set (770) FX 1 third MFX 1 bke. cpo (C.A.) MO	4.20 p.m. (*T.W.Th. 28/7 to 27/8).	Exeter Ctl.	6 24
FO	Berth	*3-set (770) 1 third 3 lav. set	4.20 p.m. (*com 3/7).	Exeter Ctl.	6 24
FO	Berth	3-set (770) 1 bke. cpo. (new)	1. 0 p.m.	Waterloo	7 9
FX	Berth	1 bke. cpo. (C.A.)	6.40 p.m.	Halwill	8 6
—	Berth	1 bke. cpo. (C.A.) 1 bke. cpo. (new)	3. 0 p.m.	Waterloo	9 1

TORRINGTON (SO).

Dep.	Station	Stock	Time	Station	Arr.
a.m. 6 25	Petrockstow	2 bke. cpos. (C.A.)	—	Berth	—
7 0	Salisbury Barnstaple Jc.	3 lav. set 1 third 1 bke. cpo. (new)	—	Berth	—
8 10 R	Waterloo	1 third 3-set (770) 3-set (770)	—	Berth	—
8 52	Halwill	1 third 3-set (770)	7.55 a.m.	Petrockstow	8 32
9 20 R	Waterloo	1 third 3-set (770)	7. 3 a.m.	Berth Barnstaple Jc. R.P. (until 27/6) Berth (com. 4/7).	— 7 43 —

TORRINGTON (SX)—continued.

Dep.	From	Stock	Time	To	Arr.
p.m. 5 46	Barnstaple Jc. ...	1 bke. cpo. (C.A.) **FO** / 2-set (63/75) (4)	4.35 p.m. / 11. 5 a.m.	Petrockstow / Waterloo ...	5 12 **MO** / 4 5
7 40	Exeter Ctl. ...	1 P.M.V. (4)	{ 11.19 a.m. / 11.23 a.m. / 10.18 a.m. / 4.28 p.m. }	Barnstaple Jc. / Barnstaple Jc. / Barnstaple Jc. / Barnstaple Jc.	11 53 **MO** / 11 58 **MX** / 10 51 / 4 58
—	Paddington / Barnstaple Jc. ...	1 W.R. van / 2 lav. set ...			
8 26	Barnstaple Jc. ...	1 bke. cpo. (C.A.) **FO** / 1 bke. cpo. (new) **FX**	6.40 p.m. / 1. 0 p.m.	Halwill / Waterloo ...	8 6 / 7 9
TWT (until 23/7 & com. 1/9)	Berth ...	1 third ...	11.23 a.m.	Barnstaple Jc. ...	11 58
FX ...	Berth ...	1 bke. cpo. (new)	11. 0 a.m.	Waterloo ...	4 5
FO ...	Berth ...	3-set (770)	4.56 p.m.	Barnstaple Jc. ...	5 29
—	Berth ...	*1 third / 3-set (770) **FX** / 1 third **MFX** / 1 bke. cpo. (C.A.) **MO**	4.20 p.m. (*T.W.Th.)	Exeter Ctl. (28/7 to 27/8.)	6 24
FO ...	Berth ...	*3-set (770) / 1 third / 3 lav. set ...	4.20 p.m.	Exeter Ctl. (*com 3/7)	6 24
FO ...	Berth ...	3-set (770) / 1 bke. cpo. (new)	1. 0 p.m.	Waterloo ...	7 9
FX ...	Berth ...	1 bke. cpo. (C.A.) ...	6.40 p.m.	Halwill ...	8 6
—	Berth ...	1 bke. cpo. (C.A.) / 1 bke. cpo. (new)	3. 0 p.m.	Waterloo ...	9 1

TORRINGTON (SO).

Dep.	From	Stock	Time	To	Arr.
a.m. 6 25	Petrockstow ...	2 bke. cpos. (C.A.) ...	—	Berth... ...	—
7 0	Salisbury / Barnstaple Jc. ...	3 lav. set / 1 third / 1 bke. cpo. (new) ...	—	Berth... ...	—
8 10 **R**	Waterloo ...	1 third / 3-set (770) / 3-set (770)	—	Berth... ...	—
8 52	Halwill ...	1 bke. cpo. (C.A.) ...	7.55 a.m.	Petrockstow	8 32
9 20 **R**	Waterloo ...	1 third / 3-set (770)	7. 3 a.m.	Berth / Barnstaple Jc. R.P. (until 27/6) / Berth (com. 4/7.)	7 43 / —

TORRINGTON (SO)—continued.

Dep.	To	Stock	Time	Final dest.	Arr.
a.m. 10 48 (Until 27/6)	Waterloo ...	1 third / 3-set (770)	—	Berth... / Waterloo ...	— / 7 24
10 48 **R** (4/7 to 29/8)	Waterloo ...	1 bke. cpo. (new) / 1 third / 3-set (770)	1.35 a.m. / 12.35 a.m.	Waterloo ...	6 34
10 48 **R** (com. 5/9)	Waterloo ...	1 third / 1 bke. cpo. (new) / 1 bke. cpo. (new) / 3-set (770)	1.35 a.m. / 12.35 a.m.	Berth... / Waterloo ...	— / 7 24 / 6 34 / 7 24
11 55	Barnstaple Jc. ...	2 lav. set ...	10.12 a.m.	Barnstaple Jc. ...	10 45
p.m. 12 35 **R** ...	Waterloo ...	*1 third / 2-set (63/75) / 3 lav. set ...	7. 3 a.m. / 8.14 a.m.	Berth... / Barnstaple Jc. / Barnstaple Jc. (*Com 4/7)	7 43 / 8 45
1 38 **R** ...	Waterloo ...	1 third / 1 bke. cpo. (new)	11.35 a.m.	Barnstaple Jc. ...	12 14
2 7 (until 27/6)	Waterloo / Barnstaple Jc. ...	1 bke cpo (new) / 1 bke. cpo. (C.A.)	10.52 a.m.	Berth... / Halwill F.P. ...	12 18 / 1 27
2 7 (com. 4/7.)	Waterloo / Barnstaple Jc. ...	1 bke. cpo. (new) / 3-set (770)	7.40 a.m.	Berth... / Waterloo ...	1 58
2 47 ...	Barnstaple Jc. ...	4 W.R. carrs.	1.28 p.m.	Barnstaple Jc. ...	
4 38	Barnstaple Jc. / Exeter Central / Totnes W.R.	2-set (63/75) / 2 lav. set / 1 P.M.V. (4) / 1 P.M.V. (4)	8.35 a.m. / 2. 0 p.m.	Waterloo... / Barnstaple Jc. / Berth...	2 31 / 2 31
4 40	Halwill ...	1 bke. cpo. (C.A.) ...	10.52 p.m.	Halwill R.P. ...	12 18
5 46 ...	Barnstaple Jc. ...	2-set (63/75) / 1 third	11. 0 a.m.	Waterloo ...	4 30
7 40 ...	Exeter Ctl. ...	1 news van B.	1.25 p.m. (Com. 5/9) / 1.35 a.m. (Until 29/8)	Waterloo... / Waterloo ...	7 24 / 7 24
8 26	Paddington / Barnstaple Jc. ...	1 W.R. van / 4-set ...	10.12 a.m. / 4.22 p.m.	Barnstaple Jc. / Exeter Ctl. ...	10 45 / 6 24
(com. 4/7)	Berth ...	1 bke. cpo. (C.A.)	6.40 p.m.	Halwill ...	8 6
—	Berth ...	1 bke. cpo. (C.A.)	10.52 a.m.	Halwill F.P. ...	12 18
—	Berth ...	3 set (770) ...	10.15 a.m.	Waterloo ...	3 41

WADEBRIDGE (SX)—continued.

—	Berth ...	1 third	9. 0 a.m.	Bodmin General ...	9 18
—	Berth ...	2-set *3-set (770) FO	8.40 p.m.	Padstow (*com 3/7) ...	8 54
—	Berth ...	2-set	10.5 p.m.	Padstow ...	10 14

WADEBRIDGE (SO).

a.m.	Berth ...	2-set	—	Berth...	—
6 55	Berth ...	2-set	—	Berth...	—
8 3	Berth ...	3-set (770) 1 third	—	Berth...	┐
8 5 R (com. 4/7)	Waterloo ...				
9 48	Bodmin North ...	2-set	8.45 a.m.	Bodmin North...	9 4
noon 12 0	Bodmin Road W.R. ...	2 W.R. set	10.10 a.m.	Bodmin Rd. W.R. F.P.	10 58
p.m. 1 25	Bodmin Road W.R. ...	2 W.R. set	12.40 p.m.	BodminRoad W.R. ...	1 10
1 45	Padstow ...	2-set 2-set	11.30 a.m. 10.10 a.m.	Padstow ... Bodmin Rd. W.R. R.P.	11 44 10 58
3 28	Bodmin Road W.R. ...	2 W.R. set	2.32 p.m.	Bodmin Road W.R. ...	3 10
5 11	Bodmin North ...	2-set	4.40 p.m.	Bodmin North ...	4 49
5 56	Bodmin Road W.R. ...	2 W.R. set	4.55 p.m.	Bodmin Road W.R. ...	5 37
6 12	Bodmin North ...	2-set	5.36 p.m.	Bodmin North ...	5 55
7 5	Bodmin Road W.R. ...	2 W.R. set	6.17 p.m.	Bodmin Road W.R. ...	6 47
8 42	Bodmin Road W.R. ...	2 W.R. set	7.10 p.m.	Bodmin Road W.R. ...	8 0
—	Berth ...	2-set	8.40 p.m.	Berth ...	8 54
—	Berth ...	2-set	10. 5 p.m.	Padstow ...	10 14

YEOFORD (WEEKDAYS).

a.m. 3 20 MO	Exeter Ctl. ...	1 stove van (400/1) 1 bke. cpo. (C.A.)	IV25 a.m.	Plymouth Friary ... Berth...	3V18 —
3F35	Plymouth Friary ... Bude ... Padstow ...	1 B.Y. (stove) (400/1) 1 B.Y. 1 van B.	2F 6 a.m.	Exeter Ctl. R.P. ...	3F26
3F46	Ilfracombe ... Barnstaple Jc. Torrington ...	1 van B. 1 van B. 1 van B.	2F 6 a.m.	Exeter Ctl. F.P. ...	3F26
SO	Berth ...	1 bke. cpo. (C.A.)	10.37 a.m.	Barnstaple Jc. ...	11 46

TORRINGTON (SO)—continued.

—	Berth ...	2 thirds (until 29/8) 1 bke. cpo. (C.A.) (until 27/6), 3-set (770) (com. 4/7)	4.56 p.m.	Barnstaple Jc. ...	5 29
—	Berth ...	2 lav. set	4.22 p.m.	Exeter Central ...	6 24
—	Berth ...	2-set (63/75) 2-set (63/75)	1. 0 p.m.	Waterloo ...	7 9
—	Berth ...	1 third 1 bke. cpo. (new)	3. 0 p.m.	Waterloo ...	9 1

WADEBRIDGE (SX).

a.m. 6 55	Bodmin North ...	1 third MX 2-set	—	Berth ...	—
7 51	Padstow ...	2-set 1 third (until 27/6)	7.22 a.m. —	Bodmin North... Berth...	7 41 —
8 3	Bodmin North ...	2-set	—	Berth ...	—
9 48	Padstow ...	2-set	9. 0 a.m.	Bodmin General ...	9 18
10 30	Bodmin North ...	2-set	8.45 a.m.	Bodmin North ...	9 4
11 10	Bodmin Road W.R. ...	2 W.R. set	10.10 a.m.	Bodmin Road W.R. ...	10 58
p.m. 12 28	Bodmin North ...	2-set	11.20 a.m.	Bodmin North...	11 39
1 25	Bodmin Road W.R. ...	2 W.R. set	11.55 a.m.	Bodmin Road ...	12 25
1 45	Padstow ...	2-set	10.55 a.m.	Padstow ...	11 4
3 12	Bodmin North ...	2-set	2.55 p.m.	Padstow F.P. ...	3 4
3 20	Exeter Ctl. ... Waterloo ... Derby ...	2-set 1 news Van " B ", 1 P.M.V. (4) *1 P.M.V. (4)	2.55 p.m.	Padstow R.P. ...	3 4
		(* As required)			
3 28	Bodmin Road W.R. ...	2 W.R. set	2.32 p.m.	Bodmin Road W.R. ...	3 10
4†43	Bodmin General ...	2 W.R. set	4. 8 p.m.	Bodmin General ...	4 27
5 18	Bodmin North ...	2-set	5. 6 p.m.	Padstow ...	5 15
5 24	Padstow ...	2-set	4.23 p.m.	Bodmin North...	4 42
5 35	Bodmin General ...	2 W.R. set	4.32 p.m.	Bodmin Road W.R. ...	5 7
6 18	Bodmin North ...	2-set	5.48 p.m.	Bodmin North...	6 7
7 5	Bodmin Road W.R. ...	2 W.R. set	6.17 p.m.	Bodmin Road W.R. ...	6 47
8 42	Bodmin Road W.R. ...	2 W.R. set	7.10 p.m.	Bodmin Road W.R. ...	8 0

84

YEOVIL TOWN (SO)—continued

Time	Station	Formation	Station	Time	Time
a.m. 10 35	Yeovil Jc.	P. & P. set	Yeovil Jc.	10.25 a.m.	10 29
10 55	Yeovil Jc.	P. & P. set	Yeovil Jc.	10.45 a.m.	10 49
11 20	Yeovil Jc.	P. & P. set	Yeovil Jc.	11. 8 a.m.	11 12
11 52	Yeovil Jc.	P. & P. set	Yeovil Jc.	11.42 a.m.	11 46
p.m. 12 19	Yeovil Jc.	P. & P. set	Yeovil Jc.	12. 9 p.m.	12 13
1 10	Yeovil Jc.	P. & P. set	Yeovil Jc.	12.30 p.m.	12 34
1 25	Yeovil Jc.	3-set	Salisbury	11.14 a.m.	12 47
1 56	Yeovil Jc.	P. & P. set	Yeovil Jc.	1.38 p.m.	1 42
2 30	Yeovil Jc.	P. & P. set	Yeovil Jc.	2.15 p.m.	2 19
2 56	Yeovil Jc.	P. & P. set	Yeovil Jc.	2.46 p.m.	2 50
3 30	Yeovil Jc.	P. & P. set	Yeovil Jc.	3.10 p.m.	3 14
4 5	Salisbury	1 News van B.	Waterloo	1.25 a.m.	4 17
		3-set	Exeter Ctl.	1. 8 p.m.	3 45
4 19	Yeovil Jc.	P. & P. set	Yeovil Jc.	4. 0 p.m.	4 4
5 0	Yeovil Jc.	P. & P. set	Yeovil Jc.	4.35 p.m.	4 39
5 26	Yeovil Jc.	P. & P. set	Yeovil Jc.	5.12 p.m.	5 16
5V40	Clapham Jc. / Gravesend	1 Van B. / 1 B.Y. (stove)	Gravesend Ctl.	2V48 p.m.	9V 5
5 50	Yeovil Jc.	P. & P. set	Yeovil Jc.	5.35 p.m.	5 39
6 20	Yeovil Jc.	P. & P. set	Yeovil Jc.	6. 8 p.m.	6 12
7 0	Yeovil Jc.	P. & P. set	Yeovil Jc.	6.33 p.m.	6 37
7 40	Yeovil Jc.	P. & P. set	Yeovil Jc.	7.14 p.m.	7 18
8 10	Yeovil Jc.	P. & P. set	Yeovil Jc.	7.53 p.m.	7 57
8 41	Yeovil Jc.	P. & P. set	Yeovil Jc.	8.27 p.m.	8 31
9 22	Yeovil Jc.	P. & P. set	Yeovil Jc.	8.56 p.m.	9 0
—	Berth	P. & P. set	Yeovil Jc.	9.40 p.m.	9 44
—	Berth	3-set (770) / 3-set / 1 third	Yeovil Jc.	9†50 p.m.	9†55
—	Berth	3-set / 2 thirds	Waterloo	6.54 p.m.	11 34

85

AXMINSTER (SUN.)

Time	Station	Time	Formation	Station	Time
a.m. 11 1	Lyme Regis	10.40 a.m.	2 lav. set	Lyme Regis	a.m. 11 11
11 58	Lyme Regis	11.37 a.m.	2 lav. set	Lyme Regis	p.m. 12 6
12 54	Lyme Regis	12.33 p.m.	2 lav. set	Lyme Regis	1 0
p.m. 2 11	Lyme Regis	1.50 p.m.	2 lav. set	Lyme Regis	2 23
3 11	Lyme Regis	2.50 p.m.	2 lav. set	Lyme Regis	3 20
4 16	Lyme Regis	3.55 p.m.	2 lav. set	Lyme Regis	4 25
5 17	Lyme Regis	4.56 p.m.	2 lav. set	Lyme Regis	5 50
7 6 / 6V28	Lyme Regis	6.45 p.m. / 5V20 p.m.	2 lav. set / 1 bke. cpo. (new) (until 28/6)	Lyme Regis / Exeter Ctl.	7 18
8 16	Lyme Regis	7.55 p.m.	2 lav. set	Lyme Regis	8 22
9 11	Lyme Regis	8.50 p.m.	2 lav. set	Lyme Regis	9 25
10 14	Lyme Regis	9.53 p.m.	2 lav. set	Lyme Regis	10 25

BARNSTAPLE JC. (SUN.)

Time	Station	Time	Formation	Station	Time
a.m. 9 35	Bideford	8.55 a.m.	2-set (63/75)	Torrington	9 25
			2 thirds		
10 35 R	Waterloo	9.50 a.m.	1 third	Ilfracombe	10 30
			5-set		
10 40	Ilfracombe	10. 2 a.m.	2 thirds	Bideford	10 21
			2-set (63/75)		
p.m. 12 5	Ilfracombe	—	4 W.R. set	Berth.	—
			4-set		
12 13	Torrington	10.16 a.m.	3-set (770)	Exeter Ctl. R.P.	11 58
2 45 R	Waterloo	10.16 a.m.	1 third	Exeter Ctl. F.P.	11 58
		—	1 bke. cpo. (C.A.)	Berth.	—
3 10	Ilfracombe	2. 0 p.m.	1 third	Ilfracombe	2 39
			5-set		
3 15	Torrington	1.55 p.m.	1 third	Torrington	2 25
			2-set (63/75)		
4 50	Torrington	10.45 a.m.	3-set (770)	Waterloo F.P.	3 5
		10.45 a.m.		Waterloo R.P.	3 5
5 5	Ilfracombe	11. 5 a.m.	2 thirds	Waterloo R.P.	4 28
		11. 5 a.m.	2-set (63/75)	Waterloo F.P.	4 28

CALLINGTON (SUN.).

	From	Set	Arr.	Berth / To	Dep.
a.m.					
8 15	Bere Alston	2-set "A"	—	Berth...	—
11 35	Bere Alston	2-set "A"	9.26 a.m.	Bere Alston	10 8
p.m.					
6 30	Bere Alston	2-set "A"	12.27 p.m.	Bere Alston	1 9
9 10	Bere Alston	2-set "A"	7.21 p.m.	Bere Alston	8 2
—	Berth	2-set "A"	10. 5 p.m.	Bere Alston	10 47

EXETER CENTRAL (SUN.).

Formation of Exeter—Exmouth 5-Coach sets:—

2 lav. thirds
*2 lav. set
1 lav. third
*From Nos. 8, 10, 13, 14, 15, 17 and 20.

	From	Set	Arr.	Berth / To	Dep.
a.m.					
8V25	Exeter St. Davids	Vans / 1 Van B. (stove)	—	Berth...	—
8 35	Honiton	3 lav. set	—	Berth...	—
9 55	Sidmouth	2 lav. set	—	Berth...	—
10 0	Exmouth	5 lav. set	9.15 a.m.	Exmouth	9 47
10 16	Barnstaple Jc. / Ilfracombe	1 bke. compo (new) / 1 third / 1 third / 3-set (770)	—	Berth...	—
10 38	Plymouth Friary / Okehampton	1 third / 3 lav. set / 2-set (Com. 19/7) / 1 P.M.V. (4)	9.23 a.m. / 9V0 a.m.	Berth... / Honiton / Berth... / Exeter St. Davids	9 54 / 9V 3
11 0	Waterloo	1 News van B. / 2 thirds / 3-set (770) / 1 refreshment sal. / 1 kit. buff. car (7) / 1 third	8.20 a.m.	Berth... / Plymouth Friary / Berth...	10 47
11 20	Exmouth	2 lav. set / 5 lav. set	—	Berth...	—
11 50	Waterloo	1 bke. compo. (new) / 1 open third / 1 rest. car (14) / 1 third / 5-set / 2-thirds / 2-set (63/75)	9.50 a.m. / 10. 2 a.m.	Ilfracombe / Bideford	11 44 / 11 44

BARNSTAPLE JC. (SUN.).—continued.

	From	Set	Arr.	Berth / To	Dep.
p.m.					
6 59	Exeter Ctl.	1 third / 3-set (770) / 2-set (63/75) / 2 lav. set	6.15 p.m. / 6.14 p.m.	Ilfracombe / Torrington	6 53 / 6 44
8 5	Torrington	2 lav. set	—	Berth...	—
9 51	Ilfracombe	2 thirds / 3-set (770)	4. 0 p.m.	Waterloo F.P.	9 46
9 56	Torrington	1 third / 1 bke. cpo. (new)	4. 0 p.m.	Waterloo R.P.	9 46
—	Berth	1 bke. cpo. (new)	10.16 a.m.	Exeter Ctl. F.P.	11 58
—	Berth	3-set (770)	11.55 a.m.	Torrington	12 25
—	Berth	2 lav. set	9. 5 p.m.	Torrington	9 35
—	Berth	2 thirds / 2-set (63/75)	9.10 p.m.	Ilfracombe	9 48

BERE ALSTON (SUN.).

	From	Set	Arr.	To	Dep.
a.m.					
9 26	Callington	2-set "A"	8.15 a.m.	Callington	8 57
p.m.					
12 27	Callington	2-set "A"	11.35 a.m.	Callington	12 16
7 21	Callington	2-set "A"	6.30 p.m.	Callington	7 10
10 5	Callington	2-set "A"	9.10 p.m.	Callington	9 51

BIDEFORD (SUN.).

	From	Set	Arr.	To	Dep.
a.m.					
10 2 R	Waterloo	2 thirds / 2-set (63/75)	9.35 a.m.	Barnstaple Jc.	9 52

BUDE (SUN.).

	From	Set	Arr.	Berth / To	Dep.
a.m.					
9 45 R	Waterloo	2-set (63/75)	—	Berth...	—
11 15	Halwill	2-set	—	Berth... Halwill	11 3
p.m.					
2 32	Okehampton	2-set	10.29 a.m.	Okehampton	12 58
6 42	Okehampton	2-set	11.50 a.m.	Waterloo R.P.	5 18
—	Berth	1 third / 1 bke. cpo. (new)	11. 0 a.m.	Waterloo F.P.	5 18
—	Berth	2-set	9.23 p.m.	Okehampton	10 29

EXETER CENTRAL (SUN.)—continued

Arr.	From	Formation	To	Dep.	Arr.
p.m. 4 14	Waterloo ...	1 bke. cpo. (new) ...	Waterloo R.P....	10.45 a.m. ...	1 56
		1 third ...			
		1 refreshment sal. ..			
		1 kitch. buff car (3)			
		1 third ...			
4 44	Waterloo ...	5-set ...	Ilfracombe ...	2. 0 p.m. ...	4 8
		1 third ...	Torrington ...	1.55 p.m. ...	4 8
		2-set (63/75) ...	Waterloo R.P. ...	11. 5 a.m. ...	3 0
		1 bke. cpo. (new) ...			
		1 open third ...			
		1 rest. car (17) ...	Ilfracombe ...	2.45 p.m. ...	4 38
4 56	Waterloo ...	4-set ...			
		5-set ...			
		1 bke. cpo. (new) ...	Waterloo R.P. ...	11. 0 a.m. ...	2 45
		1 third ...			
		1 refresh. sal ...			
		1 kitchen buffet car (2)			
		1 third ...	Plymouth Friary	2.50 p.m. ...	4 49
		3-set (770) ...			
5 10	Exmouth ...	4-set ...	Berth...	—	—
		2 lav. thirds ...	Exmouth	4.20 p.m. ...	4 50
		5 lav. set ...			
5 15	Ilfracombe ...	3-set (770) ...	Salisbury F.P. ...	1.54 p.m. ...	4 58
5V20 (Milk & Pcls.)	Waterloo ...	Vans ...	Berth...	—	—
	Templecombe	1 van B. (stove) ...			
	Axminster	1 bke. cpo. (new) ...	Plymouth Friary F.P.	11.40 a.m. ...	2 10
		1 bke. cpo. (new) ...	Berth...	—	—
		(until 28/6).			
5 25	Plymouth Friary ...	3-set (770) ...	Berth...	—	—
		3-set (770) ...			
6 16	Exmouth ...	5 lav. set ...	Berth...	—	—
6 52 Excn. (21/6, 19/7, 9/8,23/8, 6/9.)	Waterloo ...	5-set ...	Exmouth ...	2† 5 p.m. ...	2†28
		1 open third ...	Waterloo F.P. ...	9.22 a.m. ...	1 16
		1 rest. car (27) ...			
		3-set (770) ...			
		2 thirds ...			
7 15	Exmouth ...	2 lav. set ...	Exmouth ...	6.15 p.m. ...	6 45
		5 lav. set ...			
7 20	Salisbury ...	3-set ...	Ilfracombe	9. 5 a.m. ...	11 12
	Yeovil ...	3-set ...	Portsmouth & S. R.P.	11.40 a.m. ...	3 47
8 12	Plymouth Friary ...	2 thirds ...	Plymouth Friary M.P.	11.40 a.m. ...	2 10
		4-set ...	Waterloo F.P. ...	4. 0 p.m. ...	8 4

EXETER CENTRAL (SUN.)—continued.

Arr.	From	Formation	To	Dep.	Arr.
p.m. 12 2	Portsmouth & S....	4-set ...	Plymouth Friary ...	10. 0 a.m. ...	11 54
	Waterloo ...	1 third ...			
		4-set ...	Bude...	9.45 a.m. ...	11 54
		2-set (63/75) ...	Berth...	—	—
		1 open third ...			
		1 rest. car (30) ...			
		1 bke. cpo. (new) ...			
12 37	Honiton ...	3-set ...	Yeovil	10.10 a.m. ...	12 8
12 40 (12/7, 9/8 and 23/8)	Paignton W.R. ...	6-set (459) ...	Salisbury ...	10. 0 a.m. ...	12 32
12 45	Exmouth ...	2 lav. set ...	Berth...	—	11 32
		5 lav. set ...	Exmouth ...	11. 0 a.m. ...	—
1 22 (21/6, 19/7, 9/8, 23/8, 6/9).	Exmouth ...	5-set ...	Waterloo R.P. ...	9.22 a.m. ...	1 16
1 45	Waterloo ...	9 Pullman cars ...	Ilfracombe ...	12. 0 noon. ...	1 38
2 2	Ilfracombe ...	1 third ...	Waterloo F.P. ...	10.45 a.m. ...	1 56
		5-set ...			
		3-set (770) ...			
2 15	Exmouth ...	2 lav. set ...	Exmouth ...	12. 5 p.m. ...	12 35
		5 lav. set ...			
2 55	Plymouth Friary ...	3 thirds ...	Waterloo F.P. ...	11. 0 a.m. ...	2 45
	Bude ...	4-set ...			
		1 third ...			
		1 bke. cpo. (new) ...			
3 0	Exmouth ...	2 lav. set ...	Exmouth ...	1.45 p.m. ...	2 15
		5 lav. set ...			
3 10	Ilfracombe ...	1 third ...	Berth...	—	—
		2 thirds ...	Waterloo F.P. ...	11. 5 a.m. ...	3 0
		2-set (63/75) ...			
	Torrington ...	1 third ...			
		2-set (63/75) ...			
3 20	Salisbury ...	3 set ...	Honiton ...	1.22 p.m. ...	1 52
3 42	Exmouth ...	2 lav. set ...	Exmouth ...	2.55 p.m. ...	3 25
		5 lav. set ...			
3 42 (until 13/9)	Ilfracombe ...	9 Pullman cars ...	Waterloo ...	12. 0 noon... ...	3 35
3 53	Plymouth Friary ...	3 set ...	Portsmouth & S. F.P. ...	11.40 a.m. ...	3 47
		3-set ...			

90

EXETER CENTRAL (SUN.)—continued

		Formation		
p.m. 8 22 ...	Ilfracombe ...	1 third ...	10.10 a.m. ...	Yeovil F.P. ... 12 8
	Torrington ...	1 third ...	4. 0 p.m. ...	Waterloo M.P. ... 8 4
		3-set (770) ...		
		1 third ...		
8 26 ...	Exmouth ...	1 bke. cpo. (new) ...	7.10 p.m. ...	Exmouth ... 7 41
9 15 ...	Exmouth ...	2 lav. set ...	8.15 p.m. ...	Exmouth F.P. ... 8 47
		5 lav. set ...		
9 32 ...	Salisbury ...	5 lav. set ...	10. 0 a.m. (not 12/7, 9/8 and 23/8)	Salisbury ... 12 32
		6-set (459) ...	8. 5 p.m. (12/7, 9/8 and 23/8)	Paignton W.R. ... 23/8 9 25
10 16 ...	Exmouth ...	5 lav. set ...	9. 0 p.m. ...	Exmouth F.P. ... 9 30
11 0 ...	Exmouth ...	5 lav. set ...	5.45 p.m. ...	Exmouth F.P. ... 6 17
	Berth ...	1 van B. (stove) ...	9V 0 a.m. ...	Exeter St. Davids ... 9V 3
— ...	Berth ...	2-set ...	11.40 a.m. ...	Plymouth Friary R.P. ... 2 10
— ...	Berth ...	1 res. car. (29) ...	1.54 p.m. ...	Salisbury ... 4 58
		1 open third ...		
— ...	Berth ...	2 lav. set ...	5.45 p.m. ...	Exmouth R.P. ... 6 17
— ...	Berth ...	1 kitch. buff. car (5) ...	4. 0 p.m. ...	Waterloo R.P. ... 8 4
		1 refreshment sal. ...		
		1 bke. cpo. (new) ...		
— ...	Berth ...	1 third ...	6.15 p.m. ...	Ilfracombe ... 8 22
		3-set (770) ...	6.14 p.m. ...	Torrington ... 8 22
		2-set (63/75) ...		
		2 lav. set ...		
— ...	Berth ...	3-set ...	8.15 p.m. ...	Exmouth R.P. ... 8 47
		3-set ...	6.30 p.m. ...	Plymouth Friary ... 9 1
— ...	Berth ...	3-set (770) ...	7.15 p.m. ...	Yeovil ... 9 4
— ...	Berth ...	2 lav. set ...	9. 0 p.m. ...	Exmouth R.P. ... 9 30
— ...	Berth ...	1 bke. compo (new) ...	6. 0 p.m. ...	Waterloo ... 10 10
		3 thirds ...		
		1 kit. buff. car (7) ...		
		1 refreshment sal. ...		
		3-set (770) ...		
		2 thirds ...		
		1 bke. cpo. ...		
— ...	Berth ...	5-set ...	10.55 p.m. ...	Exmouth ... 10 45

91

EXETER CENTRAL (SUN.)—continued

		Formation		
	Berth ...	1 van B. (stove) ...	3V35 p.m. ...	Clapham Jc. ... 10V57
		1 third ...		
		1 bke. cpo. (new) ...		
	Berth ...	2 lav. set ...	10.30 p.m. ...	Sidmouth ... 11 11
	Berth ...	5 lav. set ...	10.55 p.m. ...	Exmouth ... 11 25

EXETER ST. DAVIDS (SUN.)

		Formation		
a.m. 9V 0 ...	Exeter Ctl. ...	1 P.M.V. (4) ...	7.58 p.m. ...	Exeter Ctl. ... 8 ISO
		1 van B. ...	8V25 a.m. ...	Exeter Ctl. ... 8V28
2 7 ... (via Exeter Ctl.)	Ilfracombe ... Torrington ... Plymouth Friary ...	1 P.M.V. (4) ... 1 P.M.V. (4) ... 1 P.M.V. (4) ...	7.58 p.m. ...	Exeter Ctl. ... 8 ISO

Formation of Exmouth—Exeter 5-Coach sets :—
1 lav. third
*2 lav. set
2 lav. thirds
*From Nos. 8, 10, 13, 14, 15, 17 and 20

EXMOUTH (SUN.)

		Formation		
a.m. 9 15 ...	Exeter Ctl. ...	5 lav. set ...	—	Berth ... —
10 38 ...	Sidmouth ...	1 bke. cpo. (new) ...	—	Berth ... —
		2 lav. set ...		
11 0 ...	Exeter Ctl. ...	5 lav. set ...	10. 0 a.m. ...	Exeter Ctl. ... 10 31
p.m. 12 5 ...	Exeter Ctl. ...	5 lav. set ...	11.20 a.m. ...	Exeter Ctl. ... 11 51
		2 lav. set ...		
1 32 ...	Tipton St. Johns ...	2 lav. set ...	12.10 p.m. ...	Tipton St. Johns ... 12 37
1 45 ...	Exeter Ctl. ...	5 lav. set ...	12.45 p.m. ...	Exeter Ctl. ... 1 15
		2 lav. set ...		
2† 5 ... (21/6, 19/7, 9/8, 23/8, 6/9).	Exeter Ctl. ...	5 set ...	9.20 a.m. ...	Waterloo ... 1 43
2 55 ...	Exeter Ctl. ...	5 lav. set ...	2.15 p.m. ...	Exeter Ctl. ... 2 47
		2 lav. set ...		
4 19 ...	Sidmouth ...	5 lav. set ...	2.48 p.m. ...	Tipton St. Johns ... 3 15
4 20 ...	Exeter Ctl. ...	5 lav. set ...	3. 0 p.m. ...	Exeter Ctl. R.P. ... 3 31
5 45 ...	Exeter Ctl. ...	5 lav. set ...	5.10 p.m. ...	Exeter Ctl. ... 5 39
		2 lav. set ...		
6 15 ...	Exeter Ctl. ...	5 lav. set ...	3.42 p.m. ...	Exeter Ctl. ... 4 11
		2 lav. set ...		
6 52 ...	Sidmouth ...	2 lav. set ...	5.27 p.m. ...	Sidmouth ... 6 12

WORKING TIME TABLES

PASSENGER TRAINS

WESTERN DISTRICT JUNE 1953

The timings shown on this page WILL NOT APPLY ON SATURDAYS, 13th June to 19th September, 1953.

 SALISBURY, EXETER, PLYMOUTH, ILFRACOMBE AND TORRINGTON LINES

Distance from Waterloo m.	c.	DOWN WEEKDAYS			MX 1,55 a.m. Pass. & Mail Eastleigh to Yeovil Town ■				1.25 a.m. Newspaper and Pass. train Waterloo ■A				MX 1.55 a.m. Pass. & Mail Eastleigh to Yeovil Town		CD Pass. News & Mail Yeovil Town		SX Workers (Not advertised)		MX Parcels	
			arr. a.m.	dep. a.m.	arr. a.m.	dep. a.m.			arr. a.m.	dep. a.m.	arr. a.m.	dep. a.m.	arr. a.m.	dep. a.m.	arr. a.m.	dep. a.m.	arr. a.m.	dep. a.m.	arr. a.m.	dep a.m.
83	56	**Salisbury**			2 36	2 50			3 11	3 19						3 30				
86	17	Wilton South													3 36	3 40				
91	78	Dinton											←	—	3C49	3 50				
96	23	Tisbury													3 57	3 59				
101	24	Semley													4 7½	4 11				
105	31	Gillingham			3 20	3 25									4 17	4 21				
112	15	**Templecombe**			3 35	3 55							3 35	3 55	4 30½	4 38				
114	48	Milborne Port													4 43½	4 44½				
118	22	Sherborne			——	→							4 6	4 10	4 50	4 55				
122	69	**Yeovil Jct.**							4A4	4 7			4 18	4 28	5D 3	5 15				
125	08	Sutton Bingham							Through coaches to Plymouth, Padstow, Torrington and Ilfracombe											
131	53	Crewkerne																		
139	58	Chard Jct.																		
144	66	Axminster																		
148	08	Seaton Jct.														–				
155	01	Honiton																		
159	49	Sidmouth Jct.								4 47										
163	30	Whimple																		
167	04	Broad Clyst																		
168	74	Pinhoe																		
170	56	Exmouth Jct.								4 57										5 26
171	22	St. James' Park Halt																		
171	60	**Exeter Central**							5 0	5 9	5 0	5 18							5 29	
172	34	Do. (St. Davids)							5 12	5 16	5 21	5 28								
173	57	Cowley Jct.								5 19		5 31			Mixed Launceston					
176	58	Newton St. Cyres																		
179	28	Crediton									5 39	5 41								
182	79	**Yeoford**									5 48	5 49			arr. a.m.	dep. a.m.				
183	76	Coleford Jct.								5 33		5 51								
187	61	Bow																		
190	72	North Tawton																		
193	58	Sampford C'nay																		
197	33	**Okehampton**							5 55	6 0						6 27		6 58	arr. a.m.	dep. a.m.
199	37	Quarry Halt															7 4	7† 6		
200	05	Meldon Jct.														6 41	7† 9			
204	09	Bridestowe							6 13	6 14										
207	26	Lydford																		7 5
208	52	Brentor																	7 8	7 9
213	59	**Tavistock North**		6 0					6 29	6 57									7 17	7 20
220	15	Bere Alston	6 10½	6 15					7 7½	7 9									7 30½	7 35
223	00	Bere Ferrers	6 20	6 21					7 14	7 15									7 40	7 41
224	73	Tamerton Foliot	6 25	6 25½																
227	14	St. Budeaux, Vic. Rd.	6 29½	6 30½					7 22	7 23									7 48	7 49
228	52	Ford	6 33½	6 34½					7 26	7 28									7 52	7 53
229	54	**Devonport, Kings Rd.**	6 37½	6 39					7 31	7 33									7 56	7 57
230	25	Devonport Jct.		6 41						7 35										7 59
230	71	**Plymouth (N. Rd.)**	6 43	6 45					7 37	7 41									8 1	8 2
232	31	Lipson Jct.		6 49						7 45										8 6
232	68	Mount Gould Jct.		6 50						7 46										8 7
233	05	Friary Jct.		6 50½						7 46½										8 7½
233	79	**Plymouth (Friary)**	6 53						7 49										8 10	
185	75	Copplestone (K)							Not to arrive Devonport before 7.30 a.m.		5 55	5 56							Through coaches from Gunnislake attached at Bere Alston	
187	47	Morchard Rd. (K)									5 59	6 0								
189	76	Lapford (K)									6 4	6 5								
193	68	Eggesford (K)									6 11	6 12								
197	64	Kings Nympton (K) (T)									6X18	6 19	arr. a.m.	dep. a.m.						
200	55	Portsmouth A. (T)									6 24	6 25								
204	67	Umberleigh (T)									6 31	6 32								
207	17	Chapelton																		
211	43	**Barnstaple Jct.** (T)									6 41			6 57						
212	19	Barnstaple Town (T) (T)											7 0	7 1						
212	32	Pottington Box (T)												7 2						
216	45	Wrafton											7 8	7 9						
217	39	Braunton											7 11	7 14						
223	29	Mortehoe & Woolacombe											7 31	7 34			arr. a.m.	dep. a.m.		
226	39	**Ilfracombe**											7 42							
—	—	**Barnstaple Jct** (K)										6 50						7 8		
214	15	Fremington (K)									6 55	6 57					7 13	7 14		
217	76	Instow (K)									7 3	7 5					7X20	7 25		
220	06	Bideford (Goods) (K)															7 29	7 33		
220	46	**Bideford (New)** (K)									7X10	7 19					7 35	7 39		
225	55	**Torrington** (K) (T)									7 28						7 48			

Clear road to be kept for this train

A—Stop at West End of Yeovil Jc. and not advertised.
C—Stop at Dinton not advertised
D—Time allowed at Yeovil Jc. for eng ine to turn.

The timings shown on this page WILL NOT APPLY ON SATURDAYS, 13th June to 19th September, 1953,

SALISBURY, EXETER, PLYMOUTH, ILFRACOMBE AND TORRINGTON LINES

DOWN WEEKDAYS							MX Q Parcels								6.20 a.m. Yeovil Town ▲		MO 4.0 p.m. (Suns.) Churns Gravesend to Yeovil Town ■		A	
			arr. a.m.	dep. a.m.	arr. a.m.	dep. a.m.	arr. a.m.	dep. a.m.	arr. a.m.	dep. a.m.	arr. a.m.	dep. a.m.	arr. a.m.	dep. a.m.	arr. a.m.	dep. a.m.	arr. a.m.	dep. a.m.	arr. a.m.	dep. a.m.
Salisbury																	4 7	5 0		
Wilton South																				
Dinton																				
Tisbury																	5 25	5 30		
Semley																	5 40	5 50		
Gillingham																	6 0	6 12		
Templecombe																	6 22	7 22		
Milborne Port																	——	→		
Sherborne																				
Yeovil Jct.								5 32							6 25	6 28				
Sutton Bingham																				
Crewkerne															6 41	6 44				
Chard Jct.															6 57	6 59				
Axminster								6 8							7W 6	7 9				
Seaton Jct.															7 15	7 18				
Honiton															7 32	7 34½				
Sidmouth Jct.								6 38							7 41	7 45				
Whimple															7 51	7 52				
Broad Clyst															7 57½	7 58½				
Pinhoe															8 2½	8 3½				
Exmouth Jct.								6 55								8 7½				
St. James' Park Halt															8 9	8 9½				
Exeter Central							6 58							7 35	8 11	8 20				8 41
Do. (St. Davids)													7 38	7 46	8 23	8 31			8 44	8 52
Cowley Jct.														7 49		8 34				8 55
Newton St. Cyres													7 54	7 55	8 39	8 40				
Crediton													8 0	8 1	8 45	8 48			9 3	9 4
Yeoford													8 8	8 9	8 55	8 58			9 11	9 12
Coleford Jct.																9 0				9 14
Bow													8 17	8 18					9 21	9 22
North Tawton													8 24	8 25					9 28	9 29
Sampford C'nay													8 31	8 32					9 35	9 36
Okehampton													8 40	8 45					9 44	48
Quarry Halt													8 52	8 53						
Meldon Jct.														8 55						
Bridestowe													9 0	9 0½					10 1	10 2
Lydford													9 6½	9 7½					10 8	10 9
Brentor													9 10½	9 11					10 12	10 13
Tavistock North				7 50								8 46	9 19	9 21					10 21	10 24
Bere Alston			8 0½	8 5							8 57		9 31½	9 33					10 34½	10 39
Bere Ferrers			8 10	8 11									9 37	9 40					10 44	10 45
Tamerton Foliot			8 15	8 16									9 44	9 45					10 49	10 50
St. Budeaux, Vic. Rd.			8 20	8 21									9 49	9 50					10 54	10 55
Ford			8 24	8 25									9 53	9 54					10 58	10 59
Devonport, Kings Rd.			8 28	8 32									9 57	10 0					11 2	11 5
Devonport Jct.				8 34										10 2						11 7
Plymouth (N. Rd.)			8 36	8 38									10 4	10 7					11A 9	11 17
Lipson Jct.				8 42										10 11						11 21
Mount Gould Jct.				8 43										10 12						11 22
Friary Jct.				8 43½										10 12½						11 22½
Plymouth (Friary)			8 46										10 15						11 25	
Copplestone															9 4	9 6				
Morchard Rd.															9 9	9 11				
Lapford															9 15	9 20				
Eggesford															9X26	9 32				
Kings Nympton										8 28					9 38	9 38½				
Portsmouth A.									8 33	8 34					9 43	9 44				
Umberleigh									8 40	8 41					9 50	9 51				
Chapelton									8 45	8 46					9 55	9 56				
Barnstaple Jct.						8 0			8 52						10 2	10 9				
Barnstaple Town					8 3	8 4									10 12	10 14				
Pottington Box						8 5										10 15				
Wrafton					8 11	8 12									10 21	10 22				
Braunton					8 14	8 18									10 24	10 26				
Mortehoe & Woolacombe					8 35	8 38									10 43	10 44				
Ilfracombe					8 46										10 52					
Barnstaple Jct.						8 2										10 18				
Fremington					8 7	8 8									10 23	10 24				
Instow					8 14	8 15									10 30	10 31				
Bideford (Goods)																				
Bideford (New)					8X20	8 24									10X36	10 42				
Torrington					8 33										10 51					

A—Advertised arrival at Plymouth North Road 11.12 a.m.

9 SALISBURY, EXETER, PLYMOUTH, ILFRACOMBE AND TORRINGTON LINES

DOWN — WEEKDAYS

Stations:

Salisbury
Wilton South
Dinton
Tisbury
Semley
Gillingham
Templecombe
Milborne Port
Sherborne
Yeovil Jct.
Sutton Bingham
Crewkerne
Chard Jct.
Axminster
Seaton Jct.
Honiton
Sidmouth Jct.
Whimple
Broad Clyst
Pinhoe
Exmouth Jct.
St. James' Park Halt
Exeter Central
Do. (St. Davids)
Cowley Jct.
Newton St. Cyres
Crediton
Yeoford
Coleford Jct.

Bow
North Tawton
Sampford C'nay
Okehampton
Quarry Halt
Meldon Jct.
Bridestowe
Lydford
Brentor
Tavistock North
Bere Alston
Bere Ferrers
Tamerton Foliot
St. Budeaux, Vic. Rd.
Ford
Devonport, Kings Rd.
Devonport Jct. (N. Rd.)
Lipson Jct.
Mount Gould Jct.
Friary Jct.
Plymouth (Friary)

Copplestone
Morchard Rd.
Lapford
Eggesford
Kings Nympton
Portsmouth A.
Umberleigh
Chapelton
Barnstaple Jct.
Barnstaple Town
Pottington Box
Wrafton
Braunton
Morthoe & Woolacombe
Ilfracombe

Barnstaple Jct.
Fremington
Instow
Bideford (Goods)
Bideford (New)
Torrington

A—Change engines at Yeovil Jct.

---

8 SALISBURY, EXETER, PLYMOUTH, ILFRACOMBE AND TORRINGTON LINES

DOWN — WEEKDAYS

Stations:

Salisbury
Wilton South
Dinton
Tisbury
Semley
Gillingham
Templecombe
Milborne Port
Sherborne
Yeovil Jct.
Sutton Bingham
Crewkerne
Chard Jct.
Axminster
Seaton Jct.
Honiton
Sidmouth Jct.
Whimple
Broad Clyst
Pinhoe
Exmouth Jct.
St. James' Park Halt
Exeter Central
Do. (St. Davids)
Cowley Jct.
Newton St. Cyres
Crediton
Yeoford
Coleford Jct.

Bow
North Tawton
Sampford C'nay
Okehampton
Meldon Jct.
Bridestowe
Lydford
Brentor
Tavistock North
Bere Alston
Bere Ferrers
Tamerton Foliot
St. Budeaux, Vic. Rd.
Ford
Devonport, Kings Rd.
Devonport Jct. (N. Rd.)
Mpson Jct.
Mount Gould Jct.
Friary Jct.
Plymouth (Friary)

Copplestone
Morchard Rd.
Lapford
Eggesford
Kings Nympton
Portsmouth A.
Umberleigh
Chapelton
Barnstaple Jct.
Barnstaple Town
Pottington Box
Wrafton
Braunton
Morthoe & Woolacombe
Ilfracombe

Barnstaple Jct.
Fremington
Instow
Bideford (Goods)
Bideford (New)
Torrington

328

The timings shown on this page WILL NOT APPLY ON SATURDAYS, 13th June to 19th September, 1953.

10 SALISBURY, EXETER, PLYMOUTH, ILFRACOMBE AND TORRINGTON LINES

DOWN WEEKDAYS																				
															MO					
	11.0 a.m. Waterloo						11.0 a.m. Waterloo						11.5 a.m. Waterloo (Not advertised)		Engine					
	■						■						■						A	
	arr. p.m.	dep. p.m.	arr. p.m.	dep. p.m.	arr. p.m.	dep. p.m.	arr. p.m.	dep. p.m.	arr. p.m.	dep. p.m.	arr. p.m.	dep. p.m.	arr. p.m.	dep. p.m.	arr. p.m.	dep. p.m.	arr. p.m.	dep. p.m.	arr. p.m.	dep. p.m.
Salisbury	12 23	12 28					12 23	12 28					12 32	1238						
Wilton South															After working 1.35 p.m. MO Sidmouth					
Dinton																				
Tisbury	Commences 21st September						Until 18th September only													
Semley																				
Gillingham																				
Templecombe																				
Milborne Port																				
Sherborne																				
Yeovil Jct.		1 9						1 9						1 19						
Sutton Bingham	Through coaches to Ilfracombe, Torrington, Padstow, Bude, Plymouth, Exmouth and Sidmouth.						Through coaches to Padstow, Bude and Plymouth, also Ilfracombe Torrington, Exmouth and Sidmouth when 11.5 a.m. Waterloo not running.						Through coaches to Ilfracombe & Torrington Exmouth & Sidmouth							
Crewkerne																				
Chard Jct.																				
Axminster																				2 5
Seaton Jct.																			2 11	2 12
Honiton																			2 27	2 28
Sidmouth Jct.	1 47	1 51					1 47	1 51					1 57	2 1		2‖15			2 35	2 36
Whimple																			2 42	2 42½
Broad Clyst																			2 48	2 49
Pinhoe																			2 53	2 54
Exmouth Jct.		2 2						2 2						2 12	2‖35					2 58
St. James' Park Halt																				3A0
Exeter Central	2 5	2 11	2 5	2 19			2 5	2 11			2 5	2 21	2 15						3 2	
Do. (St. Davids)	2 14	2 18	2 22	2 26			2 14	2 18			2 24	2 27								
Cowley Jct.		2 21		2 29				2 21				2 30	Form 2.21 p.m.							
Newton St. Cyres																				
Crediton																	Until 18th Sept. only			
Yeoford																				
Coleford Jct.		2 35		2 43				2 35				2 44								
Bow													Mondays and Fridays only 8th June to 24th July, Mondays to Fridays 27th July, to 28th Aug. and Mondays and Fridays only, 31st Aug. to 18th Sept. and "Q"							
North Tawton			2 55	2 56			2 47	2 48											arr. p.m.	dep. p.m.
Sampford C'nay																				
Okehampton			3 8	3 12	3 8	3 22	3 0	3 4	3 0	3 12								3 20		3 32
Quarry Halt																				
Meldon Jct.				3 20		3 30		3 12		3 20										
Bridestowe																	3 33	3 34	3 45	3 46
Lydford			To Padstow and Bude.				To Padstow and Bude.										3 40	3 40½	3 52	3 53
Brentor																	3 43½	3 44	3 56	3 57
Tavistock North					3 47	3 48			3 37	3 40							3 52	3 53	4 5	4 6
Bere Alston																	4 3½	4 5	4 16½	4 18
Bere Ferrers																	4 10	4 11	4 23	4 24
Tamerton Foliot																	4 15	4 16	4 28	4 29
St. Budeaux, Vic. Rd.																	4 20	4 21	4 33	4 34
Ford																	4 24	4 25	4 37	4 38
Devonport, Kings Rd.					4 14	4 16			4 6	4 11							4 28	4 30	4 41	4 44
Devonport Jct.						4 18				4 13								4 32		4 46
Plymouth (N. Rd.)					4 20	4 22			4 15	4 17							4 34	4 38	4 48	4 52
Lipson Jct.						4 26				4 21					15th June to 14th Sept. only			4 42		4 56
Mount Gould Jct.						4 27				4 22								4 43		4 57
Friary Jct.						4 27½				4 22½								4 43½		4 57½
Plymouth (Friary)					4 30				4 25								4 46		5 0	
Copplestone		2 38										2 47								
Morchard Rd.		2 40½										2 49½							Commences 21st Sept.	
Lapford		2 44										2 53								
Eggesford	2 50	2 51									2 59	3 0								
Kings Nympton		2 57										3 6								
Portsmouth A.		3 2										3 11								
Umberleigh		3 7										3 16								
Chapelton																				
Barnstaple Jct.	3 16	3 20									3 25	3 29								
Barnstaple Town	3 23	3 24									3 32	3 33								
Pottington Box		3 25										3 34								
Wrafton	3 31	3 32									3 40	3 41								
Braunton	3 34	3 36									3 43	3 45								
Mortehoe & Woolacombe	3 53	3 54									4 2	4 3								
Ilfracombe	4 2										4 11									
Barnstaple Jct.		3 25										3 34								
Fremington	3 30	3 31									3 39	3 40								
Instow	3 37	3 38									3 46	3 47								
Bideford (Goods)																				
Bideford (New)	3 43	3 48									3 52	3 56								
Torrington	3 57										4 5									

A—Call at St. James' Park Halt on Saturdays only

The timings shown on this page WILL NOT APPLY ON SATURDAYS, 13th June to 19th September, 1953.

SALISBURY, EXETER, PLYMOUTH, ILFRACOMBE AND TORRINGTON LINES 11

DOWN WEEKDAYS																				
					Q		FX		FO		FO		FO		FO					
	To Padstow				Engine and Brake Van				To Exeter Central		Engine		12.0 noon Waterloo				To Bude			
			AC				AC		AC				D							
	arr. p.m.	dep. p.m.	arr. p.m.	dep. p.m.	arr. p.m.	dep. p.m.	arr. p.m.	dep. p.m.	arr. p.m.	dep. p.m.	arr. p.m.	dep. p.m.	arr. p.m.	dep. p.m.	arr. p.m.	dep. p.m.	arr. p.m.	dep. p.m.	arr. p.m.	dep. p.m.
Salisbury				12 36				12 46		1246		1‖24		1 42						
Wilton South			1242	1242½			1252	1252½	1252	1252½	1‖30		1D47	1 53						
Dinton			1251½	1252			1 1½	1 2	1 1½	1 2	Work 12.0 noon Waterloo		"DEVON BELLE" Pullman Cars only							
Tisbury			1259	1 0			1 9	1 10	1 9	1 10										
Semley			1 8½	1 9½			1 18½	1 19½	1 18½	1 19½										
Gillingham			1 15½	1 17			1 25½	1 27	1 25½	1 27										
Templecombe			1 26½	1 29			1 36½	1 39	1 36½	1 39										
Milborne Port			1 34½	1 35½			1 44½	1 45½	1 44½	1 45½										
Sherborne			1 41	1 42			1 51	1 52	1 51	1 52										
Yeovil Jct.			1A49	1 56			1A59	2 6	1A59	2 6				2 33						
Sutton Bingham																				
Crewkerne	Until 18th Sept. only.		2 8	2 10			2 18	2 20	2 18	2 20										
Chard Jct.			2 22	2 24			2 32	2 34	2 32	2 34										
Axminster			2 31	2 34			2 41	2 44	2 41	2 44										
Seaton Jct.			2C40	2 44			2C50	2 54	2C50	3 10										
Honiton			2 59	3 0			3 9	3 10												
Sidmouth Jct.			3 6½	3 9			3 16½	3 19	→				3 16	3 19						
Whimple																				
Broad Clyst																				
Pinhoe																				
Exmouth Jct.				3 22				3 32						3 32						
St. James' Park Halt																				
Exeter Central			3 25			3†30	3 35						3 35	3 42						3 50
Do. (St. Davids)					3 33	3 35							3 45	3 47					3 53	3 55
Cowley Jct.			Commences 21st Sept			3 38								3 50						3 58
Newton St. Cyres																			4 3	4 3½
Crediton					3†48		Until 17th Sept. only.										Commences 21st Sept.		4 8½	4 9½
Yeoford																			4 16½	4 17½
Coleford Jct.														4 4						4 19½
Bow					Work 5.36. p.m. Q Milk														4 26½	4 27
North Tawton																			4 33	4 33½
Sampford C'nay																			4 39½	4 40
Okehampton		3 55							Until 18th September only.									4 27	4 48	
Quarry Halt																				
Meldon Jct.		4 4																4 35		
Bridestowe																				
Lydford																				
Brentor																				
Tavistock North																				
Bere Alston																				
Bere Ferrers																				
Tamerton Foliot																				
St. Budeaux, Vic. Rd.																				
Ford																				
Devonport, Kings Rd.																				
Devonport Jct.																				
Plymouth (N. Rd.)																				
Lipson Jct.																				
Mount Gould Jct.																				
Friary Jct.																				
Plymouth (Friary)																				
Copplestone														4 7						
Morchard Rd.														4 10						
Lapford														4 13						
Eggesford														4 19X						
Kings Nympton														4 24½X						
Portsmouth A.														4 29						
Umberleigh														4 34						
Chapelton																				
Barnstaple Jct.													4 43	4 45						
Barnstaple Town													4 48	4 49						
Pottington Box														4 50						
Wrafton																				
Braunton													4 57	5 1						
Mortehoe & Woolacombe					arr. p.m.	dep. p.m.							5 18	5 19						
Ilfracombe													5 27							
Barnstaple Jct.						4 28										4 56				
Fremington					4X33	4 34									5X1	5 6				
Instow					4 40	4 41									5 12	5 13				
Bideford (Goods)																				
Bideford (New)					4X46	4 49									5X18	5 20				
Torrington					4 58										5 29					

A—Changes engines at Yeovil Jc.
C—Convey through coach, Waterloo to Seaton.
D—Stop at Wilton South to change engines, and not advertised.

The timings shown on this page WILL NOT APPLY ON SATURDAYS, 13th June to 19th September, 1953.

SALISBURY, EXETER, PLYMOUTH, ILFRACOMBE AND TORRINGTON LINES

DOWN WEEKDAYS	FO				SO												SX		SO	
	12.46 p.m. Salisbury				Engine		11.30 a.m. Brighton												3.43 p.m. Sidmouth	
							▲ A										C		C	
	arr. p.m.	dep. p.m.	arr. p.m.	dep. p.m.	arr. p.m.	dep. p.m.	arr. p.m.	dep. p.m.	arr. p.m.	dep. p.m.	arr. p.m.	dep. p.m.			arr. p.m.	dep. p.m.	arr. p.m.	dep. p.m.	arr. p.m.	dep. p.m.
Salisbury							1 58	2 3												
Wilton South																				
Dinton																				
Tisbury																				
Semley																				
Gillingham	Until 18th Sept. only.																Runs 5 mins. later on Fridays until 18th Sept.			
Templecombe							2 37	2 40												
Milborne Port																				
Sherborne							2 51	2 53												
Yeovil Jct.							3W 1	3 4												
Sutton Bingham																				
Crewkerne																				
Chard Jct.																				
Axminster	←						3 31	3 33												
Seaton Jct.	2 50	3 10																		
Honiton	3 25	3 26				3‖34												4 0		
Sidmouth Jct.	3 32½	3 36			3‖42												4 7	4C 8	4 7	4C 8
Whimple																	4 13½	4 14½	4 13½	4 14½
Broad Clyst					Work 3.53 p.m. to Sidmouth												4 20	4 20½	4 20	4 20½
Pinhoe																	4 24½	4 25	4 24½	4 25
Exmouth Jct.		3 50						4 4										4 29		4 29
St. James' Park Halt																				
Exeter Central	3 53						4 7	4A12		4 20							4 32		4 32	
Do. (St. Davids)							4 15	4 18	4 23	4 28										
Cowley Jct.								4 21		4 31										
Newton St. Cyres									4 36	4 37										
Crediton									4 42	4 43										
Yeoford									4 50	4 52										
Coleford Jct.								4 35		4 54										
Bow																				
North Tawton																				
Sampford C'nay																				
Okehampton							4W56	4 59												
Quarry Halt																				
Meldon Jct.																				
Bridestowe																				
Lydford																				
Brentor												5 30								
Tavistock North				4 25			5 24	5 25			5 38	5 39								
Bere Alston			4 35½	4 36½			5 35½	5 36½			5 49½	5 51								
Bere Ferrers			4 41½	4 42½							5 56	5 57								
Tamerton Foliot			4 46½	4 47																
St. Budeaux, Vic. Rd.			4 51	4 52							6 4	6 5								
Ford			4 57½	4 59							6 8	6 9								
Devonport, Kings Rd.			5 2	5 4			5 53	5 55			6 12	6 13								
Devonport Jct.				5 6				5 57				6 15								
Plymouth (N. Rd.)			5 8	5 9			5 59	6 3			6 17	6 18								
Lipson Jct.				5 13				6 7				6 22								
Mount Gould Jct.				5 14				6 8				6 23								
Friary Jct.				5 14½				6 8½				6 23½								
Plymouth (Friary)			5 17				6 11				6 26									
Copplestone									4 58	4 58½										
Morchard Rd.									5 1½	5 2										
Lapford									5 6	5 7										
Eggesford									5X13	5 14										
Kings Nympton					arr. p.m.	dep. p.m.			5 20	5 21										
Portsmouth A.									5 26	5 27										
Umberleigh									5 33	5 34										
Chapelton									5 38	5 39										
Barnstaple Jct.						5 15			5 46							6 0				
Barnstaple Town					5 18	5 19									6 3	6 5				
Pottington Box						5 20										6 6				
Wrafton					5 26	5 27									6 12	6 13				
Braunton					5 29	5 30									6 15	6 16				
Mortehoe & Woolacombe					5 47	5 48									6 33	6 34				
Ilfracombe					5 56										6 42					
Barnstaple Jct.										5 52										
Fremington									5X57	5 58										
Instow									6X 4	6 7										
Bideford (Goods)																				
Bideford (New)									6 12	6 15										
Torrington									6 24											

A—Advertised departure Exeter Central 4.10 p.m.
C—Advertised departure Sidmouth Jct. 4.8 p.m.

The timings shown on this page WILL NOT APPLY ON SATURDAYS, 13th June to 19th September, 1953.

SALISBURY, EXETER, PLYMOUTH, ILFRACOMBE AND TORRINGTON LINES

DOWN WEEKDAYS					SX		SX Q		Q								MO			
	1.0 p.m. Waterloo				Engine		Empties of 4.20 p.m. Sidmouth Jct.		1.5 p.m. Waterloo								Engine		Engine	
	⌧										A D				C					
	arr. p.m.	dep. p.m.	arr. p.m.	dep. p.m.	arr. p.m.	dep. p.m.	arr. p.m.	dep. p.m.	arr. p.m.	dep. p.m.	arr. p.m.	dep. p.m.	arr. p.m.	dep. p.m.	arr. p.m.	dep. p.m.	arr. p.m.	dep. p.m.	arr.* p.m.	dep. p.m.
Salisbury	2 39	2 45							2 51	2 58	Rear portion of 1.0 p.m. Waterloo					2 55		3‖13		
Wilton South															3 1	3 2	3‖19			
Dinton															3 11	3 12	Work 12.0 noon Ilfracombe			
Tisbury															3 19	3 20				
Semley															3 28½	3 31½				
Gillingham															3 37½	3 39½				4‖ 5
Templecombe	3 19	3 23			After Working 3.43 p.m. Sidmouth				3 32			3 36			3 49	3 53			4‖13	
Milborne Port															3 58½	3 59½	15th June to 14th Sept. only			
Sherborne	3 34	3 35							Form 3.36 p.m.						4 5	4 7				
Yeovil Jct.	3 43	3 46					Runs during school periods only				3 54	3 57			4C14	4 21				
Sutton Bingham	Through coaches to Plymouth, Ilfracombe, Torrington and Templecombe														4 26	4 27				
Crewkerne											4 9	4 10			4 37	4 38				
Chard Jct.											4 22	4 23			4 50	4 51				
Axminster											4 30	4 34			4 58	4 59				
Seaton Jct.											4 40	4 42			5 4	5 5				
Honiton								4†35			4 57	4 59			5 20	5 22				
Sidmouth Jct.						4‖35	4†43				5 6	5 8			5 28½	5 30				
Whimple											5 14	5 15			5 36	5 38				
Broad Clyst											5 21	5 22			5 43½	5 44				
Pinhoe											5 26	5 27			5 47½	5 48½				
Exmouth Jct.		4 38				4 52						5 31				5 52				
St. James' Park Halt												5D33				5 54				
Exeter Central	4 41	4 48	4 41	5 5	4‖55						5 35			5 52	5 56		FO			
Do. (St. Davids)	4 51	4 54	5 8	5 12									5 55	6 1						
Cowley Jct.		4 57		5 15										6 4						
Newton St. Cyres			5 20	5 20½									6 9	6 10			Empty			
Crediton			5 25½	5 26½									6 15	6 16						
Yeoford	5 10	5 12	5 33½	5 35							To Padstow.		6 23	6 24	Runs 10 mins. later when 1.5 p.m. Q Waterloo runs		arr. p.m.	dep. p.m.		
Coleford Jct.		5 14		5 37										6 26						
Bow									arr. p.m.	dep. p.m.	arr. p.m.	dep. p.m.	6 33	6 34						
North Tawton	5 26	5 27											6 40	6 41						
Sampford C'nay													6 47	6 48						
Okehampton	5 39	5 43										5 51	6 56							
Quarry Halt																				
Meldon Jct.												5 59								
Bridestowe	5 57	5 58																		
Lydford	6 4	6 5																		
Brentor																				
Tavistock North	6 16	6 18								6 55							Until 18th Sept. only.			
Bere Alston	6 28½	6 29½							7 5½	7 7										
Bere Ferrers									7 12	7 13										
Tamerton Foliot									7 17	7 18										
St. Budeaux, Vic. Rd.	6 41½	6 42½							7 22	7 23								7†53		
Ford									7 26	7 27										
Devonport, Kings Rd.	6 47½	6 50							7 30	7 32								7 58		
Devonport Jct.		6 52								7 34								8 0		
Plymouth (N. Rd.)	6 54	6 57							7 36	7 37								8 2		
Lipson Jct.		7 1								7 41								8 6		
Mount Gould Jct.		7 2								7 42								8 7		
Friary Jct.		7 2½								7 42½								8 7½		
Plymouth (Friary)	7 5								7 45								8†10			
Copplestone			5 41	5 41½																
Morchard Rd.			5X44½	5 45																
Lapford			5 49	5 50																
Eggesford			5 56	5 57																
Kings Nympton			6X 3	6 6																
Portsmouth A.			6 11	6 12																
Umberleigh			6 18	6 19																
Chapelton																				
Barnstaple Jct.			6 30	6 35																
Barnstaple Town			6 38	6 39																
Pottington Box				6 40																
Wrafton			6 46	6 47																
Braunton			6 49	6 51																
Mortehoe & Woolacombe			7 8	7 9																
Ilfracombe			7 17																	
Barnstaple Jct.				6 40																
Fremington			6 45	6 46																
Instow			6 52	6 53																
Bideford (Goods)																				
Bideford (New)			6 58	7 0																
Torrington			7 9																	

A—Conveys through coach Waterloo to Lyme Regis until 18th September.
D—Call at St. James Park Halt Mondays to Fridays only
C—Change engines at Yeovil Jct.

SALISBURY, EXETER, PLYMOUTH, ILFRACOMBE AND TORRINGTON LINES 15

DOWN WEEKDAYS	3.54 p.m. Milk Tanks Clapham Jct. Exeter C.	Exeter Ctl.		5.0 p.m. Waterloo to Exeter Ctl.		FO 5.35 p.m. Waterloo		SX 6.0 p.m. Waterloo		SO 6.0 p.m. Waterloo		SO Engine	SO Engine	FSO To Seaton		5.0 p.m. Waterloo	
	arr. p.m.	dep. p.m.		arr. p.m.	dep. p.m.	arr. p.m.	dep. p.m.	arr. p.m.	dep. p.m.	arr. p.m.	dep. p.m.	arr. dep. p.m.	arr. dep. p.m.	arr. p.m.	dep. p.m.	arr. p.m.	dep. p.m.
Salisbury	6 27	6 40		7 0	7 6	7 29	7 35	7 44	7 50	7 44	7 50					8 1	8 9
Wilton South																	9 0
Dinton																9 5	9 6
Tisbury			7 10	7 20			7 23	7 24		8 17		8 17					9 16	9 18
Semley							7 33	7 35								9 31	9 33
Gillingham			7 35	7 6			7 41	7 43	8 18		8 18					9 40	9 42
Templecombe					8 0	8 10	7 53	7 55	8 28	8 30	8 28	8 30				10 4	10 5
Milborne Port					8 9		8 2										
Sherborne					8 18		8 13	8 15	8 40	8 41	8 40	8 41				10 9	10 10
Yeovil Jct.							8 25	8 26	8 48	8 50	8 48	8 50				10 19	10 13
Sutton Bingham							8 33	8 38								10 25	10 27
Crewkerne							9 6	9 7	9 18		9 18					10 31	10 32
Chard Jct.																10 36	
Axminster	8 19																
Seaton Jct.	8 27								9 43	9 44	9 43	9 44	9 39	9 42			
Honiton	8 30																
Sidmouth Jct.	8 37						9 41										
Whimple	8 43																
Broad Clyst	8 48								9 56		9 56						
Pinhoe	8 49																
Exmouth Jct.	8 53								9 59	10 6	9 59	10 6					
St. James' Park Halt									10 9	10 12	10 9	10 12			SO		
Exeter Central	8 56						9 44		10 10	10 15	10 10	10 15				10 39	
Do. (St. Davids)							Through Coaches to Exeter Central and Yeovil Town		10 23	10 24	10 23	10 24					
Cowley Jct.									10 30	10 32	10 30	10 32					
Newton St. Cyres																	
Crediton									10 34		10 34						
Yeoford																	
Coleford Jct.																	
Bow			SX Engine A		SX				10 55	10 57	10 46	10 47	After working 10.30 p.m. Friary		After working 9.15 p.m. Plymouth		
North Tawton									10 59	11	11						
Sampford C'nay			arr. dep. p.m.														
Okehampton			10A35	10 40					11 22	11 24	11 26	11 27	11 45		11 30		
Quarry Halt									11 37½	11 38½	11 37½	11 38½					
Meldon Jct.																	
Bridestowe									11 46	11 47	11 50	11 51					
Lydford									11 52	11 56	11 58						
Brentor									11 58	12 0							
Tavistock North									12C 0	12 2	12 7				12 15		
Bere Alston											12 9				12 17		
Bere Ferrers											12 12				12 23		
Tamerton Foliot											12 12				12 24½		
St. Budeaux, Vic. Rd.																	
Ford																	
Devonport, Kings Rd.									12 10		12 10				12 27		
Devonport (N. Rd.)																	
Plymouth (N. Rd.)			11 2														
Lipson Jct.			11 5														
Mount Gould Jct.			11 9														
Friary Jct.			11 10½														
Plymouth (Friary)			11 13														
Copplestone													Guard to collect tickets and extinguish lights at Broad Clyst		Guard to collect tickets and extinguish lights at		
Morchard Rd.																	
Lapford																	
Eggesford																	
Kings Nympton																	
Portsmouth A.																	
Umberleigh																	
Chapelton																	
Barnstaple Jct.																	
Barnstaple Town																	
Pottington Box																	
Wrafton																	
Braunton																	
Mortehoe & Woolacombe																	
Ilfracombe																	
Barnstaple Jct.																	
Fremington																	
Instow																	
Bideford (Goods)																	
Bideford (New)																	
Torrington																	

A—Attach at Bere Alston engine of 9.15 p.m. freight from Callington.
C—Advertised arrival time Plymouth North Road 12.2 mdt.

14 SALISBURY, EXETER, PLYMOUTH, ILFRACOMBE AND TORRINGTON LINES

DOWN WEEKDAYS	3.0 p.m. Waterloo		Q 3.5 p.m. Waterloo		To Launceston and Bude			W.R. Engine			SX 9.22 p.m. Engine Plymouth Millbay W.R.		SX
	arr. p.m.	dep. p.m.	arr. p.m.	dep. p.m.	arr. p.m.	dep. p.m.	arr. p.m.	dep. p.m.	arr. p.m.	dep. p.m.	arr. dep. p.m.	arr. p.m.	dep. p.m.
Salisbury	4 42	4 49	4 52	4 59									
Wilton South	Through coaches to Plymouth, Ilfracombe, Torrington and Templecombe								Rear portion of 3.0 p.m. Waterloo		4 56 5 3		8 7
Dinton											5 12 5 13		8 15
Tisbury									5 39		5 20 5 21		8 24
Semley			Form 5.39 p.m.						5 45½		5 30 5 32		8 30
Gillingham	5 23 5 27		5 33						5 53		5 38 5 40		8 38
Templecombe	Load 10 Bogies Templecombe to Exeter Cent.								6 0 6 7		5 50		8 40
Milborne Port									6 33 6 34				
Sherborne									6 41 6 50				
Yeovil Jct.	6 20 6 23		6 35						6 49 6 50				8 47 8 48
Sutton Bingham									7 12 7 14				8 54
Crewkerne									7 20½ 7 21½				9 0 9 2
Chard Jct.							7 10		7 27				9 10
Axminster									7 32				
Seaton Jct.	6 38 6 46 6 38					6 58 6 59	7 12		7 36			9 28 9 34½	9 15
Honiton	6 55 6 52 7 4					7 4						9 35	
Sidmouth Jct.						7 39							
Whimple												9 47½ 9 48½	
Broad Clyst												9 50 10 6	
Pinhoe	7 3 7 4 7 15 7 16											10 5	
Exmouth Jct.	7 11 7 12 7 23 7 24												
St. James' Park Halt												10 10 10 13	10 6
Exeter Central	7 14 7 26							7 45			After working 7.32 p.m. Newton Abbot W.R.	10 16 10 23	
Do. (St. Davids)								7 48				10 20 10 23	
Cowley Jct.							7 39					10 27	10 33
Newton St. Cyres												10 33	
Crediton											9 26	10 34	
Yeoford											9 30 9 31	10 34½	9 30 9 31
Coleford Jct.											9 34	10 37	
Bow	7 30 7 31												
North Tawton	7 34 7 35												
Sampford C'nay	7 46 7 47		7 47										
Okehampton	7 51 7 52		7 55										
Quarry Halt	8 6 8 7												
Meldon Jct.	8 11 8 12												
Bridestowe	8 19 8 26												
Lydford	8 29 8 30												
Brentor	8 37 8 38												
Tavistock North	8 34 8 36 8 40 8 42								8 35½ 8 37			8 47 8 48	
Bere Alston	8 46 8 47								8 43 8 48			8 54 8 57	
Bere Ferrers	8 50								8 52 8 53			9 2 9 3	
Tamerton Foliot									8 56 8 57			9 7 9 9	
St. Budeaux, Vic. Rd.									9 0 9 3			9 9 9 14	
Ford									9 9		9 26	9 17	
Devonport, Kings Rd.									9 13		9 30		
Devonport (N. Rd.)									9 14½		9 31		
Plymouth (N. Rd.)									9 17		9 31½		
Lipson Jct.													
Mount Gould Jct.													
Friary Jct.													
Plymouth (Friary)													
Copplestone	8 32											Guard to collect tickets and extinguish lights at Brentor	
Morchard Rd.	8 38						Guard to collect tickets at Chapelton						
Lapford	8 44 8 45												
Eggesford													
Kings Nympton													
Portsmouth A.													
Umberleigh													
Chapelton													
Barnstaple Jct.													
Barnstaple Town													
Pottington Box													
Wrafton													
Braunton													
Mortehoe & Woolacombe													
Ilfracombe													
Barnstaple Jct.	8 37 8 46												
Fremington	8X44 8 47												
Instow													
Bideford (Goods)	8 50 8 52												
Bideford (New)	9 1												
Torrington													

A—Call at Lydford on Fridays, when required, and run 3 minutes later to Plymouth Friary.

The timings on this page WILL APPLY ON SATURDAYS ONLY, 13th June to 19th September, 1953, INCLUSIVE.

SALISBURY, EXETER, PLYMOUTH, ILFRACOMBE AND TORRINGTON LINES 17

DOWN

Station	11.0 p.m. (Fridays) Waterloo	12.35 a.m. Waterloo	1.55 a.m. Pass. and Mail Eastleigh to Yeovil (T.)	Engine to Bude	1.25 a.m. News and Pass. Waterloo	1.35 a.m. News and Pass. Waterloo	Parcels	1.55 a.m. Pass. & Mail Eastleigh to Yeovil (T.)
Salisbury	12 57		2 50		3 11 3 19	3 23 3 30		
Wilton South								3 35 4 5
Dinton								
Tisbury								
Semley								
Gillingham								
Templecombe		2 10 2 20	2 36		3 11 3 19	3 23		4 16 4 20
Milborne Port			3 25 3 35					4 28 4 38
Sherborne	1 49	3 15	3 35 4 5			4 17		
Yeovil Jct.					4 4 4 7			
Sutton Bingham								
Crewkerne								
Chard Jct.								
Axminster	2 20	3 43			4 47	4 57		
Seaton Jct.								
Honiton								
Sidmouth Jct.								
Whimple								
Broad Clyst						5 9		
Pinhoe		4 17			4 57			
Exmouth Jct.	3 0						5 26	
St. James' Park Halt								
Exeter Central	3 3 3 16	4 20 4 30			5 0 5 5	5 12	5 29	
Do. (St. Davids)	3 19 3 21	4 33 4 37			5 12 5 16	5 18 a.m.		
Cowley Jct.	3 24	4 40						
Newton St. Cyres								5 18 5 28
Crediton	3 42	4 55	5 4		5 33		5 21	5 39 5 41
Yeoford							5 28	5 48 5 49
Coleford Jct.								5 51
Bow								
North Tawton				Until 27th June only				
Sampford C'nay				5 42				
Okehampton		5 19 5 27			5 55 6 0	4 57		
Quarry Halt								
Meldon		5 37		5 52				
Bridestowe					6 13 6 14	Until 29th August only		
Lydford								
Brentor								
Tavistock North					6 29 6 57			
Bere Alston					6 43 7 14 7 15			
Bere Ferrers					6 25			
Tamerton Foliot					6 29			
St. Budeaux Vic. Rd.					6 37 7 26 7 28			
Devonport Kings Rd.				6 20 a.m. Barnstaple Victoria Road W.R.	6 37 7 32 7 33			
Devonport Jct.					6 39 7 35			
Plymouth (N. Rd.)					6 43 7 37 7 41			
Lipson Jct.					6 45			
Mount Gould Jct.					6 49 7 45 7 46½			
Friary Jct.					6 50			
Plymouth (Friary)					6 53 7 49	Not to arrive Devonport before 7.30 a.m.		
Copplestone	3 46				5 55 5 56			
Morchard Rd.	3 49				5 59 6 0			6 50 6 55
Lapford	3 53				6 4			6 56 7 3
Eggesford	3 59				6 12			6 58
Kings Nympton	4 5				6 18 6 19			6 41 7 3
Portsmouth A.	4 10				6 24 6 25		7 0 6 57	7 15 7 23
Umberleigh	4 16				6 31 6 32		7 2	7 8 7 15
Chapelton					6 41		7 4 7 9	7X 8 7X 15
Barnstaple Jct.	4 26 4 36			6 25 6 30	6 45		7 6 7 2	7 24 7 29
Barnstaple Town	4 39 4 41			6 33	6 58		7 8 7 9	7 34 7 43
Pottington Box	4 42			6 34				
Wrafton					6 7		7 31 7 34	
Braunton	4 50 4 55				6 41			
Mortehoe & Woolacombe	5 12 5 14				6 33 6 43			
Ilfracombe	5 22				6 14 6 34			
Barnstaple Jct.				Worked by B.R. Engine	6 7 6 14		Runs 3 mins. later	7 3 7 9
Fremington					6 15			7X 15 7 19
Instow					6 20 6 25		5.32 a.m.	7 23 7 27
Bideford (Goods)				Form 8.25 a.m.	6 34		Q from Exeter Cen. runs	7 29 7 34
Bideford (New)							7 31 7 34	
Torrington							7 42	

A—Stop at west end of Yeovil Jc. and not advertised.

The timings shown on this page WILL NOT APPLY ON SATURDAYS, 13th June to 19th September, 1953.

DOWN WEEKDAY

Station	3.54 p.m. Milk Tanks, Clapham Jct.	6.54 p.m. Waterloo to Yeovil Town	10.20 p.m. Sidmouth	Empties of 11.5 p.m. Exeter Central
Salisbury		9 46 9 55		
Wilton South		10 1 10 12		
Dinton		10 11 10 20		
Tisbury		10 19 10 30		
Semley	9 6	10 29 10 37		
Gillingham	7 35	10 36 10 50		
Templecombe	9 30 9 50	10 47 10 54		
Milborne Port		10 56 11 3		
Sherborne		11 11 21		
Yeovil Jct.	10 18 10 33			
Sutton Bingham	10 48 11 2			
Crewkerne	11 24A			
Chard Jct.			10 41	
Axminster	11 43A		11 0	
Seaton Jct.	11 46		11 3	
Honiton			11 26	
Sidmouth Jct.			11 29	11 47
Whimple			Runs 10 mins. later on Saturdays	11 54
Broad Clyst				12 12
Pinhoe				12 12½
Exeter Central				12½ 15

A—On Saturdays, depart Seaton Jct. 11.12 p.m. and run 10 minutes later.
B—Advertised departure Templecombe 8.56 p.m.

The timings on this page WILL APPLY ON SATURDAYS ONLY,
13th June to 19th September, 1953, INCLUSIVE.

19 SALISBURY, EXETER, PLYMOUTH, ILFRACOMBE AND TORRINGTON LINES

DOWN

Station	8.30 a.m. Taunton W.R.	2.59 p.m. (Fridays) Churns Gravesend to Yeovil T.	To Yeovil Town	7.40 a.m. Yeovil Town	Empties of 8.0 a.m. Exeter Cent.	9.22 a.m. Exmouth (Not advertised)	2.58 p.m. (Fridays) Churns Gravesend to Yeovil T.	To Tavistock South, W.R.

Salisbury
Wilton South
Dinton
Tisbury
Semley
Gillingham
Templecombe
Milborne Port
Sherborne
Yeovil Jct.
Sutton Bingham
Crewkerne
Chard Jct.
Axminster
Seaton Jct.
Honiton
Sidmouth Jct.
Whimple
Broad Clyst
Pinhoe
Exmouth Jct.
St. James' Park Halt
Exeter Central
Do. (St. Davids)
Cowley Jct.
Newton St. Cyres
Crediton
Yeoford
Coleford Jct.
Bow
North Tawton
Sampford C'nay
Okehampton
Quarry Halt
Meldon Jct.
Bridestowe
Lydford
Brentor
Tavistock North
Bere Alston
Bere Ferrers
Tamerton Foliot
St. Budeaux, Vic. Rd.
Ford
Devonport, Kings Rd.
Plymouth (N. Rd.)
Lipson Jct.
Mount Gould Jct.
Friary Jct.
Plymouth (Friary)
Copplestone
Morchard Rd.
Lapford
Eggesford
Kings Nympton
Portsmouth A.
Umberleigh
Chapelton
Barnstaple Jct.
Barnstaple Town
Pottington Box
Wrafton
Braunton
Mortehoe & Woolacombe
Ilfracombe
Barnstaple Jct.
Fremington
Instow
Bideford (Goods)
Bideford (New)
Torrington

A—Advertised arrival at Plymouth North Road 11.12 a.m.

The timings on this page WILL APPLY ON SATURDAYS ONLY,
13th June to 19th September, 1953, INCLUSIVE.

18 SALISBURY, EXETER, PLYMOUTH, ILFRACOMBE AND TORRINGTON LINES

DOWN

Station	Pass., News and Mail Yeovil Town	Newspaper and Pass.	5.20 a.m. Taunton W.R.	Parcels	6.20 a.m. Yeovil Town

Salisbury
Wilton South
Dinton
Tisbury
Semley
Gillingham
Templecombe
Milborne Port
Sherborne
Yeovil Jct.
Sutton Bingham
Crewkerne
Chard Jct.
Axminster
Seaton Jct.
Honiton
Sidmouth Jct.
Whimple
Broad Clyst
Pinhoe
Exmouth Jct.
St. James' Park Halt
Exeter Central
Do. (St. Davids)
Cowley Jct.
Newton St. Cyres
Crediton
Yeoford
Coleford Jct.
Bow
North Tawton
Sampford C'nay
Okehampton
Quarry Halt
Meldon Jct.
Bridestowe
Lydford
Brentor
Tavistock North
Bere Alston
Bere Ferrers
Tamerton Foliot
St. Budeaux, Vic. Rd.
Ford
Devonport, Kings Rd.
Plymouth (N. Rd.)
Lipson Jct.
Mount Gould Jct.
Friary Jct.
Plymouth (Friary)
Copplestone
Morchard Rd.
Lapford
Eggesford
Kings Nympton
Portsmouth A.
Umberleigh
Chapelton
Barnstaple Jct.
Barnstaple Town
Pottington Box
Wrafton
Braunton
Mortehoe & Woolacombe
Ilfracombe
Barnstaple Jct.
Fremington
Instow
Bideford (Goods)
Bideford (New)
Torrington

A—Stop at Dinton not to be advertised; time allowed at Yeovil Jct. for engine to turn.

333

SATURDAYS ONLY.

The timings on this page WILL APPLY ON SATURDAYS ONLY, 13th June to 19th September, 1953, INCLUSIVE.

20 SALISBURY, EXETER, PLYMOUTH, ILFRACOMBE AND TORRINGTON LINES

DOWN			To Ilfracombe		6.33 a.m. Woking		Milk		7.33 a.m. Waterloo to Padstow and Bude		7.40 a.m. Waterloo		7.45 a.m. Salisbury						Engine	
					■				A		■									
			arr. a.m.	dep. a.m.	arr. a.m.	dep. a.m.	arr. a.m.	dep. a.m.	arr. a.m.	dep. a.m.	arr. a.m.	dep. a.m.	arr. a.m.	dep. a.m.	arr. a.m.	dep. a.m.	arr. a.m.	dep. a.m.	arr. a.m.	dep. a.m.
Salisbury				7 45	8 44½	8 50			9 19	9 25	9 29	9 35								
Wilton South			7 51	7 52½	8 56	8 57			Through		Through									
Dinton			8 1½	8 3	9 6	9 7			Coaches to		Coaches to									
Tisbury			8 10	8 12	9 14	9 15			Padstow		Ilfracombe									
Semley			8 20½	8 23½	9 24	9 26			and Bude		and									
Gillingham			8 29½	8 33½	9 32	9 35					Torrington									
Templecombe			8 43	8 50	9 45														After	
Milborne Port			8 55½	8 56½															working	
Sherborne			9 2	9 4															10.10 a.m.	
Yeovil Jct.			9 11	9 17					10	10	10	20							Seaton	
Sutton Bingham			9 22	9 23																
Crewkerne			9 33	9 35																
Chard Jct.			9 48	9 53																
Axminster			10 0	10 5				10 22												
Seaton Jct.			1011	1014			10 29													11‖ 0
Honiton			1029	1031																
Sidmouth Jct.			1037½	1041												11 19			11‖22	
Whimple															11 25	11 26			Work	
Broad Clyst															11 32	11 33			12.10 p.m.	
Pinhoe															11 37	11 38			to	
Exmouth Jct.			10	54					11	7	11	17			11	42			Exeter	
St. James' Park Halt													←	—					Central	
Exeter Central			10 57	11 39					11 10	11A16	11 20	11 26	10 57	11 39	11 45			11 49		
Do. (St. Davids)			——	→					11 19	11 24	11 29	11 36	11 42	11 47			11 52	11 57		
Cowley Jct.									11	27	11	39	11	50			12	0		
Newton St. Cyres																	12 5	12 6		
Crediton													11 58	11 59			12 11	12 14		
Yeoford													12 6	12 8			12 21	12 23		
Coleford Jct.									11	41	11	52	12	10			12	25		
Bow																	12 32	12 33		
North Tawton																	12 39	12 40		
Sampford C'nay																	12 46	12 47		
Okehampton									12 3	12 8							12 55	1 0		
Quarry Halt																				
Meldon Jct.									12	17										
Bridestowe																	1 16	1 17		
Lydford																	1 23	1 24		
Brentor																	1 27	1 28		
Tavistock North																	1 38	1 39		
Bere Alston									Commences 4th July								1 49½	1 53		
Bere Ferrers																	1 58	1 59		
Tamerton Foliot																	2 3	2 4		
St. Budeaux, Vic. Rd.																	2 8	2 9		
Ford																	2 12	2 13		
Devonport, Kings Rd.																	2 16	2 19		
Devonport Jct.																	2	21		
Plymouth (N. Rd.)																	2 23	2 27		
Lipson Jct.																	2	31		
Mount Gould Jct.																	2	32		
Friary Jct.																	2	32½		
Plymouth (Friary)																	2 35			
Copplestone											11	55	12 14	12 16			Call at			
Morchard Rd.											11	58	12 19	12 20			Quarry			
Lapford											12X 2	12 5	12 24	12 25			Halt to			
Eggesford											12	11	12 31	12 32			set down			
Kings Nympton											12	16½	12 38	12X43			wives of			
Portsmouth A.											12	21	12X48	12 54			Railway			
Umberleigh											12	26	1 0	1 1			employees			
Chapelton													1 5	1 6			Time			
Barnstaple Jct.											12 36	12 41	1 12	1 20			allowed for			
Barnstaple Town											12 44	12 46	1 23	1 25			this stop			
Pottington Box											12	47	1	26						
Wrafton											12 53	12 54	1 32	1 33						
Braunton											12 56	1 0	1 35	1 38						
Mortehoe & Woolacombe											1 17	1 19	1 55	1 57						
Ilfracombe											1 27		2 5							
Barnstaple Jct.												12 54		1 28						
Fremington											12X59	1 3	1 33	1 34						
Instow											1 9	1 10	1 40	1 41						
Bideford (Goods)																				
Bideford (New)											1 15	1 18	1X46	1 49						
Torrington											1 27		1 58							

A—Advertised departure Exeter Central 11.16 a.m

The timings on this page WILL APPLY ON SATURDAYS ONLY, 13th June to 19th September, 1953, INCLUSIVE.

SATURDAYS ONLY.

SALISBURY, EXETER, PLYMOUTH, ILFRACOMBE AND TORRINGTON LINES 21

DOWN	8.5 a.m Waterloo to Exmouth and Sidmouth		Engine		Engine		8.22 a.m. Waterloo		8.35 a.m. Waterloo				Engine		9.3 a.m. Portsm'th & S'sea		8.54 a.m. Waterloo			
	■						■		▲C						■		■A			
	arr. a.m.	dep. a.m.	arr. a.m.	dep. a.m.	arr. a.m.	dep. a.m.	arr. a.m.	dep. a.m.	arr. a.m.	dep. a.m.	arr. p.m.	dep. p.m.	arr. p.m.	dep. noon	arr. a.m.	dep. a.m.	arr. a.m.	dep. a.m.	arr. p.m.	dep. p.m.
Salisbury	9 47	9 53			After		10 3	10 10	10 26	10 32					10 41	10 47	10 50	10 56		
Wilton South	Through				working				Through								Through			
Dinton	coaches to				6.33 a.m.				coaches to								Coaches			
Tisbury	Exmouth,				Woking				Ilfracombe								to Ilfra-			
Semley	Sidmouth								& Torr'ton								combe and			
Gillingham	Seaton and								10 59	11 0			After				Plymouth			
Templecombe	Lyme		After			10‖32			11 10	11 12			working				11 30	11 33		
Milborne Port	Regis		working										10.22 a.m.							
Sherborne			8.5 a.m.										Milk				11 43	11 45		
Yeovil Jct.	10	34	Waterloo		10‖52		11	0	11	25			Axminster		11 33	11 36	11	51		
Sutton Bingham																				
Crewkerne																				
Chard Jct.																				
Axminster	11 0	11 4													12 4	12 7				
Seaton Jct.	11 10	11 14												12‖ 0			12A22	12 24		
Honiton	11 29	11 30											12 15	12 32			12 39	12 41		
Sidmouth Jct.	11 37	11 43		11‖38			11	50	12	5		1210	12	40	12 31	12 33	12A48	12 50		
Whimple											1216	1217								
Broad Clyst											1222½	1223								
Pinhoe											1226½	1227½								
Exmouth Jct.			11‖53				12	1	12	17	12	31	12‖55		12	45	1	2		
St. James' Park Halt												1233								
Exeter Central							12 4	12 10	12 20	12 26	1235				12 48	12 56	1 5	1 12	1 5	1 25
Do. (St. Davids)							12 13	12 17	12 29	12 34					12 59	1 4	1 15	1 22	1 28	1 32
Cowley Jct.							12	20	12	37					1	7	1	26	1	35
Newton St. Cyres																			1 40	1 41
Crediton			To Bude												1 15	1 16			1 46	1 48
Yeoford			and												1 23	1 24	1 38	1 39		
Coleford Jct.			Launceston				12	35	12	53					1	26	1	41	1	56
Bow	Com-		arr. p.m.	dep. p.m.															2 3	2 4
North Tawton	mences																		2 10	2 11
Sampford C'nay	4th																			
Okehampton	July			1 18											1 46	1 49			2 23	2 27
Quarry Halt							Until													
Meldon Jct.			1	27			29th													
Bridestowe							August													
Lydford							only													
Brentor																				
Tavistock North															2 14	2 16			2 52	2 55
Bere Alston															2 26½	2 28			3 5½	3 7
Bere Ferrers																				
Tamerton Foliot																				
St. Budeaux, Vic. Rd.																			3 19	3 20
Ford																				
Devonport, Kings Rd.															2 46	2 48			3 25	3 29
Devonport Jct.															2	50			3	31
Plymouth (N. Rd.)															2 52	2 55			3 33	3 35
Lipson Jct.															2	59			3	39
Mount Gould Jct.															3	0			3	40
Friary Jct.															3	0½			3	40½
Plymouth (Friary)															3 3				3 43	
Copplestone							12	38	12X55	12C58							1 45	1 46		
Morchard Rd.							12	41	1	1							1 49	1 50		
Lapford							12 45	12X52	1 5	1X10							1 54	1 55		
Eggesford							12 58	1X 5	1 16	1 18							2X 1	2 3		
Kings Nympton							1	11	1	24							2 9	2 10		
Portsmouth A.							1	15	1	29							2 16	2 17		
Umberleigh							1	20	1	34							2 23	2 24		
Chapelton																	2 28	2 29		
Barnstaple Jct.							1 29	1 34	1 44	1 52							2 36	2 39		
Barnstaple Town							1 37	1 39	1 55	1 58							2 42	2 43		
Pottington Box							1	40	1	59							2	44		
Wrafton							1 46	1 48	2 5	2 7							2 50	2 51		
Braunton							1 50	1 54	2 9	2 14							2 53	2 56		
Mortehoe & Woolacombe							2 11	2 13	2 31	2 33							3 13	3 14		
Ilfracombe							2 21		2 41								3 22			
Barnstaple Jct.										2 0										
Fremington									2X 5	2 6										
Instow									2 12	2 13										
Bideford (Goods)																				
Bideford (New)									2X18	2 22										
Torrington									2 31											

A—Call at Seaton Jct. and Sidmouth Jct. to take up passengers only.

C—Stop at Copplestone not advertised.

SATURDAYS ONLY

The timings on this page WILL APPLY ON SATURDAYS ONLY, 13th June to 19th September, 1953, INCLUSIVE.

22 SALISBURY, EXETER, PLYMOUTH, ILFRACOMBE AND TORRINGTON LINES

DOWN	9.0 a.m. Waterloo to Sidm'th and Exmouth		Engine				To Yeovil Town		10.15 a.m. Waterloo ▲		10.35 a.m. Waterloo to Padstow and Bude ▣		Engine				10.45 a.m. Waterloo to Seaton		11.0 a.m. Waterloo A▣	
	arr. a.m.	dep a.m.	arr p.m.	dep. p.m.	arr. p.m.	dep. a.m.	arr. a.m.	dep. a.m	arr. a.m.	dep. a.m.	arr. p.m.	dep. p.m.	arr. p.m.	dep. p.m.	arr. p.m.	dep. p.m.	arr. p.m.	dep. p.m	arr. p.m.	dep. p.m.
Salisbury	11 0	11 6						11 14	11 48	11 54	12 5	12 11					12 16	12 22	12 31	12 38
Wilton South	Through						11 20	11 21	Through										Through	
Dinton	coaches to						11 30	11 31	coaches to		Through								coaches to	
Tisbury	Sidmouth		After				11 38	11 39	Ilfracombe		coaches						Through		Ilfracombe	
Semley	and		working				11 47½	11 48½	and		to Padstow						coaches		and	
Gillingham	Exmouth		9.0 a.m.				11 54½	11 56½	Torrington		and Bude						to		Torrington	
Templecombe	11 40	11 44	Waterloo			11 57	12 6	12 8	12 28	12 31							Seaton			
Milborne Port							12 14	12 15									and			
Sherborne					12 8	12 9	12 21	12 22									Lyme Regis			
Yeovil Jct.	12 0	12 4			12 16	12 18	12 29	12 42		12 44		12 55						1 7		1 23
Sutton Bingham					12 23	12 24														
Crewkerne					12 34	12 35														
Chard Jct.					12 47	12 48														
Axminster	12 32	12 34			12 55									1‖28			1 34	1 39		1 50
Seaton Jct.	12 40	12 44			Form								1‖34				1 45	1 55		
Honiton					2.8 p.m.											1 45				
Sidmouth Jct.	1 5	1 11		1‖7	to Exeter										1 52				2A 7	2 12
Whimple					Ctl.															
Broad Clyst																				
Pinhoe													Work							
Exmouth Jct.			1‖25							1 37		1 52	1.55 p.m.							2 25
St. James' Park Halt													to Seaton,							
Exeter Central									1 40	1 47	1 55	2 1							2 28	2 36
Do. (St. Davids)									1 50	1 53	2 4	2 9							2 39	2 43
Cowley Jct.										1 56		2 13								2 46
Newton St. Cyres																				
Crediton																				
Yeoford																				
Coleford Jct.										2 11		2 27								3 0
Bow																				
North Tawton																				
Sampford C'nay																				
Okehampton																				
Quarry Halt																				
Meldon Jct.												2 53								
Bridestowe																				
Lydford																				
Brentor																				
Tavistock North																				
Bere Alston																				
Bere Ferrers																				
Tamerton Foliot																				
St. Budeaux, Vic. Rd.																				
Ford																				
Devonport, Kings Rd.																				
Devonport Jct.																				
Plymouth (N. Rd.)																				
Lipson Jct.																				
Mount Gould Jct.																				
Friary Jct.																				
Plymouth (Friary)																				
Copplestone										2 15	12.50 p.m.									3 3
Morchard Rd.										2 19X	Taunton									3 6
Lapford										2 22	W.R.									3 9X
Eggesford										2 27½	◆								3 15	3 17
Kings Nympton										2 33										3 23X
Portsmouth A.										2 37	arr. p.m.	dep. p.m.								3 29
Umberleigh										2 42										3 35
Chapelton																				
Barnstaple Jct.									2 51	2 56	3 0	3 9							3 45	3 51
Barnstaple Town									2 59	3 1	3 12	3 14							3 54	3 55
Pottington Box										3 2		3 15								3 56
Wrafton											3 21	3 23							4 2	4 3
Braunton									3 9	3 13	3 25	3 29							4 5	4 9
Mortehoe & Woolacombe									3 30	3 32	3 46	3 48							4 26	4 28
Ilfracombe									3 40		3 56								4 36	
Barnstaple Jct.										3 8										4 58
Fremington									3X13	3 16									4 3	4 4
Instow									3 22	3 23									4 10	4 11
Bideford (Goods)																				
Bideford (New)									3 28	3 32									4 16	4 21
Torrington									3 41										4 30	

A—Take up passengers only at Sidmouth Jct.

SATURDAYS ONLY

The timings on this page WILL APPLY ON SATURDAYS ONLY, 13th June to 19th September, 1953, INCLUSIVE.

SALISBURY, EXETER, PLYMOUTH, ILFRACOMBE AND TORRINGTON LINES 23

DOWN	11.15 a.m. Waterloo ▲		2.26 p.m. Taunton W.R. ◆				To Exeter Cent.		Engine		11.45 a.m. Waterloo to Exmouth & Sidmouth ▣		Engine				12.0 noon Waterloo C			
	arr. p.m.	dep. p.m.	arr. p.m.	dep. p.m.	arr. p.m.	dep. p.m.	arr. p.m.	dep. p.m.	arr. p.m.	dep. p.m.	arr. p.m.	dep. p.m.	arr. p.m.	dep. p.m.	arr. p.m.	dep. p.m.	arr. p.m.	dep. p.m.	arr. p.m.	dep. p.m.
Salisbury	12 42	12 48						12 56		1‖10	1 21	1 27						1 42		
Wilton South	Through								1‖16		Through						1C47	1 53		
Dinton	coaches to						1 9	1 10	Work		coaches to									
Tisbury	Plymouth,						1 17	1 18	12.0 noon		Exmouth &						"DEVON			
Semley	Padstow						1 27	1 28	Waterloo		Sidmouth						BELLE"			
Gillingham	and Bude						1 34	1 36									Pullman			
Templecombe							1 45	1 47			2 1	2 3					cars only			
Milborne Port							1 52½	1 53½												
Sherborne							1 59	2 0												
Yeovil Jct.		1 34					2 7	2 47				2 16						2 33		
Sutton Bingham							—	→												
Crewkerne																				
Chard Jct.													After							
Axminster						2 8							working							
Seaton Jct.					2 14	2 16							11.45 a.m.							
Honiton					2 32	2 33							Waterloo							
Sidmouth Jct.					2 40	2 42					2 59	3 4		3‖2			3 16	3 19		
Whimple					2 48	2 48½														
Broad Clyst					2 54	2 55														
Pinhoe					2 59	3 0														
Exmouth Jct.		2 36				3 4							3‖22					3 32		
St. James' Park Halt						3 6														
Exeter Central	2 39	2 46			3 8		To										3 35	3 42		
Do. (St. Davids)	2 49	2 52					Padstow										3 45	3 47		
Cowley Jct.		2 55																3 50		
Newton St. Cyres							D													
Crediton																				
Yeoford							arr. p.m.	dep. p.m.												
Coleford Jct.		3 9																4 4		
Bow																				
North Tawton	3 21	3 22																		
Sampford C'nay																				
Okehampton	3 34	3 38						3 55												
Quarry Halt																				
Meldon Jct.								4 4												
Bridestowe	3 51	3 52																		
Lydford	3 58	3 59																		
Brentor	4 2	4 3																		
Tavistock North	4 11	4 12														4 25				
Bere Alston															4 35½	4 36½				
Bere Ferrers															4 41½	4 42½				
Tamerton Foliot															4 46½	4 47				
St. Budeaux, Vic. Rd.															4 51	4 52				
Ford															4 57½	4 59				
Devonport, Kings Rd.	4 38	4 41													5 2	5 4				
Devonport Jct.		4 43														5 6				
Plymouth (N. Rd.)	4 45	4 48													5 8	5 9				
Lipson Jct.		4 52														5 13				
Mount Gould Jct.		4 53														5 14				
Friary Jct.		4 53½														5 14½				
Plymouth (Friary)	4 56														5 17					
Copplestone																		4 7		
Morchard Rd.																		4 10X		
Lapford																		4 13		
Eggesford			20th June															4 19X		
Kings Nympton			to															4 24½		
Portsmouth A.			5th															4 29		
Umberleigh			Sept.															4 34		
Chapelton			only																	
Barnstaple Jct			4 25	4 28													4 43	4 45		
Barnstaple Town			4 31	4 32													4 48	4 49		
Pottington Box				4 33														4 50		
Wrafton																				
Braunton			4 40	4 44													4 57	5 1		
Mortehoe & Woolacombe			5 1	5 2													5 18	5 19		
Ilfracombe			5 10														5 27			
Barnstaple Jct.																				4 56
Fremington																			5 X1	5 6
Instow																			5X12	5 13
Bideford (Goods)																				
Bideford (New)																			5 18	5 20
Torrington																			5 29	

C—Stop at Wilton South to change engines and not advertised.
D—Conveys through coaches from Waterloo.

The timings on this page WILL APPLY ON SATURDAYS ONLY, 13th June to 19th September, 1953, INCLUSIVE.

 SALISBURY, EXETER, ILFRACOMBE, PLYMOUTH AND TORRINGTON LINES

DOWN	Engine		12.15 p.m. P'mouth & S'sea		12.56 p.m. Salisbury to Exeter Central		2‖32 p.m. Engine Sidmouth		11.30 a.m. Brighton				3.9 p.m. Sidmouth		12.56 p.m. Salisbury		Engine		1.0 p.m. Waterloo	
			▲						▲						A				■	
	arr. p.m.	dep. p.m.	arr. p.m.	dep. p.m.	arr. p.m.	dep. p.m.	arr. p.m.	dep. p.m.	arr. p.m.	dep. p.m.	arr. p.m.	dep. p.m.	arr. p.m.	dep. p.m.	arr. p.m.	dep. p.m.	arr. p.m.	dep. p.m.	arr. p.m.	dep. p.m.*
Salisbury			1 49	1 55					1 58	2 3									2 39	2 45
Wilton South																				Through coaches to Plymouth' Ilfracombe & Torr't'n
Dinton																				
Tisbury																				
Semley																				
Gillingham																	Com-mences 11th July			
Templecombe					←	—			2 37	2 40									3 19	3 23
Milborne Port																				
Sherborne									2 51	2 53									3 34	3 35
Yeovil Jct.			2 39	2 42	2 7	2 47			3 1	3 4									3 43	3 46
Sutton Bingham																				
Crewkerne					2 59	3 1														
Chard Jct.					3 13	3 15									←	—				
Axminster					3 22	3 24			3 31	3 33								3‖50		
Seaton Jct.		3‖20			3 30	3 46									3 30	3A46				
Honiton															4 1	4 3				
Sidmouth Jct.	3‖44				—	→	2‖53	3‖35					3 36	3 57	4 9½	4 11	4 19	4 30		
Whimple													4 3	4 4						
Broad Clyst													4 10	4 11						
Pinhoe	Assist												4 15	4 16						
Exmouth Jct.	3.57 p.m.			3 44			3‖55			4 4				4 20		4 24	4‖50			4 38
St. James' Park Halt	from																			
Exeter Central	Sidmouth		3 47	3 55					4 7	4 12		4 22	4 23		4 27				4 41	4 48
Do. (St. Davids)	Jct.		3 58	4 2					4 15	4 18	4 25	4 28							4 51	4 54
Cowley Jct.				4 5						4 21		4 31								4 57
Newton St. Cyres											4 36	4 37								
Crediton			4 13	4 14							4 42	4 43								
Yeoford											4 50	4 52							5 10	5 12
Coleford Jct.				4 22						4 35		4 54								5 14
Bow																				
North Tawton																			5 26	5 27
Sampford C'nay																				
Okehampton									4 56	4 59									5 39	5 43
Quarry Halt																				
Meldon Jct.																				
Bridestowe																			5 57	5 58
Lydford																			6 4	6 5
Brentor																		5 32		
Tavistock North									5 24	5 25							5 40	5 43	6 16	6 18
Bere Alston									5 35½	5 36½							5 53½	5 56	6 28½	6 29½
Bere Ferrers																	6 1	6 2		
Tamerton Foliot																				
St. Budeaux, Vic. Rd.							3.36 p.m. Taunton W.R.										6 9	6 10	6 41½	6 42½
Ford																	6 13	6 14		
Devonport, Kings Rd.									5 53	5 55							6 17	6 18	6 47½	6 50
Devonport Jct.										5 57								6 20		6 52
Plymouth (N. Rd.)							◆		5 59	6 3							6 22	6 26	6 54	6 57
Lipson Jct.										6 7								6 30		7 1
Mount Gould Jct.										6 8								6 31		7 2
Friary Jct.							arr. p.m.	dep. p.m.		6 8½								6 31½		7 2½
Plymouth (Friary)									6 11								6 34		7 5	
Copplestone				4 25			Until 12th Sept. only				4 58	4 58½								
Morchard Rd.				4 28							5 1½	5 2								
Lapford				4 31X							5 6	5 7								
Eggesford				4 37							5 13	5 14								
Kings Nympton				4 42½							5 20	5 21								
Portsmouth A.				4 47							5 26	5 27	arr. p.m.	dep. p.m.						
Umberleigh				4 52							5 33	5 34								
Chapelton											5 38	5 39								
Barnstaple Jct.			5 2	5 12			5 20	5 30			5 46			6 0						
Barnstaple Town			5 15	5 16			5 33	5 35					6 3	6 5						
Pottington Box				5 17				5 36						6 6						
Wrafton			5 23	5 24			5 42	5 44					6 12	6 13						
Braunton			5 26	5 29			5 46	5 50					6 15	6 16						
Mortehoe & Woolacombe			5 46	5 48			6 7	6 8					6 33	6 34						
Ilfracombe			5 56				6 16						6 42							
Barnstaple Jct.												5 52								
Fremington											5 57	5 58								
Instow											6X 4	6 7								
Bideford (Goods)																				
Bideford (New)											6 12	6 15								
Torrington											6 24									

A—Attach assistant engine at Seaton Jct. (after working 2.35 p.m. Seaton),

The Timings on this page WILL APPLY ON SATURDAYS ONLY, 13th June to 19th September, 1953, INCLUSIVE.

SALISBURY, EXETER, PLYMOUTH, ILFRACOMBE AND TORRINGTON LINES

DOWN	4.0 p.m. Engines (2) Sidmouth				To Padstow		1.5 p.m. Waterloo						Engine Yeovil Town		Engine		3.0 p.m. Waterloo			
							■										■			
	arr. p.m.	dep. p.m.	arr. p.m.	dep. p.m.	arr. p.m.	dep. p.m.	arr. p.m.	dep. p.m.	arr. p.m.	dep. p.m.	arr. p.m.	dep. p.m.	arr. p.m.	dep. p.m.	arr. p.m.	dep. p.m.	arr. p.m.	dep. p.m.	arr. p.m.	dep. p.m.
Salisbury							2 50	2 59				3 5				3‖13	4 42	4 49		
Wilton South											3 11	3 12			3‖19		Through coaches to Plymouth, Ilfracombe Torrington			
Dinton											3 21	3 22								
Tisbury											3 29	3 30			Work 12.0 noon Ilfracombe					
Semley											3 38½	3 41½		4‖5						
Gillingham											3 47½	3 49½								
Templecombe							3 33	3 38			3 59	4 3		4 25			5 23	5 27		
Milborne Port											4 8½	4 9½								
Sherborne											4 15	4 17								
Yeovil Jct.							3 56	4 0			4 24	4 31	4‖45	5‖5			Load, 10 Bogies Temple-combe to Exeter Central			
Sutton Bingham											4 36	4 37								
Crewkerne							4 13	4 14			4 47	4 48								
Chard Jct.							4 27	4 28			5 0	5 1								
Axminster							4 35	4 37			5 8	5 9								
Seaton Jct.							4 43	4 45			5 14	5 15								
Honiton							5 0	5 2			5 30	5 32								
Sidmouth Jct.	4‖25	4‖35					5 9	5 11			5 38½	5 40					6 20	6 23		
Whimple							5 17	5 18			5 46	5 47								
Broad Clyst							5 24	5 25			5 52½	5 53								
Pinhoe							5 29	5 30			5 56½	5 57½								
Exmouth Jct.	4‖55							5 34				6 1						6 35		
St. James' Park Halt												6 3								
Exeter Central			4 41	5 5			5 37			5 52	6 5						6 38	6◆46	6 38	6 57
Do. (St. Davids)			5 8	5 12					5 55	6 1							6 49	6 52	7 0	7 4
Cowley Jct.				5 15						6 4								6 55		7 7
Newton St. Cyres			5 20	5 20½					6 9	6 10										
Crediton			5 25½	5 26½					6 15	6 16							7 3	7 4	7 15	7 16
Yeoford			5 33½	5 35					6 23	6 24							7 11	7 12	7 23	7 24
Coleford Jct.				5 37						6 26								7 14		7 26
Bow									6 33	6 34					arr. p.m.	dep. p.m.				
North Tawton									6 40	6 41										
Sampford C'nay									6 47	6 48										
Okehampton						5 51			6 56								7 34	7 37		
Quarry Halt																				
Meldon Jct.						5 59														
Bridestowe																	7 50	7 51		
Lydford																				
Brentor																				
Tavistock North																6 55	8 6	8 8		
Bere Alston															7 5½	7 7			Guard to collect tickets at Chapelton	
Bere Ferrers															7 12	7 13				
Tamerton Foliot															7 17	7 18				
St. Budeaux, Vic. Rd.															7 22	7 23				
Ford															7 26	7 27				
Devonport, Kings Rd.															7 30	7 32	8 34	8 36		
Devonport Jct.																7 34		8 38		
Plymouth (N. Rd.)															7 36	7 37	8 40	8 42		
Lipson Jct.							4.35 p.m. Taunton W.R.									7 41		8 46		
Mount Gould Jct.																7 42		8 47		
Friary Jct.																7 42½		8 47½		
Plymouth (Friary)															7 45		8 50			
Copplestone			5 41	5 41½			arr. p.m.	dep. p.m.											7 30	7 31
Morchard Rd.			5 44½	5 45															7 34	7 35
Lapford			5 49	5 50															7 39	7 40
Eggesford			5 56	5 57			Worked by S.R. engine												7X46	7 47
Kings Nympton			6X 3	6 6															7 53	7 54
Portsmouth A.			6 11	6 12															7 59	8 0
Umberleigh			6 18	6 19															8 6	8 7
Chapelton																			8 11	8 12
Barnstaple Jct.			6 30	6 35			6 50	6 55											8 19	8 26
Barnstaple Town			6 38	6 39			6 58	6 59											8 29	8 30
Pottington Box				6 40				7 0												8 31
Wrafton			6 46	6 47			7 6	7 7											8 37	8 38
Braunton			6 49	6 51			7 9	7 11											8 40	8 42
Mortehoe & Woolacombe			7 8	7 9			7 28	7 29											8 59	9 0
Ilfracombe			7 17				7 37												9 8	
Barnstaple Jct.				6 40																8 32
Fremington			6 45	6 46															8 37	8 38
Instow			6 52	6 53															8X44	8 45
Bideford (Goods)																				
Bideford (New)			6 58	7 0															8 50	8 52
Torrington			7 9																9 1	

The timings on this page WILL APPLY ON SATURDAYS ONLY, 13th June to 19th September, 1953, INCLUSIVE.

SALISBURY, EXETER, PLYMOUTH, ILFRACOMBE AND TORRINGTON LINES 27

DOWN	6.0 p.m. Waterloo arr.	dep.	Engine arr.	dep.	To Seaton arr.	dep.	5.0 p.m. Waterloo arr.	dep.	10.20 p.m. Sidmouth arr.	dep.	3.54 p.m. Milk Tanks Clapham Jct. arr.	dep.	A arr.	dep.	6.54 p.m. Waterloo to Yeovil Town arr.	dep.	Empties of 11.5 p.m. Exeter Cent. arr.	dep.
	p.m.	p.m.	p.m.	p.m.	p.m.	p.m.	p.m.	p.m.	p.m.	p.m.	p.m.	p.m.	p.m.	p.m.	p.m.	p.m.	p.m.	p.m.
Salisbury	7 44	7 50											7 56		9 46	9 55		
Wilton South																10 2		
Dinton													8 2	8 13	10 11	10 12		
Tisbury													8 20	8 21	10 19	10 20		
Semley													8 30	8 31	10 29	10 30		
Gillingham	8 17	8 18											8 37	8 39	10 36	10 37		
Templecombe	8 28	8 30									7 35		8A56	8A56	10 47	10 50		
Milborne Port								8 18					8 49		10 56	10 57		
Sherborne	8 48	8 50						9 6			9 30	9 50	9 11	11 3	11 3	11 4		
Yeovil Jct.								9 16	9 18			9 509	9 20		11 11	11 21		
Sutton Bingham								9 19										
Crewkerne	9 18	9 19						9 31	9 33		10 18	10 33						
Chard Jct.					9 33	9 42		9 40	9 42									
Axminster	9 43	9 44			9 39	9 42		9 48	9 49		10 48	11 12						
Seaton Jct.												11 34						
Honiton								10 4	10 5									
Sidmouth Jct.								10 11	10 13	10 41	10 43							
Whimple								10 19	10 20	11	11 18							
Broad Clyst	9 43	9 44						10 26	10 32	11	11 0							
Pinhoe								10 36				11 53						
Exmouth Jct.	9 56										11 36							
St. James' Park Halt																		
Exeter Central	9 59	10 6			10 39			10 39		11 3		11 56					11 47	
Do. (St. Davids)	10 9	10 12															11 54	
Cowley Jct.	10 15																	
Newton St. Cyres											11 39						12 2	
Crediton	10 31	10 32			Engine arr. dep. p.m.												12 12	
Yeoford	10 31	10 32															12+15	
Coleford Jct.	10 34																	
Bow			After working 10.30 p.m. Plymouth Friary															
North Tawton											Guard to collect tickets and extinguish lights at Broad Clyst							
Sampford C'nay																		
Quarry Halt																		
Meldon Jct.	10 46	10 47																
Bridestowe	10 59	11		11 45														
Lydford																		
Brentor																		
Tavistock North	11 26	11 27			12 15													
Bere Alston	11 37½	11 38½			12 17													
Bere Ferrers					12 19													
Tamerton Foliot																		
St. Budeaux, Vic. Rd.	11 50	11 51			12 24													
Ford					12 24½													
Devonport, Kings Rd.	11 56	11 58			12 50													
Devonport Jct.	12 0	12 4			12 52													
Plymouth (N. Rd.)	12 2	12 4			12 53													
Lipson Jct.	12 2				12 57													
Mount Gould Jct.	12 2				12 58													
Friary Jct.	12 2				12 58½													
Plymouth (Friary)	12 12			12½27	1													
Copplestone																		
Morchard Rd.																		
Lapford																		
Eggesford																		
Kings Nympton																		
Portsmouth A.																		
Umberleigh																		
Chapelton																		
Barnstaple Jct.																		
Barnstaple Town																		
Pottington Box																		
Wrafton																		
Braunton																		
Morcehoe & Woolacombe																		
Ilfracombe																		
Barnstaple Jct.																		
Fremington																		
Instow																		
Bideford (Goods)																		
Bideford (New)																		
Torrington																		

A—Advertised departure Templecombe 8.56 p.m.

---

26 SALISBURY, EXETER, PLYMOUTH, ILFRACOMBE AND TORRINGTON LINES

The timings on this page WILL APPLY ON SATURDAYS ONLY, 13th June to 19th September, 1953, INCLUSIVE.

DOWN	To Bude and Launceston arr.	dep.		arr.	dep.	3.5 p.m. Waterloo arr.	dep.	arr.	dep.	arr.	dep.	3.54 p.m. Milk Tanks Clapham Jc to Exeter Central arr.	dep.	5.0 p.m. Waterloo to Exeter Central arr.	dep.	Engine arr.	dep.
	p.m.	p.m.		p.m.	p.m.	p.m.	p.m.	p.m.	p.m.	p.m.	p.m.	p.m.	p.m.	p.m.	p.m.	p.m.	p.m.
Salisbury						4 52	5 0					6 32		7 0	7 6		Commences 4th July
Wilton South							5 7										
Dinton						5 13	5 14										
Tisbury						5 23	5 24					7 10	7 20	7 23	7 35		
Semley						5 31	5 32							7 37	7 43		
Gillingham						5 41	5 42							7 51	7 56		
Templecombe						5 48	5 50					7 35	9 6	8 2	8 0	8 18	8+15
Milborne Port														8 18	8 19		
Sherborne						5 34	5 39										8 35
Yeovil Jct.						5 51	5 53										
Sutton Bingham						6 0	6 3										
Crewkerne						6 19	6 20										
Chard Jct.						6 33	6 34										After working 3.25 p.m. Exeter Cent
Axminster						6 41	6 43										
Seaton Jct.						6 49	6 50										
Honiton						7 6	7 12½	7 55									
Sidmouth Jct.						7 14	7 20½	8 1	8 15								
Whimple						7 26½	7 27	8 19	8 20								
Broad Clyst						7 31	7 32	8 26	8 27							Guard to collect tickets and extinguish lights at Brentor	
Pinhoe							7 36	8 36	8 37								
Exmouth Jct.								8 43	8 44								
St. James' Park Halt								8 48	8 49								
Exeter Central							7 39	8 53	8 56			7 35	9 6	8 2	8 18	8 18	8 35
Do. (St. Davids)								8 10	8 7								
Cowley Jct.									8 18								
Newton St. Cyres								8 23	8 24								
Crediton								8 37	8 38								
Yeoford									8 40								
Coleford Jct.																	
Bow								8 47	8 48								After working Exeter Cent
North Tawton								8 54	8 55								
Sampford C'nay								9	9								
Okehampton	7 47							9 10	9 15								
Quarry Halt																	
Meldon Jct.	7 55			8 35				9 28	9 35								
Bridestowe				8 42	8 43			9 34	9 35								
Lydford	6 38			8 47	8 48			9 39	9 48								
Brentor	6 46			8 52	8 53			9 5	10 6								
Tavistock North	6 55	6 59		8 56	8 57			10 5	10 6								
Bere Alston		7 3	9	9 0	9 3			10 12	10 13								
Bere Ferrers		7 4		9 5				10 16	10 17								
Tamerton Foliot			9 7	9 9		9½10		10 20	10 23								
St. Budeaux, Vic. Rd.	7 8		9 13			9 26		10 25									
Ford	7 10		9 14			9 30		10 27	10 29								
Devonport, Kings Rd.	7 12		9 14½			9 34	9 36	10 33	10 34								
Devonport Jct.			9 17			9 26	9 38	10 34	10 34½								
Plymouth (N. Rd.)						9 30	9 40										
Lipson Jct.						9 31	9 45										
Mount Gould Jct.						9 34	9 48										
Friary Jct.																	
Plymouth (Friary)																	
Copplestone																	
Morchard Rd.																	
Lapford																	
Eggesford																	
Kings Nympton																	
Portsmouth A.																	
Umberleigh																	
Chapelton																	
Barnstaple Jct.																	
Barnstaple Town																	
Pottington Box																	
Wrafton																	
Braunton																	
Morcehoe & Woolacombe																	
Ilfracombe																	
Barnstaple Jct.																	
Fremington																	
Instow																	
Bideford (Goods)																	
Bideford (New)																	
Torrington																	

DOWN — SUNDAYS

Train No.	Empty Milk Tanks	Engine		3.58 p.m. (Sat.) Churns Gravesend to Yeovil T.	9.45 a.m. Parcels Yeovil Town	10.10 a.m. Yeovil Town	263 Excursion	263 Continuation of Exon Excursion Salisbury
	arr./dep. a.m.	arr./dep. a.m.	arr./dep. a.m.	arr./dep. a.m.	arr./dep. a.m.	arr./dep. a.m.	arr./dep. a.m.	arr./dep. p.m.
Salisbury							10 0	
Wilton South							10 6 / 10 6½	
Dinton							10 16	
Tisbury							10 23 / 10 24	
Semley							10 32½ / 10 33	
Gillingham				4 27 / 5 12			10 39 / 10 40	
Templecombe				5 37 / 5 42			10 50 / 10 51	
Milborne Port				5 52 / 6 37			10 57 / 10 58	
Sherborne				6 27 / 6 37			11 4 / 11 5	
Yeovil Jct.				6 47 / 7 17			11 13 / 11 15	12th July, 9th and 23rd Aug. only
Sutton Bingham				7 27 / 8 0	9 50 / 9 52	10 15 / 10 17	11 27 / 11 28	
Crewkerne				8C 8 / 8 32	9 57 / 9 58	10 20 / 10 23		
Chard Jct.					10 25 / 10 30	10 34 / 10 37		
Axminster					10 38 / 10 43	10 50 / 10 54		
Seaton Jct.		9 59			10 46 / 11 0	11 2 / 11 ??	11 46 / 11 47	
Honiton		10 0 / 10 7			10 19 / 10 51	11 18 / 11 21	11 53 / 11 54	
Sidmouth Jct.	9|55	10 7			10 23 / 11 28	11 28 / 11 31	12 15 / 12 17	
Whimple						11 42 / 11 42		
Broad Clyst				10 36 / 10 38	11 40	11 48 / 11 49		
Pinhoe		10|18 A		10 46 / 10 52	11 43	11 55 / 11 56		
Exmouth Jct.				10 54		12 0 / 12 1	12 29	12 32 / 12|40
St. James' Park Halt						12 5 / 12 5		12|41 / 12 58
Exeter Central	10|18					12 8	12 32	To Paignton W.R.

(To Bude)

Do. (St. Davids)				10 57 / 10 58				Available for ordinary passengers
Cowley (St. Davids)				11 6 / 11 8				
Newton St. Cyres				11 10				
Crediton				11 18 / 11 25	11 50			
Yeoford				11 24 / 11 41	11 58	Until 20th Sept. only		
Coleford Jct.				11 37 / 11 41				
Bow				11 54 / 11 54½				
North Tawton				12 0 / 12 1				
Sampford C'nay				12 12½ / 12 14				
Okehampton				12 25 / 12 45				
Quarry Halt				12 30½ / 12 31				
Meldon Jct.								
Bridestowe				12 37 / 12 37½				
Brentor				12 40 / 12 41				
Tavistock North				12 44 / 12 46				
Bere Alston				12 50 / 12 53				
Bere Ferrers				12 57				
St. Budeaux, Vic. Rd.				12 58				
Ford				12 58½				
Devonport, Kings Rd.								
Devonport Jct.								
Plymouth (N. Rd.)								
Lipson Jct.								
Mount Gould Jct.								
Friary Jct.								
Plymouth (Friary)								
Copplestone				10 58 / 10 59				
Morchard Rd.				11X 7 / 11 8				
Lapford				11 17 / 11 18				
Eggesford				11 31 / 11 31				
Kings Nympton				11 31 / 11 32				
Portsmouth A.				11 35 / 11 36				
Umberleigh				11 50 / 11 51				
Chapelton				11 58				
Barnstaple Jct.				12 40 / 12 41				
Barnstaple Town				12 44 / 12 44				
Pottington Box				12 46 / 12 48				
Wrafton				12 50 / 12 53				
Braunton				12 57				
Mortehoe & Woolacombe				12 58½				
Instow				12|18 / 12 13				
Bideford (New)				12 27 / 12 28				
Torrington				12 46 / 12 37				

A—Change enginemen with 8.20 a.m. Plymouth Friary and 10.38 a.m. Exeter Central.
C—Time allowed at Yeovil Jc. for engine to turn.
D—Connect with 12.5 p.m. Exmouth, due Exeter Central 12.35 p.m.

---

28 SALISBURY, EXETER, PLYMOUTH, ILFRACOMBE AND TORRINGTON LINES

DOWN — SUNDAYS

Station	Empty Milk Tanks	Engine	1.55 a.m. Pass. and Mails Eastleigh to Yeovil Town	1.35 a.m. Pass. and News Waterloo to Yeovil Town		
	arr./dep. a.m.	arr./dep. a.m.	arr./dep. a.m.	arr./dep. a.m.	arr./dep. a.m.	arr./dep. a.m.
Salisbury			2 36 / 2 50			
Wilton South						
Dinton			3 3 / 3 13	3 40 / 3 57		
Tisbury				4C10 / 4 11		
Semley				4 18 / 4 20		
Gillingham			3 29 / 3 33	4 35 / 4 44		
Templecombe			3 44 / 3 48	4 54 / 5 4		
Milborne Port						
Sherborne	8 54		3 59 / 4 2	5 15 / 5 20		
Yeovil Jct.			4 11 / 4 24	5|28 / 5 40		
Sutton Bingham						
Crewkerne			*Extra vehicles not to be attached at, or for, Tisbury, Gillingham, Templecombe and Sherborne*	*Engine and Brake van*		
Chard Jct.						
Axminster						
Seaton Jct.						
Honiton	7 20			8|25 /		
Sidmouth Jct.	7 23 / 7 28			8|28		Until 20th Sept. only
Whimple	7 31			9.0 a.m. Work		9 23
Broad Clyst				Parcels		9 29 / 9 30
Pinhoe	7 39 / 7 49					9 35½ / 9 36½
Exmouth Jct.						9 42 / 9 43
St. James' Park Halt						9 46½ / 9 47½
Exeter Central	7 57					9 51
Do. (St. Davids)						9 54
Cowley						
Newton St. Cyres						
Crediton						
Yeoford						
Coleford Jct.						

Station	Engine			
	arr./dep. a.m.	arr./dep. a.m.	arr./dep. a.m.	arr./dep. a.m.
Bow				
North Tawton				
Sampford C'nay		8 30		
Okehampton		8 43 / 8 43½		
Quarry Halt		8 49 / 8 54		
Meldon Jct.		8 53 / 9 15½		
Bridestowe		9 20½ / 9 33		
Lydford		9 35 / 9 35½		
Brentor		9 43 / 9 40		
Tavistock North		9 43 / 9 46		
Bere Alston		9 50 / 9 53		
Bere Ferrers		9 58		
St. Budeaux, Vic. Rd.		9 58½		
Ford		10 1		
Devonport, Kings Rd.				
Devonport Jct.				
Plymouth (N. Rd.)				
Lipson Jct.				
Mount Gould Jct.				
Friary Jct.				
Plymouth (Friary)				

Station	Engine			
Copplestone	8 4		Commences 27th Sept.	
Morchard Rd.	8 8 / 8 18			
Lapford	8 24			
Eggesford	8 30			
Kings Nympton	8 35		7 55	
Portsmouth A.	8 42		7 59	Until 20th Sept. only
Umberleigh				8|20
Chapelton				8 23 / 8 24
Barnstaple Jct.			8 7	8 32
Barnstaple Town			8 24	8 49
Pottington Box			8|32	8|57
Wrafton				
Braunton				
Mortehoe & Woolacombe				
Ilfracombe				
Barnstaple Jct.	9 55	Work 9.5 a.m.	Work 9.50 a.m.	9 35 / 9 40½
Fremington	10 0			9 40 / 9 46½
Instow	10X 6 / 10 9			9 52
Bideford (New)	10 14			
Torrington	10 24			

A—Guard to issue and collect tickets at Tamerton Foliot.
C—Stop at Dinton not advertised.
F—Time allowed at Yeovil Jct. for engine to turn.

Train Nos.	202												Q					
DOWN SUNDAYS	9.22 a.m. Excursion Waterloo to Exmouth						10.45 a.m. Waterloo		Engine		2.30 p.m. Milk Lifton, W.R.		Engine and Brake Van		11.0 a.m. Waterloo		To Bude	
	■						■				◆				A			
	arr. a.m.	dep. a.m.	arr. p.m.	dep. p.m.	arr. p.m.	dep. p.m.	arr. p.m.	dep. p.m.	arr. p.m.	dep. p.m.	arr. p.m.	dep. p.m.	arr. p.m.	dep. p.m.	arr. p.m.	dep. p.m.	arr. p.m.	dep. p.m.
Salisbury	11 3	11 8					12 12	12 18		12‖42					12 48	12 54		
Wilton South							Through coaches to Ilfracombe and Torrington		12‖48						Through coaches to Plymouth, Bude, (Summer) also Ilfracombe and Torrington when 11.5 a.m. Waterloo not running.			
Dinton																		
Tisbury			Until 20th Sept. only.		Com-mences 27th Sept.													
Semley																		
Gillingham									Work 12.0 noon Waterloo									
Templecombe																		
Milborne Port																		
Sherborne	11 50	11 51																
Yeovil Jct.	11 58	12 0						1 2								1 41		
Sutton Bingham																		
Crewkerne																		
Chard Jct.							Until 20th Sept. only		Until 13th Sept. only									
Axminster	12 28	12 30																
Seaton Jct.	12 36	12 38																
Honiton				1 22		1 27												
Sidmouth Jct.	12 59	1 1	1 28	1 29	1 33	1 34									2 24	2 29		
Whimple			1 34½	1 35	1 39½	1 40												
Broad Clyst			1 40½	1 41	1 45½	1 46												
Pinhoe			1 44½	1 45	1 49½	1 50												
Exmouth Jct.		1 13		1 49		1 54		1 53								2 42		
St. James' Park Halt																		
Exeter Central	1 16	1 22	1 52		1 57		1 56	2 2						2†50	2 45	2 55		
Do. (St. Davids)							2 5	2 9					2 53	2 54	2 58	3A 6		
Cowley Jct.								2 12						2 57		3 9		
Newton St. Cyres																		
Crediton																		
Yeoford																		
Coleford Jct.								2 26						3 12		3 23		
Bow	21st June, 19th July, 9th and 23rd Aug. and 6th Sept. only																	
North Tawton																		
Sampford C'nay											From Western Region							
Okehampton															3 45	3 49		4 15
Quarry Halt																		
Meldon Jct.																		4 23
Bridestowe																		
Lydford											2 45	2 52						
Brentor																		
Tavistock North												3 5			4 14	4 16		
Bere Alston															4 26½	4 27½		
Bere Ferrers																		
Tamerton Foliot																		
St. Budeaux, Vic. Rd.																		
Ford																		
Devonport, Kings Rd.												3 36			4 44	4 46		
Devonport Jct.												3 38				4 48		
Plymouth (N. Rd.)											3 40				4 50	4 53		
Lipson Jct.																4 57		
Mount Gould Jct.											27th Sept. 1953 to 21st Mar. 1954					4 58		
Friary Jct.																4 58½		
Plymouth (Friary)															5 1			
Copplestone								2 29						3 15				
Morchard Rd.								2 32					3X19	3 27				
Lapford								2 35					3†31					
Eggesford								2 41										
Kings Nympton								2 46½										
Portsmouth A.								2 51										
Umberleigh								2 56										
Chapelton																		
Barnstaple Jct.							3 5	3 10										
Barnstaple Town							3 13	3 15										
Pottington Box								3 16										
Wrafton							3 22	3 23										
Braunton							3 25	3 29										
Mortehoe & Woolacombe							3 46	3 48										
Ilfracombe							3 56											
Barnstaple Jct								3 15										
Fremington							3 20	3 21										
Instow							3 27	3 28										
Bideford (New)							3 33	3 37										
Torrington							3 46											

A—Advertised departure Exeter St. David's 3.6 p.m.

DOWN SUNDAYS			11.5 a.m. Waterloo to Ilfra-combe		Engine		11.40 a.m. Portsm'th & Southsea		11.40 a.m. Portsm'th & S'sea to Plymouth		12.0 noon Waterloo				11.5 a.m. Waterloo		11.40 a.m. Portsm'th & S'sea			
							■		■		A									
	arr. p.m.	dep. p.m.	arr. p.m.	dep. p.m.	arr. p.m.	dep. p.m.	arr. p.m.	dep. p.m.	arr. p.m.	dep. p.m.	arr. p.m.	dep. p.m.	arr. p.m.	dep. p.m.	arr. p.m.	dep. p.m.	arr. p.m.	dep. p.m.	arr. p.m.	dep. p.m.
Salisbury			12 57	1 3			1 17	1 24	1 17	1 24		1 42								
Wilton South			Through coaches to Ilfra-combe and Torring-ton.								1A47	1 53								
Dinton																				
Tisbury							Com-mences 27th Sept.		Until 20th Sept. only											
Semley											Until 13th Sept. only									
Gillingham																	Until 20th Sept. only			
Templecombe																				
Milborne Port																				
Sherborne							2 6	2 7	2 6	2 7										
Yeovil Jct.				1 49			2 14	2 16	2 14	2 16		2 33								
Sutton Bingham											"DEVON BELLE" Pullman cars only								Com-mences 27th Sept.	
Crewkerne					After working 2.0 p.m. Sidmouth															
Chard Jct.																	←			
Axminster			2 15	2 17			2 42	2 44	2 42	2 44										
Seaton Jct			2 23	2 25			2 50	2 52	2 50	3 7							2 50	3 7		
Honiton	Com-mences 27th Sept.						3 7	3 8	→								3 22	3 23		
Sidmouth Jct.			Until 20th Sept. only			2‖55	3 15	3 17			3 16	3 19					3 30	3 32		
Whimple																				
Broad Clyst																				
Pinhoe																				
Exmouth Jct.				2 57	3‖15			3 29				3 32						3 44		
St. James' Park Halt																				
Exeter Central	2 45	3 10	3 0	3 10			3 32	3 38			3 35	3 42					3 47	3 53		4 8
Do. (St. Davids)	3 13	3 17	3 13	3 16	Until 20th Sept. only		3 41	3 46			3 45	3 47					3 56	3 59	4 11	4 14
Cowley Jct.		3 20		3 19				3 49				3 50						4 2		4 17
Newton St. Cyres																				
Crediton			3 27	3 28			3 57	3 58									4 10	4 11	4 25	4 27
Yeoford							4 5	4 6									4 18	4 19	4 34	4 35
Coleford Jct.		3 34		3 36				4 8				4 4						4 21		4 37
Bow																				
North Tawton																				
Sampford C'nay																				
Okehampton							4 30	4 32									4 43	4 45		
Quarry Halt																				
Meldon Jct.																				
Bridestowe																				
Lydford																				
Brentor																				
Tavistock North							4 57	4 58									5 10	5 11		
Bere Alston							5 8½	5 10									5 21½	5 23		
Bere Ferrers							5 15	5 16									5 28	5 29		
Tamerton Foliot																				
St. Budeaux, Vic. Rd.							5 22	5 23									5 35	5 36		
Ford																				
Devonport, Kings Rd.							5 28	5 30									5 41	5 44		
Devonport Jct.								5 32										5 46		
Plymouth (N. Rd.)							5 34	5 37									5 48	5 51		
Lipson Jct.								5 41										5 55		
Mount Gould Jct.								5 42										5 56		
Friary Jct.								5 42½										5 56½		
Plymouth (Friary)							5 45										5 59			
Copplestone		3 37	3 40	3 41								4 7							4 41	4 42
Morchard Rd.		3 40	3 44	3 45								4 10X							4 45	4 46
Lapford		3 43	3 49	3 50								4 13	Until 20th Sept. only		Until 20th Sept. only				4 50	4 51
Eggesford	3 49	3 50	3X56	3 59								4 19							4 57	4 58
Kings Nympton		3 56	4 5	4 5½								4 24½							5 4	5 5
Portsmouth A.		4 0½	4 10½	4 11								4 29							5 10	5 11
Umberleigh		4 5½	4 17	4 17½								4 34							5 17	5 18
Chapelton			4 21½	4 22											←				5 22	5 23
Barnstaple Jct.	4 15	4 22	4 28	5 5							4 43	4 45			4 28	5 5			5 29	
Barnstaple Town	4 25	4 26	→								4 48	4 49			5 8	5 9				
Pottington Box		4 27										4 50				5 10				
Wrafton	4 33	4 34													5 16	5 17				
Braunton	4 36	4 38									4 57	5 1			5 19	5 22				
Mortehoe & Woolacombe	4 55	4 58									5 18	5 19			5 39	5 41				
Ilfracombe	5 6										5 27				5 49					
Barnstaple Jct.		4 25												4 50						
Fremington	4 30	4 31											4 55	4 56						
Instow	4 37	4 38											5 2	5 3						
Bideford (New)	4 43	4 46											5 8	5 10						
Torrington	4 55												5 19							

A—Stop at Wilton South to change engines, and not advertised.

32 SALISBURY, EXETER, PLYMOUTH, ILFRACOMBE AND TORRINGTON LINES

DOWN SUNDAYS	5.30 p.m. Milk Lifton W.R. ♦				4.5 p.m. Sidmouth				Engine				Engine				4.0 p.m. Waterloo			
	arr. p.m.	dep. p.m.	arr. p.m.	dep p.m.	arr. p.m.	dep. p.m.	arr. p.m.	dep. p.m.	arr. p.m.	dep. p.m.	arr. p.m.	dep. p.m.	arr. p.m.	dep. p.m.	arr. p.m.	dep. p.m.	arr. p.m.	dep. p.m.	arr p.m.	dep. p.m.
Salisbury				1 40				1 54						3‖13			5 42	5 49		
Wilton South			1 46	1 47			2 0	2 1					3‖19				Through coaches to Plymouth, Ilfracombe and Torrington			
Dinton			1 56	1 57			2 10	2 11					Work 12.0 noon Ilfracombe							
Tisbury			2 4	2 5			2 18	2 19	After working 4.5 p.m. Sidmouth											
Semley			2 13½	2 15			2 27½	2 29												
Gillingham			2 21	2 23			2 35	2 37												
Templecombe			2 32½	2 35			2 46½	2 49												
Milborne Port			2 40½	2 41½			2 54½	2 55½												
Sherborne			2 47	2 48	Commences 18th April 1954		3 1	3 2	Until 20th Sept. only								6 33	6 34		
Yeovil Jct.			2 55	3 0			3 9	3 14									6 41	6 43		
Sutton Bingham			3 5	3 6			3 19	3 20												
Crewkerne			3 16	3 19			3 30	3 33												
Chard Jct.			3 32	3 34			3 46	3 48					Until 20th Sept. only							
Axminster			3 41	3 44			3 55	3 58									7 11	7 13		
Seaton Jct.			3 50	3 52			4 4	4 6									7 19	7 21		
Honiton			4 7	4 8			4 21	4 22									7 37	7 38		
Sidmouth Jct.			4 14½	4 18	4 26	4 30	4 28½	4 32		4‖45							7 45	7 48		
Whimple			4 24	4 25	4 36	4 37½	4 38	4 39												
Broad Clyst			4 31	4 34	4 43½	4 44	4 45	4 46												
Pinhoe			4 38	4 39	4 48	4 49	4 50	4 51												
Exmouth Jct.				4 43		4 53		4 55	5‖5									8 1		
St. James' Park Halt																				
Exeter Central			4 46		4 56		4 58	5 15				5 25					8 4	8 12	8 4	8 22
Do. (St. Davids)							5 18	5 22			5 28	5 33					8 15	8 19	8 25	8 29
Cowley Jct.	27th Sept. 1953 to 21st Mar. 1954							5 25				5 36						8 22		8 32
Newton St. Cyres																				
Crediton			Commences 27th Sept.				5 33	5 34			5 44	5 45					8 30	8 31	8 39	8 41
Yeoford							5 41	5 42			5 53	5 54					8 38	8 39	8 48	8 49
Coleford Jct.								5 44				5 56						8 41		8 51
Bow											6 4	6 5					8 48	8 49		
North Tawton											6 12	6 13					8 56	8 57		
Sampford C'nay	From Western Region																			
Okehampton			Guard to light platform lamps at Broad Clyst								6 25	6 30					9 9	9 13		
Quarry Halt							Until 20th Sept. only													
Meldon Jct.																				
Bridestowe											6 43	6 44					9 26	9 27		
Lydford	5 45	6 0									6 50	6 51					9 33	9 34		
Brentor											6 54	6 55					9 37	9 38		
Tavistock North		6 13									7 3	7 4					9 46	9 49		
Bere Alston											7 14½	7 17					9 59½	10 1		
Bere Ferrers											7 22	7 23					10 6	10 7		
Tamerton Foliot											7 27	7 28								
St. Budeaux, Vic. Rd.											7 32	7 33					10 13	10 14		
Ford											7 36	7 37					10 17	10 18		
Devonport, Kings Rd.		6 48									7 40	7 43					10 21	10 23		
Devonport Jct.		6 50										7 45						10 25		
Plymouth (N. Rd.)	6 52										7 47	7 50					10 27	10 29		
Lipson Jct.												7 54						10 33		
Mount Gould Jct.												7 55						10 34		
Friary Jct.												7 55½						10 34½		
Plymouth (Friary)											7 58						10 37			
Copplestone							5 48	5 49			Guard issues and collects tickets at Tamerton Foliot								8 55	8 55½
Morchard Rd.							5 52	5 53											8 58½	8 59
Lapford							5 57	5 58											9 3	9 4
Eggesford							6 5	6 6											9 11	9 12
Kings Nympton							6 13	6 14											9 19	9 20
Portsmouth A.							6 19	6 20											9 25	9 26
Umberleigh							6 27	6 28									Guard to collect tickets and extinguish lights at Brentor		9 33	9 34
Chapelton															Until 20th Sept. only.				9 38	9 39
Barnstaple Jct.							6 38	6 42											9 46	9 51
Barnstaple Town							6 45	6 46											9 54	9 55
Pottington Box								6 47												9 56
Wrafton							6 53	6 54											10 2	10 3
Braunton							6 56	6 58											10 5	10 7
Mortehoe & Woolacombe							7 15	7 17											10 24	10 25
Ilfracombe							7 25												10 33	
Barnstaple Jct.																8 5				9 56
Fremington															8 10	8 11			10 1	10 2
Instow															8 17	8 18			10 8	10 9
Bideford (New)															8 23	8 25			10 14	10 16
Torrington															8 34				10 25	

TORRINGTON, ILFRACOMBE, PLYMOUTH, EXETER AND SALISBURY LINES 33

DOWN SUNDAYS	To Bude				Engine						7.15 p.m. Yeovil Town									
	arr. p.m.	dep. p.m.			arr. p.m.	dep. p.m.					arr. p.m.	dep. p.m.								
Salisbury																				
Wilton South																				
Dinton																				
Tisbury																				
Semley																				
Gillingham																				
Templecombe																				
Milborne Port																				
Sherborne					12th July, 9th and 23rd Aug. only															
Yeovil Jct.											7 20	7 22								
Sutton Bingham											7 27	7 28								
Crewkerne											7 39	7 40								
Chard Jct.											7 53	7 55								
Axminster											8 3	8 4								
Seaton Jct.											8 10	8 12								
Honiton											8 28	8 29								
Sidmouth Jct.											8 36	8 38								
Whimple											8 44	8 45								
Broad Clyst											8 51	8 52								
Pinhoe											8 56	8 57								
Exmouth Jct.						8‖48						9 1								
St. James' Park Halt																				
Exeter Central					8 52	8 55					9 4									
Do. (St. Davids)					8‖58															
Cowley Jct.																				
Newton St. Cyres																				
Crediton	Until 20th Sept. only																			
Yeoford																				
Coleford Jct.																				
Bow																				
North Tawton																				
Sampford C'nay					*Work 9.22 p.m. Excn. to Salisbury*															
Okehampton		9 23																		
Quarry Halt																				
Meldon Jct.		9 31																		
Bridestowe																				
Lydford																				
Brentor																				
Tavistock North																				
Bere Alston																				
Bere Ferrers																				
Tamerton Foliot																				
St. Budeaux, Vic. Rd.																				
Ford																				
Devonport, Kings Rd.																				
Devonport Jct.																				
Plymouth (N. Rd.)																				
Lipson Jct.																				
Mount Gould Jct.																				
Friary Jct.																				
Plymouth (Friary)																				
Copplestone																				
Morchard Rd.																				
Lapford																				
Eggesford																				
Kings Nympton																				
Portsmouth A.																				
Umberleigh																				
Chapelton																				
Barnstaple Jct.																				
Barnstaple Town																				
Pottington Box																				
Wrafton																				
Braunton																				
Mortehoe & Woolacombe																				
Ilfracombe																				
Barnstaple Jct.																				
Fremington																				
Instow																				
Bideford (New)																				
Torrington																				

TORRINGTON, ILFRACOMBE, PLYMOUTH, EXETER AND SALISBURY LINES

The timings shown on this page WILL NOT APPLY ON SATURDAYS, 13th June to 19th September, 1953.

UP WEEKDAYS

Distances			UP WEEKDAYS	News	6.28 a.m. Yeovil Town	7.10 a.m. Yeovil Town to Waterloo	MX Parcels & Fish	Empty

Stations listed (UP WEEKDAYS):
Torrington, Bideford (New), Instow, Fremington, Barnstaple Jct., Ilfracombe, Mortehoe & Wollacombe, Braunton, Wrafton, Pottington Box, Barnstaple Town, Barnstaple Jct., Chapelton, Umberleigh, Portsmouth A., Kings Nympton, Eggesford, Lapford, Morchard Rd., Copplestone, Plymouth (Friary), Friary, Mount Gould Jct., Lipson Jct., Plymouth (N. Rd.), Devonport, Kings Rd., Ford, St. Budeaux, Vic. Rd., Tamerton Foliot, Bere Ferrers, Bere Alston, Tavistock North, Brentor, Lydford, Bridestowe, Meldon Jct., Okehampton, Quarry Halt, Sampford C'nay, North Tawton, Bow, Coleford Jct., Yeoford, Crediton, Newton St. Cyres, Cowley (St. David's), Exeter (St. David's), Exeter Central, St. James' Park Halt, Exmouth Jct., Pinhoe, Broad Clyst, Whimple, Sidmouth Jct., Honiton, Seaton Jct., Axminster, Chard Jct., Crewkerne, Sutton Bingham, Yeovil Jct., Sherborne, Milborne Port, Templecombe, Semley, Tisbury, Dinton, Wilton South, Salisbury, Waterloo

News column selected times: 1 25, 1 27, 1 28, 1 29, 1 33, 1 35, 1 37, 1 39, 2A 5, 2 32, 3 0, 3 16, 3 18 3 20, 3 26 3 28, 3 41 3 44, 3A47 3m50, 3m53

6.28 a.m. Yeovil Town times: 6 32, 6 33, 6 6 41½6 50, 6 55

7.10 a.m. Yeovil Town to Waterloo times: 7 15 7 22, 7 29 7 30, 7 37½7 38, 7 43½7 44½, 7 53½7 54½, 8 8 13, 8 12 8 18, 8 19 8 27 8 28, 8 33 8 42, 1116

Empty column: 5 50, 6 20, 6 11 5, 5 35

Note: News for Bow and North Tawton to be taken to Yeoford and returned by 1.38 a.m. Exmouth Jct. Sidings

A—May convey up to 12 oil fed wagons between Devonport (Kings Road) and Exeter Central; vac. fitted wagons to be formed next to news van.

SALISBURY, EXETER, PLYMOUTH, ILFRACOMBE AND TORRINGTON LINES

DOWN SUNDAYS

Train No.	3.35 p.m. Milk Tanks Clapham Jct.	3.35 p.m. Milk Tanks Clapham Jct.	6.0 p.m. Waterloo	10.30 Sidmouth	8.12 p.m. Waterloo Yeovil Town

Stations listed (DOWN SUNDAYS):
Salisbury, Wilton South, Dinton, Tisbury, Semley, Gillingham, Templecombe, Milborne Port, Sherborne, Yeovil Jct., Sutton Bingham, Crewkerne, Chard Jct., Axminster, Seaton Jct., Honiton, Sidmouth Jct., Whimple, Broad Clyst, Pinhoe, Exmouth Jct., St. James' Park Halt, Exeter Central, Exeter (St. David's), Cowley Jct., Newton St. Cyres, Crediton, Yeoford, Coleford Jct., Bow, North Tawton, Sampford C'nay, Okehampton, Quarry Halt, Meldon Jct., Bridestowe, Lydford, Brentor, Tavistock North, Bere Alston, Bere Ferrers, Tamerton Foliot, Ford, St. Budeaux, Vic. Rd., Devonport, Kings Rd., Devonport Jct., Plymouth (N. Rd.), Lipson Jct., Mount Gould Jct., Friary, Plymouth (Friary), Copplestone, Morchard Rd., Lapford, Eggesford, Kings Nympton, Portsmouth A., Umberleigh, Chapelton, Barnstaple Jct., Barnstaple Town, Pottington Box, Wrafton, Braunton, Mortehoe & Woolacombe, Ilfracombe, Barnstaple Jct., Fremington, Instow, Bideford (New), Torrington

A—Detach milk tanks for Seaton Jct. at Axminster.

The timings shown on this page WILL NOT APPLY ON SATURDAYS, 13th June to 19th September, 1953.

TORRINGTON, ILFRACOMBE, PLYMOUTH, EXETER AND SALISBURY LINES

UP WEEKDAYS	To Sidmouth				To Waterloo				Q 8.8 a.m. Yeovil Town to Waterloo		A				To Waterloo		To Sidmouth			
					▣										▣					
	arr. a.m.	dep. a.m.	arr. a.m.	dep. a.m.	arr. a.m.	dep. a.m.	arr. a.m.	dep. a.m.	arr. a.m.	dep. a.m.	arr. a.m.	dep. a.m.	arr. a.m.	dep. a.m.	arr. a.m.	dep. a.m.	arr. a.m.	dep. a.m.	arr. a.m.	dep. a.m.
Torrington																				
Bideford (New)																				
Instow																				
Fremington																				
Barnstaple Jct.																				
Ilfracombe																				
Mortehoe & Woolacombe																				
Braunton																				
Wrafton																				
Pottington Box																				
Barnstaple Town																				
Barnstaple Jct.																				
Chapelton																				
Umberleigh																				
Portsmouth A.																				
Kings Nympton																				
Eggesford																				
Lapford																				
Morchard Rd.																				
Copplestone																				
Plymouth (Friary)																				
Friary Jct.																				
Mount Gould Jct.																				
Lipson Jct.																				
Plymouth (N. Rd.)																				
Devonport Jct.																				
Devonport, Kings Rd.																				
Ford																				
St. Budeaux, Vic. Rd.																				
Tamerton Foliot																				
Bere Ferrers																				
Bere Alston																				
Tavistock North																				
Brentor																				
Lydford																				
Bridestowe																				
Meldon Jct.																				
Quarry Halt																				
Okehampton																				
Sampford C'nay																				
North Tawton																				
Bow																				
Coleford Jct.															Load					
Yeoford															8 bogies					
Crediton															Exeter Ctl.					
Newton St. Cyres															to					
Cowley Jct.															Salisbury					
Exeter (St. David's)																				
Exeter Central		6 0				6 30						6 40				7 30		7 34		8 0
St. James' Park Halt												6 42						7 36		8 2½
Exmouth Jct.		6 3										6 44						7 38		8 5
Pinhoe	6 6	6 7									6 47	6 47½					7 41	7 42	8 8	8 8½
Broad Clyst	6 11	6 12									6 51½	6 52					7 45	7 46	8 11½	8 12
Whimple	6 19	6 20									6 59	7 0					7 53	7 54	8 18½	8 19½
Sidmouth Jct.	6 27	6 32			6 48	6 49					7 7	7 8			7 46	7 47	8 1	8 7	8 26	8 30
Honiton					6 56½	7 0					7 16	7 17							8 38	
Seaton Jct.					7 11	7 14					7A28	7 31					6.30 a.m.			
Axminster					7 19	7 22					7 36				8 5	8 6	Exeter C.			
Chard Jct.					7 30	7 33											to			
Crewkerne					7 46	7 49											Waterloo			
Sutton Bingham					7 57½	7 58											▣			
Yeovil Jct.					8 3	8 6			8 13	8 20					8 31	8 32	arr. a.m.	dep. a.m.		
Sherborne					8 13	8 15									8 39	8 40				
Milborne Port					8 22½	8 23											←			
Templecombe					8 28	9 3			8 36	8 38					8 50	8 52	8 28	9 3		
Gillingham					——→				8 47	8 49					9 1	9 2	9 12	9 14		
Semley								8 35									9 22½	9 23½		
Tisbury							8 42	8 43									9 30½	9 31½		
Dinton							8 49	8 50									9 37½	9 39		
Wilton South							8 58	8 59									9 47	9 48		
Salisbury							9 4		9 15	9 21					9 27	9 33	9 53	10 1		
Waterloo									11 0						11 8		12 19			

A—Change enginemen at Seaton Jct.

The timings shown on this page WILL NOT APPLY ON SATURDAYS, 13th June to 19th September, 1953.

TORRINGTON, ILFRACOMBE, PLYMOUTH, EXETER AND SALISBURY LINES

UP WEEKDAYS	Empty												To Templecombe						8.20 a.m. Launceston	
					▲				▲				A						C	
	arr. a.m.	dep. a.m.	arr. a.m.	dep. a.m.	arr. a.m.	dep. a.m.			arr. a.m.	dep. a.m.			arr. a.m.	dep. a.m.	arr. a.m.	dep. a.m.	arr. a.m.	dep. a.m.	arr. a.m.	dep. a.m.
Torrington										7 6										
Bideford (New)									7X15	7 17										
Instow									7X22	7 22½										
Fremington									7 29½	7 30										
Barnstaple Jct.																				
Ilfracombe																				
Mortehoe & Woolacombe																				
Braunton																				
Wrafton																				
Pottington Box																				
Barnstaple Town																				
Barnstaple Jct.		7†30							7 35	7 41										
Chapelton									7 47	7 47½										
Umberleigh		7 40							7 52½	7 53										
Portsmouth A.		7 46							7 59	7 59½										
Kings Nympton	7†51								8X 4½	8 5										
Eggesford	Form								8 11	8 12										
Lapford	8.28 a.m.								8 18	8 19										
Morchard Rd.	to								8 24	8 24½										
Copplestone	Barnstaple Jct.								8 28½	8 29										
Plymouth (Friary)				5 58		6 10										7 8		7 34		
Friary Jct.				6 0		6 12										7 10		7 36		
Mount Gould Jct.				6 1		6 13										7 11		7 37		
Lipson Jct.				6 2		6 14										7 12		7 38		
Plymouth (N. Rd.)			6 6	6 8	6 18	6 20									7 16	7 19	7 42	7 43		
Devonport Jct.				6 10		6 22										7 21		7 45		
Devonport, Kings Rd.			6 11	6 12	6 23	6 24									7 22	7 27	7 46	7 48		
Ford			6 15	6 15½	6 27	6 27½									7 30	7 31	7 51	7 52		
St. Budeaux, Vic. Rd.			6 19½	6 20	6 31½	6 32									7 35	7 36	7 56	7 57		
Tamerton Foliot	SX														7 40	7 41	8 1	8 2		
Bere Ferrers					6 39	6 39½									7 46	7 47	8 7	8 8		
Bere Alston	Empty		6 35	6 36½	6 48½	6 49½									7 56	8 2	8 17	8 19½		
Tavistock North			6 48		7 0½	7 2									8 13½	8 15	8 31			
Brentor	arr. a.m.	dep. a.m.			7 13	7 13½									8 26	8 26½				
Lydford					7 17½	7 18									8 30½	8 31				
Bridestowe					7 25	7 25½									8 38	8 39				
Meldon Jct.		7†16				7 33½										8 47			9 13	
Quarry Halt					7 34½	7 35½														C
Okehampton	7†21				7 39½	7 43									8 51	8 53			9C17	
Sampford C'nay					7 49	7 49½									8 59	8 59½				
North Tawton					7 54½	7 55									9 4½	9 6				
Bow					8 1	8 1½									9 12	9 13				
Coleford Jct.						8 7½				8 32			Through coach Seaton to Waterloo			9 19				
Yeoford					8 9½	8 10½			8 34	8 35					9 21	9 22				
Crediton					8 16½	8 17½			8 41	8 42					9 28	9 29				
Newton St. Cyres					8 22½	8 23			8 47	8 48					9 34	9 35				
Cowley Jct.						8 28				8 53						9 40				
Exeter (St. David's)					8 31	8 36			8 56	9 0					9 43	9 48				
Exeter Central					8 39	8 48			9 3					9 33	9 51					
St. James' Park Halt																				
Exmouth Jct.						8 51								9 36						
Pinhoe					8 54	8 54½							9 39	9 39½						
Broad Clyst					8 57½	8 58							9 42½	9 43						
Whimple					9 5	9 5½							9 50	9 50½						
Sidmouth Jct.					9 12½	9 15							9 57½	9 59						
Honiton					9 23	9 25							10 7	10 9						
Seaton Jct.					9 36	9 38							10 20	10 24						
Axminster					9W43	9 46							10 29	10 31						
Chard Jct.					9 54	9 56							10 39	10 41						
Crewkerne					10 9	10 12							10 54	10 56						
Sutton Bingham					10 21	10 22														
Yeovil Jct.					10W27	10 31							11A8	11 19						
Sherborne					10 38	10 40														
Milborne Port					10 48	10 49							——→							
Templecombe					10 54	10 58														
Gillingham					11 7	11 10														
Semley					11 19	11 20														
Tisbury					11 27	11 28														
Dinton					11 35	11 36														
Wilton South					11 45	11 46														
Salisbury					11 51															
Waterloo																				

A—Change engines at Yeovil Jct.

C—Call at Quarry Halt to take up wives of Railway employees on Saturdays and arrive Okehampton 9.20 a.m.

The timings shown on this page WILL NOT APPLY ON SATURDAYS, 13th June to 19th September, 1953.

TORRINGTON, ILFRACOMBE, PLYMOUTH, EXETER AND SALISBURY LINES

UP WEEKDAYS	MFO To Waterloo ■		9.33 a.m. Exeter Ctl. C		To Waterloo		To Waterloo ■		SXQ Engine		SO				W.R. Engine		▲D		▲D	
	arr. a.m.	dep. a.m.	arr. a.m.	dep. a.m.	arr. a.m.	dep. a.m.	arr. a.m.	dep. a.m.	arr. a.m.	dep. a.m.	arr. a.m.	dep. a.m.	arr. p.m.	dep. p.m.	arr. a.m.	dep. a.m.	arr. a.m.	arr. a.m.	arr. a.m.	dep. a.m.
Torrington					...	8 10											...	8 53	...	8 53
Bideford (New)					8X19	8 22											9 2	9 4	9 2	9 4
Instow					8 27	8 28											9 9	9 10	9 9	9 10
Fremington					8 35	8 36											9 17	9 18	9 17	9 18
Barnstaple Jct.					8 41	...											9 23	...	9 23	...
Ilfracombe						8 10												8 55		8 55
Mortehoe & Woolacombe					8 22	8 24											9 7	9 8	9 7	9 8
Braunton					8 34	8 36											9 18	9 19	9 18	9 19
Wrafton					8 38	8 39											9 21	9 22	9 21	9 22
Pottington Box	24th July					8 45												9 28		9 28
Barnstaple Town	to				8 46	8 48											9 29	9 30	9 29	9 30
Barnstaple Jct.	18th Sept.				8 51	8 56											9 33	9 39	9 33	9 39
Chapelton	only				9 2	9 3											9 45	9 46	9 45	9 46
Umberleigh	and Q				9 8	9 9											9 51	9 52	9 51	9 52
Portsmouth A.					9 15	9 16											9 58	9 58½	9 58	9 58½
Kings Nympton					9 22	9 23											10 3½	10 4	10 3½	10 4
Eggesford					9X29	9 31											10 10	10 11	10 10	10 11
Lapford					9 37	9 38											10X17	10 18	10X17	10 18
Morchard Rd.						9 43X											10X23	1023½	10X23	1023½
Copplestone						9 46											1027½	10 28	1027½	10 28
Plymouth (Friary)							...	8 15									Until 18th Sept. only		Commences 21st Sept.	
Friary Jct.								8 17												
Mount Gould Jct.								8 18												
Lipson Jct.								8 19												
Plymouth (N. Rd.)							8 23	8 26												
Devonport Jct.								8 28												
Devonport, Kings Rd.							8 29	8 31												
Ford																				
St. Budeaux, Vic. Rd.																			Through coach Yeovil Town to Waterloo	
Tamerton Foliot																	Through coaches from Lyme Regis and Yeovil Town to Waterloo			
Bere Ferrers																				
Bere Alston																				
Tavistock North							8 58	9 0												
Brentor																				
Lydford							9 13	9 13½												
Bridestowe																				
Meldon Jct.								9 27												
Quarry Halt																				
Okehampton							9 31	9 35												
Sampford C'nay	*Formed of 8.10 a.m. Ilfracombe*																			
North Tawton							9 45	9 45½												
Bow																				
Coleford Jct.						9 48		9 54										10 31		10 31
Yeoford							9 56	9 57									10 33	10 34	10 33	10 34
Crediton							10 3	10 4									10 40	10 41	10 40	10 41
Newton St. Cyres																	10 46	10 47	10 46	10 47
Cowley Jct.						10 0		10 13										10 52		10 52
Exeter (St. David's)			Through coach Seaton to Waterloo		10 3	10 8	10 16	10 20								10‖48	10 55	11 1	10 55	11 1
Exeter Central	...	*10 17*			10 11	10 30	10 23	10 30			...	*10 42*			10‖51	...	11 4	11 14	11 4	11 14
St. James' Park Halt															Work 11.47 a.m. to Plymouth Friary					
Exmouth Jct.												*10 45*						11 17		11 17
Pinhoe											*10 48*	*10 49*					11 20	1120½	11 20	1120½
Broad Clyst											*10 52*	*10 53*					...	...	1123½	11 24
Whimple											*11 0*	*11 1*					1129½	11 30	11 30	11 31
Sidmouth Jct.		*10 33*			...	...	10 48	10 55			*11 8*	*11 10*					11 37	11 38	11 38	11 39
Honiton					Through coaches from Exmouth, Sidmouth Ilfracombe, Torrington Plymouth and Seaton					*11‖15*	*11 18*		Until 18th Sept. only				11 45	11 47	11 46	11 48
Seaton Jct.									*11‖26*	...					...	...	11 58	12 0	11 59	12 3
Axminster																	12 5	12 9	12 8	12 12
Chard Jct.									*Perform Shunting*						arr. p.m.	dep. p.m.	12 17	12 19	12 20	12 22
Crewkerne			←														12 32	12 34	12 35	12 37
Sutton Bingham																				
Yeovil Jct.		*11 14*	11 8	11C19				11 38							Commences 21st Sept.		12D46	12 52	12D49	12 55
Sherborne			11 26	11C28													12 59	1 0	1 2	1 4
Milborne Port			11 35	11C36															1 11	1 12
Templecombe	*11 26*	*11 29*	11 41	...			11 50	11 55					...	12 50	...	12 55	1 11	1 13	1 17	1 19
Gillingham													12 59	1 1	1 4	1 6	1 22	1 23	1 28	1 30
Semley													1 10	1 11	1 15	1 16				
Tisbury													1 18	1 19	1 23	1 24				
Dinton													1 25	1 26	1 30	1 31				
Wilton South													1 34	1 35	1 39	1 40				
Salisbury	*12 2*	*12 8*					12 28	12 34					1 40	...	1 45	...	1 49	...	1 56	...
Waterloo	*1 37*						2 15													

C—Advertised departure Yeovil Jct. 11.15, Sherborne 11.24, Milborne Port 11.31 a.m.

D—Change engines at Yeovil Jct.

The timings shown on this page WILL NOT APPLY ON SATURDAYS, 13th June to 19th September, 1953.

TORRINGTON, ILFRACOMBE, PLYMOUTH, EXETER AND SALISBURY LINES

UP WEEKDAYS	Engine		8.30 a.m. Padstow		MO Engine to Sidmouth		To Waterloo		To Waterloo		9.35 a.m. Padstow to Waterloo ■		To Waterloo ■		SX		Engine		To Brighton and P'mouth & S'sea ▲	
	arr. a.m.	dep. a.m.	arr. a.m.	dep. a.m.	arr. p.m.	dep. p.m.	arr. a.m.	dep. a.m.	arr. a.m.	dep. a.m.	arr. a.m.	dep. a.m.	arr. a.m.	dep. a.m.	arr. p.m.	dep. p.m.	arr. p.m.	dep. p.m.	arr. a.m.	dep. a.m.
Torrington											Until 18th Sept. only		...	10 30						
Bideford (New)													10X39	10 44						
Instow													10 49	10 50						
Fremington													10 57	10 58						
Barnstaple Jct.													11 3	...						
Ilfracombe		10‖15									Terminate at Exeter Cent. on Tuesdays, Weds. and Thursd'ys 9th June to 23rd July also 1st to 17th Sept.		...	10 30						
Mortehoe & Woolacombe		10 27											10 42	10 44						
Braunton		10 37											10 54	10 57						
Wrafton													10 59	11 1						
Pottington Box		10 45												11 7						
Barnstaple Town		10 46											11 8	11 10						
Barnstaple Jct.	10‖50												11 13	11 18						
Chapelton	Will not run on Mondays 15th June to 14th Sept.																			
Umberleigh														11 28						
Portsmouth A.														11 33						
Kings Nympton							Commences 21st Sept.							11 38X						
Eggesford									Until 18th Sept. only				11 44	11 45						
Lapford														11 51						
Morchard Rd.														11 54						
Copplestone														11 57						
Plymouth (Friary)							...	9 45	...	9 50									...	11 0
Friary Jct.								9 47		9 52										11 2
Mount Gould Jct.								9 48		9 53										11 3
Lipson Jct.								9 49		9 54										11 4
Plymouth (N. Rd.)							9 53	9 57	9 58	10 2									11 8	11 10
Devonport Jct.								9 59		10 4										11 12
Devonport, Kings Rd.							10 0	10 4	10 5	10 9			Through coaches from Ilfracombe, and Torrington also Padstow Bude and Plymouth when 9.35 a.m. Padstow terminates at Exeter Cen.						11 13	11 14
Ford																				
St. Budeaux, Vic. Rd.							10 9	10 10	10 14	10 15										
Tamerton Foliot											Through coaches from Padstow Bude and Plymouth									
Bere Ferrers																				
Bere Alston							10 24	1025½	10 29	1030½										
Tavistock North							10 37	10 38	10 42	10 43									11 41	11 42
Brentor																				
Lydford							10 51	1051½	10 56	1056½										
Bridestowe							10 58	10 59	11 3½	11 4										
Meldon Jct.				10 53				11 7		11 12		11 26								12 5
Quarry Halt																				
Okehampton			10 57	11 2			11 11	11 15	11 16	11 34	11 30	11 34							12 9	12 12
Sampford C'nay			11 8	11 9			11 21	1121½												
North Tawton			11 14	11 15			1126½	11 27												
Bow			11 21	11 22			11 33	1133½												
Coleford Jct.				11 28	15th June to 14th Sept. only			11 39½				11 50		11 59						12 28
Yeoford			11 30	11 32			1141½	1142½					12 1	12 2						
Crediton			11 38	11 40			1148½	11 49												
Newton St. Cyres																				
Cowley Jct.				11 48				11 57				12 2		12 14						12 40
Exeter (St. David's)			11 51	11 55			12 0	12 4			12 5	12 9	12 17	12 21					12 44	12 49
Exeter Central			11 58	...			12 7	12 30			12 12	12 18	12 24	12 30	...	12 35			12 52	1 0
St. James' Park Halt																				
Exmouth Jct.			Terminate at Okehampton commencing 21st Sept.		...	*12‖5*										12 38				
Pinhoe															12 41	1241½				
Broad Clyst															1244½	...				
Whimple																				
Sidmouth Jct.					*12‖23*	*12‖27*							12 48	12 50	FO					
Honiton																				
Seaton Jct.															*Engine*					
Axminster																			1 34	1 36
Chard Jct.																				
Crewkerne																				
Sutton Bingham															arr. p.m.	dep. p.m.				
Yeovil Jct.												1 16		1 29					2 3	2 6
Sherborne																				
Milborne Port																				
Templecombe															*After working 12.0 noon Waterloo*					
Gillingham																		2‖50		
Semley																	3‖ 0			
Tisbury																				
Dinton																				
Wilton South																*2‖10*				
Salisbury											1 57	2 3	2 9	2 15	*2‖15*	...			2 49	2 55
Waterloo											3 32		3 40		Until 18th Sept. only					

TORRINGTON, ILFRACOMBE, PLYMOUTH, EXETER AND SALISBURY LINES 41

UP WEEKDAYS

Station	4.5 p.m. Yeovil Town	12.45 p.m. Padstow	Scholars (Not advertised) SX	To Waterloo	2·48 p.m. Empty Launceston SO	5.40 p.m. Milk Yeovil T. to Gravesend via Woking	To Portsm'th & Southsea
Torrington							
Bideford (New)							
Instow							
Fremington							
Barnstaple Jct.							
Ilfracombe							2 23
Morrehoe & Woolacombe							2 25
Braunton							2 26
Wrafton							
Pottington Box							
Barnstaple Town							2 31 2 33
Barnstaple Jct.				2 15			2 36 2 39
Chapelton				2 27			2 43
Umberleigh				2 33			2 47 2 48
Portsmouth A.				2 41			
Kings Nympton							2 56 2 58
Eggesford							3 7 3 10
Lapford							3 34 3 35
Morchard Rd.							3 39 3 39
Copplestone							3 46 3 47
Plymouth (Friary)	2 15			2 20			
Friary Jct.	2 17			2 44			
Mount Gould Jct.	2 18			2 46			
Lipson Jct.	2 19			2 47			
Plymouth (N. Rd.)	2 25 2 25		2 13	2 53			
Devonport, Kings Rd.	2 31		2 28	3 1			2 36 2 39
Ford				3 5			2 42 2 43
St. Budeaux, Vic. Rd.				3 12			2 47 2 48
Tamerton Foliot				3 16			
Bere Ferrers	2 58		2 58	3 17			
Bere Alston	3 0		3 0	3 18			2 56 2 58
Tavistock North				3 29			3 7 3 10
Brentor				3 34			3 21 3 23
Lydford				3 40			3 33 3 35
Bridestowe				3 47			3 39 3 39
Meldon Jct.	3 23		3 23	3 52			3 46 3 47
Quarry Halt							
Okehampton	3 27 3 32		3 27 3 32	3 55	3 49		3 59 4 4 5
Sampford C'nay							4 11 4 12
North Tawton							4 17 4 18
Bow							4 24 4 25
Coleford Jct.							4 31
Crediton	3 48		3 48	3 57			4 33 4 36
Newton St. Cyres	4 1		4 1	4 4			4 42 4 44
Cowley Jct.	4 8		4 8	4 6			
Exeter (St. David's)	4 11		4 11	4 14			4 53
Exeter Central	4 30		4 30	4 21	4 35		4 56 5 5 5 2
St. James' Park Halt				4 30			
Pinhoe							4 38
Broad Clyst							4 41 4 42
Whimple							4 54 4 56
Sidmouth Jct.							5 3 5 5
Honiton							5 13 5 15
Seaton Jct.							5 25 5 28
Axminster							5 35 5 38
Chard Jct.							5 45 5 46
Crewkerne							5 45 6 6 10
Yeovil Jct.							6 31
Sutton Bingham							5 52 6 39 6 43
Yeovil Jct.							6 32 6 47 6 52
Sherborne							6 57 7 6
Milborne Port							7 15 7 18
Templecombe							7 26 7 29
Gillingham							7 35 7 37
Semley							
Tisbury							
Dinton							
Salisbury				5 30 5 33	5 45 6 45 7 45		7 54 8 16
Wilton South				5 51	6 32		
Waterloo				8 25			

Through coaches (from Plym'th, Padstow Ilfracombe & Torr'ton

A—Change engines at Yeovil Jct.
B—Advertised departure Crewkerne 4.50 p.m.

---

40 TORRINGTON, ILFRACOMBE, PLYMOUTH, EXETER AND SALISBURY LINES

UP WEEKDAYS

Station	MO To Salisbury	MO To Waterloo	SO	MO	MO 1.6 p.m. Exeter Central	A To Waterloo	To Waterloo	SO	Engine to Plymouth Millbay W.R.
Torrington									
Bideford (New)	11 55								
Instow	12 4 12 11								
Fremington	12 19 12 20								
Barnstaple Jct.	12 25								
Ilfracombe									
Morrehoe & Woolacombe									
Braunton									
Wrafton									
Pottington Box									
Barnstaple Town	12 32 12 33								
Barnstaple Jct.	12 36 12 38								
Chapelton									
Umberleigh	12 48								
Portsmouth A.	12 58								
Kings Nympton	1 3								
Eggesford	1 8								
Lapford	1 14								
Morchard Rd.									
Copplestone					2 15				
Plymouth (Friary)					2 18	11 35	12 8	12 8	11 27
Friary Jct.					2 21	11 37	12 10	12 10	11 29
Mount Gould Jct.					2 25	11 46	12 18	12 18	11 31
Lipson Jct.					2 27	11 48	12 20	12 20	11 36
Plymouth (N. Rd.)					2 28 2 31	11 52	12 16 12 21	12 16 12 21	10 8
Devonport, Kings Rd.						11 55	12 22	12 22	10 10
Ford						12 2	12 26	12 26	12 12
St. Budeaux, Vic. Rd.						12 6	12 31	12 31	12 16
Tamerton Foliot						12 11	12 36	12 36	12 18
Bere Ferrers						12 21	12 47	12 47	12 21
Bere Alston						12 23	12 51	12 51	12 24
Tavistock North					2 58	12 34	12 58	12 58	12 32
Brentor						12 47	1 0	1 0	12 39
Lydford						12 54	1 9		1 56
Bridestowe					3 2	1 0			2 12
Meldon Jct.					3 23				
Quarry Halt									
Okehampton					3 27 3 32				
Sampford C'nay									
North Tawton									
Bow									
Coleford Jct.		1 16			3 48	1 57		SX Engine	
Crediton		1 28	1 50	9		2 4			
Newton St. Cyres		1 35			4 1	2 11			
Cowley Jct.		1 45			4 8	2 13			
Exeter (St. David's)					4 11	2 16 2 23	2 48		
Exeter Central	1 6	3 3	2 2	9	4 30	2 30	3 6	3 11 5	
St. James' Park Halt							3 13		
Pinhoe									
Broad Clyst				1 12	3 57		3 44		
Whimple				2 17	4 1		3 55		
Sidmouth Jct.				2 37	4 18				
Honiton				3 52	4 28				
Seaton Jct.				4 13	4 35				
Axminster				4 18					
Chard Jct.									
Crewkerne									
Yeovil Jct.									
Sutton Bingham									
Sherborne									
Milborne Port									
Templecombe									
Gillingham									
Semley									
Tisbury									
Dinton									
Salisbury		5 20		4 32	4 35		6 33		
Wilton South									
Waterloo									

'DEVON BELLE' Pullman cars only

Through coaches from Plymouth Ilfracombe & Torr'ton

A—Change engines at Yeovil Jct.
C—Stop at Wilton South to change engines, and not advertised.

TORRINGTON, ILFRACOMBE, PLYMOUTH, EXETER AND SALISBURY LINES 43

UP WEEKDAYS	SO 3.15 p.m. Padstow	SO Milk	SX 2.55 p.m. Perishables and Pass. Padstow		MO Empty Exmouth	Milk Clapham Jct.	To Eastleigh A		To Gunnislake SX	
	arr. / dep.		arr. / dep.		arr.	dep.	arr. / dep.		arr. / dep.	
Torrington (New)				4 38			4♦40 4 42		4 53 4 55	
Bideford (New)			4X47	4 51			4 43		4 56	
Instow			4 56	4 57			4 44		4 57	
Fremington			5X 6	5 4			4 48 4 52		5 1 5 2	
Barnstaple Jct.			5 10	5 10			4 55 4 58		5 4	
Ilfracombe				4 48			5 6 5 7		5 15 5 16	
Mortehoe & Woolacombe			5 0	5 11					5 25 5 26	
Braunton			5 15	5 16			5 37 5 39½		5 33 5 34	
Wrafton			5 22	5 25			5 55 5 56		6 1	
Pottington Box				5 25			6 12			
Barnstaple Town			5 23	5 28						
Barnstaple Jct.			5 43	5 49						
Chapelton			5 48	5 58			6 16 6 19½			
Umberleigh			6 5	6 5			6 25 6 26			
Portsmouth A.			6 12	6 12			6 37 6 38			
Kings Nympton			6 20	6 21						
Eggesford			6 26	6 27						
Lapford			6 31	6 32						
Morchard Rd.										
Copplestone										
Plymouth (Friary)			5 50				6 44			
Friary Jct.							6 56 6 59			
Mount Gould Jct.							7 7 10			
Lipson Jct.			5 54 5 58				7 13 7 21			
Plymouth (N. Rd.)			6 14	6 35			7♦247X50			
Devonport Jct.			6 29	6 37	6 39		7 3			
Devonport, Kings Rd.			6 26	6 35						
Ford			6 38	6 48	6 51		7 56 7 57			
St. Budeaux, Vic. Rd.				7 0			8 7 8 8			
Tamerton Foliot				6 54	7 3	7 26	8 15 8 19			
Bere Ferrers							8 26 8 28			
Bere Alston							8 39 8 41			
Tavistock North							8 48 8 49			
Brentor							8 57 9 0			
Lydford							9 15 9 16			
Bridestowe										
Meldon Jct.		Until 14th Sept. only					9 30 9 39			
Quarry Halt							9 46 9 48			
Okehampton							9 55 9 56½			
Sampford C'nay							10 1 10 4½			
North Tawton				7♦ 8 7♦11			10 15 10 17			
Bow				7 22			10 25 10 27			
Coleford Jct.							10 34 10 35			
Yeoford										
Crediton										
Newton St. Cyres										
Cowley Jct.										
Exeter (St. David's)			7 53							
Exeter Central			8 12							
St. James' Park Halt										
Exmouth Jct.										
Pinhoe										
Broad Clyst										
Whimple										
Sidmouth Jct.										
Honiton										
Seaton Jct.										
Axminster										
Chard Jct.										
Crewkerne										
Sutton Bingham										
Yeovil Jct.										
Sherborne										
Milborne Port							9 5			
Templecombe										
Gillingham										
Semley										
Tisbury										
Dinton										
Wilton South										
Salisbury							9 50	10 5	10 52	11 10
Waterloo									3 53	

A—Must not convey empty stock for Salisbury and stations beyond.

42 TORRINGTON, ILFRACOMBE, PLYMOUTH, EXETER AND SALISBURY LINES

UP WEEKDAYS	Milk and Parcels Waterloo C		FO		3.18 p.m. Bude (3.13 p.m. com. 21st Sept.)		To Waterloo		5.40 p.m. Milk Yeovil Town to Gravesend, via Woking		Milk Q		Q	
	arr.	dep.	arr.	dep.	arr.	dep.	arr.	dep.	arr.	dep.	arr.	dep.	arr.	dep.
Torrington (New)			2 47	2 47										4 5
Bideford (New)	2 56	3 1	2 56	3 1									4 8	4 8
Instow	3 6	3 7	3 6	3 7										4 9
Fremington	3X14	3 17	3X14	3 17									4 13	4 15
Barnstaple Jct.	3 22		3 22											4 17
Ilfracombe	3 0	3 0	3 12	3 13			3 50						4 18	4 20
Mortehoe & Woolacombe	3 12	3 13	3 23	3 26			3 52						4 23	4 24
Braunton	3 23	3 28	3 28	3 29			3 54						4 28	4 29
Wrafton		3 35	3 35	3 37			4 4						4 33	4 34
Pottington Box	3 36	3 37	3 40	3 47									4 44	4 54½
Barnstaple Town	3 40	3 47	3 53	3 54		Will not run on Fridays, 12th June to 18th Sept.	3 58	4 5					4 49	5 10
Barnstaple Jct.	3 53	3 54	3 7	4 8			4 5	4 7					5 21	
Chapelton	3 7	3 9	4 14	4 15										
Umberleigh	4 14	4 15	4 24	4 26			4 34	4 35						
Portsmouth A.	4 24	4 26	4 30	4 31										
Kings Nympton	4 30	4 31	4 40	4 41		4 33								
Eggesford	4 40	4 41	4 46	4 47		4 37	4 58							
Lapford	4 46	4 47	4 51	4 55										
Morchard Rd.														
Copplestone														
Plymouth (Friary)				4 58				5 2						
Friary Jct.			4 50	5 1			5 24 5 25	5 5						
Mount Gould Jct.			4 58	5 5			5 40 5 48	5 6						
Lipson Jct.	Conveys passengers between Yeovil Jct. and Semley		5 15	5 21			5 55							
Plymouth (N. Rd.)			5 24	5 31			5 22		5 48	5 36				
Devonport Jct.							5 24 5 25		5 52	5 48				
Devonport, Kings Rd.							5 40 5 48		6 3					
Ford							5 55							
St. Budeaux, Vic. Rd.				5 38			6 13 6 15						6 18	
Tamerton Foliot				5 41 5 46			6 31 6 32						6 21 6 22	
Bere Ferrers				5 42			6 37 6 39						6 25 6 26	
Bere Alston				5 52 5 53									6 33 6 34	
Tavistock North				5 59 6 1									6 41 6 42	
Brentor													6 49 6 50	
Lydford							7 7 7 11						7 7 2	
Bridestowe							7 27 7 30		6 45	7 45			7 7	
Meldon Jct.														6 15
Quarry Halt														
Okehampton														
Sampford C'nay														
North Tawton														
Bow														
Coleford Jct.			4 48	4 52			7 27 7 30		6 45	7 45				
Yeoford			4 58	5 1										
Crediton			5 8	5 12										
Newton St. Cyres			5 15	5 21										
Cowley Jct.			5 24	5 31			Through coaches from Ilfracombe & Plymouth							
Exeter (St. David's)	5 25	5 18												
Exeter Central	5C45	5C29												
St. James' Park Halt	5 45	5 55												
Exmouth Jct.	6 7	6 26												
Pinhoe	6 17	6 40												
Broad Clyst	6 40	6 45												
Whimple														
Sidmouth Jct.														
Honiton														
Seaton Jct.														
Axminster														
Chard Jct.														
Crewkerne														
Sutton Bingham														
Yeovil Jct.	6 59	8 23												
Sherborne	8 31	8 33												
Milborne Port	8 41	8 42												
Templecombe	8 47	9 20												
Gillingham	9 31	9 41												
Semley	9 50	10 0												
Tisbury														
Dinton														
Wilton South	10 25	10 40												
Salisbury	a.m. 2 32	10 40							6 45	8 27	8 37			
Waterloo											10 8			

C—Time allowed, when required, for unloading stores at Honiton Incline signal box, between Honiton and Seaton Jct.

The timings shown on this page WILL NOT APPLY ON SATURDAYS, 13th June to 19th September, 1953.

44 TORRINGTON, ILFRACOMBE, PLYMOUTH, EXETER AND SALISBURY LINES

UP WEEKDAYS	FSO 9 3 p.m. Seaton		Mixed				FO Engine		Engine		6.0 p.m. Padstow			▲		8 30 p.m. Engine Halwill	
	arr. p.m.	dep. p.m.	arr. p.m.	dep. p.m.	arr. p.m.	dep. p.m.	arr. p.m.	dep. p.m.	arr. p.m.	dep. p.m.	arr. p.m.	dep. p.m.	arr. p.m.	dep. p.m.	arr. p.m.	dep. p.m.
Torrington																
Bideford (New)	5 55	5 46		5 45												
Instow	5X 3	5 58		5 58												
Fremington	6 13	6 6		6 12												
Barnstaple Jct.	6 19	6 14		6 15												
Ilfracombe			5 57		6 21											
Mortehoe & Woolacombe			6 14	6 12	6 25											
Braunton			6 22	6 21	6 28				7 12	7 10						
Wrafton			6 28						7 22	7 13						
Pottington Box										7 14						
Barnstaple Town										7 23						
Barnstaple Jct.								Until 18th Sept. only	7 30				7 18	7 12		
Chapelton								7 11 0	7 31	7 11				7 11		
Umberleigh								7 7 2		7 7			7 24	7 17		
Portsmouth A.								7 7 3		7 8			7 30	7 27		
Kings Nympton								7 7 8		7 11			7 34	7 30½		
Eggesford								7 11 6	7 11 34				7 37	7 35		
Lapford								Work 7 153 p.m. to Plymouth Friary					7 44	7 39		
Morchard Rd.								4½ to Plymouth					7 54	7 45		
Copplestone													7 56			
Plymouth (Friary)	5 11		6 11					Work 8.26 p.m. to Ilfracombe			On Mondays calls at Quarry Halt 8.26½ to take up workmen and arr. Oke-hampton 8.32 p.m.		8 20	8 2½		
Friary Jct.	5 13		6 14										8 26	8 26		
Mount Gould Jct.	5 14		6 15													
Lipson Jct.	5 15		6 21										8 34	8 32		
Plymouth (N. Rd.)	5 19	5 21	6 19	6 21									8 42	8 42		
Devonport, Kings Rd.	5 23		6 24	6 31												
Devonport Jct.			6 34	6 35							8 46	8 25	8 46			
Ford	5 24		6 39	6 40							8 58		8 58			
St. Budeaux, Vic. Rd.	5 34		6 44	6 45							9 5		9 5			
Tamerton Foliot	5 35		6 51	6 53							9 11		9 12			
Bere Ferrers	5 39		7 2	7												
Bere Alston	5 40		7 16													
Tavistock North	5 44	5 44½													Commences 21st Sept.	8 54
Brentor	5 49½												9 18	9 20	9 11 0	
Lydford	5 50½	5 50½											9 20	9 22		
Bridestowe	6 12															
Meldon Jct.													9 34	9 37		
Okehampton													9 45	9 48		
Quarry Halt																
Sampford C'nay																
North Tawton																
Bow																
Coleford Jct.																
Yeoford													9 19	9 18		
Crediton													9 28	9 23		
Newton St. Cyres																
Cowley Jct.																
Exeter (St. David's)																
St. James' Park Halt																
Exmouth Jct.																
Pinhoe													Guard to collect tickets and extinguish lights at Brentor, Mondays to Fridays			
Broad Clyst																
Whimple																
Sidmouth Jct.																
Honiton																
Seaton Jct.																
Axminster																
Chard Jct.																
Crewkerne																
Sutton Bingham																
Yeovil Jct.																
Sherborne																
Milborne Port																
Templecombe																
Gillingham																
Semley																
Tisbury																
Dinton																
Wilton South																
Salisbury																
Waterloo																

The timings shown on this page WILL NOT APPLY ON SATURDAYS, 13th June to 19th September, 1953.

TORRINGTON, ILFRACOMBE, PLYMOUTH, EXETER AND SALISBURY LINES 45

UP WEEKDAYS	SX		SO			SX		SO		SO		W.R. Engine to Laira W.R.		W.R. Engine to Laira W.R.		SXQ		SO	
	arr. p.m.	dep. p.m.	arr. p.m.	dep. p.m.	arr. p.m.	dep. p.m.	arr. p.m.	dep. p.m.	arr. p.m.	dep. p.m.	arr. p.m.	dep. p.m.	arr. p.m.	dep. p.m.	arr. p.m.	dep. p.m.	arr. p.m.	dep. p.m.
Torrington																		
Bideford (New)																		
Instow																		
Fremington																		
Barnstaple Jct.																		
Ilfracombe	7 49	7 40				8 35	8 26											
Mortehoe & Woolacombe	7 58	7 53	7 45			8X42	8 37	Until 18th Sept. only	8 30									
Braunton	8 6	7 59	8			8 53	8 46		8 43									
Wrafton	8 12	8 7	8 9			8 59	8 54		8 57									
Pottington Box			8 18															
Barnstaple Town	8 19	8 21					9		9 6									
Barnstaple Jct.	8 24	8 30					9		9									
Chapelton	8 36	8 37	Guard to collect tickets at Chapelton				9		9									
Umberleigh	8 41	8 43																
Portsmouth A.	8 49	8 56																
Kings Nympton	9 3	9 5																
Eggesford	9 12	9 14																
Lapford	9 19	9 20																
Morchard Rd.	9 23	9 25																
Copplestone																		
Plymouth (Friary)			9 15		9 15							9 20		9 30					
Friary Jct.			9 17		9 17							9 23		9 33					
Mount Gould Jct.			9 18		9 18							9 25		9 34					
Lipson Jct.			9 18		9 18														
Plymouth (N. Rd.)			9 23	9 26	9 23	9 26						After working 3.0 p.m. Waterloo		After working 8.25 p.m. Tavistock North					
Devonport, Kings Rd.				9 28		9 28													
Devonport Jct.			9 29	9 31	9 29	9 31													
Ford			9 34	9 35	9 34	9 35													
St. Budeaux, Vic. Rd.			9 39	9 40	9 39	9 40													
Tamerton Foliot			9 44	9 45	9 44	9 45													
Bere Ferrers			9 50	9 51	9 50	9 51													
Bere Alston			10 0	10 1	10 0	10 1													
Tavistock North			10 13		1013														
Brentor			1013		10 3	10 21													
Lydford					10 10	10 21													
Bridestowe					10 37	10 36		Guard to collect tickets and extinguish lights at Brentor and Bridestowe											
Meldon Jct.					10 45	10 47													
Okehampton					10 55														
Quarry Halt																		
Sampford C'nay					10 59														
North Tawton																		
Bow																		
Coleford Jct.																		
Yeoford																		
Crediton																		
Newton St. Cyres																		
Cowley Jct.								10 18							12 15				
Exeter (St. David's)																		
St. James' Park Halt								10 21	1026						12 30				
Exmouth Jct.								1029	1031						12 33/2 35				
Pinhoe								1037	1039						12 38/2 40				
Broad Clyst								1046	1048						12 41/3 45				
Whimple								1055		Guard to collect tickets and extinguish lights at Broad Clyst									
Sidmouth Jct.																		
Honiton																		
Seaton Jct.																		
Axminster																		
Chard Jct.																		
Crewkerne																		
Sutton Bingham																		
Yeovil Jct.																		
Sherborne																		
Milborne Port																		
Templecombe																		
Gillingham																		
Semley																		
Tisbury																		
Dinton																		
Wilton South																		
Salisbury																		
Waterloo																		

A—Work 11.55 p.m. SXQ Stone train from Okehampton, when running.

SATURDAYS ONLY

The timings on this page WILL APPLY ON SATURDAYS ONLY,
13th June to 19th September, 1953, INCLUSIVE.

The timings on this page WILL APPLY ON SATURDAYS ONLY,
13th June to 19th September, 1953, INCLUSIVE.

SATURDAYS ONLY

46 TORRINGTON, ILFRACOMBE, PLYMOUTH, EXETER AND SALISBURY LINES

UP	News C		6.28 a.m. Yeovil Town		Parcels and Fish		To Sidmouth		7.10 a.m. Yeovil Town to Waterloo ✠		Engine to Seaton A		To Waterloo		Engine				Empty	
	arr. a.m.	dep. a.m.	arr. a.m.	dep. a.m.	arr. a.m.	dep. a.m.	arr. a.m.	dep. a.m.	arr. a.m.	dep. a.m.	arr. a.m.	dep. a.m.	arr. a.m.	dep. a.m.	arr. a.m.	dep. a.m.	arr. a.m.	dep. a.m.	arr. a.m.	dep. a.m.
Torrington	...	...													...	...				
Bideford (New)	...	...			...	...									...	...				
Instow	...	...													...	...				
Fremington	...	...													...	...				
Barnstaple Jct.	...	...													...	...				
Ilfracombe	News for																			
Mortehoe & Woolacombe	Bow and																			
Heddon Mill Crossing	North																			
Braunton	Tawton to																			
Wrafton	be taken to																			
Pottington Box	Yeoford																			
Barnstaple Town	and																			
Barnstaple Jct.	returned																			
Chapelton	by																			
Umberleigh	1.38 a.m.																			
Portsmouth A.	Exmouth																			
Kings Nympton	Jct. Sdgs																			
Eggesford																				
Lapford																				
Morchard Rd.																				
Copplestone																				
Plymouth (Friary)		1 25																		
Friary Jct.		1 27																		
Mount Gould Jct.		1 28																		
Lipson Jct.		1 29																		
Plymouth (N. Rd.)	1 33	1 35																		
Devonport Jct.		1 37																		
Devonport, Kings Rd.	1 39	2C 5																		
Ford																				
St. Budeaux, Vic. Rd.																				
Tamerton Foliot																				
Bere Ferrers																		5 50		
Bere Alston																		6 5	6†20	
Tavistock North		2 32													7 0	7 2				
Brentor																				
Lydford															6†35					
Bridestowe															Form					
Meldon Jct.															7.5 a.m.					
Quarry Halt															to					
Okehampton		3 0													Plymouth					
Sampford C'nay																				
North Tawton																				
Bow																				
Coleford Jct.		3 16																		
Yeoford	3 18	3 20																		
Crediton	3 26	3 28																		
Newton St. Cyres																				
Cowley Jct.		3 38																		
Exeter (St. David's)	3 41	3 44				5 0														
Exeter Central	3C47				5 3				6 0				6 30			6 40				
St. James' Park Halt																6 42				
Exmouth Jct.							6 3				6 15				6 55	6 44				
Pinhoe							6 6	6 7								6 47	6 47½			
Broad Clyst							6 11	6 12								6 51½	6 52			
Whimple							6 19	6 20								6 59	7 0			
Sidmouth Jct.							6 27	6 32			6A38	6 39	6 48	6 49	7 22	7 7	7 8			
Honiton													6 56½	7 0		7 16	7 17			
Seaton Jct.											7 0	7 30	7 11	7 14		7 28	7 31			
Axminster													7 19	7 22	7 55	7 36				
Chard Jct.													7 30	7 33	Assist					
Crewkerne													7 46	7 49	8.32 a.m.					
Sutton Bingham													7 57½	7 58	to Lyme					
Yeovil Jct.			6 32	6 33					7 15	7 22			8 3	8 6	Regis					
Sherborne			6 41	6 41½					7 29	7 30			8 13	8 15					arr. a.m.	dep. a.m.
Milborne Port			6 49½	6 50					7 37½	7 38			8 22½	8 23						
Templecombe			6 55						7 43	7 44½			8 28	9 3						
Gillingham									7 53½	7 54½			8 28	9 3 →						
Semley									8 3	8 5										8 35
Tisbury									8 12	8 13									8 42	8 43
Dinton									8 19	8 19½									8 49	8 50
Wilton South									8 27½	8 28									8 58	8 59
Salisbury									8 33	8 42									9 4	
Waterloo									1116											

A—Detach engine for 7.45 a.m. Freight, Sidmouth Jct. to Sidmouth.
C—May convey up to 12 oil fed wagons between Devonport Kings Road and Exeter Central, vac. fitted wagons to be formed next to news van.

TORRINGTON, ILFRACOMBE, PLYMOUTH, EXETER AND SALISBURY LINES 47

UP	8.8 a.m. Yeovil Town to Waterloo ✠		To Waterloo ✠		6.30 a.m. Exeter Cent. to Waterloo ✠		To Sidmouth								9.0 a.m. Seaton to Waterloo ▲					
	arr. a.m.	dep. a.m.	arr. a.m.	dep. a.m.	arr. a.m.	dep. a.m.	arr. a.m.	dep. a.m.	arr. a.m.	dep. a.m.	arr. a.m.	dep. a.m.	arr. a.m.	dep. a.m.	arr. a.m.	dep. a.m.	arr. a.m.	dep. a.m.	arr. a.m.	dep. a.m.
Torrington	...																			
Bideford (New)																				
Instow																				
Fremington																				
Barnstaple Jct.																				
Ilfracombe																				
Mortehoe & Woolacombe																				
Heddon Mill Crossing																				
Braunton																				
Wrafton																				
Pottington Box																				
Barnstaple Town																				
Barnstaple Jct.																				
Chapelton																				
Umberleigh																				
Portsmouth A.																				
Kings Nympton																				
Eggesford																				
Lapford																				
Morchard Rd.																				
Copplestone																				
Plymouth (Friary)											5 58									6 10
Friary Jct.											6 0									6 12
Mount Gould Jct.											6 1									6 13
Lipson Jct.											6 2									6 14
Plymouth (N. Rd.)									6 6	6 8									6 18	6 20
Devonport Jct.										6 10										6 22
Devonport, Kings Rd.									6 11	6 12									6 23	6 24
Ford									6 15	6 15½									6 27	6 27½
St. Budeaux, Vic. Rd.									6 19½	6 20									6 31½	6 32
Tamerton Foliot																				
Bere Ferrers									6 39	6 39½										
Bere Alston									6 48½	6 49½									6 35	6 36½
Tavistock North									7 0½	7 2									6 48	
Brentor									7 13	7 13½										
Lydford									7 17½	7 18										
Bridestowe									7 25	7 25½										
Meldon Jct.					Load				7 33½											
Quarry Halt					8 bogies				7 34½	7 35½										
Okehampton					Exeter				7 39½	7 43										
Sampford C'nay					Cent. to				7 49	7 49½										
North Tawton					Salisbury				7 54½	7 55										
Bow									8 1	8 1½										
Coleford Jct.																			8 7½	
Yeoford																		8 9½	8 10½	
Crediton																		8 16½	8 17½	
Newton St. Cyres																Through		8 22½	8 23	
Cowley Jct.																coaches			8 28	
Exeter (St. David's)																from		8 31	8 36	
Exeter Central				7 30					7 34		8 0				8 30	Lyme		8 39	8 48	
St. James' Park Halt									7 36		8 2½					Regis				
Exmouth Jct.									7 38		8 5								8 51	
Pinhoe									7 41	7 42	8 8	8 8½						8 54	8 54½	
Broad Clyst									7 45	7 46	8 11½	8 12						8 57½	8 58	
Whimple									7 53	7 54	8 18½	8 19½						9 5	9 5½	
Sidmouth Jct.									8 1	8 7	8 26	8 30						9 12½	9 14	
Honiton				7 46	7 47						8 38							9 22	9 23	
Seaton Jct.	4th July										8 38		8 47	8 49				9 34	9 36	
Axminster	to												8W57	9 0				9 41	9 43	
Chard Jct.	29th Aug.		8 5	8 6									9 11					9 51	9 53	
Crewkerne	only															Attach		10 6	10 8	
Sutton Bingham																to		10 17	10 18	
Yeovil Jct.	8 13	8 20	8 31	8 32									9 59			9.0 a.m.		10 23	10 27	
Sherborne			8 39	8 40												Seaton		10 34	10 37	
Milborne Port																		10 45	10 46	
Templecombe	8 36	8 38	8 50	8 52	8 28	9												10 50	10 51	
Gillingham	8 47	8 49	9 1	9 2	9 12	9 14							10 12					10 40	10 43	
Semley					9 22½	9 23½												10 52	10 55	
Tisbury					9 30½	9 31½												11 2	11 3	
Dinton					9 37½	9 39												11 10	11 11	
Wilton South					9 47	9 48												11 20	11 21	
Salisbury	9 14	9 21	9 27	9 33	9 53	10 1										10 45	10 51	11 26	
Waterloo	11 0		11 8		p.m. 12 19											p.m. 1235				

A—Detach engine for 7.45 a.m. Freight, Sidmouth Jct. to Sidmouth.
C—May convey up to 12 oil fed wagons between Devonport Kings Road and Exeter Central, vac. fitted wagons to be formed next to news van.

49 TORRINGTON, ILFRACOMBE, PLYMOUTH, EXETER AND SALISBURY LINES

The timings on this page WILL APPLY ON SATURDAYS ONLY, 13th June to 19th September, 1953, INCLUSIVE.

UP

Station	To Waterloo	To Waterloo	To Waterloo	To Bristol (Temple Meads) W.R. A	To Waterloo	To Waterloo	To Cardiff B	7.0 a.m. Torrington	8.5 a.m. Wadebridge to Waterloo

Stations (UP):
Torrington, Bideford (New), Instow, Fremington, Barnstaple Jct., Ilfracombe, Mortehoe & Woolacombe, Braunton, Wrafton, Pottington Box, Barnstaple Town, Barnstaple Jct., Chapelton, Umberleigh, Portsmouth A., Kings Nympton, Eggesford, Lapford, Morchard Rd., Copplestone, Plymouth (Friary), Friary Jct., Mount Gould Jct., Lipson Jct., Plymouth (N. Rd.), Devonport Jct., Devonport, Kings Rd., Ford, St. Budeaux, Vic. Rd., Tamerton Foliot, Bere Ferrers, Bere Alston, Tavistock North, Brentor, Lydford, Bridestowe, Quarry Halt, Okehampton, Sampford C'nay, North Tawton, Bow, Coleford Jct., Crediton, Newton St. Cyres, Exeter (St. David's), Exeter Central, St. James' Park Halt, Exmouth Jct., Pinhoe, Broad Clyst, Whimple, Sidmouth Jct., Honiton, Seaton Jct., Axminster, Chard Jct., Crewkerne, Sutton Bingham, Yeovil Jct., Sherborne, Milborne Port, Templecombe, Gillingham, Semley, Tisbury, Dinton, Wilton South, Salisbury, Waterloo

A — Extended to Manchester (Exchange) commencing 4th July.
B — Advertised departure Braunton 9.50 a.m.

Notes within columns: "Worked by S.R. Engine", "To Western Region", "Commences 4th July", "Through coaches from Torr'gt'n & Ilfracombe", "Through coaches from Wadebridge"

---

48 TORRINGTON, ILFRACOMBE, PLYMOUTH, EXETER AND SALISBURY LINES

The timings on this page WILL APPLY ON SATURDAYS ONLY, 13th June to 19th September, 1953, INCLUSIVE.

UP

Station	Empty	To Salisbury AA	W.R. Engine	Two Engines	9.25 a.m. Sidmouth to Waterloo	7.0 a.m. Torrington to Salisbury	8.20 a.m. Launceston	9.8 a.m. Exmouth to Waterloo

Stations (UP):
Torrington, Bideford (New), Instow, Fremington, Barnstaple Jct., Ilfracombe, Mortehoe & Woolacombe, Braunton, Wrafton, Pottington Box, Barnstaple Town, Barnstaple Jct., Chapelton, Umberleigh, Portsmouth A., Kings Nympton, Eggesford, Lapford, Morchard Rd., Copplestone, Plymouth (Friary), Friary Jct., Mount Gould Jct., Lipson Jct., Plymouth (N. Rd.), Devonport Jct., Devonport, Kings Rd., Ford, St. Budeaux, Vic. Rd., Bere Ferrers, Bere Alston, Tavistock North, Brentor, Lydford, Bridestowe, Meldon Jct., Quarry Halt, Okehampton, Sampford C'nay, North Tawton, Bow, Coleford Jct., Crediton, Newton St. Cyres, Cowley Bridge Jct., Exeter (St. David's), Exeter Central, St. James' Park Halt, Exmouth Jct., Pinhoe, Broad Clyst, Whimple, Sidmouth Jct., Honiton, Seaton Jct., Axminster, Chard Jct., Crewkerne, Sutton Bingham, Yeovil Jct., Sherborne, Milborne Port, Templecombe, Gillingham, Semley, Tisbury, Dinton, Wilton South, Salisbury, Waterloo

A — Change engines at Barnstaple Jct.

Notes within columns: "Form 8.28 a.m. to Barnstaple Jct.", "Work 9.55 to Exeter St. Davids", "Work 9.25 a.m. to Sidmouth and 9.8 a.m. Exmouth", "Through coaches from Exmouth"

The timings on this page WILL APPLY ON SATURDAYS ONLY,
13th June to 19th September, 1953, INCLUSIVE.

51 TORRINGTON, ILFRACOMBE, PLYMOUTH, EXETER AND SALISBURY LINES

UP	2.15 p.m. Yeovil Jct.		Engine		10.45 a.m. Padstow to Waterloo	11.45 a.m. Bude to Waterloo	To Waterloo		To Waterloo		To Yeovil Town	To Salisbury		To Brighton	
	arr. p.m.	dep. p.m.	arr. p.m.	dep. p.m.	arr. p.m.	arr. p.m.	arr. p.m.	dep. noon	arr. p.m.	arr. a.m.	dep. p.m.	arr. p.m.	dep. p.m.	arr. a.m.	dep. a.m.
Torrington															
Bideford (New)															
Instow															
Fremington															
Barnstaple Jct.															
Ilfracombe							12 0	12 0		11 55					11 0
Mortehoe & Woolacombe							12 12	12 13		12 4					11 3
Braunton							12 23	12 24		12 11					11 12
Wrafton										12 25					12 20
Pottington Box															
Barnstaple Town							12 31	12 31						8 10	8 8
Barnstaple Jct.							12 32	12 33							8 14
							12 36	12 38							
Chapelton															
Umberleigh								12 48					11 0		
Portsmouth A.								12 58					11 3		
Kings Nympton													8 10		
Eggesford								1 8X					11 12		
Lapford								1 14					12 20		
Morchard Rd.															
Copplestone															
Plymouth (Friary)													11 0		
Friary Jct.													11 3		
Mount Gould Jct.															
Lipson Jct.													11 8 10		
Plymouth (N. Rd.)													11 12		
Devonport Jct.													11 13 14		
Devonport, Kings Rd.															
Ford															
St. Budeaux, Vic. Rd.															
Tamerton Foliot															
Bere Ferrers													11 41 11 42		
Bere Alston															
Tavistock North													12 5		
Brentor															
Lydford															
Bridestowe															
Meldon Jct.															
Okehampton				'DEVON BELLE' Pullman cars only	Commences 4th July								12 9 12 12		
Sampford C'nay															
North Tawton															
Bow															
Coleford Jct.						12 54 1 0	12 59						12 28		
Yeoford						1 3		1 16							
Crediton															
Newton St. Cyres															
Cowley Jct.			1 29	1 20			1 28			1 2			12 40		
Exeter (St. David's)			1 31	1 24			1 35		1 15	1 12			12 49		
Exeter Central			1 40	1 31			1 45		1 23	1 30			12 52 1 0		
St. James Park Halt				1 40											
Exmouth Jct.			1 53	1 48			1 38								
Pinhoe			1 56	1 58											
Broad Clyst			2 4	2 12											
Whimple									1 47						
Sidmouth Jct.															
Honiton					2 29			2 50							
Seaton Jct.												2 15			
Axminster												2 25			
Chard Jct.									2 3 2 5	2 34 2 36		2 30			2 4 2 7
Crewkerne															
Sutton Bingham															
Yeovil Jct.						2 15									
Sherborne															
Milborne Port					3 10	3 0									
Templecombe															
Gillingham					3 23	3 13			3 10 3 26			2 49 2 55			
Semley															
Tisbur															
Dinton			3 30	3 38											3 30
Wilton South			3 39	3 46	4 1 3	3 52 3 58	3A31 3 38		3A11 3						3 39 3 41
Salisbury			3 45	3 56	4 2										3 56
Waterloo			4 1 4 1	4 20	4 7 4 8	5 37	5 20		5 42						4 25

A—Stop at Wilton South to change engines, and not advertised.

53 TORRINGTON ILFRACOMBE PLYMOUTH EXETER AND SALISBURY LINES

The timings on this page WILL APPLY ON SATURDAYS ONLY,
13th June to 19th September, 1953, INCLUSIVE.

UP

		1.0 p.m. Paddow		3.25 p.m. Exeter C.		To Waterloo		To Waterloo		2.48 p.m. Engine Launceston		5.40 p.m. Milk, Yeovil Town to Gravesend via Woking		To Portsm'th & Southsea						
		arr. p.m.	dep. p.m.	arr. p.m.	dep. p.m.	arr. p.m.	dep. p.m.	arr. p.m.	dep. p.m.	arr. p.m.	dep. p.m.	arr. p.m.	dep. p.m.	arr. p.m.	dep. p.m.	arr. p.m.	dep. p.m.	arr. p.m.	dep. p.m.		
Torrington																2 56	2 47				
Bideford (New)																3	3 1				
Instow																3 6	3 8				
Fremington																3X14					
Barnstaple Jct.																3 20	3 15				
Ilfracombe						2 7		2 10									2 55				
Mortehoe & Woolacombe						2 21	2 21	2 23								3 7	3 8				
Braunton								2 36								3 18	3 20				
Wrafton						2 36		2 39								3 22	3 23				
Pottington Box								2 45									3 29				
Barnstaple Town						2 10	2 23	2 46								3 30	3 31				
Barnstaple Jct.						2 22	2 36	2 50	2 55							3 34	3 41				
Chapelton						2 33	2 45									3 37	3 48				
Umberleigh						2 46		3 7								3 53	3 54				
Portsmouth A.						2 50	2 55	3 8								4 4					
Kings Nympton								3 16								4X16					
Eggesford						3X22		3 24								4 8	4 22				
Lapford						3 3		3 32								4X28	4 34				
Morchard Rd.						3 38		3 39								4 39	4 40				
Copplestone						3 44		3 47								4 44	4 47				
Plymouth (Friary)						2 7		2 25													
Friary Jct.						2 21		2 28						Empty train will run in this timing on 4th and 11th July							
Mount Gould Jct.								2 38													
Lipson Jct.								2 39													
Plymouth (N. Rd.)						2X16		2 43	2 45												
Devonport Jct.						2 35		2 47													
Devonport, Kings Rd.						2 41		2 48	2 50												
Ford								2 58	2 59												
St. Budeaux, Vic. Rd.								3 7													
Tamerton Foliot								3 17													
Bere Ferrers								3 31													
Bere Alston								3 33½													
Tavistock North								3 45													
Brentor								3 56½													
Lydford								3 57													
Bridestowe																					
Meldon Jct.																					
Okehampton								4 9	4 14			3 49									
Sampford C'nay								4 20													
North Tawton								4 25½													
Bow								4 32½	4 33												
Coleford Jct.						4 4		4 41													
Crediton						4 11		4 44	4 44					4 39							
Newton St. Cyres																					
Cowley Jct.								4 56	5					4 54							
Exeter (St. David's)						4 17		5	5					5 9							
Exeter Central						4 30		5 33						5 14							
St. James' Park Halt										4 35				4B8							
Pinhoe														4 41	4 42						
Broad Clyst														4 46	4 47						
Whimple														4 54	4 55						
Sidmouth Jct.														5 5	5 15						
Honiton														5 13	5 30						
Seaton Jct.														5 36	5 38						
Axminster														5 46	6 10						
Chard Jct.														6 19	6 20						
Crewkerne														6 25	6 31						
Sutton Bingham														6 36	6 43						
Yeovil Jct.														6 39	6 52		5 45	5 52			
Sherborne														6 51	6 57		6 22	6 39			
Milborne Port														7 15	7 17		6 32	6 45			
Templecombe														7 26½	7 29		6 45	6 47			
Gillingham														7 36	7 37						
Semley																					
Tisbury																					
Dinton																					
Wilton South																					
Salisbury														7 54	8 16						

Through coaches from Ilfracombe, Torrington, Plymouth and Padstow.

---

52 TORRINGTON, ILFRACOMBE, PLYMOUTH, EXETER AND SALISBURY LINES

The timings on this page WILL APPLY ON SATURDAYS ONLY,
13th June to 19th September, 1953, INCLUSIVE.

UP

		1.8 p.m. Exeter Cent. to Yeovil Town		To Waterloo		To Waterloo		Engine		4.5 p.m. Yeovil Town		To Waterloo		Engine		To Waterloo	
		arr. p.m.	dep. p.m.	arr. a.m.	dep. a.m.	arr. p.m.	dep. p.m.	arr. p.m.	dep. p.m.	arr. p.m.	dep. p.m.	arr. p.m.	dep. p.m.	arr. p.m.	dep. p.m.	arr. p.m.	dep. p.m.
Torrington				11 35	11 37				12 8			12 35	12 48		1 38	1 51		
Bideford (New)				11 38				12 11			12 47	12 54		1 57			
Instow				11 39				12 14				2		2 2			
Fremington				11 43	11 46			12 16	12 18			1 45				
Barnstaple Jct.				11 48	11 52			12 20	12 22		12 35	1 59		2 14			
Ilfracombe				11 55	12 6			12 26			1 13	2 6		2 22			
Mortehoe & Woolacombe				12 2	12 12			12 35			1 18					
Braunton				12 6	12 22			12 42			1 27	2 30				
Wrafton				12 22	12 24			12 42			1 33					
Pottington Box					12 51			12 57½			1 39					
Barnstaple Town				12 2	12 6			12 49			1 47					
Barnstaple Jct.				12 49	12 50			2 1	2						
Chapelton				12 54											
Umberleigh															
Portsmouth A.															
Kings Nympton							Com- mences 11th July								
Eggesford															
Lapford															
Morchard Rd.															
Copplestone															
Plymouth (Friary)				12 8		12 8				12 47	1 45				
Friary Jct.				12 11		12 11				12 59	1 59				
Mount Gould Jct.				12 14		12 14				2 2					
Lipson Jct.				12 16	12 18	12 16	12 18								
Plymouth (N. Rd.)				12 20	12 22	1 16	1 18				1 13	2 13			
Devonport Jct.				12 26		1 21					1 18				
Devonport, Kings Rd.				12 35		1 27	1 28			2 43	2 43				
Ford				12 41		1 37				2 50	2 50				
St. Budeaux, Vic. Rd.				12 42		1 47									
Tamerton Foliot				12 49		1 56				2 54			2 50			
Bere Ferrers						2 12				2X12					
Bere Alston															
Brentor							To Temple- combe			3X12		3X18			
Lydford															
Bridestowe															
Quarry Halt								3 2							
Meldon Jct.															
Okehampton				12 15	12 22				3½ 2			3 17		3 2			
Sampford C'nay				12 28											
Samford Courtenay				12 31				Work 4.0 p.m. to Sid- mouth							
North Tawton				12 34											
Bow				12 41											
Coleford Jct.				12 15					B	3 25	3 28		3 27	3 31		
Crediton				12 19	12 20					3 28	3 32		3 37	3 39		
Newton St. Cyres				12 23						3 33	3 34					
Cowley Jct.				2 48	2 50					3 40	4 1		3 48			
Exeter (St. David's)				2 16	2 23					4 18	4 20		3 51	3 55		
Exeter Central				2 23	2 30			3½ 17		4B56	4 20	4B36		3 58	4 5		
St. James' Park Halt										4 24	5 12				
Pinhoe								Work 5.18 p.m. milk		4 31	4 32				
Broad Clyst										4 37	4 38				
Whimple										4 44	4 45				
Sidmouth Jct.							2 42	3½ 45		4 54	4 57		3½ 45			
Honiton										5 5	5 11				
Seaton Jct.										5 18	5 25				
Axminster				2 50	2 55					5 25	5 27				
Chard Jct.				2 58	3 0	3 52	3 58			5 35	5 37				
Crewkerne				3 14	3 7		4 8	4 10		4 2					
Sutton Bingham				3 16											
Yeovil Jct.				3 24½	3 14	4 1	3 46	3 48	4 22	4 18	4 20		4 29	4 55		5 19		
Sherborne				3 30	3 40	4 45	3 55	3 57		4 24	4 28	4 29		4 55			
Milborne Port										4 32	4 33				
Templecombe				3 52	3 58					4 45	4 55		5	5		
Gillingham										5	5 12				
Semley										5 1					
Tisbury										5 18	5 19				
Dinton				4 35	4 41		4 54	5 1				5 53		
Wilton South				4 45										
Salisbury				6 24	6 40					5 25	5 35		5	6 0		
Waterloo										5 37	5 42		7 38			

Through coaches from Seaton & Lyme Regis.

Through coaches from Ilfr'mbe or Torrington.

Through coaches from Ilfr'mbe or Torrington and Padstow.

A—Advertised departure Axminster 2.45 p.m.
B—Advertised departure Crewkerne 4.43 p.m.

55 TORRINGTON, ILFRACOMBE, PLYMOUTH, EXETER AND SALISBURY LINES

The timings on this page WILL APPLY ON SATURDAYS ONLY,
13th June to 19th September, 1953, INCLUSIVE.

UP		3.15 p.m. Padstow		To Eastleigh	To Taunton	9.3 p.m. Seaton		Mixed		6.0 p.m. Padstow
	arr. p.m.	dep. p.m.	arr. p.m.	dep. p.m.	arr. p.m.	dep. p.m.	arr. p.m.	dep. p.m.	arr. p.m.	dep. p.m.
Torrington (New)								5 45			
Bideford (New)	4 38							5 46	5 57		
Instow	4 47	4 51						6 6	5 58		
Fremington	4 56	4 57						6 6	6 14		
Barnstaple Jct.	5X4	5 5						6 14	6 15		
	5 10							6 19	6 25		
Ilfracombe		4 48						6 22		
Mortehoe & Woolacombe	5 0							6 28		
Braunton	5 11	5 13						6 11		
Wrafton	5 15	5 15					5 11	6 13		
Pottington Box		5 22					5 13	6 14		
Barnstaple Town	5 23	5 25					5 14	6 15		
Barnstaple Jct.	5 28	5 35			5 15	5 11	5 21		
Chapelton	5 42	5 43			5 28	5 13	6 19	6 21		
Umberleigh	5 48	5 49			5 40	5 21	6 23		
Portsmouth A.	5 56	5 58			5 49	5 35	6 24	6 31		
Kings Nympton	6X4	6 1			5 51	5 40	6 34	6 35		
Eggesford	6 13	6 13			5 6 0	5 44	6 44	6 45		
Lapford	6 20	6 21				6 12	6 51	6 51		
Morchard Rd.	6 26	6 27					7 2	7 4½		
Copplestone	6 31	6 32					7 16		
Plymouth (Friary)				4 40				
Friary Jct.				4 42				
Mount Gould Jct.				4 43				
Lipson Jct.				4 46				
Plymouth (N. Rd.)				4 48 4 52				
Devonport Jct.				4 54				
Devonport, Kings Rd.				4 55 4 58				
Ford				5 5				
St. Budeaux, Vic. Rd.				5 6				
Tamerton Foliot								
Bere Ferrers				5 21 5 26				
Bere Alston				5 25 5 31				
Tavistock North				5 33				
Brentor				5 44				
Lydford				6 12				
Bridestowe								
Meldon Jct.				6 16 6 19½				
Okehampton				6 25 6 26				
Quarry Halt				6 30 6 31				
Sampford C'nay				6 37½ 6 38				
North Tawton								
Bow								
Coleford Jct.	6 35		6 44					
Yeoford	6 37 6 39		6 46 6 50					
Crediton			6 56 6 59					
Newton St. Cyres	6 51		7 4 7 5					
Cowley Jct.	6 54 7 0		7 10					
Exeter (St. David's)	7 3		7 13 7 21					
Exeter Central			7 24 7X50					
St. James' Park Halt								
Exmouth Jct.			7 56 7 57					
Pinhoe			8 0 8 1					
Broad Clyst			8 7 8 8½					
Whimple			8 15 8 19					
Sidmouth Jct.			8 26 8 28					
Honiton			8 39 8 41					
Seaton Jct.			8 57 9 0	9 19				
Axminster			8 59 9 16	9 23				
Chard Jct.			9 13	9 28				
Crewkerne								
Sutton Bingham			9 30 9 39					
Yeovil Jct.			9 46 9 48					
Sherborne			9 55½ 9 56½					
Milborne Port			10 1 10A 6					
Templecombe			10 25 10 27					
Gillingham			10 34 10 35					
Semley								
Tisbury								
Dinton								
Wilton South								
Salisbury			10 52 11 10					
Waterloo			a.m. 3 53					

A—Must not convey empty stock for Salisbury and stations beyond.

---

54 TORRINGTON, ILFRACOMBE, PLYMOUTH, EXETER AND SALISBURY LINES

The timings on this page WILL APPLY ON SATURDAYS ONLY,
13th June to 19th September, 1953, INCLUSIVE.

UP	Milk and Parcels, Waterloo	3.13 p.m. Bude	To Waterloo	Milk	Empty		5.40 p.m. Milk Yeovil Town to Gravesend via Woking	Engine	Milk Tanks Clapham Jct.	3.35 p.m. Engine Padstow
	arr. dep. p.m.	arr. dep. p.m.	arr. dep. p.m.	arr. dep. p.m.	arr. dep. p.m.		dep. p.m.	dep. p.m.	arr. dep. p.m.	arr. dep. p.m.
Torrington										
Bideford (New)					3 25 3 37 3 40					
Instow			3 50 3 52							
Fremington			3 53 3 54							
Barnstaple Jct.			3 58 4 4	4 0 4 1 4 5			Commences 4th July			
Ilfracombe			4 7			4 5				
Mortehoe & Woolacombe						4 7				
Braunton						4 9				
Wrafton						4 17				
Pottington Box										
Barnstaple Town						4 13 4 18				
Barnstaple Jct.			4 34 4 35			4 24 4 33			5 57	6 16 6 6
Chapelton						4 34				
Umberleigh						4 44 4 54½				
Portsmouth A.						5 6				
Kings Nympton						5 10				
Eggesford			4 58			5 21				
Lapford										
Morchard Rd.										
Copplestone			5 2 5 6						6 25	
Plymouth (Friary)		4 33								
Friary Jct.										
Mount Gould Jct.										
Lipson Jct.										
Plymouth (N. Rd.)		4 37								
Devonport Jct.										
Devonport, Kings Rd.				5 36		6 18				
Ford						6 21 6 22				
St. Budeaux, Vic. Rd.						6 33 6 34				
Tamerton Foliot						6 49 6 50				
Bere Ferrers				5 48		7 2				
Bere Alston				5 52 6 0		7 7				
Tavistock North				6 3					6 40 6 47	
Brentor									6 43 6 50	
Lydford									6 52	
Bridestowe								Until 27th June only		
Meldon Jct.										
Okehampton		5 35 5 37			6 15		6 45 7 45		6 48	6 55
North Tawton										
Bow										
Coleford Jct.										
Yeoford			5 22 5 24 5 25							
Crediton		5 38 5 40								
Newton St. Cyres	5 25	5 41 5 45	5 45 5 48							
Cowley Jct.	5 40	5 42 5 46	5 52 5 55							
Exeter (St. David's)	6 0	5 46 5 53	6 1 6 3							
Exeter Central	6 17	5 9	6 13 6 15			6 27	7 27 7 35			
St. James' Park Halt	6 40		6 31 6 32							
Exmouth Jct.			6 37 6 39							
Pinhoe										
Broad Clyst	6 59		7 7 7 11							
Whimple	8 23									
Sidmouth Jct.	8 33		7 27 7 30			8 27 8 37		8 8 8 11	7 27 7 35	
Honiton	8 42		7 27 7 30 Through coaches from Ilfracombe & Plymouth					8 8 8 28	8 8	
Seaton Jct.	8 47							8X20 8 28		
Axminster	9 20									
Chard Jct.	9 31		8 3 8 9						9 5	
Crewkerne	9 41									
Sutton Bingham	9 50									
Yeovil Jct.	10 0							9 15	9 50	10 5
Sherborne										
Milborne Port										
Templecombe	10 25 10 40		10 8			9 37			10 5	
Gillingham										
Semley										
Tisbury										
Dinton										
Wilton South										
Salisbury										
Waterloo	2 32									

TORRINGTON, ILFRACOMBE, PLYMOUTH, EXETER AND SALISBURY LINES

UP — SUNDAYS

	7.0 a.m. Yeovil Town	To Sidmouth	To Sidmouth	Parcels and Fish	To Sidmouth		11.40 a.m. Yeovil Town	To Yeovil Town	To Waterloo		

(Detailed Sunday timings for:)

Torrington, Bideford (New), Instow, Fremington, Barnstaple Jct., Ilfracombe, Mortehoe & Woolacombe, Braunton, Wrafton, Pottington Box, Barnstaple Town, Barnstaple Jct., Chapelton, Umberleigh, Portsmouth A., Kings Nympton, Eggesford, Lapford, Morchard Rd., Copplestone, Plymouth (Friary), Friary Jct., Mount Gould Jct., Plymouth (N. Rd.), Devonport Jct., Devonport, Kings Rd., Ford, St. Budeaux, Vic. Rd., Tamerton Foliot, Bere Ferrers, Bere Alston, Tavistock North, Brentor, Bridestowe, Lydford, Meldon Jct., Okehampton, Sampford C'nay, North Tawton, Bow, Coleford Jct., Yeoford, Crediton, Newton St. Cyres, Cowley Jct., Exeter (St. David's), Exeter Central, St. James' Park Halt, Exmouth Jct., Pinhoe, Broad Clyst, Whimple, Sidmouth Jct., Honiton, Seaton Jct., Axminster, Chard Jct., Crewkerne, Sutton Bingham, Yeovil Jct., Sherborne, Milborne Port, Templecombe, Gillingham, Semley, Dinton, Tisbury, Wilton South, Salisbury, Waterloo.

Notes: "Guard issues and collects tickets at Tamerton Foliot", "Commences 18th April 1954", "Until 20th Sept. only", "Formed of 8.20 a.m. Plymouth Friary", "Until 20th Sept. only and 'Q'".

The timings on this page WILL APPLY ON SATURDAYS ONLY, 13th June to 19th September, 1953, INCLUSIVE.

UP

	To Taunton	To Taunton	Empties of 4.35 p.m. Taunton W.R.		W.R. Engine to Laira W.R.	W.R. Engine to Laira, W.R.	

(Detailed Saturday timings for the same station list:)

Torrington, Bideford (New), Instow, Fremington, Barnstaple Jct., Ilfracombe, Mortehoe & Woolacombe, Braunton, Wrafton, Pottington Box, Barnstaple Town, Barnstaple Jct., Chapelton, Umberleigh, Portsmouth A., Eggesford, Lapford, Morchard Rd., Copplestone, Plymouth (Friary), Friary Jct., Mount Gould Jct., Plymouth (N. Rd.), Devonport Jct., Devonport, Kings Rd., Ford, St. Budeaux, Vic. Rd., Tamerton Foliot, Bere Ferrers, Bere Alston, Tavistock North, Brentor, Bridestowe, Lydford, Meldon Jct., Okehampton, Sampford C'nay, North Tawton, Bow, Coleford Jct., Yeoford, Crediton, Newton St. Cyres, Cowley Jct., Exeter (St. David's), Exeter Central, St. James' Park Halt, Exmouth Jct., Pinhoe, Broad Clyst, Whimple, Sidmouth Jct., Honiton, Seaton Jct., Axminster, Chard Jct., Crewkerne, Sutton Bingham, Yeovil Jct., Sherborne, Milborne Port, Templecombe, Gillingham, Semley, Dinton, Tisbury, Wilton South, Salisbury, Waterloo.

Notes: "Until 12th Sept. only", "To Western Region", "Guard to collect tickets at Chapelton", "Worked by S.R. Engine", "Empty", "For berthing", "After working 3.0 p.m. Waterloo", "After working 8.25 p.m. Tavistock North", "Guard to collect and extinguish lights at Brentor and Bridestowe", "Guard to collect tickets and extinguish lights at Broad Clyst".

TORRINGTON, ILFRACOMBE, PLYMOUTH, EXETER AND SALISBURY LINES

UP SUNDAYS

UP SUNDAYS	Engine		To Waterloo		To Waterloo A		Engine		To Waterloo A		3.45 p.m. Yeovil Town to Waterloo	
	arr. p.m.	dep. p.m.	arr. p.m.	dep. p.m.	arr. p.m.	dep. noon	arr. p.m.	dep. p.m.	arr. a.m.	dep. a.m.	arr. p.m.	dep. p.m.
Torrington (New)			11 55					11 40				
Bideford (New)			12 4	12 2			11 42	11 42				
Instow			12 11	12 9			11 43	11 43				
Fremington			12 19	12 20			11 44	11 44				
Barnstaple Jct.			12 25				11 48	11 50				
Ilfracombe					12 12 0	12 0	11 52					
Mortehoe & Woolacombe					12 12 13	12 13	11 53	11 55				
Braunton					12 23 12 24		11 58	11 59				
Wrafton							12 3	12 3				
Potington Box					12 12 33	12 33						
Barnstaple Town					12 36 12 38	12 38						
Barnstaple Jct						12 48						
Chapelton						12 53						
Umberleigh						12 58						
Portsmouth A						1 8						
Kings Nympton						1 14						
Eggesford												
Lapford												
Morchard Rd												
Copplestone												
Plymouth (Friary)					"DEVON BELLE" Pullman Cars only							
Friary Jct												
Mount Gould Jct												
Lipson Jct												
Plymouth (N Rd)												
Devonport Jct												
Devonport. Kings Rd.												
Ford												
St Budeaux Vic Rd												
Tamerton Foliot												
Bere Ferrers												
Bere Alston												
Tavistock North				Engine								
Brentor												
Lydford												
Bridestowe												
Meldon Jct												
Okehampton												
Sampford C'nay												
North Tawton												
Bow												
Coleford Jct	Until 13th Sept. only						Until 20th Sept. only					
Yeoford								1 38		1 40 42		
Crediton					1 16					1 48 51		
Newton St Cyres												
Cowley Jct			12 37				1 59			2 2		
Exeter (St David's)				12 42 12 43		1 28 35				2 2 7		
Exeter Central			12 40	12 45	12 48	1 31 38				2 10		
St James' Park Halt			12 46 12 43	12 51	12 51 12 52	1 38 45						
Exmouth Jct			12 47	12 58	12 59							
Pinhoe			12 53	12 51								
Broad Clyst				12 57	1 6							
Whimple			1 8	1 13	Commences 27th Sept.							
Sidmouth Jct	Until 20th Sept. only						After working 12.0 noon Waterloo		After working 12.0 noon Ilfracombe			
Honiton												
Seaton Jct					2 3					3 50	3 57	
Axminster											4 6	
Chard Jct										4 20	4 15	
Crewkerne							2 50			4 32	4 22	
Sutton Bingham											4 34	
Yeovil Jct					3 3		3 3			4 55	4 48	
Sherborne										5 1	4 56	
Milborne Port										5 5 14		
Templecombe			2 10 5							5 19 30		
Gillingham												
Semley												
Tisbury												
Dinton						3A31 3 38	3 46					
Wilton South					3 46	3 51						
Salisbury					5 20						7 24	
Waterloo												

A—Stop at Wilton South to change engines, and not advertised.

TORRINGTON, ILFRACOMBE, PLYMOUTH, EXETER AND SALISBURY LINES

Train No. UP SUNDAYS	Engine		9.45 a.m. Bude		To Waterloo A		To Waterloo A		To Waterloo Q		To Portsmouth and Waterloo		To Waterloo		To Waterloo and Portsmouth		To Portsmo'th Q		To Waterloo Q	
	arr. a.m.	dep. a.m.	arr. a.m.	dep. a.m.	arr. a.m.	dep. a.m.	arr. a.m.	dep. a.m.	arr. p.m.	dep. p.m.	arr. p.m.	dep. p.m.	arr. p.m.	dep. p.m.	arr. p.m.	dep. p.m.	arr. p.m.	dep. p.m.	arr. p.m.	dep. p.m.
Torrington (New)					10 2	10 2														
Bideford (New)					10 7	10 8														
Instow					10 15	10 16														
Fremington					10 21															
Barnstaple Jct.																				
Ilfracombe					9 50	9 50														
Mortehoe & Woolacombe					10 4	10 4														
Braunton					10 14	10 16														
Wrafton					10 18	10 19														
Potington Box					10 25				Through coaches from Bude to Waterloo		10 0	10 0								
Barnstaple Town					10 26	10 27					10 3	10 3								
Barnstaple Jct					10 30	10 35					10 4	10 4								
Chapelton											10 8	10 8								
Umberleigh					10 45	10 45					10 10	10 10								
Portsmouth A					10 57	10 57					10 13	10 13								
Kings Nympton					1X12	1X12					10 15	10 15								
Eggesford					11A 9															
Lapford					16½	16½														
Morchard Rd					11 3															
Copplestone					19½	19½														
Plymouth (Friary)							Until 20th Sept. only				Until 20th Sept. only									
Friary Jct																				
Mount Gould Jct																				
Lipson Jct																				
Plymouth (N Rd)																				
Devonport Jct																				
Devonport. Kings Rd.									Formed of 9.50 a.m. Ilfracombe											
Ford																				
St Budeaux Vic Rd																				
Tamerton Foliot																				
Bere Ferrers																				
Bere Alston																				
Tavistock North				10 53					Formed of rear portion of 10.0 a.m. Plymouth											
Brentor																				
Lydford																				
Bridestowe				10 57																
Meldon Jct																				
Okehampton																				
Sampford C'nay																				
North Tawton																				
Bow																				
Coleford Jct							Commences 27th Sept.				10 42 10 43		10 42 10 43		Commences 27 Sept.					
Yeoford		11	11																		
Crediton		11 20																		
Newton St Cyres		11 23 24																		
Cowley Jct		11 27							11 50		11 10 11 15		11 10 11 15		11 10 11 15					
Exeter (St David's)					11 34				11 44		11 31		11 31		11 31				12 12	
Exeter Central				11 22	11 37 11 41		11 22		1 44		11 43 11 51		11 43 11 51		11 43 11 51					
St James' Park Halt					11 44 11 50				1 23		11 54 12 2		11 54 12 2		11 54 12 2					
Exmouth Jct					44 12 2															
Pinhoe											Will not apply when 12.12 p.m. Exeter Cent. to Waterloo runs									
Broad Clyst																				
Whimple																				
Sidmouth Jct																				
Honiton																				
Seaton Jct									12 55 12 57		12 36 12 39		12 36 12 39		12 36 12 39				12 46 12 49	
Axminster																				
Chard Jct						Through coaches from Ilfracombe and Bideford														
Crewkerne									1 50		1 7 1 10		1 7 1 10		1 7 1 10				1 17 1 20	
Sutton Bingham																				
Yeovil Jct																				
Sherborne																				
Milborne Port											{ 1 54 2 1		1 54 2 1		1 54		1 54		2 2	
Templecombe									1 44 1 50		2 3		2 3		2 9		3 49		2 7 3 54	
Gillingham									3 23		3 54		3 54							
Semley																				
Tisbury																				
Dinton																				
Wilton South																				
Salisbury																				
Waterloo																				

A—Stop at Lapford not advertised.

UP SUNDAYS

Train Nos.	To Waterloo	To Waterloo Q	To Waterloo Q	Milk Q (arr.)	Milk Q (dep.)	6.15 p.m. Milk Yeovil Town to Clapham Jct. (arr.)	6.15 p.m. Milk Yeovil Town to Clapham Jct. (dep.)	Milk Waterloo (arr.)	Milk Waterloo (dep.)	209 Return Excn. to Waterloo D (arr.)	209 Return Excn. to Waterloo D (dep.)	To Yeovil Town A (arr.)	To Yeovil Town A (dep.)
	p.m.	p.m.	p.m.	p.m.	p.m.	p.m.	p.m.	p.m.	p.m.	p.m.	p.m.	p.m.	p.m.
Torrington													
Bideford (New)													
Instow													
Fremington													
Barnstaple Jct.													
Ilfracombe	2 45												
Morthoe & Woolacombe	2 57	2 59											
Braunton	3 11	3 14											
Wrafton													
Pottington Box	3 20												
Barnstaple Town	3 21	3 23											
Barnstaple Jct.	3 26	3 31											
Chapelton	3 41												
Umberleigh	3 46												
Portsmouth A													
Kings Nympton	3X5 3 58												
Eggesford													
Lapford	4X7 4 11				4 25								
Morchard Rd	4 14				4 30								
Copplestone													
Plymouth (Friary)		2 50											
Friary Jct		2 52											
Mount Gould Jct		2 53											
Lipson Jct		2 54											
Plymouth (N Rd)		2 58 3 1											
Devonport Jct		3 4 3 7											
Devonport, Kings Rd		3 4 3 7											
Ford													
St Budeaux, Vic Rd													
Tamerton Foliot													
Bere Ferrers		3 24 3 26	Commences 27th Sept.										
Bere Alston		3 37 3 40											
Tavistock North		4 7 4 11											
Brentor													
Lydford													
Bridestowe													
Meldon Jct													
Okehampton													
Sampford C'nay													
North Tawton													
Bow		4 27	4 34										
Coleford Jct	4 16		4 42										
Yeoford													
Crediton													
Newton St Cyres	4 28	4 39	4 50										
Cowley Jct	4 31 4 35	4 42 4 46	5 1										
Exeter (St David's)	4 38 4 44	4 49 4 56	5 8										
Exeter Central								5 20	5 29				
St James' Park Halt											7 26 7 30		7 20
Exmouth Jct										7 7	7 31		7 23
Pinhoe	5 21	5 14	5 17					5 45	5 50	7 37	7 38		7 26
Broad Clyst							7 13	5 55	5 58				7 31
Whimple								6 6	6 12	7 9	7 10		7 38
Sidmouth Jct	5 25	5 24 5 26	5 39				7 29	6 8	6 23	7 36	7 45		8 8
Honiton							7 32	6 20	6 40	7 37	7 50		8 12
Seaton Jct								7 12	7 16				8 17
Axminster								7 30					8 28
Chard Jct		5W53 5 59	6 12			6 20	6 30	7 52	8C53 9C11				8 43
Crewkerne	5 54 5 58	6 38	6 22			6 38	6 50		9C35				8 53
Sutton Bingham		6 29	6 31										8 59
Yeovil Jct	6 28	6 31	6 44			7	7 30	8C35		8 33			9A10
Sherborne								9 4					
Milborne Port								9C13					
Templecombe	7 1	7 10	7 16			8 12	8 21	9 55	9 35	9 10 9 16			
Gillingham	7 7	7 15							a.m.				
Semley								2 22		11 12			
Tisbury													
Dinton													
Wilton South													
Salisbury	8 43	8 43	9 15										
Waterloo													

Runs as passenger train, Exeter Central to Chard Jct. (Not advertised). Guard to light platform lamps at Broad Clyst.

21st June, 19th July, 9th and 23rd Aug. and 6th Sept. only

Commences 27th Sept.

Until 20th Sept. only

UP SUNDAYS

Station	12.15 p.m. Empty Milk Tanks Millbay W.R. to Lifton, W.R. (arr.)	12.15 p.m. Empty Milk Tanks Millbay W.R. to Lifton, W.R. (dep.)	To Salisbury (arr.)	To Salisbury (dep.)	To Waterloo (arr.)	To Waterloo (dep.)	3.20 p.m. Exeter Ctl. (arr.)	3.20 p.m. Exeter Ctl. (dep.)	2.37 p.m. Launceston (arr.)	2.37 p.m. Launceston (dep.)	2.32 p.m. Bude (arr.)	2.32 p.m. Bude (dep.)
	p.m.	p.m.	p.m.	p.m.	p.m.	p.m.	p.m.	p.m.	p.m.	p.m.	p.m.	p.m.
Torrington												
Bideford (New)												
Instow												
Fremington												
Barnstaple Jct.					1 55	2 7						
Ilfracombe					2 13							
Morthoe & Woolacombe					2 20							
Braunton					2 25							
Wrafton												
Pottington Box	12 19				2 10							
Barnstaple Town	12 20				2 12							
Barnstaple Jct.					2 27 2 34							
Chapelton					2 35							
Umberleigh			3 1 5		2 52							
Portsmouth A					2 57							
Kings Nympton					3 4							
Eggesford					3 17							
Lapford					3 24							
Morchard Rd					3 30							
Copplestone					3 35							
Plymouth (Friary)												
Friary Jct	12 52											
Mount Gould Jct												
Lipson Jct												
Plymouth (N Rd)												
Devonport Jct												
Devonport, Kings Rd												
Ford												
St Budeaux, Vic Rd												
Tamerton Foliot												
Bere Ferrers												
Bere Alston												
Tavistock North	7 15											
Brentor		7 To W.R.										
Lydford												
Bridestowe												
Meldon Jct												
Okehampton												
Sampford C'nay												
North Tawton												
Bow										3 23	3 27	3 40 3 44
Coleford Jct												
Yeoford												
Crediton			3 20									
Newton St Cyres			3 26 3 23									
Cowley Jct			3 31 3 32									
Exeter (St David's)			3 40		3 40 3 43							
Exeter Central	3 1/5		3 49		3 49 3 50							
St James' Park Halt					3 58							
Exmouth Jct			4 1		4 5							
Pinhoe		3 23	4 8		4 8 4 14							
Broad Clyst			4 13									
Whimple			4 18									
Sidmouth Jct	3 43 4 25		4 32		4 31 4 33							
Honiton	4 37		4 45									
Seaton Jct		5 10	4 57									
Axminster			4 58									
Chard Jct			5 3 5 29		5 17 5 19		5 29					
Crewkerne	5 37 5 55				5 26 5 28		5 37 5 39					
Sutton Bingham							5 47 5 48					
Yeovil Jct					5 40 5 41		6 6 6 11					
Sherborne							6 20 6 21					
Milborne Port							6 28					
Templecombe		Until 1st April 1954			Through coaches from Ilfracombe and Torrington		6 36 6 37					
Gillingham					6 14 6 20		6 46 6 47					
Semley					7 49		6 52					
Tisbury												
Dinton												
Wilton South												
Salisbury												
Waterloo												

Perform shunting (milk tanks) at Seaton Jc. and Chard Jc.

Engine Yeovil Town

27th Sept. 1953 to 21st Mar. 1954

Until 20th Sept. only

A—Depart Yeovil Jct. 9.3 p.m., commencing 27th September.

C—When 6.52 p.m. Return Excursion Exeter Ctl. to Waterloo runs, dep. Templecombe 8.45 p.m., and run 10 minutes later to Salisbury.

D—Connect with 6.15 p.m. Exmouth due 6.45 p.m.

Page 63 — UP SUNDAYS

Station	263 Return Excn. to Salisbury (A)	263 Return Excursion (A)	(Commences 27th Sept.)	(Until 20th Sept. only)	(Until 20th Sept. only)
Torrington					
Bideford (New)				9 10	9 14
Instow				9 23	9 22
Fremington					9 21
Barnstaple Jct.				9 37	9 29
Ilfracombe					
Mortehoe & Woolacombe					
Braunton					
Wrafton					
Pottington Box					
Barnstaple Town					
Barnstaple Jct.				9 43	9 44
Chapelton					
Umberleigh					
Portsmouth A.					
Kings Nympton					
Eggesford					
Lapford					
Morchard Rd.					
Copplestone					
Plymouth (Friary)					9 15
Friary Jct.					9 17
Mount Gould Jct.					9 18
Lipson Jct.					9 19
Plymouth (N. Rd.)					9 23
Devonport, Kings Rd.					9 27
Devonport Jct.					9 28
Ford					9 30
St. Budeaux, Vic. Rd.					9 34
Tamerton Foliot					9 39
Bere Ferrers					9 44
Bere Alston					9 50
Tavistock North					9 59
Brentor					10 10
Lydford					10 23
Bridestowe					10 29
Meldon Jct.					10 37
Quarry Halt					10 47
Okehampton					10 51
Sampford C'nay					
North Tawton					
Bow					
Coleford Jct.					
Yeoford				9 35	
Crediton					
Newton St. Cyres					
Cowley					
Exeter (St. David's)				9 38	
Exeter Central				9 41	
St. James' Park Halt				9 46	
Exmouth Jct.				9 48	
Pinhoe				9 55	
Broad Clyst				10 3	
Whimple				10 12	
Sidmouth Jct.					
Honiton					
Seaton Jct.					
Axminster					
Chard Jct.					
Crewkerne					
Sutton Bingham					
Yeovil Jct.					
Sherborne					
Milborne Port					
Templecombe					
Gillingham					
Semley					
Tisbury					
Dinton					
Wilton South					
Salisbury					
Waterloo					

A—Connect with 9.0 p.m. Exmouth, due 9.30 p.m.

Page 62 — UP SUNDAYS

Station	Empty Milk Tanks to Ilfracombe WR	Return Excursion (A)	Milk Clapham Jct. (Q)		Engine	6 42 p.m. Bude
Torrington						
Bideford (New)			5 40 5 49			
Instow			5 57			
Fremington			6 4			
Barnstaple Jct.				6 23 6 14		
Ilfracombe				6 27 6 15		
Mortehoe & Woolacombe				6 38 6 28		6 30
Braunton				6 39		6 32
Wrafton				6 42		6 34
Pottington Box			6 18	6 48		
Barnstaple Town				6 49 6 50		6 38
Barnstaple Jct.			6 29	6 53 6 59		6 40
Chapelton			6 35	7 5 7 6		6 43
Umberleigh			6 40	7 11 7 12		6 45
Portsmouth A.			6 46	7 19		6 49
Kings Nympton				7 24 7 25		6 54
Eggesford			6 52 7 12	7 31 7 32		6 58
Lapford			7 17	7 38		7 4
Morchard Rd.			7 21	7 48 7 49		
Copplestone						
Plymouth (Friary)						
Friary Jct.						6 30
Mount Gould Jct.						6 32
Lipson Jct.						6 34
Plymouth (N. Rd.)	4 0					6 38
Devonport, Kings Rd.	4 3					6 42
Devonport Jct.						6 45
Ford						6 49
St. Budeaux, Vic. Rd.						6 54
Tamerton Foliot						6 58
Bere Ferrers						7 4
Bere Alston	4 33					7 13
Tavistock North						7 27
Brentor						7 40
Lydford	4 48 4 55					7 44
Bridestowe						7 52
Meldon Jct.						8
Quarry Halt						
Okehampton						
Sampford C'nay						
North Tawton				7 49		
Bow						
Coleford Jct.						
Yeoford			7 25	7 52		8 5
Crediton			7 33 7 37	7 54 8 1		8 8
Newton St. Cyres				8 2		8 13
Cowley						8 25
Exeter (St. David's)			7 48 7 52	8 10		
Exeter Central			7 55 8 5	8 13 8 19		8 32
St. James' Park Halt				8 22		8 36
Exmouth Jct.						8 42 8 43
Pinhoe						
Broad Clyst						8 51
Whimple						8 54 8 58
Sidmouth Jct.			9 20			9 1
Honiton						
Seaton Jct.		9 11				
Axminster		9 20 9 12				
Chard Jct.		9 27 9 21				
Crewkerne		9 37 9 38				
Sutton Bingham		9 47 9 48				
Yeovil Jct.		9 55 9 56	9 39 9 54			
Sherborne						
Milborne Port						
Templecombe		10 3 10 4				
Gillingham		10 13 10 14				
Semley		10 19				
Tisbury						
Dinton						
Wilton South			10 36 10 41			
Salisbury						
Waterloo						

SALISBURY, EXETER, PLYMOUTH, ILFRACOMBE AND TORRINGTON.

5

Distance from Nine Elms	Distance (m. c.)	DOWN WEEKDAYS.	Speed Tables arr. h.m.	dep. h.m.	arr. h.m.	dep. h.m.	MX SX 6.0 p.m. Temple-combe arr. mdt.	dep. a.m.	To Launceston MX arr. a.m.	dep. a.m.	To Launceston MO Trip arr. a.m.	dep. a.m.	To Launceston MO arr. a.m.	dep. a.m.	arr. a.m.	dep. a.m.
82	—	Salisbury	0 0												1 38	
84	58	Salisbury West Yard													1 45	1 55
90	39	Wilton South													2 0	2 5
94	04	Dinton														
99	65	Tisbury														
103	72	Semley		1 10											2 32	3 35
113	56	Gillingham													2 35	3 39
113	09	Milborne Port	1 5													
116	63	Templecombe	1 40													
121	31	Sherborne													3 56	3 58
123	49	Yeovil Jct.	1 45												4 16	4 25
133	30	Sutton Bingham							Freight & Mail as from Okehamp-ton							4 38	4 40
133	19	Hewish Sdg.								12 38		12 21		12 45 12 54			
138	27	Chard Jct.	2 43	2 45								12 59 1 0			
143	49	Axminster							12 1			1 26 2 35			
150	33	Seaton Jct.							8 12 13 12 28			3 39			
158	10	Honiton Inc. Box.	3 35	3 40					8 12 18 13 22						
161	42	Sidmouth Jct.							24 12 9d						
165	45	Whimple							12 57						
167	35	Broad Clyst													
169	13	Pinhoe	4 10	4 20		Continued from Page No. 14.									
170	28	Exmouth Jct. Sdgs.	4 27	4 30		12 0			3 10 4 0		3 20 4 0				
170	75	Exmouth Jct.	4 35	4 40					1 19 2 25		4 14				
		Exeter Central							1 4						
		Exeter (St. David's)	4 44						2 57						
172	18	Cowley Jct.													
176	19	Newton St. Cyres	5 5	5 10											
181	40	Crediton	5 14												
182	37	Yeoford													
		Coleford Jct.													
186	22	Bow													
189	33	North Tawton													
195	19	Sampford Courtenay													
198	03	Quarry Sig. Box	5 55	6 0		12 0									
198	46	Meldon Jct.													
202	50	Bridestowe													
205	60	Lydford													
206	33	Brentor	6 40	6 45		2 40 2 50									
218	56	Tavistock North													
218	50	Bere Alston													
221	41	Bere Ferrers													
224	52	Ernesettle Sdg.				3 30 4									
224	55	St. Budeaux (Vict. Rd.)	7 25 7 30			4 6									
228	33	Devonport (Kings Rd.)	7 36			4 10									
229	32	Plymouth (N. Rd.)	7 40			4 16									
230	29	Lipson Jct.	7 42			4 19									
231	46	Mount Gould Jct.	7 43			4 22									
232	40	Priory Jct.													
		Plymouth (Friary)	7 46												
184	36	Copplestone			5 30										
186	08	Morchard Road			5 34			6 26 6 30							
187	37	Lapford			5 51			6 34							
192	29	Eggesford			5 58			6 35							
196	25	King's Nympton			6 11										
202	58	South Molton A.							6 40					6 40	
203	13	Umberleigh							6 44					6 48	
205	50	Chapelton							0 44					6 53	
210	04	Barnstaple Jct.			6 26 6 30				6 50 4					6 56	
210	60	Barnstaple Town			6 34 6 35				7 14					7 8	
210	73	Pottington Box													
215	01	Wrafton													
215	40	Heddon Mill Crossing													
218	22	Mortehoe & W'combe													
225	00	Ilfracombe			7 14										
212	56	Barnstaple Jct.			6 40										
215	75	Instow			6 48										
218	47	Bideford (Goods)			6 53										
219	07	Bideford (New)			6 56										
224	16	Hartlett's Sdg.			7 8										
		Torrington			7 8										

87

BERE ALSTON AND CALLINGTON BRANCH—continued

A—Conveys Callington wagons only.

DOWN

SUNDAYS	Mixed A arr. a.m.	dep. a.m.	arr. p.m.	dep. p.m.	arr. p.m.	dep. p.m.	arr. p.m.	dep. p.m.
Bere Alston	9 26		12 27		7 21		10 5	
Calstock	9 32 9 34		12 33 12 35		7 27 7 35		10 10 10 13	
Gunnislake	9 49 9 52		12 52 12 58		7 41 7 42		10 35 10 26	
Chilsworthy	9 51 9 52		12 58 7 58		7 50 7 51		10 31 10 31	
Latchley	9 56 9 57		12 57 12 58		7 55 7 56		10 35 10 36	
Luckett	10 2 10 2		1 2		8 2		10 40 10 41	
Callington	10 8		1 9		7		10 47	

UP

SUNDAYS	Mixed arr. a.m.	dep. a.m.	arr. a.m.	dep. a.m.	arr. p.m.	dep. p.m.	arr. p.m.	dep. p.m.
Callington		8 15		11 35		6 30		9 10
Luckett	8 21 8 22		11 41 11 46		6 36 6 36		9 16 9 16	
Latchley	8 26 8 27		11 46 11 46		6 45 6 46		9 26 9 27	
Chilsworthy	8 31 8 32		11 50 11 51		6 46 6 50		9 30 9 31	
Gunnislake	8 35 8 36		11 54 12 7		6 49 7 3		9 43 9 44	
Calstock	8 48 8 50		12 16 12 19		7		9 51	
Bere Alston	8 57							

HALWILL AND TORRINGTON BRANCH

WEEK-DAYS

Distance (M. C.)		Mixed (Conveys Workmen) arr. a.m.	dep. a.m.	Mixed arr. a.m.	dep. a.m.	SX Mixed arr. a.m.	dep. a.m.	SO Mixed arr. a.m.	dep. a.m.
—	58	Torrington		6 25		8 52		4 16 4 17		4 40 4 49
4	42	Watergate Halt	6 32	6 33	8 59 9 4		4 21 4 22		4 47 5 7
5	49	Yarde Halt	6 46 6 48		9 13 9 14		4 31 4 44		5 15 5 16
7	68	Dunsbear Halt	6 52 6 55		9 28 9 29		4 41 4 53		5 26 5 38
12	46	Petrockstow			9 38 9 39		4 51 5 5		5 35 5 57
17	56	Meeth Halt			9 48 9 50		4 51 5 6		5 56 6
20	47	Hatherleigh			10 8 10 9		5 21		6 6
		Hole			10 18					
		Halwill								

WEEKDAYS

Distance (M. C.)		Mixed arr. a.m.	dep. a.m.	SO Mixed 13th June to 19th Sept. only arr. a.m.	dep. a.m.	SX Mixed (Conveys Workmen) arr. p.m.	dep. p.m.	Mixed arr. p.m.	dep. p.m.
—	36	Halwill				10 52		4 35		6 40
3	07	Hole			10 49 10 50	11 2		4 44 4 45	6 49 6 50	
5	71	Hatherleigh	8 4		11 40	11 23	4 50 4 51		7 17 7 18	
8	37	Meeth Halt	8 10 8 11		11 46 11 47	11 52	5 4 5 5		7 27 7 28	
12	59	Petrockstow	8 24 8 25		11 56 11 57	12 0	5 12		7 37 7 38	
14	78	Dunsbear Halt	8 32		X29 11 30	12 11			7 44 7 45	
16	05	Yarde Halt			11 45 11 45				7 58 7 59	
18	69	Watergate Halt			11 58 11 59				8 6	
20	47	Torrington			12 6					

Will not run on Saturdays 13th June to 19th Sept.

SALISBURY, EXETER, PLYMOUTH, ILFRACOMBE AND TORRINGTON.

DOWN. WEEKDAYS.

Station	MO To Torrington	7.4 p.m. FX / 7.30 p.m. FO Basingstoke	12.35 a.m. / 12.15 a.m. MX Salisbury to Torrington C	MO	MX 10.0 p.m. SX Nine Elms SF A	G 10.0 p.m. SX Nine Elms SF A
	arr. dep. a.m.	arr. dep. a.m.	arr. dep. a.m.	arr. dep. a.m.	arr. dep. a.m.	arr. dep. a.m.
Salisbury						
Salisbury West Yard	12 35			1 25	12 40 12 41	12 40 12 41
Wilton South					12 55 1 10	12 55 1 10
Dinton						
Tisbury						
Semley						
Gillingham	1 40 1 55				2 5	2 5
Templecombe						
Milborne Port				2 30	2 5 3 10	2 5 3 10
Sherborne						
Yeovil Jct.	2 25 2 30			3 40 4 32	3 40 4A32	3 40 4A32
Sutton Bingham						
Crewkerne						
Hewish Siding			Will not run on Saturdays 13th June to 19th Sept.	5 27 5 45	5A27 5E45	5A27 5 45
Chard Jct.	3 26 3 40			5 55 6 5	5 55 6 6	5 55 6 27
Axminster						
Seaton Jct.						
Honiton Inc. Bx.				6 35 6 50	6 35 6 50	6 57 7 8
Honiton				6 50 6 9	6 53 6 9	7 17 7 54
Sidmouth Jct.				7 17 7 29	7 17 7 29	8 2 8 14
Whimple						
Broad Clyst						
Pinhoe						
Exmouth Jct. Sdgs.	4 45 6 0	3 40 5 35	(4M33 / 4M045 6 0)	7 45	7 45	8 30
Exmouth Jct. Box		5 42 5 46	6 7 6 9			
Exeter Central		5 51 5 55	6 14 6 15		6 48	
Exeter (St. David's)					6 53 6 54	
Exeter (St. Dav. Yd.)			6 19		6 56 7 16	Alternative timing
Cowley Jct.						
Newton St. Cyres		5 59				5.32 a.m.
Crediton				7 10 7 30		MX G Parcels
Yeoford		6 21 6 33	6 41 7 9	7 30 8 40 9 5		Yeovil Jct.
Coleford Jct.		6 37	7 13			runs.
Bow						
North Tawton						
Sampford O'nay						
Okehampton		7 18 7 43		Stop each weekday at Bridge No. 149 near 106¼ mp. between Eggesford and Kings Nympton to set down cans of drinking water.		
Quarry Sig. Box						
Meldon Jct.						
Bridestowe						
Lydford						
Brentor						
Tavistock North		8 23 8 31				
Bere Alston						
Bere Ferrers						
St. Budeaux (Vic. Rd.)						
Devonport (Kings Rd.)		9 11 9 41		Timing will not apply when		
Devonport Jct.		9 47				
Plymouth (N. Rd.)		9 53		5.32 a.m.		
Mount Gould Jct.		9 55		MX G		
Lipson Jct.		9 56		Parcels		
Plymouth (Friary)		9 59		Yeovil Jct. runs.		
Copplestone			7 24		9 21 9 30	
Morchard Road			7 28		9X38 9 47	
Lapford			7 33		9X65 10S10	
Eggesford			7X41 7 44		10 4 10 9	
King's Nympton			7X51 8 12		12X17 12S55	
Portsmouth A.			8 25		12X17 12S55	
Umberleigh					1 28 1 22	
Chapelton					1 54 1 45	
Barnstaple Jct.			8 39 9025			
Barnstaple Town						
Pottington Box						
Wrafton						
Braunton						
Heddon Mill Crossing						
Mortehoe & W'combe						
Ilfracombe						
Barnstaple Jct.						
Fremington						
Instow						
Bideford (Goods)						
Bideford (New)						
Bartlett's Sdg.						
Torrington						

A—On Saturdays until 19th September depart Yeovil Jct. 4.25 a.m. and arrive Axminster 5.20 a.m.
B—Depart 9.12 a.m. on Saturdays 13th June to 19th September.

SALISBURY, EXETER, PLYMOUTH, ILFRACOMBE AND TORRINGTON.

DOWN. WEEKDAYS.

Station	MO Engine.	Freight and Mail.	Freight & Mail to Bude.	9.10 p.m. SX Nine Elms SF	Mixed Launceston.	To Bude.	MX	SO To Torrington SF	MX To Torrington SF
	arr. dep. a.m.	arr. dep. a.m.	arr. dep. a.m.	dep. p.m.	arr. dep. a.m.	arr. dep. a.m.	arr. dep. a.m.	arr. dep. a.m.	dep. a.m.
Salisbury				11 37 11 45				12 15	12 15
Salisbury West Yard	1M55			12 35					Will not run on Saturdays 13th June 19th Sept.
Wilton South									
Dinton									
Tisbury									
Semley				12 51					2 15
Gillingham	1 49 1 60							1 20 1 50	2 15
Templecombe	1 53 1 54			1 30					
Milborne Port	1156 2 10	2 10				3 30			
Sherborne	1156 (2 25)								
Yeovil Jct.				2				3 5	3 8 3 28
Sutton Bingham									
Crewkerne									
Hewish Siding									
Chard Jct.						3 37 3 39			
Axminster		3 17	4 37	3 40		3 44 3 45		3 40	
Seaton Jct.			4 51			3 47 4 12			
Honiton Inc. Bx.									
Honiton		3 15							
Sidmouth Jct.	3 15 3 46	3 26 3 30		4 2		4 16			
Whimple	3 24 3 50			4 5		4 46		4 5	4 33
Broad Clyst						6 50			
Pinhoe									
Exmouth Jct. Sdgs.						4 37		4 5 6 0	4 5 6 0
Exmouth Jct. Box							4 0		
Exeter Central						7V13 7V24	4 4 13		
Exeter (St. David's)					9 41		4 13		
Exeter (St. Dav. Yd.)							4 16 (G 0)		
Cowley Jct.									
Newton St. Cyres									
Crediton		4 38 4 40		4 20					
Yeoford		4 55		4 5					
Coleford Jct.									
Bow									
North Tawton									
Sampford O'nay									
Okehampton					6 27 7 47 8 10				
Quarry Sig. Box									
Meldon Jct.					8 41	8 24			
Bridestove									
Lydford				5 38					
Brentor								6.58 a.m. Laira.	
Tavistock North									
Bere Alston									
Bere Ferrers				6 19				arr. dep. a.m.	dep. a.m.
St. Budeaux (Vic. Rd.)				6 21				7 0	7 0
Ernesettle Sidings				6 25				7 1	7 1
Devonport (Kings Rd.)				6 31					
Devonport Jct.				6 33				7 4	7 4
Plymouth (N. Rd.)				6 34					
Mount Gould Jct.									
Lipson Jct.									
Friary Jct.									
Plymouth (Friary)				6 37					
Copplestone		3 57						5 40	6 38
Morchard Road		4 1						5 44 6 42	6 42
Lapford		4 4 6						5 45 6 43	6 43
Eggesford		4 14 4 16							
King's Nympton		4 23						5 54 6 52	6 52
Portsmouth A.		4 29						6 0 6 58	6 58
Umberleigh		4 38 4 40						6 11 7 6	7 6
Chapelton		4 55						6 14 7 12	7 7 12
Barnstaple Jct.								6 24	
Barnstaple Town									
Pottington Box									
Wrafton									
Braunton									
Heddon Mill Crossing									
Mortehoe & W'combe									
Ilfracombe									
Barnstaple Jct.		5 15							Will not run on Saturdays 13th June 19th Sept.
Fremington		5 22							
Instow		5 29 5 30							
Bideford (Goods)		5 38 5 48							
Bideford (New)		5 51 5 56							
Bartlett's Sdg.									
Torrington		6 8							

SALISBURY, EXETER, PLYMOUTH, ILFRACOMBE AND TORRINGTON.

DOWN. WEEKDAYS.

Station	Engine.	Stone Empties.	To Wadebridge.	Engine.	To Wadebridge.	SO	SO
Salisbury							★ 9 56 / 10 15
Salisbury West Yard							10 26 / 10 36
Wilton South							10E46 / 11 25
Dinton							
Tisbury							
Semley							
Gillingham							
Templecombe							11 39
Milborne Port							11E36 / 12 27
Sherborne							
Yeovil Jct.							12 42 / 1 0
Sutton Bingham							1 15 / 2 17
Crewkerne							
Hewish Siding		Will not run Saturdays 13th June to 19th Sept.	Until 19th Sept. only.		Will not run on Saturdays 13th June to 19th Sept	Commences 26th Sept.	2 29 / 2 49
Chard Jct.		7 32					2 47 / 2 58
Axminster		7 38 / 7 50					3 0 / 3 17
Seaton Jct.		7 54 / 7 57					3 9
Honiton Inc. Bx.							3 12
Honiton		8 2					
Sidmouth Jct.							
Whimple							
Broad Clyst							
Pinhoe		8 31					9 30 / 9 34
Exmouth Jct. Sdgs.		(8012) 8 31					
Exmouth Jct.	Will not run Saturdays 13th June to 19th Sept.	8 37					
Exeter Central	9J18 (10J10)	9 26	10 4		10 4		
Exeter (St. David's)	9J24 (10J10)	9 40 (9J56)	10 58		10 55		
Exeter (St. Dav. Yd.)							
Newton St. Cyres							
Cowley Jct.							
Crediton							
Yeoford							
Coleford Jct.							
Bow					(1236)		
North Tawton							
Sampford C'nay							
Okehampton	(8 49)		10 44	1 13	12 56	10J30	10 26 / 10 36
Quarry Sig. Box	9J24 (10J10)			1 17		10J37 (10J28)	10E46 / 11 25
Meldon Jct.		11 39	10 53	1 22			
Bridestowe				1 23			11 39
Lydford				1 23½			
Brentor							
Tavistock North				1 26			12 42 / 1 0
Bere Alston			9J20 p.m. W.R. Engine Laira.				1 15 / 2 17
Bere Ferrers							
Brunestele Sidings							
St. Budeaux (Vic. Rd.)			2 22 / 2 23				2 29 / 2 39
Devonport (Kings Rd.)			2J26 (2 58)				2 47 / 2 58
Devonport Jct.							3 0
Plymouth (N. Rd.)							3 9
Lipson Jct.							3 12
Mount Gould Jct.							
Friary Jct.							
Plymouth (Friary)							

Station	SO	SO	
Copplestone			
Morchard Road			
Lapford		12.35 a.m. MO	8 39 / 9 12
Eggesford	SO	12.15 a.m. MX Salisbury.	9 31 / 9 41
King's Nympton	12.15 a.m. Salisbury.		9 49 / 10 52
Portsmouth A.			10 50X7 / 10 52
Umberleigh			11 E 11X7
Chapelton		Will not run on Saturdays 13th June to 19th Sept.	8 11 / 10X55 / 11 13
Barnstaple Jct.	Until 19th Sept. only.	Will not run on Saturdays 13th June to 19th Sept.	9J50 / 11 14 / 11 31
Barnstaple Town			0 53
Pottington Box			10J1 / 11 33
Wrafton			
Braunton			
Heddon Mill Crossing	9A42		
Mortehoe & W'combe	A		
Ilfracombe	9A50		

Station			
Barnstaple Jct.			
Instow			
Fremington			
Bideford (Goods)			
Bideford (New)			
Bartlett's Sdg.			
Torrington			

A.—When required on Saturdays, 13th June to 19th September, start at 9.37 a.m. and arrive Fremington 9.45 a.m.

Western.—B.

SALISBURY, EXETER, PLYMOUTH, ILFRACOMBE AND TORRINGTON.

DOWN. WEEKDAYS.

Station	From Keyham Dockyard. SO G	To Eggesford. SO	12.33 a.m. Stone Empties Woking. SX G	From Keyham Dockyard. SX G	G	Engine. SO	SO	SX
Salisbury								
Salisbury West Yard			3 55					
Wilton South			3 48					
Dinton								
Tisbury								
Semley								
Gillingham			4E55 / 5 20		Alternative timing when 5.32 a.m. MX G Pds. Yeovil Jct. runs.			
Templecombe								
Milborne Port			5 50 / 6 37					
Sherborne								9 5
Yeovil Jct.					5 40 / 5 57			
Sutton Bingham		Until 19th Sept. only.			5 A			
Crewkerne		6 42 / 6 48		5 55 / 6 20	6 5 / 6 22	Call at Broom Crossing to unload Churn of drinking water.	Call at Broom Crossing to unload Churn of drinking water.	9 38 / 10 0
Hewish Siding		6 53 / 6 54	7 27	6 41	6 43 / 7 21			10 5 / 11 8
Chard Jct.		7 19 / 7 16		7 45	7 45 / 7 31			11 35
Axminster								
Seaton Jct.								
Honiton Inc. Bx.			8 12 / 8 35	5 30				
Honiton		7 30 / 7 40						
Sidmouth Jct.		8 49 / 12 15						
Whimple								11 49 / 12 6
Broad Clyst				5 55 / 6 20				12 12 / 12 31
Pinhoe						After Freight Shunting.	After Freight Shunting.	12 39 / 12 58
Exmouth Jct. Sdgs.			9 5			11J59	11J59	
Exmouth Jct.						11 54	11 54	1 8
Exeter Central	10 13 / 10 23			10 45 / 11 15	11 5 / 11 25	11 50	11 50	1 10
Exeter (St. David's)	10 30			11 22	11 32	12 0½	12 0½	1 11
Exeter (St. Dav. Yd.)								
Newton St. Cyres						12J1 / 3		1 14
Cowley Jct.								
Crediton								
Yeoford								
Coleford Jct.								
Bow	From Western Region East.		SX From Keyham Dockyard.	From Western Region East.		12.5 p.m. Laira.		
North Tawton								
Sampford C'nay								
Okehampton	10.50 a.m. Laira to Cattewater.							
Quarry Sig. Box								
Meldon Jct.	10 52							
Bridestowe								
Lydford								
Brentor						12 7 / 12 8		
Tavistock North								
Bere Alston								
Bere Ferrers								
Brunestele Sidings								
St. Budeaux (Vic. Rd.)								
Devonport (Kings Rd.)								
Devonport Jct.								
Plymouth (N. Rd.)								
Lipson Jct.								
Mount Gould Jct.								
Friary Jct.								
Plymouth (Friary)								

Station			
Copplestone	SX From W.R. via St. Budeaux East.	Timing will not apply when G service runs.	
Morchard Road			
Lapford			
Eggesford	1.25 a.m.		
King's Nympton			
Portsmouth A.			
Umberleigh			
Chapelton			
Barnstaple Jct.			
Barnstaple Town			
Pottington Box			
Wrafton			
Braunton			
Heddon Mill Crossing			
Mortehoe & W'combe			
Ilfracombe			

Station			
Barnstaple Jct.			
Instow			
Fremington			
Bideford (Goods)			
Bideford (New)			
Bartlett's Sdg.			
Torrington			

A.—Sutton Bingham Signal Box to be open for this service.

SALISBURY, EXETER, PLYMOUTH, ILFRACOMBE AND TORRINGTON.

DOWN. WEEKDAYS.	Stone Empties. G arr. dep. a.m. a.m.	A ★ arr. dep. a.m. a.m.	SO arr. dep. a.m. a.m.	Engine. G arr. dep. a.m. a.m.	Engine. G arr. dep. p.m. p.m.	Engine. F arr. dep. p.m. p.m.	G CD arr. dep. p.m. p.m.	SO To Gilling-ham. arr. dep.	SO To Temple-combe. ★ arr. dep.	arr. dep. a.m.	arr. dep. p.m. p.m.
Salisbury West Yard											
Salisbury (West)											
Wilton South	Will not run on Saturdays 13th June to 19th Sept.			Will not run on Saturdays 13th June to 19th Sept.				6 20 7 43	6 30 8 0	Will not run on Saturdays 13th June to 19th Sept.	Will not run on Saturdays 13th June to 19th Sept.
Dinton											
Tisbury								6 45			
Semley											
Gillingham								6 45			
Templecombe									6 56 8 0		
Milborne Port											
Sherborne								Until 19th Sept. only.			12 17 19
Yeovil Jct.											12 10
Sutton Bingham											12 24 32
Crewkerne											12 34 (1 45)
Hewish Siding											
Chard Jct.											
Axminster											
Seaton Jct.	10 38					1 9 (1F30)	11 50				
Honiton Inc. Bx.	10 8 10 36		(10.52) 11 20	11 44 11 57	11 57 1 F30 (9F55)	1 9 (1F30)	11 57 12 9			12 13 15	
Honiton	10 40 10 44		11 26	12 0 12 55	12 9 12 12	1F36 (9F55)	12 4 12 6			12 24 12 32	
Sidmouth Jct.							12 10			12 34 (1 45)	
Whimple	10 49			12 8							
Broad Clyst											
Pinhoe				12 30			12 23 12 26				
Exmouth Jct. Sdgs.	10 38			Perform shunting.	12 31		12 38 1 0				
Exmouth Jct.					12 31		1 4				
Exeter Central (St. David's)											
Exeter (St. David's)											
Exeter (St. Dav. Yd.)											
Cowley Jct.											
Newton St. Cyres											
Crediton											
Yeoford	11 18					12 31	1 45 2 20	SX 5.0 p.m. Laira to Cattewater		11 57	
Coleford Jct.	12 13										
Bow	12 27 (12 (57)										
North Tawton							3 0 3 10				
Sampford Chay											
Okehampton								EB p.m. 5 2			
Quarry Sig. Box							4 18				
Meldon Jct.							4 20 4 23				
Bridestowe							4 29				
Lydford							4 31				
Brentor							4 32				
Tavistock North							Will not run on Saturdays 13th June to 19th Sept.				
Bere Alston											
Bere Ferrers											
Ernesettle Sidings											
St. Budeaux (Vic. Rd.)											
Devonport (Kings Rd.)											
Plymouth (N. Rd.)											
Lipson Jct.											
Mount Gould Jct.											
Friary Jct.											
Plymouth (Friary)											
Copplestone			Will not run on Saturdays 13th June to 19th Sept.								
Morchard Road											
Lapford							SX Engine.				
Eggesford											
King's Nympton											
Portsmouth A.			Worked by Freming-ton shunting engine.					SO arr. dep. p.m. p.m.			
Umberleigh											
Chapelton								2‖ 5			
Barnstaple Jct.								2‖ 5			
Podington Box											
Barnstaple Town								Perform Shunting.			
Wrafton											
Braunton											
Heddon Mill Crossing											
Mortehoe & W'combe											
Ilfracombe											
Barnstaple Jct.	11A37 11A45 (11.51)									11 57 12 5 (1222)	
Fremington											
Instow	Will not run on Saturdays 13th June to 19th Sept.		SO ★							Until 19th Sept. only.	
Bideford (Goods)											
Bideford (New)											
Bartlett's Sdg.											
Torrington											

A—On Mondays, 14th June to 14th September, start at 11.35 a.m. and arrive Instow 11.43 a.m.
C—On Saturdays, 13th June to 19th September, depart Chard Jc. 10.6 a.m. depart Devonport (King's Road 4.25 a.m. and run 7 minutes later.
D—Commencing 21st Sept. depart Quarry Sig. Box 3.17.
F—Convey empty wagons, when required and arrive Quarry Signal Box 1.40 p.m.

SALISBURY, EXETER, PLYMOUTH, ILFRACOMBE AND TORRINGTON.

DOWN. WEEKDAYS.	SX arr. dep. a.m.	3.45 p.m. Laira. ◆ dep. p.m.	6.35 a.m. Exmouth Jct. Sdgs. arr. dep. a.m. a.m.	Stone Empties. arr. dep. a.m. a.m.	12.20 a.m. Eastleigh. MX ★ arr. dep. a.m. a.m.	To Exmouth Jct. Sdgs. MO ★ arr. dep.	11.58 p.m. Feltham. MX ★ AC arr. dep. a.m. a.m.	SO arr. dep. a.m. a.m.	SO arr. dep. a.m.
Salisbury West Yard									
Salisbury (West)					1 30				
Wilton South	9 50 9 50				1 45 4 31 4 30		4 35 4 55		9 0 9 0 (9 40)
Dinton	10 6 10 23								
Tisbury	10 34 10 44								
Semley	10E54 10 30								Until 19th Sept. only.
Gillingham							6 5 6 40		
Templecombe	11 44		Until 19th Sept. only.				6 7 15		
Milborne Port	11 54 12 15				5 35 5 55		7 1 7 25 8 10		
Sherborne	12 22 12 37				6 35 7 5		8 35 8 58	Will not run on Saturdays 13th June to 19th Sept.	
Yeovil Jct.	12 52 1 14			Will not run on Saturdays 13th June to 19th Sept.	0V16 6 25		9 8		
Sutton Bingham	1 29 2 10						8 35 8 58		
Crewkerne	2 17 2 27				8 0 8 16		9 23 0A43 10E10		
Hewish Siding					8 26	8 35	9A55 10E50 11C20		
Chard Jct.	2 39 3 40						10 50 11C20		
Axminster	3 7				9 30 9 38		Terminate at Axminster on Saturdays 13th June to 19th Sept.	10 36	
Seaton Jct.	3 9					9 43		10 40	
Honiton Inc. Bx.	3 13			9 55				10 49 11 10	
Honiton	3 18		8 40 12 13 11	9 15	10 5			11 47	10 42
Sidmouth Jct.	3 19							12 11 12 4	10 46
Whimple	3 21							12 30	10 47
Broad Clyst	3 22								
Pinhoe	3 25			9 22 9 30	9 57				
Exmouth Jct. Sdgs.				9 30 9 54					
Exmouth Jct.					10 19				
Exeter Central (St. David's)			10 12	10 5 10 13					
Exeter (St. David's)			15 11	10 11					
Exeter (St. Dav. Yd.)				10 20 11 35	10 48				
Cowley Jct.				4‖7 12 32					
Newton St. Cyres			12 19	12 36					
Crediton									
Yeoford	9 30								
Coleford Jct.	9 34								
Bow									
North Tawton									
Sampford Chay			Convey churns of drinking water from Lapford to cottages near Lapford up distant signal.						
Okehampton				11 43 11 57 (12‖25)					
Quarry Sig. Box									
Meldon Jct.									
Bridestowe									
Lydford									
Brentor									
Tavistock North									
Bere Alston									
Bere Ferrers									
Ernesettle Sidings									
St. Budeaux (Vic. Rd.)									
Devonport (Kings Rd.)									
Plymouth (N. Rd.)									
Lipson Jct.									
Mount Gould Jct.		3 47							
Friary Jct.		3 49							
Plymouth (Friary)		3 51							
Copplestone			1‖X27 1‖X 8 1S35 2 39 (3 17)	1X 2‖2 44 1X 6 1 27 1S35 2X30 2 39 (3 17)					
Morchard Road									
Lapford									
Eggesford									
King's Nympton									
Portsmouth A.									
Umberleigh									
Chapelton									
Barnstaple Jct.									
Portington Box									
Barnstaple Town									
Wrafton									
Braunton									
Heddon Mill Crossing									
Mortehoe & W'combe									
Ilfracombe									
Barnstaple Jct.									
Fremington									
Instow									
Bideford (Goods)									
Bideford (New)									
Bartlett's Sdg.									
Torrington									

A—On Saturdays, 13th June to 19th September, depart Chard Jc. 10.6 a.m. and arrive Axminster 10.18 a.m.
C—On Saturdays commencing 26th Sept. depart Seaton Jct. 11.18 a.m.

SALISBURY, EXETER, PLYMOUTH, ILFRACOMBE AND TORRINGTON.

DOWN. WEEKDAYS.

(upper table, columns headed:)

Station	6.30 a.m. Salisbury.	5.40 a.m. Stone Empties Three Bdgs.	FO	SXⒼ	C	SXⒼ	SO	SX	SO	SX 8.55 p.m. Laira.

Stations (top table):
Salisbury
Salisbury West Yard
Wilton South
Dinton
Tisbury
Semley
Gillingham
Templecombe
Milborne Port
Sherborne
Sutton Bingham
Yeovil Jct.
Crewkerne
Hewish Siding
Chard Jct.
Axminster
Seaton Jct.
Honiton Inc. Bx.
Honiton
Sidmouth Jct.
Whimple
Broad Clyst
Pinhoe
Exmouth Jct. Sdgs.
Exmouth Jct. Box
Exeter Central
Exeter (St. David's)
Exeter (St. Dav. Yd.)
Cowley Jct.
Newton St. Cyres
Crediton
Yeoford
Coleford Jct.

Bow
North Tawton
Sampford C'nay
Okehampton
Quarry Sig. Box
Meldon Jct.
Bridestowe
Lydford
Brentor
Tavistock North
Bere Alston
Bere Ferrers
St. Budeaux (Vic. Rd.)
Devonport (Kings Rd.)
Devonport (N. Rd.)
Plymouth (N. Rd.)
Lipson Jct.
Mount Gould Jct.
Friary Jct.
Plymouth (Friary)

Copplestone
Morchard Road
Lapford
Eggesford
King's Nympton
Portsmouth A.
Umberleigh
Chapelton
Barnstaple Jct.
Barnstaple Town
Pottington Box
Wrafton
Braunton
Heddon Mill Crossing
Mortehoe & W'combe
Ilfracombe

Barnstaple Jct.
Fremington
Instow
Bideford (Goods)
Bideford (New)
Bartlett's Sdg.
Torrington

SALISBURY, EXETER, PLYMOUTH, ILFRACOMBE AND TORRINGTON.

12 DOWN. WEEKDAYS.

(lower table, columns headed:)

SOⒼ 9.45 a.m. Feltham.	MO&Ⓖ	MXⒼ 4.56 a.m. Basing-stoke (empty cattle wagons).	MX	SX	MX	SXⒼ Motive Power Dept. Coal.	C	MO	SO 6.30 a.m. Salisbury.

SALISBURY, EXETER, PLYMOUTH, ILFRACOMBE AND TORRINGTON.   15

DOWN. WEEKDAYS.	10.45 a.m. Feltham. SF	SX Trip.	SX	Engine.	9.45 a.m. Stone Empties Tonbridge. SX Q	7.20 p.m. Redbridge Yard (C.C.E. Dept. Material). Q	SO Engine Yeovil. A	SX 6.55 a.m. Templecombe.	7.4 p.m. FX 7.30 p.m. FO Basingstoke. C ★
	arr. dep. p.m.	arr. dep. a.m.	arr. dep. a.m.	arr. dep. a.m.	arr. dep. a.m.	arr. dep. a.m.	arr. dep. a.m.	arr. a.m.	arr. dep. p.m.
Salisbury									9 25 9 30
Salisbury West Yard	3 44 3 45								9 50 10 35
Wilton South	3 59 5 15								
Dinton South									
Tisbury									
Semley									
Gillingham							8 52		a.m. 11 40 12 5
Templecombe	6 20 6 35					8 46			
Milborne Port						9 52 9 57	9 A55		1C15
Sherborne	7 5 7 15		8 15		9 30				12 35
Yeovil	7 42 7 30		8 35 (9 10)		10 0 10 15	10 20	10A15 10A20	7 42 10 45	2C15 2 35
Sutton Bingham	7 45							10 55	
Crewkerne			Will not run on Fridays 12th June to 18th Sept.					11 17	
Hewish Siding							Run 15 mins. later when 7.20 a.m. Redbridge runs.	11 27	
Chard Jct.	8 13	8 43	9 55		11 10 11 30 11 15 11 30			11 43	3 40
Axminster	8 25	8 55						5	
Seaton Jct.		10 35 10 45 10 54 11 40		12 E10 12 20	12 E10 12 20			12 55	
Honiton Inc. Bx.					a.m.				
Honiton									
Sidmouth Jct.	9 25	11 55 12 10		12 52	12 52			1 25	5 35
Whimple									
Broad Clyst			Terminate at Yeovil Jct. on Saturdays.	Timing not available when 7.20 p.m. Q Stone Empties runs.					
Pinhoe		12 2							
Exmouth Jct. Sdgs.							Redbridge runs.		
Exmouth Jct.				9.45 a.m. SX Q					
Exeter Central				Tonbridge runs.					
Exeter (St. David's)									

TORRINGTON, ILFRACOMBE, PLYMOUTH, EXETER AND SALISBURY.

UP. WEEKDAYS.

	MO	MO	MO	MX	MO	SF.A	Speed Tables			
		5|45 a.m. Engine Yeovil.	5|25 a.m. Yeovil.			4&40 p.m. Wadebridge. ★SF.A.				

Stations (distances m. c.):

Torrington, Bideford (New), Bideford (Goods), Instow, East Yelland Sdg., Fremington, Barnstaple Jct.

Ilfracombe, Mortehoe & W'combe, Heddon Mill Crossing, Braunton, Wrafton, Pottington Box, Barnstaple Town, Shapland & P. Sdg., Barnstaple Jct., Chapelton, Umberleigh, Portsmouth A., King's Nympton, Eggesford, Lapford, Morchard Road, Copplestone.

Plymouth (Friary), Friary Jct., Mount Gould Jct., Lipson Jct., Plymouth (Nth. Rd.), Devonport (Kings Rd.), St. Budeaux (Vic. Rd.), Bere Ferrers, Bere Alston, Tavistock North, Wilmistone Sdg., Brentor, Lydford, Bridestowe, Meldon Jct., Quarry Sig. Box, Okehampton, Sampford Cray, North Tawton, Bow.

Coleford Jct., Yeoford, Crediton, Newton St. Cyres, Cowley Jct., Exeter (St. Dav. Yd.), Exeter (St. David's), Exeter Central, Exeter Oil Gds. Yd., Exmouth Jct. Yd., Exmouth Jct. Sdgs, Poltimore Sdg., Min. of Food Sdg., Pinhoe, Broad Clyst, Whimple, Sidmouth Jct., Honiton, Seaton Jct., Axminster, Chard Jct., Crewkerne, Sutton Bingham, Yeovil Jct., Sherborne, Milborne Port, Templecombe, Gillingham, Semley, Tisbury, Chilmark Sdg., Dinton, Wilton South, Salisbury, Salisbury East Yard.

A.—On Saturdays 13th June to 19th September, depart Tisbury 5.37 a.m., Chilmark Sidings arrive 5.45 a.m., depart Tisbury 5.57 a.m., Dinton arrive 6.5 a.m., depart 6.20 a.m., Salisbury arrive 6.40 a.m., depart 6.50 a.m., Salisbury East Yard arrive 6.54 a.m.

C.—Starts at 4.50 p.m. on Mondays to Fridays until 18th September and at 4.22 p.m. on Saturdays to 19th September.

SALISBURY, EXETER, PLYMOUTH, ILFRACOMBE AND TORRINGTON.

DOWN. SUNDAYS.

										W.R. Freight to Laira.		
	7.45 p.m. Yeovil Jct.	7.30 p.m. (Sats.) Redbridge Yard (C.C.E. Dept. material).	7.4 p.m. (Sats.) Basingstoke	9.10 p.m. (Sats.) Nine Elms ★ SF	8.45 p.m. (Sats.) Feltham	12.23 a.m. Stone Empties Woking.				◆ A		★

Stations:

Salisbury, Salisbury West Yard, Wilton South, Dinton, Tisbury, Semley, Gillingham, Milborne Port, Sherborne, Yeovil Jct., Crewkerne, Chard Jct., Axminster, Seaton Jct., Honiton, Sidmouth Jct., Whimple, Broad Clyst, Pinhoe, Exmouth Jct. Sdgs., Exeter Central, Exeter (St. David's), Exeter (St. Dav. Yd.), Cowley Jct., Newton St. Cyres, Crediton, Yeoford, Coleford Jct.

Bow, North Tawton, Sampford Cray, Okehampton, Quarry Sig. Box, Meldon Jct., Lydford, Brentor, Tavistock North, Bere Alston, Bere Ferrers, St. Budeaux (Vic. Rd.), Devonport (Kings Rd.), Devonport Jct., Lipson Jct., Mount Gould Jct., Friary Jct., Plymouth (Friary).

Copplestone, Morchard Road, Lapford, Eggesford, Portsmouth A., King's Nympton, Umberleigh, Chapelton, Barnstaple Jct., Barnstaple Town, Pottington Box, Wrafton, Braunton, Heddon Mill Crossing, Mortehoe & W'combe, Ilfracombe.

Barnstaple Jct., Fremington, Instow, Bideford (Goods), Bideford (New), Torrington.

A—Take up Pilot Guard.

C.—Saturday nights.

UP. WEEKDAYS.	5|55 a.m. Engine Yeovil. arr. dep. a.m. a.m.	SO 10.0 p.m. (Fridays) Plymouth Friary. ★ arr. dep. a.m. a.m.	10.0 p.m. SA Plymouth Friary. ★A arr. dep. a.m. a.m.	MX Trip. arr. dep. a.m. a.m.	MX arr. dep. a.m. a.m.	Q Engine. arr. dep. a.m. a.m.	SO ★ arr. dep. a.m. a.m.	SO Q arr. dep. a.m. a.m.	Q arr. dep. a.m. a.m.	★ arr. dep. a.m. a.m.
Torrington	... ...	... ...	... ...	... ...	... ...	... ...	... ...	... ...	... ...	... ...
Bideford (New)	... ...	... ...	... ...	... ...	... ...	... ...	... ...	... ...	... ...	... ...
Bideford (Goods)	... ...	... ...	... ...	... ...	... ...	... ...	... ...	... ...	... ...	... ...
Instow	... ...	... ...	... ...	... ...	... ...	... ...	... ...	... ...	... ...	... ...
East Yelland Sdg.	... ...	... ...	... ...	... ...	... ...	... ...	... ...	... ...	... ...	... ...
Fremington	... ...	... ...	... ...	... ...	... ...	... ...	... ...	... ...	... ...	... ...
Barnstaple Jct.	... ...	... ...	... ...	... ...	... ...	... ...	... ...	... ...	... ...	... ...
Ilfracombe	... ...	... ...	... ...	... ...	... ...	... ...	... ...	... ...	... ...	... ...
Mortehoe & W'combe	... ...	... ...	... ...	... ...	... ...	... ...	... ...	... ...	... ...	... ...
Heddon Mill Crossing	... ...	... ...	... ...	... ...	... ...	... ...	... ...	... ...	... ...	... ...
Braunton	... ...	... ...	... ...	... ...	... ...	... ...	... ...	... ...	... ...	... ...
Wrafton	... ...	... ...	... ...	... ...	... ...	... ...	... ...	... ...	... ...	... ...
Pottington Box	... ...	... ...	... ...	... ...	... ...	... ...	... ...	... ...	... ...	... ...
Barnstaple Town	... ...	... ...	... ...	... ...	... ...	... ...	... ...	... ...	... ...	... ...
Shapland & P. Sdg.	... ...	... ...	... ...	... ...	... ...	... ...	... ...	... ...	... ...	... ...
Barnstaple Jct.	... ...	... ...	... ...	... ...	... ...	... ...	... ...	... ...	... ...	... ...
Chapelton	... ...	... ...	... ...	... ...	... ...	... ...	... ...	... ...	... ...	... ...
Umberleigh	... ...	... ...	... ...	... ...	... ...	... ...	... ...	... ...	... ...	... ...
Portsmouth A.	... ...	... ...	... ...	... ...	... ...	... ...	... ...	... ...	... ...	... ...
King's Nympton	... ...	... ...	... ...	... ...	... ...	... ...	... ...	... ...	... ...	... ...
Eggesford	... ...	... ...	... ...	... ...	... ...	... ...	... ...	... ...	... ...	... ...
Lapford	... ...	... ...	... ...	... ...	... ...	... ...	... ...	... ...	... ...	... ...
Morchard Road	... ...	... ...	... ...	... ...	... ...	... ...	... ...	... ...	... ...	... ...
Copplestone	... ...	... ...	... ...	... ...	... ...	... ...	... ...	... ...	... ...	... ...
Plymouth (Friary)	... ...	... ...	... ...	... ...	... ...	... ...	... ...	... ...	... ...	... ...
Friary Jct.	... ...	... ...	... ...	... ...	... ...	... ...	... ...	... ...	... ...	... ...
Mount Gould Jct.	... ...	... ...	... ...	... ...	... ...	... ...	... ...	... ...	... ...	... ...
Lipson Jct.	... ...	... ...	... ...	... ...	... ...	... ...	... ...	... ...	... ...	... ...
Plymouth (Nth Rd.)	... ...	... ...	... ...	... ...	... ...	... ...	... ...	... ...	... ...	... ...
Devonport Jct.	... ...	... ...	... ...	... ...	... ...	... ...	... ...	... ...	... ...	... ...
Devonport (Kings Rd.)	... ...	... ...	... ...	... ...	... ...	... ...	... ...	... ...	... ...	... ...
St. Budeaux (Vic. Rd.)	... ...	... ...	... ...	... ...	... ...	... ...	... ...	... ...	... ...	... ...
Bere Ferrers	... ...	... ...	... ...	... ...	... ...	... ...	... ...	... ...	... ...	... ...
Bere Alston	... ...	... ...	... ...	... ...	... ...	... ...	... ...	... ...	... ...	... ...
Tavistock North	... ...	... ...	... ...	... ...	... ...	... ...	... ...	... ...	... ...	... ...
Wilminstone Sdg.	... ...	... ...	... ...	... ...	... ...	... ...	... ...	... ...	... ...	... ...
Brentor	... ...	... ...	... ...	... ...	... ...	... ...	... ...	... ...	... ...	... ...
Lydford	... ...	... ...	... ...	... ...	... ...	... ...	... ...	... ...	... ...	... ...
Bridestowe	... ...	... ...	Start from	... ...	... ...	... ...	... ...	... ...	... ...	... ...
Meldon Jct.	... ...	... ...	Exmouth	... ...	... ...	... ...	... ...	... ...	... ...	... ...
Quarry Sig. Box	... ...	... ...	Jct. Sdgs.	... ...	... ...	... ...	... ...	... ...	... ...	... ...
Okehampton	... ...	... ...	on	... ...	... ...	... ...	... ...	... ...	... ...	... ...
Sampford C'nay	... ...	... ...	Mondays.	... ...	... ...	... ...	... ...	... ...	... ...	... ...
North Tawton	... ...	... ...	... ...	... ...	... ...	... ...	... ...	... ...	... ...	... ...
Bow	... ...	... ...	... ...	... ...	... ...	... ...	... ...	... ...	... ...	... ...
Coleford Jc.	... ...	... ...	... ...	... ...	... ...	... ...	... ...	... ...	... ...	Will not
Yeoford	... ...	... ...	... ...	... ...	... ...	... ...	... ...	... ...	... ...	run on
Crediton	... ...	Until	Will not	... ...	... ...	... ...	Until	... ...	... ...	Saturdays
Newton St. Cyres	... ...	19th Sept.	run on	... ...	... ...	... ...	19th Sept.	... ...	... ...	13th June
Cowley Jct.	... ...	only.	Saturdays	... ...	... ...	... ...	only.	... ...	... ...	to
Exeter (St. Dav. Yd.)	... ...		13th June	... ...	... ...	... ...		... ...	... ...	19th Sept.
Exeter (St. David's)	... ...		to	... ...	4 5	... ...		... ...	... ...	
Exeter Central	... ...		19th Sept.	... ...		... ...		... ...	... ...	
Exeter Ctl. Gds. Yd.	... ...			... ...		... ...		4 30	... ...	4 30
Exmouth Jct.	... ...	2 45 3 45	2 45 4	4 10	... ...	... ...		4 30	... ...	4 30
Exmouth Jct. Sdgs.	... ...				... ...	... ...			... ...	
Poltimore Sdg.	... ...				... ...	... ...			... ...	
Min. of Food Sdg.	... ...				... ...	... ...			... ...	
Pinhoe	... ...				... ...	... ...			... ...	
Broad Clyst	... ...	4 10	4 29		... ...	... ...	4 55 5 35		... ...	4 55 5 35
Whimple	... ...	4 24	4 43A		Will not	5 50 6 0		... ...	5 50 6 0	
Sidmouth Jct.	... ...	4 41	5 0A		run on	6 17 8 7		... ...	Timing	6 17 8 50
Honiton	... ...	4E47 5 22	5A 6 5 40	SO	Saturdays	8E14 8 48		... ...	not	8E57 10 0
Seaton Jct.	... ...	5 38 5 53	5 56 6 15		13th June			... ...	available	
Axminster	... ...	6 15 6 25	6 41 7 24	arr. dep.	to			... ...	on	
Chard Jct.	... ...			a.m. a.m.	19th Sept.			(9058) 10 8	Saturdays	
Crewkerne	6|| 0 6|| 1	6 45 8 42	7 43 8 42			9 43		10 16	13th June	10 55 11 45
Sutton Bingham	6||10 (10||30)	8 53 9 8	8 53 9 8						to	11 56 12 16
Yeovil Jct.		9 28	9 28 9 43	(9 10)	9 40 (9 35) 10.13				19th Sept.	12 31 12 36
Sherborne				9 47	10 20					12 15 12 45
Milborne Port			10E13 10 16							
Templecombe			10 26 10 36		Will not					
Gillingham			10 44 10 59		run on					
Semley			11 6||11 14		Saturdays					
Tisbury					13th June					
Chilmark Sdg.				Until	to				1 20 1 32	
Dinton				19th Sept.	19th Sept.				1 37	
Wilton South			11 35 11 39	only.						
Salisbury			11 43			12||13				
Salisbury East Yard										

n—On Mondays, call at Honiton 4.44—4.49 a.m. (unload news and mails only), pass Seaton Jc. 5.6 a.m. arr. Axminster 5.12 a.m.

UP. WEEKDAYS.	SO Engine. arr. dep. a.m. a.m.	Engine. arr. dep. a.m. a.m.	★ arr. dep. a.m. a.m.	★ arr. dep. a.m. p.m.	SO ★ Engine. arr. dep. a.m. a.m.	★ arr. dep. a.m. a.m.	Engine. arr. dep. a.m. a.m.	A Stone. arr. dep. p.m. p.m.	Freight or Engine Laira. arr. dep. a.m. a.m.
Torrington	... ...	... ...	... ...	... ...	... ...	... 6||40	... ...	... ...	... ...
Bideford (New)	... ...	... ...	... ...	... ...	... ...	6||49	... ...	... ...	... ...
Bideford (Goods)	... ...	... ...	... ...	... ...	... ...	6||52	... ...	... ...	... ...
Instow	... ...	... ...	... ...	... ...	... ...	Perform	... ...	... ...	... ...
East Yelland Sdg.	... ...	... ...	... ...	... ...	... ...	shunting.	... ...	... ...	... ...
Fremington	... ...	... ...	... ...	... ...	... ...		... ...	... ...	... ...
Barnstaple Jct.	... ...	... ...	... ...	... ...	... ...		... ...	... ...	... ...
Ilfracombe	... ...	... ...	... ...	... ...	... ...	Will not	... ...	... ...	... ...
Mortehoe & W'combe	... ...	... ...	... ...	... ...	... ...	run on	... ...	... ...	... ...
Heddon Mill Crossing	... ...	... ...	... ...	... ...	... ...	Saturdays	... ...	... ...	... ...
Braunton	... ...	... ...	... ...	... ...	... ...	13th June	... ...	... ...	... ...
Wrafton	... ...	... ...	... ...	... ...	... ...	to	... ...	... ...	... ...
Pottington Box	... ...	... ...	... ...	... ...	... ...	19th Sept.	... ...	... ...	... ...
Barnstaple Town	... ...	... ...	... ...	... ...	... ...		... ...	... ...	... ...
Shapland & P. Sdg.	... ...	... ...	... ...	... ...	... ...		... ...	... ...	... ...
Barnstaple Jct.	... ...	... ...	... ...	... ...	... ...	4 50	... ...	... ...	... ...
Chapelton	... ...	... ...	... ...	... ...	... ...	5 5 5 25	... ...	... ...	... ...
Umberleigh	... ...	... ...	... ...	... ...	... ...	5 37 5 55	... ...	... ...	... ...
Portsmouth A.	... ...	... ...	... ...	... ...	... ...	6X 4 6 45	... ...	... ...	... ...
King's Nympton	... ...	... ...	... ...	... ...	... ...	6X57 7 48	... ...	... ...	... ...
Eggesford	... ...	... ...	... ...	... ...	... ...	7 58	... ...	... ...	... ...
Lapford	... ...	... ...	... ...	... ...	... ...	8 8	... ...	... ...	... ...
Morchard Road	... ...	... ...	... ...	... ...	... ...	8 14	... ...	... ...	... ...
Copplestone	... ...	... ...	... ...	... ...	... ...		... ...	... ...	... ...
Plymouth (Friary)	... ...	... ...	2 0	4 15	... ...	... ...	5||28	... ...	6 20
Friary Jct.	... ...	... ...	2 3	4 18	... ...	... ...	5 30	... ...	6||23
Mount Gould Jct.	... ...	... ...	2 4	4 19	... ...	... ...	5 31	... ...	6||24
Lipson Jct.	... ...	... ...	2 7	4 21	... ...	... ...	5 32	... ...	... ...
Plymouth (Nth Rd.)	... ...	... ...	2 13	4 27	... ...	... ...	5 37	... ...	... ...
Devonport Jct.	... ...	... ...	2 15	4 29	... ...	... ...	5 39	... ...	... ...
Devonport (Kings Rd.)	... ...	... ...	2 17 2 38	4 31 4 44	... ...	... ...	Will not	... ...	... ...
St. Budeaux (Vic. Rd.)	... ...	... ...			... ...	... ...	run on	... ...	... ...
Bere Ferrers	... ...	... ...		5 10	... ...	... ...	Saturdays	... ...	... ...
Bere Alston	... ...	... ...			... ...	... ...	13th June	... ...	... ...
Tavistock North	... ...	... ...	3 19 3 22		... ...	... ...	to	... ...	... ...
Wilminstone Sdg.	... ...	... ...			... ...	... ...	19th Sept.	... ...	... ...
Brentor	... ...	... ...			... ...	... ...	Perform	... ...	... ...
Lydford	... ...	... ...			... ...	... ...	Shunting.	... ...	... ...
Bridestowe	... ...	... ...	3 58		... ...	... ...	Q	... ...	... ...
Meldon Jct.	... ...	... ...			... ...	... ...	Engine.	... ...	... ...
Quarry Sig. Box	... ...	... ...			... ...	... ...	arr. dep.	... ...	... ...
Okehampton	... ...	... ...	4 6 4 42		... ...	... ...	a.m. a.m.	... ...	... ...
Sampford C'nay	... ...	... ...			... ...	... ...	(9||40) 9||55 (9||24) 10 16	... ...	... ...
North Tawton	... ...	... ...			... ...	... ...	10|| 0 10A24 10 26	... ...	... ...
Bow	... ...	... ...			... ...	... ...	Will not	... ...	... ...
							run on		
Coleford Jct.	... ...	... ...	5 6		... ...	8 18	Saturdays	10 57	... ...
Yeoford	... ...	... ...	5 9 5 25	Q	... ...	8 21 9 2	13th June		Engine
Crediton	... ...	... ...	5 33 5 43		... ...		to		arr. dep.
Newton St. Cyres	... ...	... ...		★	arr. dep.		19th Sept.		p.m. p.m.
Cowley Jct.	... ...	... ...	5 58		a.m. a.m.	9 24		11 23	
Exeter (St. Dav. Yd.)	... ...	... ...	6 1 6 30		Until	9 27 10 22			
Exeter (St. David's)	... ...	... ...	6 33 6 42		19th Sept.	10 25 10 31		11 28 11 35	
Exeter Central	... ...	... ...	6 47 6 51	arr. dep.	only.	10 36 10 39		11 40 11 45	
Exeter Ctl. Gds. Yd.	... ...	... ...	6 53 7 22	a.m. a.m.		10 41 10 59			
Exmouth Jct.	5||45	6||20						11 50	
Exmouth Jct. Sdgs.			7 27		7 45	9 25 11 3			
Poltimore Sdg.				7 51 8 10	9 1 9 29 9 31 9 58		SX		
Min. of Food Sdg.				8 12 (8Q31)	9 31 9 58 10 0 10 50				
Pinhoe					10 0 10 40 10 52 (1120)				
Broad Clyst					10 46 (1145)				
Whimple							SX		
Sidmouth Jct.	6|| 3 (7 15)	6||38 (7 45)			Will not		Engine.		
Honiton					run on		arr. dep.		
Seaton Jct.					Saturdays		a.m. p.m.	Commences	
Axminster					13th June			21st Sept.	
Chard Jct.	Until	Will not			to		(1020) 11 50		
Crewkerne	19th Sept.	run on			19th Sept.		12 2 12 17	Until	
Sutton Bingham	only.	Saturdays					12 24	18th Sept.	
Yeovil Jct.		13th June						only.	
Sherborne		to							
Milborne Port		19th Sept.						11|| 0	11|| 5
Templecombe								1||10 (4 35)	11||15 (4 35)
Gillingham								Perform	Perform
Semley								freight	freight
Tisbury								shunting.	shunting.
Chilmark Sdg.									
Dinton									
Wilton South									
Salisbury									
Salisbury East Yard									

A—Change Guards.

TORRINGTON, ILFRACOMBE, PLYMOUTH, EXETER AND SALISBURY.

UP. WEEKDAYS.

Station	Engine	SO Engine	A	SO Engine	CD	SO	Engine	SF★F
	arr. a.m. / dep. a.m.	arr. a.m. / dep. a.m.	arr. p.m. / dep. p.m.	arr. p.m. / dep. p.m.	arr. a.m. / dep. a.m.	arr. p.m. / dep. p.m.	arr. p.m. / dep. p.m.	arr. a.m. / dep. a.m.
Torrington					(11 45)			
Bideford (New)	10 2 / 10 55				11 C 51 / 12 5 12 22			
Bideford (Goods)	11 E 4 / 11 X 7	11 X 40 / 11 40			11 C 55 / 12 C 7 12 26 12 33			
Instow	11 10	11 49			12 C 12 / 12 D 32 12 43			
East Yelland Sdg.	After Shunting.				12 040	12 51		
Fremington		12 11 / 11 56						
Barnstaple Jct.	Will not run on Saturdays 13th June to 19th Sept.	12 1			Will not run on Saturdays 13th June to 19th Sept.	Until 19th Sept. only.		
Ilfracombe		Until 19th Sept. only.						
Mortehoe & W'combe								
Heddon Mill Crossing								
Braunton								
Wrafton								
Pottington Box								
Barnstaple Town								
Shapland & P. Sdg.								
Barnstaple Jct.								
Chapelton								
Umberleigh								
Portsmouth A.								
King's Nympton								
Eggesford								
Lapford								
Morchard Road								
Copplestone								
Plymouth (Friary)								
Friary Jc.								
Mount Gould Jct.								
Lipson Jct.								
Plymouth (Nth. Rd.)					Will not run on Saturdays 13th June to 19th Sept.			
Devonport Jct.								
Devonport (Kings Rd.)								
St. Budeaux (Vic. Rd.)								
Bere Ferrers								
Bere Alston								
Tavistock North								
Willminstone Sdg.								
Brentor					(12 27) / 12 57			
Lydford					1 1 / 1 2			
Bridestowe								
Meldon Jct.								
Quarry Sig. Box								
Okehampton								
Sampford Crnay								
North Tawton								
Bow								
Coleford Jct.								
Yeoford					SO			
Crediton					4 40 p.m. Engine Yeovl.			1 F 50
Newton St. Cyres								
Cowley Jct.						arr. p.m. / dep. p.m.		
Exeter (St. Davr. Yd.)								
Exeter (St. David's)			4 C 55 / 5 C 5			4 45 / 4 46		2 F 50
Exeter Central			5 A 15 / 5 A 15					4 5 / 4 15
Exeter Cntl. Gds. Yd.								
Exmouth Jct.			4 30					4 35 / 4 55
Exmouth Jct. Sdgs.			Will not run on Saturdays 13th June to 19th Sept.			5 1 6 (5 30)	Until 19th Sept. only.	
Poltimore Sdg.								
Pinhoe								
Broad Clyst								5 25 / 5 10
Whimple								
Sidmouth Jct.								
Honiton								
Seaton Jct.								
Axminster								
Chard Jct.								
Crewkerne								
Sutton Bingham								
Yeovil Jct.			4 32					
Sherborne								
Milborne Port								
Templecombe								
Gillingham								
Semley								
Tisbury								
Chilmark Sdg.								
Dinton								6 7 / 7 10
Wilton South								7 / 7 35
Salisbury								7 15 / 7 16 7 45 / 7 48
Salisbury East Yard								7 20 / 7 52

A—Arrive Templecombe 5.0 p.m. when not required to call at Milborne Port.
C—On Mondays, 15th June to 14th September, start at 11.49 a.m. and run 2 minutes earlier to Fremington.
D—Terminate at Fremington when engine required for shunting purposes.
F—On Saturdays commencing 26th September, start at 2.0 p.m. and arrive Axminster 3.0 p.m.

TORRINGTON, ILFRACOMBE, PLYMOUTH, EXETER AND SALISBURY.

UP. WEEKDAYS.

Station	SX To Salisbury East Yard.	SX To Temple-combe.	SO To Keyham Dockyard.	Stone.	Engine.	SX To Keyham Dockyard.	SX To Keyham Dockyard.	SO	EB To Laira.
	arr. p.m. / dep. p.m.	arr. p.m. / dep. p.m.	arr. a.m. / dep. a.m.	arr. a.m. / dep. a.m.	arr. p.m. / dep. p.m.	arr. a.m. / dep. a.m.	arr. a.m. / dep. a.m.	arr. a.m. / dep. a.m.	arr. a.m. / dep. a.m.
Torrington									
Bideford (New)				12 10					
Bideford (Goods)				12 51 / 12 55					
Instow				1 0					
East Yelland Sdg.									
Fremington				1 14 / 1 14					
Barnstaple Jct.				1 25					
Ilfracombe						Worked by Devonport Shunting Engine.	Worked by Devonport Shunting Engine.	8 20	
Mortehoe & W'combe								8 23 / 8 24	
Heddon Mill Crossing								8 26	
Braunton								8 32 / 8 34	
Wrafton					Timing available until 21st Sept.				
Pottington Box									
Barnstaple Town							8 49 / 8 55	8 36 / 8 50	
Shapland & P. Sdg.								9 1	
Barnstaple Jct.				2 30 / 2 35	Worked by Devonport Shunting Engine.	9 16 / 9 50		9 20 / 9 28	
Chapelton						10 / 10 5	9 35 / 9 50	9 43	
Umberleigh								10 / 9 53	
Portsmouth A.								10 / 10 5	
King's Nympton				3 35 / 3 58	To Western Region via St. Budeaux East.	To Western Region via St. Budeaux East.	To Western Region via St. Budeaux East.	10 11	
Eggesford									
Lapford									
Morchard Road									
Copplestone									
Plymouth (Friary)				4 28				11 25 / 12	10 10
Friary Jc.				4 55				11 28	10 13
Mount Gould Jct.									10 14
Lipson Jct.								11 36	
Plymouth (Nth. Rd.)			(11 57) 12 30	(11 57) 12 25				11 40 / 12 51	
Devonport Jct.			12 30	12 30				12 46 / 12 51	
Devonport (Kings Rd.)								12 51	
St. Budeaux (Vic. Rd.)								12 58	
Bere Ferrers								1 3	
Bere Alston								1 5 / 1 10	
Tavistock North					SX To Temple-combe.			1 25 / 12 / 1 25	
Willminstone Sdg.									
Brentor								1 40 / 1 45	
Lydford								1 55 / 1 42	
Bridestowe								2 1 / 2 7	
Meldon Jct.								2 29	
Quarry Sig. Box									
Okehampton					1 35			2 27 / 2 30	
Sampford Crnay								2 / 2 56	
North Tawton						Timing will not apply when 9.50 a.m. service runs.		2 / 3 19	
Bow									
Coleford Jct.									
Yeoford								3 38	
Crediton					1 53 / 1 53			3 / 4 25	
Newton St. Cyres								4 34 / 4 38	
Cowley Jct.									
Exeter (St. Davr. Yd.)									
Exeter (St. David's)					2 51 / 2 51			4 43	
Exeter Central				Commences 21st Sept.					
Exeter Cntl. Gds. Yd.								4 43	
Exmouth Jct.									
Exmouth Jct. Sdgs.	1 20								
Poltimore Sdg.									
Pinhoe									
Broad Clyst									
Whimple									
Sidmouth Jct.									
Honiton									
Seaton Jct.									
Axminster									
Chard Jct.	1 38 / 2 30								
Crewkerne									
Sutton Bingham									
Yeovil Jct.	Will not run on Saturdays 13th June to 19th Sept.	Until 18th Sept.							
Sherborne									
Milborne Port									
Templecombe									
Gillingham	(11 55) / 4 35			6 / 6 43					
Semley	4 51 / 5 35								
Tisbury	5 45 / 5 55			6 58 / 7 3					
Chilmark Sdg.									
Dinton									
Wilton South	6 7 / 7 10			7 3					
Salisbury									
Salisbury East Yard									

TORRINGTON, ILFRACOMBE, PLYMOUTH, EXETER AND SALISBURY.

UP. WEEKDAYS. (Table 23)

Column headings (left to right): — | SO (To Exmouth Jct. Sdgs.) | SX (Stone.) | SX Ⓠ (Stone.) | — (12.45 p.m. Torrington to Nine Elms. ★CSF) | D | To Lairs. | SX | Trip | SO

Station										
Torrington										
Bideford (New)	2 37 / 3 26									
Bideford (Goods)	2 51 / 3 26									
Instow	3 35									
East Yelland Sdg.	3 43 / 4 11									
Fremington	4 14 / 4 29									
Barnstaple Jct.	4 88 / 4 30									
Ilfracombe		12 44		2 29 / 3 20			11 5			
Mortehoe & W'combe		12 47		3CS29 3CS33			11 9			
Heddon Mill Crossing		12 48		3C40 4S 9			11 11			
Braunton		12 50		4X20 4 30			11 17			
Wrafton		12 56		4 38 5X15			11 19			
Pottington Box		12 58		5 25 5 35			11 21			
Barnstaple Town		1 0 1 54		5 43 5X46			11 21 12			
Shapland & P. Sdg.	4 43			5 53						
Barnstaple Jct.		2 19 3 33					12 33 1 10			
Chapelton		3 9 4 5					1 27 1 49			
Umberleigh										
Portsmouth A.		4S25 4 53					2 33 2 56			
King's Nympton		5 16					3 4 3 15			
Eggesford							3 23			
Lapford							3 28			
Morchard Road						11 40 / 11 44				
Copplestone						11 43				
Plymouth (Friary)				Will not run between Torrington and Exmouth Jct. Sdgs. on Saturdays 13th June to 19th Sept.	4 56D		4 25 5 36	6		
Friary Jct.					4 D59		5 44 5 54			
Mount Gould Jct.										
Lipson Jct.							6 10			
Plymouth (Nth. Rd.)										
Devonport Jct.										
Devonport (Kings Rd.)										
St. Budeaux (Vic. Rd.)					★ASF	SX	6 14 6 17	6 14		
Bere Ferrers							6 22 6 25			
Bere Alston							6 30	6		
Tavistock North										
Wilmistone Sdg.										
Brentor										
Lydford										
Bridestowe										
Meldon Jct.										
Quarry Sig. Box										
Sampford C'nay										
Okehampton		5 26 5 43	4 22	5 57 5 59						3 50
North Tawton										4 2 4 20
Bow			4 30	6 44						4 28 5 6
Coleford Jct.									Com-mences 26th Sept.	4 5 16 5 30
Crediton				6 47 6 52	7 5				3 50	5 40 6 0
Newton St. Cyres				6 57 7 5	7 5					6E25 7 35
Cowley Jct.										7 52 8 15
Exeter (St. David's Yd.)										
Exeter (St. David's)										
Exeter Central				7 10 8 30	7 23 7 37				8 55 9 15	8 55
Exeter Cll. Gds. Yd.					8 23					
Exmouth Jct.									9 45	9 45
Exmouth Jct. Sdgs.										
Pinhoe										
Broad Clyst										
Whimple										
Sidmouth Jct.										
Honiton										
Axminster										
Chard Jct.										
Crewkerne										
Sutton Bingham										
Yeovil Jct.				9 55 10A48						
Sherborne										
Milborne Port										
Templecombe										
Gillingham										
Semley										
Tisbury										
Dinton										
Wilton South										
Salisbury										
Salisbury East Yard										

TORRINGTON, ILFRACOMBE, PLYMOUTH, EXETER AND SALISBURY.

UP. WEEKDAYS. (Table 22)

Column headings (left to right): SO (Engine.) | SO (A) | — (Engine. After Shunting) | SX (1.35 p.m. Exmouth Jct. Sdgs.) | — (To Nine Elms.) | SX | SO | Ⓠ (Stone. Salisbury.) | SO (1||2 p.m. Halwill.) | — (9.45 a.m. Budo.) | SX | SO

Station												
Torrington												
Bideford (New)	12|50											
Bideford (Goods)	12|55											
Instow												
East Yelland Sdg.	1|| 1|| 2				12 45 / 1 55						
Fremington				1||40	1 0 / 1 57							
Barnstaple Jct.	1||36			1||36	2 13 / 3 21 2 29 / 3 20							
Ilfracombe	Commences 26th Sept.				Will not run between Torrington and Exmouth Jct. Sdgs. on Saturdays 13th June to 19th Sept.							
Mortehoe & W'combe												
Heddon Mill Crossing												
Braunton												
Wrafton												
Pottington Box												
Barnstaple Town												
Shapland & P. Sdg.												
Barnstaple Jct.												
Chapelton												
Umberleigh												
Portsmouth A.												
King's Nympton								Until 11th July only.				
Eggesford												
Lapford												
Morchard Road												
Copplestone												
Plymouth (Friary)									1||55			
Friary Jct.									2 19			
Mount Gould Jct.									1|21	1||25		
Lipson Jct.				SX	MXⒼ							3 50	3 50
Plymouth (Nth. Rd.)												
Devonport Jct.												
Devonport (Kings Rd.)												
St. Budeaux (Vic. Rd.)					Engine.				Trip.			
Bere Ferrers					2|| 6				C			
Bere Alston												
Tavistock North					2 26			2 36			4 4 58	4 4 20
Wilmistone Sdg.								3 3	2C52		5 15 5 30	4 28 5 6
Brentor					2 29 / 2 37 2 34 / 2 35			3 8 3 13 3 13 3 29	2C57		5 40 6 40	5 16 6 40
Lydford					2||38			3 35			6 40	6E25 7 45
Bridestowe											6 45 7 45	7 52 8 20
Meldon Jct.											7E 2||	8 55 9 15
Quarry Sig. Box											8 17	
Sampford C'nay								4 5			8 47	9 45
Okehampton										2 14		9 40
North Tawton												
Bow												
Coleford Jct.												
Crediton												
Newton St. Cyres										Engine.		
Cowley Jct.												
Exeter (St. David's Yd.)			1 45							2|40 4|| 7		
Exeter (St. David's)			1 48 / 1 53							4||14 (5 36		
Exeter Central			1 58 / 2									
Exeter Cll. Gds. Yd.												
Exmouth Jct.	2 7									Until 19th Sept. only.		
Exmouth Jct. Sdgs.										Perform Freight shunting.		
Pinhoe												
Broad Clyst												
Whimple											4 2 4 20	
Sidmouth Jct.											4 28 5 6	
Honiton				SO							5 16 5 30	
Axminster											5 40 6 0	
Chard Jct.			(5|0) 5 30								6E25 7 45	
Crewkerne			5 16 6 15								7 52 8 20	
Sutton Bingham			5 31 6 45								8 25	
Yeovil Jct.			5 55 7 10								8 55 9 15	
Sherborne	5 5											
Milborne Port											9 45	
Templecombe												
Gillingham												
Semley												
Tisbury			7 22 8 25									
Dinton			7 48 9 0									
Wilton South												
Salisbury			8 6 8 55									
Salisbury East Yard												

A—Arrive 2.13 p.m. on Saturdays, 13th June to 19th September.
C—On Saturdays 13th June to 19th September, start at 3.5 p.m. and arrive Exmouth Sidings 3.10 p.m.

365

TORRINGTON, ILFRACOMBE, PLYMOUTH, EXETER AND SALISBURY.

UP. WEEKDAYS.	To Feltham. SX SF★	Empty Wagons. SX ★	5.45 p.m. Plymouth Docks. SO ◆	To Laira.	12.44 p.m. Plymouth Friary. SO ★	1.55 p.m. Stone Quarry. Q A★	12.45 p.m. Torrington to Nine Elms. SF★	11.35 a.m. Wade-bridge. F	7.5 p.m. Exmouth Jct. Sdgs. C.SF ★
Torrington									
Bideford (New)									
Bideford (Goods)									
Instow									
East Yelland Sdg.									
Fremington									
Barnstaple Jct.									
Ilfracombe									
Mortehoe & W'coombe									
Heddon Mill Crossing									
Braunton									
Wrafton									
Pottington Box									
Barnstaple Town									
Barnstaple Jct.									
Shapland & P. Sdg.									
Chapelton									
Umberleigh									
Portsmouth A.									
King's Nympton									
Eggesford									
Lapford									
Morchard Road									
Copplestone									
Plymouth (Friary)									
Friary Jct.									
Mount Gould Jct.									
Lipson Jct.									
Plymouth (Nth Rd.)									
Devonport Jct.									
Devonport (Kings Rd.)									
St. Budeaux (Vic. Rd.)									
Bere Ferrers									
Bere Alston									
Tavistock North									
Wilminstone Sdg.									
Brentor									
Lydford									
Bridestowe									
Meldon Jct.									
Quarry Sig. Box									
Okehampton									
Sampford C'nay									
North Tawton									
Bow									
Coleford Jct.									
Yeoford									
Crediton									
Newton St. Cyres									
Cowley Jct.									
Exeter (St. Dav. Yd.)									
Exeter (St. David's)									
Exeter Central									
Exeter Chl. Gds. Yd.									
Exmouth Jct. Sdgs.									
Pinhoe									
Broad Clyst									
Whimple									
Sidmouth Jct.									
Honiton									
Seaton Jct.									
Axminster									
Chard Jct.									
Crewkerne									
Sutton Bingham									
Yeovil Jct.									
Sherborne									
Milborne Port									
Templecombe									
Gillingham									
Semley									
Tisbury									
Dinton									
Wilton South									
Salisbury									
Salisbury East Yard									
Nine Elms									

A—When 9.10 p.m. when not required to call at Shapland & Petter's Sdg., depart Axminster 10.15 p.m.
Q—Livestock Exeter Central to Salisbury runs, depart Yeovil Jct. 11.0 p.m. and arrive Templecombe 11.30 p.m.
Q—Livestock Exeter Central to Salisbury runs depart Yeovil Jct. 11.0 p.m.
D—On Saturdays after 13th June to 19th September start at 11.40 a.m. On Mondays to Fridays (Summer) when 4.27 p.m.
Okehampton to Bude does not run, Meldon Jn. 9/0 p.m. and arr. Okehampton 9.10 p.m.

TORRINGTON, ILFRACOMBE, PLYMOUTH, EXETER AND SALISBURY.

UP. WEEKDAYS.	To Laira.	SO	SX	SX	SO	Mixed.	SX	1.20 p.m. Bude.	SX Engine.
Torrington									
Bideford (New)									
Bideford (Goods)									
Instow									
East Yelland Sdg.									
Fremington									
Barnstaple Jct.									
Ilfracombe									
Mortehoe & W'coombe									
Heddon Mill Crossing									
Braunton									
Wrafton									
Pottington Box									
Barnstaple Town									
Barnstaple Jct.									
Shapland & P. Sdg.									
Chapelton									
Umberleigh									
Portsmouth A.									
King's Nympton									
Eggesford									
Lapford									
Morchard Road									
Copplestone									
Plymouth (Friary)									
Friary Jct.									
Mount Gould Jct.									
Lipson Jct.									
Plymouth (Nth Rd.)									
Devonport Jct.									
Devonport (Kings Rd.)									
St. Budeaux (Vic. Rd.)									
Bere Ferrers									
Bere Alston									
Tavistock North									
Wilminstone Sdg.									
Brentor									
Lydford									
Bridestowe									
Meldon Jct.									
Quarry Sig. Box									
Okehampton									
Sampford C'nay									
North Tawton									
Bow									
Coleford Jct.									
Yeoford									
Crediton									
Newton St. Cyres									
Cowley Jct.									
Exeter (St. Dav. Yd.)									
Exeter (St. David's)									
Exeter Central									
Exeter Chl. Gds. Yd.									
Exmouth Jct. Sdgs.									
Pinhoe									
Broad Clyst									
Whimple									
Sidmouth Jct.									
Honiton									
Seaton Jct.									
Axminster									
Chard Jct.									
Crewkerne									
Sutton Bingham									
Yeovil Jct.									
Sherborne									
Milborne Port									
Templecombe									
Gillingham									
Semley									
Tisbury									
Dinton									
Wilton South									
Salisbury									
Salisbury East Yard									

A—Arrive 7.0 p.m. when not required to call at Shapland & Petter's Sdg.
C—On Fridays until 18th Sept. start at 5|11 p.m. and arrive Barnstaple Jct. 5|16 p.m.

TORRINGTON, ILFRACOMBE, PLYMOUTH, EXETER AND SALISBURY.

UP. WEEKDAYS.

Station
Torrington
Bideford (New)
Bideford (Goods)
Instow
East Yelland Sidg.
Fremington
Barnstaple Jct.
Ilfracombe
Mortehoe & W'combe
Heddon Mill Crossing
Braunton
Wrafton
Pottington Box
Barnstaple T. P. Sdg.
Barnstaple Town
Barnstaple Jct.
Chapelton
Umberleigh
Portsmouth A.
King's Nympton
Eggesford
Lapford
Morchard Road
Copplestone
Plymouth (Friary)
Friary Jct.
Mount Gould Jct.
Lipson Jct.
Plymouth (Nth Rd.)
Devonport Jct.
Devonport (Kings Rd.)
St. Budeaux (Vic. Rd.)
Bere Ferrers
Bere Alston
Tavistock North
Wilmistone Sdg.
Brentor
Lydford
Bridestowe
Meldon Jct.
Quarry Sig. Box
Okehampton
Sampford Cosy
North Tawton
Bow
Coleford Jct.
Yeoford
Crediton
Newton St. Cyres
Cowley Jct.
Exeter (St. Dav. Yd.)
Exeter (St. David's)
Exeter Central
Exeter Ctl. Gds. Yd.
Exmouth Jct. Sigs.
Pinhoe
Broad Clyst
Whimple
Sidmouth Jct.
Honiton
Seaton Jct.
Axminster
Chard Jct.
Crewkerne
Sutton Bingham
Yeovil Jct.
Sherborne
Milborne Port
Templecombe
Gillingham
Semley
Tisbury
Dinton
Wilton South
Salisbury
Salisbury East Yard

A—Starts at 4.50 p.m. Mondays to Fridays until 18th September and at 4.22 p.m. on Saturdays until 19th September.

TORRINGTON, ILFRACOMBE, PLYMOUTH, EXETER AND SALISBURY.

UP. WEEKDAYS. (continued)

Station
Torrington
Bideford (New)
Bideford (Goods)
Instow
East Yelland Sidg.
Fremington
Barnstaple Jct.
Ilfracombe
Mortehoe & W'combe
Heddon Mill Crossing
Braunton
Wrafton
Pottington Box
Barnstaple T. P. Sdg.
Barnstaple Town
Barnstaple Jct.
Chapelton
Umberleigh
Portsmouth A.
King's Nympton
Eggesford
Lapford
Morchard Road
Copplestone
Plymouth (Friary)
Friary Jct.
Mount Gould Jct.
Lipson Jct.
Plymouth (Nth Rd.)
Devonport Jct.
Devonport (Kings Rd.)
St. Budeaux (Vic. Rd.)
Bere Ferrers
Bere Alston
Tavistock North
Wilmistone Sdg.
Brentor
Lydford
Bridestowe
Meldon Jct.
Quarry Sig. Box
Okehampton
Sampford Cosy
North Tawton
Bow
Coleford Jct.
Yeoford
Crediton
Newton St. Cyres
Cowley Jct.
Exeter (St. Dav. Yd.)
Exeter (St. David's)
Exeter Central
Exeter Ctl. Gds. Yd.
Exmouth Jct. Sigs.
Pinhoe
Broad Clyst
Whimple
Sidmouth Jct.
Honiton
Seaton Jct.
Axminster
Chard Jct.
Crewkerne
Sutton Bingham
Yeovil Jct.
Sherborne
Milborne Port
Templecombe
Gillingham
Tisbury
Dinton
Wilton South
Salisbury
Salisbury East Yard
Nine Elms

A—When 9.10 p.m. Q Livestock Exeter Central to Salisbury runs depart Axminster 10.15 p.m. and arrive Yeovil Jct. 11.10 p.m.

B—Arrive Barnstaple Jct. 7.54 p.m. when not required to call at Shunland Siding.

D—On Fridays 12th June to 18th September, Bideford (New) arrive 6X14 p.m., depart 6.19 p.m. and arrive Bideford Goods 5.22 p.m.

TORRINGTON, ILFRACOMBE, PLYMOUTH, EXETER AND SALISBURY.

UP. SUNDAYS.	Q		Engine.		Engine.				Engine.		7.5 p.m. (Sats.) Exmouth Jct. Sdgs. C		1.55 p.m. (Sats.) Stone Meldon Quarry. Q C		4.5 p.m. (Sats. Summer). 5.0 p.m. (Sats. Winter). Torrington. C		4.5 p.m. W.R. Freight Laira. ◆ A			
	arr. p.m.	dep. p.m.	arr. a.m.	dep. a.m.	arr. a.m.	dep. a.m.			arr. mdt.	dep. a.m.	arr. p.m.	dep. p.m.	arr. p.m.	dep. a.m.	arr. a.m.	dep. a.m.	arr. p.m.	dep. p.m.		
Torrington	...	...	...	...	...	...	...	...	...	...	...	...	...	...	...	...	...	...	...	...
Bideford (New)	...	...	...	...	...	...	...	...	...	...	...	...	...	...	...	...	...	...	...	...
Bideford (Goods)	...	...	...	...	...	...	...	...	...	...	...	...	...	...	...	...	...	...	...	...
Instow	...	...	...	...	...	...	...	...	...	...	...	...	...	...	...	...	...	...	...	...
East Yelland Sdg.	...	...	...	...	...	...	...	...	...	...	...	...	...	...	...	...	...	...	...	...
Fremington	...	...	...	...	...	...	...	...	...	...	...	...	...	...	...	...	...	...	...	...
Barnstaple Jct.	...	...	...	...	...	...	...	...	...	...	...	...	...	...	...	...	...	...	...	...
Ilfracombe	...	...	...	...	...	...	...	...	...	...	...	...	...	...	...	...	...	...	...	...
Mortehoe & W'combe	...	...	...	...	...	...	...	...	...	...	...	...	...	...	...	...	...	...	...	...
Heddon Mill Crossing	...	...	...	...	...	...	...	...	...	...	...	...	...	...	...	...	...	...	...	...
Braunton	...	...	...	...	...	...	...	...	...	...	...	...	...	...	...	...	...	...	...	...
Wrafton	...	...	...	...	...	...	...	...	...	...	...	...	...	...	...	...	...	...	...	...
Pottington Box	...	...	...	...	...	...	...	...	...	...	...	...	...	...	...	...	...	...	...	...
Barnstaple Town	...	...	...	...	...	...	...	...	...	...	...	...	...	...	...	...	...	...	...	...
Barnstaple Jct.	...	...	...	...	...	...	...	...	...	...	...	...	...	...	...	...	...	...	...	...
Chapelton	...	...	...	...	...	...	...	...	...	...	...	...	...	...	...	...	...	...	...	...
Umberleigh	...	...	...	...	...	...	...	...	...	...	...	...	...	...	...	...	...	...	...	...
Portsmouth A.	...	...	...	...	...	...	...	...	...	...	...	...	...	...	...	...	...	...	...	...
King's Nympton	...	...	...	...	...	...	...	...	...	...	...	...	...	...	...	...	...	...	...	...
Eggesford	...	...	...	...	...	...	...	...	...	...	...	...	...	...	...	...	...	...	...	...
Lapford	...	...	...	...	...	...	...	...	...	...	...	...	...	...	...	...	...	...	...	...
Morchard Road	...	...	...	...	...	...	...	...	...	...	...	...	...	...	...	...	...	...	...	...
Copplestone	...	...	...	...	...	...	...	...	...	...	...	...	...	...	...	...	...	...	...	...
Plymouth (Friary)	...	*11 30*	...	...	...	...	...	...	...	...	...	...	...	...	...	...	From Western Region		...	...
Friary Jct.	*11 32*		...	...	...	...	...	...	...	...	...	...	...	...	...	...			...	...
Mount Gould Jct.	*11 33*		...	...	...	...	...	...	...	...	...	...	...	...	...	...			...	...
Lipson Jct.	*11 35*		...	...	...	...	...	...	...	...	...	...	...	...	...	...	4 11		...	...
Plymouth (Nth Rd.)	*11 41*		...	...	...	...	...	...	...	...	...	...	...	...	...	...	4A17	4 18	...	...
Devonport Jct.	*11 43*		...	...	...	...	...	...	...	...	...	...	...	...	...	...	4 20		...	...
Devonport (Kings Rd.)	*11 44*	*12 5*	...	...	...	...	...	...	...	...	...	...	...	...	...	...	4 23		...	...
Ford	...	...	...	...	...	...	...	...	...	...	...	...	...	...	...	...	...	...	...	...
St. Budeaux (Vic. Rd.)	...	...	...	...	...	...	...	...	...	...	...	...	...	...	...	...	...	...	...	...
Bere Ferrers	...	...	...	...	...	...	...	...	...	...	...	...	...	...	...	...	...	...	...	...
Bere Alston	*12 45*	*12 55*	...	...	...	...	...	...	...	...	...	...	...	...	...	...	...	...	...	...
Tavistock North	...	...	...	...	...	...	...	...	Commences 27th September.		...	...	...	...	...	...	5	5	...	...
Brentor	...	...	...	...	...	...	...	...			...	...	...	...	...	...	...	...	...	...
Lydford	...	...	...	...	...	...	...	...			...	...	...	...	...	...	...	...	...	...
Bridestowe	...	...	...	...	...	...	...	...	...	...	...	...	...	...	...	...	...	...	...	...
Meldon Jct.	...	*1 45*					...	...	...	...	...	...	...	...	...	...	...	...	...	...
Quarry Halt	...	...	Until 20th Sept. only.		Com-mences 27th Sept.		...	...	...	...	...	...	...	...	...	...	...	...	...	...
Okehampton	*1 55*	...					...	...	(12 0)	12‖56	...	...	...	...	...	...	5 55	6 15	...	...
Sampford C'nay	...	...					...	...	...	...	...	...	...	...	...	...	...	...	...	...
North Tawton	...	...					...	...	...	...	...	...	...	...	...	...	...	...	...	...
Bow	...	...	...	...	...	...	...	...	...	...	...	...	...	...	...	...	...	...	...	...
Coleford Jct.	...	...	...	...	...	...	...	...	...	...	...	...	...	...	...	...	...	...	...	...
Yeoford	...	...	...	12‖ 5	...	12‖55	...	...		1 26	...	...	...	...	...	...		6 42	...	...
Crediton	...	...	...	...	...	...	...	...	...	...	...	...	...	...	...	...	...	...	...	...
Newton St. Cyres	...	...	...	...	...	...	...	...	...	...	...	...	...	...	...	...	...	...	...	...
Cowley Jct.	...	...	12 25		1 15		...	...	1 46		...	...	...	...	...	...		7 4	...	...
Exeter St. Dav. Yd.	...	...	...	...	...	...	...	...	...	...	...	...	...	...	...	...	7 7	...	...	...
Exeter (St. David's)	...	...	12 28	12 30	1 18	1 20	...	...	1 49	1 51	...	...	...	...	...	...	...	...	...	...
Exeter Central	...	...	12 33	12 35	1 23	1 25	...	...	1 54	1 55	...	...	...	...	...	...	...	...	...	...
Exeter Ctl. Gds. Yd.	...	...	...	...	...	...	...	...	...	...	...	...	...	...	...	...	...	...	...	...
Exmouth Jct.	...	...	12‖40	...	1‖30	...	...	...	2‖ 0	...	...	...	...	...	...	...	...	...	...	...
Exmouth Jct. Sdgs.	...	...	...	...	...	...	...	...	...	...	...	...	...	...	...	...	...	...	...	...
Pinhoe	...	...	...	...	...	...	...	...	...	...	...	...	...	...	...	...	...	...	...	...
Broad Clyst	...	...	...	...	...	...	...	...	...	...	...	...	Will not run on Sundays 14th June to 20th Sept.		...	...	...	...	...	...
Whimple	...	...	...	...	...	...	...	...	...	...	...	...			...	...	...	...	...	...
Sidmouth Jct.	...	...	...	...	...	...	...	...	...	...	...	...			...	...	...	...	...	...
Honiton	...	...	...	...	...	...	...	...	...	...	...	...			←		...	...	...	...
Seaton Jct.	...	...	...	...	...	...	...	...	...	...	...	...			p.m.		...	...	...	...
Axminster	...	...	...	...	...	...	...	...	...	...	...	...			11 45C		...	...	...	...
Chard Jct.	...	...	...	...	...	...	...	...	...	...	...	...	...	...	...	...	...	...	...	...
Crewkerne	...	...	...	...	...	...	...	...	...	...	...	...	...	...	...	...	...	...	...	...
Sutton Bingham	...	...	...	...	...	...	...	...	...	...	...	...	...	...	a.m.	a.m.	...	...	...	...
Yeovil Jct.	...	...	...	...	...	...	...	...	...	...	...	...	...	...	12 35	12 45	...	...	...	...
Sherborne	...	...	...	...	...	...	...	...	...	...	←		←		...	...	...	...	...	...
Milborne Port	...	...	...	...	...	...	...	...	...	...	...	...	...	...	...	...	...	...	...	...
Templecombe	...	...	...	...	...	...	...	...	...	...	11C18	11C55	*11C58*	*12 12*	1 15	1 45	...	...	...	...
Gillingham	...	...	...	...	...	...	...	...	...	...	...	...	...	...	...	...	...	...	...	...
Semley	...	...	...	...	...	...	...	...	...	...	...	...	...	...	...	...	...	...	...	...
Tisbury	...	...	...	...	...	...	...	...	...	...	...	...	...	...	...	...	...	...	...	...
Dinton	...	...	...	...	...	...	...	...	...	...	...	...	...	...	...	...	...	...	...	...
Wilton South	...	...	...	...	...	...	...	...	...	...	a.m.	a.m.	a.m.	...	...	...	...	...	...	...
Salisbury	...	...	...	...	...	...	...	...	...	...	1 0	1 1	*1 19*	...	3 0	3 8	...	...	...	...
Salisbury East Yard	...	...	...	...	...	...	...	...	...	...	1 5	...	...	...	3 12	3 30	...	...	...	...
Nine Elms	...	...	...	...	...	...	...	...	...	...	...	...	...	...	7 17	...	...	...	...	...

A—Set down Pilot Guard.
C—Saturday nights.

HALWILL AND TORRINGTON BRANCH.

Distance.		WEEKDAYS.	Mixed (Conveys Workmen)		Q				Mixed.		F		SO Q EB		SX		SX Mixed.		SO Mixed.	
m.	c.		arr. a.m.	dep. a.m.	arr. a.m.	dep. a.m.			arr. a.m.	dep. a.m.	arr. a.m.	dep. a.m.	arr. p.m.	dep. p.m.	arr. p.m.	dep. p.m.	arr. p.m.	dep. p.m.	arr. p.m.	dep. p.m.
—	—	**Torrington** Ⓣ	...	6 25	...	...	...	...	...	8 52	...	10 30	...	*12 25*	...	1 0	...	3 55	...	*4 40*
1	58	Watergate Halt	6 32	6 33	...	...	...	...	8 59	9 0	10 37	10 42	...	...	...	...	4 2	4 3	*4 47*	*4 48*
4	42	Yarde Halt	6 46	6 48	...	...	...	...	9 13	9 14	...	...	...	...	...	...	4 16	4 17	*5 1*	*5 2*
5	49	Dunsbear Halt	6 52	6 55	...	...	...	...	9 18	9 19	...	...	...	...	...	...	4 21	4 22	*5 6*	*5 7*
5	72	Marland Clay Co.'s Sdg.	...	...	*(7 25)*	*7 35*	...	...	...	...	11 1	11 11	...	...	1 25	1 35	...	...	...	...
7	68	Petrockstow Ⓣ	7 4	(7 55)	*7 45*	...	...	...	9 28	9 29	11X21	12 6	*12 55*	*(1 15)*	1 45	(1 55)	4X31	4 32	*5 16*	*5 17*
9	56	Meeth Clay Co.'s Sdg.	...	...	...	...	...	...	...	...	12 12	12 27	...	...	...	...	...	...	...	...
10	46	Meeth Halt	...	...	...	...	...	...	9 38	9 39	...	...	...	...	...	...	4 41	4 42	*5 26*	*5 27*
12	56	Hatherleigh Ⓣ	...	...	...	...	...	...	9 48	9 50	12 39	1 11	...	...	...	...	4 51	4 53	*5 36*	*5 38*
17	40	Hole Ⓣ	...	...	...	...	...	...	10 8	10 9	1 29	1F39	...	...	...	...	5 11	5 12	*5 56*	*5 57*
20	47	**Halwill** Ⓣ	...	...	...	...	...	...	10 18	...	1F48	...	...	...	...	...	5 21	...	*6 6*	...

		WEEKDAYS.	Q		Mixed.		Mixed. C				SO Mixed. D			SO Q		SX A	
m.	c.		arr. a.m.	dep. a.m.	arr. a.m.	dep. a.m.	arr. a.m.	dep. a.m.			arr. a.m.	dep. a.m.		arr. p.m.	dep. p.m.	arr. p.m.	dep. p.m.
—	—	**Halwill** Ⓣ	...	...	...	...	...	10 40	...	...	...	*10 52*	...	...	...	...	...
3	07	Hole Ⓣ	...	...	...	...	10 49	10 50	...	...	*11 1*	*11 2*	...	...	...	...	...
7	71	Hatherleigh Ⓣ	...	...	...	...	11 7	11 11	...	...	*11 19*	*11 23*	...	...	...	Conveys Workmen.	
10	01	Meeth Halt	...	...	...	...	11 20	11 20½	...	...	*11 32*	*11 32½*	...	...	...		
10	71	Meeth Clay Co.'s Sdg.	...	...	...	...	...	...	...	...	...	...	...	...	...	...	...
12	59	Petrockstow Ⓣ	...	*7 14*	(7 4)	7 55	11X29½	11 30½	...	...	*11 41½*	*11 42½*	...	*(12 55)*	*1 15*	(1 45)	1 55
14	55	Marland Clay Co.'s Sdg.	*7 25*	*(7 35)*	...	...	...	...	...	...	...	...	...	...	...	...	...
14	78	Dunsbear Halt			8 4	8 5	11 39½	11 40	...	...	*11 51½*	*11 52½*	...	...	...	2 4	2A14
16	05	Yarde Halt	...	...	8 10	8 11	11 45	11 45½	...	...	*11 57*	*11 57½*	...	...	...	2A19	2A20
18	69	Watergate Halt	...	...	8 24	8 25	11 58½	11 59	...	...	*12 10½*	*12 11*	...	...	...	...	...
20	47	**Torrington** Ⓣ	...	...	8 32	...	12 6	...	...	...	*12 18*	...	...	*1 42*	...	2A38	...

WEEKDAYS.	SX			SO		SX Q					SX Mixed (Conveys Workmen)		SX Q		Mixed.			
	arr. p.m.	dep. p.m.		arr. p.m.	dep. p.m.	arr. p.m.	dep. p.m.				arr. p.m.	dep. p.m.	arr. p.m.	dep. p.m.	arr. p.m.	dep. p.m.		
Halwill Ⓣ	...	2 20	*Will not apply when 2.35 p.m.* SX Q *runs.*	...	*2 20*	...	*2 35*	*Will apply when 10.30 a.m. Torrington revised from Hole.*	...	...	...	...	...	...	...	6 40	...	...
Hole Ⓣ	2 29	2 39		*2 29*	*2 39*	*2 44*	*2 54*		...	...	...	...	...	...	6 49	6 50	...	...
Hatherleigh Ⓣ	2 55	3 12		*2 55*	*3 2*	*3 10*	*3 27*		...	...	...	...	...	...	7 7	7 9	...	...
Meeth Halt	3 22	3 27		...	...	*3 37*	*3 42*		...	...	...	...	...	...	7 18	7 19	...	...
Meeth Clay Co.'s Sdg.	3 29	3 39		*3 14*	*3 24*	*3 44*	*3 54*		...	...	...	...	...	...	...	...	...	...
Petrockstow Ⓣ	3X45	(4.35)		*3 30*	*3 45*	*4 0*	*(4 35)*		...	...	{ (3 45)	4 35	*(4 31)*	*5 15*	7 28	7 29	...	...
Marland Clay Co.'s Sdg.	...	...		...	...	...	...		...	...	{ (4 00)	...	...	...	...	...	...	...
Dunsbear Halt	...	...		...	...	...	...		...	...	4 44	4 45	...	...	7 38	7 39	...	...
Yarde Halt	...	...		...	...	...	...		...	...	4 50	4 51	...	...	7 44	7 45	...	...
Watergate Halt	...	...		...	...	...	...		...	...	5 4	5 5	...	...	7 58	7 59	...	...
Torrington Ⓣ	...	...		*4 12*	...	...	...		...	...	5 12	...	*5 42*	...	8 6	...	...	...

A—When not required to attach or detach at Dunsbear Siding depart 2.5 p.m., Yarde Halt arrive 2.10 p.m., depart 2.11 p.m. and arrive Torrington 2.29 p.m.

C—Will not run on Saturdays 13th June to 19th September.

D—Until 19th September only.

F—When required to attach livestock, depart Hole 1.54 p.m. and arrive Halwill 2.3 p.m.

BARNSTAPLE JUNCTION AND BARNSTAPLE (VICTORIA ROAD) (Western Region).

(Distance 1 Mile 61 Chains)

WEEKDAYS.		D	A		C	D	A
	◆	SO ◆		◆	◆	SO	◆
	a.m.	a.m.	a.m.	a.m.	p.m.	p.m.	p.m.
B'staple (Vic. Rd.) Ⓢ dep.	7 20	*8‖20*	9 45	10 40	5 50	*7‖0*	7 3
B'staple Jct. Ⓢ arr.	7 25	*8‖25*	9 50	10 45	5 55	*7‖5*	7 8

WEEKDAYS.		A	A	D		D	D	A
	◆	S.R. Eng.	◆	SO ◆	◆	SO ◆	SO	◆
	a.m.	a.m.	a.m.	p.m.	p.m.	p.m.	p.m.	p.m.
B'staple Jct. Ⓢ dep.	8 0	9‖ 5	11 5	*11 16*	5 8	*5 22*	*7‖ 8*	7 30
B'staple (Vic. Rd.) Ⓢ arr.	8 5	9‖10	11 10	*11 21*	5 13	*5 27*	*7‖13*	7 35

A—Will not run on Saturdays 13th June to 19th September.

C—On Saturdays until 19th September start at 5.52 p.m. and arrive Barnstaple Jc. 5.57 p.m.

D—Until 19th September only.